WISCONSIN
COMMUNITY TREASURES

Wisconsin State Capitol, Madison WI

by Damon Neal
and Lynda Kusick

a part of the Morgan & Chase Treasure Series
www.treasuresof.com

MORGAN & CHASE PUBLISHING INC.

Morgan & Chase Publishing, Inc.
531 Parsons Drive, Medford, Oregon 97501
(888) 557-9328
www.treasuresof.com

Printed and bound by Taylor Specialty Books—Dallas TX
First edition 2007
ISBN: 978-1-933989-13-6

I gratefully acknowledge the contributions of the many people involved in the writing and production of this book. Their tireless dedication to this endeavour has been inspirational.
—Damon Neal, *Publisher*

The Morgan & Chase Publishing Home Team

Operations Department:
V.P. of Operations—Cindy Tilley Faubion
Travel Writer Liaison—Anne Boydston
Shipping & Receiving—Virginia Arias
Human Resources Coordinator—Heather Allen
Customer Service Relations—Casey Faubion, Terrie West, Sue Buda, Marie Manson
IT Engineer—Ray Ackerman
Receptionist—Shauna O'Callahan

Production Department:
Proof Editors—Avery Brown, Clarice Rodriguez
Editor/Writers—Gregory Scott, Robyn Sutherland
House Writers—Megan Glomb, Prairie Smallwood
Photo Coordinator—Wendy L. Gay
Photo Assistant—Donna Lindley
Photo Editor—Mary Murdock
Graphic Design Team—C.S. Rowan, Jesse Gifford, Tamara Cornett, Jacob Kristof, Michael Frye

Administrative Department:
CFO—Emily Wilke
Accounting Assistants—Danielle Barkley, David Grundvig, Cari Qualls, Tiffany Myers
Website Designer—Molly Bermea
Website Software Developer—Ben Ford

Contributing Writers:
Mary Beth Lee, Lynda Kusick, Mark Allen Deruiter, Nancy Backhaus, Anne Marie Schmidt, Dusty Alexander, Paul Hadella, Mary Knepp, Chris McCrellis-Mitchell, Laura Young, Todd Wels, Jennifer Buckner, Carol Bevis,Amber Dusk, Alexis McKenna, Maggie McClellen, Nancy McClain, Marek Alday, Particia Smith, Kate Zdrojewski

Special Recognition to:
Pam Hamilton, David Smigelski, John Gaffey, Chris Rose-Merkle, Gene Mitts

To my favorite songwriter and husband of 23 years, Geno. Thank you for letting me travel our home state to help complete this book.

To my three sons, Moriah (Moe), Kendrick and Logan—my treasures. May you always know your mother's heart is for you. Loving you, praying for you, and carrying your hurts as my own.

In doing these interviews over the last year, I've met many warm-hearted, passionate people who have truly made treasures of their lives' work. They've invested time, money and their creative energy to make it special for you. May you enjoy reading about them and paying them visits as much as I have enjoyed featuring them.

—Anne Marie Schmidt

How to use this book

Wisconsin Community Treasures is divided by city and category. Categories range from accommodations to wineries, with headings such as attractions, bakeries, galleries, home, recreation, restaurants and shopping in between.

In the index, all of these Treasures are listed alphabetically by name as well as by the city where you can visit them.

We have provided contact information for every Treasure in the book.
These are places and businesses that we encourage you to visit on your travels through Wisconsin.

We sincerely hope you find this book to be both beautiful and useful.

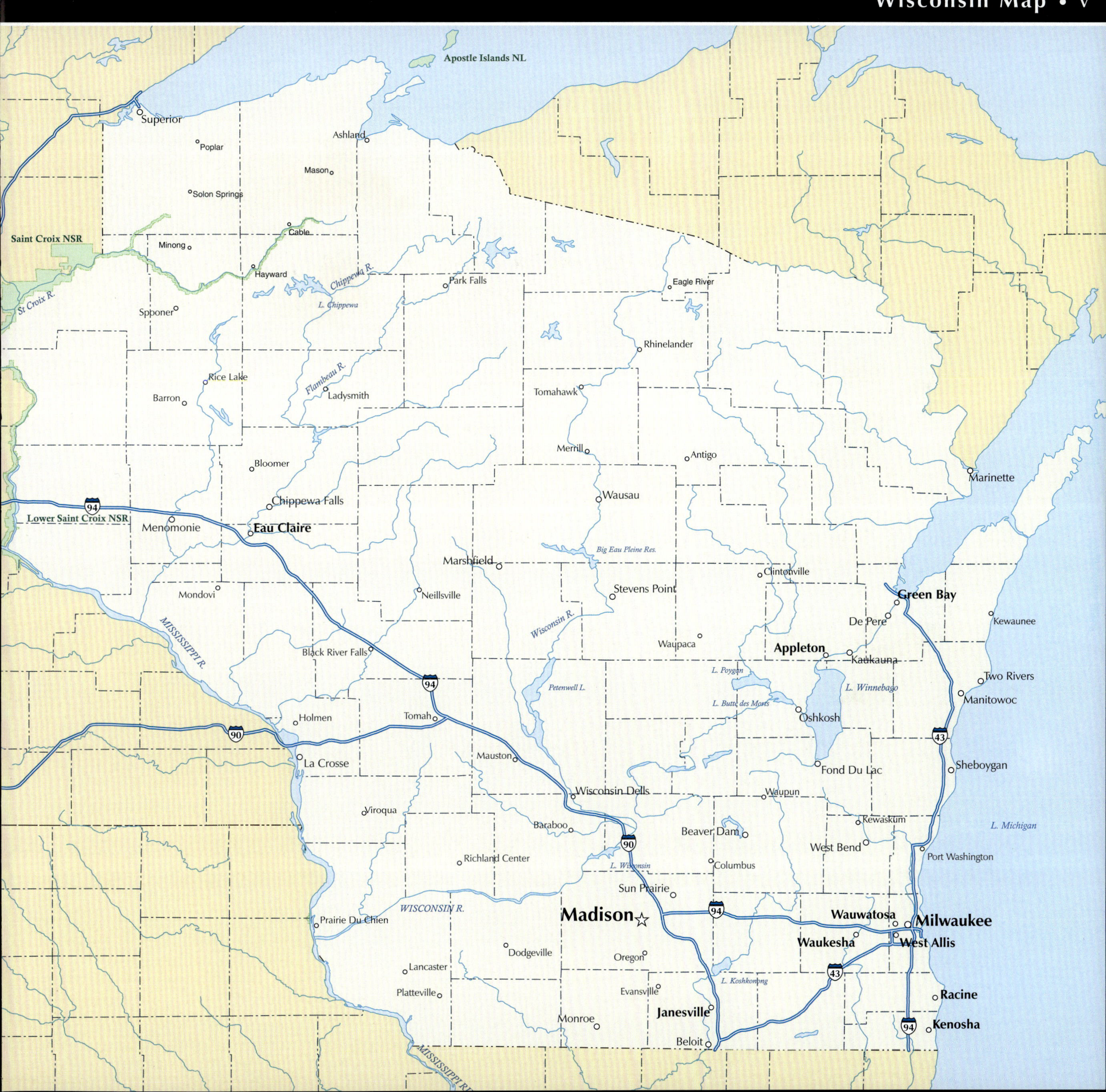
Apostle Islands NL
Superior
Poplar
Ashland
Mason
Solon Springs
Saint Croix NSR
Cable
Minong
Hayward
Chippewa R.
St Croix R.
Park Falls
Eagle River
L. Chippewa
Spooner
Rhinelander
Rice Lake
Flambeau R.
Ladysmith
Barron
Tomahawk
Merrill
Antigo
Bloomer
Marinette
Wausau
Chippewa Falls
94
Lower Saint Croix NSR
Menomonie
Eau Claire
Big Eau Pleine Res.
Marshfield
Clintonville
Mondovi
Neillsville
Stevens Point
Green Bay
MISSISSIPPI R.
Kewaunee
De Pere
Wisconsin R.
Waupaca
Black River Falls
Appleton
Kaukauna
L. Poygan
Two Rivers
L. Winnebago
Petenwell L.
Manitowoc
L. Butte des Morts
Holmen
Tomah
Oshkosh
90
43
La Crosse
Mauston
Sheboygan
Fond Du Lac
Wisconsin Dells
Waupun
Viroqua
Kewaskum
Baraboo
L. Michigan
Beaver Dam
West Bend
Port Washington
Richland Center
L. Wisconsin
Columbus
Sun Prairie
WISCONSIN R.
Madison
Wauwatosa
Milwaukee
Prairie Du Chien
Waukesha
West Allis
Dodgeville
Oregon
Lancaster
L. Koshkonong
Platteville
Evansville
Racine
Janesville
Monroe
Kenosha
Beloit
MISSISSIPPI R.

WISCONSIN AT A GLANCE:

Admitted to the Union: 1848, the 30th state
Population (2006): 5,556,506
Largest City: Milwaukee, 578,887
Largest Metro Area: Milwaukee, 1,753,355
Highest Point: Timms Hill, 1,951 feet

Animal: Badger
Bird: Robin
Fish: Muskellunge
Flower: Wood Violet (*Viola papilionacea*)
Fossil: Trilobite
Mineral: Galena
Motto: Forward

Foreword

Welcome to *Community Treasures of Wisconsin*. This book is a resource that can guide you to some of the best places in the State of Wisconsin, one of the most beautiful places in North America. Wisconsin is a state of great diversity, from cosmopolitan Milwaukee and Madison through the breathtaking, peaceful beauty of the north woods.

In 1634, Jean Nicolet of France became Wisconsin's first European explorer, landing near Green Bay. At that time, Chippewa, Ho-Chunk, Menominee, Sac and Fox lived in the area. Yankees were among the first non-Indian settlers to arrive, and New Yorkers brought the dairy industry to the territory. Wisconsin joined the Union in 1848 and massive immigration followed, including Germans but also Scandinavians, Irish, Poles and others. Many African Americans came in the 20th century. Today, Wisconsin continues to have one of America's strongest German heritages, but the state celebrates all of its many peoples with its world-famous ethnic festivals.

Wisconsin has a cultural scene well out of proportion to its population. Art, music and theater cluster in Madison, which is not only the state capital but the home of the University of Wisconsin, one of the most important academic institutions in the world. In Milwaukee, you must see the Milwaukee Art Museum, with its stunning architecture that is now a state emblem. Milwaukee's Summerfest is the world's largest music festival, according to *Guinness World Records*. Architect Frank Lloyd Wright was a Wisconsin native and his Taliesin studio remains a major draw. A different kind of attraction is Lambeau Field, home of the Green Bay Packers. And for thrills, nothing beats the EAA AirVenture Oshkosh air show.

In preparing this book, we talked to literally thousands of business people about their products, their services and their vision. We stayed at bed & breakfasts and dined at fine restaurants. We visited spas in the Lake Country, strolled galleries in Milwaukee and picked out trendy outfits in Lake Geneva. We rode the Ducks at Wisconsin Dells and inspected the trolls in Mt. Horeb. We ate hot dogs in Kenosha and celebrated cranberries in Warrens. You are holding the result of our efforts in your hands. *Community Treasures of Wisconsin* is a 502-page compilation of the best places in Wisconsin to eat, shop, play, explore, learn and relax. We did the legwork. All you have to do now is enjoy.

—Cindy Tilley Faubion

ALTOONA

The settlement of Altoona began in 1881 when the Chicago, St. Paul, Minneapolis and Omaha Railway selected the site for a new terminal to replace the overcrowded existing terminal in Eau Claire. Residents began moving into East Eau Claire in early 1882. However, confusion between the Eau Claire and East Eau Claire stations quickly caused the railroad to rename the new terminal Altoona. Altoona incorporated as a city in 1887. Continued growth in both Altoona and Eau Claire over the past century has left the two cities adjacent to one another. Altoona is bounded on the north by Lake Altoona and the picturesque Eau Claire River. The city is developing River Prairie, an exceptional mixed-use planned community on the Eau Claire.

PLACES TO GO

- Lake Altoona County Park
  Beach Road
  (715) 834-9042

THINGS TO DO

June

- Cinder City Days
  (715) 834-5671

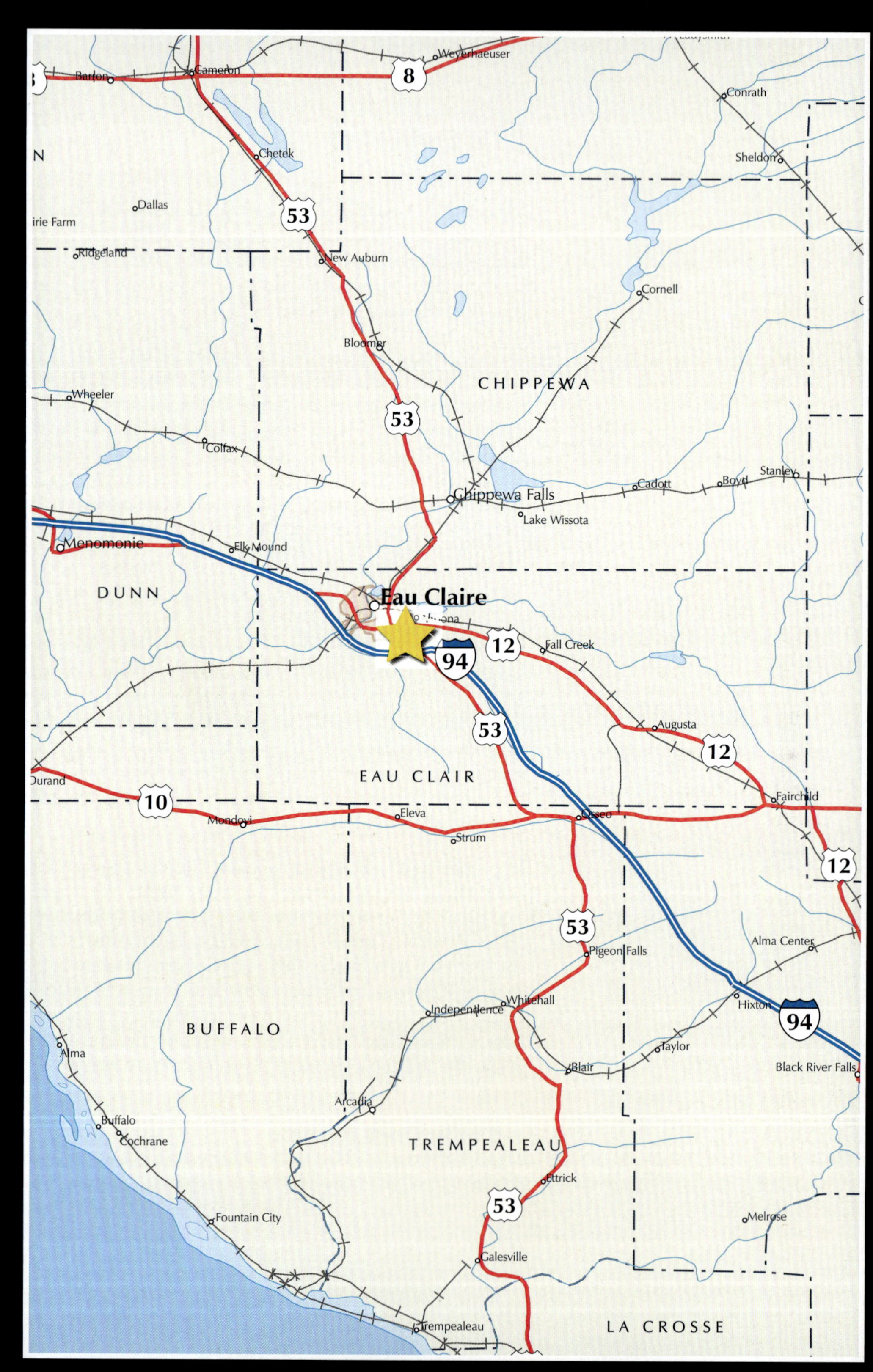

Eau Claire Golf & Country Club

RECREATION

If golf is your game, membership in the Eau Claire Golf & Country Club allows you to play a course known as one of the finest and most challenging in the upper Midwest. The course's history of championship play dates back to 1967, when it first hosted the Wisconsin State Open, and continues to the present. The Wisconsin State Senior Open was contested here in 2006, and the State Open will be held here in 2008. Club members also enjoy reciprocity with five other private courses in the region, as well as the benefit of using the state-of-the-art practice facility at Eau Claire. In fact, a golf membership entitles individuals and families to the full range of amenities that the club offers. That means not only tennis on lighted courts and a family-oriented swimming facility with hot tub, but dining privileges as well. A second category of membership includes all privileges except golf; a third offers dining privileges only. Dining at Eau Claire is a cause for celebration, thanks to Chef Casey Anderson, who lends his creative touch to such dinner entrées as pecan crusted pork chops, fresh pistachio sea scallops and a Sicilian vegetable strudel. Breakfast, lunch and catering services are also available. Consider a membership in the Eau Claire Golf & Country Club, bringing premier private club amenities to the Chippewa Valley since 1901.

828 Clubview Lane, Altoona WI
(715) 836-8420
www.ecgcc.com

BEAVER DAM

Midway between Madison, Milwaukee and the Fox River cities, Beaver Dam is on the shores of beautiful Beaver Dam Lake. The lake, more than 10 square miles in size, provides great fishing and recreational opportunities. Beaver Dam is home to 18 municipal parks, with several Dodge County Parks nearby. Parks along the lake contain fishing piers, boat ramps and picnic areas. The community is also home to the Beaver Dam Family Center and Ice Arena which hosts hockey and figure skating events for seven months out of the year.

PLACES TO GO

- Beaver Dam Family Center
  609 Gould Street
  (920) 885-5430
- Crystal Lake Park
  W8064 State Route 33
  (920) 885-9931
- Derge County Park
  N8379 County Road CP
  (920) 887-0365
- Dodge County
  Historical Society and Museum
  105 Park Avenue
  (920) 887-1266
- Swan City Park and Pool
  316 E South Street
  (920) 885-9781

THINGS TO DO

July

- Beaver Dam Lake Days
  www.beaverdamlakedays.com

August

- Dodge County Fair
  www.dodgecountyfairgrounds.com

September

- Oktoberfest
  (920) 887-8879

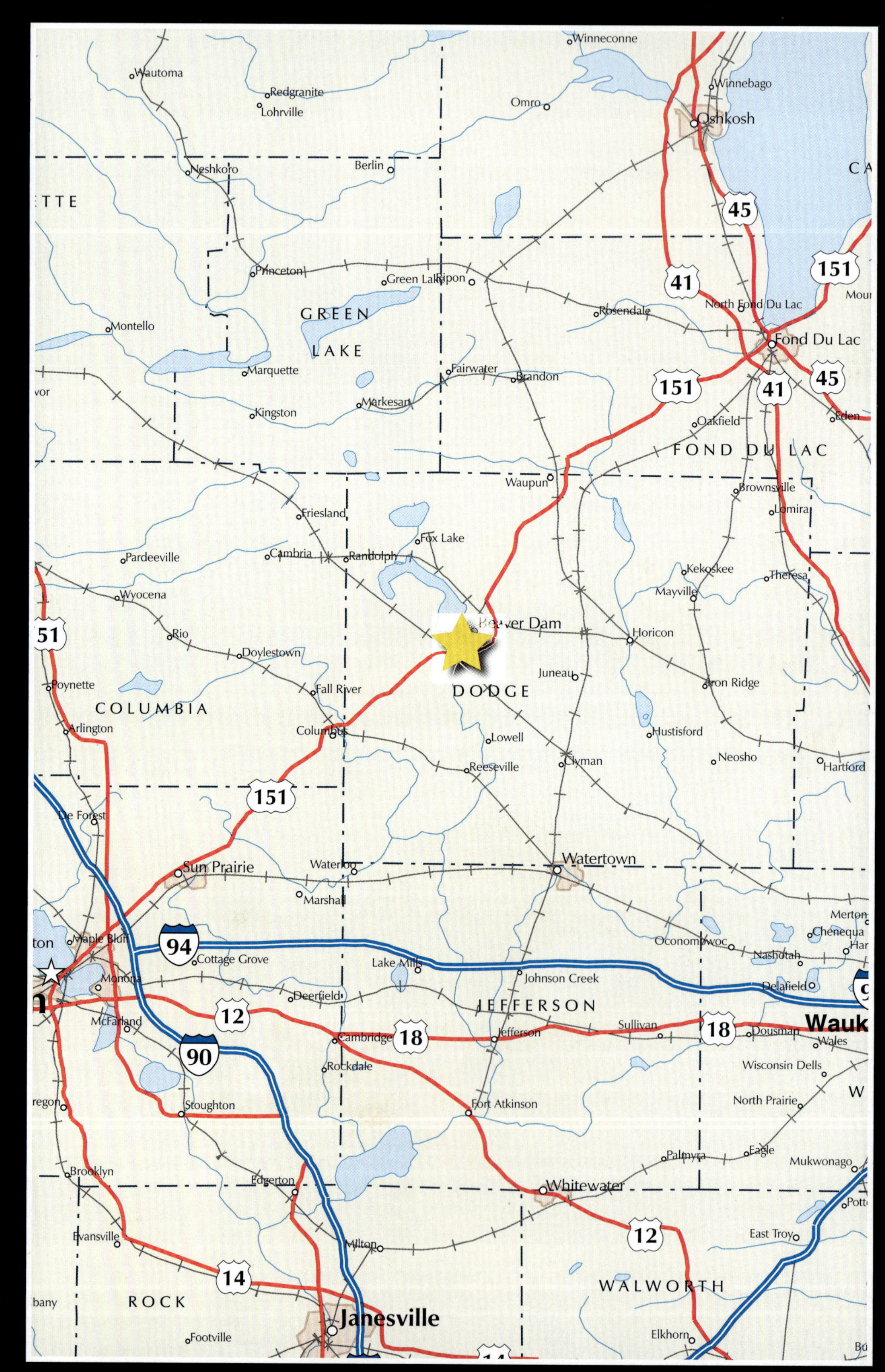

Nancy's Notions

ARTS & CRAFTS

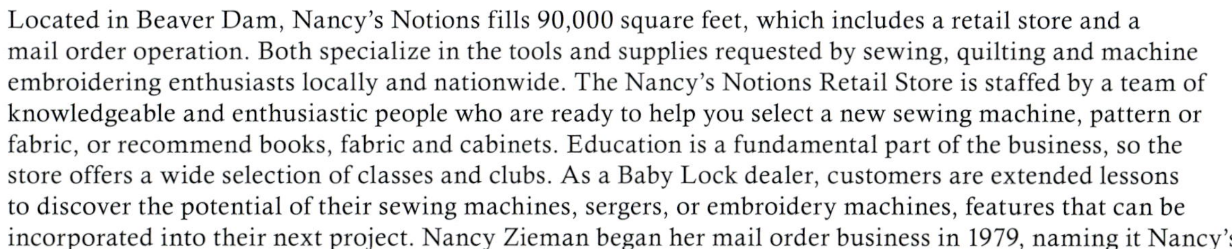

Located in Beaver Dam, Nancy's Notions fills 90,000 square feet, which includes a retail store and a mail order operation. Both specialize in the tools and supplies requested by sewing, quilting and machine embroidering enthusiasts locally and nationwide. The Nancy's Notions Retail Store is staffed by a team of knowledgeable and enthusiastic people who are ready to help you select a new sewing machine, pattern or fabric, or recommend books, fabric and cabinets. Education is a fundamental part of the business, so the store offers a wide selection of classes and clubs. As a Baby Lock dealer, customers are extended lessons to discover the potential of their sewing machines, sergers, or embroidery machines, features that can be incorporated into their next project. Nancy Zieman began her mail order business in 1979, naming it Nancy's Notions. Today, a Nancy's Notions Catalog is mailed monthly to 200,000 prospects and buyers. With an active web site as well, more than 7,000 products are available to customers. In 1982, Nancy started her television show, *Sewing with Nancy*. Now seen on 90 percent of public television Stations, on Create TV and web cast at www.quiltersnewsnetwork, this how-to program continues to demonstrate new techniques and products that make sewing, quilting and machine embroidery a rewarding occupation and hobby for millions. Nancy has authored many books. Her newest title is *Serge with Confidence,* published by Krause Books. For sewing inspiration, education, tools and more, visit Nancy's Notions.

333 Beichl Avenue, Beaver Dam WI
(800) 833-0690 (mail order) or (800) 725-0361 (retail store)
www.nancysnotions.com

Charter Raceway Park, Beaver Dam

ATTRACTIONS

Charter Raceway Park, Beaver Dam, a one-third mile banked oval track, is one of the best clay track facilities in the Midwest, boasting an average of 130 to 150 cars participating each week at this family-oriented venue. Well-known race car drivers, such as Tony Stewart, Kasey Kahn, Kenny Schrader and Steve Kinser, have competed at the Park. The Park draws drivers from all over the United States, Canada and other countries. Drivers have come to compete from as far away as Australia and Japan. Races take place every Saturday night with some specials on holidays and weekdays. Members of the Charter High-Speed Card promotion enjoy reduced rates, plus promotional and other incentives. Travelers are always welcome and overnight dry camping is free. Five regular weekly divisions along with special events make up the yearly schedule of events at the Park. Weekly divisions include Modifieds, Street Stocks, INEX Legends, Grand Nationals and the entry level, four-cylinder division of Dirt Devils. Special events at the Park include the World of Outlaw Sprints and Late Models, IRA Sprints, Badger Midgets, MSA Sprints and Mini-Sprints. Experience the action and excitement at Charter Raceway Park, Beaver Dam.

N7086 Raceway Road, Beaver Dam WI
(920) 887-1600
www.wismotorsports.net

Wayland Academy

BUSINESS & SERVICES

Wayland Academy is an independent, coeducational, college preparatory boarding and day school that fosters strong character and a lifelong love of learning. The Academy offers multiple leadership opportunities through participation in community service, athletics, extracurricular programs, student government, or even as a Senior Prefect, Wayland's highest student leadership position. Furthermore, Wayland's boarding environment fosters a sense of place and belonging and, thanks in part to the mentoring program, each pupil maintains close contact with a faculty member throughout his or her high school life. The ongoing alumni participation in events ranging from community service projects to reunion weekends demonstrates the fact that the Wayland experience remains with students long after they have left the campus. Within the Wayland family, character emerges alongside challenging and relevant academic discipline. With a high percentage of advanced degrees, the talented and inspiring faculty teach multiple honors and Advanced Placement classes along with creative curricula throughout the Liberal Arts education that makes the learning process rewarding from freshman to senior year. Meanwhile, Wayland's low student-to-faculty ratio allows students to get the one-on-one attention that they need. With the majority of the faculty living on or near campus, teachers are available to students at all hours of the day and night. The diverse and talented student body represents 12 states and 10 countries, and each year 100 percent of the graduating seniors receive acceptances to colleges across the nation. To prepare your student for excellence in college and beyond, contact Wayland Academy.

101 N University Avenue, Beaver Dam WI
(800) 860-7725 ***www.wayland.org***

Crystal Creek Dairy House

MARKETS & DELIS

Like many others who grew up near Beaver Dam, Lois Cramer first came to the Crystal Creek Dairy House on a school field trip many years ago. Now, Lois and her husband Bob, along with Roxanne Cramer, own this restaurant and dairy, known for its delicious cheese and ice cream. The dairy offers an extensive selection of cheeses, cheese spreads, sausages and other gourmet foods. One of the top sellers is the Wisconsin Blue, a semi-soft cheese with a rich, pungent flavor. The aged Cheddar, Colby and Swiss are popular choices. After visiting the dairy, stay for lunch or dinner at the on-site restaurant. Happy customers say the rich, creamy shakes made with homemade ice cream are the perfect complement to a burger and fries. Enjoy your meal on one of the three gazebos near the blooming flowers, one of Lois's other passions. The relaxing sound of running water in the background comes from Crystal Creek, the inspiration for the dairy's name. The dairy ships its delicious cheeses and other fine foods worldwide, so you can bring the taste of Wisconsin home with you. Come to Crystal Creek Dairy House for homemade cheese and ice cream in a fun and wholesome atmosphere.

W7790 Highway 33 E, Beaver Dam WI
(920) 887-2806

Bayside Supper Club

RESTAURANTS & CAFÉS

The Bayside Supper Club is your banquet specialist in Beaver Dam. The business is family owned and operated, and since 1988, Mike Kuzniewicz and his wife, Doreen, have taken pride in providing hands-on service aimed at quality and integrity. Their four sons all help out in the family business. The Supper Club's banquet facility has seating for as many as 450 people, and hosts many wedding and anniversary dinners, as well as fundraising banquets and charity events. Many local organizations schedule breakfast or dinner meetings at the Bayside. The house specialty is prime rib. On Friday, you can enjoy a chicken, fish and seafood buffet. On Sunday, come for brunch. The Supper Club also offers a full bar. The Kuzniewicz family contributes to the community by supporting local charities and service organizations. In particular, they support wildlife conservation efforts. Whether you have scheduled a special event or simply want a great meal, try the Bayside Supper Club.

W9231 County Highway G, Beaver Dam WI
(920) 887-0505

PLACES TO GO

- Dousman Stagecoach Inn Museum
  1075 Pilgrim Parkway
  (262) 782-4057
- Fox Brook County Park
  2925 N Barker Road
- Mitchell Park
  19900 River Road
- Sunset Playhouse
  800 N Elm Grove Road, Elm Grove
  (262) 782-4430
- Wilson Center for the Arts
  19805 W Capitol Drive
  (262) 781-9520
- Wirth Park
  2585 Pilgrim Road

THINGS TO DO

May
- Civil War Reenactment
  Dousman Stagecoach Inn
  (262) 782-4057

June
- Brookfield Days
  Mitchell Park
  (262) 789-7339

July
- 4th of July Celebration
  Mitchell Park
  (262) 796-6675

August
- Stonewood Village Art Fair
  (262) 538-3810

September
- Hidden River Art Festival
  Wilson Center for the Arts
  (262) 781-9470

December
- Christmas at the Inn
  Dousman Stagecoach Inn
  (262) 782-4057

BROOKFIELD AND ELM GROVE

Between 1850 and World War II, the Town of Brookfield remained a quiet agricultural community. The rural atmosphere attracted one notorious resident: Al Capone established a residence and distillery on Brookfield Road. A more respectable citizen, born in 1839, was Caroline Ingalls, mother of Laura Ingalls Wilder. After World War II, development in Brookfield took off, and the city was incorporated in 1954. Today, Brookfield covers almost 27 square miles, numbers 40,000 residents, and is a major business, retail and industrial hub. Brookfield's daytime population soars to more than 75,000 due to business activity within the city. The value of the real estate in Brookfield is the third-highest in the state, after only Milwaukee and Madison. You can take in a show at the Sharon Lynne Wilson Center for the Arts or catch a glimpse of the past at the Dousman Stagecoach Inn, a historic farmhouse and inn built in 1847. Brookfield entirely surrounds the pleasant village of Elm Grove, with which it shares a school district.

Mike Crivello's Camera Center

ARTS & CRAFTS

Longtime Milwaukee residents recognize and can probably sing the jingle: Mike Crivello's World, a Wonderful World of Cameras. Family owned, Mike Crivello's Camera Center first opened in 1969 and still supplies the latest in photographic equipment and services. The experienced and knowledgeable employees, all avid photographers, help customers select the right equipment and address their photographic concerns. The store provides basic services, such as in-house 35mm color processing and enlargements, E-6 processing and prints from digital media. Home ordering of prints from digital files is also available. Contact the store for your *free* software. Slide duplication, digital print restoration and slide generation for PowerPoint presentations are also available. Mike Crivello's can take care of specialized photographic needs, such as digital imaging services, film transfer and tape duplication. The shop has Kodak Image Centers for do-it-yourself prints or enlargements. The Brookfield superstore carries thousands of accessories, from camera bags to tripods and from filters to dark room supplies. For your convenience, Mike Crivello's also has locations in Whitefish Bay and Shorewood. Mike was a video photographer for Channel 12 television and won several Emmy awards before purchasing his first store. It is worth a trip to Brookfield to see what is in stock, including hard-to-find items no one else seems to have. The photographic industry is like a fast moving wave, and Mike Crivello's Camera and Imaging Centers is riding the crest. Mike invites you to hop on and join the fun.

18110 W Bluemound Road, Brookfield WI
(262) 782-4303 ***www.mikecrivellos.com***

Photo by Walter J. Roob

China Doll

ARTS & CRAFTS

Cynthia Guilette opened China Doll in 1988 and operated it while traveling extensively throughout the United States, Canada and Italy for more than eight years, teaching doll making along the way. Cynthia eventually returned home to stay and now offers her expertise in an inviting and hands-on atmosphere. Like most little girls, Cynthia loved dolls. Later in life, after learning the art of fine china painting, she began making porcelain dolls. Her delicate work soon gained popularity all over the country and shone in a one-woman show at the Rahr-West Art Museum in Manitowoc and other prominent venues. While Cynthia enjoys creating dolls, she loves sharing the art of doll making with others. China Doll offers classes and seminars on the finer points of doll making, as well as classes in hand-painted china. As a Doll Artisan Guild instructor, Cynthia offers outstanding education and uses Seeley products, a line of fine doll-making supplies. If you have ever experienced the panic of a child's favorite doll losing a limb or other malady, you know the value of the shop's doll hospital. Whether it is a Barbie or American Girl doll from today or one that children played with generations ago, the doll hospital can repair, clean and repaint it. Cynthia also offers appraisals, informing owners of the history and value of an individual doll. Come to China Doll and let Cynthia share her passion for doll making with you.

655 N Brookfield Road, Brookfield WI
(262) 787-1921

Eclectica and The Bead Studio

ARTS & CRAFTS

Irina Miech first became interested in beading and jewelry design while on a business trip in Morocco. Soon she was designing jewelry and selling it through galleries and museum shops, which led to opening her own store, Eclectica. Over the next sixteen years, Eclectica moved to its present location in the Galleria West Shopping Center and then proceeded to expand several times. It is now one of the largest bead stores in the United States, and houses a tremendous variety of beading supplies, including semi-precious stone, crystal and pearls from all over the world. In 2005, The Bead Studio opened next door to Eclectica. The Bead Studio is devoted to jewelry-making kits designed by Irina and features a large, well-lit workspace where customers can create jewelry of their own. The Bead Studio is also known for its Precious Metal Clay (PMC) workspace. PMC consists of small particles of fine silver or gold, suspended in an organic binder. When fired in a kiln, the organic binder burns away, revealing the beauty of fine silver. While experimenting with PMC, Irina immediately noticed its unique ability to capture the beauty of nature and she began developing her own style, with organic elements figuring prominently in her designs. She became a certified instructor and now teaches many classes in that medium. Irina has also authored two books, *Metal Clay for Beaders* and *More Metal Clay for Beaders*. Stop by Eclectica or The Bead Studio and peruse the phenomenal selection or visit them on the web.

18900 W Bluemound Road #148,
Brookfield WI
(262) 641-0910
www.eclecticabeads.com

Sharon Lynne Wilson Center for the Arts

ATTRACTIONS

The Sharon Lynne Wilson Center for the Arts is the leading venue for music, theater and the visual arts in western metropolitan Milwaukee. It also serves as a major resource for the Elmbrook public schools. The Wilson Center sits at the edge of the woods in Brookfield's Mitchell Park. The city of Brookfield provided the site, but all other resources were assembled through local fund-raising. The center, first conceived in 1993, became a reality in 2002. Thousands attended a grand dedication ceremony featuring the Milwaukee Symphony Orchestra and soprano Audra McDonald. This performance inaugurated the acoustically impressive Kuttemperoor Auditorium, with seating for 619. Each Wilson Center concert season includes an impressive slate of performances by top singers, dance troupes and jazz musicians. The Milwaukee Symphony Orchestra continues to perform regularly. Other performance spaces include a flexible Studio Theater with a 160-person capacity and the Gerlach Outdoor Theater, suitable for informal concerts or combined with the Studio Theater for indoor/outdoor events. A grand hall and multi-purpose studio add to the multi-purpose performance capabilities. Groups such as the Milwaukee Art Museum, Milwaukee Ballet Company and the Wisconsin Conservatory of Music conduct classes here. Students can attend a summer arts camp sponsored by these institutions. Paintings and sculptures are found throughout the building. The upper level Ploch Art Gallery provides exhibit and reception space. The diverse programming of the Wilson Center ensures your pleasure, whether you seek a matinee or a thrilling night out.

19805 W Capitol Drive, Brookfield WI
Box office: (262) 781-9520
Main phone: (262) 781-9470
www.wilson-center.com

Photo by Larry D'Attilio

Scotty's Car Care

AUTO

For more than 40 years, drivers have entrusted their cars to Scotty's Car Care for maintenance and repair. "Our number one priority is safety for your precious cargo," say owners John and Laurie Bluemel, who purchased the Brookfield business from the original owners in 2003. Though Scotty's began as a radiator and air conditioning service store, it has expanded into a full-service garage. Now, whether you need work on an engine or transmission, Scotty's is ready with quality parts and expert technicians to meet your needs. The highly trained technicians can also handle axle and brake issues, as well as providing care for your shocks, struts and exhaust systems. Scotty's is a fully equipped Firestone tire dealer. Customers appreciate the friendly and dependable staff as well as the cookies available for munching while they wait. Those bringing their vehicles to Scotty's for repairs are eligible for free local towing from Mayfair Towing, which is also owned by John and Laurie. Scotty's offers a free shuttle service to get you where you need to go while your vehicle is being repaired. "We service every vehicle as if it was our own," John says. Come to Scotty's Car Care, where you and your vehicle will be pampered like royalty.

12465 W Lisbon Road, Brookfield WI
(262) 781-2060

American Imports

AUTO

The owners and staff at American Imports in Brookfield know their customers as well as they know their Hondas, Toyotas, Mazdas and Nissans. They use their knowledge to bring you the kind of honest answers, affordable prices and quality auto repair that every car owner hopes to find. Yes, you can take any Asian import here for repair as well as some domestic cars and light trucks. Owner Jeff Jans and his wife, Cindy, concentrate on building strong relationships with their customers and ensuring that you deal with the same person throughout your experience. "We will fix it right the first time and on time," says Jeff. Established in 1998, American Imports, with its eight-year record as an AAA approved shop, offers ASE-certified mechanics who use the latest diagnostic equipment. This full-service facility can handle everything from an oil change to major engine repair. "We're here to help people," says Jeff, who believes in bringing his Christian values into his family business. American Imports offers 24-hour towing, fleet service discounts and special financing that allows you to pay for your repairs in 90 days without incurring an interest charge. You can even use a free loaner car while your car is being fixed. The folks at American Imports provide a 100 percent guarantee on all services. For Automotive Repair by People Who Care, come to American Imports.

4225 N 124th Street, Brookfield WI
(262) 783-5020
www.americanimportsautorepair.com

Sunshine Adoption Inc.

BUSINESS & SERVICES

The adoption specialists at Sunshine Adoption are experts in international adoptions. They match children in need of loving homes with families in need of children to love. After their adoption of Anya from a Russian orphanage, Steven and Aimee Klundt were so moved by the plight of the children left behind that they responded by starting Sunshine Adoption in Elm Grove, a charitable organization and a Wisconsin-state licensed child placement agency. Sunshine has helped many Wisconsin families complete their adoptions of children from Russia, Ukraine, Kazakhstan, Guatemala, Colombia and China. Children from Nepal, India, Brazil and Taiwan will soon be added to this list. Sunshine's staff and social workers help families with paperwork, travel, translation and post-adoption services. Sunshine Adoption also provides direct assistance to children in orphanages as they await adoption. Funding for the agency comes from client fees and private grants and donations. Sunshine considers all applicants, regardless of financial concerns. In fact, Sunshine can suggest resources that aid in defraying adoption-related expenses. If you are prepared to add a child to your family, contact Sunshine Adoption to help you get the process started.

910 Elm Grove Road, Suite 34, Elm Grove WI
(262) 796-9898
www.sunshineadoption.org

Woller-Anger & Company, LLC

BUSINESS & SERVICES

Does looking for the best insurance policy to fit your needs bring on bouts of frustration and anxiety? When you want an insurance advisor who is working for your benefit, consider Woller-Anger & Company, an independent insurance agency started in 1984 by Ervin C. Woller, Jr. and Robert M. Anger. From the beginning and through the development of specialized departments, Woller-Anger clients have enjoyed the best possible combination of ideas, current knowledge and technology to meet individual needs. Clients have access to an impressive array of financially strong, reputable insurance companies and a staff of insurance professionals to serve them. All of the agency's service representatives are licensed insurance agents, committed to prompt and efficient handling of questions or claims. The Woller-Anger team participates in continuing education programs as well as in-house training. You can have confidence in your relationship, knowing that agents at Woller-Anger do not work for a single insurance company—they work for you. The insurance experts at Woller-Anger want to provide you the best insurance value possible. To do this, they identify the risks you face, and then tailor a risk management program to your individual needs. The company is proud of its achievements, including such awards as the 2005 Presidential Award from the West Bend Mutual Insurance Company. Keep your calm while the team at Woller-Anger & Company finds the right insurance policies for you.

930 Elm Grove Road, Elm Grove WI
(262) 789-2500
www.wolleranger.com

Majesty Mortgage

BUSINESS & SERVICES

Do you want to buy a home, but feel overwhelmed by the loan process, the small print, the risk? David, Nick and Jim MacCudden of family-owned Majesty Mortgage want to help. With more than 60 years combined experience in residential and commercial lending, the MacCuddens know and serve all of Wisconsin. Focusing on the relationship between the client and the lenders is their priority as they search for a specific solution for each mortgage situation. Services here include closings that are stress-free with guaranteed costs and no surprises or unexpected fees. The MacCuddens' access to more than 60 different lenders allows them to find the lowest interest rates for you and to close on loans in a fast and efficient manner. The MacCuddens use their extensive resources and experience to find you the best opportunity. They are comfortable with the full range of financing needs, so you can rest assured that new homes, first homes and refinancing are transactions they know well. Weekly updates from start to finish keep customers apprised of every aspect of their loan process. Ninety percent of the MacCuddens' business is based on referrals from satisfied customers. David, Nick and Jim want your loan process to be the most relaxed part of your purchasing transaction. Give them a call, and put a team of experts to work for you.

740 Pilgrim Way, Suite 102, Elm Grove WI
(262) 785-1363
www.majestymortgage.com

WhimsiKidz Inc

FASHION

"Because there's no excuse not to be cute"—that's the motto Heidi Swan-Mikich uses for her winsome boutique and salon, WhimsiKidz, Inc. Heidi, a hair stylist of 21 years, opened this favored Elm Grove children's boutique in 2000 with the help of her husband, Tom. Heidi's family has owned Swan Interiors, a community landmark, for more than 60 years, and the customer-focused, service-driven attitude she learned there has followed her to her new enterprise, where she dedicates herself to complete customer satisfaction. Whimsikidz, Inc. offers a full line of children's clothing, including heirloom quality baptismal and communion wear. The boutique further offers big brother and big sister gifts, diaper bags and baby accessories, along with puppets, toys and an array of books and puzzles. In the salon, Cuts for Kidz, young visitors find child-sized chairs, engaging videos and whimsical capes and décor. Each member of the salon's talented style team has been exclusively cutting children's hair for a minimum of seven years, and the team focuses on making kids feel happy and relaxed while they're receiving a terrific hair cut that is perfect for their personalities and lifestyles. To help moms with their own styling abilities, the salon offers *Hair-do* workshops. New classes are formed regularly. WhimsiKidz and its employees assist with fundraising fashion shows for community schools and charity organizations and provide haircuts for patients at the Children's Hospital. Cuts for Kidz welcomes children who are wheelchair bound or have other special needs. Let your child's cute side come out with a trip to WhimsiKidz.

12898 W Bluemound Road, Elm Grove WI
(262) 785-9012
www.whimsikidz.com

Church & Chapel Funeral Service

BUSINESS & SERVICES

More and more families in the metropolitan Milwaukee area have come to trust Church & Chapel Funeral Service to make final arrangements for their loved ones. Ted and Pam Larsen, owners of Church and Chapel Funeral Service, believe that families need to feel comfortable with all aspects of funeral arrangements, which is why Church & Chapel will help you make arrangements from the privacy of your own home or church. As the Church & Chapel name suggests, you may use the church or chapel of your choice for funeral services. The caring, professional staff at Church & Chapel can make either burial or cremation arrangements without unnecessary expenses. In many cases, the charges run nearly half of what you might expect to pay. The business got its start arranging for funeral services at nursing homes, cemetery chapels and other venues. As their business grew, the Larsens realized that Church & Chapel needed to have its own funeral homes, and they now have seven convenient locations in the metro area. The staff at Church & Chapel recommends preplanning. This allows individuals to make their own decisions and spares family members from decision-making during a difficult time. Offering funeral services is a family tradition for the Larsens. Ted's father and uncle were funeral directors, and he has a brother in the profession as well. For sensitive, thorough arrangements, consult Church & Chapel Funeral Service.

1875 N Calhoun Road, Brookfield WI
(262) 827-0659 (Milwaukee) or (262) 549-0659 (Waukesha)
http://churchandchapel.com

Heritage Printing

BUSINESS & SERVICES

Heritage Printing is one of the largest independent printing companies in the United States. Their focus is on short run, full-color printing and mailing/fulfillment services. A business-to-business company, a significant part of their work comes from producing marketing materials for corporations throughout Southeastern Wisconsin. Owner Terry Tarillion and Executive Vice President Bob Wendt have developed the experience needed to produce the highest quality products. Terry opened Heritage Printing at the start of the trend toward short run printing, his company being one of the first in Milwaukee to provide such service. Many of the employees have been with the company for more than 20 years, and the entire staff at Heritage Printing strives to provide exceptional customer service. Heritage Printing is completely digital and is housed in a beautiful new facility. It has received several industry awards for printing quality. Recognizing the latest trends in business needs, Heritage Printing has branched out into developing web applications for businesses that want to order printing over the Internet. For a superior communications resource to help your business, visit Heritage Printing, where the high quality work makes it a true community treasure.

3575 N 124th Street, Brookfield WI
(262) 790-5000
www.clickheritage.com

Suiters Distinctive Clothiers

FASHION

Suiters Distinctive Clothiers is the best men's clothing store in the region. Owner Bruce Magnuson and President Perry Newsom have taken 5,000 square feet of space inside the Brookfield Towne Centre and created an immaculate display of exquisite and distinctive menswear that is quite unlike anything most men have experienced. When you enter, you will think you are at a men's club. You will notice seating in front of a fireplace. You will be offered either coffee or a glass of wine. You can watch a game on their large screen television. The vintage, black-and-white photos of Hollywood stars dressed in their finest attire are designed to inspire your fashion sense. The goal at Suiters is to be the best men's store in the Midwest. With lines such as Canali, Paul & Shark, Hart Schaffner Marx and the new collection by David Chu, Suiters lives up to that goal. Suiters features high-quality suits, a large selection of sportswear and a shoe department. If they don't have what you need in stock, they will place special orders. Whether you're looking for business casual, boardroom executive, or stylish sportswear, this elegant store is your place. For a relaxing shopping experience that will send you home in style, visit Suiters Distinctive Clothiers.

3885 N Brookfield Road, Brookfield WI
(262) 754-2801
www.suiterslimited.com

Mio Bella

GALLERIES & FINE ART

Take home original art and the story behind the art at Brookfield's Mio Bella, a store designed to mimic the look and feel of an art festival. Owners Laura Staton and Julia Jaegersberg enjoyed attending art festivals together during their years in the advertising business. They opened the store in 2004, marrying their love of art and their shared marketing backgrounds. The store's name, meaning "my beautiful" in Italian, was inspired by the name Isabella, a name belonging to both of their daughters. Mio Bella features an array of original art from artists in Wisconsin and beyond. The store is a sensory delight with art hanging from walls and ceilings and gracing the floors. Besides paintings and sculpture, the shopper will find gallery-quality selections of touchable objects. Look for hand-blown lamps, jewelry, fiber art and handbags. Check out the government chop marks on antique furniture from northern China. A friend goes to Asia to hand-select these one-of-a-kind pieces for the store. Mio Bella stocks inventory in a variety of price ranges in hopes of helping a broad range of customers put art in their lives. This is a great place to pick up a ready-to-go gift with artistic packaging or to browse in the exciting atmosphere while enjoying bottled water and cookies. Take time to read the biographies of the artists, and take home an artist profile with each purchase at Mio Bella, where every day is an art festival.

18905 W Capitol Drive,
Brookfield WI
(262) 781-6707
www.miobella.net

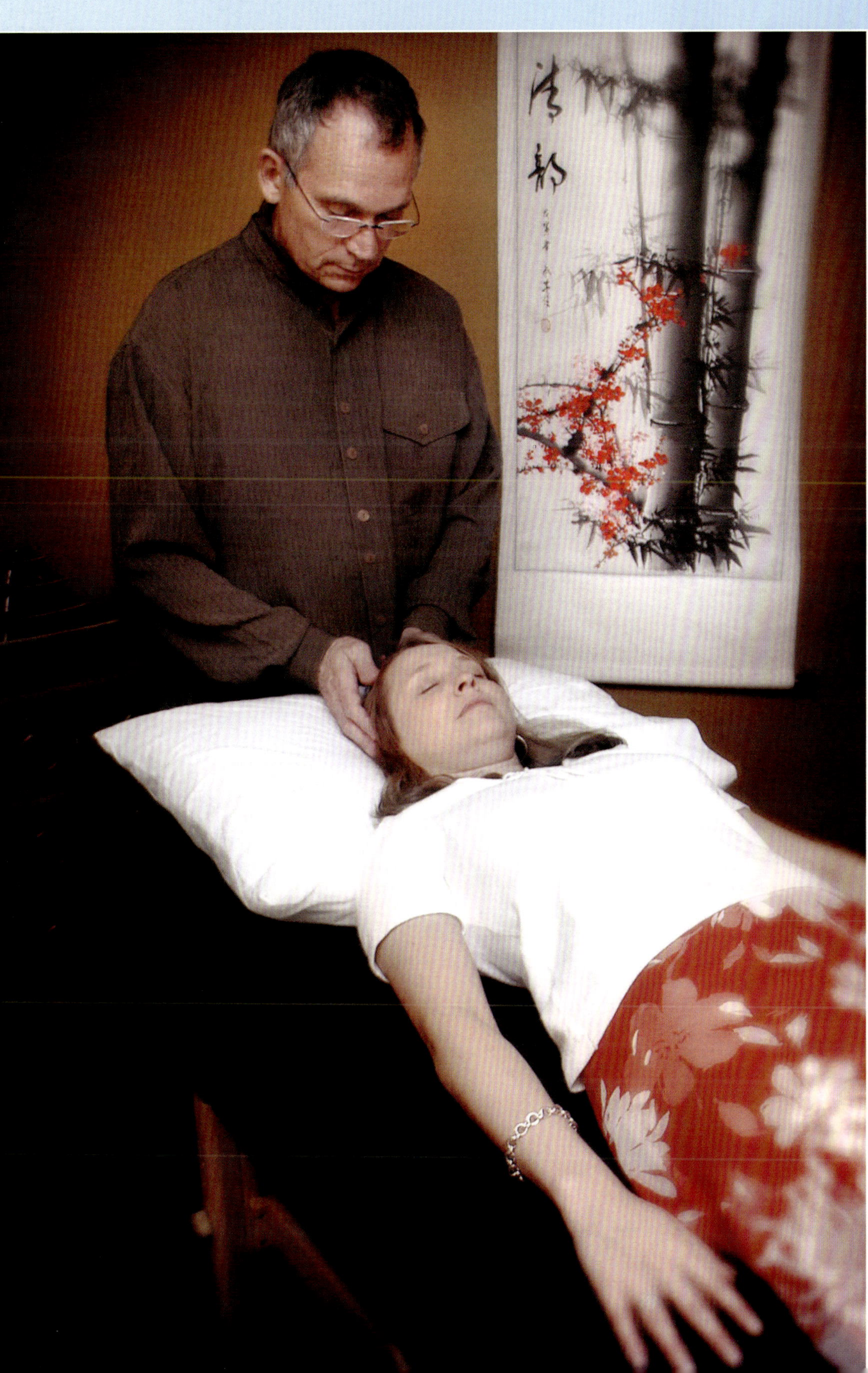

Kindo Integrated Health Center

HEALTH & BEAUTY

Acupuncture is a 3,000-year-old proven Asian therapy. Digital Infrared Thermal Imaging is a cutting-edge diagnostic tool that provides thermal pictures of inflammation, the precursor to disease. When used together, as they are at Kindo Integrated Health Center in Elm Grove, this ancient method and modern technology guide the body into harmony so that symptoms resolve naturally. More than 70,000 patients have been treated at Kindo—people come from near and far to find relief here from back pain, arthritis and many other ailments. In addition to acupuncture, the doctors at Kindo practice low level laser therapy, a modern needle-less approach to acupuncture. They perform acupressure and assist patients with stretching and joint mobilization. They also administer Chinese herbal formulas that are based on a 5,000-year-old system of healing. Chinese medicine has treated more people on the planet than all other forms of medicine combined. Besides being a leader in patient treatment, Kindo is also a training facility, where students come to be taught by founder Arthur Rapkin, Doctor of Oriental Medicine. Dr. Rapkin has 20 years of experience and is regarded as one of the leading acupuncturists in the United States. For freedom from pain with little to no side effects, consider treatment at Kindo Integrated Health Center.

890 Elm Grove Road, Elm Grove WI
(262) 827-4000
www.kindocenter.com

Salon Nouveaux

HEALTH & BEAUTY

Robert and Colette Kowalik met when she was his stylist at a premier salon in Wisconsin. In 2002, they purchased Salon Nouveaux and transformed it into an Aveda Concept Salon and Spa. Salon Nouveaux strictly adheres to the Aveda philosophy, providing a complete sensory experience utilizing the best products on earth. The Salon Nouveaux approach is very personal and comprehensive. Its focus is to create beautiful images, one face at a time. A beverage is served while you wait for your appointment. Essential oils, aromatherapy and massage are employed to create a sense of complete well-being. One of the services offered by Salon Nouveaux is the Private Affair bridal service, which allows an entire bridal party to reserve the salon and all its services. For parties of four or more, Colette will close the entire salon to focus on you and your guests. Start the most important day of your life with the attention you deserve. The salon will be open to your family, friends or photographers. Colette will focus on all details and cater the event to make it an experience fit for a bride. For young girls, the Princess Party lets girls experience an updo, while teaching them about appropriate makeup use and the development of positive self-image. As a community service, Salon Nouveaux participates in the Locks of Love program, which donates hair to provide wigs for children suffering from rare diseases. Also, the salon works with local women's shelters to help those in need. Immerse yourself in the Aveda beauty concept and the personal attention of Salon Nouveaux. Call today and experience the difference.

21075 Swenson Drive, Brookfield WI
(262) 798-1090
www.salon-nouveaux.net

Barstool Central

HOME & GARDEN

When you've narrowed your shopping focus to barstools, come to the folks who open up a world of barstool options. Family owned, Barstool Central represents several manufacturers and has more than 300 barstools on display. Owners Ruth and Tom Stout and their friendly staff can assist with finishes and fabrics, stool heights or space constraints. Bring in samples of your countertops, flooring, tiles and paint colors, and they will help you find stools to complement your décor. Each manufacturer has different metal finishes and fabric choices, and some can upholster stools with a customer's own fabric. The light and spacious showroom displays stools ranging from casual to formal and modern to vintage. Current trends feature metal finishes that coordinate with the woods in your home. The Stouts' personal favorite is the swivel stool that allows you to eat, entertain or watch television without leaving your seat at the bar. The showroom's individual vignettes help customers visualize an overall decorating scheme. Ruth and Tom want customers to be happy with their choices, so they will allow you to try out a stool at home. Barstool Central has opened its inventory to include pub tables, bars, wall art and wine accessories. Stop by Barstool Central and see what this family owned store can do to enhance your home's entertainment options.

13665 W Capitol Drive, Brookfield WI
(262) 754-8989
www.barstoolcentral.com

Bazaar Home Decorating Center

HOME & GARDEN

Let Bazaar Home Decorating Center in Brookfield make your interior design dreams come true. Bazaar Home Decorating Center was founded in 1969 by Al and Alice Anheuser and is currently owned and operated by son Tom. Al, who worked for a fabric mill, started the business as an outlet selling remnants and eventually transformed it into the area's premiere destination for fine drapery and upholstery fabrics. For over 30 years this service-driven business has been Waukesha County's prime resource for decorator fabrics, window treatments and decorating accessories. Bazaar can create custom window treatments and bedding products for your home or help you select custom wood blinds, cellular shades and other desirable window treatments. Bazaar Home Decorating Center's professional design team, with more than 30 years combined experience in the field, can come to your home or office and assist you in choosing the designs and fabrics best suited to your interior. Additionally, the company's install team, which boasts more than 40 years of combined experience, is on hand to complete your order with timely and professional services. Beyond customization services and designer fabrics and services, Bazaar also carries some unusual accessory pieces, including mirrors and clocks, to further turn your decorating fantasies into vivid reality. Bazaar's focus on providing superior services at affordable prices has earned it an unsurpassed reputation for excellence. Shop where the designers shop and experience stress-free decorating with a visit to Bazaar Home Decorating Center.

21950 Watertown Road, Brookfield WI
(262) 784-2448
www.bazaarhdc.com

Design Resource Center

HOME & GARDEN

Jolene Steigerwald developed Design Resource Center because she was missing a centralized location for gathering samples and swatches when she was starting her design business 18 years ago. Her one-store-one-source concept has blossomed, bringing together all the materials and consultants needed for any interior or exterior remodel or new construction project. The lower level houses samples of materials used in the design and building process. The upper floor features lighting, furniture and rugs, along with art and accessories. Interior design is Jolene's passion, and she is always on the cutting edge of new developments in the industry. Very involved with the community, she serves on the board of interior design for a local technical college. She also teaches and continuously advances her own education in the interior design field. Her focus on personalizing each individual's home and on complete customer satisfaction has led to a business based mainly on referrals. With 10 skilled designers on staff who specialize in everything from flooring to window treatments and florals, Design Resource Center and Jolene's bed and bath store, European Comforts, have the resources you need to turn your home into a magnificent reflection of your tastes and lifestyle.

890 Elm Grove Road, Elm Grove WI
(262) 797-7883
www.drcdesign.com

P.M. Bedroom Gallery

HOME & GARDEN

All of us are familiar with the American Dream, of those shining stars among us who visualize a goal and strive toward success with single-minded determination. P. M. Bedroom Gallery, which was envisioned by brothers Arvid and Ben Huth in 1993, is the fulfillment of such a dream. The two farm-raised brothers sold seven cows and two snowmobiles, in addition to borrowing $10,000 from their parents, before heading off to the big city of Milwaukee, where on July 31, 1993, they hoisted their first Open-for-Business sign and began a legacy of exceptional quality and service that remains unmatched today. P.M. Bedroom Gallery offers more than 200 unique bedroom sets and is the largest bedroom furniture store in the nation. Here you can find numerous options that will allow you to customize the bedroom set of your dreams. P.M. Bedroom Gallery carries only American made furniture; 90 percent of its inventory is made in Wisconsin, and all items have been masterfully crafted to last for generations. When selecting a piece, customers often have the option of customizing what type of wood is used, which stain color they would like and what type of handles best suit their taste. Additionally, many pieces have secret compartments built in, and some beds can accommodate drawer storage. P.M. Bedroom Gallery also offers a multitude of accessories, including lamps and accent pieces, along with private label mattresses. Create the bedroom of your dreams, with furniture that will last a lifetime, at P.M. Bedroom Gallery.

17300 W Bluemound Road, Brookfield WI
(262) 827-9464
8380 W Layton Avenue, Greenfield WI
(414) 425-8888
www.pmbedroomgallery.com

Brookfield Gardens Assisted Living

LIFESTYLE DESTINATIONS

Brookfield Gardens Assisted Living offers more than just a beautiful place to live. It provides compassionate and quality care for older adults and is licensed by the State of Wisconsin as a Community Based Residential Facility (CBRF). The staff recognizes how difficult it is to move away from home and the facility provides space for residents to embrace their independence and individuality so they can make a seamless transition to the Brookfield community. The friendly, cheery indoor and outdoor environments invite relaxation and enjoyment. Residents enjoy private suites tucked into a neighborhood setting and surrounded by comfortable gathering rooms, intimate dining rooms and cozy spas. Social gatherings and outings introduce residents to new friends through music, laughter and fellowship. Brookfield encourages residents to participate in daily events as well as special celebrations. The Brookfield Gardens staff is trained to support a lifestyle of wellness and enrichment in a friendly environment. Safety and security are the top priorities at Brookfield Gardens and a registered nurse is onsite Monday through Friday from 8 am to 9 pm, and is on call 24 hours a day. Most importantly, staff members want residents to feel happy in their new surroundings and to live as comfortably and independently as possible. Brookfield Gardens Assisted Living invites you to a carefree community with all the comforts of home.

660 Woelfel Road, Brookfield WI
(262) 789-7499
www.brookfieldgardens.com

Angelina's Deli

MARKETS & DELIS

Named in honor of the Floryance family's great cook, Grandma Angelina, Angelina's Deli is where Brookfield's gourmet cooks and gourmet lovers turn for the foods of the Mediterranean. Imported olive oils and tahini spreads from Greece join Italian pastas and amaretti cookies from Italy and fresh Italian bread from Milwaukee. Lunchtime favorites here include tasty hot and cold subs made on freshly baked rolls, salads, lasagnas and avancini rice balls, filled with cheeses, mushrooms or beef. Angelina's is a family affair, opened by Jerry Floryance, Sr. and his son Peter in 1997. Jerry's wife, Carol, son Gerry, Jr. and daughter Paula also help out in the store, which is open seven days a week. Jerry Sr. started in the food business while still attending college. He worked as a manager for Herb Kohl and another deli before opening Angelina's. He strives for freshness and fair prices and sets a standard that keeps customers returning for such specialties as the Friday carry-out fish fry, a traditional Christmas lasagna with spicy Italian sausage and Sunday's Slovenian sausage, from Angelina's recipe. Dessert is another deli specialty, and Angelina's on-site bakery concocts totally tempting cannoli, tiramisu, cookies and pies. Customers can eat in, take out or have food and party trays delivered. *Milwaukee Magazine* readers knew a good thing when they voted Angelina's Deli as the best new deli with Italian flair in the western suburbs. Angelina's family invites you to come and enjoy the family atmosphere and many delicacies at Angelina's Deli.

15655 W North Avenue, Brookfield WI (262) 938-9038

Brookfield Hills Golf Course

RECREATION & FITNESS

Just 15 minutes west of Milwaukee lies the challenging 18-hole Brookfield Hills Golf Course. This par-62 executive course is open to the public, and local residents know it as a fun gathering place. With quality conditions and greens that are manicured to country club standards, this course offers both 9-hole and 18-hole games. Long tee boxes and large greens make the course appealing to all levels of players. If you're looking for practice, take advantage of the pitching and putting greens. You'll find electric carts, club rentals and pull carts. Senior citizen rates apply before 3 p.m. Monday through Friday. You can be assured of your tee time with an advance reservation. Whether you are interested in a league, outing play or a round of golf after work, Brookfield Hills is prepared to meet your needs. Leon Storm has owned and operated this quality course for 35 years. Along with his children and partners, he guarantees a golfing experience that will leave you hungry for return visits. The clubhouse will keep you supplied with free coffee every morning and other liquid refreshments throughout the day. Visit Brookfield Hills, where the play is challenging and the access, just two blocks south of Brookfield Square Mall, is convenient.

16075 Pinehurst Drive, Brookfield WI
(262) 782-0885
www.brookfieldhillsgolfcourse.com

YogAsylum Inc

RECREATION & FITNESS

YogAsylum is the end result of great intention, conscious planning and a love of life. Practices here support personal growth, health and well-being—elements that owner Pam Bliss thoroughly considered when she created the center. Pam developed a strong vision for a functional space suited to healing practices. She applied the design principles of feng shui, along with eco-friendly materials and soundproofing, to promote a harmonious environment. A staff of professional, accredited instructors with international training inspires students to move along their own personal paths, using practices that benefit mind, body and spirit. YogAsylum brings together the community with classes, workshops, energy work and bodywork. The facility offers a boutique and hosts concerts and lectures. Choices for personal growth include a full range of yoga and exercise systems, as well as meditation and reiki, a Japanese system for enlightenment and hand-on healing. Yoga classes are appropriate for children as young as four and adults of any age. YogAsylum even hosts yoga birthday parties for kids. Various class configurations suit people with different interests and expertise. For an enriching experience, come home to YogAsylum.

3815 N Brookfield Road, Suite 101, Brookfield WI
(262) 781-8102

Elite Fitness and Racquet Clubs

RECREATION & FITNESS

Elite Fitness and Racquet Clubs are just what you need for your journey to health. Once you get acquainted with the four first-rate facilities, the only question that remains is which club to join. With two clubs in Brookfield, one in Glendale and one in Mequon, convenience is assured. If your travels require a choice of locales, you can join all four clubs with a Passport membership. After managing a club for 12 years, Elite's owner, Kay Yuppek, decided that it was time to begin her own venture. Her vision for Elite Fitness is in the letters of the name: E = Energy, L=Living it, I=Innovation, T=Teaching it, and E= Excellence. Elite's commitment to its membership is evident in its staff of educated and certified professionals, its competitive and social events and its emphasis on fitness as a way of life. As an involved local owner, Kay seeks comfort, safety and convenience at each facility. You'll find biomechanically correct equipment, a basketball court based on a design by Harvard University psychologists and a lap pool free of chlorine. You don't have to know a sport to give it a try with Elite's many lesson options. Children start their journey to health and fitness here with supervised activities and instruction, parties, child size fitness equipment, summer camps and day care. Kay and her husband, Richard, invite you to try any of the Elite clubs. They promise that their clubs are so outstanding that they can only be compared to each other.

600 N Barker Road, Brookfield WI
(262) 786-3330
www.eliteclubs.com

Western Racquet Club

RECREATION & FITNESS

With 14 outdoor tennis courts and excellent swimming, dining and fitness facilities, Western Racquet Club is a love match for families and individuals looking for a private club. The club, located on 16 beautiful acres in Elm Grove, opened in 1960, with the goal of providing top-notch tennis and swimming. The club features 14 outdoor tennis courts, including three clay courts and three championship style courts. You'll also find several indoor courts here. The junior tennis program includes many of the state's top ranked junior players. The club's Olympic-size swimming pool is the site of many organized events, including a summer children's swim program and group and private swimming lessons. The club also forms teams in water polo, diving and synchronized swimming. To keep you in tip-top shape for your sport, the racquet club offers an up-to-date fitness center with classes in yoga, Pilates and weight training. You can ease sore muscles with a massage, whirlpool bath or a trip to the sauna. Both the locker rooms and the clubhouse have recently been renovated. Club members enjoy dining in the club's formal and casual dining rooms, where cuisine is prepared by an award winning chef. Parents appreciate the nursery and childcare facilities here as well as the friendly and knowledgeable staff. For a private club experience geared toward families, come to Western Racquet Club. You will experience the difference.

1800 Highland Drive, Elm Grove WI
(262) 786-7060
www.westernracquetclub.com

B & G Golf, Bowling & Racket Sports

RECREATION & FITNESS

For almost 50 years, three generations of the Storts family has been developing personal relationships with customers at B & G Golf, Bowling & Racket Sports. They know the games you play, the equipment you need and the services you value most, which accounts for B & G's four locations—two in Brookfield, one in Delafield and one in Mequon. This full-service sporting goods retailer carries hundreds of golf clubs and golf bags. Browsers can try out the clubs in the golf club fitting area before they buy. The staff will professionally fit all equipment to each customer to assure every individual gets the greatest enjoyment possible from their golf game. You can also arrange for private lessons with a PGA professional. For those who prefer tennis, racquetball or bowling, B & G is ready with necessary equipment and special ordering. B & G can fit you with a racquet that delivers power without wrist fatigue. You could set up the better part of a bowling alley or be the envy of your bowling league with equipment from B & G. Name-brand apparel, shoes and every conceivable accessory fill the B & G shelves. B & G also provides repair services for your sporting equipment. When you need sporting equipment or advice, visit the experts at B & G Golf, Bowling & Racket Sports.

19035 W Bluemound Road, Brookfield WI
(262) 782-2201
www.bggolf.com

Saffron Indian Bistro

RESTAURANTS & CAFÉS

If you want to take a culinary journey through India, then Saffron Indian Bistro is the place to go. After Dr. Kailas helped a friend expand his Indian restaurant, he realized that this was exactly the business he wanted to operate himself. So, he purchased Saffron Indian Bistro in 2005. In the short time since opening, the Saffron Bistro has already earned a 25 out of 30 star rating from Zagat Survey. Saffron Indian Bistro has also been rated as one of the top 30 restaurants in Milwaukee by Dennis Getto, a renowned restaurant critic, who rated the restaurant three and half out of four stars in June 2006. One of the many keys to Kailas' success is his unusual use of spices, especially the expensive and rare saffron. The pungent smell of saffron, ginger and curry suffuse this beautiful restaurant. The elegant dining room with handmade silk tapestries on the walls and silk Indian linens on the tables envelops you in its exotic décor. Saffron Indian Bistro offers a divinely delicious Indian menu, authentically prepared right down to the use of their clay tandoori oven. The lamb, poultry, seafood and rabbit selections are delectable choices, served with 10 different varieties of Indian breads. If you are vegetarian, never fear; a full vegetarian menu is also available, made to your specifications. You will even find a saffron flavored ice cream for dessert. Save yourself the airfare and spend a truly elegant evening in India sampling this ancient culture's exquisite food and heritage.

17395 W Bluemound Road, Brookfield WI
(262) 784-1332

goo goo gaa gaa

SHOPPING

Getting ready for a new baby has changed over the past few years, with many parents wanting more stylish apparel and luxurious surroundings for their new arrival. Goo goo gaa gaa has become a destination store for all of Southeastern Wisconsin and Northern Illinois. Tom and Ginny Gerczak opened the store to fill a void in the children's marketplace in Milwaukee. They decided on the store's catchy name after running across the phrase while reading to their children. Infants will goo goo and parents will go gaa gaa over the distinctive small-size fashions from the store. Styles range from right-off-the-runway coordinates, precious layette wear and glitzy yet sweet toddler clothes in sizes up to 6X for boys and girls. Christening and special occasion wear are also featured. Dress up the baby's room with distinctive furniture, crib bedding and linens, and accessories. Cozy slip-covered chairs are available for those late nights in the nursery. The inviting shop has play area for children, which makes the shopping more fun for kids and less stressful for adults. The store offers creative specialty toys that your youngsters will adore. Create your dream nursery or find the perfect shower gift at goo goo gaa gaa. It has a fabulous baby-loving staff to assist you who will gladly wrap your purchase in signature complimentary gift wrap.

18905 W Capitol Drive, Brookfield WI
(262) 790-6890
www.googoogaagaa.com

Kubichek Office Products

SHOPPING

John Kubichek knows what service is all about. While growing up, he watched his father Frank sell and repair manual typewriters and adding machines from his shop in the Manhattan Building in downtown Milwaukee. After graduating from college with a business degree, he witnessed technological innovations in office machines including electronic typewriters, calculators, analog copiers, fax machines and laser printers. It became apparent to John that the future of office automation was changing. Stand-alone, single-purpose machines evolved into today's interconnected multifunctional devices, and Kubichek Office Products is positioned at the forefront of these advancements. It stocks digital products from Kyocera-Mita, Ricoh, Gestetner, Konica Minolta, Okidata and Samsung. A vast inventory of parts and supplies plus a service staff of more than 30 technicians enables the shop to quickly and completely maintain and supply any of your office machines. With three stores, in Brookfield, West Bend and Madison, and the most complete lines of digital equipment available, you will be able to count on the store for all of your office equipment needs. For over 70 years, old-fashioned personalized service and state-of-the-art equipment has been the standard at Kubichek Office Products. Visit soon to bring the best of both worlds into your business life.

12530 W Burleigh Road, Brookfield WI
(262) 754-0700 or (866) 228-4100
www.kubichek.com

Elm Grove Village Flower Shop

SHOPPING

The Elm Grove Village Flower Shop offers customers fresh floral and custom silk arrangements, unique gifts and a bit of the unexpected to beautify their homes. The store opened in 1955, and owner Peggy Hofstad purchased the shop in 2001. Peggy, who has an art background, imparts her distinctive style and experience to the products, often using vibrant colors and uncommon flowers. Many of the fresh herbs and organic flowers get their start in local gardens. The locally grown Asiatic lilies last two to three times longer than traditional lilies, and the flower shop also uses filtered water to keep the arrangements looking fresh even longer. That kind of detail is important to Peggy and her flower designers, who readily admit to having very high standards about the quality of their flowers. The shop offers distinctive wedding arrangements and lovely memorial flowers. The shop also offers a wide range of gifts to accompany the bouquets, which can be delivered on the same day the order is placed. Visit the Elm Grove Village Flower Shop for original floral designs with pizzazz.

13458 Watertown Plank Road,
Elm Grove WI
(262) 782-8380 or (877) 223-1200

Female cardinal

CAMBRIDGE

The village of Cambridge is nestled among farm fields in south-central Wisconsin. Scottish and Norwegian farmers settled the surrounding area. Inside Victorian storefronts and century-old buildings on Main Street lie charming shops and galleries. You'll find pottery and furniture, crafts and folk art, coffees and candies. Bed and breakfast establishments are all over. Famous people from Cambridge include Matt Kenseth, 2003 NASCAR Winston Cup champion.

PLACES TO GO

- Cam-Rock County Park
  68 County Highway B
- Lake Ripley Park
  N4310 Park Road
- Matt Kenseth Museum & Fan Club
  700 Kenseth Way
  (866) 878-1717

THINGS TO DO

May

- Renaissance Faire
  Lake Ripley Park
  www.cambridgeareaems.com/ren_faire.htm

June

- Cambridge Pottery Festival
  Lake Ripley Park
  www.cambridgepotteryfestival.org

August

- Utica Festival
  Utica Community Association Park
  (608) 423-4727

September

- Fall Harvest Festival
  Downtown
  (608) 423-3780

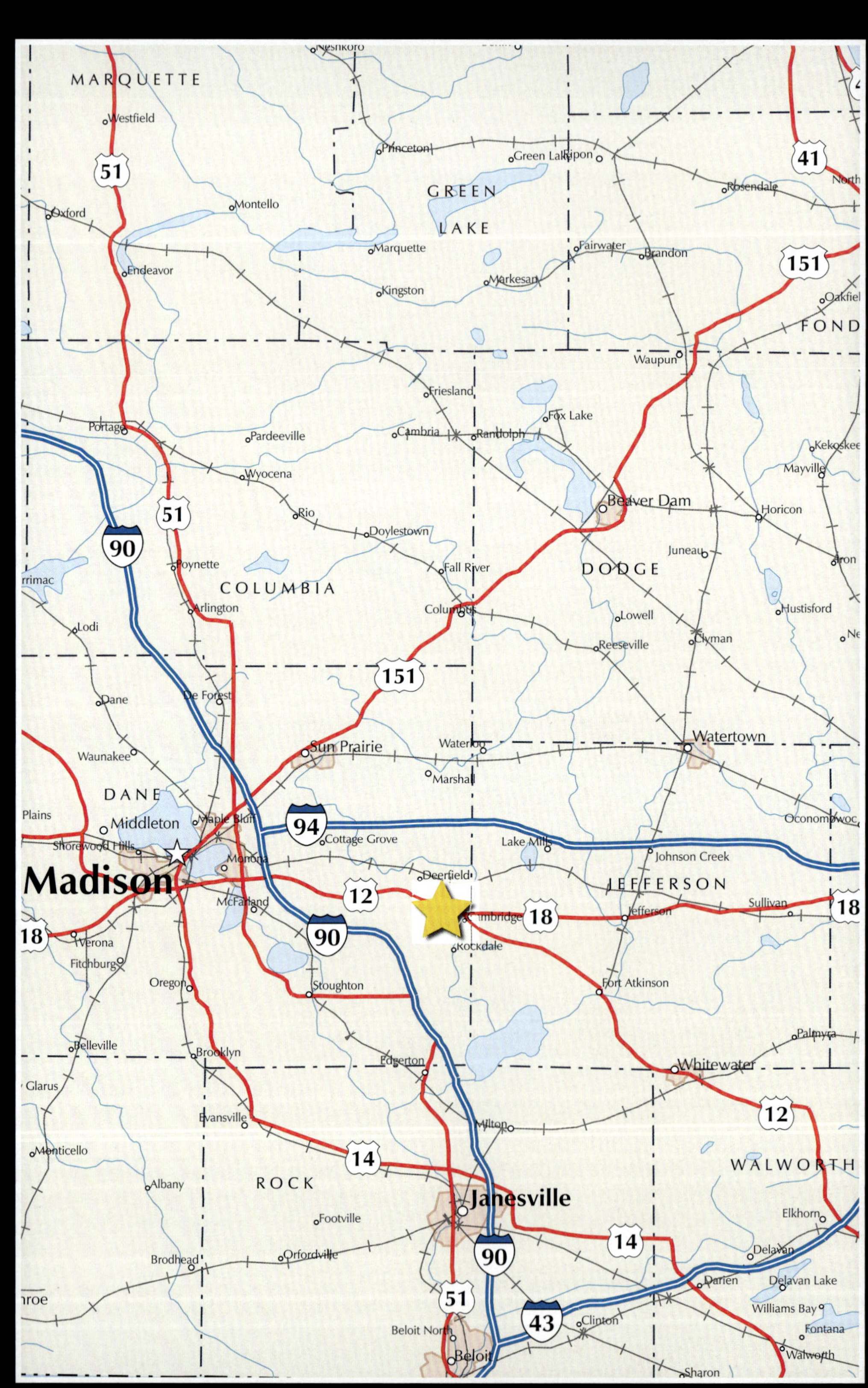

Cambridge House Bed & Breakfast

ACCOMMODATIONS

Jeff and Linda Leoni long desired to own a bed and breakfast. Jeff had been involved in the restaurant business, while Linda fondly recalled her grandmother's little cottage bed and breakfast. So they were thrilled when they purchased Cambridge House in 2003. This multi-themed getaway is located in the heart of central Wisconsin, an hour from Milwaukee, 20 minutes from Madison and two hours from downtown Chicago. Every room at the Cambridge House Bed & Breakfast has special touches to make guests as comfortable as possible, including in-room Jacuzzis and décor designed to give the feel of an exotic home away from home. Jeff and Linda have given each room a specific theme to create an extraordinary ambience. You can schedule an in-room massage, or relaxing manicure or pedicure, to help you feel pampered. Cheese baskets and champagne are available, along with a wide range of beverages to enhance your experience, such as freshly ground coffee, various teas and fruit juices. Regardless of your preferred method of being spoiled, Cambridge House Bed & Breakfast is an ideal choice for your next B&B excursion.

123 E Main Street, Cambridge WI
(608) 423-7008
www.cambridgehouse-inn.com

The Garment Shop

FASHION

Quality clothing at reasonable prices is the way that The Garment Shop's proprietor Jan Carpenter looks at her business, and a visit to her establishment shows she means it. Jan takes the time to get to know her customers and how she might best meet their needs. Her primary focus is to provide service that you just can't find anymore. The Garment Shop has been offering old-fashioned customer service since 1978. Jan has been active in the retail women's clothing business for many years, and she liked it so much she bought the shop. The primary focus of The Garment Shop is women's apparel, such as the vintage style April Cornell line, Tribal (Canadian) and Woolrich garments. Jan also offers children's clothing options and a number of men's items, as well as accessories ranging from Minnetonka sandals to attractive jewelry. Customers visiting The Garment Shop can also check out the new Cream City Gallery and Gifts in the same historic building, making for an even more enjoyable experience. For a worthwhile shopping excursion, stop by and visit Jan for the special touch of service that has become her hallmark over the years at The Garment Shop.

125 W Main Street, Cambridge WI
(608) 423-3740

Purple Wood Violets

CEDARBURG

Cedarburg boasts amenities that include the last covered bridge in Wisconsin, the Interurban Trail and a historic downtown. Cedarburg is a noted tourist destination that prides itself on century-old buildings and small businesses. The community benefits from many parks and much green space, even in the downtown area. Originally, Cedarburg was a stop for travelers on the Green Bay Trail. More and more families decided to stay put at this stop, and soon they established a small Irish/German community at New Dublin, now the Hamilton Historic District. Today, the downtown boasts historic buildings occupied by independent businesses, often specializing in arts and crafts. The Cedar Creek Winery and the Woolen Mill in which it is located are a popular stop. Both offer tours.

PLACES TO GO

- Cedarburg Woolen Mill
  W62 N580 Washington Avenue
  (262) 377-0345
- Covered Bridge Park
  7600 Cedar Creek Road

THINGS TO DO

February

- Winter Festival
  www.cedarburgfestivals.org/Winterfestival.htm

June

- Strawberry Festival
  www.cedarburgfestivals.org/Strawberry.html
- Plein Air Contest (art)
  www.cedarburgartistsguild.com/

July

- Hometown Parade and July 4th Celebration
  (800) 237-2874

August

- Ozaukee County Fair
  Fairgrounds www.ozaukeecountyfair.com

September

- Wine & Harvest Festival
  www.cedarburgfestivals.org/WineHarvest.htm

Legacy Scrapbooks

ARTS & CRAFTS

Legacy Scrapbooks is the largest scrapbooking store in the North Shore, and will help you preserve your heritage for generations to come by providing a full line of scrapbook products, a knowledgeable staff and classes to improve your skills. The design team is helpful and creative and ready to answer any scrapbook question. They always keep up to date on the latest techniques, designs and products. If you have never scrapped before, they can help you get started. For the experienced scrapper, they can show you how to get organized and, more importantly, how easy it is to stay organized. Owners Colleen and Kim make sure that the store has a positive environment where customers can focus on their work during classes and let go of the stresses of the day as they relax and have fun. Come in on Friday night and join the Midnight Crop which includes snacks, beverages and dinner. Stop by Saturday for a free Make & Take project. Twice a year Legacy holds a Scrap-a-Thon which takes place from 8 a.m. to midnight, with breakfast, lunch and dinner provided in addition to snacks, beverages, goodie bags and door prizes. You can come in any time to complete projects in the workroom and use the tools, punches and die cutter. You can even host your own scrapbooking party. Named one of the top 150 places to shop by *Milwaukee Magazine*, Legacy Scrapbooks is the place to indulge your creative nature.

W62 N542 Washington Avenue,
Cedarburg WI
(262) 377-3642
www.legacy-scrapbooks.com

Giralté Gems and Beads

ARTS & CRAFTS

Giralté Gems and Beads is a supply haven for beaders and jewelry makers in the Cedarburg area. Artist and owner Marge Giralté, who launched her enterprise in 1998, makes sure all her bins are fully stocked for everyone's artistic pleasure. Her inventory is extensive, and includes Cloisonné beads, Czech pressed-glass, seed beads, art glass and Japanese cylinder beads. You'll find wood, bone and hand-blown glass beads, along with precious wires, hemp and leather stringing supplies. Get help with instructional videos and CDs, or schedule private lessons with Marge herself. Marge had been a hairdresser for 27 years before she launched Giralté Gems and Beads. Handcrafting was second nature to her. When the chemicals from hairdressing got to her, the artist in her did what she knew best, beadwork. Marge was the owner of C3 gifts, where she represented herself along with more than 40 Wisconsin artists. Her favorite kind of beading is the intricate seed bead work represented in her amulet bags and neckpieces, which may take as much as 70 hours each. Marge makes a limited selection of jewelry for sale and gets many orders for custom work for weddings and special occasions. The best part of her job is helping customers pick out shapes and colors for their own creations. She is positive that everyone can learn beading with a little instruction and the inspiration of her colorful store.

W62 N580 Washington Avenue, Cedarburg WI
(888) 689-0558 or (262) 375-5501
www.giraltegemsandbeads.com

Cedarburg Preschool

BUSINESS & SERVICES

Cedarburg Preschool has been providing a warm and accepting learning environment for children aged three to five since 1965. This nonprofit organization is parent-owned, state licensed and accredited by the National Association for the Education of Young Children. The school offers half-day programs based on the philosophy that play activity is the most effective way to give children the foundations needed for learning the three Rs. Each year the school enrolls about 150 children and groups them into classes of 14, 16 or 18 students with two teachers per class. A child at this school develops a strong self-image and learns how to have good relationships with adults and peers while being exposed to the basics of math, language, science and reading. Each classroom is divided into separate areas of interest and has room for both quiet and active play. The space has been carefully designed to encourage curiosity, resourcefulness and pleasure. Children have opportunities to develop their social abilities along with music, art and creative dramatics through the use of puppets and other playthings. Cedarburg Preschool assesses a child's development annually and works closely with parents in every aspect of childcare. To put your children on a path of learning that will guide them for life, investigate the possibilities at Cedarburg Preschool.

W68N563 Evergreen Boulevard, Cedarburg WI
(262) 375-0160
www.cedarburgpreschool.com

Jung Furniture

HOME & GARDEN

Fine quality furniture at fair prices is waiting for you at Jung Furniture in Cedarburg. Owner Raymond Jung is the fourth generation in the furniture business. His great-grandfather Gustav started selling furniture in 1908 and built the store in 1913 as a combination furniture store and funeral parlor. In 1964, the store received an addition. Raymond focuses on furniture and accessories from both small and large manufacturers who still take pride in craftsmanship and stand behind their products. His showroom changes constantly to show off his selections, which must meet his rigorous standards for quality to appear here. You'll find furniture for every room in your home as well as area rugs, mattresses and lamps. Make that family room a dream-come-true with an entertainment center, comfortable upholstered pieces and a good-looking coffee table. Perhaps you've always dreamed of an office with a roll-top desk or prefer an armoire for your computer. You'll find practical and attractive dining sets, kitchen pieces, fine wooden fireplace mantels and bedroom sets that combine traditional styling with modern comfort. For furnishings that will stand the test of time, come to Jung's Furniture and put 100 years of furniture expertise at your disposal.

W62 N604 Washington Avenue,
Cedarburg WI (262) 377-2950
www.jungfurniture.com

Prairie Gardens

HOME & GARDEN

The staff members at Prairie Gardens believe in happy plants and happy people. They stock big, healthy plants and have the experience to answer any questions you may have. Prairie Gardens can help you make your garden a success, regardless of how experienced you are. Owners Ken and Judi Kowalke will help you choose the right plants for your specific garden conditions. The Kowalkes left their careers in the Chicago area to pursue their dream of owning their own business. In 2004, those dreams became reality. Their roomy store is a complete gardening and floral center that also carries garden tools and books. In addition, the shop carries home décor items, including candles and brand-name gifts. The covered yard features an amazing selection of annual container gardens, hanging baskets, perennials and shrubs, all specially grown to withstand the harsh Wisconsin winters. Holidays are one of the best times to visit. In the autumn, the kids will love the pumpkin patch, hay-bale maze, ducks and bunnies. At Christmas time, they can get their picture taken with Santa and get up-close and personal with his reindeer. Moms and dads alike will love the selection of indoor and outdoor decorations. Whatever the time of year, Prairie Gardens will help you transform your yard into a place that welcomes you when you come home.

8504 State Highway 60, Cedarburg WI
(262) 377-2500
www.prairiegardener.com

The Pagoda Fine Jewelry

FASHION

If you seek distinctive jewelry and personal attention, just look for the red roof in the center of Cedarburg. The Pagoda Fine Jewelry is hard to miss, and with your first visit you'll find it impossible to forget. The Pagoda offers original pieces that you won't find anywhere else. Each of the three owners brings her own special talents to the business. This means more variety, selection and service for their customers. Designer Debra LaValley uses her degree in art metals to carve and cast one-of-a-kind art nouveau pieces. Catherine Laing is a jewelry designer and fabricator with an art degree from Cornell College, who specializes in pieces with a Scandinavian feel. Paula Luba is a graduate gemologist who focuses on appraisals, jewelry repairs and working with outside designers whose work reflects the Pagoda spirit. The Pagoda owners cater to their customers and take on commissions that other jewelry shops avoid. For a special shopping experience and that perfect piece of jewelry, visit The Pagoda Fine Jewelry.

N58 W6189 Columbia Road,
Cedarburg WI
(262) 376-8730

Morton's

RESTAURANTS & CAFÉS

For casual tavern dining and Wisconsin tradition with a full service restaurant menu, Morton's is the place to be. When you enter this historic 1905 building, you will immediately be struck by the style. There are kitsch pieces covering every interior wall. You will definitely have to visit more than once to see it all. Beyond the décor, Morton's is definitely best known for its food. Everything here is homemade and chef Tim Ryan is known for his original recipes and specialty dinners. Favorites here include the brats, sausages and build-your-own hamburgers, which begin with a 14-ounce patty. This is one of the few places left where you can still order your burger rare. Business partner Chris Morton runs the tavern portion of the operation. His Bloody Marys are well worth a stop. On Wednesday, it's Mexican food night and local entertainment is featured, which could be anything from blues and bluegrass to jazz. Another popular day to visit is Thursday, when you can enjoy the pasta bar that's open for both lunch and dinner. Friday, of course, is Fish Fry night. Come for the Sunday brunch, when you can try the popular Surf and Turf Bloody Mary. Start your meal with an appetizer, such as the coconut Cajun crusted shrimp, and try a specialty like the jalapeno blue cheese bratwurst or the delicious blackened swordfish for your main course. No matter what you choose, you won't go home hungry from Morton's.

N56 W6339 Center Street, Cedarburg WI
(262) 377-4779

C. Wiesler's

RESTAURANTS & CAFÉS

C. Wiesler's is one of the original taverns of Cedarburg, and the historic town is rightfully proud of this refreshing saloon and eatery. Conrad Wiesler, the original owner, erected the building in 1885, and at three stories, it was one of Cedarburg's original skyscrapers. Mike and Teri Jackson bought the building in 1988 and restored it. The floors and walls are original. Sidle up to the bar, which dates to 1892, and rest your foot on a real brass rail. The restaurant booths are from a 1930s drug store soda fountain. In season, you can drink and dine on the outdoor sun-and-fun deck. Come to experience the authentic atmosphere and the marvelous selection of beers on tap. You will stay for the food. The lively, creative kitchen, staffed by a crack culinary crew, prepares irresistible appetizers and succulent sandwiches. You can enjoy salads, subs or stuffed tomatoes. A full grill menu features the house special Wies-Burger. Paninis are grilled to perfection. Friday brings an incredible fish fry, one of the best fries around. Oh, and there is pizza. See and be seen at Cedarburg's premier weekend hang-out. Find your place in history at C. Wiesler's. How could it get any better?

W61 N493 Washington Avenue,
Cedarburg WI
(262) 377-8833

Klug's Creekside Inn

RESTAURANTS & CAFÉS

They say that variety is the spice of life, and variety is just what you'll find at Klug's Creekside Inn on scenic Cedar Creek. For lunch you will find traditional fare such as salads, sandwiches, pastas, stir fries and smaller portion meals. You will likely take awhile to decide on dinner as the choices are plentiful. The restaurant features a regular menu of seafood, poultry, meat and vegetarian dishes, in addition to sandwiches and burgers. Tuesday night the menu expands to include even more variety, with combo specials that let you try two popular entrées for one low price. On Wednesdays and Sundays, Klug's offers traditional German fare, including a German Sampler Platter. Thursday is Rib Night, where you can sample the signature prime rib for a discounted price. On Friday, enjoy the Friday Night Fish Fry and the seafood buffet. On Sunday mornings you can enjoy brunch. Klug's also takes pride in their page-long wine list, and the staff is happy to make suggestions. Even if you're not feeling very social, Klug's has you covered, because you can order your food to go. Keep them in mind for catering, too. Klug's Creekside Inn is at the forefront of the casual fine dining movement. Come see why locals keep coming back and tourists can't say enough.

N58 W6194 Columbia Road, Cedarburg WI
(262) 377-0660
www.foodspot.com/klugs

Tomaso's

RESTAURANTS & CAFÉS

Tomaso's offers a full menu of traditional Italian fare, good service and a fair price. An educator for 11 years, Ray Thomas had always wanted his own business, and the opportunity presented itself in 1976 when he purchased De Quardos Restaurant. At that point, it had already been a Cedarburg staple for 20 years. Ray changed the name, but he retained manager Jim Hoberg's services and the original menu, adding a few enhancements as time went on. In 2002, the business began to franchise and other locations sprang up in Mequon and West Bend. Upon Ray's retirement in April of 2005, the restaurants traditions were continued by his two children Scott and Nicole. Ingredients are always fresh at Tomaso's, with only the best meats and sauces. Known for its great pizza, Tomaso's thin crust pies were voted number one by *Milwaukee Magazine.* If you're not in the mood for pizza, you can choose from pasta, spaghetti, sandwiches and lasagna, in addition to a terrific appetizer selection and a full bar. Take advantage of the daily specials. Tomaso's participates in a number of local festivals, including June's Strawberry Festival and the Wine Harvest Festival in September. For these special events, Tomaso's offers pizza by the slice, as well as homemade ice cream using an old-fashioned John Deere ice cream maker. For good food, variety and a place to gather with good friends, visit Tomaso's.

W63 N688 Washington Avenue, Cedarburg WI (262) 377-7630

Romano's Pizzeria

RESTAURANTS & CAFÉS

Romano's Pizzeria offers specialty and gourmet pizzas sure to get you out of your pizza rut. When you enter, you'll see the upscale Italian décor and recognize immediately that this isn't the same old pizza place. Everything on the menu tastes as good as it sounds, and the wonderful smells that fill the restaurant will only make your decision on what to eat that much tougher. Try one of the Romano's wraps or a hand-tossed pizza made to order, and watch it being made right before your eyes. You can also make your own pizza creation by starting with your choice of a hearty white or honey wheat crust, then choose from one of six sauces, meats and veggies, and pick one or more of seven different cheeses. Romano's also offers delicious stromboli, calzones and pizza rolls, in addition to the more traditional sides such as salad, breadsticks and chicken strips or wings. This family-oriented restaurant offers dine in, carry out and free delivery, plus a game room. You can even set up a pizza party for the kids where they can toss their own pizza crust and top it with their favorite toppings, plus choose a beverage and have cinnamon breadsticks for dessert. Romano's is not just a pizza place, its people are members of the community. The owners are always involved in local endeavors. At Romano's Pizzeria, you'll stop for a slice and become a regular customer.

W63 N540 Hanover Avenue, Cedarburg WI
(262) 375-9921

Wayne's Drive In

RESTAURANTS & CAFÉS

Jump in your hot rod, put on your leather jacket and head to Wayne's Drive In, where it is always the 1950s. From April to November, enjoy made-to-order, high quality quarter-pound burgers, cheeseburgers and chicken sandwiches. For liquid refreshment, enjoy Sprecher root beer and Cedar Crest ice cream from the fountain, or try a delicious malt, shake, sundae or banana split. From Memorial Day through Labor Day, you can be served right at your car by one of Wayne's skating carhops. If you would prefer to eat indoors, the malt shop theme carries over inside as well, from the red and silver sparkle vinyl booths and round red stools at the chrome soda fountain, to the black-and-white checkered floor and the jukebox that pipes music into the parking lot. Come with your classic car on Thursday night for Cruise Night, which often attracts as many as 1,000 people. Classic Chevys and Fords easily fill the 100-space parking lot, and overflow hot rods fill the street as far as the eye can see. To add to the fun, there is a DJ, giveaways for the show cars and Hula Hoop contests for the kids. Even if you don't own a classic car, you're welcome to enjoy a juicy special recipe burger and fries. Take a step back in time at Wayne's Drive In.

1331 Covered Bridge Road, Cedarburg WI
(262) 375-9999
www.waynesdrivein.com

The Gem Shop, Inc.

SHOPPING

The largest rock shop and lapidary in the Midwest is The Gem Shop, boasting more than 200,000 pounds of in-stock rough rock. This is a global business with the connections and knowledge to support it. Owner Eugene Mueller says he is "dedicated to revealing the beauty of the mineral world," and he feels that this is his mission in the rock business. The Gem Shop carries everything from agates to fine jaspers in the rough and polished specimens, books, rock tumblers, other lapidary equipment. Discover stone beads, findings, minerals and fossils. You will also find interesting gift items made from rock, such as bookends, wind chimes, carvings and lamps. Customers benefit from The Gem Shop's direct connection with the source of many rocks, including some that are mined by Gene himself. The Gem Shop has many customers with a variety of interests, such as lapidary hobbyists, custom jewelry designers, specimen collectors, and bead and jewelry manufacturers. The Gem Shop has been in business for 36 years. Eugene is considered to be an expert in his field, having been featured in numerous journals and magazines. He has also won three AGTA Cutting Edge awards for his lapidary skills. The Gem Shop is an active supporter of the Cedarburg Community Scholarship Fund and other local events. Free tours are offered to groups that are interested in the lapidary arts. For all your rock and mineral needs, visit The Gem Shop in Cedarburg. Both wholesale and retail inquiries are welcome.

W64 N723 Washington Avenue, Cedarburg WI
(262) 377-4666
www.thegemshop.com

Cedar Creek Trading Post

SHOPPING

Cedar Creek Trading Post adds an old-fashioned general store to the mix of shops at Cedar Creek Settlement. Famous for freshly popped Amish-grown black popcorn, the trading post also carries a variety of other gourmet specialty foods, plus toys and games for the kids. Among the specialties at this three-story shop are diverse teas, jams and jellies, plus fudge and chocolates by South Bend Chocolate Company. Mealtime is certain to be more interesting with help from the trading post's selection of Door County coffees as well as cookbooks and spices. Kids will be as amused as you are by the selections here, plus they get to pick a prize when you make a purchase. Customers appreciate the free samples and gift wrapping, while religious praise music adds a special tone to the shopping environment. While visiting Cedar Creek Settlement, be sure to visit the trading post's sister store, Robin's Nest Antiques and Gifts. You'll find Victorian and country antiques and vintage jewelry alongside European fine arts cards, soaps and handcrafted linens. For enjoyable shopping in a historic setting, visit Cedar Creek Trading Post and Robin's Nest.

N70 W6340 Bridge Road, Cedarburg WI
(262) 377-0400 (Cedar Creek Trading Post)
(262) 377-3444 (Robin's Nest)

Newberry Thicket

SHOPPING

Newberry Thicket is a one-of-a-kind shop where you will encounter an enchanting array of woodland creatures that seem to come alive the moment you look at them. Owner Bunnie Werth is an artist who has captured the essence of fantasy and nature. Bunnie began by creating collectible rabbit ornaments out of clay and wire, and dressed them in tiny overcoats and boots. After selling them at the local artists' co-op, she later wanted to expand on the concept. Newberry Thicket is the magical result. Vines surround you as you enter the world of rabbits, goats, knitting lambs and prancing ponies. Dollhouse furniture and miniature gardens add to the fun. Her creek-side location in the Cedarcreek Settlement couldn't be more perfect. You can wander through her inspired realm and take a little piece of Newberry Thicket home with you. It's a shopping experience for the young-at-heart.

N70 W6340 Bridge Road, Cedarburg WI
(262) 375-4386
www.cedarcreeksettlement.com

Leap of Faith

SHOPPING

Patricia Lietzke speaks for all entrepreneurs in calling her business Leap of Faith, though her prospects when she began in 1997 were perhaps more tenuous than most. After all, the world is not often kind to artists who wish to earn a living through their art. From its beginnings as Patricia's studio and gallery, Leap of Faith has evolved into what it is today, a shop in the Cedar Creek Settlement of Cedarburg where visitors can find art and gifts with meaning, thought and creativity. Patricia wants folks to be inspired as they peruse the many items that celebrate life, love, family and friendship. These include gifts with wise sayings, uplifting books and pretty jewelry. Patricia and her daughter, Amy Wills, create many of the things that you see in Leap of Faith, which is truly a family business. Amy also manages the store and helps with the buying, while Patricia's other daughter, Karin Kinzel, works here part-time. Patricia still keeps a studio above the store, where she teaches Touch Drawing classes by appointment. As Leap of Faith approaches its 10th anniversary, Patricia can look back knowing that she made the right move when she decided to go for it. For meaningful gifts from a positive person, visit Leap of Faith today.

N70 W6340 Bridge Road, Second Floor, Cedarburg WI
(888) 703-0245

Copper Falls State Park located in Mellen

PLACES TO GO

- Chippewa Falls Museum of Industry and Technology
  21 E Grand Avenue
  (715) 720-9206
- Cook-Rutledge Mansion
  505 W Grand Avenue
  (715) 723-7181
- Heyde Center for the Arts
  3 N High Street
  (715) 726-9000
- The James Sheeley House Restaurant
  236 W River Street
  (715) 726-0561
- Lake Wissota State Park
  18127 County Highway O
  (715) 382-4574

THINGS TO DO

February

- Kiwanis Wine, Beer & Cheese Gala
  Avalon Hotel
  715-579-9180

June

- June Dairy Days
  Northern Wisconsin Fair Grounds
  (715) 723-0331
- Country Fest
  Cadott
  (800) 326-FEST (3378)

June-July

- Wisconsin Renaissance Faire
  www.wirenfaire.com

July

- Rock Fest
  Cadott
  www.rock-fest.com
- Northern Wisconsin State Fair
  www.norwisstatefair.com

August

- Pure Water Days/Heritage Fun Fest
  (715) 723-7858

September

- Oktoberfest
  www.chippewachamber.org/oktoberfest.asp

CHIPPEWA FALLS

Time has named Chippewa Falls one of the top ten small towns in America. The National Trust for Historic Preservation has named Chippewa Falls one of the Trust's Dozen Distinctive Destinations, in part due to the Main Street Historic District, which is listed in the National Register of Historic Places. The city is also the birthplace of Seymour Cray and the home of the original Cray Research, which pioneered the supercomputer. The Jacob Leinenkugel Brewing Company is here, as well as the Heyde Center for the Arts, a venue for regional, national and international artists and performers.

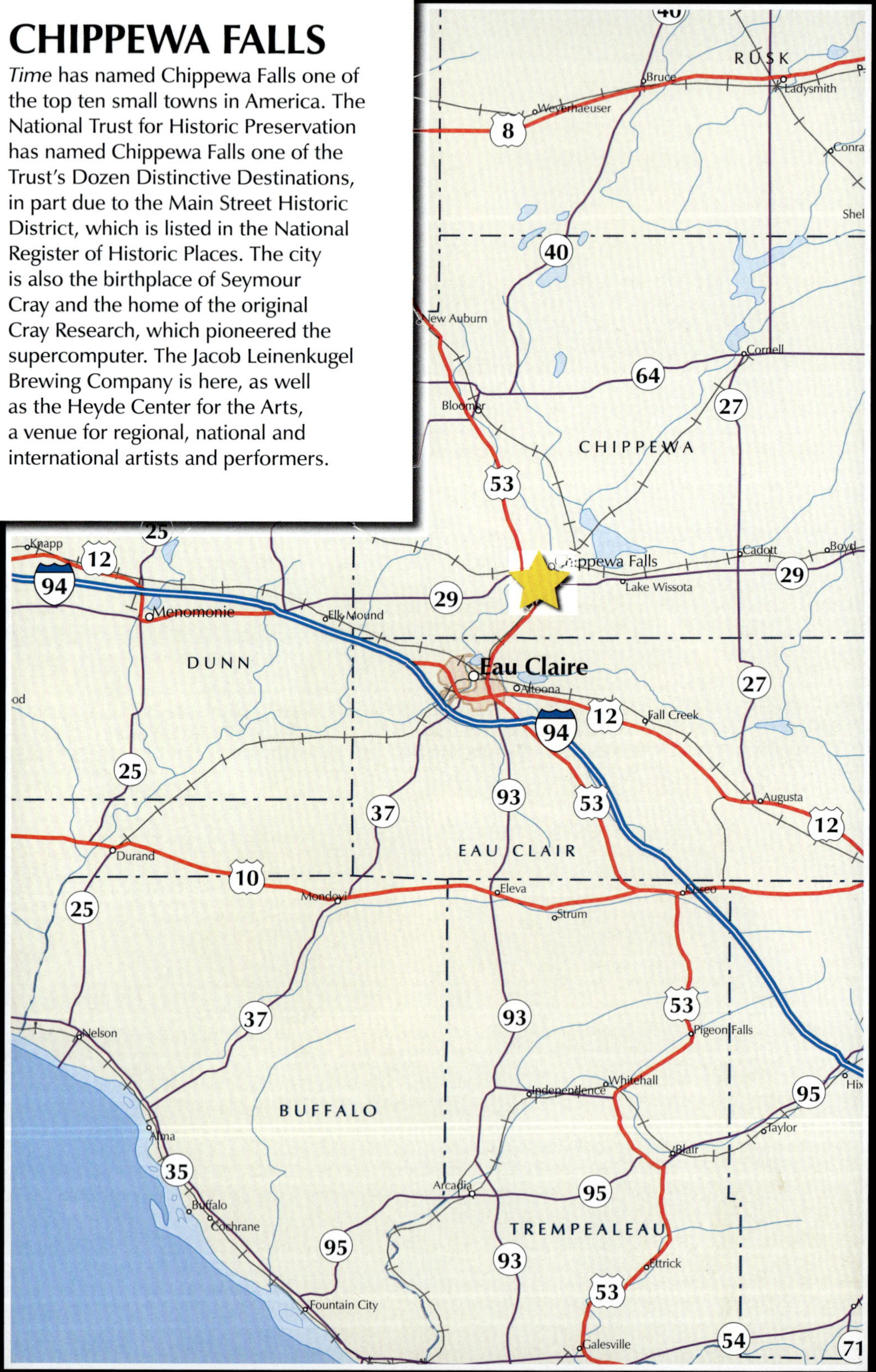

Pleasant View Bed & Breakfast

ACCOMMODATIONS

With its great view of the clear, sparkling waters of Lake Wissota, it's obvious how Pleasant View Bed & Breakfast got its name. Owners Mike and Jeanine Adams purchased the home in 1993 and completely renovated it. Any of the five themed guest rooms show off their labor of love. For a rustic cabin quality, choose the Northwoods room with its canoe paddle, crosscut saws and deer rack. If you like the sea, the nautical theme of the Wind & Waves room will appeal with its netting and deck access. The Secret Garden room features a cozy fireplace and floral décor, while Cozy Corner showcases family heirlooms from the turn of the century. Finally, Hidden Harbor reminds guests of a Cape Cod cottage. Many rooms offer whirlpool tubs, and all possess private baths. Mike and Jeanine serve up a delicious breakfast every morning and will take requests and work around dietary restrictions. Business travelers appreciate Pleasant View's wireless Internet access. The Adams have played host to everyone from out-of-state honeymooners to television celebrity Joan Rivers. For comfort, courtesy and lakefront views, come to Pleasant View Bed & Breakfast.

16649 96th Avenue, Chippewa Falls, WI
(715) 382-4401 or (866) WISSOTA (947-7682)
www.pleasantviewbb.com

Petersons' Lafayette Orchard

ATTRACTIONS

The folks at Petersons' Lafayette Orchard are so sure you'll love their crisp, juicy apples that they'll let you adopt one of their trees. For just $40, the 30-acre Chippewa Falls orchard will let you put your name on one of their many trees and possess every bit of succulent fruit that grows on it. Not only that, you'll be free to bring your family and friends to have a picnic around it during the harvest season. Petersons' Lafayette Orchard is the only orchard in the area to grow the signature Akane apple, which is equally great for eating fresh, baking and dehydrating. The Akane is just one of the 18 varieties grown here, including the sweet Honey Crisp. On weekends, the melodic sounds of live music join the gentle rustling of the leaves. Petersons' also offers pony rides for the young and young-at-heart. You'll find exclusive gifts at the fully stocked gift shop. Peterson's is a huge pick-your-own orchard, so come and pick a bushel this fall. For a few apples to make a pie or a whole tree full of apples to last year-round, plan a visit to Petersons' Lafayette Orchard.

19589 County Highway Oo, Chippewa Falls WI
(715) 720-1313

Olson's Ice Cream & Deli

FUN FOODS

It's nice to know that even in our fast-paced world a few things manage not only to endure but to remain as good as they always were. Take Olson's Ice Cream & Deli, for example, which has served its signature *Homaid* ice cream from the same location in downtown Chippewa Falls since 1944. The ice cream is made fresh daily on the premises, just as it was on the very first day that the parlor opened its doors. New flavors have been added over the years, but the recipes pretty much stick to the original way of doing things. That means that the 22 flavors available at any one time are always made with fresh milk, cream and high quality flavoring ingredients, never with powders or cheap substitutes. The business was founded by A.J. Olson, and you will still find an Olson or two behind the counter or in the production area. Beloved by locals and tourists alike, Olson's has been featured in *Wisconsin West Magazine* and is included in the ice cream lover's invaluable travel guide, *The Very Best Ice Cream & Where to Find It.* For a double scoop of old-fashioned flavor, drop by Olson's Ice Cream & Deli.

611 N Bridge Street, Chippewa Falls WI
(715) 723-4331

High Shores Supper Club

RESTAURANTS & CAFÉS

Dining at the High Shores Supper Club on Lake Wissota has been a Chippewa Falls tradition since 1994. The restaurant has 220 feet of shoreline with five docks, so boaters find it easy to pull right up. The entire south wall inside High Shores is glass, providing a view of the water from just about every table. As you might guess, seafood is well represented on the menu, whether it's king crab from the seas of Alaska or blue gill and perch from the waters of Canada. A full range of beef, pork and poultry choices are also available, including prime rib and roast duckling, as well as vegetarian dishes. Homemade soup and salad bar accompany each entrée. The champagne breakfast buffet on Sunday features all the traditional breakfast favorites, fruits and desserts. The restaurant is tastefully decorated throughout with a musical instrument motif, glass top tables and candlelight. The waterfalls and flower gardens create an ambience for all to enjoy either on the porch or the deck. Exclusive to the area, a champagne dinner cruise is offered from May to October, featuring a scenic pontoon ride, as well as a five-course romantic dinner. It doesn't matter whether you arrive by boat or car; the important thing is that you bring your appetite for fine food with you when you choose High Shores Supper Club.

17985 County Highway X,
Chippewa Falls WI
(715) 723-9854
www.highshores.com

COTTAGE GROVE

Cottage Grove, a fast growing suburb of Madison, took its name in 1849 because the first house built in the township was set among a grove of oak trees. Farming was the main occupation from then until the middle of the 20th century. Today, Cottage Grove boasts 10 parks and open space areas totaling 133 acres. Additionally, the school district maintains a 68-acre School Forest with trails and educational opportunities. McCarthy County Park is located just north of the village. Downtown, the Glacial Drumlin State Trail begins its 51-mile course through rolling farmland and small towns on its route to Waukesha. A major expansion is underway in the form of the Arrowwood Community, a mix of primarily senior housing, offices and retail space on the east side. When the project is complete in 2012, up to 600 people will live in the 40-acre development.

PLACES TO GO

- McCarthy Youth and Conservation Park
  4911 County Highway TT
- Norman Vethe School Forest
  299 Taylor Street

THINGS TO DO

May

- Fireman's Festival
  (608) 575-3879

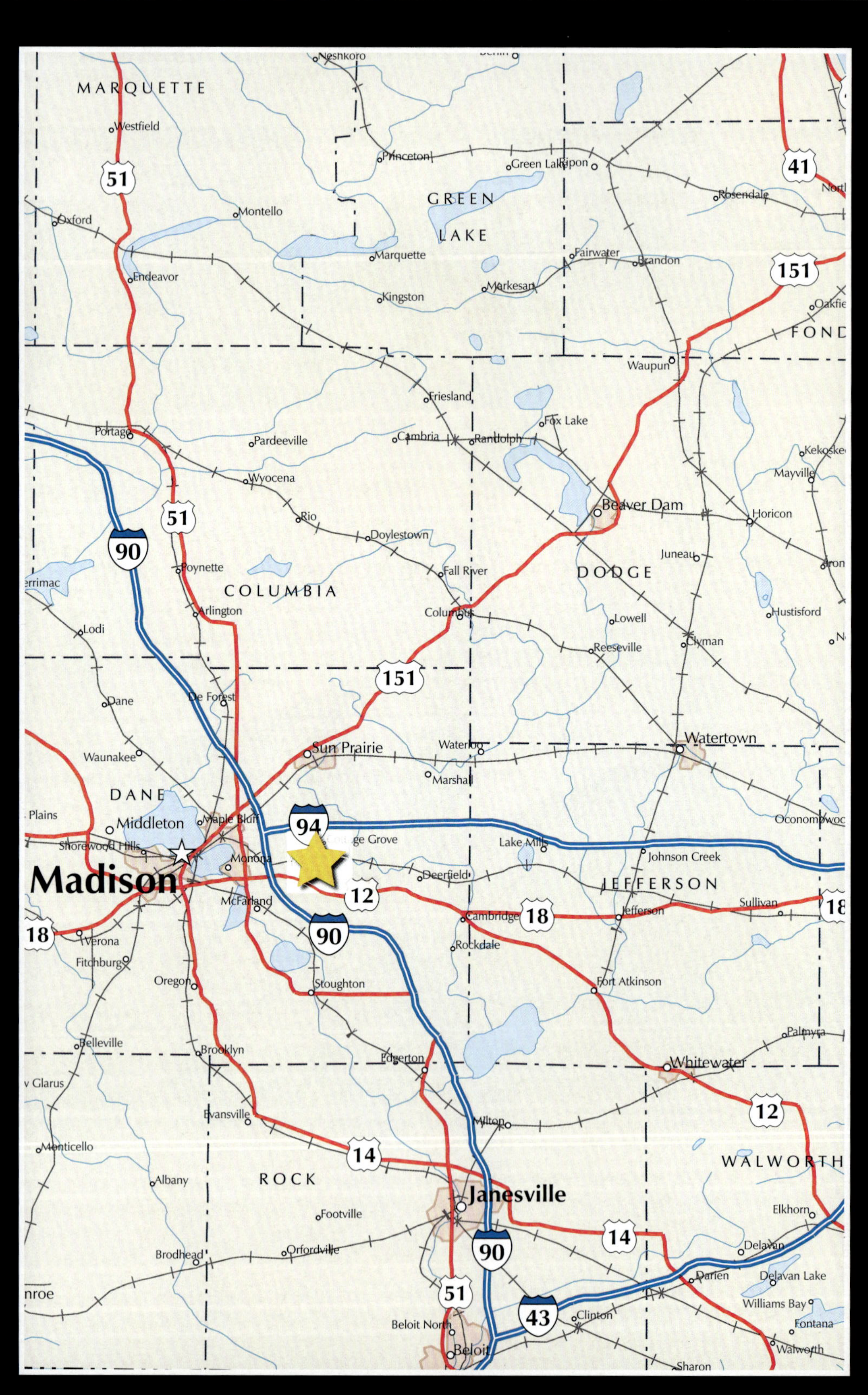

The Oaks Golf Course

RECREATION & FITNESS

The Oaks Golf Course opened in June 2003 and has been earning accolades ever since. *Golf Digest* fell in love with the public facility, listing The Oaks as number five on the list of America's Best New Affordable Golf Courses, and giving it a four-and-one-half star rating in the list of Best Places to Play. Owner John G. Blaska is justifiably proud of his creation and admits, "People started to laugh…about the farmer who was starting a golf course. They were as shocked with me as they were with the guy in Field of Dreams who built a baseball park in his field." Open to the public, The Oaks features 165 acres of wildlife, wetlands, fescue and rolling terrain. The Koshkonong Creek intermingles with several holes. New to the course is a state-of-the-art GPS system, built right into the golf car's dash, which adds tremendous enjoyment to the round. Distance to the flag, professional tips, food and beverage ordering, plus real-time scoring, all increase enjoyment. General Manager and PGA Professional Jason Manke has also been part of the project since inception. "We're proud of what we've all created here. Equally, we're happy to be able to share it because of the value and accessibility." The Oakleaf Restaurant is open from mid-morning until the last golfer leaves and offers a bistro-style menu, a bar with the finest locally crafted beers on tap, and a classic Wisconsin fish fry. For a round that can be enjoyed by all, on a beautiful layout, Bring Your Game to The Oaks.

4740 Pierceville Road, Cottage Grove WI
(608) 837-4774 ***www.golftheoaks.com***

DELAVAN

Delavan is a historical circus town. In 1847, the Mabie brothers, proprietors of the U.S. Olympic Circus, then the largest traveling show in America, chose Delavan for their winter quarters, a year before Wisconsin attained statehood. More than 26 circuses wintered in Delavan by the late 19th century. P.T. Barnum founded his circus, the Greatest Show on Earth, in Delavan in 1871. The Lake Lawn Resort, on the shores of Delavan Lake, is on the site of the old Mabie circus. Main Street sports a statue of Delavan's most infamous resident: Romeo, the Killer Elephant, responsible for five deaths. Andes Candies, maker of the Andes Chocolate Mint, set up shop in Delavan in 1921. Owned by Tootsie Roll Industries since 2000, the popular after-dinner mints are manufactured in Delavan to this day. Delavan is home to no less than six structures designed by Frank Lloyd Wright. It also hosts the Wisconsin School for the Deaf, situated high on a hill overlooking the town.

PLACES TO GO

- Congdon Park and Rotary Gardens
  Geneva Street at I-43
- Paul Lange Arboretum
  Terrace Street at Lake Comus
- Veteran's Memorial Park
  Terrace Street and Richmond Road at Lake Comus

THINGS TO DO

January

- Delavan's Winterfest
  www.delavanwi.org/winterfest.html

July

- July 4th Celebration
  (262) 728-5095
- Jammin in the Gardens
  Rotary Gardens (262) 740-1150

September

- Scarecrow Fest
  www.delavanwi.org/scarecrow.html
- Darien Corn Fest
  Darien
  www.dariencornfest.com

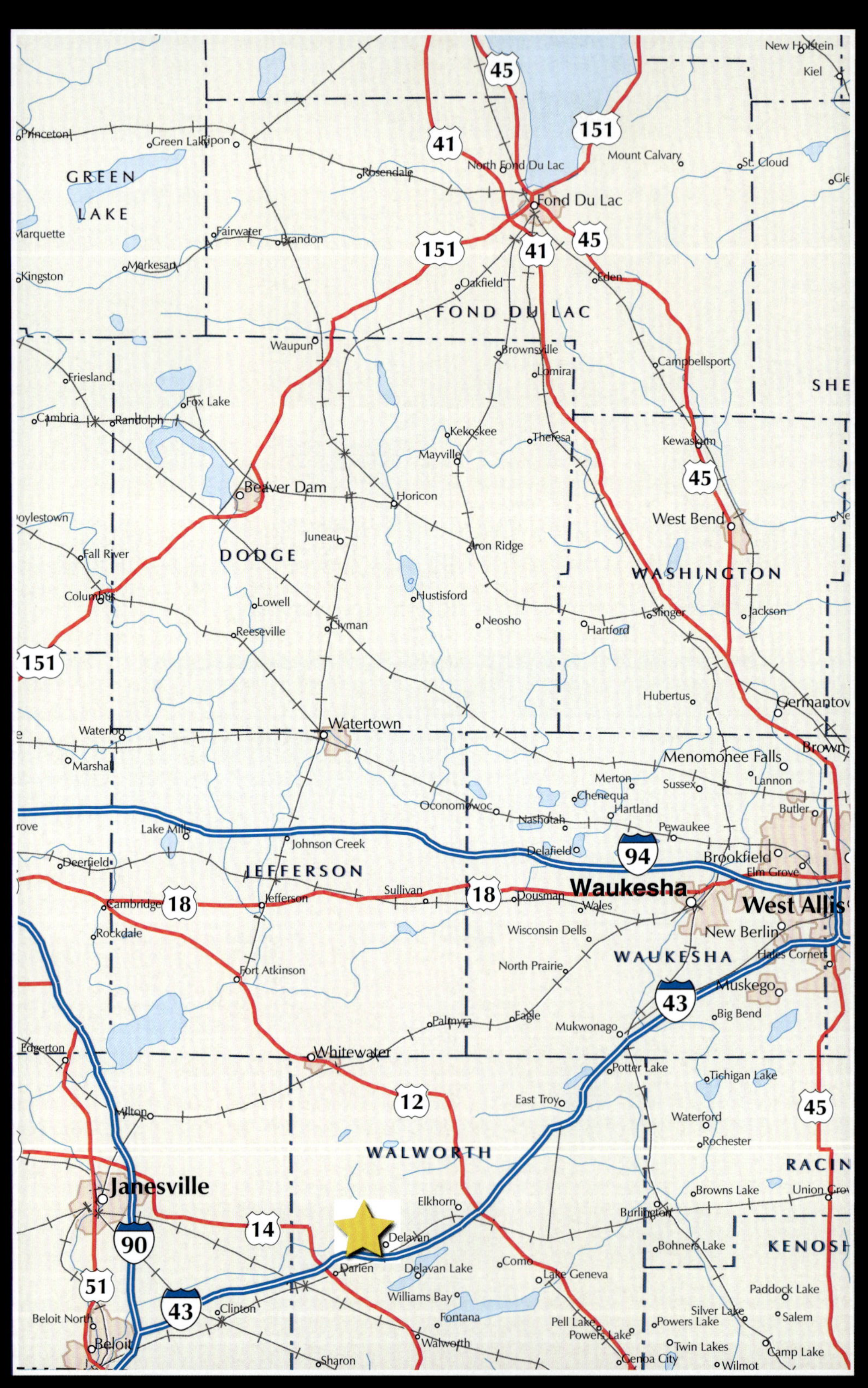

The Allyn Mansion

ACCOMMODATIONS

It may be the 21st century outside, but when you spend the night at the Allyn Mansion in Delavan, you're enveloped in 1885 grandeur. The inn won a grand prize from the National Trust in its Great American Home Awards in 1992 for the restoration work done by owners Ron Markwell and Joe Johnson. When you look at the grand 13-foot ceilings on the first floor, the antique fixtures and the authentic Victorian furniture and décor, you'll see why. What you would never guess is that the building, which was built for the wealthy Allyn family in the 1880s, once served as a nursing home and then as a furniture store. Joe and Ron restored the mansion to its previous glory, and you can experience that Victorian splendor in one of eight luxurious bedrooms. Six of the bedrooms feature private bathrooms, and five offer fireplaces. A century-old Steinway piano dominates each of the parlors. Ron and Joe are both retired schoolteachers who chose to become innkeepers to continue being active and productive members of their community. They treat their guests to a wine and cheese social hour in the evening and a full breakfast on antique china and sterling flatware in the morning. Allyn Mansion invites 21st century visitors to come and get a taste of Victorian style and elegance.

511 E Walworth Avenue, Delavan WI
(262) 728-9090
www.allynmansion.com

The Duck Inn

RESTAURANTS & CAFÉS

In the 1920s, patrons at the Duck Inn literally had to duck in to the speakeasy ever so unobtrusively. Today, you can duck in proudly and spread the good news among your friends, because the Duck Inn serves substantial meals in the supper club tradition. The Delavan restaurant started as a place to drink during Prohibition. When the dry spell ended, Wisconsin issued liquor licenses with the contingency that an establishment had to serve food, and the Duck Inn was legally reborn as a supper club. Since 1994, Owner Jeff Karbash has been restoring the Duck Inn to its original splendor, complete with three dining rooms featuring warm wood tones. With a name like the Duck Inn, it's natural that a big portion of the menu is reserved for poultry, including such favorites as apple brandy glazed duck and a half roasted duck on wild rice. You'll also find delicious steaks, pork, shrimp and seafood, along with opportunities to create your own combination dinner. The Duck Inn caters many private parties in two of its dining rooms. The Drake Room comfortably holds up to 100 people in a room with soaring ceilings and an impressive stone fireplace, while the smaller Duck Room handles up to 70 diners. Head to the bar for a martini, Old-Fashioned cocktail, a Manhattan or one of the Duck Inn's specialty drinks. Experience a traditional supper club with a visit to the Duck Inn.

CR-A and Highway 89, Delavan WI
(608) 883-6988
www.duckinndelavan.com

Photo by Mark Sadowski

EAGLE

Eagle is the home of Old World Wisconsin, America's largest outdoor museum of rural life. Old World Wisconsin contains 69 historic buildings in the pristine southern Kettle Moraine State Forest. It portrays the daily lives of 19th and early 20th century Wisconsin farmers, villagers and other pioneers on 10 ethnic farmsteads and an 1870s crossroads village. Ethnic groups represented include German, Finnish, Polish, Yankee, African-American and others. The museum offers hands-on activities, heirloom gardens, a restaurant and gift shop, a tram service and more.

PLACES TO GO

- Kettle Moraine State Forest–Southern Unit
  S91 W39091 State Route 59
  (262) 594-6200
- Old World Wisconsin
  S103 W37890 Highway 67
  (262) 594-6300

THINGS TO DO

June

- Swedish Midsommar Celebration
  Old World Wisconsin
  (262) 594-6300

August

- Little House on the Prairie Day
  Old World Wisconsin
  (262) 594-6300
- Old World Wisconsin Fair
  Old World Wisconsin
  (262) 594-6300

September

- Civil War Encampment
  Old World Wisconsin
  (262) 594-6300

October

- Autumn on the Farms
  Old World Wisconsin
  262-594-6300

The Civil War Encampment at Old World Wisconsin
Photo by Anna

Beckwith-Design, LLC

BUSINESS

Do you want to build a new home or add on to an existing one, but are unsure where to start? Beckwith-Design recommends that you start your project with a plan. Beckwith-Design is an independent design firm that specializes in custom new homes, additions and remodeling. Its design team can help you develop a plan to maximize the use of your space and save money on construction. Beckwith-Design team members listen to you and can turn your vision into a reality. They do not impose a style on clients, but are always ready with creative ideas when that is necessary. In the end, you have plans drawn by professionals who understand building codes, industry standards and construction procedures. At Beckwith-Design, you own the plans. You can take them to contractors and obtain competitive bids. Because the contractors are all bidding to the same design, you can easily see who is offering the best deal. The Beckwith-Design team is used to working with contractors, and if you like, Beckwith-Design can continue to be your advocate throughout the life of the project. Scott Beckwith, the senior designer, has more than 20 years of experience in construction management and design. He has a BS in building construction management and an MS in engineering management. Scott's brother Kurt is the director of sales and has a BS in business and in architectural drafting construction technology. Call Beckwith-Design for a free initial consultation on your project.

S103 W37879 Betts Road, Eagle WI
(262) 594-3940
www.beckwith-design.com

Photo © Windy Oaks Aquatics

Windy Oaks Aquatics

HOME & GARDEN

Create a secret garden getaway right in your own backyard with the help of Windy Oaks Aquatics, where you will find everything you need to create stunning aquascapes and ponds that are an ideal place to relax and unwind at the end of a busy day. Let Marilyn Buscher and her professional staff help you design magical water gardens filled with flowers and colorful fish. Marilyn's business, which she founded in 1972, originally operated as a traditional greenhouse. When she was unable to find any water plants in the area for her backyard pond, she changed tactics and began offering a wide variety of pond plants to the Midwest's gardening community. From there, she expanded into pond equipment and pond maintenance services, including installation, landscaping and upkeep. Marilyn travels to the rainforests of Brazil for some of her exotic seedpods, such as the Victoria, a native Brazilian water lily that grows up to six feet in diameter. Windy Oaks further offers a variety of delightful pond fish, such as koi, shubunkin and sarassas. The water gardens at Windy Oaks Aquatics have been featured in *Country Living* magazine and on the *Great Lakes Gardener*, a popular Wisconsin cable television program. During the second weekend of October, Windy Oaks hosts a four-studio art show that features the work of various local artists, including Marilyn herself, who designs and builds metal sculptures in her spare time. Design the aquascape of your dreams with a visit to Windy Oaks Aquatics.

W377 S10677 Betts Road, Eagle WI
(262) 594-3033
www.windyoaksaquatics.com

PLACES TO GO

- Carson Park
  Carson Park Drive
- Children's Museum of Eau Claire
  220 S Barstow Street
  (715) 832-KIDS (5437)
- Chippewa Valley Museum and Anderson Log House
  1204 Carson Park Drive
  (715) 834-7871
- Chippewa Valley Railroad
  3750 Rimridge Road
  (888) 523-3866
- Eau Claire Regional Arts Center
  316 Eau Claire Street
  (715) 832-2787
- Paul Bunyan Logging Camp
  110 Carson Park Drive
  (715) 835-6200

THINGS TO DO

January

- Eau Claire Ragtime Festival
  First Congregational Church
  www.ecragtime.org

February

- Eau Claire Polar Plunge
  Half Moon Beach, Carson Park
  www.specialolympicswisconsin.org/plunge_a3.asp
- Home and Garden Show
  Indoor Sports Center
  (715) 835-2526

July

- Country Jam USA
  www.countryjam.com

September

- Clearwater Beer Festival
  County Expo Center
  www.ecwijaycees.org/cwbfhome.htm

EAU CLAIRE

Eau Claire, incorporated in 1872, currently has a population of more than 65,000, and it is the heart of a metropolitan area of almost 200,000. The lumber industry drove Eau Claire's growth in the late 19th century. Today, the community has a diverse and expanding economic base in manufacturing, information technologies, health care and retail trade. Colleges include the University of Wisconsin-Eau Claire. The city is the home of the Menards home improvement stores and Silver Spring Gardens, the world's largest grower and producer of horseradish products. Eau Claire is French for clear water, referring to the Eau Claire River. It is pronounced as if it were spelled O'Clare. In 1996, Eau Claire was rated the safest city in America. It remains in the top ten today. Famous Eau Claire natives include sisters Ann Landers and Abby van Buren.

Photo by lisaschaos

The Atrium Bed and Breakfast

ACCOMMODATIONS

A beautiful atrium full of trees, flowering vines and a fountain would make any inn special. At the Atrium Bed & Breakfast in Eau Claire, this skylighted central lounge is just one part of a peaceful and rejuvenating experience. Stained glass windows rescued from an 1850s church add brilliance to the guest rooms and commons areas. What's more, this house with three guest rooms and a two-room suite sits amid 15 acres in western Wisconsin's Chippewa Valley. Wildlife, birds and wildflowers abound here. If you come in the spring, you will find the woods in bloom with trillium and violets. Owners Dick and Celia Stoltz invite guests to follow the winding trails along Otter Creek and enjoy a picnic on the little sandy beach. A homemade breakfast, which may include cappuccino chip muffins and a Wisconsin cheese and egg bake, gets you ready for your ramblings. If you would prefer to stay put, you will find a seat in the patio gardens or the double hammock in the wildflower glen most welcoming. For an inn where the scenery is just as lovely indoors as it is out, try the Atrium Bed and Breakfast.

5572 Prill Road, Eau Claire WI
(715) 833-9045
www.atriumbb.com

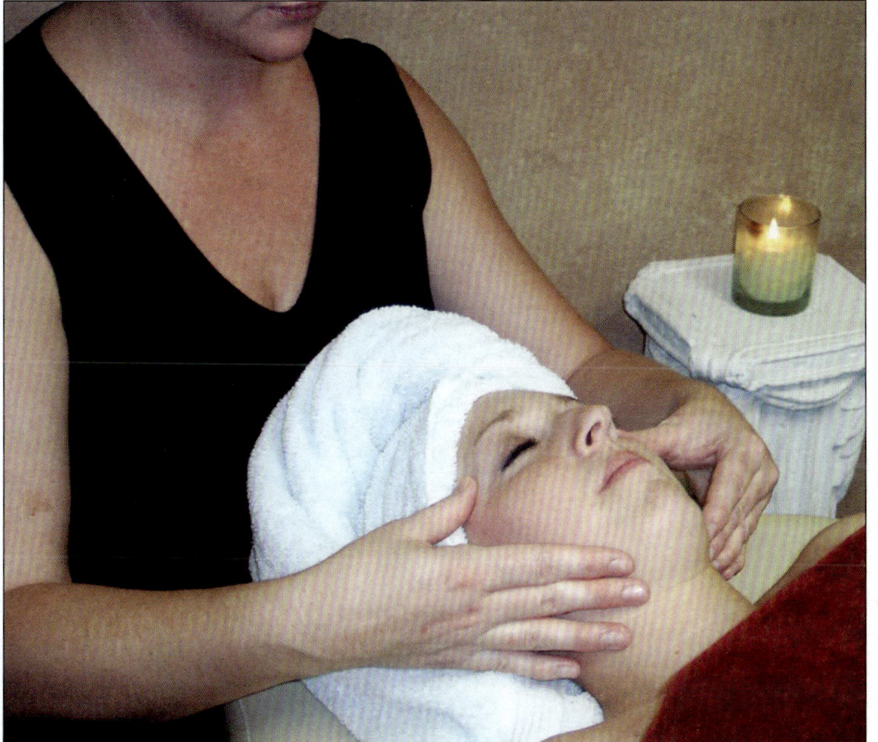

Nicole's Salon, Spa & Tanning

HEALTH & BEAUTY

For more than 10 years, the staff at Nicole's Salon, Spa & Tanning in Eau Claire has had one goal—to make customers look and feel beautiful. To this end, owner Nicole Kuhnert starts by relaxing her clients with warm, soothing surroundings. The special pampering at Nicole's helps the pressures of daily life melt away, at least for a while. You can dissolve the tensions still further with a massage and facial, then carry on with a pedicure or manicure or maybe both. Nicole's stylists will help you find the look that fits the way you feel—traditional or conservative, possibly a little daring. A successful hairstyle and color brings out your self-image while still allowing you to live in your busy world, putting as much or as little effort as you can afford to give to your hair each day. At Nicole's everything you need to accomplish your look is within your reach. Once you have the waves, perms or color of your dreams, you can choose to get extra smooth with body waxing or complement the new you with a glow from one of the salon's six tanning beds. Nicole has worked to bring a set of delights together that will make your visit extraordinary. "If you feel great, we've accomplished our mission," says Nicole. "It's a pleasure to be a part of that." The next time you need to improve your look and your state of mind, visit Nicole's Salon, Spa & Tanning.

1037 W Clairemont Avenue, Eau Claire WI
(715) 835-3510

Norske Nook

RESTAURANTS & CAFÉS

Lots of attention hasn't stopped owner Jerry Bechard from focusing on good old-fashioned hometown cooking at the newest Norske Nook in Eau Claire. Norske Nook began humbly in 1973 as a small town eatery in Osseo. The name Norske Nook means *Norwegian corner* and honored the retired Norwegian farmers who came in at the same time each day. Since *Esquire* magazine named Norske Nook one of the nation's Ten Best Restaurants and the farm wife who founded the restaurant gave David Letterman a lesson on pie making, Norske Nook has become nationally known. It now boasts locations in Osseo, Rice Lake, Hayward and Eau Claire. One of the restaurant's signature creations is the *lefse* wrap, which uses Norwegian flatbread in combination with such American favorites as cod and steak. The Denver lefse puts the ingredients of a Denver omelette on the flatbread and covers the combination with hollandaise sauce. The breakfast, lunch and dinner menus feature many signature meals as well as hearty burgers and pizza. You can enjoy a slice of pie any time of day or buy a whole pie to go at Norske Nook. Bakers rise early each morning to create as many as 30 pie varieties, each with a hand rolled crust and tasty fillings of fruit, creams and cheese. Norske Nook is a first place winner in the National Pie Championship. The Eau Claire Norske Nook is conveniently located next to Northwoods Brew Pub Grill, a place devoted to Jerry's passion for microbrews. For down-home eating from a restaurant that has become famous, visit Norske Nook.

3560 Oakwood Mall Drive,
Eau Claire WI
(715) 552-0510
www.norskenook.com

Northwoods Brewpub and Grill

RESTAURANTS & CAFÉS

Imagine you have been hiking for hours in the woods, and you are tired, hungry and thirsty, when you spot a lodge up ahead that wasn't mentioned in any of the trail guides. You hurry through the door to find people laughing and having a good time, all of them kicked back on log furniture and enjoying pints of beer. "Welcome to Northwoods Brewpub and Grill," says the greeter. "We have more than a dozen microbrewed beers on tap. Would you like to try something light, our White Weasel golden ale, perhaps? It looks like you could use something heartier, the Red Cedar Red or even the Poplar Porter." Subtract the part about getting lost in the woods, and this scene is no dream. Northwoods has been quenching thirsts with its handcrafted beers and satisfying appetites with its grill favorites since 1997. The décor really will make you feel like you are in a lodge in the woods. Founder and owner Jerry Bechard began brewing beer at home in the 1980s and testing it on his friends, all of whom agreed that people would pay to drink beer this good. The crowds who gather at Northwoods prove that his buddies were right. Jerry also owns the restaurant adjoining Northwoods called the Norske Nook, a place that offers more than one way to satisfy your appetite—with fine dinners, burgers, pizzas and over 30 varieties of pie. For your pint of microbrew at the end of the trail, hike into the Northwoods Brewpub and Grill today.

3560 Oakwood Mall Drive, Eau Claire WI
(715) 552-0510
www.northwoodsbrewpub.com

EDGERTON

Edgerton's nickname is Tobacco City U.S.A. because it was at one time a front-runner in the tobacco industry. Farmers in the region still grow a fairly large tobacco crop. At one time, 40 tobacco warehouses dotted the streets of Edgerton, and Queen Anne-style mansions on Washington Street testified to the wealth of the tobacco merchants. The town's founders named it for a 19th century railroad engineer, Benjamin Edgerton. When approached about the use of his name, Edgerton recommended caution. "You better wait until after I'm dead. I might do something to discredit the name." Edgerton was also home to the famous art potter Pauline Jacobus and her husband, Oscar Jacobus, who were active from the 1880s through the 1900s. Today, galleries throughout the world prize Pauline Pottery. The author Sterling North also hailed from Edgerton.

PLACES TO GO

- Central Park
  Swift Street
- Race Track Park
  Stoughton Road
- The Sterling North Home
  409 W Rollin Street
  (608) 884-3074

THINGS TO DO

July

- Edgerton's Heritage Days
  www.tobaccoheritagedays.com

August

- Rock River Thresheree
  Threshermen's Park
  www.thresheree.org
- Afternoon in the Park
  Racetrack Park
  (608) 884-3731

September

- Chilimania
  www.chilimania.com
- Applefest

www.edgertonwisconsin.com/applefest

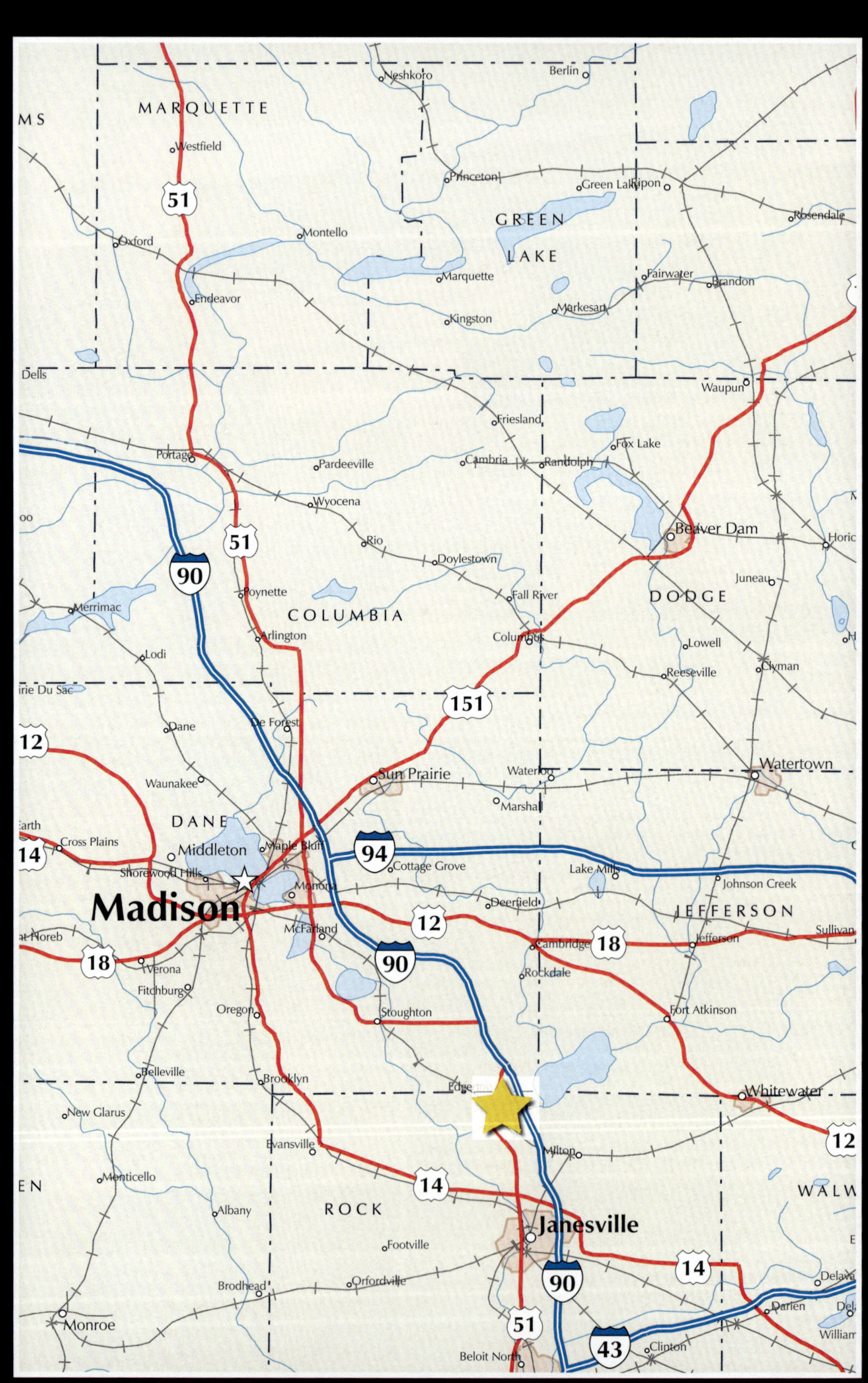

Coachman's Golf Resort

ACCOMMODATIONS

Tucked away in the heartland of southern Wisconsin, Coachman's Golf Resort blends comfortable accommodations, a casual dining restaurant and a regulation 27 holes of golf into one attractive package. Owners Mark Johnson and Lydia Moore, who are brother and sister, carry on a family tradition at Coachman's. Their father Eldon Johnson opened Coachman's Golf Resort upon return from military service in World War II. All packages feature a hotel room adjoining the golf course and unlimited golf. Suites come with fireplaces, televisions and VCRs as well as refrigerators, microwaves and coffee makers. You'll also enjoy the swimming pool, golf pro shop and massage therapy. Homer Fieldhouse designed all three nine-hole golf courses to bring out the best in players while allowing neophyte golfers to keep up. The dining room serves gourmet specialties in an English country inn environment and features a wine list that's been recognized by *Wine Spectator* magazine. The Wisconsin Restaurant Association has recognized the resort, and *Discover Wisconsin* magazine has featured it. Coachman's Golf Resort prides itself on having just what you need to make your affair memorable. As host to your special occasion, meeting, or party, they offer excellent catering services. Perfect for class reunions, wedding receptions, holiday parties and family get-togethers, the banquet facilities hold up to 175 people. Come join the legions of loyal customers who appreciate a great golf getaway at Coachman's Golf Resort, Where Everything is on Course.

984 County Highway A, Edgerton WI
(608) 884-8484 or (800) 940-8485
www.coachmans.com

EGG HARBOR

In the Door County resort region, Egg Harbor offers great golfing, swimming, sandy beaches, a deep-water harbor for sailing, concerts in the park, festivals, and more than 100 boutiques and shops. Meticulously groomed gardens and streetscapes complement restored historic buildings. The village is named for a legendary egg battle that took place in 1825. The battle began when the men of a trading flotilla began throwing hardtack at each other while approaching a spot of land. This escalated into a battle of eggs, which stopped only for want of ammunition, when the men laughed until exhausted. The next morning the battlefield was strewn with eggshells, speeches were made, and the spot was formally christened Egg Harbor.

PLACES TO GO

- Egg Harbor Fun Park
  7340 State Route 42
  (920) 868-9417

THINGS TO DO

May

- Brat Fry
  Harbor View Park

July

- Egg Harbor Fireworks and Parade
  Harbor View Park
  (920) 868-3717

Birch Creek Music Performance Center

ATTRACTIONS

In the fields and woods of Door County lies a beautiful stone and wood barn transformed into a performance hall, and farm buildings remodeled as classrooms and dormitories. This is Birch Creek Music Performance Center, a summer music academy. Birch Creek provides intensive performance-based instruction to promising young musicians. Because of the performance orientation, Birch Creek presents more than 30 concerts from June to mid-August. These concerts have become popular tourist attractions, anticipated by visitors and local residents. Guest performers often participate in the student concerts. Birch Creek students study one of three musical genres: symphony, percussion and steel band, or big band jazz. Birch Creek also provides free outreach concerts at community sites, such as parks, churches and nursing home facilities. Volunteers from the local community help make the Birch Creek experience possible. Birch Creek has a student-teacher ratio of 2 to 1. The faculty comes from universities and schools of music throughout the country, from the University of Colorado to Indiana University. The 200 students of Birch Creek come from all over the country. Most are from 14 to 18 years old. A scholarship program is available. Even if you do not know a young musician who can take advantage of the Birch Creek Music Performance Center's summer program, if you are nearby in the summer, you will want to take in one of Birch Creek's excellent concerts.

3821 County Highway E, Egg Harbor WI
(920) 868-3763
www.birchcreek.org

ELKHORN

Elkhorn was recently rated number 14 on a list of the 100 best small towns in America based on each community's quality of life. The Walworth County seat, Elkhorn is one of the fastest growing towns in Wisconsin. A quaint downtown shopping district blends with new commercial development, and new residential communities complement existing historic structures. The Walworth County Fair in Elkton has been named one of the 25 best county fairs in the country. Band instrument manufacturing was one of Elkhorn's first industries and today both the Getzen Company and the Frank Holton Band Instrument Company continue this tradition. Elkhorn's annual Christmas Card parade has gained national recognition.

PLACES TO GO

- Sunset Park
  699 W Walworth Street
- Webster House Museum
  9 E Rockwell Street
  (262) 723-4248

THINGS TO DO

June

- Harley Fest
  (262) 723-9997

July

- Elkhorn's Star Spangled Celebration
  Sunset Park
  (262) 723-5788

August

- Festival of Summer
  Downtown
  (262) 723-5788

August-September

- Walworth County Fair
  www.walworthcountyfair.com

October

- Oktoberfest
  Downtown
  (262) 723-5788

December

- Elkhorn Christmas Card Parade
  www.elkhorn-wi.org/parade.php

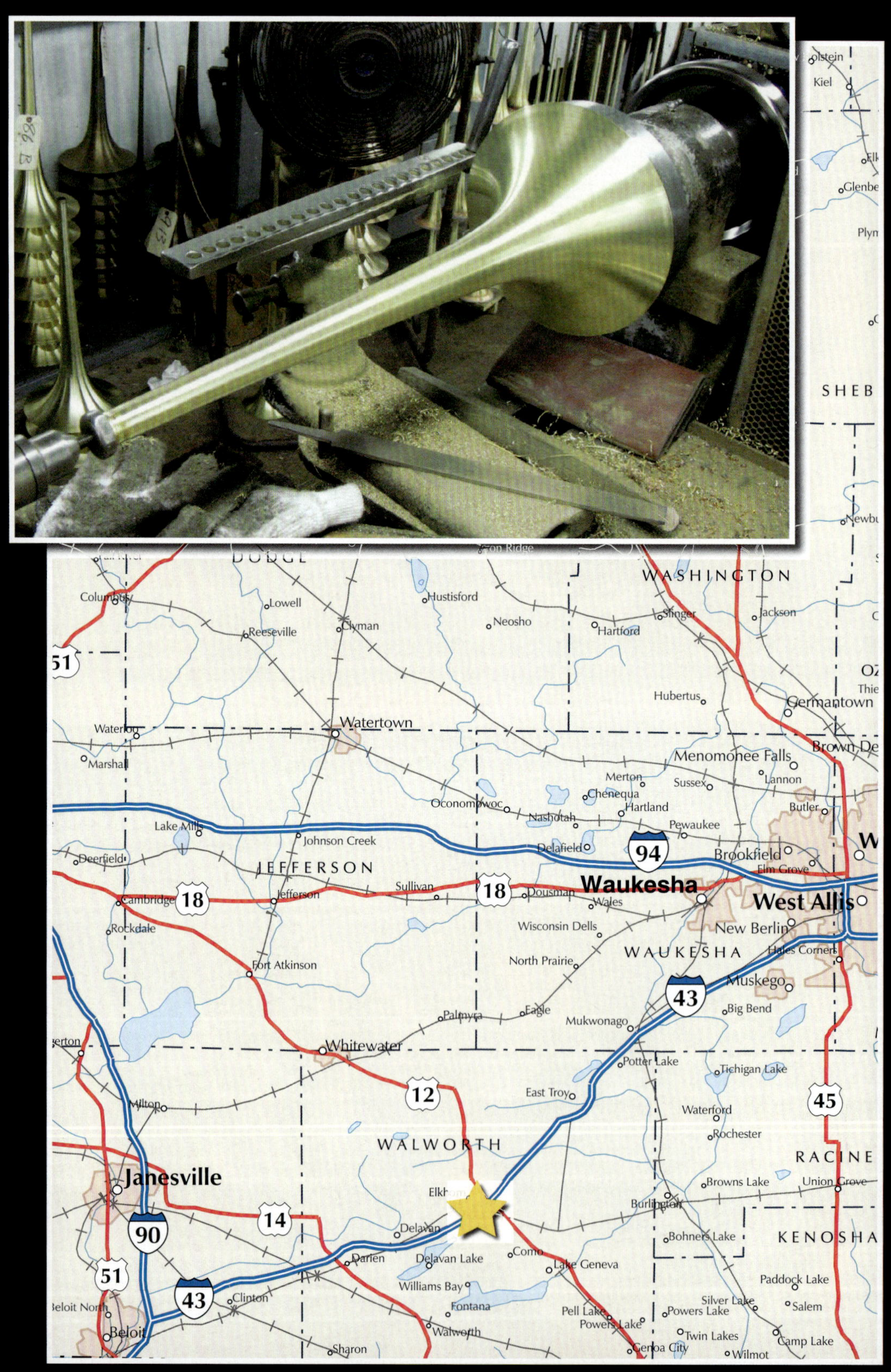

Trombone on lathe in Elkhorn instrument factory
Photo by Daniel Rossi

Kirchoff's Florist & Greenhouses

HOME & GARDEN

When you do business at Kirchoff's Florist & Greenhouses, you'll have a team of growers and a team of floral designers at your disposal. Manny and Jan Kirchoff insisted on growing their own plants for their florist business from the start. In 1976, they operated the business with the support of one greenhouse and soon added a second greenhouse to their backyard. In 1987, they moved their facility to its present location in Elkhorn and now grow their year-round plant needs from six greenhouses. Many facets of the Kirchoff's operation stand out, including their insistence on using water from their well to grow most of their plants, with the exception of the houseplants. One greenhouse is dedicated solely to houseplants, including a fine selection of cymbidium orchids. The Kirchoffs grow greenery, annual flowering plants, perennial landscape plants, hanging baskets and vegetables. They also carry soils, fertilizers and seeds to meet the needs of the home gardener. Seasonal specialties include poinsettias, Easter lilies and azaleas. Whether you're in the market for a singular floral arrangement or planning a wedding, funeral or party, the professional designers are ready to put their creativity to work for you. They'll also time their deliveries to meet your needs. Jan no longer works as a nurse, but she continues to provide tender loving care to her plants and her customers. When you have a need for flowers or greenery, in a pot or cut and arranged, come to Kirchoff's.

420 E Court Street, Elkhorn WI
(262) 723-5505 or (800) 275-4907
www.kirchoffsflorist.com

FISH CREEK

Door County is a natural peninsula often called the Cape Cod of the Midwest. *Money Magazine* has named it one of the top 10 vacation destinations in North America. Plunk in the middle of this beautiful, natural retreat is the little village of Fish Creek, with its tidy, freshly painted buildings. Look around and see the shoreline, bluffs overlooking the deep waters of Lake Michigan and offshore islands. Next to the town you'll find what may be the most wonderful public park for year round activities in Wisconsin—Peninsula State Park. Fish Creek has been a vacation destination for more than 100 years, and several of its original inns are still in operation. Fish Creek's oldest unchanged residence, the Alexander Noble House, was built in 1874 and is open for tours.

PLACES TO GO

- Alexander Noble House
  Main Street
  (920) 868-2091
- Peninsula State Park
  9462 Shore Road
  (920) 868-3258

THINGS TO DO

February

- Fish Creek Winter Games
  Clark Park
  (920) 868-2316
- Kites over the Bay
  (888) 535-KITE (5483)

July

- Fish Creek Fest and Fireworks
  Clark Park
  (920) 868-2316

August

- Peninsula Music Festival
  Door Community Auditorium
  www.musicfestival.com

Photo by Kim Scarborough

Fred & Company

FASHION

Offering a large selection of footwear and a unique selection of women's apparel, Fred & Company is a favorite Door County shopping destination for mothers and daughters alike. Guests can browse distinct collections of daily wear by Mod-O-Doc, Free People, French Connection, April Cornell and other specialty lines. A store favorite is the denim collection by AG Jean, which offers fashionable styles wearable by all body types. The knowledgeable staff can assist you in creating complete outfits or finding a special piece for your wardrobe. The store's expanded footwear selections offer everything from the season's hottest styles to everyday comfort footwear. Be sure to check out the latest styles from Dansko, Frye, Indigo, Reef and Yellow Box. Proprietor Terry Goettelman is on hand most days to welcome visitors to her charming Fish Creek boutique. Don't be surprised if you are also met at the front door by official store greeter Ruby, Terry's dog. Ruby has been welcoming guests to the shop since she was eight weeks old. Some customers stop in just to say hello and see Ruby while on vacation. Come and enjoy a truly unique shopping experience.

4143 Main Street, Fish Creek WI
(920) 868-2338 www.shopfred.com

FITCHBURG

With more than 22,000 people, Fitchburg is a growing suburb of Madison. Fitchburg is a great town for cyclists: several of the best-known Madison area bike trails wind through Fitchburg and surrounding communities. The first permanent settlers were the Vroman brothers, William, George and Joseph. They were Netherlands immigrants who came to the area to work on the State Capitol but turned to farming. An Irish heritage figures prominently in Fitchburg's history and settlement as well. Many descendants of those first families still live in Fitchburg. The city has five sites on the National Register of Historic Places. They include Fox Hall, a Greek revival style stone house built in 1856; the Mann House (Quivey's Grove restaurant) built in 1855; and the Italianate McCoy House built between 1857 and 1861. Other buildings of historic interest include the Oscar Mayer Observatory. Built in 1878, it was moved to Fitchburg in 1960.

PLACES TO GO

- Goodland Park
  2862 Waubesa Avenue, Madison
- McGaw Park
  5236 Lacy Road
- McKee Farms Park
  2881 Mickelson Parkway

THINGS TO DO

April

- Capital City Jazz Fest
  Madison Quality Inn & Suites
  www.madisonjazz.com/jazzfest

May

- Fitchburg Days Festival
  McKee Farms Park
  www.fitchburgdays.com

June

- Festa Italia
  McKee Farms Park
  www.iwcmadison.com/festa

November

- Berbee Derby (run and walk)
  www.berbeederby.com

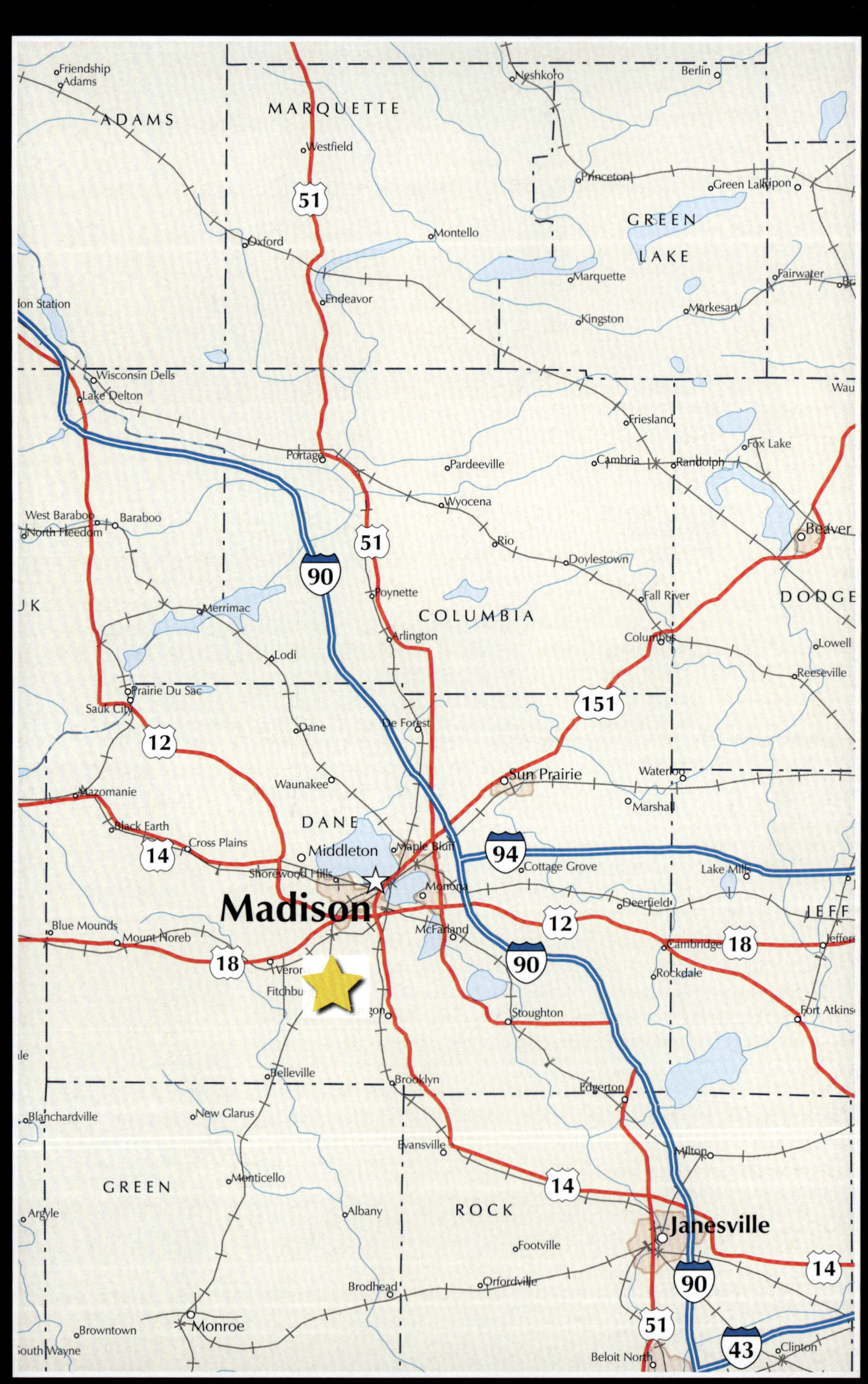

Eplegaarden

ATTRACTIONS

In an age of high tech gadgets and over-scheduling, Eplegaarden stands out as a place where the pace of life is slower and the entire family can enjoy good, old-fashioned farm fun. Owners Vern and Betty Forest founded the Norwegian-themed 105-acre farm in 1993. Since then they have planted a whopping 5,000 apple trees representing more than 100 different varieties, along with other produce that includes raspberries, peaches, pumpkins, gourds, squash and corn galore. When you arrive at the farm, stop by Ole and Lena's Informashun Stashun to see what is available for *plukkin*. Next, take one of the 60 wheelbarrows or wagons out to the field, where you can pluck the perfect apple or pumpkin for yourself. The farm is home to the Wisconsin Sesquicentennial Barn, celebrating 150 years of the state's past. Eplegaarden offers many fall festivities including Harold Potterson's Horrific Haunts for Little Wizards, homemade apple cider and horse-drawn hay rides. Bring a blanket to spread out and enjoy folk music under the apple trees, or reserve the orchard for your next birthday party, family reunion or other gathering. As the slogan has it, Velkommen til Eplegaarden, Da Apple Orchard vit da Norvegian Exposure.

2227 Fitchburg Road, Fitchburg WI
(608) 845-5966
www.eplegaarden.com

Escape du Monde

HEALTH AND BEAUTY

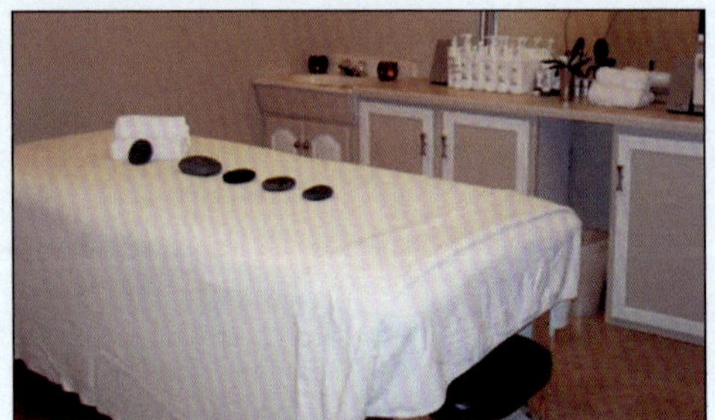

Escape du Monde greets entering patrons with warm tones, fresh flowers and a soothing wall fountain as an invitation to escape from the hectic outside world. You may arrive tired after a long day, but a massage, body wrap or new hairstyle by experienced professionals will leave you rejuvenated. Owners Marie Cerrajero and Beth Gilpin offer a full range of spa and salon treatments using all natural products. Marie and Beth continually train their stylists and aestheticians in the latest treatments and techniques, which ensures your look is always up-to-date. Featured product lines include Aquage, a line inspired by the sea which uses a blend of organic seaweeds and algae, as well as Kenra, a high performance hair care line with pharmaceutical grade ingredients. The licensed aestheticians offer a range of facials, including those with renewing properties of alpha-hydroxy acids, facials geared for a gentlemen's skin, and facials for acne-prone skin. Dermalogica and Cellex-C products are used for treatments and available for purchase. Enjoy the stress relief of a therapeutic deep tissue or stone massage. Full body waxing, restorative body wraps, pedicures and manicures complete the pampering. The salon keeps its doors open into the evening several days a week to accommodate the busy lives of its clients. Make an appointment at Escape du Monde, where you will be able to see and feel the difference in your looks and in your mind.

5973 Executive Drive, Fitchburg WI
(608) 273-6060
www.escapedumonde.com

Barriques

MARKET & DELIS

If your idea of the basic food groups is chocolate, wine, coffee and cheese, then Barriques is your paradise. Barriques offers a club for each of these four. Become a member, and you receive a different selection from around the world each month. The fabulous four are also on the menu at Barriques' bistro-style market. With the mellow sounds of jazz in the background, Barriques provides an upscale yet relaxing environment in which to indulge your appetite for your brand of soul food. Here, along with sandwiches and salads, you'll find cheese and meat platters, which you can wash down with a beer or a glass of wine chosen from the Wall of 100. See the specialty drinks menu board at the counter for all the tasty combinations that can be made with coffee. People have been known to drop by Barriques for coffee in the morning and wine in the evening. Port by the glass and margaritas are also available. Barriques offers a full catering menu that includes its coffees, artisanal cheeses and such dessert specialties as New York cheesecake and chocolate-covered strawberries. For food and drink to make you merry, owners Finn Berge and Matt Weygandt invite you to Barriques.

5957 McKee Road, Fitchburg WI
(608) 277-9463
www.barriquesmarket.com

Nine Springs Golf Course

RECREATION

The Nine Springs Golf Course in the heart of Fitchburg covers 55 acres dotted with mature oaks and bisected by a flowing creek. The nine-hole, par 30 layout has enough hazards to challenge skilled players, yet is friendly enough for people just learning the game. With its small greens, water that comes into play on six of the nine holes, and stately trees guarding three of the short par threes, solid precise shot making is the name of the game. The three par-fours let you use your woods and long irons, and with bunkers throughout the course, you might find yourself working on sand shots as well. Nine Springs boasts a sandwich bar that offers daily specials and a weekday golf and luncheon special. Nine Springs offers lessons for all levels. Beginners can benefit from group lessons, and advanced players can take private instruction from the knowledgeable and friendly staff. The Nine Springs short-game practice facilities are open to all, including a large chipping green with practice bunker and a lighted putting green. Next time you want to grab a quick nine, hit Nine Springs Golf Course, a tidy little golf getaway in the heart of Fitchburg.

2201 Trace Way Drive, Fitchburg WI
(608) 271-5877
http://ninespringsgolfcourse.com

The Great Dane Pub

WINES, BREWS, PUBS & CLUBS

Europe may be the birthplace of the brew pub, but American brew pubs are in their halcyon days, and the Great Dane Pub and Brewing Company in Fitchburg is one of the best. The Great Dane Pub has racked up nearly 150 awards nationally for its beer and food, and one visit will show you why. The first Great Dane was started in Madison by Eliot Butler and Rob LoBreglio, who moved into the famous old Fess Hotel in 1994. They opened the Fitchburg location in 2002. They brew their beers in strict accordance with traditional guidelines, using the finest raw ingredients from around the globe. You'll always find at least 10 different styles, and sometimes as many as 15, all made on the premises. The atmosphere at The Great Dane is friendly and the décor is both upscale and comfortable, with outdoor seating and a menu of pub favorites that are as well prepared as the brews. The Great Dane serves Sunday brunch, a Friday night fish-fry featuring fresh walleye, and homemade desserts. The next time you are in Fitchburg, make plans to visit The Great Dane Pub, one of the best modern examples of a centuries-old tradition.

2980 Cahill Main, Fitchburg WI
(608) 442-9000
www.greatdanepub.com

FONTANA

On Geneva Lake, Fontana offers the peace and serenity of a small town with the recreational opportunities of a resort community. On summer weekends, the town's population may soar from just under 2,000 souls to as many as 7,000. The town is named for its many springs. Nature lovers will enjoy any of three annotated walks in the Fontana Fen conservation area, home to the calcareous fen. This rare type of wetland prairie has an internal ground water system that supports only a few specialized plants.

PLACES TO GO

- Fontana Fen
  Main Street and Dewey Avenue

THINGS TO DO

July

- 4th of July Fireworks
  Lakefront
  (262) 275-5102

September

- Antique Classic Boat Show
  The Abbey Resort
  (262) 275-6811
- Lake Geneva Classic Car Rally
  www.classiccarrally.net

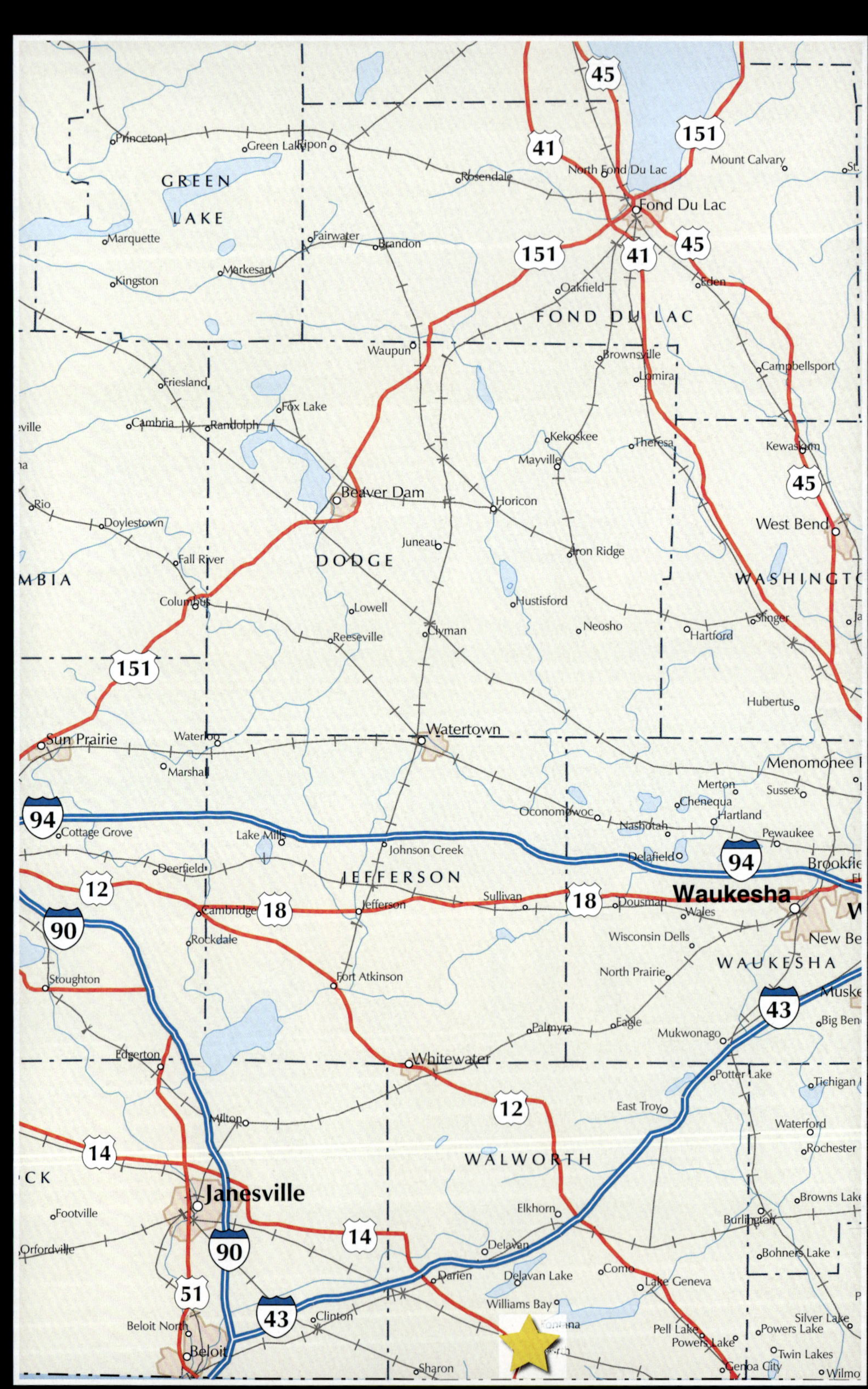

The Abbey Resort

ACCOMMODATIONS

A $40 million renovation the Abbey Resort continues its 40-plus year tradition on Lake Geneva. The 90-acre resort offers 334 luxurious rooms, 40,000 square feet of meeting space, nine distinct cafés and restaurant outlets and a private 407-slip marina. Getting out on this exceptional lake was never easier, thanks to charter tours and a ski school. Groups of two to 15 guests can enjoy a cruise aboard the 32-foot Abbey Gale yacht. After an exciting day of water sports or para-sailing, guests have a choice of restaurants. At the Fontana Grill, you'll enjoy your steak or chops with a view of the marina and the resort's lawns. The Abbey's landmark A-Frame holds the redesigned Porto restaurant, offering a menu with seasonal selections that showcase the flavors of northern Italy, France, Spain and Greece. For a laid-back Key West atmosphere, you'll appreciate the Waterfront, where your burgers, wraps and tropical drinks come with a spectacular harbor view. The Abbey's concierge staff can help you find the right activity for you any time of the year. Perhaps your interests will take you to the Fontana Spa for a massage or a full day of pampering. The Abbey staff also can arrange a tee time at one of several area golf courses. The Kids Club supervises younger guests with numerous fun activities, including a Kid's Night Out, which features an evening of crafts, games and a movie complete with a pizza party. Put all the pleasures of Lake Geneva at your fingertips with a stay at the Abbey Resort.

269 Fontana Boulevard, Fontana WI
(262) 275-9000 or (800) 709-1323
www.TheAbbeyResort.com

Gordy's on Lake Geneva in Fontana

RECREATION & FITNESS

Gordy's on Lake Geneva in Fontana is the largest commercially owned property on the lake and offers a full slate of marine goods and services. Company President Tom Whowell was 15 years old when his father Gordy launched the business in 1955 as a seasonal boat ride and rental operation. Since then, three generations of Whowells have pitched in to create a powerful family tradition and an international reputation. Today, Gordy's offers a marina; boat sales, service and storage; and a ski and wakeboard school. You'll find a pro shop featuring the famous Gordy Gear, a bait shop, and a seasonal deli and ice cream shop. You can dock your boat at one of the three piers and visit the celebrated Boat House Restaurant or rent a boat from Gordy's by the hour or the day. Private parties enjoy the spectacular Cobalt Lounge, which comfortably holds up to 50 people. Many groups renting the lounge also take advantage of the private charter cruise boat, the *Diamond Lady*. Gordy's not only offers many services, it offers superior ones. In 2005, its Cobalt boat dealership earned a ranking of 15th in *Boating Industry* magazine's listing of the top 100 dealers. It has also repeatedly received Cobalt Dealership Awards for annual sales in excess of $1 million. The Lake Geneva Area Convention and Visitor's Bureau awarded Gordy's a hospitality award for its outstanding contribution to the boating industry. Come enjoy what Whowell family tradition can do for you at Gordy's on Lake Geneva in Fontana.

320 Lake Avenue, Fontana WI
(262) 275-2163
www.gordysboats.com

FORT ATKINSON

Surrounded by some of the world's finest dairy herds, Fort Atkinson is set against the beautiful backdrop of Lake Koshkonong and the Rock and Bark Rivers. Fort Atkinson is a growing community—*Money Magazine* has named it one of America's Hottest Little Boomtowns. The city grew up on the site of a 19th century fort originally called Fort Koshkonong. It was renamed to honor General Henry Atkinson, who served in the War of 1812 and the Black Hawk War. Fort Atkinson's largest employer and anchor of the tourism industry is the Fireside Dinner Theatre. The city also boasts high-tech industry, upscale shops and a striking downtown riverside.

PLACES TO GO

- Hoard Historical Museum and National Dairy Shrine
  407 Merchants Avenue
  (920) 563-7769
- Rock River Park
  1300 Lillian Street

THINGS TO DO

May

- Buckskinner Rendezvous
  Rock River Park
  (888) 733-3678

June

- Baseball Fest and Marketplace
  Jones Park
  (414) 698-5559

July

- Old Fashioned Ice Cream Social
  Hoard Museum
  (920) 563-7769

Hoard Historical Museum

ATTRACTIONS

For 50 years, the Hoard Historical Museum has preserved the past for future generations. Under the direction of the Fort Atkinson Historical Society, the museum collects and preserves the treasures of the area. The museum is located in a home built during the Civil War by a prominent local businessman. Frank and Luella Hoard purchased the home in 1906. When Luella passed away in 1956, her two children donated the home to the city of Fort Atkinson to be used as a museum. The museum's name honors Frank's father, William Dempster Hoard, former governor of Wisconsin and father of the Wisconsin dairy industry. The museum is home to the National Dairy Shrine Visitors Center with a multimedia show that captures the past, present and future of dairy farming. The Indian Artifact Room features more than 4,000 archaeological artifacts that detail the prehistory of the American Indians who lived in the Jefferson County area. The Lincoln Era Library and Exhibit chronicles President Lincoln's participation in the Black Hawk War of 1832 and his influence on Jefferson County. The historical society sponsors a variety of free events that enrich the community. Events include the Civil War History Program, Mary Hoard Art Show, the longest running local art show in the state of Wisconsin, the Holiday Open House and the 4th of July Ice Cream Social. The museum is closed Mondays; admission is free. Visit the Hoard Historical Museum, and learn more about the fascinating history of the Fort Atkinson area and the families who built it.

407 Merchants Avenue, Fort Atkinson WI
(902) 563-7769
www.hoardmuseum.org

GERMANTOWN

As its name suggests, Germantown was a pioneer settlement known for German immigrants and German culture. Dheinsville, established in 1842, is Germantown's oldest crossroads settlement. The spot is a park and historical center today. Half-timber (*fachwerk*) buildings reflect the original construction methods of early settlers from the Hunsruck area of Germany. The Dheinsville commercial center is composed of log, quarried limestone, brick and clapboard buildings dating from early settlement through the Victorian era. Germantown retains its *Gemütlichkeit* today, but it is also one of the fastest-growing suburbs in the Milwaukee area.

PLACES TO GO

- Bast Bell Museum
  W18780 Holy Hill Road
  (262) 628-3170
- Dheinsville Settlement
  Six-way Crossroads and Holy Hill Road
  (262) 628-3170
- Homestead Hollow Park
  Freistadt Road

THINGS TO DO

June

- Worldwide Wine-Tasting Party
  Bast Bell Museum
  (262) 628-3170

September

- Oktoberfest
  Dheinsville Settlement Park
  (262) 628-3170
- Fall Country Art & Craft Fair
  St. John United Church of Christ
  (262) 251-0640

Cake & Bake

BAKERIES, COFFEE & TEA

Lynn Zehms and Chris Bulgren remind you that life is short, so eat dessert first. They are the dessert experts at Cake & Bake in the Germantown Marketplace, and they want you to think of their store whenever you think of cake. Their custom decorated masterpieces have been adding to the fun at parties and weddings since 1998. Selling cakes and such other scrumptious desserts as éclairs, cookies and cupcakes is just part of what Lynn and Chris do at Cake & Bake. They also teach cake decorating and candy making with special theme classes to complement the season. Prepare for Christmas, for example, with a two-and-a-half-hour class on making Christmas candy, decorating Christmas cookies or creating gingerbread houses. Basic cake decorating classes are held throughout the year in a two-day mini-course or a more extensive four-week course. Cake & Bake also carries a full line of cake decorating equipment, cookie cutters and other baking supplies. Need some dough to go? Lynn and Chris will sell you ready-to-bake frozen dough to make everything from breads and muffins to cinnamon buns, cookies and strudels. If it's already past noon and you haven't had dessert yet, then it's time to head to Cake & Bake.

W164 N11271 Squire Drive,
Germantown WI
(262) 502-1219
www.cakeandbake.com

The Parlor

HEALTH & BEAUTY

If you've ever watched a professional dance team perform during breaks in a basketball game, you know that their routines provide a real aerobic challenge. Their hair gets quite a workout, too, yet it always looks good. Ask Ann Weber and her staff at The Parlor in Germantown how that's possible. The Parlor is the official salon of the Milwaukee Bucks' Energee! Dance Team, so the stylists here are experts on cutting and maintaining hair for active lifestyles. They'll put some bounce in your hair and make sure it stays that way no matter how many cartwheels you turn. They also like working on naturally curly hair. The Parlor has been featured as a Top Salon in *Milwaukee Magazine*, where it was recognized for its outstanding hair services. It has also been highlighted in local papers for fundraising, local magazines for makeovers, and on curly hair websites. Ann worked for other salons for 11 years before fulfilling her dream of opening her own salon in 2001. She keeps the atmosphere at The Parlor fun but very professional, which also sums up each Energee! performance. Root for the Bucks, and feel like a million bucks with salon services from The Parlor.

W161 N11629 Church Street, Germantown WI
(262) 253-6800

The Flower Source

HOME & GARDEN

As you peruse the two acres of greenhouses full of roses, annuals and perennials at the Flower Source in Germantown, consider that owner Kostas Koutantzis can hardly recall a day in his life that didn't involve entering a greenhouse. His family's home back in his native Greece was surrounded by them. The family has been in the flower business since 1905. Kostas recalls that there was no time for playing soccer or any other sports when he was growing up. He, his two brothers and their sister were too busy learning the names of the flowers and plants. At dinner every night, conversation would turn to the needs of the plants and the related subjects of insect control, diseases and the market. The parents invited the children to help solve the problems that arose in the business. Inevitably Kostas went to school in Florence, Italy to study horticulture. Today, Kostas can overlook never being given the chance to become a soccer star as he presides over the Flower Source, a business success story since 1982. In addition to the greenhouses brimming with flowers, the Flower Source features acres of display area. There, you will find shrubs as well such garden décor as arbors, birdbaths and benches. The outstanding service from the knowledgeable staff is a Flower Source trademark. For flowers by the thousands from a man who knows their names by heart, visit the Flower Source today.

W156 N11124 Pilgrim Road, Germantown WI
(262) 251-ROSE (7673)
www.flower-source.com

Sneakers Health & Fitness

RECREATION & FITNESS

Sneakers Health & Fitness is Germantown's upscale adult fitness center. Sneakers provides top-notch equipment, excellent customer service and the classes and training you need to meet your personal fitness goals. Sneakers is proud to offer Bodybugg, the world's most intelligent calorie management system. The Sneakers facility is bright and clean. A large cardiovascular area features cross-trainer machines, elliptical trainers, treadmills, steppers and bikes. Selectorized (that is, adjustable) weight machines as well as free weights help build muscle and strength. Classrooms feature state-of-the-art hardwood floors, sound systems and equipment such as steps, weights, power bands and mats. The clean and spacious locker rooms feature free towel service, shampoo, conditioner and hair dryers. Permanent lockers are available. Well-attended classes include Basic Exercise and Strength Training (BEAST), Power Pump strength training and the Studio Cycling classes with Schwinn spinning bikes. The 15-minute Crunch Time classes are also popular. Membership is month-by-month and there are no contracts. Childcare is available. Sneakers is the brainchild of Mark Miller, a marketing major with a life-long passion for fitness. Join Mark at Sneakers Health & Fitness, where you can develop a training plan that is right for you.

W175 N11162 Stonewood Drive, Germantown WI
(262) 502-1800
www.sneakersfit.com

Vintage Fine Wine Selections

WINES, BREWS, PUBS & CLUBS

After years of dreaming, planning and educating himself about wine, John Edwards opened Vintage Fine Wine Selections in 2005. John has been involved in the wine business for more than 25 years, starting out as the wine and spirits buyer for his family's restaurant and eventually working his way up to be a state manager for Gallo Winery. Having his own Germantown wine shop lets him share the expertise he acquired during his career in wine sales. John enjoys helping customers with their selections and expanding their horizons. Vintage Fine Wine Selections carries more than 400 domestic and imported wines as well as 60 varieties of imported and microbrewed beers. You'll find an assortment of wine accessories and glassware in the shop. Vintage features wine sampling and discussion on Thursday, Friday and Saturday afternoons. Monthly wine classes often feature a special guest speaker and opportunities to expand your wine knowledge. Beer classes are held from time to time, too. Members of the Wine Club receive two special wine selections each month, held for them at the shop. The club offers a great way to take advantage of expert guidance while venturing into new wine territory. For John Edwards, wine is a journey, not a destination. Join him and develop your own expertise at Vintage Fine Wine Selections.

N112 W16700 Mequon Road,
Germantown WI
(262) 250-1602
www.vintagegermantown.com

PLACES TO GO

- Kletzsch Park
  6560 N Milwaukee River Parkway
- Lincoln Park
  1301 W Hampton Avenue
- Old Heidelberg Park
  700 W Lexington Boulevard
  (414) 964-0300

THINGS TO DO

June

- Scottish Fest/Highland Games
  Old Heidelberg Park
  (262) 796-0807

July

- Glendale Days—A 4th of July Festival
  www.glendale-wi.org/days.htm
- Greater Milwaukee Open
  www.usbankchampionship.com
- Bavarian Volkfest
  Old Heidelberg Park
  (414) 964-4221

September

- Octoberfest
  Old Heidelberg Park
  (414) 964-4221

GLENDALE

Glendale, the last six square miles of the old Town of Milwaukee to incorporate as its own city, straddles the banks of the Milwaukee River. The city is home to more than a dozen well-known corporate names that occupy its two major industrial parks. In 1953, Glendale was one of the first cities in the nation to construct a shopping center and, 20 years later, to enclose it as an indoor shopping mall. The Bayshore Mall continues to be a fashionable destination for area shoppers, offering locally-owned stores and brand names not found in other malls. The Glendale Centre, a mixed-use area, gains distinctive character from the city's signature décor, expressed in street lighting, banners, markers and paving. The 318-acre Lincoln Park includes an outdoor swimming pool, nine-hole golf course, baseball and softball diamonds and a performing arts pavilion. Kletzsch Park, at 119 acres, features a terraced waterfall, wooded terrain, and extensive open spaces dotted with ancient Indian burial mounds. During the eight weeks of summer, the Glendale Recreation Department sponsors a free weekly concert series, Music in the Glen.

Brass Bell Music Store

ARTS & CRAFTS

In 2006, Brass Bell Music Store celebrated 35 years as a family-owned, full-service music store serving the Milwaukee area. Alan Gaulke, a band director, spent a great deal of time trying to locate instruments for his students before eventually opening the store. He has since passed the reins to owner and daughter Tristann Rieck and son Todd Gaulke. Brass Bell sells, rents and services educator-recommended, brand-name band and orchestra instruments as well as rock band instruments. You'll find related accessories, such as instrument cases, oils and sheet music, in the large 7,400-square-foot facility. Three available qualities and rental price ranges for band and orchestra instruments ensure that every student, from beginner to advanced, will find a suitable instrument. Tristann, who plays French horn in several community orchestras, loves to see people becoming involved with music and wants Brass Bell to be the music store they count on. More than 50 instructors teach private lessons and group classes in Brass Bell's 16 studios. Brass Bell offers lessons in all instruments for any age and any skill level. The recital hall hosts many exciting events, and a variety of musicians, including aspiring rock bands, use the practice rooms. When music matters, find what you need under one roof at Brass Bell Music Store.

210 W Silver Spring Drive, Glendale WI (414) 963-1000 *www.brassbellmusic.com*

GRAFTON

Quiet, tree-lined Grafton is one of the oldest communities in Ozaukee County. Timothy Wooden purchased the 145 acres that would become Grafton's business district in 1838. Settlers, mainly of German descent, had the area under development within two years. They built lumber and grist mills on the rapids of the Milwaukee River. They found vast limestone deposits underlying the region, and in 1846, Wooden established the first limestone quarry. By 1900, Wisconsin ranked third nationally in lime production. You can still see remains of the Milwaukee Falls Lime Company quarries and reefs in Lime Kiln Park. A pavilion that looks like an old railroad depot hosts performing arts here. During the 1920s, the Milwaukee Northern Interurban Railroad carried early country, jazz and blues musicians to Grafton to record for the legendary Paramount Records. Lime Kiln Park is now the site of an annual blues festival commemorating this heritage. Downtown on the square, a museum dedicated to Paramount Records is under construction as part of a comprehensive revitalization project. The Milwaukee River, which flows through the heart of the city, is the site of an annual canoe race.

PLACES TO GO

- Centennial Park
  1370 17th Avenue
- Lime Kiln Park
  2020 S Green Bay Road

THINGS TO DO

April
- Downriver Canoe Race
  (262) 377-1650

July
- Holidaze 4th of July Celebration
  Lime Kiln Park
  (262) 377-1650

September
- Paramount Blues Festival
  Lime Kiln Park
  (262) 377-1650

Timeless Trenz

HEALTH & BEAUTY

From everyday hair and nail care to luxurious pampering, Timeless Trenz offers a full-service salon experience for men and women that will prepare you to attend any occasion looking stylish. The Grafton salon also features a boutique with a variety of gifts and accessories. Included is a wide range of jewelry such as custom-made stones, gems and fine diamonds. The owners, Jennifer Salmon and Mary Jo Lorenz, have been friends for over 15 years and bring that sense of affability and style to the salon. Timeless Trenz offers a complete menu of services which include everything from basic haircuts to texture treatments, such as permanent waves or highlights to give individual special effects. Enhance your final look by visiting their Nail Spa Suite, located inside the salon. Their nail tech offers a healthy alternative to nail enhancements with ultraviolet light gel nail product. If you're looking for a more artistic statement, try varieties of nail art to complete your look. For more in-depth care, treat yourself to a paraffin manicure or a deluxe spa pedicure. You'll have no problem relaxing and putting yourself into the capable hands of the expert staff in this upscale, comfortable environment. Those looking to bring a bit of the salon experience home with them will appreciate the array of pampering products for body and hair care. Other treasures you may find here include candles, all occasion cards, photo or art prints, and hand-sewn handbags and scarves. Gift certificates are available year-round for your personal gift giving. For a full salon experience that never goes out of style, come to Timeless Trenz.

1209 11th Avenue, Grafton WI
(262) 387-1209 (Jennifer)
or (262) 376-1209 (Mary Jo)

GREENFIELD

Settlers from New England named Greenfield after Greenfield, Massachusetts, and in honor of its vast green fields. Greenfield originally covered 36 square miles of the Milwaukee area. Beginning in 1902, portions of Greenfield that wanted city services began incorporating or asking to be annexed by Milwaukee. West Allis (1902), West Milwaukee (1906), Greendale (1938), Hales Corners (1952) and the southwest side of the City of Milwaukee resulted. Greenfield today is a third of its original size. A little-known fact is that the city purposefully has no sidewalks. Greenfield's original Honey Creek Settlement is now the site of the Greenfield Historical Society. The grounds preserve the 1832 Finan-Gabel-Bodamer Log Cabin, dedicated as a museum in 1969. Also on the site is the Montag-Boogk Cream City Brick Home. The house is an example of the famous Milwaukee cream-colored brick.

PLACES TO GO

- Konkel Park
  5151 W Layton Avenue
- Honey Creek Settlement
  56th Street and W Layton Avenue

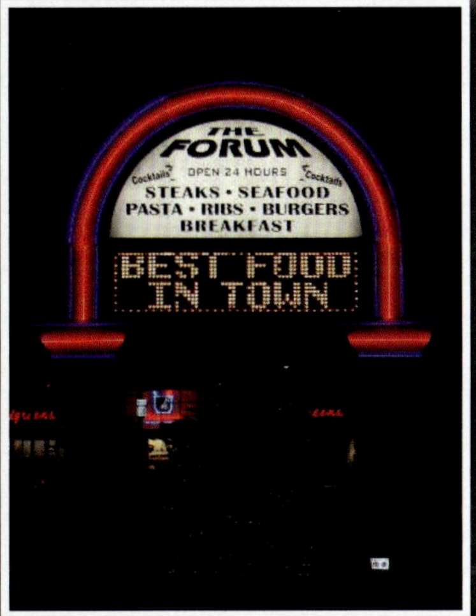

Forum Restaurant

RESTAURANTS & CAFÉS

Sam Diamantopoulos, owner of the Forum Restaurant, invites guests into a 200-seat dining area that is true to the meaning of the word forum as a meeting place. Centrally located just 10 minutes from downtown Milwaukee or the airport, on the southwest corner of Highway 100 and Layton Avenue, the Forum feeds droves of hungry people 24 hours a day, seven days a week. Generous breakfast portions are a main attraction as are the free desserts that complete such traditional Forum family meals as steak, fish, meatloaf and pasta. Its size notwithstanding, the Forum is a place with personality, defined by a rich cherry wood interior. The spectacular U-shaped pie case, imported from Italy, marks the entrance into the seating area in grand style. The muffins, pies and cakes on display within the case come straight from the Forum's in-house bakery. Sam and the rest of his family, which includes his father Peter, his mother Georgia and his sister Voula, are Greek immigrants living the American dream of turning hard work and a great product into a successful business. The tremendous customer loyalty which the Forum enjoys speaks for itself. For your meeting and perhaps some new friends, try the Forum Restaurant.

4711 S 108th Street, Greenfield WI
(414) 529-4001

HALES CORNERS

Hales Corners, three square miles of Milwaukee County, is named for its original white settlers, brothers Seneca and William Hale and their father Ebenezer. In 1837, the Hales each claimed 160 acres of property on three of the four corners at the intersection of Janesville Road and 108th Street. The settlement grew as an agricultural center. Hales Corners is home to 600-acre Whitnall Park, which includes the world-famous Boerner Botanical Gardens. Charles Whitnall, secretary of the Milwaukee County Parks Commission from its inception in 1941, conceived of the park as nature resort where city dwellers could commune with gardens, lakes and streams. Historical landmarks in Hales Corners include the original Hale summer kitchen and the 1924 Ben Hunt log cabin.

PLACES TO GO

- Ben Hunt Cabin
  (414) 425-6040
- Boerner Botanical Gardens
  9400 Boerner Drive
  (414) 525-5600
- Whitnall Park
  5879 S 92nd Street
  (414) 257-5100

THINGS TO DO

June

- Arts & Crafts Show
  Sacred Heart School of Theology
  (414) 425-7208

September

- Labor Day Art and Craft Fair
  Sacred Heart School of Theology
  (414) 425-7208

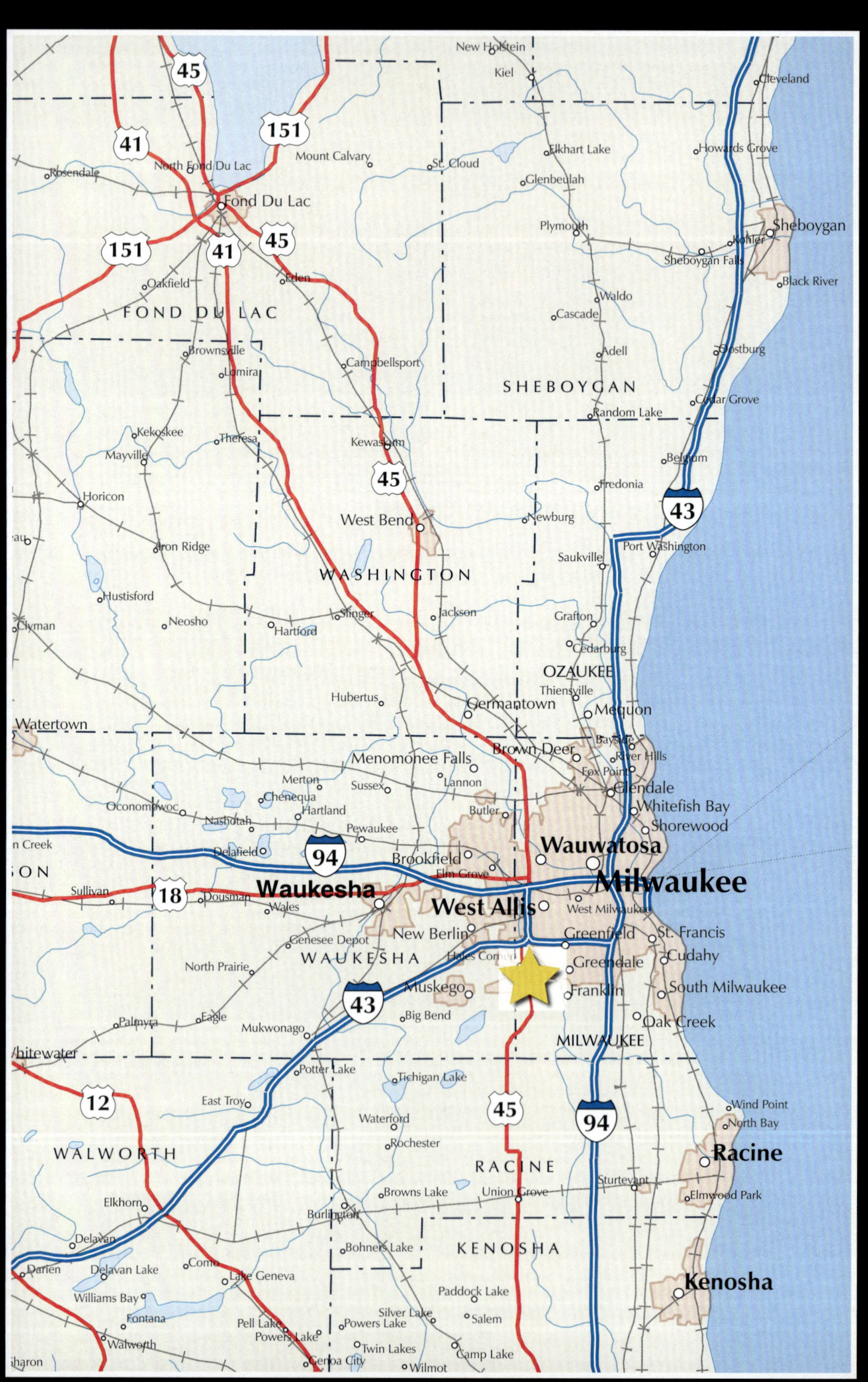

Corners Pet and Grooming

ANIMALS & PETS

Heidi Wilson's future was marked since the time she slept with a jar of worms when she was a little girl. Her love of all animals great and small drove her to take in strays, to work for the Elmbrook Humane Society, and finally in 2000, to purchase Corners Pet and Grooming. The business has been around since 1975, and the first thing Heidi did was double its size, so that it now offers a full gamut of supplies and grooming services as well as a large variety of animals. Along with dogs and cats, Corners carries fish, amphibians and exotics. It will not only sell you a cockatiel or parakeet and provide you with the information you need to be a responsible pet owner, but it will also tend to your bird's maintenance from nails to beak to wings. The store's two full-time groomers will bathe your dog and clean your hamster's teeth. Corners is the place to find healthful food for whatever pet you own. Heidi and her staff are committed to upholding the highest standards in the pet profession, starting with maintaining a pleasant, clean environment for their animals and customers. For a store where love of animals meets love of service, go to Corners Pet and Grooming.

5430 S 108th Street, Hales Corners WI
(414) 425-PETS (7387)
www.cornerspet.com

Bead Needs

ARTS & CRAFTS

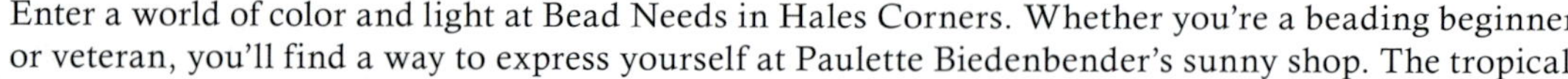

Enter a world of color and light at Bead Needs in Hales Corners. Whether you're a beading beginner or veteran, you'll find a way to express yourself at Paulette Biedenbender's sunny shop. The tropical mural serves as a colorful backdrop for the rainbow hues of fine Japanese Toho seed beads and whimsical ceramic beads from Jangles. Choose from silver Bali beads, vintage German beads and dazzling Swarovski crystal beads from Austria. You'll be able to stock up on beading supplies, too, and can find the right wire, pliers or string for your latest project. Classes teach beginners basic bead stringing and design, while more experienced beaders can perfect their stitches with the help of Alice Korach, founding editor of *Bead & Button* magazine. Bead Needs also offers special parties and events. A Bridal Beading party offers a relaxing and creative escape from hectic wedding planning as bride and bridesmaids, mothers and friends create jewelry and accessories. Ladies Night Out offers a chance for your favorite friends to craft perfect cuff bracelets or sparkling necklaces. Girls and Girl Scouts can also indulge in the need to bead through scheduled classes or as part of a scout meeting. Whether you need a necklace restrung or crave creative expression in colored glass and gemstones, visit Bead Needs.

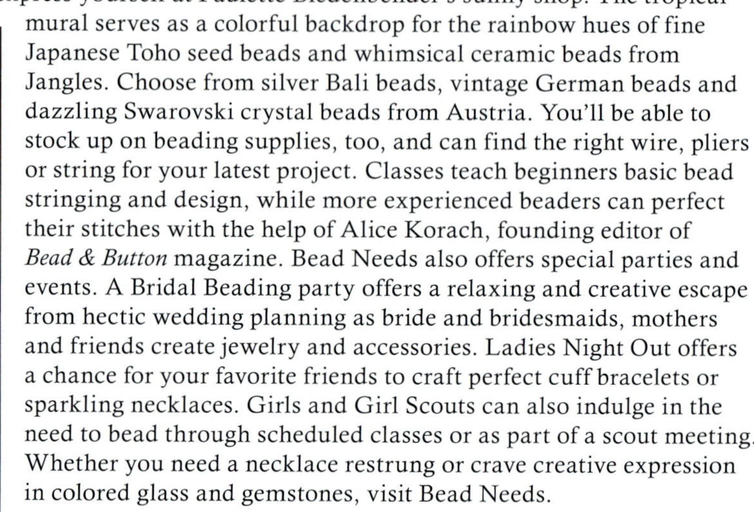

5150 S 108th Street, Hales Corners WI
(414) 529-5211
www.beadneedsllc.com

Wheel & Sprocket

RECREATION & FITNESS

Visiting any of the six Wheel & Sprocket stores in Wisconsin is like going to a cycling fair. From kids' tricycles to $10,000 exotics, Wheel & Sprocket brings you the world of cycling in all of its variety. With close to 1,000 bikes on display at each location, it's fascinating just to look at all of the possibilities. In addition to a large selection of road and mountain bikes, you will find tandems, recumbents and even one-wheel exercise bikes. The dealers represented read like a Who's Who of industry leaders, with Wisconsin's own Trek topping a list that includes Schwinn, Gary Fisher and racing cycle specialist Lemond. However, it's more than just volume of sales that has earned Wheel & Sprocket Retailer of the Year awards from the bicycle industry. The company's 150 very dedicated employees don't see themselves as representing a business so much as a cause. Promoting cycling as a positive lifestyle choice starts at the top with the president of Wheel & Sprocket, Chris Kegel, who started biking on his paper route at the age of 13 and was one of the store's first employees in the early 1970s. Every year the company raises more than $1 million for charity. For what's happening in the world of cycling, go to Wheel & Sprocket.

5722 S 108th Street, Hales Corners WI
(414) 529-6600 or (800) 362-4537
www.wheelandsprocket.com

That's Amoré

RESTAURANTS & CAFÉS

Many folks in the Milwaukee area have developed a love affair with That's Amoré in Hales Corners. This restaurant offers large portions of authentic Italian cuisine in a casual atmosphere. The appetizers, which can function as mini-meals, include such favorites as mozzarella marinara, eggplant roll-ups and grilled calamari. The sandwich menu is loaded with variety, from the relatively light chicken parmigiana to the hearty Dino Cheesesteak, a prime rib topped with mushrooms, onions, green peppers and plenty of mozzarella. The entrées at That's Amoré feature both original recipes and traditional dishes. Consider such delights as the Sicilian steak with its coating of homemade bread crumbs or the Crabby Chicken, topped with crabmeat and Alfredo sauce and served over pasta. The Nonno Tonys, as seen on *The Sopranos*, toss sautéed potatoes, bacon, Italian sausage, mushrooms and green peppers with spaghetti. Each night brings a different special, such as the Monday all-you-can-eat shrimp, the Friday fish fry and the Thursday Pig-out Day with its special pork menu. Families appreciate the children's menu and the special kids' price on Tuesdays. AOL members voted That's Amoré Best of the Burbs in 2002 and best for Family-Friendly Italian Comfort Food in 2005. Owner Joe LoPiparo and his father Antonio are at the restaurant every day. The LoPiparo family came from Sicily in the 1950s; they maintain close ties with Italy through visits, and all family members speak Italian. For authentic Italian food and generous proportions, come to That's Amoré.

5080 S 108th Street, Hales Corners WI
(414) 425-7150
www.foodspot.com/thatsamore

PLACES TO GO

- Loew Lake Unit, Kettle Moraine State Forest
  St. Augustine Road
  (262) 670-3400
- Pike Lake Unit, Kettle Moraine State Forest
  3544 Kettle Moraine Road
  (262) 670-3400
- Wisconsin Automotive Museum
  147 N Rural Street
  (262) 673-7999

THINGS TO DO

March

- It's A Spring Thing Craft Fair
  St. Kilian School
  (262) 673-4308

August

- American Accents:
  A Festival of Fine Arts and Crafts
  Willowbrook Park
  (262) 673-0708

September

- Rendezvous and Buckskinner's Encampment
  (800) TAN-HIDE (826-4433)

HARTFORD

Hartford is on the edge of the Kettle Moraine Forest, a natural wonder of glacial landforms that attracts thousands of visitors. Hartford encompasses the Loew Lake and Pike Lake units of the forest. A kame, or hill left by glacial melt, rises 1,300 feet above Pike Lake, offering dramatic views. James and Charles Rossman built a dam and sawmill here in the 1840s. Rossman's Saw Mill brought steady growth to Hartford. In 1855, the Milwaukee-LaCrosse rail line came through—this was the main line between Minneapolis and Chicago for more than 50 years. The W.B. Place & Company tannery, established in 1866, still sells leather goods in Hartford. Each September, the company hosts a Rendezvous and Buckskinner's Encampment. In the early 1900s, the Kissel Motor Car Company built cars in Hartford. Tourists can see a large collection of vintage Kissels and other historic autos at the Hartford Heritage Auto Museum. Hartford's attractive downtown boasts historic buildings, specialty boutiques and many antique shops. It is ornamented with brick paving and old-style benches.

Schauer Arts & Activities Center

ATTRACTIONS

The Schauer Arts & Activities Center boasts a professional quality theater, art gallery and meeting spaces that make it a hub for cultural arts and entertainment in the central Kettle Moraine region, as well as a charming venue for private functions. Fred and Bea Schauer envisioned the building, originally a 1918 canning factory, as a place for the community to come together to develop, support and promote the arts. In 2000, after five years of hard work by many community-minded folks, their dream became reality. The 571-seat Ruth A. Knoll Theater with state-of-the-art acoustics spotlights local, national and international talent. In the Suckow Family Art Gallery, hardwood floors and original wood beams remain from the building's early days. The public can explore rotating exhibits of photography, painting and other artwork. If someone in your family has an artistic bent, consider enrolling them in the Community School of the Arts performing and visual arts classes for all ages. The Center includes ample space for social events, such as weddings, receptions or business functions. Huge windows in the 4,000-square-foot Pike's Peak community room overlook Jordan Park, the Rubicon River and beautiful downtown Hartford, providing a spectacular backdrop for any occasion. Visit the Schauer Arts & Activities Center, conveniently located between Milwaukee, Madison and Green Bay, at a virtual Crossroads of Art and Entertainment.

147 N Rural Street, Hartford WI
(262) 670-0560 ext. 201
www.schauercenter.org

Chandelier Ballroom

BUSINESS & SERVICES

A distinctive space full of history and elegance, the Chandelier Ballroom adds a special touch to any important function. The ballroom, built in 1928, hosted such big band performers as Lawrence Welk, Guy Lombardo and the Dorsey Brothers. This musical hot spot underwent several name changes and once served as a camp for prisoners of war. In 1949, Marty Zivko purchased the ballroom and brought in numerous local and national music groups to perform on a regular basis. The Hartford Rotary Foundation purchased the building in 1996 and spearheaded an ambitious $1 million renovation, and the community came together with generous donations of time and money to restore the building to its former grandeur. The Hartford Historic Preservation Foundation now owns the ballroom, which is listed on the National Register of Historic Places. The Chandelier's crown jewel is the Signicast Great Hall, a large octagonal ballroom with a ceiling that rises to a lofty peak in the center of the room. A German art deco chandelier, surrounded by 28 smaller chandeliers, casts a magical light over the original maple floors, which are perfect for dancing the night away. With a seating capacity of 600, the great hall offers plenty of room for a large wedding, trade show or other gala event. If you would like to provide guests with a more intimate setting, the Steel Craft Fireside Room features an inviting stone fireplace surrounded by wood paneled walls and a full bar. Give your next event a sense of history while making new memories at the Chandelier Ballroom.

150 Jefferson Avenue, Hartford WI
(262) 673-4946
www.chandelierballroom.com

Mickey's Fresh Frozen Custard

FUN FOODS

Mickey's Fresh Frozen Custard offers a tantalizing array of ice cream treats along with sandwich specialties, hamburgers and Chicago-style hot dogs. In fact, you'll find just about everything but diet food. In 1993, Kim and Jeff Mueller bought the shop from the original owners, who had employed Kim while she attended college. Having also worked for Eddy's Grand Ice Cream for seven years and sometimes working simultaneously at both ice cream shops, Kim knew she would enjoy the business. Her emphasis has always been on using the best and freshest ingredients, and she believes presentation is everything. The food must be delicious and look good, too. She picks her own strawberries from a local grower's field and uses pure vanilla extract in the custard. Mickey's is known for its turtle sundaes, which come fully loaded with crunchy pecans roasted in salt and butter. The malts are still made with old-fashioned malt powder. Healthy hamburgers feature low-fat beef from steers raised on Jeff's family farm. The Muellers employ about 15 people during their March to October season. Kim caters area events, such as company picnics, balloon rallies and various charity fundraisers. Mickey's has become a favorite community hangout, and Thursday night is cruise night, an opportunity to see many classic cars parked outside. For great-tasting food in a fun, friendly atmosphere, cruise by Mickey's Fresh Frozen Custard and indulge in something cool and creamy.

675 Grand Avenue, Hartford WI (262) 670-2663

hbor tells neighbor about LENNOX heating comfort!
LENNOX
Aire-Flo Heating
JOHN THIELMANN & SON

John Thielmann & Son

HOME & GARDEN

When you turn to John Thielmann & Son for your heating and air conditioning needs, you will get a business that has spent 77 years making homes comfortable. John Thielmann & Son provides all your heating and cooling needs, as well as air quality systems, sheet metal services and repair of all makes and models of heating and cooling units. In 1929, John Thielmann founded the family business, servicing boilers and oil furnaces. His son Walter soon joined forces with him, building the business into what it is today. Together, John and Walter became the local representatives of the Lennox Furnace Company. The family tradition continued with Walter's sons, Paul and Tom, who started helping in the shop when they were still in grade school. Paul took over the business in 1969 and introduced air conditioning. Tom rejoined the business as a service technician in 1977 and continues to serve as the company's office and service manager. Now, under the ownership of Brad Smith, the company's high standards of quality and customer service remain steadfast. One of the oldest Lennox dealers in the state, John Thielmann & Son recently earned the Lennox 60-Year Award. Generations of loyal customers return to the company for the focus on quality products and carefully performed installations. Let the experts at John Thielmann & Son put their years of experience into making your home feel just right

501 W Sumner Street, Hartford WI
(262) 673-2500

The Mole Hole of Hartford

SHOPPING

Mother and daughter Claudia and Krysta Deede relished browsing through their favorite gift shop, the Mole Hole of Hartford. There, they knew they could find the perfect treasure for everyone on their gift list. When they heard the store was closing, Claudia and Krysta decided to purchase it together and continue to provide shoppers with gifts, collectibles and home accents. The store's featured lines of collectibles include Wee Forest Folk, tiny painted mice filled with personality, and Department 56 lighted villages, carefully detailed miniature porcelain houses. The Mole Hole carries gifts for the bride and groom, as well as the bouncing baby. Friendly service and thoughtful extras, such as complimentary gift wrapping and a bridal registry, make the items easy to choose and give. Claudia and Krysta place a great deal of importance on giving back to the community and support several nonprofit organizations, including the American Cancer Society, Hartford Food Pantry and Shop with a Cop, which pairs needy children with police officers for a day of holiday shopping. Come visit the Mole Hole of Hartford and see for yourself why Claudia and Krysta worked to keep this charming store open.

100 N Main Street, Hartford WI
(262) 670-1400
www.moleholehartford.com

Expedition Supply Ski-Cycle-Sporting Goods

RECREATION & FITNESS

Expedition Supply is a true bicycle shop. Offering expert advice and personal service, it specializes in creating cycling awareness throughout the southeastern part of the state. Owner Mike Raasch started at the age of 15 working part-time at the local bike shop and eventually purchased the business in 1996. Mike combines traditional philosophy with century-old technique that has been handed down through many generations of bicycle shops. Today in two locations, Expedition Supply is staffed with some of the area's most talented and creative bicycle technicians who are willing to answer questions, give technical advice and even tell a good story. Whether you prefer a leisurely stroll along a bike path, or to go screaming downhill, Expo covers the full spectrum. For the BMX crew, Expedition Supply carries the latest in frames, forks, clothing, shoes and accessories. It doesn't stop here. Expo carries the top name brand skateboards and accessories as well. When winter hits, there is no slowing down—Expedition Supply covers your winter sporting needs with snowboards, alpine skis, cross-country skis, snowshoes and outerwear. Mike believes it is important to give back to the community and Expo donates time, products and services to many local charities. The store sponsors a mountain bike team and a snowboard team that compete throughout the state. Race over to either Expedition Supply location for everything you need to get active.

20 W Sumner Street, Hartford WI (262) 673-7303
108 S Center Street, Beaver Dam WI (920) 821-2000
www.expeditionsupply.com

Design Originals Floral

SHOPPING

Design Originals Floral in Hartford opened in 1989, but Owner Charlene Jung started in the business many years earlier. Working for a florist for eight years gave her hands-on experience, and graduating from a floral program at Lakeshore College in Cleveland prepared her to open her own business. A natural artist with flowers, Charlene strives to put creativity into everything that goes out the door, which means no two designs are ever alike, unless by customer request. She offers seasonal discounts, including specials on roses in June and on foliage plants in March. As a full-service florist, Charlene provides timely delivery and innovative floral designs for any occasion. She specializes in weddings, handling everything from flowers to tuxedo rentals. Design Originals also stocks greeting cards, plush animals, baby gifts, lots of home décor items, as well as balloons and balloon bouquets. Charlene offers in-home consultations, custom silk arrangements and plant rentals for home and office. An avid supporter of numerous charitable and community functions, she donates many dozens of roses on Good Neighbor Day, with the stipulation that the receiver keeps only one rose and gives the other 11 away to friends and neighbors. Charlene's artistry and merchandise selection guarantee you'll find original ways to honor special occasions when you stop in at Design Originals Floral.

15 N Main Street, Hartford WI
(262) 673-6844
www.designoriginalsfloral.com

Robin, Wisconsin state bird

HUBERTUS

Hubertus is an unincorporated community located within the Town of Richfield and Town of Erin in Washington County. Early settlers to the area were farmers attracted by the soil in Richfield, which is well-watered by streams of the Rock River system. Two battling glaciers, the Green Bay and Michigan, had disrupted the land, leaving a striking landscape. A driving tour of Hubertus provides dramatic views of this landscape. The community of Hubertus arose alongside a former railroad that brought passengers to the Basilica of Holy Hill. The Basilica, with its accompanying National Shrine of Mary, Help of Christians, continues to attract pilgrims from near and far. Home to the Holy Hill Monastery, the neo-romanesque church, with its priceless stained glass windows and magnificent mosaics, sits at one of the highest points in the state. Thousands of visitors climb to the top of the observation tower inside one of the spires for a spectacular view. In addition to religious services, Holy Hill hosts community events and has a gift store and cafeteria.

PLACES TO GO

- Basilica of Holy Hill
  1525 Carmel Road
  (262) 628-1838

THINGS TO DO

September

- Holy Hill Arts Festival
  Holy Hill Monastery
  (262) 628-1838

Photos by Curtis Waltz/aerialscapes.com

Country Coffee House and the Farm at Holy Hill

ATTRACTIONS

Relax and enjoy a cup of gourmet coffee inside an original 1890s farm house. Driving onto the 10-acre property immediately reduces the stress of busy city life. Owners Marc and Lee Ann Steffens opened their business two years ago, after discovering this land in the heart of the Kettle Moraine. They knew it was the perfect place for their combined coffee house, gift barn, country market and farm. Sip a steaming hot specialty drink or a refreshing fruit smoothie as you wander the grounds. Find a shady spot under the trees to eat a snack or sandwich. Inside the coffee house discover paintings, pottery, jewelry, home décor and other items handcrafted by the area's creative artisans. The country market offers fresh eggs from the farm's free-roaming chickens, organic meat and produce, jams, jellies and specialty cheeses. Visitors love the tasty difference of golden yolks, which are part of the hearty farm breakfast. Quiche, fresh baked goods, organic yogurt and granola round out the selection. The lunch menu features delicious specialty sandwiches. The favorite is locally made focaccia bread filled with a variety of meats, salads, or cheeses, then grilled panini style. In the fall, celebrate harvest time at the farm. Pumpkins, hay bales, gourds and other seasonal items offer a natural approach to decorating. A petting zoo and other activities welcome kids. Find distinctive treasures and gifts while shopping in the gift barn. Come to the Country Coffee House and the Farm at Holy Hill for wholesome fun the entire family will enjoy.

4231 Highway 167, Hubertus WI
(262) 628-4010

Alpine Retreat Supper Club

RESTAURANTS & CAFÉS

The Alpine Retreat Supper Club is so full of history and humor, it's easy to forget what makes it great: the food. The inside of this historic restaurant is decorated with mementos of the Alpine Retreat's early years, including WWI photos, a beer cap collection that strings across the bar, genuine football helmets, vintage beer bottles and more. Every item has a story behind it. Owner C.J. Klemmer has deep roots here. His parents owned the restaurant back in the 1970s, and his aunt and uncle owned it after that. C.J. and his wife, Jean, bought the business in 2002 and made it better than it ever was. Jean recently passed away, but C.J. is carrying on, doing what he does best, which is prepare delicious meals in a friendly, down-to-earth atmosphere. The Alpine Retreat is known for steaks and Friday fish frys with the best walleye you'll ever eat. C.J. also serves a fine lamb chop, great soups, and ice cream drinks that are locally famous. The Alpine Retreat has a history that reaches back to 1932. The intervening years brought world wars, the Great Depression, births, deaths and ownership changes, but the business has survived. Pieces of C.J.'s past and the restaurant's history are evident throughout this fine old establishment, including a pair of wooden shoes from C.J.'s Dutch grandfather. Visit the Alpine Retreat for a great meal, and be sure to ask about the story behind the supper club's mascot, Ira the Goose.

1380 Friess Lake Road, Hubertus WI
(262) 628-3995
www.alpineretreat.net

Fall colors from the Holy Hill Monastery tower in Wisconsin

JACKSON

Jackson is a fast-growing northern suburb of Milwaukee. In 1988, a new expressway that allowed for 30-minute commutes between the cities brought an influx of relocation to Jackson. Jackson's population grew by 99 percent during the 1990s and is projected to continue growing. A hundred years earlier, the railroad brought civilization to Jackson. German immigrant Franz Reis, who had acquired 400 acres in the hamlet, offered his property for a railroad depot. The prosperity brought by the depot allowed Franz to build Jackson's first general store, saloon and grain elevator. Citizens of Jackson gather at Jackson Park, which offers a duck pond, picnic areas and free movies and concerts in the summer.

PLACES TO GO

- Jackson Park
  3500 W Forest Home Avenue
  (414) 672-5052

THINGS TO DO

June

- Action in Jackson Family Festival
  Downtown
  (262) 677-9665

October

- Annual Fall Classic Golf Outing
  Hidden Glenn Golf Club
  (262) 387-0100

November

- It's A Stitch Craft Fair
  Heidel's Restaurant
  (262) 377-9521

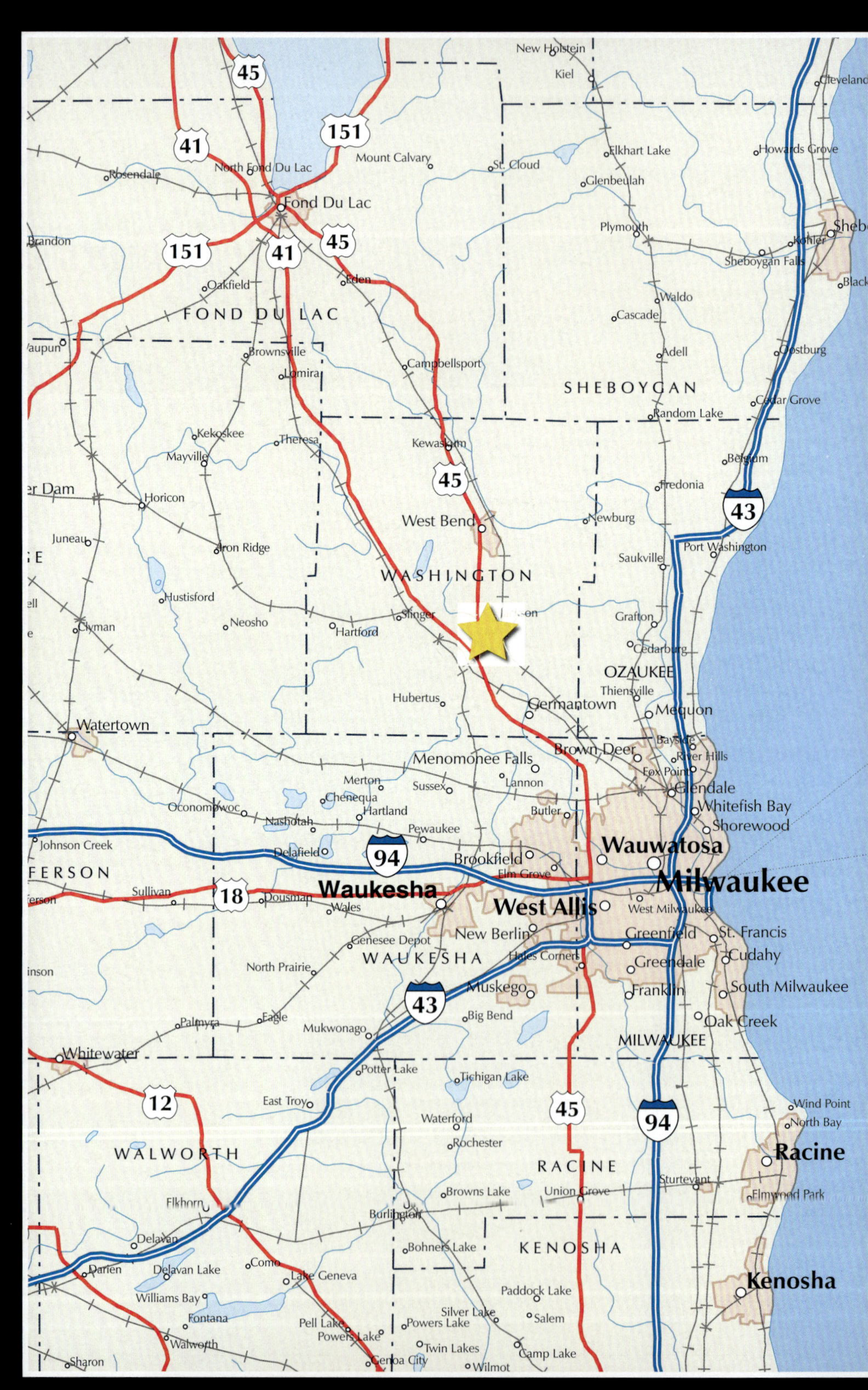

Jackson Crossing Retirement Community

LIFESTYLE DESTINATIONS

Jackson Crossing is a retirement community that offers the peace and tranquility of waterfront living, freeing you from the daily worries of maintenance and utility costs. Secure and private, Jackson Crossing gives you an assortment of floor plan choices, from a studio to a two-bedroom apartment home. Enjoy watching the wildlife from the private balcony or patio that comes with each residence. A private fishing pier, individual garden plots, putting green, walking paths along the lake, whirlpool spa, beauty parlor, wellness center, art center, computer lab, dining service, transportation, and free pharmacy delivery are just a small sampling of what sets Jackson Crossing Retirement Community apart from the rest. The Lakeshore, The Landmark and The Lodge at Jackson Crossing offer three different levels of living. The Lakeshore is an independent resort-type community. The Lodge provides a higher level of personal care. The Landmark is an assisted living program with a 24-hour nursing staff, better suited for those experiencing significant health care needs. All of the employees at Jackson Crossing are specialized professionals, with 50 percent registered nurses, and the rest certified aides. At Jackson Crossing, owner and RN Amy Lloyd keeps life simple, right on down to the billing process. No matter which accommodations you choose, quality of life is valued and promoted at every level of the Jackson Crossing Retirement Community.

N168 W22022 Main Street, Jackson WI
(262) 993-2838
www.jacksoncrossings.com

JEFFERSON

Jefferson lies between Milwaukee and Madison at the confluence of the Rock and Crawfish Rivers. The city is known for its historic buildings and German heritage. Its two rivers support recreation, and Rotary Park on the Rock River hosts free concerts in the summer. Jefferson is home to the Aztalan State Park, which preserves one of Wisconsin's most important archaeological sites. A 12th century Indian civilization left remains of a village in the park, which was marked by large, flat-topped pyramidal mounds and surrounded by a stockade. The Aztalan Museum preserves remains of a pioneer village, including a church, cabin and school, and prehistoric Indian artifacts.

PLACES TO GO

- Aztalan State Park
  County Highway Q
  (920) 648-8774
- Lake Mills/Aztalan Museum
  N6284 Highway Q
  (920) 648-4632

THINGS TO DO

July

- 4th of July Celebration
  Jefferson County Fair Park
  (920) 674-4511
- Badgerland Bluegrass Music Classic
  Fairgrounds
  (414) 961-0660
- Jefferson County Fair
  www.jeffersoncountyfairpark.com

September

- Gemuetlichkeit Days
  Fairgrounds
  www.gdays.org
- Wisconsin Sheep & Wool Festival
  Fairgrounds
  www.wisconsinsheepandwoolfestival.com

October

- Autumn Fest
  Jefferson County Fair Park
  (608) 244-8416

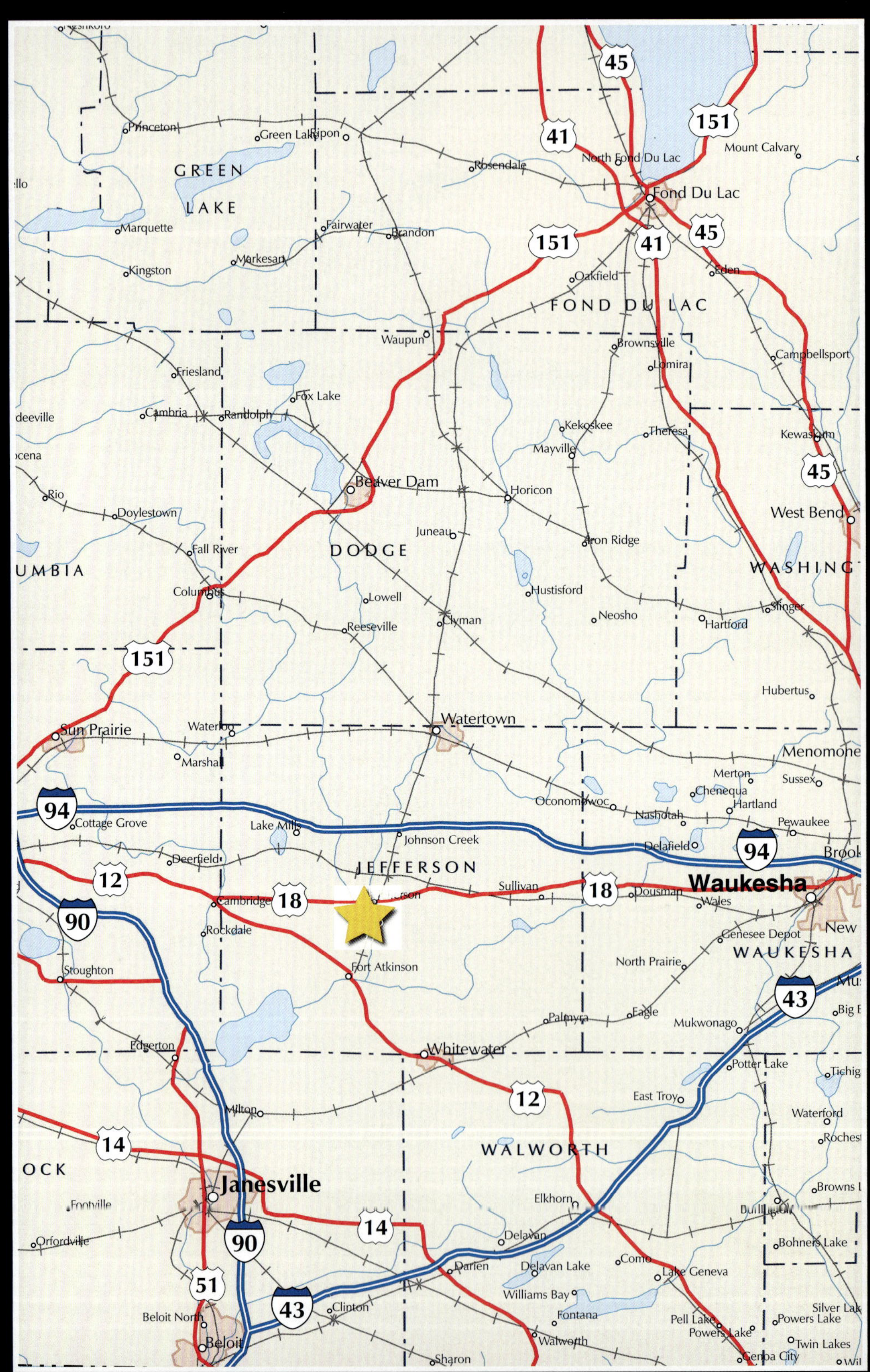

Towne Inn

RESTAURANTS & CAFÉS

A casual atmosphere, good food and great prices make Jefferson's Towne Inn the kind of place people like to go to hang out with friends after a ballgame. The restaurant serves pizzas, sandwiches and fish-and-chips, but regulars insist that if you really want a taste of Wisconsin, you should try the house specialty, the Butch Burger. It is made with a half pound of choice ground chuck and piled with your choice of tasty toppings, such as bacon, mushrooms and Swiss cheese. If you stop by on a Tuesday, the Butch Burger is half off. Towne Inn offers other great specials every day of the week, like half off the menu price for any pizza on Mondays. Owner Kevin Brumm enjoys being a part of the community, and the restaurant is proud to sponsor local athletic groups. Each year, Kevin participates in a race for charity, making him a small town business owner with a big heart, literally and figuratively. For tasty food in a friendly atmosphere, come to Towne Inn, because It's Where the Fun Begins.

124 W Rockwell, Jefferson WI
(920) 674-2547

El Chaparral Restaurant

RESTAURANTS & CAFÉS

Every day is a fiesta day at El Chaparral Restaurant, close to Highway 94 in Jefferson. Specializing in authentic Mexican cuisine, this family-owned and operated restaurant has been serving up savory dishes to hungry customers since 2000. Owners Jorge and Glory Baker offer a menu of favorites, including *Lo Favorito de la Casa* (the favorite of the house), a mouthwatering selection of meaty enchiladas, crispy chimichangas and steaming fajitas. Food isn't the only thing that's spicy at El Chaparral; everything about this restaurant adds a zesty twist to your dining experience. El Chaparral makes its home in the historic Jefferson House, which dates back to 1837 when a single room rented for $1.50 per night and a double room for $2.50. Miss Kitty's bar was located here, and the original tin and copper ceiling and beautiful mahogany wood accents continue to provide El Chaparral with its authentic charm. You can challenge yourself and your friends to a thrilling ride on the mechanical bull, enjoy live music on the weekends plus exciting karaoke nights where you can show off your singing talents. The restaurant is open seven days a week with a four-hour happy hour Monday through Friday. Stop in and be sure to say a hearty *hola* to Jorge and Glory.

135 S Main Street, Jefferson WI
(920) 674-6040

JOHNSON CREEK

Located at the intersection of Interstate 94 and State Highway 26, Johnson Creek calls itself the Crossroads with a Future. In recent years, the village has hosted many new residential and commercial developments. Johnson Creek Premium Outlets boasts 60 stores with brand names such as Adidas, Calvin Klein, Eddie Bauer, Liz Claiborne, Nike and Tommy Hilfiger, among others. The picturesque Rock River winds through the village, setting the scene for fishing and boating excursions. South of the village you can access to the Glacial Drumlin State Bike Trail, a 53-mile trail for bikers, hikers and snowmobiles.

PLACES TO GO

- Fireman's Park
  Union Street
- Jefferson County Dog Park
  Bicentennial Park
  www.co.jefferson.wi.us/dogpark
- Johnson Creek Premium Outlets
  575 W Linmar Lane
  (920) 699-4111

THINGS TO DO

August

- Creek Fest
  (920) 699-4949

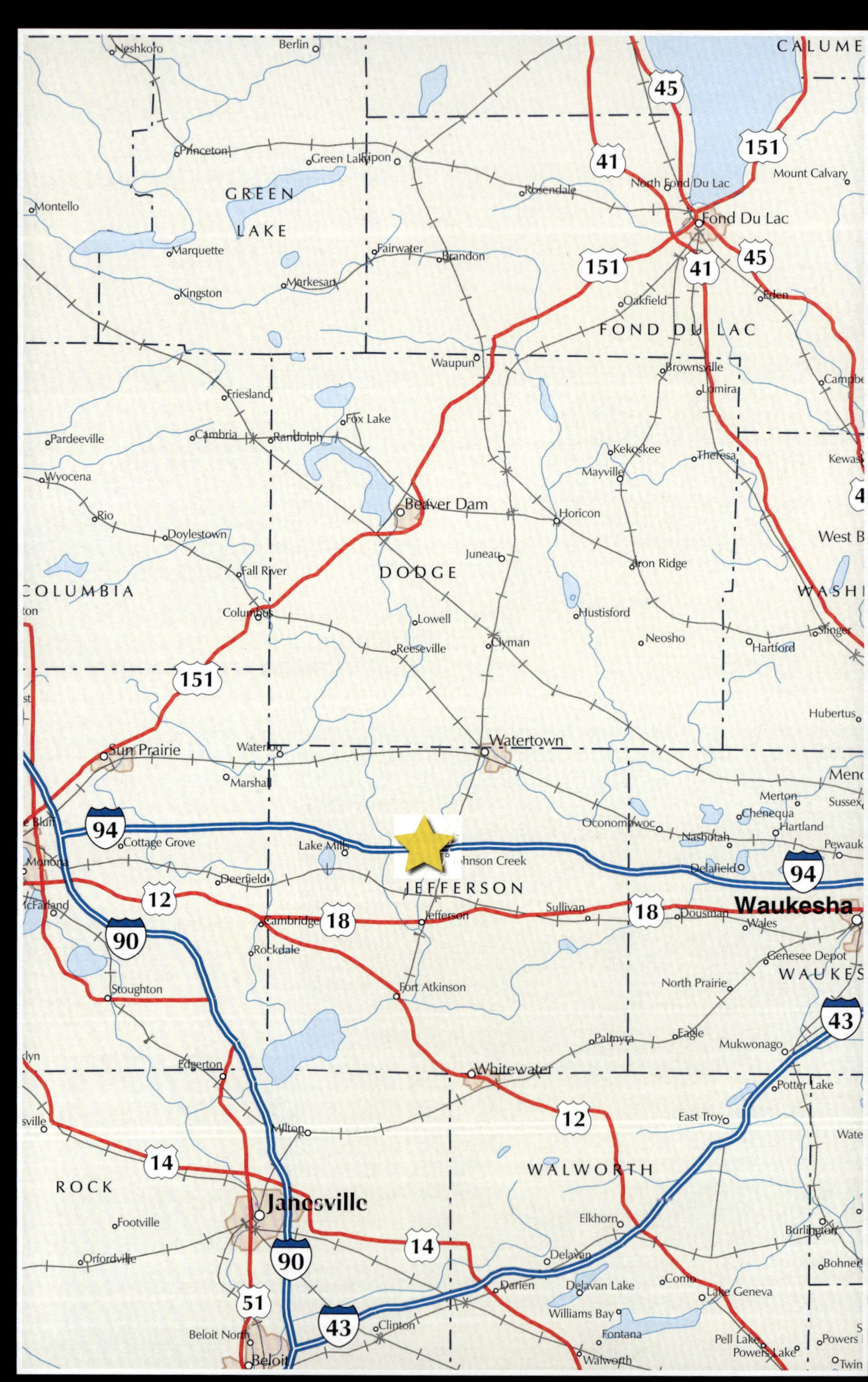

Pernat's Premium Meats

MARKETS & DELIS

Ask any deer hunter in Dodge and Jefferson County where to go for top quality deer processing, and they'll point you straight to Pernat's Premium Meats. Located off of Interstate 94 and Highway 26 in Johnson Creek, Pernat's is family owned and operated, and owners Brian and Bonnie Pernat are proud that every customer is a return customer. Pernat's processes many meats, including venison, but you don't have to be a hunter to savor Pernat's outstanding sausages. In fact, customers from all over the country enjoy Pernat's sausage products. Famous for its homemade natural casing wieners, Pernat's offers a wide selection of meats, including summer sausage, smoked Polish sausage and ring bologna. You'll also find an abundant assortment of cheeses. Brian and Bonnie are active in the community and offer fundraising opportunities for local youth athletic teams, church groups or 4-H clubs. Additionally, Pernat's hosts a weekly brat fry in cooperation with the local radio station, where an average of 1,200 brats are served up and devoured in just three hours. Whether you want to process your own meat or just want to taste the best sausages around, Pernat's is the place to go in either Johnson Creek or Juneau.

312 Milwaukee Street, Johnson Creek WI
(920) 699-6990
N4202 County Highway M, Juneau WI
(920) 386-3340

JUNEAU

Juneau is the seat of Dodge County, in a rich agricultural valley beside the Rock River. Juneau was once a virgin forest known to the Indian tribes as Waushereka, the land of foxes. The city's namesake, Paul Juneau, was the son of an Indian princess and of Solomon Juneau, the founder of Milwaukee. Being half white and half Indian, Juneau often acted as mediator in controversies between white settlers and their Indian neighbors. He was highly respected by both communities. In 1858, Juneau was accidentally shot by a boy playing with a horse pistol. His death almost caused an Indian uprising. After the Indians were convinced that it was accidental, they buried Juneau between two oak saplings, the highest honor they could grant. These oaks, his only monument, stand in the city cemetery.

PLACES TO GO

- Wild Goose State Trailhead
  4 miles S, State Highway 60

THINGS TO DO

August

- Juneau August Fest
  City Park
  www.juneauwi.org/events.cfm#August

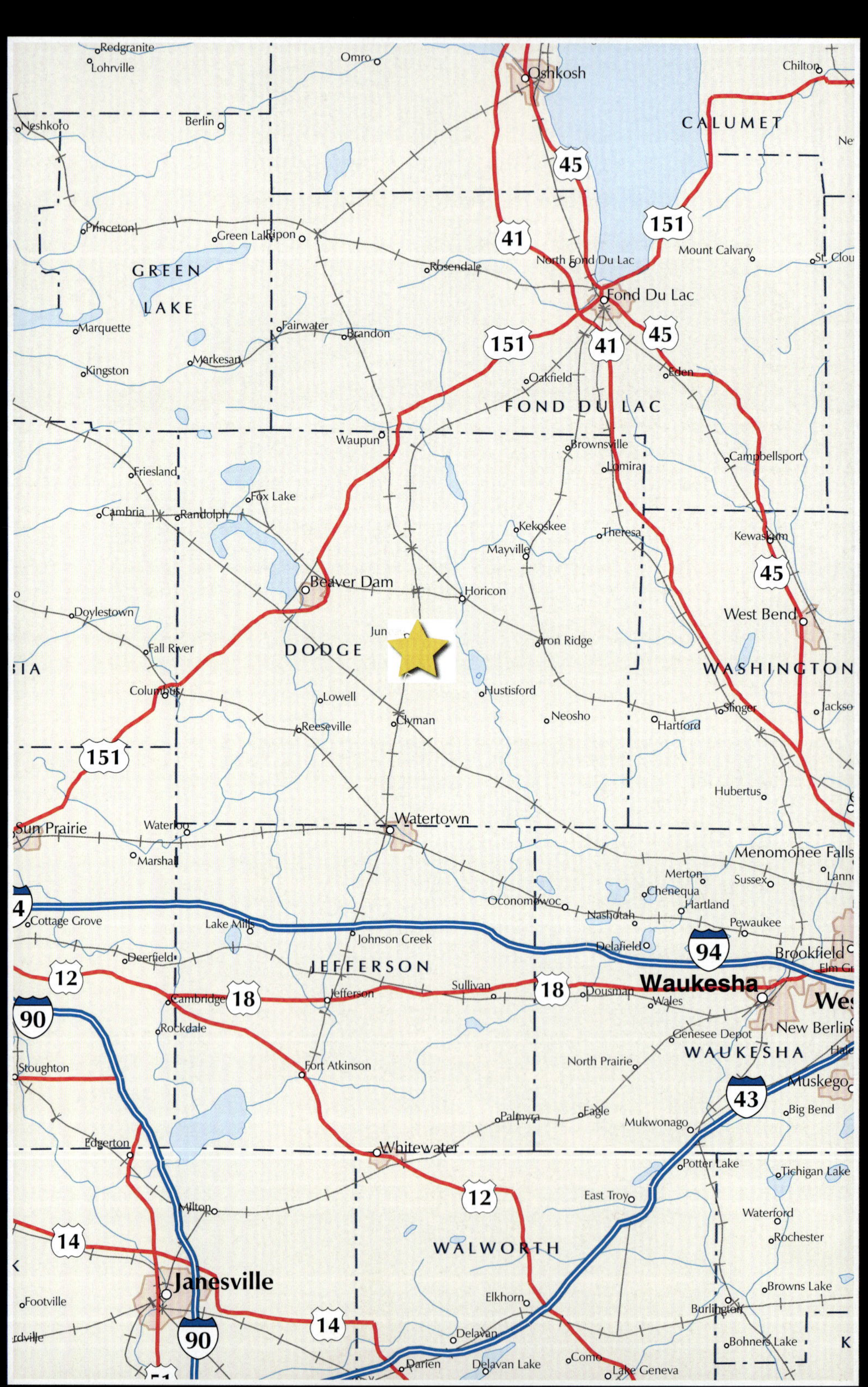

Waldvogel's Farm

ATTRACTIONS

From May through October, Waldvogel's Farm offers the freshest in produce and loads of farm fun. The peak of the season is the Fall Festival, which runs from late September through the end of October. You can take a hayride out to the pumpkin patch, navigate through a corn maze and jump in the hay barn. The Back Forty is filled with entertainments, some with a Halloween theme. If you are brave, you can pass through the Haunted Granary. You can explore the Lost Mine, slide down the Giant Mine Shaft Slide or take a ride on the Waldvogel Express farm train. Small children can race around the Trike Track. During the Fall Festival, Waldvogel's is open seven days a week. Some of the attractions at the farm are open all summer. The miniature golf course opens in July. You can visit the farm animals beginning in May. Do not miss Bunnyville or Billy Goat Mountain. Try your luck panning for real gemstones at Beaver Creek. Waldvogel's Farm Market and Bakery are open May through October. Asparagus arrives in May. June brings strawberries, tomatoes and shucked garden peas. The end of July means blueberries, cherries and sweet corn. The bakery features pies and many other tasty wares. Waldvogel's Farm is a fully functional operation that grows corn, soybeans and wheat. The farm is family-owned and family-spirited—Debbie and Phil Waldvogel are your hosts. Come harvest some family memories at Waldvogel's Farm.

N7416 County Road I, Juneau WI
(920) 885-9590
www.waldvogelfarm.com

KENOSHA

In the far southeastern corner of Wisconsin, Kenosha is the state's fourth largest city. Once an important Great Lakes shipping port, modern Kenosha has replaced the smokestacks and cargo ships of yesteryear with a revitalized landscape of parks, beaches, marinas and promenades. The city encompasses 18 miles of public Lake Michigan shoreline and nearly 800 acres of parks, where seasonal flora, public art, concerts and festivals flourish. Two lighthouses and cluster of historic buildings called the Kemper Center stand on the waterfront. The 70-acre HarborPark is the centerpiece of the waterfront, the site of Kenosha's weekly HarborMarket. An electric streetcar system connects HarborPark to a chain of Kenosha attractions, including the Kenosha Public Museum, Dinosaur Discovery Museum and Civil War Museum. Kenosha boasts four nationally listed Historic Districts, many of which claim ghosts. Kenosha's Washington Park is the home of the oldest operating velodrome (bicycle speedway) in the United States, the Washington Bowl.

Kenosha Southport Lighthouse at sunset
Photo by Richie Diesterheft

Dinosaur Discovery Museum
Photo by Richie Diesterheft

PLACES TO GO

- Anderson Arts Center
  121 66th Street
  (262) 653-0481
- Dinosaur Discovery Museum
  5608 10th Avenue
  (262)-653-4450
- HarborMarket
  200 56th Street Place de Douai
  (262) 498-4388
- Hawthorn Hollow
  Nature Sanctuary & Arboretum
  880 Green Bay Road
  (262) 552-8196
- Kemper Center
  6501 3rd Avenue
  (262) 657-6005
- Kenosha History Center
  220 51st Place
  (262) 654-5770

Civil War Monument with Old Library
Photo by Richie Diesterheft

- Kenosha Public Museum
  5500 1st Avenue
  (262) 653-4140
- Washington Bowl
  Washington Park
  www.333m.com

THINGS TO DO

June

- Good Old Summertime Art Fair
  Civic Center Park
  (262) 654-0065
- Picnic In The Park Car Show
  Kennedy Park
  (262) 620-3326
- Outta Sight Kite Flight
  Kennedy Park, 4051 5th Avenue
  (262) 653-4444
- Civil War Days
  (262) 653-4444

July

- A Kenosha Homecoming:
  Great Cars on a Great Lake
  Kennedy Park
  (262) 654-5770
- Food, Folks & Spokes
  Library Park
  (262) 654-9622 ext. 133

July-September

- Bristol Renaissance Fair
  www.renfair.com/Bristol

August

- Pike River Rendezvous
  (historical reenactment)
  (262) 843-3757
- Days of Discovery Maritime Festival
  Civic Center Park
  (262) 654-0065
- HarborPark Jazz & Blues Festival
  (262) 654-2412

September

- Walk in the Woods Art Fair
  Hawthorn Hollow
  (262) 552-8196

Bristol Renaissance Faire

ATTRACTIONS

It's 1574, and Queen Elizabeth is visiting the port of Bristol. The festival prepared in her honor is much like the Bristol Renaissance Faire. On weekends and Labor Day throughout the summer, the faire, located at the Wisconsin-Illinois border just west of Interstate 94, promises many a *hail and well met* along with opportunities to laugh and make merry with costumed magicians, jugglers, street performers and musicians. Cheer as your favorite knight jousts; feast on fish and chips, Shepherd's Pie and a tankard of ale; visit shops filled with handicrafts and artwork like those you might have encountered during this spirited age of discovery and invention. Renaissance Entertainment Corporation has created an annual event Where Fantasy Rules and celebrates 20 years of rambunctious good times in 2007. The Bristol Renaissance Faire is proof that people of all ages can find delight in a well-organized fantasy experience. The faire takes place on 30 wooded acres with open-air stages and more than 1,000 costumed performers. Activities abound for children, who are naturals at the whimsical game. Participating in the action begins when you don the clothing of a courtier or a lusty wench, just some of the costuming available for rent at the faire. Enjoy a juried art show and purchase food, furnishings, jewelry, glass, clothing and leatherwork from 180 independent merchants, offering goods from around the globe. The theme for each year's celebrations vary, but the consistent gaiety assures *we shall see thee anon* at the Bristol Renaissance Faire.

12550 120th Avenue, Kenosha WI
(847) 395-7773
www.renfair.com/bristol

Harborside Common Grounds

BAKERIES, COFFEE & TEA

Somewhere in the back of her mind, Bobbi Duczak held onto the dream of having a coffeeshop similar to the one in the long running sitcom, *Friends*. In 2000, she opened Harborside Common Grounds on the Lake Michigan waterfront, a place Where Friends Meet Friends. Bobbi knew that if she wanted Common Grounds to be a second home to her customers she needed to provide atmosphere, so this former 1920s fish market is decorated with collectibles and original local art you can purchase. The building has room to satisfy just about any grouping with a quiet adult space, a lively family space and a three-level deck overlooking the harbor. The rooms feature carved crown molding and high ceilings. Beverages go beyond coffee drinks to smoothies and hot tea served in individual teapots. Those who want something to go with that espresso drink will find baked goods, build-your-own sandwiches and ice cream. A Common Grounds sandwich is an adventure in combinations, with tempting choices of breads and fillings. In summer, the Wurst Grill opens on the back deck with bratwurst, hot dogs and grilled chicken breast. A second Common Grounds location on Lake Andrea in Pleasant Prairie is a quiet setting with the feel of a lake cottage. Make a date with friends or meet new ones at Harborside or Lakeside Common Grounds, where the welcome is warm and the Boom Brothers coffee is hot and fresh.

5159 6th Avenue (Harborside), Kenosha WI (262) 652-5111
10000 Terwall Terrace (Lakeside), Pleasant Prairie WI (262) 947-5500
www.foodspot.com/commongrounds

Gottfredsen & Nicoll

FASHION

When Leslie Thelen-Klemens was a child, the back room of Gottfredsen & Nicoll, her father's jewelry store, was her after-school hangout. When she graduated from college, her future husband John Klemens was just starting work there. Today, Leslie and John can be found at the store every day ministering to their customers' needs in much the way Rasmus Ormsted Gottfredsen did when he first opened the store in 1851. Succeeding owners have shared a love for jewelry, for this special store and for each other. A visit to this lovely shop, built in 1892 on the site of the original store, is an opportunity to experience history from the inside out, because the Klemens work in a virtual museum, surrounded by many original shop pieces, including mahogany display cases, a safe, a tin ceiling and a seven-foot glass cabinet door that opens by sliding upward. In the 1880s, Gottfredsen brought on his son-in-law, and the Nicholls family ran the jewelry store for many years. Leslie's father, Chester Thelan, began sweeping the floor for Robert Nicoll, who became like a father to him. Eventually, Chester became a certified gemologist, taking over as owner in 1951 and passing the business on to his daughter and son-in-law in the 1970s. A visit to Gottfredsen & Nicoll is your opportunity to purchase fine jewelry and gifts from people connected to the past by their love of jewelry and their dedication to this historic jewelry shop.

5708 6th Avenue, Kenosha WI
(262) 658-8833

S.J. Crystal's

FASHION

Modern lads often fail to realize that girls really do go crazy for a sharp-dressed man. You can sharpen up your look at S.J. Crystal's, Kenosha's upscale men's store. At S.J. Crystal's, the clothing is distinctive. Every item is hand picked, and the stock is always changing. Styles run from casual to suits and formal wear. You can find jeans, shorts and swimwear on the main floor. You can rent or buy a tuxedo in the lower level, which offers private, personalized service and also handles suits. S.J. Crystal's offers a full line of menswear, including shirts, slacks, sweaters, socks, shoes and belts. All items are of the highest quality, and the clothing is made of the best fabrics. Large sizes are available, and everything can be tailored on-site. Lewis Aceto, the proprietor, is one of the friendliest shopkeepers in Kenosha. You may come to S.J. Crystal's as a customer, but you will leave as a friend. The shop dates to 1900, and Lewis's father worked there in the 1950s. Lewis actually grew up in the bustling store, where the young salesmen dressed so well that girls would stop by on Friday evenings just to check them out. Lewis bought S.J. Crystal's in 1990 after working elsewhere. Today, the elegant renovated shop is the fulfillment of Lewis's dream. Come to S.J. Crystal's, and you will leave looking and feeling on top of the world.

5701 6th Avenue, Kenosha WI
(262) 656-9910

Chocolate Bliss

FUN FOODS

Chocolate may very well be the perfect food; it quells hunger, uplifts the spirit and is a delight for the senses in every way. Treat yourself to decadent taste sensations or find the perfect chocolaty gift for friends and family at Chocolate Bliss, a fine chocolate and gift boutique. Owner Kim Naegele, along with her husband, Sam, opened the specialty shop in September 2005 to bring a comprehensive selection of quality chocolates to the Kenosha area. The shop carries gourmet chocolate confections from popular shops all across the nation, like the Sweet Shop in Texas and Ethel M in Las Vegas, as well as international goodies from countries famous for their chocolate, such as Belgium and Columbia. Chocolate Bliss has a chocolate for every palate, including white, dark and milk chocolates, fudge and jumbo peanut butter cups, and a variety of turtles, caramels and haystacks. This is also the ideal place to find perfectly packaged truffles that are just the right size for party favors and place settings. In addition to quality chocolates and sugar-free chocolates, Kim stocks a terrific selection of greeting cards, chocolate themed books and gift items, and she offers a wonderful custom gift basket service. The shop's small seating area offers a welcoming place to relax with friends while sipping a delicious cup of freshly brewed Alterra coffee or Omanhene hot chocolate from Milwaukee. Find gifts for all occasions while savoring chocolate from around the globe at Chocolate Bliss.

3002 75th Street, Kenosha WI
(262) 925-8888

DeBerge's

GALLERIES & FINE ART

DeBerge's has been placing Kenosha's memories behind custom frames since 1890, when Henry F. DeBerge opened his downtown shop. The business remains in its 1926 location and retains the charm provided by wood floors, a tile ceiling and leaded windows. Kim Baas and Barb DeBerge, great granddaughters of Henry, represent the fourth generation of the DeBerge family to run this store. Both are expert framers and serve a loyal clientele who has been patronizing DeBerge's for many decades. The shop houses a full custom frame shop, which employs conservation and preservation techniques, as well as a distinctive art gallery. Beyond frames, customers can find an array of gift items, including art objects, collectibles and home décor. Each frame is a custom creation, made at the store following placement of your order. With hundreds of molding styles to choose from, customers can frame styles to suit any taste, whether contemporary or traditional. Kim and Barb also offer delivery and installation services. If you are struggling for the right presentation of your artwork, DeBerge's can arrange a private consultation at your home or business. Kim and Barb are proud to continue their family tradition of quality products and excellent service and invite you to visit DeBerge's and rediscover an old favorite.

2008 63rd Street, Kenosha WI
(262) 654-2032
www.deberges.com

Pollard Gallery

GALLERIES & FINE ART

The Rhode Center for the Arts grew in diversity and stature with the addition of the Pollard Gallery in 2004. The gallery is packed with the work of longtime Kenosha residents George and Nan Pollard, and also features some guest artists. George has completed some 5,000 charcoal and oil portraits of presidents, governors, sports stars and celebrities such as Muhammad Ali, Bob Hope and Pope John Paul II. His work hangs alongside artwork by his wife, Nan, who has illustrated more than 2,000 children's books, including *Curious George, Captain Kangaroo* and *Peter Pan*. George grew up during the Great Depression and owes his art education to his mother, who scraped together the money to send him to Layton School of Art for one semester. George graduated from the Art Institute of Pittsburgh and studied in Chicago with Fredrick Mizan, the dean of American portrait artists. World War II found him stationed in New Zealand, where he began painting his comrades and their native brides. Word of the portraits made it to his regimental commander, who ordered a portrait of Eleanor Roosevelt and later sent George to Australia to paint General Douglas MacArthur. In May 2006, George and Nan were honored by the Wisconsin Historical Society and presented the Georgia O'Keeffe Award for Distinction in the Visual Arts. At the Pollard Gallery you may view some of the Pollards' collection and purchase prints, gallery coloring books and the *Pollard Journal*, with insights into celebrities the Pollards have drawn. You will enjoy visiting the Pollard Gallery, where all donations help support this beautiful place.

Gallery photo by Sylvester Wettle

518 56th Street, Kenosha WI
(262) 657-7529
www.rhodeopera.com/pollard

Equinox, the Body and Soul Boutique

HEALTH & BEAUTY

The name *equinox* comes from the two times in the year when night and day are of equal length. Equinox, the Body and Soul Boutique seeks to introduce balance into your life—mental, physical, emotional and spiritual balance. Equinox specializes in massage and body treatments in a stress-free and calming atmosphere. When you enter, your senses get a boost from the fragrance of lavender and gentle music. Equinox suggests aromatherapy accompaniments to most treatments and makes thoughtful use of pure essential oils and flower essences. Therapeutic massage may reach the deeper tissues or, if you wish, the therapist will work the superficial muscles only, for a more relaxing experience. Hot stone massage and Reiki are other choices. Body treatments include a variety of cocoons, body polishes and body scrubs. Equinox facials employ personally blended essential oils in combination with Bioelements skin care products. Owner Maria Caravati is a certified massage therapist and flower essence practitioner. A team of trained therapists assists her, including her husband Curzio, a licensed aesthetician who performs all facials. The talented Curzio is also an organic gardener. All of the staff members at Equinox develop ongoing relationships with their clients. Maria promotes beauty in the general community by her work with flowers in downtown Kenosha. Equinox also attracts clients from places such as Alabama and Alaska, who come to experience holistic treatments to address their personal needs. Local clients and tourists alike find many reasons to return. Let Maria and the other experts at Equinox bring health and harmony to you.

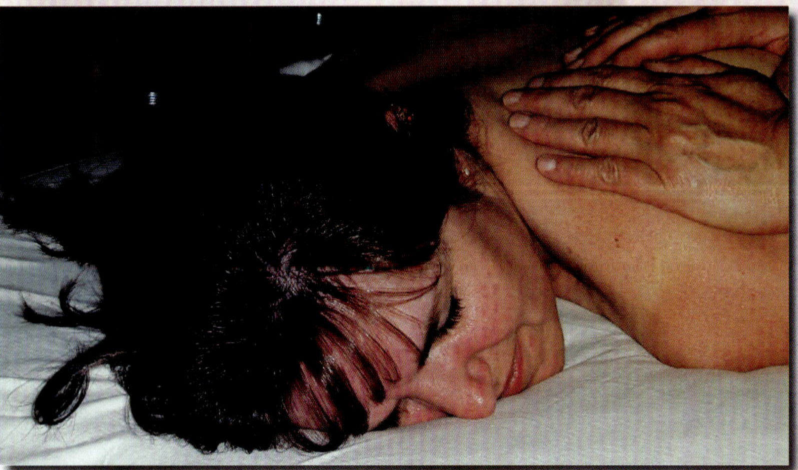

5901 6th Avenue, Kenosha WI
(262) 656-1830
www.lovequinox.com

The Pear Tree

HOME & GARDEN

Give your kitchen a fresh new look with creative accessories and décor from the Pear Tree, located inside of the Kitchen Shoppe, one of Kenosha's leading kitchen design and remodeling resources. The Pear Tree and the Kitchen Shoppe are two collaborative businesses owned and operated by Ron and Diane Dietman, with the assistance of daughter Tammie Klem and lead kitchen designer Christine Johnson. Ron opened the company in 1958 under the name R & R Construction, where he sold custom cabinetry and operated as a Wood-Mode dealer for 45 years. The company slowly evolved into a full-service kitchen design and remodeling company with Christine joining the team in 1989. Tammie and Christine are both graduates of Wood-Mode's design school and Christine has a degree in interior design. The Kitchen Shoppe offers a full range of options for updating your kitchen with custom cabinetry, granite or solid surface countertops, faucets, hardware and appliances. In 1995, they opened the Pear Tree, where you can add that finishing touch to any room with many classy accessories. Displayed in a series of inviting vignettes, you can easily picture how these items will look in your home. The shop carries decorative accent furniture, floral arrangements and Heritage Lace (special orders are welcome). You'll find butcher blocks by Boos, pot racks by Enclume and chef's soaps and aromatic sprays by Cucina. The Pear Tree also sells a huge selection of Brighton goods, such as jewelry, small leather bags, sunglasses, clocks, key rings and other great finds. The shop can provide elegant gift wrapping while you wait. Find distinctive gifts and creative design solutions at the Pear Tree.

6105 22nd Avenue, Kenosha WI
(262) 657-3304 ***www.thekitchenshoppe.com***

Garden Star

HOME & GARDEN

Imagine a statue framed by plantings at the end of your garden path or a fountain lending its cool splash to your lawn. At Garden Star, in Kenosha, Jim and Nancy Malkowski have assembled the largest selection of garden statues and fountains in the area, as well as some of the most unusual. Nancy is a people person who will gladly help you find your way around the three-acre display yard with its garden settings and hundreds of fountains. Jim is a sculptor, known in Kenosha for the giant badgers, turtles and other animal statuary at Kenosha Marina. Jim has applied his artistry to garden art and opened Garden Star in 1995. He makes many of his own molds, including those for some of his gargoyles, and sells his work at his store and at art shows. He also takes on special projects and has reproduced period pieces for historical homes. Garden Star is also the place to turn for imported bronze and granite statuary and all sorts of garden art, including planters, birdbaths and benches. Consider stepping stones, a sundial or stone benches as ways to introduce formality or fun into your private paradise. Need an oriental lantern, a folk art rabbit or a pair of classical urns? Jim and Nancy invite you to visit Garden Star between March and Christmas.

6300 120th Avenue (W Frontage Road), Kenosha WI
(262) 857-8600

Harbor MarketPlace of Kenosha

MARKETS & DELIS

Every Saturday from Memorial Day weekend to the end of October, an average of 1,500 people throng to the festive Harbor MarketPlace of Kenosha. All vendors selling vegetables and fruits grow their own products locally, and much of the produce is organic. The market displays organic meat and fish, and you can pick up such edibles as bread, salsa and mushrooms. The locally processed goods even include something for your dog, like Pampered Pup dog biscuits. The marketplace, on Kenosha's vibrant lakefront, is more than an ordinary farmers' market with almost as many artisans as food vendors. Jewelry artists display their work in many of the stalls, and you can also see photography and other art. Makers of handmade scented soaps and importers of baskets from Africa exhibit their wares. The market seeks to educate the public on the health benefits of fresh, local food. Chefs give weekly demonstrations; one vendor teaches wool spinning. Music and live entertainment vary from week to week. Special events range from a garlic growing contest and Salsa Day to Miss Wisconsin in Kenosha. The volunteers who founded the market fashioned it after some of the finest markets in America and Europe, and Market Committee Chair Ray Forgianni visited markets around the world to gather ideas. Along with Market Manager Elise Shelley and Vice-Chair Curzio Caravati, Ray invites you to come down and see one of the most exciting markets in the Midwest.

715 56th Street, Kenosha WI
(262) 498-4388
www.kenoshaharbormarketplace.com

Tenuta's Liquor & Deli

MARKETS & DELIS

Tenuta's Liquor & Deli houses a vast collection of specialty groceries, beer and liquors. The variety and quality of groceries inspires many devoted customers. One says that the store is one of the best things about Kenosha. Another travels from Washington, D.C. to shop here. Tenuta's has been a neighborhood fixture since 1950, when Italian immigrants John and Lydia Tenuta realized the dream of opening their own store. With the help of their son Ralph, and now the third generation with grandson Chris, the store has grown into the specialty market it is today. On entering, you are struck by the fragrant aromas of the food. In the deli you will find Italian prosciutto, Genoa salami, capicola, soppräsata, mortadella and homemade extra lean Italian sausage. The shop also offers a large assortment of olives, pasta salads and prepared take-home and warm Italian dinner dishes. A huge cheese case flanks the meat cases, and contains the finest Wisconsin and imported cheeses from around the world. Freezer cases hold Tenuta's own ravioli, tortellini, gnocchi and other frozen pasta items, as well as homemade pasta sauces and Italian ice creams. Grocery aisles have everything from imported olive oils and vinegars to jars of octopus and anchovies. As weather permits, the outdoor grill serves famous Italian sausages, bratwurst and other grilled favorites, with outdoor seating under the umbrellas. The liquors include cognacs, tequilas, exotic liqueurs, cordials and everything in between. An enormous cigar humidor, filled with imported cigars, sits at the front of the store. Tenuta's is unpretentious, with a hard-working and youthful staff, ready to help. Visit Tenuta's Liquor & Deli and prepare to be pleasantly surprised at the variety you will find.

3203 52nd Street, Kenosha WI
(262) 657-9001
www.tenutasdeli.com

Mars' Cheese Castle

MARKETS & DELIS

In 1947, Mario and Martha Ventura purchased an old schoolhouse in Kenosha and converted it into Mars' Cheese Castle, a local landmark for gracious service and an abundance of quality cheeses, meats and fine Wisconsin products. Mario was named in honor of Mars, the Roman god of war, and goes by the nickname Mars, as does Mario Jr., his son and managing director. Mario's love of castles is evident by the name of his store and such charming product names as the King of Clubs cheddar cheese spread and the Court Jester variety pack, filled with four distinctive cheeses and a flavorful summer sausage. Mars' Cheese Castle stocks up to 400 different cheeses at any given time, along with a choice selection of smoked meats, sausages, baked goods and condiments. The shop also offers fresh-frozen delicacies, like apple pies from the Elegant Farmer and bratwurst made especially for Mars by the Wisconsin based Usinger's Sausage Company. Ease your hunger pangs in the deli, where friendly servers create scrumptious sandwiches, tender grilled brats and juicy hamburgers, or step into the lounge and catch a local sports game while sipping away on a fabulous Bloody Mary, cold beer or one of Mars' 200-plus wines, which include 40 Wisconsin vintages. Treat your friends and family to delicious cheeses, meats and gourmet delights from Mars' Cheese Castle, where the rule is if Mario doesn't like it, they don't sell it.

2800 120th Avenue, Kenosha WI
(262) 859-2244
www.marscheese.com

House of Gerhard

RESTAURANTS & CAFÉS

Gerhard Dillner came to the United States from Germany in 1954 with a pocket full of recipes and a young family. He opened House of Gerhard in Kenosha a decade later, serving up such family recipes as pork shank, rouladen and authentic sauerkraut. Today his daughter Angie, with her husband, Richard Rudin, and their children Kyle and Sabine continue his tradition with a heaping spoonful of Old World charm and a nice portion of solid American favorites. The two dining rooms at House of Gerhard offer a choice of atmosphere. One is bright and full of windows; the other is a peek into old Germany. Kenosha residents often gather at the cozy bar for a drink and a visit. Your entrée comes complete with a complimentary appetizer of pâté and garlic toast. Authentic German dishes are popular here, along with steak, prime rib and fresh seafood choices, including the beloved seafood bouillabaisse. The restaurant bakes its homemade rolls and muffins fresh each day. If you saved room for dessert, look for House of Gerhard's signature strawberry shaum torte. Whether you are looking for *jäegerschnitzel* or a filet mignon, you'll find the food you fancy for lunch or dinner on any day but Sunday at this smoke-free restaurant. Angie and Richard invite you to House of Gerhard and wish you *guten Appetit*.

3927 75th Street, Kenosha WI
(262) 694-5212
www.foodspot.com/gerhards

Chops on the Lake

RESTAURANTS & CAFÉS

Whether you are a nervous beau about to pop the question or an executive hoping to close the biggest deal of your life, Chops on the Lake will impress your guest. As if plucked straight from New York City and set gently down at Kenosha's picturesque marina, Chops on the Lake is the quintessential metropolitan steakhouse. As your guest lays a white linen napkin across his lap or picks up her chilled salad fork, they will notice the vaulted ceilings, terrazzo floors and fountain wall that together echo the 1930s. The professional waitstaff is personable, knowledgeable and efficient. Start with an order of BBT, a favorite appetizer of *Journal Sentinel* dining critic David Getto. This big flavor appetizer combines strips of beef tenderloin with bleu cheese and a cherry tomato on crostini. For your entrée your server will present a tray of prime Allan Brothers meat for your personal selection. Chops chooses its meat for age and quality and cuts it in-house. Among the seafood selections is a free-form seafood ravioli made with shrimp, crab and lobster laid over a sheet of fresh pasta and covered with saffron cream. Did you cinch that big deal? Celebrate your victory by lingering in the lounge, where you can choose from 100 varieties of vodka for that perfect martini and listen to live music four nights a week. For steak and seafood in elegant surroundings, stop by Chops on the Lake, on the lower level of the Marina Shores building.

5722 3rd Avenue, Kenosha WI
(262) 842-0510
www.chopsonthelake.com

Ron's Place

RESTAURANTS & CAFÉS

If you are a fan of the great American hamburger, you owe it to yourself to stop at Ron's Place in Kenosha. Ron's 5X5 is a half pound of ground beef on a five-inch sesame seed bun. Clearly, Ron's supplies ample portions. You can wash this monster down with one of Ron's equally famous Long Island ice teas. Choose from 31 spirituous flavors. Microbrews are also a growing part of the drinks list here. The walleye sandwich and dinner are just one of the Wednesday or Friday menu choices. The menu is loaded with variety, from such finger foods as fried calamari or mini tacos to entrees as varied as the Cajun chicken breast and the T-Hurst Special. The T-Hurst is a ham, cheese and onion construction on top of the 5X5, named for the customer who demanded it. Ron's takes a special pride in never running out of anything on the menu. The pub is warm and cozy, and all the food is cooked in open view behind the bar. The place is always buzzing with excitement, and everyone feels at home. Ron's is a family affair, founded in 1972 by Ron Pendrick and his wife, Pat. Pat's sister, Judy Udvare, has been partnered up with Ron's for the last 20 years. Today, the owners are Tracy Murray, Ron and Pat's daughter, and Tom Plummer, who worked at the establishment for many years. For satisfying fare from lunch to late night, come to Ron's Place.

3301 52nd Street, Kenosha WI
(262) 657-5907

Boat House Pub & Eatery

RESTAURANTS & CAFÉS

Boat House Pub & Eatery, since 1992 Kenosha's only authentic waterfront pub, offers a sweeping view of Lake Michigan. Conveniently located in Kenosha's small boat harbor, Boat House is a popular stop for charter fishing cruises and provides 22 courtesy docks for guests. Owners Jim Matzur and Dean Van Daalwyk bought the building next door to expand the restaurant after they purchased the 1900s-era tavern and banquet hall. The pub boasts a full bar and offers 20 versions of Long Island tea. Nautical décor here includes gleaming brass fixtures, etched glass windows and more than 50 historical Kenosha harbor photographs. The Boat House serves lunch and dinner seven days a week with breakfast added on weekends. Seafood figures predominately in the menu, with local catches, such as whitefish, walleye pike, smelt, and lake perch, taking center stage. Juicy meats, such as chicken, pork and ribs, are smoked in-house, and steaks, brisket, pizza, salads and an array of appetizers, many with seafood, complete the menu. Try the Bread Boat, a toasted bread bowl filled with the steaming soup, chowder or house-made chili. If you're in need of lodging, too, check out the Merry Yacht Inn, an 1895 fire station right across the street. By land or by water, stop by Boat House Pub & Eatery for great food in a fun, casual atmosphere.

4917 7th Avenue, Kenosha WI
(262) 654-9922
www.foodspot.com/boathouse/index.html

Trolley Dogs

RESTAURANTS & CAFÉS

You do not have to go to Chicago to get a great Chicago style hot dog. At Trolley Dogs in downtown Kenosha, this quintessential all-American summertime favorite gets the toppings and respect it deserves. Brothers Frank and Joe Catuara opened the eatery in 2003 with the slogan Dogs So Great You'll Scrape Your Plate. Polish sausage, Italian beef and corn dogs are some of the breeds you can sample. Try chili or cheese on your dog, or for a Wisconsin variation order the Kenosha dog, covered with cheddar cheese. Try a tamale topped with chili and cheese or variations like the Mother-in-Law, a tamale on a bun, and the Trolley Dog, a dog and a tamale on the same bun. You can match everything up with fries, cheese fries or chili cheese fries. Inside the restaurant, model trolley cars on a track circle the ceiling. Frank and Joe first fell in love with hot dogs in high school when they pushed a hot dog cart in Chicago. They went on to establish careers in the world of business. A public television special on hot dog vendors inspired the brothers to open Trolley Dogs in an historic building that was once the Longshoreman's Union Hall. The location is a prime one, downtown's closest spot to the HarborPark development. The Catuaras are proud to support their youthful staff, who are some of the politest kids around. Come to Trolley Dogs, where Every Bite Is a Delight.

5501 6th Avenue, Kenosha WI
(262) 652-DOGS (3647)
www.trolleydogs.co

Mo's Coffee Lounge

RESTAURANTS & CAFÉS

Mo's Coffee Lounge is a bright and airy restaurant in the heart of the newly renovated Kenosha lakefront district. It's a good place to have a cappuccino, read the *Kenosha News* or visit with a friend or neighbor from the HarborPark development. In addition to espresso, Mo's offers chai and other teas, smoothies and power drinks. The restaurant opens at 6:30 am with traditional breakfast fare or eye-opening options, such as the Southwestern wrap with egg, cheese and salsa. Mo's makes its own granola and serves Loaded Oatmeal, which contains banana, pecans and raisins. For lunch, contemplate the Ultimate Grilled Cheese with six different cheeses on herb bread, or try a tilapia fish sandwich with bacon and cheese. Of course, you can have a cheeseburger, a BLT or soup and sandwich. The bread and salads are homemade. Mo's offers daily specials and changes those specials weekly. On Sunday afternoons, the restaurant sets up for family games. On Friday, you can lunch on salsa verde shrimp and listen to live jazz. Mo's is famous for its potato salad, which customers regularly buy in 10 to 20 pound lots. The restaurant has a banquet room that seats up to 100 and a special catering menu. Owner Grant Simmons has worked in the food business since he was 14. He loves the pace, the people and the food. Grant bought the restaurant in 2003 and changed its name from Kristi's Café to Mo's several years later. Come to Mo's Coffee Lounge, where life is good, and you may want to stay forever.

5537 6th Avenue, Kenosha WI
(262) 653-8071
www.moslounge.com

Franks Diner

RESTAURANTS & CAFÉS

Located near Harbor Park in downtown Kenosha, Franks Diner is the oldest continuously operating lunch car diner in the country. In 1926, six horses pulled the diner to its present location. In July 2006, the Kenosha City Council named the diner a local historic structure. Franks Diner is a mandatory stop for anyone campaigning for public office. It also saw many celebrities who played at the Kenosha Theater and has served everyone from the Three Stooges to Duke Ellington. The cooks grill the food right in front of you and the portions are enormous. The Original Garbage Plate, the most famous dish and a cure for hangovers, contains hash browns, hot and green peppers, ham and onions scrambled with five eggs. Fortunately for lighter eaters, you can get a half plate with three eggs. Other breakfasts are Franks Twist Bread French Toast and inventive omelettes, such as the chili and cheddar cheese omelette. Franks makes great homemade bread, cinnamon rolls and desserts. For lunch, consider the half-pound Wow Burger or the Bleu Schu Burger with blue cheese and bacon. Other possibilities are the velvety smooth Hungarian mushroom soup, baked chili, or homemade lunch specials such as the meatloaf dinner. Three women, Kris Derwae, Lynn Groleau and Chris Schwartz, bought Franks from the Franks family in 2001. The staff is friendly; food is made fresh to order and a sense of humor prevails, as evidenced by the trademarked slogan: Order What You Want, Eat What You Get. If you come to Kenosha, you must come to the legendary Franks Diner.

508 58th Street, Kenosha WI
(262) 657-1017

Little Europe at Timber Ridge

RESTAURANTS & CAFÉS

The sign on the roof of Little Europe at Timber Ridge calls out Bohemian Cooking. Inside, the European décor is simple, but the meals are positively elaborate. Bohemian cuisine has some things in common with Austrian, Hungarian and Polish fare. Pierogies stuffed with sauerkraut or cheese are classic appetizers. Sauerkraut, red cabbage and rye bread are staples. Wiener schnitzels and Old Prague-style schnitzels (pork cutlet) are perfectly breaded and fried. The stews and roasts are moist, tender and flavorful. The beef in the sauerbraten is marinated for a week. Gravies are lighter than in Germany and are often thickened with sour cream. Everything is made from scratch. Owners Miro and Bozka Gono make their own sausages and smoked meats, which they retail through their subsidiary Euro-Meats. Miro learned sausage making from his family in Slovakia when he was a little boy, and he makes the sausages using authentic European recipes and spices. Meats are smoked using cherry, hickory and apple wood chips. Miro prepares the sausages and meats in a new building, Miro's Charcoal House, which is also used for parties and catering. The whole family works in the business, and family members make sure that the restaurant is sparkling clean and the service is excellent. Come to Little Europe at Timber Ridge and enjoy the great taste of Central European cooking.

6613 120th Avenue, Kenosha WI
(262) 857-9073

tg's Restaurant & Pub

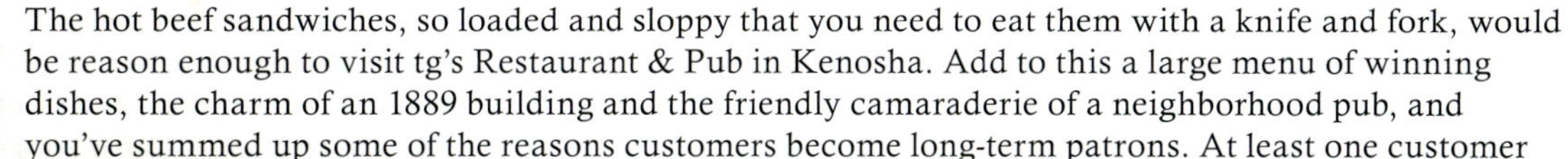

RESTAURANTS & CAFÉS

The hot beef sandwiches, so loaded and sloppy that you need to eat them with a knife and fork, would be reason enough to visit tg's Restaurant & Pub in Kenosha. Add to this a large menu of winning dishes, the charm of an 1889 building and the friendly camaraderie of a neighborhood pub, and you've summed up some of the reasons customers become long-term patrons. At least one customer has been visiting every day since the 1950s. Old photos and part of the original 1920s bar line the walls, and the pub still uses the mahogany bar built by Blatz Brewery in 1939. Prohibition appeared to squelch the pub, which advertised ice cream and shoeshines at the time, but a tunnel running to the tavern provided moonshine. Today, diners enjoy the bar or a family-friendly non-smoking dining room. Such famous guests as the Kennedy brothers have visited here. Sisters-in-law Theresa and Sherry Revis bought tg's in 2003, making good use of Theresa's experience growing up around her father's bar and Sherry's catering background. The bar offers numerous microbrews, imports and domestic beers on tap, plus specialty martinis and other drinks. Expect a three-hour happy hour, live music on most Saturdays and an open mic on Wednesdays. Beyond beef, look for homemade soups and tg's signature desserts. Friday night seafood specials offer broad appeal. Put some history and conviviality into your lunch or dinner plans with a visit to tg's Restaurant & Pub.

4120 7th Avenue, Kenosha WI
(262) 658-8080

Summers Garden

SHOPPING

Many people visit a florist only at a time of great joy, such as a wedding, or of great sorrow, such as a funeral. Denise MacDonald, owner of Summers Garden, is doing what she can to change that. While filling orders for special occasions is an important part of her Kenosha business, Denise would like to share the beauty of flowers with people on an every day basis. Believing that floral elegance should not be an extravagance but something that is affordable for everyone, she offers truly great deals at her shop. On the day that we dropped by, customers were receiving a half dozen free roses with the purchase of a dozen. That's nothing compared to Denise's gift certificate program. Buy one of these modestly priced certificates, and the recipient gets a free bouquet every month, including a Love Bunch in February and a Spooky Boo-kay in October. All he or she has to do is drop by, flash the certificate and take the beauties home. Denise looks at it as having 12 opportunities to win that person's trust and business. Besides flowers, she also offers plants, silk arrangements, fruit baskets and gifts from her shop that once was a gas station. You'll find no grit and oil stains here now, just terrific deals and wall-to-wall beauty. Make visiting Summers Garden a regular occurrence.

2122 60th Street, Kenosha WI
(262) 657-7673 or (800) 201-3075
www.myfsn.com/summersgarden

Andrea's

SHOPPING

Giacomo (Jack) Andrea left the olive groves of southern Italy for the promise of America in 1909, when he was just a teenager. He cobbled together a livelihood as a Golden Gloves pugilist and a laborer at a local mattress factory. He soon tired of the painful job of tying the raw metal mattress springs and dreamed of having his own business. Family legend has it that Jack Andrea's first store was actually a piano crate from which he sold tobacco, candies and newspapers to the factory workers. It was successful enough to enable Jack to have a real storefront by 1912. From that day, through the 1950s, Andrea's claim to fame was its candy selection and legendary homemade ice cream. Jack and his wife, Theresa, and eventually their six children, offered a bounty of sweet treats, from penny candies to hand-dipped chocolates. Using the state's finest ingredients, they manufactured small batches of rich and creamy ice cream, served at a beautiful marble soda fountain. This soda fountain is now the oldest still in use in southeastern Wisconsin. Now in the hands of third and fourth generation family members, Andrea's thrives in its original location in Kenosha's Historic Uptown neighborhood. For generations, Andrea's has been the place to go for beautiful gifts, jewelry and accessories, as well as candies, gourmet foods and premium cigars (presented in a handsome humidor). Made-from-scratch soups, malts and ice cream sodas highlight the café menu and bring friends and family together for lunch and fountain treats, continuing a tradition that Kenosha has enjoyed for almost 100 years.

2401 60th Street, Kenosha WI
(262) 657-7732
www.andreasgifts.com

Sommelier

WINES, BREWS, PUBS & CLUBS

Robert Mitchell knows about wine, and with the opening of Sommelier, residents and visitors to Kenosha are going to know about wine too. Robert's specialty wine shop, launched in 2004, offers wines from near and far and expert staff to aim you toward wines you might enjoy. All main floor wines cost $12 or less. A downstairs wine cellar, modeled after ones Robert visited in Europe, offers more expensive and vintage selections. Robert and his wife, Leslie, handpick the wines for the shop. They offer Saturday wine tastings to the public, several more elaborate events throughout the year and opportunities to book private wine tastings at your residence. Robert grew up in Kenosha and has been in the restaurant business for 20 years. He moved home from Boston when he thought Kenosha was ready for his expertise. Robert is passionate about wine and makes his shop a beautiful tribute to that passion, with exposed brick walls, lime green accents and trim created from wine corks. He sells wine art and the kinds of specialty food and drink that your guests are sure to appreciate. Look for artisan cheeses from Wisconsin, plus European cheeses and specialty crackers. Choice liquors and hard to find microbrews are also available. Robert even lets you make up your own six-pack for sampling the brews. Hone your knowledge and your palate with a visit to Sommelier, your wine steward in downtown Kenosha.

720 58th Street, Kenosha WI
(262) 925-8436

Wine Knot Bar & Bistro

WINES, BREWS, PUBS & CLUBS

Wine Knot Bar & Bistro in downtown Kenosha presents wine and food from around the world in an upscale, yet cozy, atmosphere. Terry and Allison McDonald came upon the inspiration for their establishment while visiting a wine bar in Ohio. They understand the power in pairing wine and food and help aim their customers toward delightful, though by no means mandatory, combinations. The McDonalds offer unpretentious surroundings and want you to feel comfortable when you settle in to enjoy fine food and wine. They offer more than 50 distinctive wine varieties and the expertise to help you find your favorites and experience them fully. Their facilities are available for private parties and corporate events with elements found in big-city restaurants that have been customized for a small-town environment. On Wednesday or Saturday evenings, customers enjoy live music along with their food and wine. The McDonalds suggest a matua Pinot Noir with your ahi tuna or a 10-ounce Black Angus top Sirloin paired with a Thunder from Down Under Flight. (Flights allow guests to sample three three-ounce wine portions.) Wine Knot also features special wine dinners that showcase particular wine collections. Make plans to discover the synergy between fine wines and foods at Wine Knot Bar & Bistro, where the world comes to you in a host of complementary flavors.

5611 6th Avenue, Kenosha WI
(262) 653-9580
www.wine-knot.com

LAKE COUNTRY TOWNS

Delafield, Dousman, Genesee Depot, Hartland, Nashotah, Oconomowoc and Wales

The Lake Country takes its name from the dozens of sparkling lakes carved out of the Kettle Moraine hills by glaciers 15,000 years ago. Here you will find some of the most luxurious and impressive homes in the Milwaukee area. Historically, the region was a summer getaway for well-heeled Chicago and Milwaukee families, and Oconomowoc was known as the Newport of the West. Between 1870 and 1930, hundreds of wealthy Milwaukee, Chicago and St. Louis residents took the train to Oconomowoc and other lake communities to relax at the resorts or in one of the area's many palatial houses. Lake Road in Oconomowoc was known as President's Avenue because so many presidents vacationed here, including Grant, Cleveland, McKinley, T. Roosevelt, Taft and Coolidge. Today, the Lake Country is a prized location for year-round homes. The clear lakes offer swimming, boating and fishing. Pewaukee Lake yields more fish per acre than any other lake in the state. In the winter, you can skate, ice fish or snowmobile. Oconomowoc is to the west in the district, and Delafield, Hartland and Nashotah are to the east. To the southeast lie Dousman, Genesee Depot and Wales. Local attractions include Ten Chimneys in Genesee Depot, a retreat created over 75 years ago by the revered acting team Alfred Lunt and Lynn Fontanne and now open to the public.

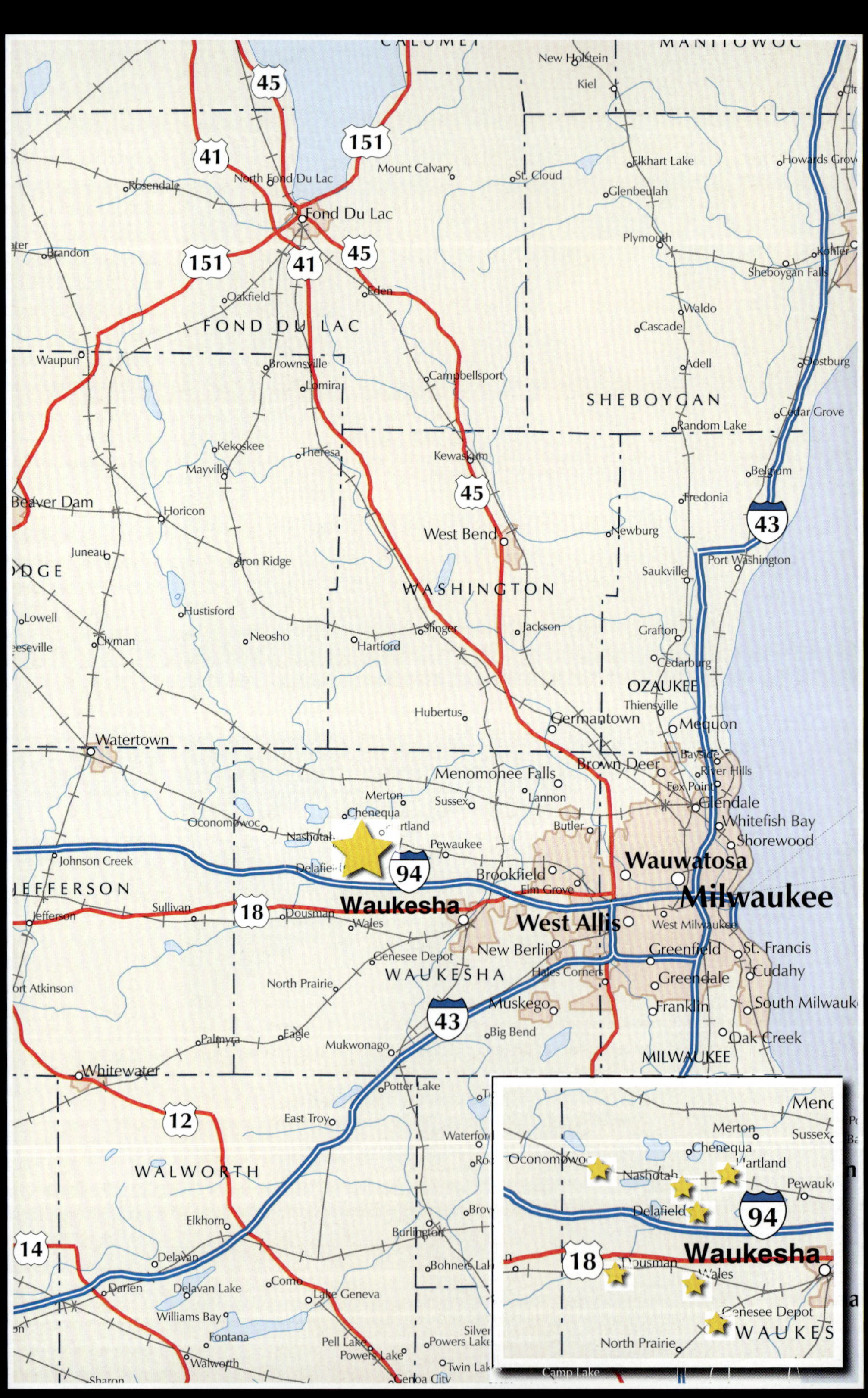

Fall in Wisconsin

PLACES TO GO

- Glacial Drumlin State Trail
  HQ: 1213 S Main Street, Lake Mills
  (920) 648-8774
- Highlands of Olympia Ski Area
  965 Cannon Gate Road, Oconomowoc
  (262) 567-6048
- Kettle Moraine State Forest-
  Lapham Peak Unit
  W329 N846 County Highway C, Delafield
  (262) 646-3025
- Naga-Waukee Park
  651 State Route 83, Hartland
- Ten Chimneys
  S43 W31575 Depot Road, Genesee Depot
  (262) 968-4161

THINGS TO DO

July

- Hartland's Hometown Celebration
  (262) 367-7059
- Delafield Days
  (262) 646-8100
- Dousman Derby Days
  www.dousmanchamber.com/derby.htm

August

- Waukesha Blues Fest
  Naga-Waukee Park
  (262) 547-1522
- Donna Lexa Memorial Art Fair
  Wales
  (262) 968-2945
- Festival Week
  Oconomowoc
  (262) 567-2666
- Oconomowoc Festival of the Arts
  Fowler Park
  www.oconomowocarts.org

Pedal'rs Inn Bed and Breakfast

ACCOMMODATIONS

Dee Nierzwicki realizes that she is the owner of not just another bed and breakfast but of a source of community pride. The magnificent three-story Victorian mansion that is now the Pedal'rs Inn Bed and Breakfast has been adding a large touch of splendor to Wales since the 1890s. Today, the hospitality that Dee extends to her guests is in keeping with the air of cordialness and refinement found throughout the house and grounds. Guests choose from four bedchambers, each with its own distinctive features. One room's highlights include a canopy bed, handcrafted fireplace and private bath with massaging jets, while the sole chamber on the third floor boasts a soaker tub for two beneath a skylight to the heavens. A king bed, wrought iron fireplace and interior balcony are other features of this grand room. Weekend lodgers enjoy a four-course gourmet breakfast, while weekday guests feast on a full American-style breakfast, often including homemade baked goods. Dee enjoys directing guests to the many attractions that make the Pedal'rs Inn an ideal retreat for all sorts of folks, including antique collectors, sports fanatics and romantics, as well as naturalists, history buffs and festival-goers. The inn's name and its charming Victorian bicycle décor were inspired by the popular biking route, the Glacial Drumlin State Trail, which runs right by the inn. Let Dee make you feel at home at Pedal'rs Inn Bed and Breakfast.

101 James Street, Wales WI (262) 968-4700 *www.pedalrsinn.com*

Merton Veterinary Clinic

ANIMALS & PETS

For your pets, going to the doctor probably feels more like visiting friends when the doctor is at Merton Veterinary Clinic, serving Hartland since 1954. The excited barking and meowing that greets them upon arrival are music sounds to their ears, telling them that this is a place where animals are happy and allowed to be themselves. Owner and Office Manager Susan Butler and her family live at the clinic. They share space with a troop of adopted dogs and cats with precious names such as Casper, Scooby, Buck and Booboo. They wander through the office and waiting room to see who has dropped by. "It's pretty much a zoo," says Susan's husband Chris Butler, who chips in when he is off duty as Waukesha County deputy sheriff. While it may get a little wild and wooly around the perimeter at Merton Clinic, the veterinary care offered at the center of this facility is thoroughly modern, and the veterinarians, led by Dr. John Cheslak, are professional and caring. Merton features state-of-the art surgery and radiology rooms. Its dietary planning for your pet is based on the latest research. You will appreciate the spaciousness of this six-acre facility, should you choose to board your pet at Merton. Staff takes your dog on an outside walk at least twice a day. You can also bring your pet's favorite blanket and toy. For first-rate care in a friendly environment, take your pet to Merton Veterinary Clinic.

N67 W28626 Sussex Road, Hartland WI
(262) 538-1280

Our Creative Outlet

ARTS & CRAFTS

Our Creative Outlet is an artist's studio where people of all ages come to play with clay. In business since 2002, the Delafield studio is the brainchild of Karen Norris, who decided to use what she learned during her days as an interior designer and decorator to open and manage an art studio. Her current focus is to give clients the opportunity for creative expression as a means of reducing their stress and improving their quality of life. Karen provides the technical expertise and materials, and her customers provide the willingness to learn and try something new. The techniques Karen teaches include raku, which involves firing pottery and putting the scalding pieces into garbage cans to cool. The unusual cooling process allows the pieces to dry in a striking range of colors. Karen also offers expertise in custom-made mosaic tiles that she joins in a variety of shapes, sizes and colors to create pictures. Our Creative Outlet offers classes for adults and children, including instruction tied to home-schooling programs. Beyond raku, Karen teaches hand-building and wheel-throwing. The studio is also available for children's parties, for open studio time and for supervised project-based sessions. Specialty workshops allow students to create a specific item, perhaps a teapot, tile or mug. Make a visit to Our Creative Outlet to take a class or buy pottery, sculpture and gifts.

329-B Genesee Street, Delafield WI
(262) 646-9921
www.ourcreativeoutlet.com

Music Dynamics of Wales

ARTS & CRAFTS

The mission of Music Dynamics of Wales is to provide music students of all ages with the skills they need to experience the fun of learning and the joy of accomplishment. Music Dynamics offers lessons in piano/keyboard, voice, guitar and other string and wind instruments. Among the company's offerings are combination private-group lessons for small groups of four to six students of about the same age and level of experience. Students in these classes receive 30 minutes of group learning followed by 15 minutes of private instruction. Music Dynamics believes that music lessons should be fun and that the small-group experience promotes that spirit. The company is licensed to offer MusikGarten, a nationally known early childhood music curriculum. Aimed at children from one and a half to six years of age, MusikGarten is a family focused approach that combines songs, movement games and instruments. Music Dynamics offers three MusikGarten classes for different age groups. In addition to acoustic pianos, Music Dynamics uses the latest Clavinova digital pianos equipped with disk drives for recording sessions. Laura Swenson, a nationally certified teacher of music, is co-owner of Music Dynamics. Laura received her Bachelor of Music degree from Alverno College and later taught at that school. She has more than 30 years of teaching experience and has served as president of the Wisconsin Music Teachers Association. For lessons that will enrich your life or the life of your child, schedule a free, no-obligation interview with Music Dynamics of Wales.

110 E Oak Crest Drive, Wales WI
(262) 968-5866
www.wmta.net/MusicDynamics

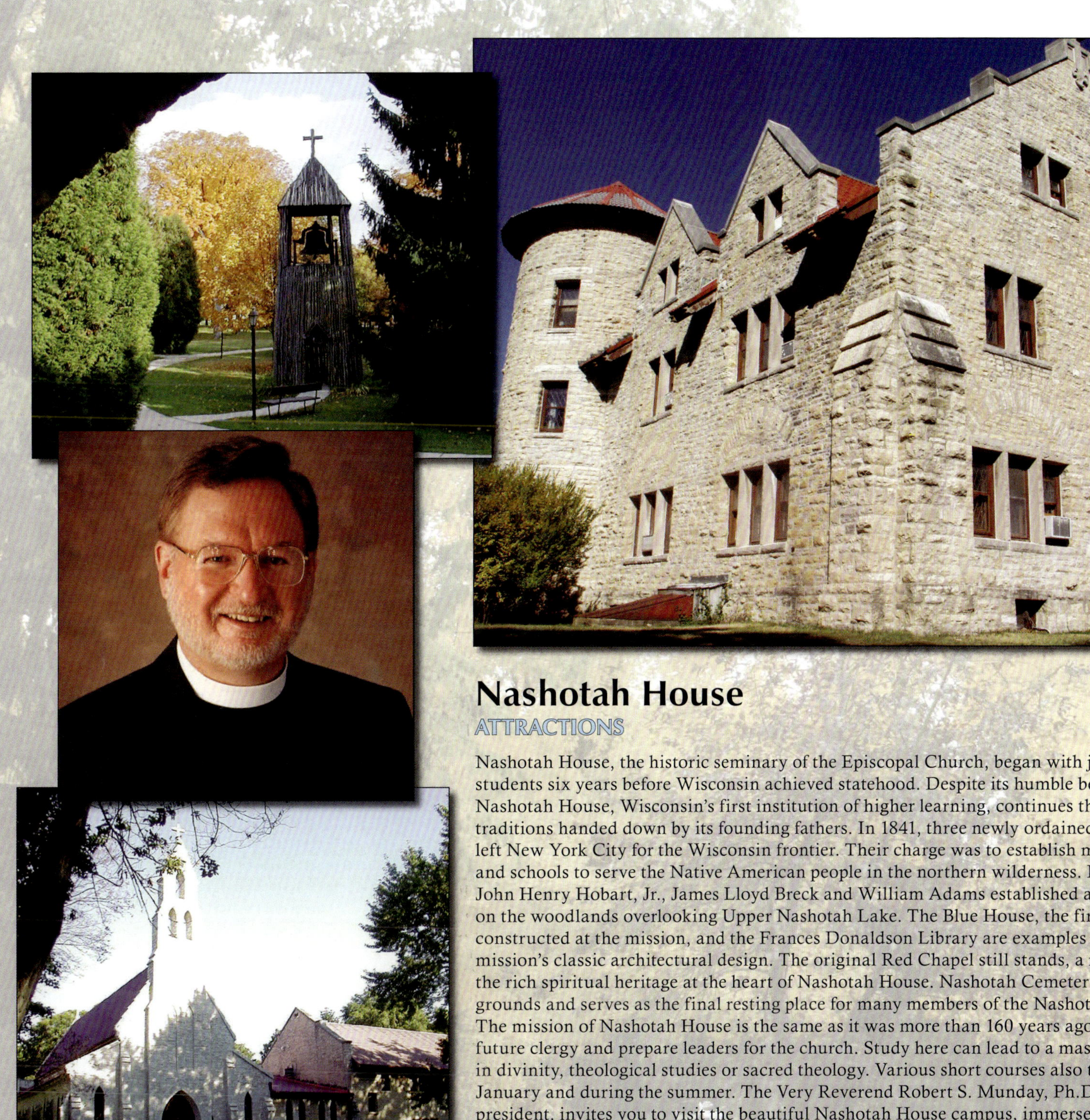

Nashotah House

ATTRACTIONS

Nashotah House, the historic seminary of the Episcopal Church, began with just three students six years before Wisconsin achieved statehood. Despite its humble beginnings, Nashotah House, Wisconsin's first institution of higher learning, continues the rich traditions handed down by its founding fathers. In 1841, three newly ordained deacons left New York City for the Wisconsin frontier. Their charge was to establish missions and schools to serve the Native American people in the northern wilderness. Founders John Henry Hobart, Jr., James Lloyd Breck and William Adams established a mission on the woodlands overlooking Upper Nashotah Lake. The Blue House, the first building constructed at the mission, and the Frances Donaldson Library are examples of the mission's classic architectural design. The original Red Chapel still stands, a reminder of the rich spiritual heritage at the heart of Nashotah House. Nashotah Cemetery overlooks the grounds and serves as the final resting place for many members of the Nashotah community. The mission of Nashotah House is the same as it was more than 160 years ago: to train future clergy and prepare leaders for the church. Study here can lead to a master's degree in divinity, theological studies or sacred theology. Various short courses also take place in January and during the summer. The Very Reverend Robert S. Munday, Ph.D., dean and president, invites you to visit the beautiful Nashotah House campus, immerse yourself in the history of the seminary and experience the passion and mission of the community.

2777 Mission Road, Nashotah WI
(262) 646-6500 or (800) 627-4682
www.nashotah.edu

Ewald Automotive Group

AUTO

With 620 associates, Ewald Automotive Group may seem like a big company, but at the core it is still a family business, selling cars from Chrysler, Ford, GM and other companies. Emil Ewald, who started the business in 1964, runs the company with his four sons, Craig, Brian, Dan, and Tom. They consider their associates part of the family and believe they are a team working together. Their guiding philosophy is the Golden Rule, "do unto others." As a result, Ewald Automotive is an admirable neighbor in the community, supporting charities and involving themselves in efforts to improve the places they live. The mission at Ewald Automotive Group is to take care of its customers. Its full service dealerships are devoted to solving transportation needs. They offer a huge selection of new and pre-owned vehicles, plus fleet and rental vehicles. The service and parts departments are unequaled in service and convenience. Ewald promises to meet or beat any estimate for comparable work, and it works with all major insurance companies. Ewald Automotive Group exhibits passion for what it does. Next time you need help with your transportation, introduce yourself to the Ewald family.

36833 W Wisconsin Avenue, Oconomowoc WI
(866) 411-2093
www.ewaldauto.com

Bartolotta Fireworks Company

BUSINESS & SERVICES

If you live in Wisconsin, you may not know the Bartolotta family personally, but there's a good chance that you have been entertained by one of their thrilling fireworks shows. As Sam Bartolotta's hobby of making fireworks grew into a business in the late 1970s, he contented himself by staging three or four shows a year. That number has grown to about 500 these days, with the Bartolotta Fireworks Company handling major events, such as Summerfest and many of Wisconsin's ethnic festivals. The company designs 75 to 100 shows throughout the state on the 4th of July alone, including the grandest of all—U.S. Bank's fireworks at the Milwaukee lakefront. That show takes two days of preparation by a staff of about 40. It also requires five miles of wire to shoot more than 5,000 shells for the 30-minute sky display, which computes to about 166 shells per minute. Don't let these numbers lead you to believe that the Bartolotta Company has gotten too big for your wedding, fundraiser or company function. The company lights up the night at small events as well, complete with such Bartolotta touches as choreographing the fireworks to music. For plenty of bang and the red glare of rockets, think of the Bartolotta Fireworks Company.

W329 S 1744 Jones Road, Delafield WI
(800) 444-5705
www.bartolottafireworks.com

KC's Driving School

BUSINESS & SERVICES

Learning to drive is one of those things we tend to take for granted. But if you stop to think about it, this often-overlooked rite of passage in our culture is one of the biggest steps any of us will take. The family that owns and operates KC's Driving School understands this importance, and they instill it in their students by treating them as family. They do more than prepare students to pass an exam. They teach road safety and defensive driving skills that will last a lifetime. The family has been providing superior-quality driver's education at reasonable prices since 1986. They now operate four locations, in Watertown, Oconomowoc, Hartland and Waukesha. KC's stands for Kathy's children, because Owner Kathy Braatz wanted to reflect the family nature of the business. Her daughter, Georgia Pirkel, is co-owner of the Watertown location. As a retired driver's license examiner, Kathy's husband, Philip, is a true asset to the company. Son Timothy opened the Oconomowoc and Hartland offices, and Anthony opened the Waukesha location. Every parent wants to feel confident that their teen is safe when they get behind the wheel. The family at KC's knows that feeling. So when you or a friend are looking for a school to teach someone you love, put your mind at ease by calling the folks at KC's Driving School.

120 N Main Street, Oconomowoc WI (262) 560-4118
215 E Main Street, Watertown WI (920) 261-1750
540 Hartbrook Drive, Hartland WI (262) 367-5004
139 W Broadway, Waukesha WI (262) 544-9199
www.kcsdrivingschool.com

Horst Dorner (left), Wolfgang Dorner (center), and Werner Dorner (right)

Dorner Manufacturing

BUSINESS & SERVICES

Dorner Manufacturing is one of the world's leading designers and manufacturers of conveyors and related equipment. Dorner is owned by three brothers, Horst, Wolfgang and Werner Dorner. Dorner opened its doors in 1965 as a tool and die shop. In the early 1970s, Horst and Wolfgang decided they needed a conveyor to efficiently remove scrap and parts from under their machines, but they couldn't find what they needed. They were informed by existing conveyor manufacturers that the devices couldn't be built small enough to fit into the pockets the Dorners needed. True to the spirit of invention and ingenuity that made them great tool and die makers, the brothers decided to solve the problem themselves. They developed and patented a new radial thrust bearing and worked with belting companies to obtain a flexible, durable belt that fit their needs. The result was the Low Profile 4100, unveiled in 1973. Within a few years, the brothers were in the conveyor business full time. Over the years Dorner expanded from steel-frame conveyors into a full line of aluminum and stainless-steel framed devices for every application you can imagine. Dorner conveyors are used in more than 1,200 different industries. The Dorners are committed to people, including those who work for them and those who buy from them. If your business is facing application challenges, visit Dorner Manufacturing. They'll help you figure out a solution.

975 Cottonwood Avenue, Hartland WI
(800) 397-8664 (inside the USA)
(262) 367-7600 (outside the USA)
www.dorner.com

Lifetime Homes Inc

BUSINESS & SERVICES

"Call us. All we need is a place to start and your imagination," says David Walsch, owner of Lifetime Homes. David's enthusiasm for his business is evident in his readiness to answer questions and talk about home building. He loves what he does and could talk about home construction all day. David began his building experience 21 years ago by working 10 years for a large home construction company doing business in Milwaukee and Waukesha counties. His expertise grew with seven additional years spent with a custom builder in southeast Wisconsin. Four years ago David spread his wings and opened his own business in the center of downtown Hartland. He is proud to be living and working in Kettle Moraine, where residents are unwilling to accept the average and strive for excellence in their schools, government and community as well as in their homes. This local insistence on excellence matches David's business philosophy, built on high standards and continual efforts to *raise the bar.* Lifetime Homes offers plans for several model homes and can reconfigure a home or make custom changes that will provide a client with a house meant to last a lifetime. It is important to David to have a positive impact on the lives he touches and this desire is evident in his relationship with his clients. Integrity is a given. Doing business with David carries a lifetime guarantee that no one will huff and puff and blow your house down. It's a promise. Come to Lifetime Homes for value and experience you can trust.

139 E Capitol Drive, Hartland WI
(262) 369-5529
www.lifetimehomesinc.com

Fill your heart with songs of love

Realty Executives-Integrity Phillips Team

BUSINESS & SERVICES

Buying or selling a piece of property is about the most important decision you can make. It really makes sense to work with professionals, which is why people call on the Phillips Team, J.R. and Mari. They specialize in single-family, duplexes and condos, as well as recreational parcels, hunting land and investment properties. J.R. is an avid hunter and sports official who enjoys finding recreational parcels for people nationwide who seek the great outdoor experiences offered by Wisconsin. Together with Mari, he services not only the Lake Country and Watertown areas, but the entire state. Most of their clients become friends, not just clients. Their own family, which consists of five girls and one boy, is a large part of their motivation to serve families both large and small. J.R. and Mari commit themselves to sharing their knowledge about real estate and they do it with integrity, sensitivity and humility. They strive to be stepping stones toward comfort, individuality and style. Gene Schmidt, executive vice president of Hand of Help Ministries, was so impressed with the fine job that the Phillips did in selling their Wisconsin Dells property that they wrote them a letter of recommendation. Walter and Linda Walk were first-time homebuyers who sent the Phillips a thank you note for being patient while taking the time to answer all the questions they had about purchasing property. David and Lana Tank never felt rushed or pressured and in the end they couldn't have been happier. Brian and Wendy Engelbrecht recommend J.R. and Mari if you want excellent service in selling or buying a home. If you are looking for or considering selling property in the Lake Country area, Watertown, or anyplace else in Wisconsin, enlist the services of the Phillips Team.

810 Cardinal Lane, Hartland WI
(920) 262-7447
www.wiphillipsteam.com

welcome

Lake Country Mortgage LLC

BUSINESS & SERVICES

Lake Country Mortgage brings a depth of experience to dealing with a broad range of financing needs. The goal of this Hartland lender is to supply customers with a level of service that develops into more than a business relationship. Whether you are purchasing, refinancing or investing, the staff will shop the market for you to find the best rate. Lake Country Mortgage offers construction loans, small-business loans and specials for first-time buyers. Assisting the credit-challenged individual is not a problem at Lake Country Mortgage—it's one of the company's strengths. "One of the most common mistakes made by consumers is not being aware of their credit scores," says company President Kevin Gifford. "Understanding how the scores affect home financing is pivotal in attaining the best mortgage rates possible." Let a loan specialist show you how lenders evaluate risk while giving you creative solutions for raising your score. "If your credit score is low," says Kevin, "don't let it be a barrier. There are methods to improve it." Whatever your financing needs, the Lake Country Mortgage team will go to work for you.

130 E Capitol Drive, Suite 1,
Hartland WI
(262) 367-9879
www.LakeCountryMortgage.net

Tim and Debbie Michelic—Realty Executives

BUSINESS & SERVICES

There is much to discover in Waukesha County's Lake Country area, just 30 minutes west of Milwaukee. Beautifully sculpted by the glaciers, featuring many lakes, parks and conveniences, Lake Country offers a wonderful lifestyle for residents of all ages. This is where Tim and Debbie Michelic chose to raise their family and to practice real estate over the past 22 years. They have assisted hundreds of families with their real estate needs. Tim and Debbie's experience and knowledge of real estate values, trends, school districts, construction and communities assures results whether you are selling or purchasing area property. Both are designated Seniors Real Estate Specialists (SRES) with expertise to assist sellers and buyers of all ages. They are also familiar with developmental and zoning issues affecting vacant land, waterfront, condominiums, commercial and transitional properties. Their current development, Mission Lakes Luxury Senior Condominiums in Okauchee, are unique waterfront condo units on Florence Lake, with an attached activity center and in a quaint village setting. Waukesha County is a great place in which to live, work and play. When your plans include a sale or purchase of real estate, an excellent choice is Tim and Debbie Michelic of Realty Executives. Call or visit their website today. They look forward to seeing you.

810 Cardinal Lane, Hartland WI
(262) 367-7656
www.TimtheRealtor.com

Midwest Accounting Service

BUSINESS & SERVICES

The day-to-day operations of a small or midsize business can be difficult under the best of circumstances, and the need to construct accounting, tax and payroll plans can only add to the stress of founding a new company or compound the organizational stresses of an existing one. Midwest Accounting Service of Wales can alleviate those stressors by offering comprehensive services for your business that are designed to help your company become stable and profitable. Midwest Accounting Services was founded in 1967 by Bert Sutkiewicz and is currently under the ownership of son Jerry Sutkiewicz, who joined the company in 1979 and purchased it in 1992. Jerry's staff consists of 20 degreed accountants and bookkeepers, who have all been with the company for quite some time and are dedicated to the ultimate success of their clients. Midwest Accounting helps businesses establish and maintain the systems and routines that are essential to the financial stability of any organization. This includes year-round tax consultations and year-end planning, along with financial statements, and business expansion and problem solving evaluations. Additionally the Midwest experts will provide you with projections, budgets, equipment and real estate planning and purchases, along with payroll services that include a myriad of extras, like direct deposit, computerized signatures and customized reports. Make sure that you are building your business on a stable foundation by working with Midwest Accounting Services, the firm that has made life a little easier for business owners since 1967.

308 E Oak Crest Drive, Wales WI
(262) 968-1717
www.midwestaccounting.net

Beverly Designs Boutique & Gallery

FASHION

Beverly Designs began with a rack of owner and artist Beverly Bartel's hand-painted clothing at the local farmer's market. Now celebrating 10 years in downtown Oconomowoc, with over 2,000 square feet of merchandise space, Beverly Designs Boutique & Gallery features novelty, casual and elegant clothing for the person who loves compliments. Resort-wear for women and children, including Fresh Produce Sportswear and Jams World, is available year-round. Try on the latest styles and colors of Crocs amazingly comfortable shoes. You'll be thrilled by the unexpected selection of gifts, toys, games and creative infant clothing. A child's play area and complimentary gift-wrapping are welcome extras. Clothing sizes range from XS to 3X. Contemporary home décor and art objects from local, national and international artists provide an art-show-in-an-hour atmosphere. Beverly Designs also features many one-of-a-kind pieces of clothing, fun accessories and artsy jewelry created by other wearable art designers. Beverly still paints her own abstract designs on clothing, and every year on the third weekend of August, Beverly Designs Artwear can be found in her booth across the street from the Oconomowoc Festival of the Arts. Thanks to Beverly's vibrant artistic vision, good eye for the most distinct merchandise and her personable staff, Beverly Designs is one place you've got to see.

149 E Wisconsin Avenue, Oconomowoc WI
(262) 567-3650 or (888) 567-3650
www.beverlydesignsllc.com

Pursenal X'pressions

FASHION

Michelle Strunsee experienced a dilemma that most women have faced and turned it into a business. For a friend's upcoming wedding, she found the perfect dress, shoes and jewelry, but did not have a purse to match. Michelle's solution was to design her own purse, which led to Pursenal X'pressions. Michelle dubbed her first bag the Posh Purse, and it is now one of her signature lines. She quickly designed three other purses, and they all proved to be so popular with friends that she opened her own studio to sell custom bags, belts and jewelry. One of the most innovative features of the store is the Build Your Own Bag, or BYOB concept. You choose the style, inner and outer fabric and accessories for your bag, and a talented seamstress sews it for you. The store also offers customers a party room for making their own BYOB creations, and it is just the place for a fun bachelorette party, baby shower or girls' night out. Pursenal X'pressions provides the space, the materials and the refreshments, and you just bring your creativity. Michelle has found so much success in Delafield that she is opening a second store in Oklahoma, to be managed by her sister, Robyn Lewis. Get your friends together for a visit to Pursenal X'Pressions, and never again worry about what purse you will wear with that special outfit.

638 Milwaukee Street, Delafield WI
(262) 646-4464
www.pursenalxpressions.com

Vosswinkel Family Cookie Company

FUN FOODS

The Vosswinkel Family Cookie Company is the result of much thought, many answered prayers, and a lot of hard work. Thirty years of Mari Vosswinkel's baking extraordinary Christmas cookies that wowed family and friends has now turned into a year 'round business for herself, husband Mark, daughters Analiese and Kaitlin, and one employee. Their unique butter cookies are individually hand shaped to resemble fruits and vegetables. The Vosswinkels now produce over 20 different varieties, each with its own exquisite flavor. Fruit cookie flavors include apple cobbler, peach, key lime pie and strawberry, while vegetables use such luscious flavors as cheesecake, crème de menthe and amaretto. The cookies are finished with airbrushed highlights and a plastic leaf or stem to create realistic miniature works of art that melt in your mouth. News has spread fast about these special cookies by word-of-mouth, plus magazine and newspaper articles. Individual and corporate orders have shipped throughout the United States, Canada and Europe, and to South Korea, Japan and Hong Kong. These tasty treats were served at a function with First Lady Laura Bush when she was in Wisconsin speaking on women in business. To mark the occasion, the Vosswinkels included cinnamon chili pepper-shaped cookies to represent her home state of Texas, corn on the cob shapes for Wisconsin and Bing cherries for Washington DC. Wherever you are, you can indulge in a beautiful tin or other gift package by contacting the Vosswinkel Family Cookie Company by telephone or website. The goal is that every package creates an event to remember.

520 W Wisconsin Ave, Oconomowoc WI
(877) 7 COOKIE (726-6543)
www.vosswinkelcookies.com

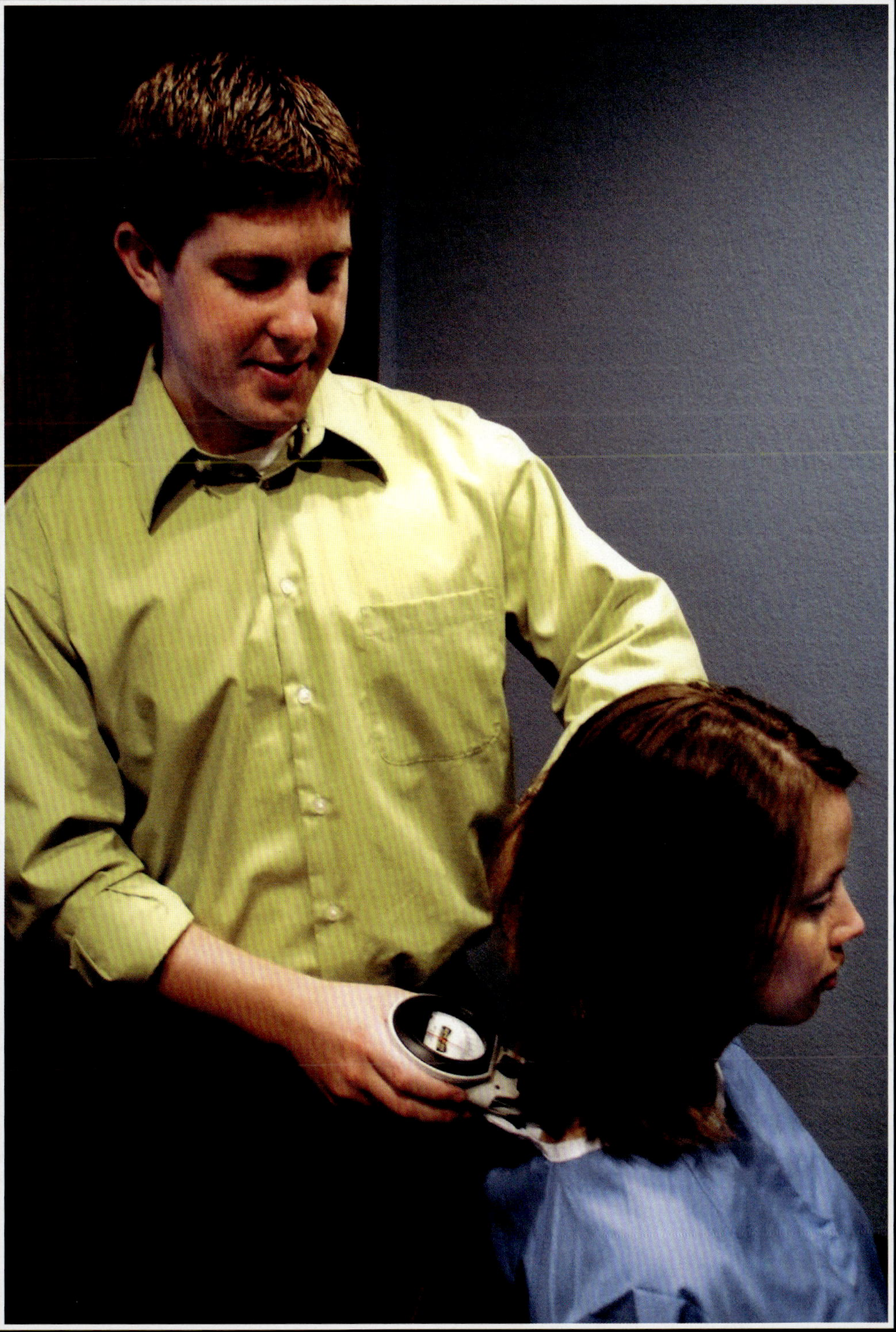

Krieser Family Chiropractic

HEALTH & BEAUTY

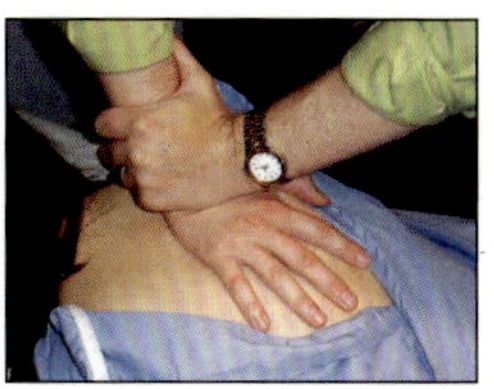

Kenneth Krieser Doctor of Chiropractic, has a passion for the chiropractic profession that was kindled when he was young. He missed 42 days of school because of sinus and respiratory troubles when he was a child. Doctors prescribed 14 medications; none were fully effective and the side effects made him tired and weak. After seeing a chiropractor and getting several adjustments, Ken and his parents saw his health improve and became chiropractic advocates. At Krieser Family Chiropractic, the philosophy is that chiropractic care allows your body the best opportunity to heal from injury as well as fight ailments and diseases. Dr. Ken provides his patients with the most precise care possible using the Gonstead method. This method uses a multi-step protocol: x-ray analysis to ensure a thorough understanding of the patient's spinal structure; palpation to detect motion, swelling and tenderness; and instrumentation to detect and monitor inflammation. This multi-step protocol ensures that Dr. Ken provides the proper adjustment in the proper way, at the proper time, thus maximizing care and recovery. The Gonstead method of treatment will correct the subluxated vertebrae in a manner that avoids excessive rotation or twisting of the spine. Dr. Ken acknowledges that his role is to restore the body's ability to heal itself naturally. Therefore, he promises to give the body time to heal, and he follows the Gonstead way of chiropractic care—find it, fix it and leave it alone. Make an appointment today, because what Krieser Family Chiropractic offers will make a difference you can feel.

1280 Brown Street, Suite F,
Oconomowoc WI
(262) 567-6700
www.krieserchiro.com

Leaves of Change

HEALTH & BEAUTY

Cindy Wilichowski has seen the future and it shows her still giving soothing massages at the age of 107. With a caring heart and healing hands, Cindy, the owner of Leaves of Change, has been helping clients feel more balanced and relaxed since 2003. At Leaves of Change, clients receive careful assessment and treatment plans designed to meet their individual needs. They choose from five different types of massage including a luxurious two-hour Swedish style treatment and the gentle Raindrop Therapy, in which 10 essential oils are dropped on the client's back and spine. This technique, designed to strengthen the immune system, may help the body fight and recover from common illnesses, such as the flu and colds, while relieving headaches, backaches and stress. There are fewer than 300 certified Fijian massage therapists in the United States and Leaves of Change has one of them. Outside of her business, Cindy continues to contribute to the wellness of her community through free workshops at health fairs and special seminars. For bodywork from someone who plans on using her gift of healing for many years to come, go to Leaves of Change.

W330 N4339 Lakeland Drive,
Nashotah WI
(262) 909-4967
www.leaves-of-change.com

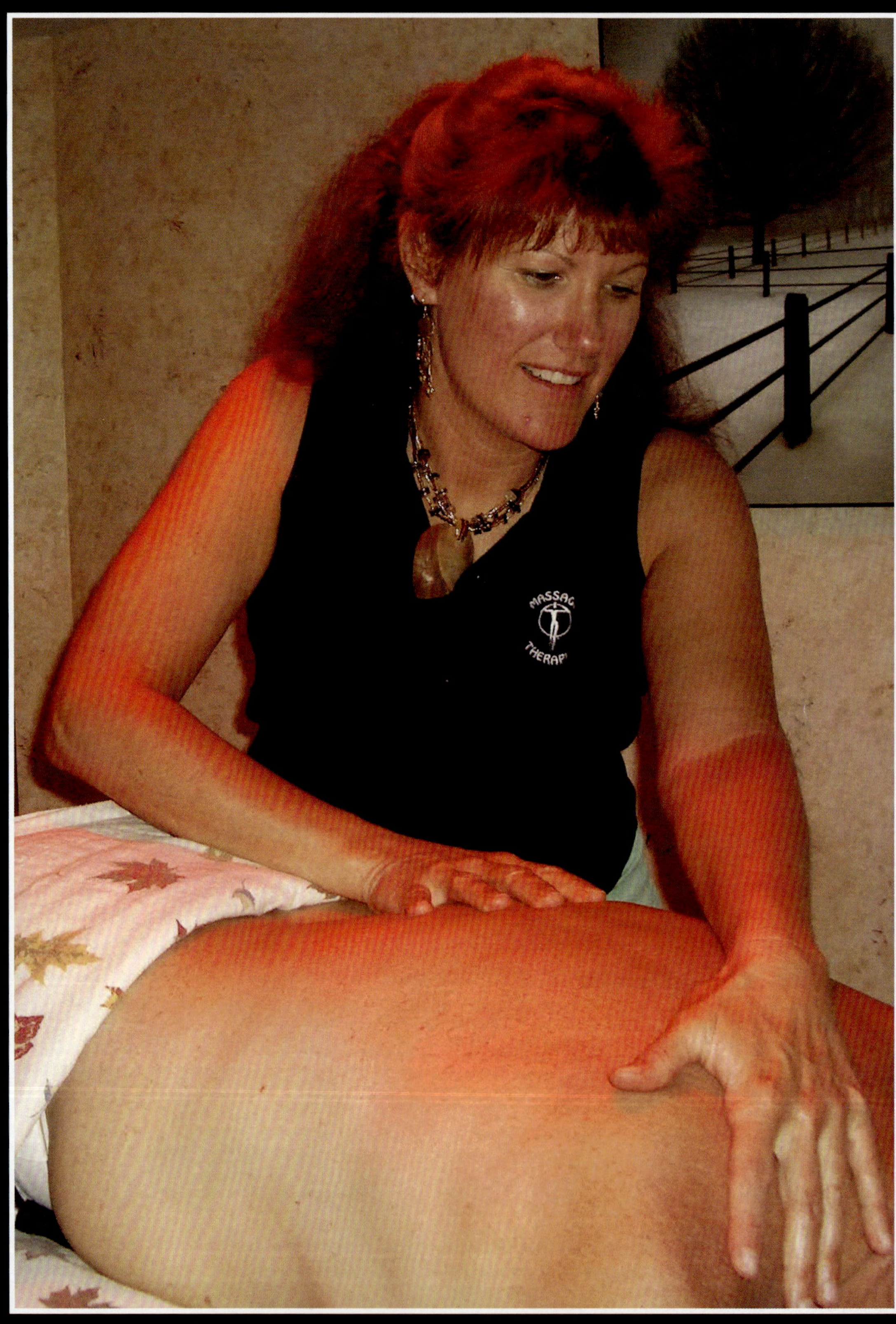

Lake Country Salons

HEALTH & BEAUTY

Theresa Tiegs and her husband, Greg, bought Lake Country Salon in 1998. Theresa had been a stylist for the former owners, but when the opportunity arose to purchase the business, the Tiegs made it happen. Things have grown from there. They opened a Pewaukee location in 2001, and then in 2004 they set up shop on Brown Street, giving them three locations to better serve the community. The growth is possible because Lake Country Salons does it all with style. Whether you want to create a signature look for yourself or just undergo a subtle change, a design team is waiting to provide options for women, men or children. If you need something striking for a special occasion, the team at Lake Country is ready. And they don't just do hair. They offer ear piercing, waxing, nail care and tanning, plus they offer great packages. Gift certificates are available, and their selection of professional salon products is impressive. Get yourself done up in style at Lake Country Salons.

1091 E Summit Avenue, Oconomowoc WI
(262) 567-0550

Heaven on Earth Massage Therapy

HEALTH & BEAUTY

When you walk into Heaven on Earth's studio, you will begin to relax immediately. Soothing music is playing, and you can hear the gentle trickle of a waterfall and birds calling in the distance. As you look around, the soft colors draw your attention to a breathtaking view of the lake. Your massage experience begins with a chocolate waiting for you on a soft blanket and warm sheets. Hot packs and aromatherapy eye pillows are offered to enhance your experience. Each one of your senses is engaged during your therapeutic massage. Deb Weiss, owner of Heaven on Earth Massage Therapy in Oconomowoc, is a state and nationally certified massage therapist. Deb offers a comfortable setting for both men and women to shed the stresses of life. She has found a special calling in helping people with chronic pain due to injuries, disease or trauma. Her goal is to help people function at a higher level. Supplemental therapies, including infrared therapy, are also offered as well as education on well-being. Come escape from life's pressures at Heaven on Earth Massage Therapy.

105 E. Wisconsin Avenue, Suite 102, Oconomowoc WI
(262) 567-9890
www.heavenonearthmt.com

Jeanne's Total Image

HEALTH & BEAUTY

Jeanne's Total Image considers your hair and your overall look in a family salon atmosphere that welcomes all ages and genders. The salon employs seven highly skilled stylists to provide cuts, perms and coloring services using the latest training and techniques. They also accept walk-ins. A visit to Jeanne's is an opportunity to indulge in beauty treatments usually reserved for spas. Polish your look with manicures, pedicures and waxing, then let the staff aesthetician perform a facial, using botanically based skin care products. If you dream of fuller lips or more dramatic eyes, the permanent makeup solutions at Jeanne's may be for you. The shop is full of top lines of hair care and therapeutic products, and even features a small gift area with such items as candles and jewelry. After many years of salon experience, owner Jeanne Walters fulfilled a dream with the opening of the salon in 2000. Come experience Jeanne's Total Image, where scientific breakthroughs lend a lift to your look and your spirit.

200 N Wales Road, Wales WI
(262) 968-1765

Lake Country Pool & Spa

HOME & GARDEN

If you dream of vacationing in your own yard in a beautiful in-ground pool, but dread the hassle of pool construction, call the pros at Lake Country Pool & Spa. Owners Keith and Amy Brouwer pledge that their staff will be with you every step of the way, from preliminary planning to site selection, permitting and construction. The company has earned a reputation for honest and on-time work. Once the Lake Country Pool & Spa crew arrives at your home to begin the job, your pool is its top priority. It finishes one pool at a time, and it consistently completes it on schedule and on budget. Keith, who has been building pools since he was 17, is on-site for every project, either building or expediting. You can choose from 12 different options for standard pool construction, from rectangles and ovals to the irregular outlines of the mountain lake design. If none of these standard patterns suits your needs, Keith and Amy will brainstorm with you to turn your idea into a custom pool. Lake Country Pool & Spa also sells and installs hot tubs. Serving the entire Lake Country from its Delafield and Hartland locations, Lake Country Pool & Spa wants to be your choice for hassle-free pool construction.

2725 Hillside Drive, Delafield WI
(262) 522-7665
600 Hartbrook Drive, Hartland WI
(262) 367-8100
www.lakecountrypoolandspa.com

Remodeling, LLC

HOME & GARDEN

Dissatisfied with your basement? Would you like your garage to be something more than a place where you store stuff? Wouldn't it be nice to sit on a back deck next summer? Remodeling, LLC can help out. Michael D. McDonald, owner of the service, handles home improvements, additions and new construction as well. Concrete flatwork and stamped concrete, foundations and floor slabs, patios and decking are among his specialties, but Mike can handle much else as well. Remodeling LLC can repair a leaky basement or refinish a recreation room. Installing and servicing windows and doors is a major line of work, as is the installation of vinyl or aluminum siding and trim. Remodeling, LLC even offers real estate brokerage services. Mike has years of experience and has been in business for himself since 2002. Let Mike and his wife, Karen, help you with your next building project. Call Remodeling, LLC.

S12 W29015 Summit Avenue, Delafield WI
(262) 968-5591

JP Kitchen Design Studio

HOME & GARDEN

Is your kitchen outdated? Does the idea of remodeling intimidate you? JP Kitchen Design Studio can help. Whether you are contemplating a remodel or are building a new house, the decisions you have to make can be overwhelming. The JP staff will take the time to educate you and help you plan a kitchen that truly fits your needs. You will see your choices projected in their Virtual Vignette digital screen that instantly shows you the results of changes to color, materials or cabinetry. JP Kitchen Studio offers custom and Legacy semi-custom cabinets as well as the work of several local custom cabinet makers. JP Kitchens specializes in smart kitchens that are wired for features such as Internet access, audio systems and intercom. Video monitering offers the peace of mind of knowing that while you are busy in the kitchen, you can watch your children play in the backyard and see the front door all at the same time. For personal service in creating the centerpiece of your home, consult JP Kitchen Design Studio.

1288 Summit Avenue, Suite 110,
Oconomowoc WI
(262) 560-1200
www.jpkitchenstudio.com

Furniture made by Dennis Bork

Photo taken at Antiquity

Antiquity Period Designs, Ltd.

HOME & GARDEN

Antiquity Period Designs, Ltd. is a unique store specializing in handmade reproduction period furniture and handcrafted period decorating accessories that contribute to the beauty of a traditional home. Dennis Bork and his wife CeCe work together to run their store. Some of the accessories they carry are hand-blown glass, hand-cast pewter and forged wrought iron. They also stock loomed rugs, period bed coverings, floor cloths and historic prints on canvas. Period lighting, both interior and exterior, as well as historic paints are offered. Antiquity Period Designs is an authorized Williamsburg Shop, the perfect place to satisfy your Williamsburg craving. Dennis is a master period furniture maker able to create heirloom pieces from circa 1650 to 1825. He uses only authentic 18th century methods such as hand-cut dovetails, mortise and tenon joinery, hand-planed boards, hand-carved moldings and ball and claw feet. Only solid woods are used, along with slotted screws and cut nails to be authentic. Finishes are hand-applied. His clients come from all over the country, even Hawaii. Just send him a photo of a cherished Queen Anne table or a Chippendale highboy, and he will reproduce it for you. Most of his pieces are custom made. In addition to Dennis' furniture, the shop also carries upholstered furniture, both formal and country, and Windsor chairs and dining tables. Walking into Antiquity Period Designs is like stepping back in time.

719 Genesee Street, Delafield WI
(262) 646-4911
www.antiquity-furniture.com
info@antiquity-furniture.com

House of Handles

HOME & GARDEN

From the front door to the back porch and every place in between, the House of Handles has what you need for opening, closing, hanging and knocking. Located in the Wal-Mart Center on Highway 83 and 94 in Delafield, House of Handles is a family-owned store specializing in decorative hardware. Since 2004, House of Handles has offered cabinet hardware and hinges, bath accessories, including showerheads and valves, and, of course, knobs of every shape and size. Owners John and Debra Rizer have more than 20 years of combined experience in the decorative hardware industry, and they work hard to make sure that House of Handles has all of the hard-to-find items you need to complete your home décor. Whether you are building new or remodeling, the staff members at House of Handles will work closely with you or your contractor to put the finishing touches on your project. They are dedicated to working within your budget to make sure you are satisfied. A fresh new look for your cabinets, bathrooms or even your front door is waiting for you at House of Handles. The store showroom has a stunning 6,000 pieces of cabinet hardware on display, including more than 100 door mounts, more than 50 bath collections and several freestanding towel racks and mirrors. John and Debra invite you to stop at House of Handles, or visit the website, to get your hands on something special.

2850 Heritage Drive, Delafield WI
(262) 646-4240
www.houseofhandlescorp.com

Klink's Karpets Inc

HOME & GARDEN

Mark Klink and Peggy Andrews are a brother and sister team whose company, Klink's Karpets, has been helping to beautify Hartland homes since 1972 with its full spectrum of residential and commercial flooring choices. Mark and Peggy are the second generation of Klinks to run Klink's Karpets. They took over the business in 1994 from their parents and founders, Francis and Judy. Mark began as a carpet installer. Peggy started as a customer relations specialist at the store. Together they know every dimension of the flooring business, from color selection and measuring to installation and care. They work hard with customers to help them choose the best flooring for their home, whether it be carpeting, tile or wood. Klink's Karpets carries the top products in the business from such trusted names as Mohawk, Shaw Carpets, Mannington vinyl and and Kährs wood flooring . Your home is your castle, so trust this second-generation family business to treat you like royalty and help you find the perfect flooring for every room.

107 North Avenue, Hartland WI
(262) 367-4670
www.klinkskarpets.com

Laue's Landscapes & Design Solutions, Inc

HOME & GARDEN

As the name implies, Laue's Landscapes, located in Genesee Depot, can undertake a variety of landscaping projects. Laue's specialty, however, is helping people discover the delights of outdoor living. R.C. and Susan Laue can provide all the essentials needed to create an outdoor living area. You can define the room with a pergola, then equip the room with a convection grill, weatherproof furniture and a fireplace or fire pit. You and your guests will never want to come inside. If all you have is a balcony, you can still equip it with a grill, furniture and a freestanding gas lantern from this versatile company. Laue's Landscapes finds many ways to redefine your outdoor spaces, including a large collection of outdoor fountains and topiary frames. The topiary frames allow you to bring unusual shapes or animals to accent your garden area. You might choose a teapot or a shoe; in animal-shaped frames, expect anything from a dachshund to a dinosaur. Laue's offers classes for adults on creating topiaries and classes for children on how to garden. For some out of the ordinary ideas on how to design your outdoor oasis, visit Laue's Landscapes & Design Solutions, Inc.

S47 W30760 Highway 59, Genesee Depot WI (262) 968-6726 *www.laues.com*

Carpets Plus Color Tile of Oconomowoc

HOME & GARDEN

Add beauty and value to your home with a little help from Carpets Plus Color Tile of Oconomowoc, where owners Eric and Tammy Rosenow and their knowledgeable staff can assist you in finding the right flooring to suit your lifestyle. Eric, a fourth generation Oconomowoc Lake area native, was raised by a family that earned its living in the flooring business and instilled in him an appreciation for the craft. Eric began in the field as a carpet installer, but later turned to tile work to focus more on using his artistic abilities to create stunning floors, fireplace surrounds, countertops and backsplashes. Eric and the staff at Carpets Plus Color Tile also offer tile showers, tubs and niches for your bathroom or kitchen. Eric isn't the only Rosenow to ply the family trade; wife Tammy is a design specialist and flooring consultant as well as being responsible for the company's promotions and in-store sales. Wayne Rosenow is the company warehouse manager and inventory controller, and Mary Alice Rosenow, who has been in flooring for more than 30 years, acts as general manager and one of Carpets Plus Color Tile's design specialists. In addition to quality carpeting and the excellent tile collection, Carpets Plus Color Tile offers natural stone, custom rugs and both cork and bamboo flooring. The Rosenows' professional sales staff and expert installers make reflooring your home simple and enjoyable, so head down to Carpets Plus Color Tile of Oconomowoc, where adding personality to your floor is the company specialty.

650 E Wisconsin Avenue, Oconomowoc WI
(262) 567-5630 or (888) 698-FLOR (3567)
www.creativeflooringwi.com

Boneck's Professional Pool Builders

HOME & GARDEN

The Boneck family has put its name behind its pools for more than 30 years. Adding a pool to your home is a major decision, and it can lead to headaches, if it is not done right or on time. With 2,000 satisfied customers as its best endorsement, Boneck's Professional Pool Builders has earned your business, if you are in the market for a beautiful in-ground pool. Each successful project begins with the right design to complement your home and lifestyle, uses only quality materials and relies on precise, skillful workmanship. This is the Boneck way. Denny Boneck has been building pools since 1975, and his sons, Brett and Barry, have worked alongside him since they were school kids. Their experience and pride show in every detail of their work. They offer a full range of options, from rectangular and oval pools to kidney and L-shaped designs. If you can't find what you have in mind in their catalog, they will personally design a pool for you. They are also committed to servicing your pool for as long as you own your home. For a pool you can enjoy for many summers to come, depend on Boneck's Professional Pool Builders.

580 E Summit Avenue (Highway 18), Wales WI
(262) 968-2440

Photo by David Omastiak

The Fabric Gallery

HOME & GARDEN

For home décor fabrics that are difficult to find at mainstream fabric stores, come to the Fabric Gallery Oconomowoc. The Fabric Gallery offers an extensive collection of designer fabrics in stock with mill direct pricing. Owners Nancy Showers and Landy Brown offer a wealth of interior design experience. The pair opened The Fabric Gallery in 2002, which now features more than 3,500 square feet of showroom space. "We can provide custom solutions for home decorating needs from start to finish," says Nancy. "Or, we can help clients who prefer to do home decorating projects on their own. Most people that visit our gallery are overwhelmed by the selection of fabrics we have in our showroom. Our designers are friendly, knowledgeable and willing to work with clients to create a unique look within their budget." The Fabric Gallery carries beautiful fabrics, in a rainbow of colors and patterns, some of which are imported from around the world. The Gallery offers custom window treatments, bedding, pillows, cushions and more. Blinds, shades and shutters made by Hunter Douglas, Graber and Kirsch are also available. In-home consulting and installation services are provided as needed. The Fabric Gallery is conveniently located in the Whitman Park Shopping Center. Drop by today, and discover terrific solutions for your home decorating needs.

1085 Summit Avenue, Oconomowoc WI
(262) 560-1100
www.fabricgallerwi.com

Lorleberg's True Value Hardware

HOME & GARDEN

No business place is better known in Oconomowoc than Lorleberg's True Value Company, hardware merchants. During its 137 years of existence it has become a household word among the local residents, as well as those in the outlying rural areas. Hugo Lorleberg, who founded the company, erected the first waterworks plant in Oconomowoc and had the first street sprinkling contract. Today, owners Jeff and Lisa Burchardt continue Hugo's tradition of customer service in a hardware store that caters to patron's needs. Lorleberg's is one of the state's leading retailers of Weber grills. It carries Stihl power tools and Simplicity equipment. Knowledgeable employees understand their stuff, so whatever your project, they can help you find what you need. Lorleberg's also offers such services as glass cutting, pipe cutting and fitting, and window screen repair. If you need keys cut or propane, they can help you with that, as well. Lorleberg's is an award-winning hardware store that also contributes to the community in numerous ways. Whether you're repairing your home, buying new tools or need a grill for your summer, Lorleberg's is the place to come.

900 E Wisconsin Avenue, Oconomowoc WI
(262) 567-0267 ***www.lorleberg.com***

Aquatica

HOME & GARDEN

With its innovative water garden techniques, Aquatica can bring tranquility and beauty to any outdoor area. After working in the pond business for more than 16 years, Dean Pipito and Aaron Worden started Aquatica in 2000. Their commitment to consumer education, experienced installers and exemplary customer service quickly earned them recognition from numerous media outlets, including features in *Green Side Up*, *Life Style West* and *I&G* magazines. Aquatica has also been featured on the *Great Lakes Gardener* television show, won numerous national Top 10 Wale's area company awards and *Home Show's* Best of Show and People's Choice awards. Aquatica is a certified Aquascape contractor, held to the highest industry standards, and can design and install any water feature for your home or business, whether you want the energy of a rushing waterfall or a quiet pond with aquatic plants. If you are a do-it-yourselfer, Aquatica offers on-site design and installation consultation and can guide you through your project. The more than 50 gardens on Aquatica's annual water garden tour inspire participants with ideas for their own homes while benefiting two very important charities, the Wildlife In Need Center in Waukesha County and the Cerebral Palsy Center of Green Bay. The Aquatica retail location offers seasonal seminars to give you firsthand instruction and education about water gardens. The stores also carry a variety of books and magazines to further your knowledge. Call or stop by Aquatica, and create your own backyard retreat.

230 James Street, Wales WI
(262) 968-5540
www.aquaticaponds.com

World of Wood

HOME & GARDEN

World of Wood in Oconomowoc is a company founded on a passion for wood. Here, artisans create the ultimate in custom wood work for the luxury home market. This includes cabinetry, furniture, moldings, doors and all sorts of specialty projects. With 23 employees, World of Wood consists of 15 skilled craftsmen, two in-house designers and other professionals, all committed to excellence. The firm's master woodworkers, who consider themselves keepers of the craft, create tomorrow's antiques by combining Old World craftsmanship with contemporary technology. The company was started by Rick and Lois Erdmann in 1975 and continues to be owned and operated by the Erdmann family. Today, son Robert Erdmann is president. Visitors who enter the World of Wood showroom immediately begin the "WoW" experience as they are surrounded by fine woodwork, including a knotty butternut home office display, a flame-grain walnut table, a French country kitchen island and myriad custom pieces. Among its many awards was the special recognition the company earned for its restoration work on an historic Italian Renaissance-style mansion on Lake Michigan. In that same fashion, World of Wood designers work closely with clients to draw out their dreams and ideas. Clients, in turn, give high praise: "It's obvious that a lot of pride and meticulous workmanship went into the project," said one client. And an architectural client proclaimed that "only one standard exists at World of Wood and that is the standard of excellence." Always fostering the relationship side of the business, World of Wood encourages clients to tour its nearby production facility during their own project's fabrication process. To see what wood can do in creating your luxury home, visit the World of Wood showroom.

148 E Wisconsin Avenue, Oconomowoc WI
(262) 567-0188 or (888) 545-0188
www.worldofwood.com

R-Farm

MARKETS & DELIS

In 1990, Mac Riemenschneider looked around and saw that there was a fierce need and demand for naturally raised, quality meats and poultry, so he fulfilled his lifelong dream of becoming a farmer and opened R-Farm. At R-Farm, animals eat grass and homegrown organic grains; the steers and fowl have access to pasture lands during warmer weather, which makes for a fresher and more flavorful end product. R-Farm sells beef, pork and chicken during the appropriate growing cycles and packages meat in portions that are easy for customers to manage, including individual cuts and variety boxes. During the summer months, the farm's chickens eat fresh grass from the pastures and Mac's special homemade grain mix. You can place an order no later than August 1 to obtain a fresh pasture-raised turkey for Thanksgiving. R-Farm offers smoked ham steaks and roasts, as well as pork sausage with such seasonings as maple or Italian. Beef comes in a wide array of popular cuts, including t-bone, porterhouse and round steaks. The farm also offers several roast options, such as English, sirloin tip and rolled rump roasts. Additional treats include preformed ground beef patties, all-beef wieners and both plain and garlic seasoned summer sausage. R-Farm also sells fresh brown eggs and an assortment of seasonal vegetables. Bring fresh flavor and quality back to your family's dinner table with meats, eggs and produce from R-Farm, where Mac sells only what he grows.

W394 S4398 Highway Z, Dousman WI
(414) 881-2098

Peak Performance

RECREATION & FITNESS

The personal trainers at Peak Performance provide workouts that far transcend the health club experience. Clients rave about the energized atmosphere, innovative exercises and guaranteed results. Have you joined countless health clubs, never to go? Are you willing to make a commitment to energizing your life, renewing your spirit and transforming your body? If so, Peak Performance is for you. Its nationally accredited professionals take an integrated approach to evaluating your fitness. They then design an individual program to improve your health and fitness. The goal is a life changing experience that gives you the power and energy to conquer the demands of life. You will definitely look great, but that is a second-level goal. Training takes a functional approach by focusing on training movements rather than isolated muscles. Your posture will improve while you build strength throughout your core (hips, abdominals, low back and shoulders). Peak Performance offers private and group training sessions in a fully equipped, state-of-the-art private studio for adults and athletes of all ages. The Corporate Health and Wellness program, geared towards medium to large corporations, creates confidence, improves energy and fosters greater workplace success. Bridal Boot Camp gets brides and grooms looking their best for their weddings and, more importantly, creates health and wellness that lasts the rest of their lives. Doug J. Krueger, owner of Peak Performance, began his career traveling to homes and schools to train clients, bringing his unique fitness philosophy wherever it was needed. Through word of mouth, his business grew rapidly to the point where he needed to open a studio and recruit additional staff. Peak Performance opened a second facility in 2006. Let Peak Performance show you how fitness can be a lifestyle.

133 Hill Street, Hartland WI
(262) 367-3742
1231 George Towne Drive, Pewaukee WI
(262) 695-6776
www.peakpt.net

Knollwood Farm Ltd.

RECREATION & FITNESS

With an equestrian program that is among the largest in the United States, Knollwood Farm Ltd. has produced many world champions. The farm's complete saddle seat riding program has something for everyone, from competitive to recreational riders. Knollwood Farm offers a Tiny Tot riding program for children as young as four, along with summer riding school for children ages seven and older. The instructional program takes place all year in either the large, heated indoor arena or in one of the two lovely outdoor arenas, depending on the season. The farm's talented instructors regularly win awards and shows throughout the United States. As a way to keep costs down, Knollwood offers group lessons, but if you desire more individualized instruction, you can arrange for private lessons. Throughout the year, Knollwood students and their families take part in special activities through the farm's chartered riding club, the Knollwood Knockouts. The farm welcomes visitors to its regularly scheduled student competitions. Information booths and show horse demonstrations are a part of each show. Owners Carol and Scott Matton, Riding School Director Nancy Turner and Assistant Director Ann Wilt invite you to visit their beautiful facility, take some lessons and improve your riding skills or simply learn more about horses.

2800 Oakwood Road, Hartland WI (262) 367-2391
www.knollwoodfarmltd.com

Lake Country Racquet and Athletic Club

RECREATION & FITNESS

From its modest beginning in 1974 as a tennis club, Lake Country Racquet and Athletic Club has grown into a multifunctional facility serving the sports and fitness needs of the Hartland community. Eight indoor tennis and three racquetball courts host everything from league and tournament play to beginner lessons. You can play basketball, wallyball and sand volleyball here, too. Swim laps in the pool, or work out in the fitness center, where you and a specialist can develop a personalized exercise program. The center has weights, treadmills and rowing machines for burning calories and toning muscles. Come with a friend or make a new one at an aerobics, kickboxing or yoga class. After your game or workout, relax in the whirlpool or sauna. Owned by the Gebhard family since it first opened its doors, Lake Country Racquet and Athletic Club is a clean facility staffed by highly qualified instructors. The club has a membership package perfect for you, whether you want the full range of the facility or just need a place to play tennis year-round in any weather. If you are not already a member, come by and let manager Judy Gebhard and her staff show you around.

560 Industrial Drive, Hartland WI
(414) 367-4999
www.lcclub.com

USA TaeKwonDo

RECREATION & FITNESS

Scott Lewandowski and his seven certified instructors impart their *Yes, I Can* attitude to each man, woman and child who enters into instruction at USA TaeKwonDo, with locations in Hartland and Wales. Scott knows a lot about resolve after 24 years in the martial arts field and six years as an Olympic sparring champion. He opened USA TaeKwonDo 14 years ago and offers a multifaceted program, which incorporates techniques from four disciplines: TaeKwonDo, hapkido, judo and jiu-jitsu. Each discipline adds a different element for a well rounded education in weaponless self-defense. TaeKwonDo is the art of kicking and punching, while hapkido teaches escaping. Falls and throws characterize judo, and jui-jitsu involves ground-grappling and the defeat of an attacker by use of the attacker's own weight and strength. The school's leadership program teaches children to become people who are prepared to be examples to others, while adults enjoy the workout and the self-defense training. Scott's passion defines his life and extends to his family members. Both his wife and two daughters hold black belts, and his son is well on his way to the same accomplishment. For a solid martial arts program that teaches discipline, confidence, focus and respect, come to USA TaeKwonDo.

725-C Industrial Court, Hartland WI
(202) 367-3595
200 W Summit Avenue, Wales WI
(262) 968-5455
www.usa-taekwondo.net

Tinus Marine Inc

RECREATION & FITNESS

The largest water sport shop in the Greater Milwaukee area, Tinus Marine in Oconomowac carries seven lines of boats for sale, everything from jet boats to cruisers. It also features a pro shop and pontoon boat rentals. It was a different world when Tinus opened its doors nearly 60 years ago. For example, a deliveryman still left milk on your door step. Harrold Tinus knows. He worked as a milkman before starting in business. He and his wife, Arlene, were the boat sales pioneers who introduced Mercury outboard motors to the area in the 1950s. They also founded the Milwaukee Marine Dealers Association. Today their sons Steve and Tim run the dealership, and a third generation, Austin and Trevor, work there. The Tinuses are proud that at least 30 fourth-generation families are still customers. With 17 lakes within a 15-mile radius of the dealership, there is a great chance that Tinus will stay headquarters for boat sales, accessories and service for generations to come. The world may change, but the urge to have fun on the water is timeless. Let Tinus get you equipped.

307 Forest Street, Oconomowoc WI
(262) 567-7533
www.tinusmarine.com

Studio One Dance Company

RECREATION & FITNESS

Kelly Heis, owner and director of Studio One Dance Company, began dancing at the age of three through a park and recreation program in Illinois. As her passion and enthusiasm for dance grew throughout the years, she studied at Winona State University earning a degree in business administration and dance, with an emphasis in management. After graduating in 2000, Kelly became the dance director at the YWCA of Waukesha. In 2004, Kelly opened her own studio in Wales. Studio One Dance Company prides itself on offering the opportunity for all to dance. Its ultimate goal is for students to develop grace, self-confidence, and creative well-being while gaining a love for dance. Studio One offers a variety of dance forms allowing students of all ages to explore the art of dance. Classes are offered for students who want to have fun. The studio also has offerings for students who want to pursue dance on a more serious level by auditioning for the Competitive Dance Company. To start dancing today, take your fancy feet to Studio One Dance Company.

543 AJ Allen Circle, Suite H, Wales WI
(262) 968-1820
www.studioonedanceco.com

Lemon Grass

RESTAURANTS & CAFÉS

At Lemon Grass in Oconomowoc, owner Choo Ng puts the focus on healthful eating, then sweetens your dining experience with artistic flair. The traditional buffet and other old ways of offering Asian restaurant food do not apply at Lemon Grass. A simple, somewhat minimalist approach to fine dining choices puts the focus here squarely on superb ingredients that please the palate and the arteries. Choo's customers appreciate the lighter, tasty fare he provides and consider it a refreshing option. His sleek black and white décor further reminds them that they are making a contemporary choice to live and eat well. Whether you prefer your food spicy, mild, sweet or savory, Lemon Grass has choices to match your tastes. The entrée names will be familiar to lovers of Asian fare, but the flavors will be more vibrant, fresher and truer than usual. For delicious Asian food made with uncompromising quality, visit Lemon Grass.

1288 Summit Avenue, Oconomowoc WI
(262) 567-7000
www.lemongrassbistro.com

Marsibiglio's

RESTAURANTS & CAFÉS

The precious recipes used for homemade pastas have been passed down in the Marsibiglio family to become part of the quality heritage of Marsibiglio's in Hartland. Takeout and delivery are popular options at this Italian restaurant, known throughout the Hartland Lake Country for its casual family atmosphere and quality pizzas, pasta and subs. The house special is a double layer pizza, one of the most popular of the 15 specialty pizzas here. Soups, salads and appetizers are available, and the kids' menu features ravioli stuffed with hot dog and cheese. The Marsibiglio family immigrated to the United States from Pretoro, Italy in 1912. Marsibiglio's uses only the best ingredients and the same high quality you would find in the pizzerias of Italy. Like the pasta, the pizza dough is handmade using family recipes. Marsibiglio descendant Kevin Martin owns the restaurant. Everyone involved with Marsibiglio's takes pride in the food and service and looks forward to sharing a slice of the Old World with you at Marsibiglio's.

139 E Capitol Drive,
Hartland WI
(262) 367-9888
www.marsibiglios.com

Marty's Pizza

RESTAURANTS & CAFÉS

Marty's Pizza first opened in 1957, and Angie and Marty Skibosh were as famous for their fabulous thin-crust pizzas as they were for their warm welcome and home-like, family atmosphere. In fact, it's a custom here that even if you move away, you still have to come back for Marty's pizza once a year, because you just can't get pizza like this anywhere else. Current owners Dick Flath and Ed Bautz have stayed true to both Marty's pizza recipe and his welcome. Marty's is where the five-foot pizza got its start, and its been a great favorite of the parties that Marty's Pizza caters for groups as large as 2,000 people. Ed and Dick are proud of the faith-based philosophy that has been the foundation of Marty's since the beginning, so they've always kept prices reasonable and the quality of the pizza terrific. They want the average family on a budget to be able to enjoy an evening out and a good meal. Marty's has both longstanding customers and employees that go back for years, because this is a restaurant that cares about the people on both sides of the counter. Whether you want to eat at the restaurant, choose carryout or have the food delivered to your workplace or home, Marty's is fully equipped to meet your needs. With its bright and friendly booths and the happy and efficient staff, Marty's is a great place to start your own tradition of coming back year after year for a great pizza.

2580 Sun Valley Drive, Delafield WI
(262) 646-3327
16680 W Bluemound Road, Brookfield WI
(262)-782-5830
www.foodspot.com/martys

A calm autumn morning in Wisconsin

PLACES TO GO

- Big Foot Beach State Park
  1452 Highway H
  (262) 248-2528
- Mountain Top at Grand Geneva
  7036 Grand Geneva Way
  (262) 248-8811

THINGS TO DO

January

- Winterfest & US National Snow Sculpting Competition
  Riviera Park and Downtown
  (800) 345-1020

June

- Honor the Fire Keepers Native American Pow-Wow
  Dunn Field
  (262) 248-2784

August

- Venetian Festival
  www.lakegenevajaycees.org/Venetian%20Fest.html
- Art in the Park
  Library Park
  genevalakeart.org/artinthepark.htm

September

- Lake Geneva Wine Festival
  www.lakegenevawinefestival.com

October

- Oktoberfest
  Downtown
  (800) 345-1020

LAKE GENEVA

Lake Geneva, an attractive resort town on the lake of the same name, has been called the Newport of the West. Since the mid-1800s, Lake Geneva has been a popular tourist destination and summer place for wealthy residents of Milwaukee and Chicago. After the Chicago fire of 1871, many families settled permanently in their summer homes in Lake Geneva. Many of these houses, now listed on the National Register of Historic Places, still stand on the wooded bluffs above the lake. Geneva Lake is the source of the White River. The town's pioneers used a 14-foot waterfall at the top of the river to power grist and sawmills. The power proved so economical that farmers brought grain from as far away as Kenosha, Milwaukee and Beloit to mill in Lake Geneva. Many of the dams and canals that once fed these mills can still be seen. Visitors enjoy tours of Geneva Lake by boat or on foot using the Potawatomi Trail. Originally used by the Potawatomi Indians, the trail offers public passage through otherwise private lakeside property. Downtown Lake Geneva offers historic buildings, quaint shops, galleries and antiques.

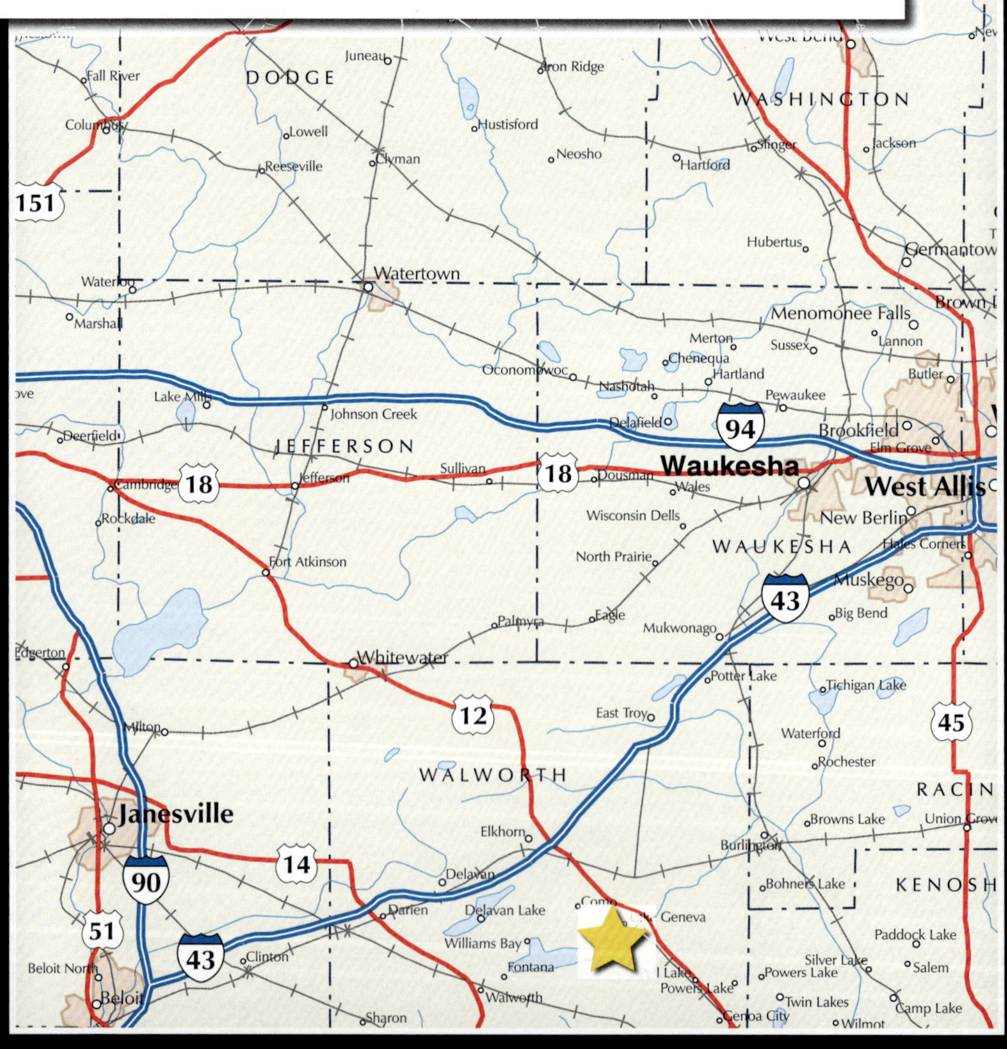

The Cove of Lake Geneva

ACCOMMODATIONS

With 222 luxurious, king-size suites steps from the shimmering lakefront, the Cove of Lake Geneva offers all the ingredients for an exceptional stay. The suites are individually owned and decorated, with the hotel management handling the rental arrangements. The suites range in size from 640 to 1,290 square feet, and each features a private balcony or patio. All offer a full kitchen, fireplace, whirlpool tub, high-speed Internet and DVD player. If you don't feel like cooking or going out, room service is available from Houlihan's Restaurant & Bar. The Cove is located in the heart of Lake Geneva, but there's plenty to do at the hotel itself. The outdoor cabaña area features a full bar, live music on the weekends and the biggest heated outdoor pool in Lake Geneva. There's a heated indoor pool, sauna and fitness room. If you're looking for a place to hold a business meeting, the Cove offers more than 8,000 square feet of space, along with catering and a meeting coordinator to make sure your event goes smoothly. The Cove is also an ideal place for weddings and reunions and has a full-time wedding coordinator on staff. The Cove's world-class service staff strives to make your visit absolutely unforgettable. The hotel opened its doors to travelers in 1996. Whether you're on vacation, traveling for business or holding an event, come to the Cove of Lake Geneva for the finest accommodations and service.

111 Center Street, Lake Geneva WI
(262) 249-9460 or (800) 770-7107
www.cove-lake-geneva.com

Photos by David Omastiak

The Grandview Restaurant & Lounge

ACCOMMODATIONS

The Grandview Restaurant & Lounge offers elegant dining on the shores of Geneva Lake. Owners Clarence and Marilyn Schawk opened the restaurant in 1990, inside the luxurious Geneva Inn. The focus at The Grandview is on contemporary American cuisine using only quality ingredients at the peak of freshness, and Executive Chef Scott Commings continually updates the menu to correspond to the changing seasons. The menu reflects the relaxed sophistication of the atmosphere with entrées such as tangerine glazed duck, Bourbon and sage brined pork loin and seared scallops and lobster. Part of the dining experience includes the artful pairing of wine with food. A series of wine dinners takes the culinary adventure a step further, with Chef Scott preparing a five-course meal that showcases a chosen wine. Consider making a weekend of it with an overnight stay at the Geneva Inn, and retreat to your room after dinner. On Saturday and Sunday, treat yourself to a champagne brunch with such inspired offerings as sun-dried tomato and blue cheese quiche and jumbo lump crab cakes. Dine at The Grandview Restaurant & Lounge, where lunch or dinner and a view prove equally enticing.

N2009 S Lake Shore Drive, Lake Geneva WI
(262) 248-5680 or (800) 441-5881
www.genevainn.com

Photos by David Omastiak

The Geneva Inn

ACCOMMODATIONS

In 1989, Clarence and Marilyn Schawk's fond memories of dining at The Old Shore Club inspired them to purchase the stately manor and share the magic of Geneva Lake with others. Built more than a century earlier, the original inn's structure could not be salvaged, so Clarence and Marilyn built a new retreat, keeping in mind the history and European-inspired charm of the first. The Geneva Inn offers guests unobtrusive elegance, from the vintage baths to four-poster beds. Many of the tastefully appointed rooms feature views of Geneva Lake from private balconies. Special touches like the thick, fluffy bathrobes and dark chocolate at bedtime make you feel pampered, and the coffee and weekday newspaper waiting outside your door in the morning start the day on a relaxing note. After that first cup of java, head down to the Grandview Restaurant for a deluxe Continental buffet breakfast, including pastries, fresh fruit, smoked meats and Wisconsin cheese. Many magazines and organizations, including *Country Inns Bed & Breakfast*, have bestowed praise on the Geneva Inn for its understated elegance and Old World charm. The annual Geneva Inn Lake Walk encourages community members to walk all or part of the 20-mile loop around the picturesque lake as a fundraiser for a local charity. Discover the allure of Geneva Lake with a visit to the Geneva Inn.

N2009 S Lakeshore Drive, Lake Geneva WI
(262) 248-5680 ***www.genevainn.com***

French Country Inn on the Lake

ACCOMMODATIONS

While you are enjoying a gorgeous view of Lake Como from your balcony at the French Country Inn, ponder the remarkable history of this building. The story begins in Denmark, where the current main guesthouse was built and then shipped to Chicago. The structure served as the Danish Pavilion at the World's Fair in 1893. The spectacular wood inlaid flooring and oak staircase at the inn are examples of the building's original handiwork. After the fair, the building was moved to its current location three and one-half miles west of downtown Lake Geneva. Through the years, it was used as a first-class restaurant, a speakeasy and even a hideout for Bugs Moran and his gang. Today the French Country Inn offers European style with an emphasis on comfort. Its 34 rooms each feature a private bath, whirlpool and fireplace. Most have skylights or cathedral ceilings, and in some a spiral staircase connects the main area to a loft. Rates include a full breakfast. Next door, the renowned Kirsch's Restaurant overlooks the lake. You rarely think of a building as well traveled, but the French Country Inn on the Lake certainly fits that description. Make it your choice for a romantic and picturesque escape.

W4190 West End Road, Lake Geneva WI
(262) 245-5220
www.frenchcountryinn.com

General Boyd's Bed & Breakfast

ACCOMMODATIONS

General Boyd's Bed & Breakfast has been in business since 1995, but its history extends back to the 19th century. Gen. John W. Boyd arrived in the Lake Geneva area in 1844 and established his six-acre farmstead in 1867, following two terms as Walworth County's first state senator. The Colonial Revival home, surrounded by rolling hills and classic timber-framed barns, belongs to Bob and Sue Morton. Sue, Gen. Boyd's great granddaughter, was raised in the home. After Sue and her sisters inherited the property, Sue and Bob decided to create this idyllic bed and breakfast and offer four comfortable rooms with private baths. The home received a perfect score after an evaluation by the Wisconsin Bed & Breakfast Association and holds a Three Diamond rating from AAA. Gen. Boyd's daughters were wonderful artists, and much of their original work is on display here, along with original pieces created by Bob Morton's family. Perennial gardens and a wildflower meadow delight guests who find many ways to enjoy their stay, from sipping coffee, tea or wine from a swing to swaying in a hammock or reading in front of the massive stone fireplace that dominates the 45-foot long living room. Big Foot State Park and Beach is just five minutes away. Fresh, delicious breakfasts here include egg dishes, cobbler and baked goods. For country tranquility, visit General Boyd's Bed & Breakfast.

W 2915 County Road BB, Lake Geneva WI
(262) 248-3543 or (888) 248-3548
www.generalboydsbb.com

Golden Oaks Mansion

ACCOMMODATIONS

People are still living like royalty in the Golden Oaks Mansion in Lake Geneva. These days the lucky occupants are guests at the luxury bed-and-breakfast instead of members of the Chicago elite who once spent summers here. Built in 1856 and regarded as one of Lake Geneva's finest landmarks, Golden Oaks Mansion makes a lavish statement in the Italianate style, beginning with the fountain, statuary and gardens that impress guests as they approach the entrance. Inside, the emphasis on high style continues with marble fireplaces, crystal chandeliers and a grand staircase. Tall windows and 14-foot ceilings add a sense of spaciousness to the overall feeling of luxury. Owner Nancy Golden (Waspi) Bell and Chef David Bell offer four queen rooms and three king suites to their guests, each room featuring its own private bath and Franklin fireplace. Breakfast is a gourmet affair that may include strawberry soup, French toast and fresh tortillas filled with sausage, mushrooms and herb cream cheese. Golden Oaks Mansion provides a special setting for weddings and large or small receptions. Whether you are planning an intimate event or an elaborate affair with up to 150 people, Nancy and her staff can accommodate your needs and will even help coordinate the music, flowers and other arrangements. For lodging or event hosting, consider the Golden Oaks Mansion, a symbol of luxury since the 1850s.

421 Baker Street, Lake Geneva WI
(262) 248-9711 or (800) 823-2921
www.goldenoaksmansion.com

Grand Geneva Resort

ACCOMMODATIONS

After checking in at the Grand Geneva Resort, the largest resort operation in the state of Wisconsin, guests are faced with a tough decision. What to do first? If you have left a stressful job behind, you might want to head straight to The Well, a full-service spa offering an array of massages and treatments. However, if the drive here has you itching for a little exercise, then you might be ready to climb the rock wall or shoot some hoops at the Sport Center. If golf is your game, which championship course should you try? Will it be the Brute, one of the longest and most challenging courses in the Midwest, or the Highlands, which Jack Nicklaus and Pete Dye originally designed? Of course, if you have arrived hungry, you will probably want to eat first, but then you must decide between the Grand Café, the Geneva Chophouse or Ristorante Brissago. What's that you say? These are the kinds of decisions that you have been waiting a long time to make? By now, you have already chosen between a room at the resort or a suite at the Timber Ridge Lodge. Probably it was the kids who talked you into staying at the latter because of its 50,000-square-foot Moose Mountain Falls waterpark. For days filled with exhilarating options, plan your next vacation at the Grand Geneva Resort.

7036 Grand Geneva Way, Lake Geneva WI
(262) 248-8811 or (888) 392-8000
www.grandgeneva.com

Roses Bed and Breakfast

ACCOMMODATIONS

When Ruth Ann Bae turned 60, she began her new life by buying a charming inn. Her guests at Roses Bed and Breakfast in Lake Geneva have been thanking her ever since. Located just one block from the lake and a short stroll to downtown, this 1920s summer cottage embodies a casual, comfortable elegance. Ruth has tastefully furnished and decorated the rooms with her own antiques, including the lovely rose prints that hang in the cozy Mary Rose Room. The inn's four guest rooms each feature a private bath and an individual personality. For the best view of the lake, choose the Lake Room. A private balcony is yours with the Red Room. The English-style Garden Room overlooks Ruth's second love, her amazing rose gardens. Did we say her second love? Yes, if there's anything that Ruth loves more than tending her flowers, it would be preparing breakfasts for her guests. The three-course breakfast served on the inn's wraparound porch is her trademark. It's just what you'll need to get yourself ready for an active day in Lake Geneva. Between an opening fruit course and ending with a treat for your sweet tooth, Ruth serves a hearty main dish that may include egg casserole, ginger pancakes, or stuffed French toast. For a present to yourself at any time of the year, book a room at Roses Bed and Breakfast.

429 S Lakeshore Drive, Lake Geneva WI
(262) 248-4344
www.rosesbnb.com

Maria's Bed & Breakfast

ACCOMMODATIONS

It seems quite appropriate that Maria's Bed & Breakfast is a Federal-Victorian style building, a style of architecture that utilizes the best aspects of the European Victorian and the American Federal styles. Just as this Lake Geneva guest house mixes European and American sensibilities, so does Maria Karvunidis herself, who moved to the United States from Germany at the age of 22 and opened her inn in 1999, creating a motif that combines European charm and the hospitality of the American heartland. Maria's winning philosophy is simple. Although sojourners will arrive as guests, they will leave as friends. The inn's main building features antiques from England and Germany, but the infrastructure has been fully renovated. Her talented companion, Edwin Carrero, was very instrumental in this process. Guest rooms each have Victorian style electric fireplaces, European featherbeds and fine linens. A separate cottage, where pets and kids are welcome, offers a stone fireplace and a seven-foot Jacuzzi tub in the bedroom. Breakfast times are flexible, and all dietary restrictions are respected. Some of the more popular breakfast items include stuffed French toast, German style crepes and leek quiches. Arrive at Maria's to experience European style, and by the time you leave, you'll know what old-fashioned American and German hospitality is all about.

512 S Wells Street, Lake Geneva WI
(262) 249-0632 or (877) 249-0632
www.mariasbandb.com

Pederson Victorian Bed & Breakfast

ACCOMMODATIONS

Kristi Cowles brings a Green philosophy to her work as owner, innkeeper and earth keeper at Pederson Victorian Bed & Breakfast in Lake Geneva, where she goes to extraordinary lengths to achieve a healthy guest environment. Kristi's vegetarian breakfasts include organic coffees and teas, dishes prepared with eggs from local farms, whole grain flours and natural sweeteners, like local honey and Wisconsin maple syrup. Kristi banishes chemicals from the premises and dries her 100 percent cotton bed linens outdoors throughout the year. Handmade quilts cover the beds in the four authentically Victorian guest rooms. Kristi's 1880 home, framed by a white picket fence, features tall windows and a scalloped Victorian porch with a swing. Seasonal arrangements adorn the home's nooks and crannies, while hardwood floors and an exterior seven-step paint process honor the home's outstanding architectural details. You won't find any televisions in this old-fashioned guest house, but Kristi is willing to entertain you with a song. She had a 17-year singing career, and if you like what you hear, she offers four CDs for sale. Kristi also owns Singing Wolf Center & Productions, which offers creative, cultural change workshops and musical concerts. Enter a world that's simpler than our own with a visit to Pederson Victorian Bed & Breakfast, the oldest Green bed and breakfast in Wisconsin.

1782 Highway 120 N, Lake Geneva WI
(262) 248-9110 or (888) 764-9653
www.pedersonvictorian.com

Photo by Kevin Adams

T.C. Smith Historic Inn

ACCOMMODATIONS

It's not every day you get to be a guest in a historic home that holds high standards, but still encourages you to relax. The T.C. Smith Historic Inn, named after a local historical figure, lies two blocks from downtown Lake Geneva. This Italianate Greek Revival masterpiece, constructed at the end of the Civil War in 1865, offers three large, handsomely appointed rooms with whirlpool tubs, fireplaces and fine period antiques. The Marks family manages to make their guests feel comfortable amid the exquisite antiques and fine art that define their décor. Although it may seem surprising, they even allow children and pets to stay here. The Marks family owned a bed-and-breakfast by the same name at a different location, but sold that home to reopen at this grand locale. They started the first inn to send the children to college, but from the first it was clear that they had found their calling. Guests can expect to be the center of attention. They can also vouch for the full breakfast, a feast in high Victorian style with a different food focus each morning. Some visitors come every year to celebrate an anniversary; others come more frequently. Plan a visit to T.C. Smith Historic Home and discover for yourself why visitors to this picturesque resort town are so loyal to this particular historic home.

834 Dodge Street, Lake Geneva WI (262) 248-1097 or (800) 423-0233 *www.tcsmithinn.com*

Lake Geneva Cruise Line

ATTRACTIONS

Enjoy the gentle warmth of the sun on your face and the caress of wind in your hair while floating across picturesque Lake Geneva on one of eight fabulous boats from the Lake Geneva Cruise Line. In 1958, father and son team Russell and William Gage purchased the Williams Bay boatyard, a winter port for excursion boats since the early 1900s. The original Lake Geneva Steamer Line dates back to 1873, and Lake Geneva Cruise Line, formerly called Gage Marine, is the oldest and largest continually operated marine business in the area. Once the Gages repaired the half-sinking boats they had purchased, they began building new excursion boats, first on their own and then teaming up with designer John Hacker to create the Gage-Hacker wood boat line. Today Lake Geneva Cruise Line continues to be the area's number one attraction and offers a full array of lake tours, as well as a marina specializing in the care and maintenance of both modern and classic boats. Current President Bill Gage and General Manager Harold Friestad are proud to offer exhilarating tours for two to 225 passengers, including the U.S. Mailboat Tour and the Geneva Bay Mansions Tour. The cruise line also offers great meal cruises and special event cruises that are ideal for birthdays, weddings or reunions. Experience Lake Geneva from the best possible vantage point with excursions from Lake Geneva Cruise Line.

812 Wrigley Drive, Lake Geneva WI
(262) 248-6206 or (800) 558-5911
www.cruiselakegeneva.com

Lake Geneva Pie Company

BAKERIES, COFFEE & TEA

What makes pie taste better if it already has a winning recipe, outstanding ingredients and meticulous preparation entirely from scratch? For owners John and Marty Adams of the Lake Geneva Pie Company, the answer is the love they put in every pie. That love is manifested by their steadfast unwillingness to compromise either food preparation or their interaction with customers. John insists he will do anything he can to meet his customers' needs. He proves his assertion through his array of selections. John serves 50 types of dessert pies, including strawberry, raspberry, blackberry and apple. You will not find any canned fillings, preservatives or lard either. If cream pies are more to your liking, you can find those, too. John and Marty also offer quiches constructed from fine ingredients like asparagus and tomato; the house quiche is a union of artichoke, bacon, ground red pepper and nutmeg. You can also select from a variety of salads, soups and sandwiches. Stop by the Lake Geneva Pie Company on your way into town and on your way out. Pie is available by the slice, or you can take a whole pie with you and enjoy it at home or on the road.

150 E Geneva Square,
Lake Geneva WI
(262) 248-5100
www.lgpie.com

Geneva Java

BAKERIES, COFFEE & TEA

Geneva Java is more than just another coffee joint. The shop is uncommonly cozy, warm and friendly. You'll feel completely at home while you savor Geneva Java's outstanding espresso. The fresh coffee is locally roasted and ground on request. Plug in your laptop and stay awhile. Along with the coffee, tea or drink of your choice, try the wonderful scones. Not only do they have great moist flavors, but you can buy them frozen in dough form and take them home to bake in your own kitchen. Of course, you can also take home baked scones and any of a variety of other tasty baked goods. Geneva Java now offers an extended lunch menu under the moniker The Artist's Café. Try the innovative sandwiches, hearty soups and fresh salads. The shop also has a selection of unique gifts. Geneva Java is a block up the street from their old location on Broad Street in the old church, which is now Geneva Village Shops, but it's still right in the heart of town. Before or after you enjoy all the activities that Lake Geneva has to offer, stop by Geneva Java, where you can sit in the outside courtyard garden while you have some refreshments and a snack.

723 Geneva Street, Lake Geneva WI
(262) 248-1010

Lake Geneva School of Cooking

BUSINESS & SERVICES

Cynthia Fueredi spent years fundraising and working at home before deciding to reinvent herself and emerging as owner of the Lake Geneva School of Cooking, a profession that allows her to share her passion for the culinary arts with classes, parties and a retail store. It seems appropriate the school is run out of a restored church parsonage since Cynthia's passion borders on the ministerial. She loves to see people coming together in the kitchen and having a great time. Businesses enjoy her corporate team building parties, which teach cooking right alongside communication, collaboration and cooperation. Incorporating cooking into a party also works well for bridal showers, birthday parties and club events. The school's kitchen exudes a warm, vibrant décor that's a perfect match for Cynthia's personality. Cynthia insists on excellent appliances, so uses Wolf and Sub-Zero products in her kitchen along with custom cabinetry by Wood-Mode. The school's two-story store gives serious cooks serious choices in kitchenware and hard to find specialty cooking tools. Available brand names include All-Clad, Le Creuset and Wusthof Cutlery. The school offers monthly classes for kids, along with adult classes for all levels of experience from novice to gourmet. Put cooking stage center in your life with a visit to Lake Geneva School of Cooking.

727 Geneva Street, Lake Geneva WI
(262) 248-3933
www.lakegenevaschoolofcooking.com

Celebration on Wells Street

BUSINESS & SERVICES

Celebration on Wells Street is the perfect place in Lake Geneva to hold a party or other catered event. Its excellence has been honored with an International Gala Award, a sign that owner Charles Lorenzi is one of the best caterers in the business. Charles, whose lineage includes a string of chefs, received his training in Europe. He moved to Lake Geneva to work in a local resort and became its catering and banquet manager. It was when he got full swing into catering parties that he discovered his true passion. Today, Celebration on Wells Street, in business for 16 years, plans and manages parties for celebrities and the ultra rich of the Chicago area. However, Charles insists he will work with any budget and offers a vast selection of menu items and bar choices, which include everything from upscale dinners to cookouts. The main dining room is an elegant room for a gathering of up to 200 people with vaulted ceilings and a striking brass Lannon fireplace. Two smaller rooms add options for cozier gatherings. Whether you are planning a business lunch buffet or an elaborate wedding, when you choose Celebration on Wells Street, you can concentrate on celebrating and leave the planning and cleanup to the professionals.

422 S Wells Street, Lake Geneva WI
(262) 248-2555
www.celebrationcatering.net

Chinawest Jewelers

FASHION

Paul and Kathy Yih of Chinawest Jewelers in Lake Geneva sell and design jewelry that originates throughout the world. Both are former college professors and delight in educating their customers while working with them to select the perfect piece of jewelry. Paul was born in Shanghai and raised in Brazil. He and Kathy met and fell in love in his adopted country while Kathy was a foreign exchange student. The couple discovered they shared a love for Brazilian gems and exquisite jewelry and decided to open their own business in 1977. Both are fluent in Portuguese, and Paul speaks Spanish and three Chinese dialects. His language facility allows him to travel to Brazil and Asia to personally select all their gems. When he returns from his many trips, he and Kathy design individual pieces using such stones as amethyst, tourmaline and rubies. They also incorporate pearls, peridot and sapphires into their designs. Custom diamond engagement rings are a Chinawest specialty. The shop's elegant interior features a Chinese motif with antique art, 250-year-old cloisonné pieces and custom-made stone boxes. Come see extraordinary jewelry in a beautiful setting at Chinawest Jewelers.

803 Main Street, Lake Geneva WI
(262) 248-0304 or (888) 231-4367
www.chinawest-jewelers.com

Leather Accents

FASHION

Leather has long been a clothing accessory as well as a durable and beautiful option for outerwear and carryalls. Leather's many useful adornments are the focus of Linda Longwell's Leather Accents in Lake Geneva. The jackets, belts and handbags showcased here promise years of beautiful service. "Our personal attention to design, excellence and quality materials lives up to the highest standards that our customers expect," says Linda, who offers products that blend quality with affordability for outstanding value. When Linda was still a teenager, she learned to tool leather from two Native American neighbors. She also learned to buy and sell leather while running a kiosk specializing in leather products. In 1977, she purchased Leather Accents and has been an anchor in the local business community ever since. Linda sells belts, handbags and backpacks as well as hats, wallets, briefcases and leather jackets for men, women and children. You'll find both suede and smooth leather products as well as specialized clothing, like that used by motorcyclists. Gift wrapping is available. For leather products from around the world, stop by Leather Accents.

717 W Main Street, Lake Geneva WI
(262) 248-0421
www.genevaleather.com

Nancy's Petites

FASHION

Finding petite sizes at department stores can be frustrating, and the limited selection of colors and styles doesn't make it any easier, which is why Nancy Quickel, owner and proprietress of Nancy's Petites, scours the fashion dens of New York and Chicago to find designs for petite customers. Nancy, a 15-year veteran in the retail clothing business, actually managed this popular Lake Geneva clothier for several years before buying the company, which she now operates with daughter Suzanne Hadley. If having a fashion consultant and a personal shopper appeals to you, you'll love Nancy's Petites. Both Nancy and Suzanne work closely with their customers to gain a feel for their individual styles and then use that knowledge to find the right outfits and accessories. The shop carries a wide selection of fashion-forward clothing from top companies, such as Lorizoni, which uses fabrics from Chanel and Gucci, as well as up-to-the-minute designs from accessory mavens like the Mary Frances line of handbags. The shop offers a distinguished array of companies such as Karen Kane, City Girl and Blue Ice and a choice selection of chic casual wear, like Vanilia Italian jeans and sportswear from Blast. There is also a full selection of sweaters and jackets in regular sizes so that the sales associate can help every size, not only petites. Enjoy old-fashioned service while stocking up on contemporary fashions that flatter your proportions at Nancy's Petites.

728 Main Street, Lake Geneva WI
(262) 248-8820

Strawberry Fields

FASHION

Strawberry Fields satisfies your fashion sense with trendy clothing while providing a festive spot to spend an afternoon in the Lake Geneva area. Owner Shari Straube believes fashion is an art, and her job as a fashion artisan is to help customers find the contemporary styles they seek. Shari strives to help customers rediscover the sense of enjoyment a garment find can produce. This focused retailer goes the extra mile to stock this season's colors and feminine styles to meet every mood, from sexy to sophisticated, then looks for further ways to give back to the citizenry that support her efforts with involvement in several Lake Geneva charities. Look for Diane Von Furstenberg dresses, the signature pick and green of the Lilly Pulitzer line or cigarette leg jeans and gaucho styles by Joe's Jeans. After a hard day's night, take the long and winding road to Strawberry Fields, where you might not be able to buy love, but you can find something spectacular to enhance your wardrobe.

707 W Main Street, Lake Geneva WI
(262) 249-8550
www.shopstrawberryfields.com

Wild & Woolly

FASHION

As you step inside Trae Torhorst's comfortable Wild & Woolly clothing shop in Lake Geneva, the casual atmosphere and trend-setting women's clothing put you at ease while exciting your inner fashion diva. Trae has lived in the Lake Geneva area for nearly three decades. Her particular fashion insights give Wild & Woolly its reputation for clothing that's well made and always comfortable. Trae's sense of fashion formed at an early age when she began experimenting with quilting, knitting and crochet. She draws on markets in New York and Las Vegas, which keeps her abreast of trends on both coasts while providing her Midwestern clientele an assortment of clothing options. Fun and funky is the focus of the Wild & Woolly boutique, where staff members know the merchandise and the tastes of their customers, who may be local residents or visitors from Chicago and beyond, thrilled to find designer labels from such companies as Flax, Vanilia, Willow and An Ren. For styles that dare to be distinctive, come to Wild & Woolly, and Never Be Afraid to Make a Statement.

225 Broad Street, Lake Geneva WI
(262) 248-9577

The Bootery

FASHION

Once upon a time, before department stores and catalogs, people bought shoes at specialized stores, where they received the shop owner's undivided attention. Thanks to the Bootery, owned and operated by Roger and Nancy Wolff, you can still receive the kind of hands-on service that assures a great fit—and fashion to boot. Roger and Nancy are dedicated to offering exeptional products and services to their loyal customers, and so are their sales staff, who provide a warm and energetic environment to shop for shoes. The duo opened their first store in Highland Park, Illinois, nearly 30 years ago. In 2005, after finding the perfect corner store in Lake Geneva, they opened a second location, which has been a rousing success. The Bootery is decorated in a classic style and features elegant architectural elements, including a fireplace, leaded glass windows and cherry wood panels, which offer a perfect backdrop for an afternoon of serious shoe shopping. While Roger is at the helm of the business, it is Nancy who is the shop's creative force, and she uses her talent to design lovely vignettes and displays of classic, eclectic and contemporary shoes. The Bootery carries all of your favorite brands, including Donald Pliner, Kors, Merrell and Ugg, as well as a choice selection of handbags and accessories. Enjoy personalized service while finding styles that will put a spring in your step at the Bootery.

771 W Main Street, Lake Geneva WI
(262) 348-1911
www.thebootery.com

The Malt Bar & Dessert Lounge

FUN FOODS

If it's charming, upscale and sweet perfection, it must be the Malt Bar & Dessert Lounge. This is an ice cream parlor where grownups can indulge their senses. Be assured your kids will love it too. After 15 years working in interior design, owner Stacy McDermott decided she wanted to recreate her childhood memories of ice cream served with an unbelievable malt. She spent years trying to find the malt of her memories and when she succeeded, she bought the rights and equipment she needed to serve her cherished delicacies in Lake Geneva. For a special treat, try the Maltochino, a partnership of malt and cappuccino. The hot chocolate with toasted marshmallows tempts many a return visit. You can watch as the staff toasts the marshmallows in front of you or opt for a malted hot chocolate. Desserts include gelato in several flavors, chocolate truffles and cream puffs. If you require lunch before indulging in sweet delights, the Malt Bar & Dessert Lounge offers healthy sandwiches, soups and salads that feature organic fruits and vegetables. A courtyard setting enhances the entire experience. Let the Malt Bar & Dessert Lounge awaken your senses and charm your inner child.

221 Broad Street, Lake Geneva WI
(262) 248-8484
www.themaltbar.com

Gilbertson's Stained Glass Studio

GALLERIES & FINE ART

Light streaming through a stained glass window stirs the emotions; it also stirs the artisans at Gilbertson's Stained Glass Studio. A tour of their work should begin in Lake Geneva, where doors and windows bear their trademark bold colors and intricate designs. Gil Gilbertson, his son Ed, and their staff, never rely on preformed models, but work with each client to develop a unique expression every time they take on a project. They have enhanced homes and businesses with wildlife scenes, floral profusion and abstract designs of striking beauty. You would need to travel extensively to see all of their work, because the Gilbertsons have satisfied clients as far away as Europe and the Grand Cayman Islands. In fact, if pressed to choose one work that could stand as his best since he started his business in 1975, Gil would probably select the three-panel underwater landscape that delights everyone who sees it at a condominium on Grand Cayman. Each panel rises seven and a half feet to reveal an ocean world full of dazzling fish, plants and even a graceful mermaid. Churchgoers feel touched by the divine when light interacts with stained glass windows. The restoration of old windows and church stained glass is a Gilbertson's specialty, accounting for about a quarter of its business. From God's house to your castle, the folks at Gilbertson's Stained Glass Studio approach each job with respect for the artistic tradition that they represent. Drop by their studio today for a consultation.

705 Madison Street,
Lake Geneva WI (Studio)
(262) 248-8022
727 Geneva Street,
Lake Geneva WI (Showroom)
(262) 248-8184
www.stainedartglass.com

Galerie Matisse

GALLERIES & FINE ART

Bob Skibitzki invites you to get lost in a world of beauty when you visit his Galerie Matisse in downtown Lake Geneva. Fine art is the focus, every piece of it selected by Bob himself. You will find hundreds of works by national and international artists as you wander through several rooms with many attractive display areas. Linger over oil paintings and sculptures in a mix of styles, sizes and prices. In business since 1976, Bob is very gratified when a piece of art finds its right owner. Because fine art has the power to enhance a person's life and home, Bob knows that selecting it is an intensely personal decision subject to second thoughts. That's why he offers a six-month exchange privilege. You are welcome to try the art in your home and exchange it at any time within six months if it doesn't work for you. Bob began collecting art while he and his wife, Sandy, were living in Europe. When they moved to Lake Geneva, Sandy's hometown, Bob decided that the city needed a fine art gallery and that he was the perfect person to start one. Visit him at Galerie Matisse, where the purpose is beauty.

830 Main Street, Lake Geneva WI
(262) 248-9264

J'Marc Graphics

GALLERIES & FINE ART

Mark Britt is never too busy at his gallery and frame shop to talk a little art with his customers. The shop is called J'Marc Graphics, and it's located in downtown Lake Geneva. Maybe you stopped in because you need something framed, and you heard that J'Marc carries more than 500 frames. It could be that you just added a new room to your home and you're looking to accent it with an original oil painting or watercolor, a limited edition print or a fine art poster. The selection at J'Marc includes work by local and national artists. While you're doing what you came to do, drop the name of a famous artist and see if Mark responds. Chances are that he will. Since 1984, Mark has been sharing his love of art with his customers. He enjoys answering questions, so please, go ahead and ask him if, in his opinion, Rembrandt was the greatest portrait artist who ever lived. Mark was an art collector before community members encouraged him to open his gallery. For good conversation, custom framing and a gallery of tastefully displayed artwork, visit J'Marc Graphics.

736 Main Street, Lake Geneva WI
(262) 248-9030 or (800) 433-2443

Geneva Art Pottery

GALLERIES & FINE ART

The story of Geneva Art Pottery begins in a small French village renowned in the art world for its style of pottery. The town is called La Borne, and Claire Berger Bailey spent 10 years there learning all she could about the art of wood firing and the use of natural ash glazes before founding Geneva Art Pottery in 1987, with her husband at the time, John. All of the stoneware on display at the gallery is made in the adjacent studio, fired at a temperature of 2,400 degrees in a 50-foot-long tunnel kiln. The finished pieces balance beauty with function and follow the La Borne tradition of deep colors, especially copper red. Visitors to the gallery may purchase pieces directly from the makers, who include not only Claire, but her current husband, Jesse Healy, and Claire's son, William. On display are bowls, dinner services and vases of all sizes, from two-inch miniatures to two-foot floor pots. They are lead free and safe for microwaves and dishwashers. Claire and her family live on the premises, and it is safe to say that their life revolves around pottery. Though she is proud of her success, she says, "It's all about art, not business." These words resonate when spoken by someone who went straight to the source for her training and committed a decade of her life to completing it. For pottery fired with passion and devotion, visit Geneva Art Pottery today.

W3403 County Road BB, Lake Geneva WI
(262) 248-9078
www.geneva-art-pottery.com

Sign of the Unicorn

GALLERIES & FINE ART

Sign of the Unicorn offers artistic treasures as fantastic as the mythical creature it honors in the gallery name. Frank and Judy Scott hand-pick all the art and crafts in the gallery. For over twenty years they have cultivated relationships with artists from the U.S. and Canada. They enjoy educating customers about everything from antique prints to the art of blowing glass. You will find varied collections from scrimshaw to Inuit sculpture. The shop carries fine-art jewelry, and a large selection of antique prints, as well as a broad collection of contemporary art glass. You can also order a custom frame for your artwork, including 22-karat gold leaf frames hand-built by Frank. Frank also offers his own hand-carved Santas for the holiday season and flame-worked glass beads—some of which Judy makes into jewelry. Garden balls of every size and style, stained glass lamps, wooden boxes, art tiles and kaleidoscopes further the possibilities of finding just what you need for a gift or for yourself. Come in and let Sign of the Unicorn show you the magic of the art within the gallery.

233 Center Street, Lake Geneva, WI
(262) 248-1141

Waterfront Gallery

GALLERIES & FINE ART

Lovers of nautical art are always pleased by the selections at the Waterfront Gallery. Owned by artist Bob Stewart, the Lake Geneva gallery has plenty of Bob's skillful paintings on display. He has sold 30,000 prints since opening the gallery in 1996. Bob studied at the Layton School of Art and spent 25 years in advertising before deciding to pursue his love of art on a full-time basis. Bob paints widely throughout Wisconsin and is well known locally for his paintings of Lake Geneva. He focuses on nautical scenes and prides himself on the accuracy of boats and other water-related detail. You'll find new, original pieces of art every year. Bob also takes 12 commissions a year, where he may paint homes, boats, pets or whatever else the buyer wishes. In addition to Bob's artwork, the gallery carries work by other local and national artists and museum quality nautical antiques, such as ships' wheels and compasses. Many model boats also grace the gallery. For artwork with Wisconsin themes from Wisconsin artists, set sail for the Waterfront Gallery.

237 Broad Street, Lake Geneva WI
(262) 248-9100

Earth, Wind and Flowers

HEALTH & BEAUTY

Deborah Werner, the founder and creator of Earth, Wind and Flowers, works to improve men, women and children's emotional and physical states through flower essences and aromatherapy. By encouraging co-creative partnerships with nature, Deborah helps others reach vibrant health by harmonizing the soul, mind and body with the support of flower remedies. Her grandfather was an avid biodynamic gardener who used rich, fertile soil and heirloom seeds. His garden served as her sanctuary. After years of studying nutrition and working as a florist, Deborah discovered her true destiny and began studying how flower essences can work in the subtle energy field, vibrationally, to help a person strengthen and recover from stress. By balancing these emotions, these remedies can assist a person to stand up to difficult challenges, heal from traumatic situations, cope with change or generally achieve more vibrant health. Deborah has co-created more than 100 remedies with plants from the woodlands, wetlands and prairies of Illinois and Wisconsin. Call ahead for a personal consultation and custom formula or register for a class or retreat and learn how flower essences can help you. Earth, Wind and Flowers is not a public center and is open by appointment only. Please check the website or call ahead for class schedules, workshops and open houses.

Lake Geneva WI
(262) 245-9853
www.earthwindflowers.com

Sparkle Soap Factory & Boutique

HEALTH & BEAUTY

In most places, receiving intensive care has a medical connotation. At the Sparkle Soap Factory & Boutique, it's the best way to describe the store's philosophy on how to treat customers. Owners Maria Halpin and Anne Marie Janikowski insist on taking the time needed to meet a customer's individual needs. Perhaps you seek just the right aroma or desire a customized product for party favors or gifts. The business manufactures and sells its own line of specialty items designed for personal care. The Shea butter creams, conditioners and shampoos are all scent-free, as are the hand sanitizers, scrubs and bar soaps. This does not mean you can't have scent, however. In fact, you have the option of choosing from 250 designer scents. Choosing a scent could be the most involved decision you make all day, and Maria and Anne Marie promise unwavering patience while you decide. All products were once made in the back room, but the company's growth now necessitates manufacture off the premises. People are not the only ones who receive intensive care here. Your pets get intensive care, too, thanks to a line of pet products that includes shampoos designed for different skin types, dry shampoos and baked pet goodies. In a world where nearly everything seems made for mass consumption, the Sparkle Soap Factory & Boutique is a refreshing change. Drop in for the individual attention you deserve.

156 ½ Broad Street, Lake Geneva WI
(262) 348-9454

Belongings

HOME & GARDEN

Each time Alice Gibson travels, she returns with fresh ideas for her shop located in downtown Lake Geneva. This intimate shop is called Belongings and features extraordinary giftware, which Alice chooses for its warmth, color and individuality. She brings Modigliani pottery and Vietri dinnerware from Italy. She brings Terre è Provence, Quimper and Limoges porcelain boxes and beautiful linens from France. Whether entertaining for a corporate event or tea with your best friends, Portugal's Casafina stoneware provides the perfect touch. Artist's tables evolve from the banks of the Danube River in Central Europe. Many items are hand-signed. Additional lines you'll find at Belongings are Memory Blocks by artist Sid Dickens, Mariposa tableware and Fruits & Passions Cucina. Also, look for fine teas, candles and more. Mike (Elsyan), Helen and Vanessa are on staff to help coordinate accessories to create a stunning new look for your table or home. Evan, Alice's grandson, is a cheerful, capable helper and likes a good conversation. Beautiful gift-wrapping is a courtesy. Belongings is sure to be that special shop you will always want to return to.

152 Center Street, Lake Geneva WI
(262) 249-8831 or (877) 440-9096

Alice & Grandson Evan
Photos by Holly Leiter

Bonnie Gardner

HOME & GARDEN

Bonnie Gardner shares her name with her business, and both are concerned with interior design. Her approach is so effective that one customer recently told her, "You not only change our environment; you change our lives." Bonnie's clients come through word-of-mouth, and these constant recommendations have taken her on interior design missions in major metropolitan areas throughout the United States. Working with large and small budgets, Bonnie will adapt her approach to meet her client's needs. She began with an art gallery where she sold her original paintings and has expanded to include furniture, mirrors and home accents as well as other fine art. Bonnie has experienced a significant amount of tragedy in her life and has discovered that exploring individual creativity is the best way to cope. In addition to her interior design work, Bonnie helps to recreate shattered inner lives through her grief counseling. She is in the process of re-introducing a popular children's program called Creative Kids Company and works with young people to develop their creativity, helping them grow in self-confidence and self-knowledge as they become more aware of their surroundings. Visit Bonnie Gardner for a comprehensive approach to redecorating your interior that could just redefine your life.

253 Center Street, Lake Geneva WI
(262) 248-0440

Cedar Fields

HOME & GARDEN

If you want your home to proclaim your love of the outdoors, then you will enjoy shopping at Cedar Fields. A whole showroom of lodge furnishings and décor awaits you in this downtown Lake Geneva specialty store. Owners Diane and Mike Garrett have created a store that reflects the way they live. For the interior of their Lake Geneva farmhouse, built in 1846, they use rich colors, warm blankets and rustic accessories. You will find everything you need at Cedar Fields to create the same look in your home, including Pendleton blankets and pillows, Old Hickory furniture and wildlife-motif lamps. Which rugs and wall hangings would work with the log bed and tables? The Garretts make it easy for you to imagine how all the pieces can come together, because they have arranged the store to look like the inside of a lodge. You will find coat racks crafted from tree trunks and even oars that can be used as attractive curtain rods. The Garretts, who belong to IACA (Indian Arts and Craft Association), carry handcrafted gift items made by Native American artists, such as dolls and authentic jewelry. For a home that says you feel at home with nature, visit Cedar Fields for furnishings and accessories.

755 W Main Street, Lake Geneva WI
(262) 248-8086
www.cedarfields.com

The Cornerstone Shoppe

HOME & GARDEN

The Cornerstone Shoppe, owned and operated by Bruce and Karin Bennett, sits comfortably on a corner in downtown Lake Geneva. The Cornerstone Shoppe is a special Lake Geneva destination specializing in home décor. It has a reputation recognized far and wide for its passion in merchandise selection, display presentation and a team dedicated to personal service. With more than 8,500 square feet of home accessories, candles, baby items, paper goods, picture frames, dishes, linens and gifts, you are sure to find that special someone the perfect gift. If you are looking to redecorate or refurnish your home, they have it all with wood furniture, area rugs, lamps, shelves and mirrors. A well-stocked Lang center, gift cards, bridal and gift registry, and in-home decorating are just a few of the services they offer. Come for a visit to the Cornerstone Shoppe on the corner of Broad and Main Streets.

214 Broad Street, Lake Geneva WI
(262) 248-6988
www.cornerstoneshoppe.com

Paper Dolls Home Furnishings

HOME & GARDEN

If you've ever longed for someone to help you with your own personal decorating style while also tackling the nuts and bolts of furniture and fabric selections plus custom window treatments, you are in need of Paper Dolls Home Furnishings in Lake Geneva. More than 20 years ago, Christine Haak and Kristi Hugunin operated a paper hanging business and moved on to selling consignment crafts to raise money to send their kids to a Christian school. This eventually led to the 11,000-square-foot showroom and home design business they operate today. At Paper Dolls you will find a fresh and constantly changing inventory that includes functional yet elegant furniture at competitive prices. The imagination of the designers helps enhance the warmth and comfort of your home. Whether you need assistance designing from blueprints or just input into original ways to embellish on what you already have, the capable interior designers here offer their assistance. "We start with quality first, sprinkle in a touch of personality and mix with designing women," says Christine. Find out what the right ingredients can mean to your surroundings with a visit to Paper Dolls Home Furnishings.

138 Geneva Square, Lake Geneva WI
(262) 248-6268
www.paperdollsinteriors.com

Pesche's Greenhouses, Floral Shop & Gift Barn

HOME & GARDEN

Pesche's roots extend all the way back to 1924 when Fred Pesche began offering flowers out of his Des Plaines, Illinois greenhouse. In 1970, Fred's son, Fred R., moved to Lake Geneva and opened a full-service flower business on a property with a 100-year-old barn and room for expansion. In 1984, grandson Robert and his wife, Mary, took over the year-round business, open seven days a week. In 2005, Robert's son, Nick, joined the management team as the fourth generation to come on board. Today, Pesche's boasts a nursery and garden center, 20 greenhouses, a barn full of gifts and antiques, and a full-scale florist shop with, as you might imagine, some very fresh blooms. Look for rose bushes, annuals and perennials in season, along with shade and fruit trees, herbs and vegetables. The garden center includes books, birdhouses, birdbaths and birdseed for enjoying wildlife. Fountains and statues found here will dress up your garden. The greenhouses give Pesche's the ability to grow more than a million plants, including tropical varieties, cacti and such blooming beauties as the 10,000 mums offered each fall. When you need fresh-cut flower arrangements for weddings, holidays or expressions of love or sympathy, Pesche's has the skill and the blooms to meet your need. Pesche's encourages browsing in their large facility, which promises, Growing for Every Season, Gifts for Every Reason. Get lost for hours in the beauty and nearly limitless plant selection at Pesche's Greenhouses, Floral Shop & Gift Barn.

W4080 Highway 50, Lake Geneva WI
(262) 245-6125
www.peschesgreenhouse.com

Klockit

HOME & GARDEN

You could order timepieces, do-it-yourself clock kits and art objects from Klockit's 60-page mail order catalogue. However, if you are in Lake Geneva, you can have the pleasure of seeing the extensive inventory and customer friendly environment for yourself. Fred and Karen Koermer opened their shop in 1984 and provide just about anything you could desire for keeping time, including grandfather clocks, cuckoo clocks, watches and kits for clocks, music boxes and weather stations. Klockit's line of clocks includes Howard Miller and Hentschel products. The shop also sells Radio Controlled and Atomic clocks and watches that match official U.S. time. Beyond clocks, look for copper weather vanes, outdoor benches and fire pits. Metal sculptures, patio heaters and solar powered garden lighting add to the Klockit phenomenon. The shop also offers clock replacement parts and tools. Fred and Karen say, "If you need anything for a clock, we have it." Klockit gives you many ways to shop for its products. You may view an online catalog or request a mail order catalog that is shared with over 500,000 households in the spring and fall. Glory in the possibilities for telling time or just plain enjoying your time when you visit with the friendly staff at Klockit.

N3211 County Road, Lake Geneva WI
(262) 248-1153 or (800) 556-2548
www.klockit.com

The Cheese Box

MARKETS & DELIS

Wisconsin is known for its cheeses and The Cheese Box in Lake Geneva is one of the finest examples of the cheese making art. The shop offers more than 65 specialty Wisconsin cheeses. The inside of the store looks much the way it did when the store opened in 1940. For over 60 years, generations of visitors have stopped to stock up on fine Wisconsin cheeses and send delicious cheese and sausage gifts to friends. Some employees go back 30 years in the company and contribute their special memories and a conspicuous sense of pride in customer service. As the oldest and last remaining cheese store in the Lakes Area, Owners Ed and Leslie Schwinn look back proudly but also look forward, knowing their product continues to be treasured by people throughout the country. Visit The Cheese Box and try on the taste of tradition.

801 S Wells Street, Lake Geneva WI
(262) 248-3440 or (800) 345-6105
www.cheesebox.com

Lake Geneva Country Meats

MARKETS & DELIS

Having enjoyed widespread recognition for its quality meat products for several decades, Lake Geneva Country Meats is a prime example of what sets a full-service butcher apart from other meat sellers in the industry. This butcher shop distinguishes itself with quality cuts of pork, beef and lamb along with such specialty items as a wide selection of legendary bratwursts. Manager Kathy Vorpagel feels that it is almost like she is opening her home to company each morning when Lake Geneva Country Meats starts the day, and the shop's reputation is due to her emphasis on providing consistent quality to every customer. Lake Geneva Country Meats is a family-run business with Kathy's husband Scott and sisters Michelle, Theresa and Barb all involved in daily operations at the shop, which was started by Kathy's parents, John and Rita Leahy, in 1965. With a slaughterhouse and processing facility on the premises, a full-service deli and an on-site German-style smokehouse, Lake Geneva Country Meats can handle everything from filling your freezer for a year to enhancing your next dinner party. In an effort to help you choose the flavors and cuts that suit you best, the shop provides plenty of samples and gladly shares recipes. The retail store also carries a full line of gourmet condiments, cheeses, crackers, breads, fresh produce, dairy products and pantry items to compliment your meat purchases. For flavorful meat and exemplary service that is truly a cut above, Kathy and her family invite you to visit Lake Geneva Country Meats.

5907 State Road 50E, Lake Geneva WI
(262) 248-3339
www.lakegenevacountrymeats.com

Geneva National Golf Club

RECREATION & FITNESS

The visions of a trio of golf legends come together at the Geneva National Golf Club. The beautiful 1,600-acre parcel is home to 54 holes of golf in three courses designed by Arnold Palmer, Lee Trevino and Gary Player. The Geneva National Clubhouse, with a massive wall of windows overlooking Lake Como, provides an ideal location for weddings and other gala affairs. The club's many amenities and golfing options make it an appealing venue for professional golfing events, as well. The developmental tour of the LPGA, the Duramed Futures Tour, includes Geneva National as one of its most anticipated stops. The challenging Palmer course traverses hilly woodlands. It's often considered the most difficult and requires golfers to hit many shots to the right side of the hole. The Trevino course is Trevino's only course in the Midwest. It features hillside views and Trevino's signature wide fairways. The Player course, opened in 2000, is the newest and most secluded of the three. Its position next to a wildlife conservation area offers a peaceful and reflective game with five par-5s that reward the big hitter. Nestled between the sixth and tenth holes of the Player course, the Hunt Club restaurant offers fine dining. The recently established Geneva National Foundation supports educational institutions in Walworth County through a variety of fundraisers held throughout the year. Experience courses designed by champions with a round—or two or three—at Geneva National Golf Club.

1221 Geneva National Avenue S,
Lake Geneva WI
(262) 245-7000
www.genevanationalresort.com

Clear Water Outdoor

RECREATION & FITNESS

If you're the kind of person who loves the outdoors or if you just like to play, then Clear Water Outdoor is the store for you. Located in downtown Lake Geneva, it carries quality brands for cycling, kayaking, cross-country skiing and many other outdoor sports. Hobie kayaks, Mountain Boy sleds, Tubbs snowshoes and Wenonah canoes share the showroom with clothing, apparel and gear from Patagonia, Cloudveil and Mountain Hardwear. Owners David and Sarah Schuster pursued active lifestyles while living in Arizona and Oregon. They are proud to bring a sense of the Westerner's enthusiasm for outdoor adventure and sports to Lake Geneva, where Sarah was born. They offer whatever it takes, including advice and rentals, to get folks off the couch and into nature. They, along with their two young children who complete Team Schu, advocate a philosophy of kindness to the environment. David and Sarah carefully select brands for their store according to a company's commitment to the same ideal. Putting philosophy into practice, the Schusters are members of Friends of Big Foot Beach State Park, a community group that provides program support and performs trail maintenance at this Lake Geneva recreational area. Before heading out to play in the great outdoors, make a stop at Clear Water Outdoor.

744 W Main Street, Lake Geneva WI
(262) 348-2420
www.clearwateroutdoor.com

Photos by Ricardo J. Praefke

Kirsch's Restaurant

RESTAURANTS & CAFÉS

Executive Chef John Bogan is sure he can keep you from even thinking about another food establishment while you are visiting Kirsch's Restaurant, located at the French Country Inn in Lake Geneva. John and Partner Jim Kirchschlager's fine food and entertainment variety make Kirsch's a place of endless surprise and delight. You'll be too busy enjoying the Sunday champagne brunches, the Tuesday tapas or the Celebration Wine Dinners to make comparisons. John is passionate about food preparation and offers French and American cuisine with a few sprinkles of Italian tossed in, as well as pronounced influences from the Hawaiian Islands and New Orleans. Wine Sommelier Roy Hanson assures that you'll find just the right wine to accompany your meal at this six-time winner of *Wine Spectator's* Award of Excellence. Expect lots of fun with your food at Kirsch's. The restaurant hosts the annual Lake Geneva Wine & Food Festival and the annual Hawaiian Ohana Festival. It's also home to several Bashes on the Bayou, including those held on Sunday of the Labor Day weekend and on Father's Day. The bashes offer live Louisiana blues and such Cajun specialties as N'Awlins Gumbo and blackened jumbo shrimp. Summer fun includes Thrill of the Grill cooking demonstrations at water's edge. Christmas events are favorites at Kirsch's and your opportunity to enjoy four-course meals while a live chorus fills the room in surround-sound fashion. Yes, the food is outstanding, and the frequent events are fun, but once you've visited Kirsch's, we think you will agree with the locals who say John Bogan's passion and infectious personality place Kirsch's in a category all its own.

W 4190 West End Road, Lake Geneva WI
(262) 245-5756
www.kirschs.com

The Red Geranium Restaurant

RESTAURANTS & CAFÉS

The Red Geranium Restaurant has a simple, yet important philosophy: "Treat each guest as if they were coming to our home as an honored guest." This vision has been maintained for more than 20 years since the family restaurant was founded by Lyle and Audrey Swatek. The restaurant setting is a refurbished home decorated in a Red Geranium motif that is bright and elegant with fireplaces and a glass-enclosed porch. The lunch menu includes anything from classic club sandwiches to signature dishes such as The Red Geranium Baked White House. For Sunday's plated brunch, enjoy a Belgian waffle or made-to-order omelette. For dinner, the list of entrée selections is extensive with seafood, beef or poultry. Regardless of what your tastes are, do not pass up the Red Geranium She Crab Soup. The extensive wine list offers more than 25 wines by the glass. For private or corporate dining experiences, the restaurant affords four different dining areas that include the octagon Garden Room, which seats up to 100 guests, or the Wine Cellar, which seats up to 22. Regardless of whether you are searching for a distinct dining experience for lunch, dinner or Sunday brunch, come as a guest to The Red Geranium, where great food and true hospitality are the philosophy for dining.

393 N Edwards Boulevard
and Highway 50 E, Lake Geneva, WI
(262) 248-3637
www.redgeraniumrestaurant.com

Gilbert's

RESTAURANTS & CAFÉS

From Oprah Winfrey to *Chicago Magazine*, noted critics are singing the praises of the elegant, all-natural fare at Gilbert's. "The survival of the world depends on the health of its inhabitants," says the Lake Geneva restaurant's executive chef and co-owner Ken Hnilo, explaining why his restaurant focuses on organic, sustainable free-range food as much as possible. Ken changes the menu every night to make sure diners can enjoy the freshest, tastiest ingredients. Ken studied under world-famous organic chef Charlie Trotter and brings every bit of what he learned to each dish. *Chicago Magazine* critic Dennis Ray Wheaton praised the organic Amish chicken with seasonal vegetables, apple wood smoked bacon and savory chicken broth. He said the beef carpaccio was the best he had ever tasted. For a real adventure, try the four-to-six course Chef's Tasting or Vegetable Tasting, wherein your table is treated to a variety of flavors. Follow that with one of the restaurant's delicious cheesecakes, which have earned the adoration of Oprah Winfrey and *Town and Country*. The bar was recognized by *Wine Spectator* with its Award of Excellence. Gilbert's is located in a spacious 30-room Victorian mansion that has been meticulously restored, with old-time Hawaiian décor combining with the Victorian style to create an attractive treat for the senses. A smiling portrait of Ken's son, Gilbert, the restaurant's namesake, greets visitors. Come to Gilbert's for an elegant dining experience you won't soon forget.

327 Wrigley Drive, Lake Geneva WI
(262) 248-6680
www.gilbertsrestaurant.com

Carvetti's of Lake Geneva

RESTAURANTS & CAFÉS

Every seasoned traveler will tell you that when you travel to a new city find the places where the locals go to eat, drink and play. In Lake Geneva, Carvetti's is just such the place. Owners Dan and Joe Caravette grew up spending their summers in Lake Geneva, so when the opportunity came to give back to the community that has given them so much they jumped at the chance. The menu features delicious huge half-pound char-burgers, refreshing salads, tasty wraps, appetizers, pasta entrées smothered in homemade sauce and an absolute must try is their signature Panini sandwiches (try the chicken pesto). A full-service bar features over 25 beers including their very own Carvetti's Lager, a local brew and favorite, along with an extensive Martini and tropical drink menu. Kick back under a palm tree with your favorite drink while relaxing on an award-winning outdoor patio, the largest in Southern Wisconsin with its very own sand volleyball court and Tiki bars. The Riverside patio has been the site for family reunions, wedding rehearsals, birthdays, anniversary parties and theme events like pig roasts, beach parties, luaus and World Championship Wrestling. When you're looking for a little entertainment, Carvetti's offers some of the biggest names around with a state-of-the-art light and sound show. Summer time is especially busy so come early and stay late. Carvetti's offers complimentary shuttle service back to area hotels. It's no wonder their customers say, "What happens in Lake Geneva starts at Carvetti's." You've got to come see why.

642 W Main Street, Lake Geneva WI
(262) 248-9752
www.carvettis.com

Hogs & Kisses

RESTAURANTS & CAFÉS

You can be sure any restaurant with a name like Hogs & Kisses has a story to tell. This Lake Geneva hotspot was started by a man who traded pork bellies on the futures market and opened a restaurant as a fun sideline. Today Hogs & Kisses acts as a neighborhood pub with a hopping night scene. A loyal local crowd can vouch for all aspects of the Hogs & Kisses experience, from the melt-in-your-mouth baby back ribs to the entertainment and the striking charm of the building. Enjoy homemade soups, char-grilled burgers or tasty sandwiches surrounded by antique architectural pieces brought from Chicago. Leaded windows, fret work and hard-to-find lighting fixtures add to the pleasures here. Hogs & Kisses acts as a hub for local nightlife. You'll find dancing to live music and disc jockey driven tunes Thursday through Saturday and acoustic guitar on other days. The lineup of talent is noteworthy, and patrons look forward to well known regional performers as well as those who command national and international audiences. Theme parties are popular here too, including Mardi Gras shindigs in the spring and reggae parties in the summer. You have to be a little bit curious about a business that bears the motto Live Well, Love Much, Laugh Often. Come by soon, and find out why so many people choose to gather at Hogs & Kisses.

149 Broad Street, Lake Geneva WI
(262) 248-7447
www.hogsandkisses.com

Scuttlebutts

RESTAURANTS & CAFÉS

Enjoying a steaming stack of Swedish pancakes from a perch above Geneva Lake could be just the break you need in your routine. Scuttlebutts restaurant provides that break in a somewhat more sophisticated way than sailors experienced when they gathered around the ship's drinking water cask, known as a scuttlebutt. The sailors were probably regaling each other with stories of their lives and gossip about others. One thing's for sure—they weren't enjoying the fantastic food choices you'll have at Scuttlebutts. Owners Steve and Emily Sundberg acquired a building across the alleyway, and local scuttlebutt had it that they were going to buy this property as well, and open a restaurant. Fortunately for Lake Geneva, they did just that and now serve up a mix of northern and southern specialties that attest to their varied backgrounds. Steve's background taught him to love Swedish meatballs and other Scandinavian delicacies, and Emily grew up enjoying traditional Midwestern cooking and her mom's unique barbecue sauce and ribs. Together, they provide a blend of American and Swedish dishes alongside their own hickory smoked ribs and southern style barbecue. Creative salads and gourmet hamburgers are popular here, and the restaurant has won readers' choice awards for its fish fry and breakfast offerings. Expect a cheery, bright atmosphere with enormous windows overlooking Geneva Lake. When you need a break from life as usual, bring yourself, your family and friends to Scuttlebutts.

831 Wrigley Drive, Lake Geneva WI
(262) 248-1111

Fleming's

SHOPPING

For the past 30 years Fleming's has been a resource for all things Irish. This delightful Lake Geneva shop is owned and operated by Kevin J. Fleming who, along with his wife, is of Irish descent. Both sets of grandparents were immigrants from that enchanted land. Kevin and his spouse visit Ireland every year, where he works directly with the owners of numerous small companies to bring back the best Ireland has to offer. A majority of Fleming's merchandise is Irish-made, including Irish teas and treats, photographs, snug children's clothing and Donegal tweeds. The shop offers pottery by Nicholas Mosse of Kilkenny, who is quickly gaining international recognition for his spongeware pottery, which is based on a 19th century Irish tradition. Look for Irish jewelry, including authentic Celtic wedding bands. Irish sweaters, blankets, pillows and throws, along with a wide range of Irish books and music, show off the bounty of the Emerald Isle. American-made Vera Bradley handbags and luggage, featuring 100 percent quilted cotton, will coordinate nicely with any Irish ensemble. Whether you are Irish or simply an admirer of these fine goods, come to Fleming's, where traditional Irish wares are sure to delight you and your family.

711 Main Street, Lake Geneva WI
(262) 248-4637 or (800) 553-2779
www.flemingsltd.com

Rag Thyme

SHOPPING

Kathy Fraser, owner of Rag Thyme, dreamed of recreating the charms of the many gift shops she visited on vacation as a child. She started off her business selling rag dolls and now offers a good deal more, including a year-round selection of Christmas items at the downstairs Snowman Stop. Kathy insists she wants her customers to enjoy their shopping experience and to feel at home. Her philosophy must be working, because customers come from miles around. The small front door may fool you, but once inside you discover a bright and airy shop with what seems like endless selection. Kathy and her staff make many of the dolls and other country crafts here. You'll also find your favorite collectibles, including Demdaco angels, Boyds and Bearington bears, and candles by Warm Glow, Swan Creek and Keeper of the Light. Jewelry, purses and gourmet foods increase the gift giving options. The handmade wood furniture is a delightful surprise, and the hand pressed flowers in glass are extremely popular. You can have your gift selection shipped anywhere in the United States or Canada or give a gift certificate and let the gift recipient have the distinct pleasure of experiencing Rag Thyme. Come on in to Rag Thyme, where you'll be greeted with complimentary Door County Coffee, fine gifts and the opportunity to experience the culmination of Kathy's dream.

719 W Main Street, Lake Geneva WI
(262) 248-4448
www.ragthyme.com

Geneva Village Shops
Geneva Village Shops
Geneva Village Shops

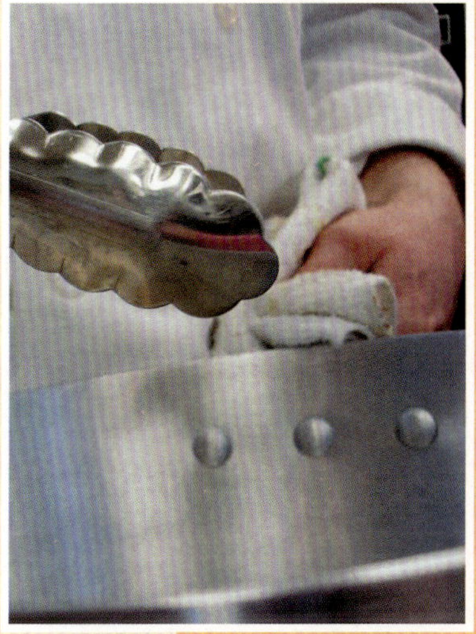

Geneva Village Shops

SHOPPING

The serious shopper can have hours of fun at the Geneva Village Shops, located one block north of Main Street in Lake Geneva. Here you will find a cluster of independently owned businesses, each with its own charm. The inspired setting for the shops is a former Baptist church, still in possession of its stained glass windows and bell tower. The connected parsonage houses the Geneva School of Cooking, a place to learn cooking, to hold a party or to buy a fine cooking tool. "If you've got the kids," say the owners of Doodlebugs Kids & Caboodle, "we've got the caboodle." In other words, parents and grandparents are invited to drop by and peruse the fine selection of clothing, furniture and toys for kids from newborn to age 14. In All Her Glory is all about the ladies. Jewelry, purses and shawls are among the featured items, along with fun boots and comfy slippers. The Geneva Artist Gallery presents the best work of local artists, everything from paintings and jewelry to photography, woodwork and sculpture. The stained glass windows and lamps are dazzling. Pray for More Stuff is a garden shop, or is it? The container plants, birdhouses and birdbaths would lead you to think so, but the unusual home accents and fine antiques that complement the garden accessories make this a shop that defies simple definition. Raining Cats and Dogs is where your pet would shop if you gave it an allowance. You get to have all the fun yourself as you pick out some treats, toys or maybe a chic collar for your pet. For a shopping excursion full of variety, visit the Geneva Village Shops.

727 Geneva Street, Lake Geneva WI

MADISON

Madison is the Wisconsin state capital, home of the University of Wisconsin, and an industrial center in its own right. These three roles have made Madison one of the fastest growing cities in the state. Magazines and books regularly list it as one of the country's best places to live. In 2003, *Forbes* ranked Madison as having the highest number of Ph.D.s per capita in the United States.

Madison was founded on the narrow isthmus between lakes Monona and Mendota, and downtown Madison remains dramatically bordered by water on either side. In 1829, James Doty, a territorial judge and land speculator, traveled through the isthmus and liked the site so much that he bought 1,200 acres. In 1836, he persuaded the territorial legislature to designate his paper city as the site for the new capital. The Wisconsin State Capitol dome stands on the ridgeline of the isthmus, visible to the whole city due to a state law that limits building heights within one mile of it.

During the summer, Capitol Square is the site of weekly farmers markets and free symphony concerts. State Street, the main downtown thoroughfare, links Capitol Square with the University of Wisconsin. The street is lined with restaurants, shops and cafés. State Street is home to Madison's arts palace, the Overture Center for the Arts, designed by internationally famous architect Cesar Pelli.

The university fosters a thriving college sports culture. The university football stadium holds some 76,000 fans and almost always fills up. The university Arboretum is home to the oldest and most varied collection of restored ecological communities in the world.

Madison supports a lively music scene, including independent rock. Music festivals range from rock, jazz and blues to electronic and world music. The Great Taste of the Midwest craft beer festival is one of Madison's biggest attractions, typically selling out within a few hours every year. Madison's premier Independence Day Celebration, Rhythm

Madison skyline at twilight

& Booms, boasts the biggest fireworks show in the Midwest. Marching bands, skydivers and F-16 fly-overs are just part of the warm-up to the show, which attracts 300,000 people every year.

PLACES TO GO

- Alliant Energy Center Exhibition Hall
  1881 Expo Mall E
  (608) 267-3976
- Camp Randall Stadium (U-W football)
  1440 Monroe Street
  (800) GO-BADGERS (462-2343)
- Capital Springs State Park and Recreation Area
  3101 Lake Farm Road
  (608) 224-3606
- Chazen Museum of Art
  800 University Avenue
  (608) 263-2246
- Henry Vilas Zoo
  702 S Randall Avenue
  (608) 266-4733
- Kohl Center (U-W basketball and hockey)
  601 W Dayton Street
  (800) 462-2343
- Madison Children's Museum
  100 State Street
  (608) 256-6445
- Olbrich Botanical Gardens
  3330 Atwood Avenue
  (608) 246-4550
- Overture Center for the Arts
  201 State Street
  (608) 258-4177
- U-W-Madison Arboretum
  1207 Seminole Highway
  (608) 263-7888
- U-W-Madison Geology Museum
  1215 W Dayton Street
  (608) 262-1412
- The Wisconsin Historical Museum
  30 N Carroll Street
  (608) 264-6555
- Wisconsin State Capitol Building
  2 E Main Street
  (608) 266-0382

THINGS TO DO

February

- International Festival
  Overture Center for the Arts
  www.overturecenter.com/international.htm

March

- Kids Expo
  Alliant Energy Center
  www.kids-expo.com
- St. Patrick's Day Parade
  Capitol Square
  www.stpatsmadison.org

April

- Wisconsin Film Festival
  www.wifilmfest.org

May

- World's Largest Bratfest
  Willow Isand at the Alliant Energy Center
  www.bratfest.com
- Madison Marathon
  www.madcitymarathon.com
- Audubon Art Fair
  Olbrich Botanical Gardens
  (608) 255-2473
- Cows on the Concourse
  State Capitol Concourse
  (608) 250-4212

July

- Rhythm & Booms
  www.rhythmandbooms.com
- Art Fair on the Square
  www.mmoca.org/events/artfair
- Art Fair off the Square
  www.artcraftwis.org/afos.html
- Dane County Fair
  Alliant Energy Center
  www.danecountyfair.com

August

- Great Taste of the Midwest
  www.mhtg.org

September

- Taste of Madison
  www.madisonfestivals.com/taste

October

- World Dairy Expo
  Alliant Energy Center
  www.worlddairyexpo.com

The capitol dome of Wisconsin

Crawdaddy Cove Holiday Inn Hotel & Suites

ACCOMMODATIONS

Whether you are a family seeking amusement or an executive seeking business services, you can find what you seek at the Holiday Inn Hotel & Suites Madison West, featuring Crawdaddy Cove Indoor Waterpark, located in Madison's west side shopping district. This luxury hotel merges such business amenities as an executive floor, business center and wireless Internet access with family-friendly suites and water play. Enjoy the irresistible indoor water park that includes the stationary S.S. *Crawdaddy* shrimp boat anchored in the wading pool, where miniature slides and water fountains entertain young adventurers. In the larger pool, buccaneers of all ages can slither down the 55-foot water slide and indulge in water basketball. After exhausting the aquatic options, escort your youngsters to a suite designed for kids, complete with a kids area equipped with bunk beds, kids desk and television. For dinner, treat the family to anything from steaks and seafood to burgers at George's Chop House, where kids 12 and under eat free. If you're traveling on business, you can count on the kind of attention and service that has earned the Holiday Inn Hotel & Suites the Quality Excellence Award from InterContinental Hotels Group. Enjoy the fitness, video game room and the Grand Piano Lobby Bar. You'll be just minutes away from biking and hiking trails, upscale shopping and an array of tempting restaurants. Nearby attractions include the Henry Vilas Zoo, the University of Wisconsin-campus and the State Capitol. For comfort, convenience and amusement, visit the Holiday Inn Hotel & Suites and Crawdaddy Cove Indoor Waterpark.

1109 Fourier Drive, Madison WI
(608) 826-0500 or (888) 522-9472
www.wiscohotels.com

The Edgewater

ACCOMMODATIONS

At The Edgewater they like to point out that the only thing they overlook is Lake Mendota. Located at the water's edge on Wisconsin Avenue, they are not kidding. The Edgewater is the only true lakefront hotel in Madison. They've been here since 1948, and through the years have had the privilege of hosting some incredible people, such as Tommy Dorsey, Bob Newhart, John Mellencamp and Bob Dylan. Anyone who has toured the Lisa Marie Airplane in Memphis has seen the wooden hangers from the Edgewater Hotel. Apparently Elvis and his pals took over two floors of The Edgewater back in the mid 1970s. Elvis liked it so much he kept the hangers. Throughout remodels, The Edgewater has kept that swank feel. You'll want to dine in the Admiralty dining room, The Edgewater's waterfront restaurant, where maitre d' David Martineau greets visitors as he has for the past 37 years. The dress code has relaxed over time, but the food remains exceptional. The floating seasonal café, The Pier, is a favorite for Friday night fish frys, paninis, chicken wings and burgers. Listen to the smooth sounds of ivory keys as you relax in front of the fireplace at The Cove Lounge. The walls are covered with more than 100 autographed pictures of famous and infamous guests who have passed through. Liberace, John Prine, Warren Zevon and Bob Denver are just a few. All the rooms at The Edgewater are large, ranging from singles to two-bedroom suites. Throughout your stay, you will be treated like royalty. They'll even have a limo pick you up at the airport if you need it. The next time you need a restful getaway in Madison, give The Edgewater a call.

666 Wisconsin Avenue, Madison WI
(800) 922-5512 or (608) 256-9071
www.theedgewater.com

Photo by Anna

Wingate Inn Madison

ACCOMMODATIONS

The Wingate Inn Madison is one of the best mid-priced hotels in Wisconsin. The hotel, adjacent to Yahara Hills Golf Course, features a complimentary hot breakfast buffet, heated indoor pool, whirlpool, fitness center and comfortable rooms at a good price. The hotel offers great packages, including our favorite, a golf package that includes 18 holes at Yahara Hills and dinner for two at Rossario's Restaurant at a ridiculously low price. Lovers will be tempted by the Romantic Getaway package, and business travelers will find both the amenities and the meeting facilities first-rate. The Wingate Inn, owned by Randy and Ingrid Ratzlaff, is located close to several fine restaurants and attractions, including Fireside Dinner Playhouse, Olbrich Botanical Gardens, Alliant Energy Center, State Street and the University of Wisconsin. The next time you're in Madison, check out the Wingate Inn.

3510 Mill Pond Road, Madison WI
(608) 224-1500 or (800) 510-3510
www.wingateinnmadison.com

The Madison Concourse Hotel and Governor's Club

ACCOMMODATIONS

The Madison Concourse Hotel and Governor's Club is Madison's premier downtown hotel. Located in the heart of downtown, The Madison Concourse Hotel represents the height of luxury, greeting you with a grand staircase that will sweep you from the lobby to one of 350 guest rooms, including the 100-room Governor's Club executive level. The private Governor's Club lounge captures the very essence of Madison, offering complimentary top-shelf cocktails, hors d'oeuvres, desserts and a continental breakfast. On the Concourse level, each newly remodeled and spacious room features a sitting area, desk, complimentary wireless Internet access and weekday newspaper. Enjoy the indoor pool, sauna, whirlpool and fitness center. With three ballrooms, The Madison Concourse Hotel provides an elegant setting for weddings and other special occasions. The Dayton Street Café serves breakfast, lunch and Sunday brunch, and nestled just behind it is Ovations, the hotel's fine dining establishment offering cuisine with Mediterranean influences. The Bar offers over 100 wines, microbrews, single malt scotches and specialty drinks. Live jazz is featured every Wednesday, Friday and Saturday night, and there is never a cover charge. Experience everything downtown Madison has to offer at The Madison Concourse Hotel and Governor's Club.

1 W Dayton Street, Madison WI
(800) 356-8293 or (608) 257-6000
www.concoursehotel.com

Hilton Madison Monona Terrace

ACCOMMODATIONS

Doing business in Madison is a pleasure when you make the Hilton Madison Monona Terrace your hotel. Frank Lloyd Wright designed Monona Terrace, Madison's premier convention facility that is attached to the hotel. Guests at the hotel reach the convention center by strolling through the skywalk. The Hilton Madison itself features four flexible meeting spaces and a staff dedicated to the success of your group event. In 2006, Corporate Report readers gave the Hilton Madison a Best of Wisconsin Business Award, while readers of Meetings MidAmerica chose it as an outstanding meeting facility, providing excellence in service. The 14-story Hilton Madison is set on the shores of scenic Lake Monona, and business travelers find the view from within the hotel quite relaxing. Indeed, whether it's providing complimentary airport pickup, concierge service or an umbrella in your room, the hotel management has seemingly thought of everything to take the stress out of your experience. Rooms and suites are richly appointed, finished in soft harvest tones and furnished with maple and mahogany desks and chairs. Adjacent to the Hilton in the historic Chancery Building, the Capitol Chophouse serves steak and seafood in a stylish environment. The Capitol Club on the 14th floor presents a regal view of Madison and surrounding lakes. Feel like you're on vacation while you're taking care of business at the Hilton Madison Monona Terrace.

9 E Wilson Street, Madison WI
(608) 260-2363 or (608) 255-5100
www.hiltonmadison.com

Baymont Inn & Suites

ACCOMMODATIONS

If you are planning an extended stay in Madison, the Baymont Inn and Suites has not only the rooms to please you, but the kind of amenities guaranteed to banish homesickness. The suites are some of the most spacious around with kitchens, oversized whirlpool tubs and free wireless Internet access. You'll find a satisfying breakfast buffet in the Old Sauk Lounge with a make-your-own waffle station, and you can return to the lounge in the evening for a complimentary drink. For some well-earned recreation, the Baymont has you covered with a fitness center, a game room and a sunlit atrium with an indoor pool. The inn, a member of the Wisco Hotel Group, provides a shuttle service to and from the Dane County Airport. Business savings and the proximity of several business parks make the Belmont particularly appealing to the business traveler. Baymont is also close to the State Capitol and the University of Wisconsin and closer than any other hotel to University Ridge Golf Course. Shoppers appreciate the nearness of the Hilldale Shopping Center, Greenway Station and the Antiques Mall of Madison. The Baymont is well placed for sightseeing, too. Within 35 miles, you'll find House on the Rock, Fireside Theater, Cave of the Mounds and the Tyrol Ski and Snowboard Area. Nearby cultural offerings include the Madison Museum of Contemporary Art and the Veterans Memorial Museum. Stay awhile, with everything you need for business and pleasure within easy reach at Baymont Inn & Suites.

8102 Excelsior Drive, Madison WI
(608) 831-7711 or (888) 522-WISC
www.wiscohotels.com

Photo by Mark Sadowski

Courtyard by Marriott Madison East

ACCOMMODATIONS

The Courtyard by Marriott Madison East offers contemporary lodging with a warm, rustic feel. Rich wood tones and marble accents grace the entrance to your home away from home. Rooms include all the amenities you might expect from a Marriott, plus refrigerators in all rooms and both wired and wireless high-speed Internet access. Rooms on the courtyard side have a view of the State Capitol building, a straight run down Washington Avenue. You can opt for one of the spacious whirlpool suites. Try sitting for a delicious lunch or dinner at the Courtyard Café, or have dinner delivered right to your room from Pizzeria Uno's Chicago Grill. If you just need a quick bite, you can pick up grab-and-go sandwiches and beverages from the 24-hour market. Enjoy the indoor pool, whirlpool and exercise room or sink into a comfortable leather chair in the evening while enjoying a beverage in the cozy lounge. The Marriott has the facilities you need for your next business function, including extensive audiovisual equipment and catering services. The Marriott is close to East Town Mall and enjoys easy access to the airport. Visit the Courtyard by Marriott. Let the staff make your trip to Madison extra special with generous accommodations, friendly service and modern conveniences.

2502 Crossroads Drive, Madison WI
(608) 661-8100
www.courtyardmadisoneast.com

Courtyard by Marriott Madison West/Middleton

ACCOMMODATIONS

The Courtyard by Marriott Madison West/Middleton offers contemporary lodging with a warm feel. Rich wood tones and marble accents grace the entrance to your home away from home. The Courtyard by Marriott is a 100 percent smoke-free hotel. Rooms and suites include all the amenities you might expect, plus refrigerators, speakerphones and wireless high-speed Internet access in all rooms. Try sitting down for a delicious breakfast at the Courtyard Café or have dinner delivered right to your room from a nearby restaurant. If you just need a quick bite, you can pick up grab-and-go sandwiches and beverages from the 24-hour market. Enjoy the indoor pool, whirlpool and exercise room or sink into a comfortable leather chair in the evening while tasting a beverage in the cozy lounge. The Courtyard by Marriott has the facilities you need for your next business function, including extensive audiovisual equipment and catering services. The Courtyard by Marriott is near Greenway Station, an open-air shopping and dining district. Downtown Middleton is a few blocks away. You have easy access to the University of Wisconsin, a quick run down University Avenue. Visit the Courtyard by Marriott. Let the staff make your trip to Madison extra special with generous accommodations, friendly service and modern conveniences.

2266 Deming Way, Madison WI
(608) 203-0100
www.courtyard.com

The Mariner's Inn

ATTRACTIONS

For more than four decades, the Mariner's Inn has been serving up succulent steak and seafood along Madison's Lake Mendota. The restaurant's founders, Bill and Betty von Rutenberg, owned a small hamburger spot in 1961 before purchasing an upscale supper club in 1966 that went on to become the Mariner's Inn. The family business continues with Bill and Betty's sons, Bill, Jack and Robert, carrying on the tradition of fine dining and hospitality begun by their parents. Begin your culinary voyage with one of the inn's signature appetizers, including a shrimp cocktail with a house-made sauce or a portobello mushroom stuffed with tenderloin steak and finished with a peppercorn sauce. From there, you can cruise to a main course of fine steak or seafood. The eight different steaks on the menu are hand cut and aged to the inn's precise specifications. The whiskey peppercorn sauce and mushroom ragout put the bacon-wrapped Chef's Tenderloin in a class by itself. Seafood dishes include Canadian lobster tails, North Atlantic salmon and five delicious shrimp entrees. The chef also turns on the creativity with such creations as the Admiral's Chicken, Mariner's Duck, and barbeque glazed bacon-wrapped pork tenderloin medallions. The Mariner's Inn's wine list has earned *Wine Spectator* magazine's Award of Excellence for four years in a row. For fine dining on the lake in a setting filled with authentic marine antiques, sail in to the Mariner's Inn.

5339 Lighthouse Bay Drive, Madison WI
(608) 246-3120
www.marinersin.com

The Nau-Ti-Gal

ATTRACTIONS

It was Betty von Rutenberg who came up with the Nau-Ti-Gal's playful name. Her sense of casual fun perfectly describes the enjoyable atmosphere at this lakefront restaurant. Readers of *Madison Magazine* honored it for the Best Brunch in Madison. The restaurant's name is a play on the word *nautical,* a reference to both the lakefront location and such succulent seafood dishes as the hand-breaded sweet baby walleye. The Nau-Ti-Gal is famous for its fish fry, featuring cod fillets served with all the trimmings. Landlubbers can indulge in the Key West chicken or one of six unique and awesome burgers. Then, there's that famous Sunday brunch, an all-you-can-eat affair that satisfies everyone with such choices as smoked salmon, prime rib and omelettes as well as pastries and desserts. The Nau-Ti-Gal with its picturesque location on Lake Mendota can handle your special event, whether you seek casual outdoor play combined with burgers and brats or a fine china affair. The outdoor facilities easily handle groups as large as 500 and offer a pleasant waterfront atmosphere for weddings, class reunions or corporate events. For food and fun, come to the Nau-Ti-Gal, one of the fine restaurants brought to you by the family-owned and operated von Rutenberg Ventures.

5360 Westport Road, Madison WI
(608) 246-3130
www.nautigal.com

Captain Bill's

ATTRACTIONS

Steak, seafood and lake scenery are on deck at Captain Bill's, a Middleton restaurant named for its founder, Bill von Rutenberg, and run by his three sons. Seafood abounds here, and you may want to start with an appetizer of house-made crab cakes so delicious they've been featured on television's Food Network. Other starters worth your consideration include fresh oysters or a lobster and crab quesadilla. If you're fishing for seafood delicacies, a tour of this menu will take you all over the world. Consider the Admiral's Swordfish, a 10-ounce grilled steak completed with sautéed lobster meat and hollandaise sauce. The fish fry with its battered cod, French fries and coleslaw is always in demand. For seafood cooked however you like, order your tuna, shrimp, salmon or mahi mahi either grilled, blackened or broiled, then pick a preferred topping, perhaps lump crab meat or one of the restaurant's signature sauces. Steaks, chicken and pasta are other worthy choices. For little ones, the Minnow's Menu includes everything from a fried shrimp plate to such kid favorites as macaroni and cheese and, of course, ice cream. Captain Bill's offers nightly specials, ranging from Monday's All-You-Can-Eat Steak Night, to Sunday's Wine Night, featuring a free bottle of wine with the purchase of any two entrées. You can choose to dine in the cozy indoors or enjoy views of Lake Mendota from a luxurious deck. For meals to suit every taste, cast off for Captain Bill's.

2701 Century Harbor Road, Middleton WI
(608) 831-7327
www.capbills.com

Betty Lou Cruises

ATTRACTIONS

Betty von Rutenberg loved the shimmering waters of Wisconsin's lakes, so her sons named the family cruise line Betty Lou Cruises in her honor. A fleet of four motoryachts leave from the Mariner's Inn on Lake Mendota and the Machinery Row building on Lake Monona. From Betty Lou's deck, the magnificent Madison skyline spreads before you, including the State Capitol, Governor's Mansion and the University of Wisconsin campus. You'll cruise past miles of lovely shoreline, including Governor Nelson State Park, and glimpse some of Wisconsin's finest lakefront estates. Passengers remaining indoors enjoy a spacious cabin with many amenities. On every cruise, the captain and crew to tend to your needs. Whether it is brunch, lunch or dinner, the buffet meals will delight all passengers with offerings from the chefs at the Mariner's Inn. Bar service is available. You can cruise day or night April through October. The fall colors cruise is a highlight every year. Additionally, the company hosts several special cruises for holidays, as well as themed cruises, which include events for beer and wine lovers. You can reserve a private group charter for a wedding, birthday or other occasion. The company also specializes in corporate events. Take in Madison's majesty from the comfort of the Betty Lou.

1001 Arboretum Drive #204, Waunakee, WI
(608) 246-3138
www.bettyloucruises.com

Cool Beans Coffee Café

BAKERIES, COFFEE & TEA

Located in Madison's East Towne area, Cool Beans Coffee Café is a sophisticated, yet welcoming alternative to the ever-present fast food establishments. Owner Lisa Stearns, a former teacher of hearing impaired children, opened Cool Beans in the summer of 2001. Cool Beans offers both great coffee and great food, featuring an expansive menu selection for breakfast, lunch and dinner. Everything is fresh and first-class, from bistro style sandwiches and unique breakfast burritos, to fresh salads, delicious soups, homemade quiches and elegant desserts. In addition to the usual assortment of tea and espresso bar drinks, Cool Beans offers all natural fruit and juice smoothies, protein shakes and house specialties such as the East Side Slide, a frozen coffee drink. The cozy and contemporary interior design sets a relaxing and embracing mood. Warmed by the double-sided fireplace, rich hardwood floors and comfy stuffed chairs, the ambience invites you to sit back and enjoy. Wireless Internet is free and a conference area that seats 16 to 20 may be reserved for parties or meetings. A special children's area allows a little rejuvenation time and during the warm weather customers can choose to sit outside on the beautiful patio. From a quiet place to enjoy a book or a friend's company, to a great spot for a casual business lunch, there's something for everyone at Cool Beans Coffee Café. Once you discover this refreshing oasis you'll make it a point to return frequently.

1748 Eagan Road, Madison WI
(608) 244-8414

JavaCat

BAKERIES, COFFEE & TEA

To call the JavaCat a coffee shop would be a serious understatement. It's a cozy shop, but it's also a bakery, gelateria, Internet café and drive-thru. Step inside and savor the exquisite coffeehouse aroma. The shop features 100 percent fair trade coffee, tea, pastries and a variety of other bakery items made fresh daily. Care for some light lunch? Try the soup and sandwich special. It comes with gelato for dessert. Owners Shari Olson and Renee Raspiller believe locally roasted, fair trade coffee, friendly atmosphere and quality service are the first steps to a successful business. "Our shop is a community living room, open to everyone," they say. Sit by the fireplace and relax, or surf the Internet for free on the computers. JavaCat has a growing reputation throughout Madison as a bright, comfortable, neighborhood coffeehouse. Gelato clearly reigns at JavaCat. The display case is the first thing that greets you as you step inside. JavaCat's gelato is made with fresh ingredients daily. The friendly staff encourages sampling several flavors to help you decide what you really want. For a coffee shop that will make you purr, try the JavaCat.

3918 Monona Drive, Madison WI
(608) 223-5553
www.javacatcoffee.com

Madison Sourdough

BAKERIES, COFFEE & TEA

Madison Sourdough's mission is simply to create world-class breads, but to an artisan baker that process is anything but simple. Owner and breadmaster Cameron Ramsay uses just three ingredients in his loaves: flour, filtered water and sea salt. The outcome depends on his years of experience and knowledge of the baker's art as well as a well-honed intuition and a feel for the bread. According to Cam, the definition of bread is fermented grain, and a baker's job is to help the wheat reach its peak experience. Blending different flours and adjusting manipulation and baking times are often necessary for a successful bake-off, and constant monitoring is a must. With workdays beginning at 1:30 am seven days a week, Madison Sourdough was a labor of love for Cameron and a responsibility he shared with his wife, BJ. After starting Madison Sourdough in 1994 and enduring six years of seven-day workweeks, Cam and BJ closed the business. For the next two years Cam toured the United States and France, where he spent considerable time exchanging techniques and knowledge with Parisian artisan bakers. Refreshed from his travels, he has reopened Madison Sourdough. In a shop filled with music and decorated with art throughout, Cam has taken up his calling once again. Come by Madison Sourdough in the Clock Tower Court and enjoy the heady aromas of the rich, flavorful breads that only a master craftsman can create.

6640 Mineral Point Road, Madison WI (608) 833-8009 ***www.madisonsourdough.com***

Oasis Day Spa

HEALTH & BEAUTY

The first time you visit the Oasis Day Spa, it may be to treat yourself to a little luxury. Once you experience a healthful, stress-reducing hour or more of services, says owner Lori Heffernon, future visits will become a lifestyle choice. For body treatments, you may choose from various massages, body wraps or exfoliation techniques. Guests can also experience the dramatic results from the Inch Loss Wrap. The Glycolic Body Exfoliation is a complete body treatment with scrub and massage that leaves skin glowing. Oasis Day Spa also offers manicures and pedicures, facials, tanning, airbrush tanning and waxing. A spa package is a great way to enjoy several relaxing and rejuvenating services. Experience how the Oasis defines Pure Bliss with a package that includes a one-hour massage, a European facial and a soothing dip in warm paraffin for hands and feet. The Steamy Wonder features a massage and aromatherapy in a steam tent. All-day packages, such as the Bridal and the Royalty, even include lunch. The Couples Package is for romantics only. Couples enjoy a one-hour massage in the same room and then share the whirlpool tub and a glass of champagne. To feel marvelous in Madison, try the Oasis Day Spa.

8016 Watts Road, Madison WI
(608) 828-9470
www.yourdayspa.com

The Ultimate Spa & Salon

HEALTH & BEAUTY

"Education is our foundation," says Deb Offerdahl, noting that her staff members at the Ultimate Spa & Salon consider ongoing training as part of their job. When we dropped by to visit, one of Deb's stylists was in New York to learn the newest cutting and coloring techniques. Sixty professionals wait to serve you at the Ultimate, a busy spa and salon with three facial treatment rooms and a full-service nail department in addition to several massage rooms and showers. Amid the classic Greek décor, you can enjoy an array of packages named after gods and goddesses. The Cupid Package, for example, combines a manicure and pedicure in the whirlpool thrones with an aromatherapy steam shower, a half-hour massage and a body treatment. It includes a light lunch. Deb's own specialty is hair. She is so good at what she does that she has been featured in *Ladies Home Journal* as one of the top stylists in the Midwest. The Ultimate has won several People's Choice awards and is the exclusive salon for the television personalities on Madison's Channel Three. One the many innovative services that the Ultimate provides is the cellulite reduction procedure called Synergie. A room at the salon known as the Secret Garden was designed to serve cancer patients. For the latest techniques and innovations in the field, visit the Ultimate Spa & Salon.

5713 Monona Drive, Madison WI
(608) 222-4174
www.ultimatespa.com

C's Specialty Foods

MARKETS & DELIS

Charlene and Michael Cherepinsky, owners of C's Specialty Foods, say that they have the largest variety of gluten-free foods in Madison. That's good news, because more and more people, approximately one in 133, are being diagnosed with gluten intolerance. If all people were alike, we wouldn't need a store like C's Specialty Foods. However, for some people to achieve and maintain optimal health, they must avoid wheat in their diet, or sugar or diary products. C's Specialty Foods meets the needs of these people. It also offers low sodium, low carb and soy-free foods, while providing choices for vegetarian, vegan and raw diets. Education is a large part of the store's mission. Daily samples allow customers to taste new products, while guest speakers and nutrition classes keep customers informed about the latest research. The staff at C's Specialty Foods provides personalized attention to make shopping easy and pleasant. It will even have your items ready for pick up if you order by phone or e-mail. If you are looking for a store that makes the connection between diet and good health, visit C's Specialty Foods.

462 Commerce Drive, Suite A,
Madison WI
(608) 829-1918
www.csspecialtyfoods.com

Nakoma Golf Club

RECREATION & FITNESS

If you long for a place where everyone knows your name, where food, sports and special occasions meet your exacting standards, this private club with a longstanding reputation for excellence is the answer to your yearning. Nakoma Golf Club will exceed your expectations with its stately English Tudor clubhouse, three fine restaurants and a choice of sporting venues, including an 18-hole golf course, four hard-surface tennis courts and a swimming pool. The club started in the 1920s and sits on Wigwam Hill, a century-old campsite for the Winnebago tribe. Nakoma is an Ojibwa word meaning *I do as I promise*, and what Nakoma promises is a warm community and first-rate amenities. The scenic 18-hole golf course, surrounded by the University of Wisconsin Arboretum, has been home to such golfing greats as two-time U.S. Open Champion Andy North and three-time winner of the Women's British Open, Sherri Steinhauer. Both PGA golf and USPTA tennis teaching professionals are available for group or private lessons. Enjoy priority tee times and take part in group play for men, women, couples and juniors. Nakoma's youth love the pool, with opportunities for competitive swimming and diving, water ballet and just plain fun. The tennis courts, lighted at night, offer casual and tournament play. While the winter puts a hold on the sports, social events and dining are a year-round pleasure at Nakoma. The club offers choices for refined, casual or quick meals and banquet facilities to accommodate groups as large as 250. Nakoma Golf Club is truly a place to feel the classic experience.

4145 Country Club Road, Madison WI
(608) 238-3141
www.nakoma.org

Dotty Dumpling's Dowry

RESTAURANTS & CAFÉS

Dotty Dumpling's Dowry focuses on selling delectable hamburgers while maintaining its status as a notable Madison landmark. Proprietor Jeff Stanley says the story of his ownership is reminiscent of Frank Capra's *It's a Wonderful Life*. On one of the earliest days of his ownership, as customers crowded the smoke-filled room, all the hanging order slips were blown into the air by an overly aggressive fan. About a week later, Jeff was trying to drain frying oil and discovered he had poured it all over the floor. These stories and others like it show that Dotty Dumpling's had a rocky beginning, but there is an ongoing happy ending that is satisfying enough to make any Hollywood director proud. To say that Jeff's restaurant sells award winning burgers may just be an understatement. His burgers have been declared the best in Madison by the *Isthmus Weekly's* readers' poll every year since 1982. They have also repeatedly been declared the best in town by the *Daily Cardinal*, the *Badger Herald* and *Madison Magazine*. The burgers have also received nationwide recognition in *USA Today*. Visit Dotty Dumpling's Dowry to see how a series of disasters became a longstanding Madison tradition while enjoying award winning food that has stood the test of time.

317 N Frances Street, Madison WI
(608) 259-0000
www.dottydumplingsdowry.com

Joey's Seafood & Grill

RESTAURANTS & CAFÉS

Founded in Canada in 1985 by legendary seafood lover Joe Klassen, Joey's Seafood & Grill has surfaced stateside in Madison. Owner Keith Stoesz had long dreamed of running his own business, and in 2005, he and his wife, Erin, opened their own franchise. This innovative restaurant serves up fresh, high-end seafood almost as quickly as fast food eateries, but in the kind of friendly, energetic atmosphere you'd typically find in a neighborhood seafood place. The diverse menu offers a multitude of choices, and diners can watch as chefs prepare their order in the open kitchen. Every type of seafood imaginable is represented here, along with multiple choices of preparation methods. Homemade sauces include remoulade, tarragon aioli, mango mandarin orange and lime mustard. From homemade crab cakes to calamari tacos and Joey's Special Jambalaya, there's something for every taste, whether traditional or adventurous. Joey's celebrates Fridays with a fish fry and also features daily chalkboard specials. For those who don't fancy something finny, the restaurant offers steaks and pasta as well. For mouthwatering seafood in a fun and friendly atmosphere, pack up the family and head down to Joey's Seafood & Grill. You'll be hooked.

6602 Mineral Point Road, Madison, WI
(608) 829-0093 ***www.joeysseafood.com***

The Madison Club

RESTAURANTS & CAFÉS

Established in 1909, the Madison Club has provided its members an elegant venue to enjoy fine dining, fantastic social events and other private functions for almost 100 years. The Club features sixteen private rooms for members to reserve for personal and professional events, and also two terrific dining rooms. Chuchill's fine dining room is an elegant space that overlooks Lake Monona and highlights a wonderful variety of gourmet cuisine, while TR's Pub & Grille is a more casual option for appetizers and happy hour specials after work or before a Badger game. The Madison Club also offers many special events and activities throughout the year including cooking and dance classes, card playing nights, holiday brunches, wine tastings, comedy and trivia nights, weekend trips and luncheon speakers. Additionally, members enjoy premiere seating at Overture events, special rates at the Hilton Hotel-Monona Terrace, and reciprocal privileges with over 200 private clubs across the world. Dining menus, membership information and event details are available on the Madison Club's website.

5 E Wilson Street, Madison WI
(608) 255-4861
www.madisonclub.org

Capitol Chophouse

RESTAURANTS & CAFÉS

Capitol Chophouse prides itself on spectacular steak, seafood and style. The *Milwaukee Journal Sentinel* praised this downtown Madison restaurant's food and stylish atmosphere as "a cut above." The secret to the mouthwatering menu is in the ingredients. All of the beef is hand selected from Allen Brothers of Chicago and aged 28 days for maximum flavor. The produce is locally grown and bought from Dane County farmers' markets. The fish is line-caught, which does less damage to the meat than nets. It's never been frozen, which preserves flavor and texture. Whether it's a New York strip, a rib eye or tenderloin, Capitol Chophouse will grill it to perfection. Not in the mood for beef? Try the slow-roasted Alaskan halibut. The locally raised Willow Creek Farms Berkshire pork with apricot and curry chutney is another favorite as is the gouda-stuffed bone-in chicken breast. Capitol Chophouse received recognition from *Wine Spectator* magazine for its extensive wine list. The friendly staff helps patrons find wines to complement their meals. Among the particularly tempting desserts are raspberry charlotte with ladyfinger lemon mousse or fresh raspberries and blackberries with raspberry purée. For special occasions, Capitol Chophouse features three private dining rooms for groups between four and 40 people. For all-American cuisine, make your reservations online or by telephone for Capitol Chophouse.

9 E Wilson Street, Madison WI
(608) 255-0165
www.capitolchophouse.com

The Brass Ring

RESTAURANTS & CAFÉS

The Brass Ring is a restaurant, bar and pool hall extraordinaire. Its name is derived from carousel rides that rose to popularity from 1880 to 1920, and refers to a brass ring that dangled above riders. Lucky riders able to snatch the ring gained an additional ride for free. Gaining the brass ring now has come to represent obtaining any worthy prize, and Larry Walsh, the Brass Ring's proprietor, strives to make customers feel like prizewinners here. The Brass Ring is a prizewinner in its own right as winner of a 2006 vote for Madison's best nightspot. The restaurant focuses on upscale pub food, such as burgers, chicken dishes and steak sandwiches, with more than two dozen entrée choices. The bar is constructed of several strikingly beautiful wood varieties, including paduke, curly maple and cherry wood. The restaurant offers 10 premium beers along with single malt scotches and upscale tequilas. Larry designed the pool hall area to treat players to excellent equipment and a lack of interruptions or obstructions. You'll find eight Diamond Professional pool tables here. The Brass Ring hosts an 8-ball league, a 9-ball league and a beginner's league for couples. The 1915 building housing the Brass Ring has been beautifully restored to hold several Madison businesses. Photographs displayed here take a nostalgic look at Madison's history. Visit the Brass Ring for outstanding pub fare, fine spirits and a game of pool.

701 E Washington Avenue, Suite 104, Madison WI
(608) 256-9359
www.thebrassringmadison.com

Benvenuto's

RESTAURANTS & CAFÉS

In 1999, Madison's Northside Planning Council asked residents what the area needed. They answered: an Italian restaurant. Local leaders invited Brian Dominick, owner of the wildly successful Benvenuto's in Beaver Dam, to expand into Madison. The new Benvenuto's opened in 2003, the same year that Beaver Dam residents voted the original restaurant the best in the county. Enormously popular, Benvenuto's has it all—great Italian and American food at reasonable prices, excellent service and a cheerful family ambience. Enter to find an Italian town square with faux balconies and laundry hanging from clotheslines. You are immediately served crusty, herbed Italian bread with olive oil for dipping. The menu is wide-ranging. You can order a huge, homemade calzone, spinach lasagna or chicken tetrazzini. If you prefer an American entrée, Benvenuto's has steak, fried fish and many other standards. The pizza flies out of the oven, of course. The house special pie has three meats, four veggies and four cheeses. No matter what you order, you will probably take some of it home. Benvenuto's success comes from careful planning and cultivation of its employees. Brian hires only the best applicants, including many with disabilities, and provides health insurance to everyone. Employee turnover is as low as 13 percent a year, unbelievable in the restaurant business. Benvenuto's now has a location in Fitchburg, poshly decorated but with the same service and menu. Visit one of the three Benvenuto's soon to see what the fuss is about.

1849 Northport Drive, Madison WI (608) 241-1144
2949 Triverton Pike Drive, Fitchburg WI (608) 278-7800
831 Park Avenue, Beaver Dam WI (920) 887-7994
www.benvenutos.com

Eno Vino Wine Bar & Bistro

RESTAURANTS & CAFÉS

Readers of *Madison Magazine* voted EnoVino Wine Bar & Bistro the Best New Restaurant in 2005 and it's easy to see why. Owner Alfredo Teuschler and Managing Partner Patrick Quinlan have created an elegant environment that encourages conversation and camaraderie with warm earth tones and cozy leather seating. For the wine lover, Eno Vino offers more than 275 wines by the bottle, 45 of which are poured by the glass. The wine list recently received an Award of Excellence from *Wine Spectato*r magazine for the impressive and diverse wine selection that is offered. For those that are not into wine, you need not worry. Eno Vino Wine Bar & Bistro also boasts a full bar, featuring local and imported beer selections. Specialty cocktails and martinis are created by Beverage Director Robert Fedorovich. Eno Vino features international fare, freshly prepared in full view by a James Beard Award Winner, Chef Michael Peterson, and his staff. On the eclectic and forward thinking menu, which rotates seasonally, you are sure to find unusual soups and salads, tempting tapas and decadent desserts. So if you hunger for delicious food, fine wine and ambience you can sink into, make reservations to visit Eno Vino Wine Bar & Bistro.

601 Junction Road, Madison WI
(608) 664-9565
www.eno-vino.com

Essen Haus German Restaurant

RESTAURANTS & CAFÉS

Enjoy a true taste of Germany with a visit to Essen Haus German Restaurant, where Eat, Drink and Be Merry is more than motto; it's a way of life. Robert Worm founded the original Essen Haus in Madison in 1984. He has since made quite a name for the place with recognition as the Best of Bars by the Food Network and as one of America's Top Tasty Destinations by *Martha Stewart Living* magazine. Robert's second Essen Haus is part of the delightful Bavarian Village and Chalet complex in the heart of downtown Wisconsin Dells. Here you can view the German glockenspiel that reenacts the Pied Piper of Hamelin legend every half hour and tour the outdoor biergarten. When you're finished with your tour, head inside Essen Haus for an authentic German meal served up by friendly staff members dressed in traditional German attire, complete with dirndls and lederhosen. Specialties of the house include the roast pork, along with the Wiener schnitzel, hühner schnitzel, and the wurst teller, a combination sausage plate featuring bratwurst, Thuringer and knockwurst. Essen Haus German Restaurant is proud to be the nation's largest seller of German draft beer in the United States and offers 12 traditional German beers on tap, as well as an extensive selection of domestic and imported beers and Weissbier bottles. Treat yourself to an authentic German meal without leaving the country by visiting Essen Haus German Restaurant, a Wisconsin tradition.

414 Broadway, Wisconsin Dells WI (608) 253-7766
514 E Wilsonstrasse Street, Madison WI (608) 255-4674
www.essen-haus.com

Fyfe's Corner Bistro

RESTAURANTS & CAFÉS

Fyfe's Corner Bistro is located in a historic 19th century brick building with a colorful history. The building once housed the Fuller and Johnson Plow Company, and was a flop house during the Great Depression. The circular bar came from the Chicago World's Fair in 1933. Today the venerable old building is home to one of Madison's finest restaurants. Keith Fyfe Blew and Susan Breitbach established Fyfe's Corner Bistro in 1993. Their attention to detail pays off with consistent quality in everything they do. Dennis Ghetto, restaurant critic for the *Milwaukee Journal Sentinel*, in his book *Great Wisconsin Restaurants*, named Fyfe's as one of Wisconsin's greatest restaurants. Fyfe's offers the perfect setting for a romantic evening. Cobblestone floors, candlelit tables and the works of local artists create an artistic and cozy atmosphere that is quiet, subdued and intimate. The menu is anything but ordinary. For an appetizer you may want to try Fyfe's crab cakes with cilantro-lime mayonnaise over a bed of mixed greens. Their signature steaks come from Certified Black Angus. Their Norwegian salmon, pumpkin-almond ravioli, and pan-seared Maple Leaf Farms duck breast are not to be missed. Every item on the menu, from the baked chèvre to the lamb shanks, comes with a wine suggestion from Fyfe's extensive list. For dessert, Fyfe's is famous for their flan. You may also want to try the tiramisu, Belgian chocolate cake, or key lime pie. Weekends at Fyfe's feature live music on Thursday, Friday and Saturday nights. Next time you are in Madison, head on down to Fyfe's Corner Bistro, a cornerstone of a great community.

1344 E Washington Avenue, Madison WI
(608) 251-8700
www.foodspot.com/fyfes
www.madisonoriginals.org

Gratitudes Floral & Gift Boutique

SHOPPING

"Really wonderful things start with the letter G, like gravy, golf, guacamole and Gratitudes," says longtime florist and master gardener Lori Malicki, who seized the opportunity to open a new store on Madison's west side after selling her first floral shop. Open since August 2005, Gratitudes Floral & Gift Boutique showcases the owner's whimsical sense of fun and commitment to exceptional quality and customer service. This 3,000-square-foot shop provides full floral service for weddings, funerals and corporate events as well as local and worldwide daily delivery. Gratitudes also offers a corporate vase exchange to local businesses that order on a weekly or biweekly basis, as well as gift baskets and permanent floral arrangements. Lori purchases flowers locally whenever possible and presents fresh stem designs in an open air cooler for easy viewing. Gratitudes carries an international card selection from 75 different artists, including Karen Schneider and Ashley Osborn. Uncommon gifts include a line of vintage baby clothing. An impressive array of bath and body products, guaranteed to pamper and please, make thoughtful gifts or a well-deserved treat for you. Check out the fun and flashy website, which offers an opportunity to place an order online when you can't make the trip. Visit in person when you can at Gratitudes Floral & Gift Boutique, where you are sure to find an array of floral possibilities to delight everyone's fancy.

7424 Mineral Point Road, Madison WI
(608) 833-2112
www.gratitudes.biz

J.T. Whitney's Pub & Brewery

WINES, BREWS, PUBS & CLUBS

"Beer—proof that God loves us." That quote from Benjamin Franklin describes the basic philosophy behind J.T. Whitney's Pub & Brewery in Madison. Managing partner and confessed beer guy David Bookstaff named the pub for a college buddy of his and set about giving patrons that feeling of community you get at the best British pubs. The first ingredient, naturally, was great beer, which brewmaster Rich Becker brews in abundance. Whether your tastes run to ale or stout, you'll find something to love here. The Badger Red Ale, J.T. Whitney's signature beer, is medium-bodied and smooth with a pleasant balance of malt and hops and has picked up medals at the Great American Beer Festival and World Beer Championships. Another favorite is the Black Diamond Porter, nice and dark with a bubbly, tan head. You'll generally find six to eight beers on tap. You'll also find some of Rich's authentic sodas, brewed on-site and available only at the brewery, including a not-too-sweet, but oh-so-creamy and delicious root beer. Those looking for a bite to eat with their beer will find soups, salads and sandwiches along with burgers and homemade vegetarian pizzas. A Friday all-you-can-eat fish fry is very popular. Children eat free on Monday nights. You'll find poker nights too. Enjoy a good time with your friends and award winning beer with a visit to J.T. Whitney's Pub & Brewery.

674 S Whitney Way, Madison WI
(608) 274-1776
www.jtwhitneys.com

Mackesey's Irish Pub

WINES, BREWS, PUBS & CLUBS

For more than 30 years, Mackesey's Irish Pub in Madison has been serving up brews fit for a governor or even a duke. The pub is owned by Vince and Arline Mackesey, and Mark Mackesey. The pub business is in the Mackesey blood. Arline's dad, Tony Frank, operated a pub during the Great Depression. You'll find many imported beers and Irish whiskeys here, with 14 varieties of beer on tap from which to choose. The historical building, which dates back to 1913, adds to the overall charm. Restoration work performed in 2005 improved the building while leaving its historical flavor intact. Mackesey's Irish Pub has attracted several famous people over the years. One St. Patrick's day, a Wisconsin governor and his bodyguard stopped by to enjoy a pint of Irish beer. As for the Duke? Mark's friend from drama class in college, Tom Wopat, who played Luke Duke on the television series The Dukes of Hazzard, is a favored guest at the pub. You don't need to be a Duke or governor, though, to enjoy the friendly atmosphere here. For an authentic Irish pub experience, both lively and friendly, come to Mackesey's Irish Pub.

317 State Street, Madison WI
(608) 256-6071

High Noon Saloon

WINES, BREWS, PUBS & CLUBS

The High Noon Saloon is the place to go for live music and fun in Madison. Owner Cathy Dethmers opened the club in 2004, following the demise of her previous club, O'Cayz Corral, to a fire. Like O'Cayz Corral, you'll find indie and punk bands playing here, but you'll also find local, national and international acts from just about every musical genre imaginable. A couple of recent highlights to perform at High Noon Saloon were alt-country Hank Williams III and rockabilly queen Wanda Jackson. If you feel like letting out your inner rock star, every Tuesday features karaoke with a live band called the Gomers, who have been voted Madison's Favorite Band (in one form or another) every year since 1999. The variety of acts is just one of the many things that prompted the *Isthmus Annual Manual* to declare High Noon Saloon the best live music venue in the area for several years running. The décor of High Noon Saloon lives up to its name with Southwest influences. The building has a retro, but warm, feel. If you don't feel like being right in the middle of things, you can observe the action from a second-story balcony. If you're looking for great food and beverages to help you rock the night away, try some of the Glass Nickel pizza, sold by the slice, or a drink from the saloon's well-stocked bar. For live music and a great social scene, come on in to High Noon Saloon.

701 E Washington Avenue, Madison WI
(608) 268-1122
www.high-noon.com

MARSHALL

In June of 1837, 45 men forged their way from Milwaukee to Madison to begin construction of the new state capitol. Three of these men, Andrew and Zenas Bird and Aaron Petrie, made a mental note of an idyllic location on the Maunesha River where they would return to build their homes. Return they did; but months of labor ended in October 1838 when an autumn prairie fire destroyed a public building and the beginnings of a sawmill. For more than a decade afterwards, the name of the village was Bird's Ruins. As it gradually grew back, it went by a variety of names, including Medina, Hanchetville and Howard City. In the mid-1880s, Madison real estate mogul Samuel Marshall purchased a large quantity of land in the now thriving village and named it Marshall.

PLACES TO GO

- Firemen's ParkPark Drive
  (608) 655-3698
- Little Amerricka (amusement park)
  700 E Main Street
  (608) 655-3181
- Riley-Deppe County Park
  870 State Route 19

THINGS TO DO

June

- Marshall Firemen's Festival
  (608) 655-3698

September

- Block Party on Main Street
  (608) 655-1666

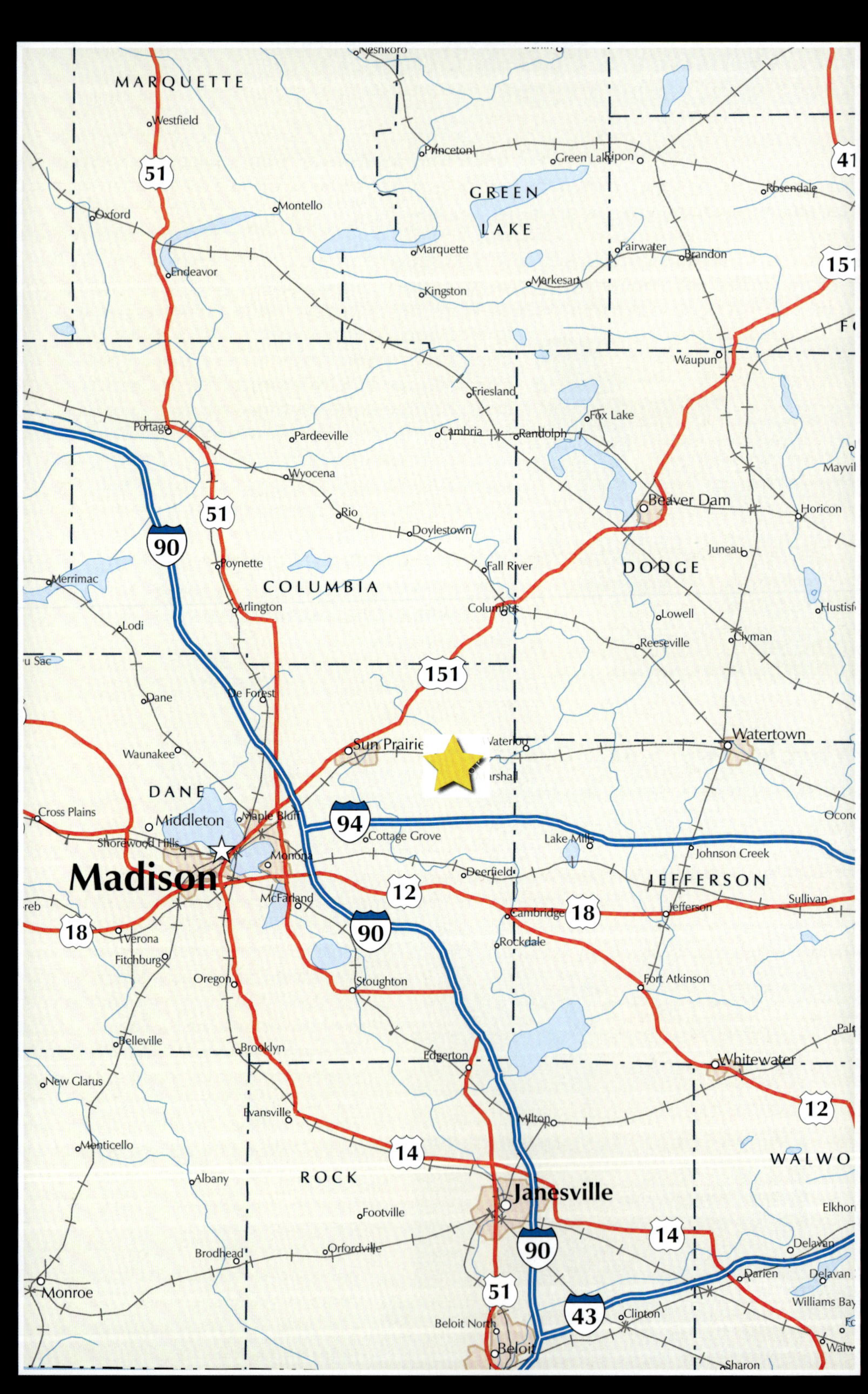

Little Amerricka

ATTRACTIONS

Hidden away in the Wisconsin cornfields of Marshall, Little Amerricka is a nostalgic family-owned amusement park straight out of the past. Owner Lee Merrick, a Marshall businessman and lifelong train enthusiast, along with General Manager Darrell Klompmaker, opened Little Amerricka in 1991 with a handful of rides, miniature golf and the Whiskey River Railway. Since that time, the park has grown to include over 25 rides and attractions, such as the classic Mad Mouse roller coaster, bumper boats and the only Wisconsin monorail. The 2007 season will give Little Amerricka its first woodie—the historic reconstruction of a junior wooden roller coaster named the Meteor. These, along with many other classic restored rides, makes Little Amerricka a perfect outing for the entire family. The Whiskey River Railway is a one-third scale, premiere light railway, where families can enjoy a 15 minute train ride through the beautiful Wisconsin countryside and catch a glimpse of the domestic and exotic animals from one of Mr. Merrick's many farms. There is nothing he enjoys more than seeing one of his beautiful steam engines and passenger cars filled with families all having a great time at Little Amerricka. Now celebrating more than 15 years, the park still remains an excellent family value. With no general admission or parking fees, guests can purchase a variety of á la carte tickets or unlimited all-day ride passes at an affordable price. Visit Little Amerricka Amusement Park for an Old Fashioned day of Big Fun.

700 E Main Street, Marshall WI
(608) 655-3181
www.littleamerricka.com

MENOMONEE FALLS

Occupying a scenic 33 square miles of small town charm, Menomonee Falls calls itself Wisconsin's largest village. The village is located in the northeastern corner of Waukesha County, a mosaic of lakes and rivers, rolling hills, forests and wetlands guarded by herons. Area pioneers originally sought the abundant waterpower of the Menomonee River's waterfalls, one of which now ornaments the village's downtown. In the later 19th century, Menomonee Falls was a significant quarrying town. Today the 16-acre former quarry is a lake in Menomonee Park, open for swimming, fishing, boating and ice-skating with concessions in the summer. History lives on in Menomonee Falls's Old Falls Village, a collection of 19th century buildings that includes a schoolhouse, railroad depot, several log homes and a dairy. The centerpiece of Old Falls, the 1858 Miller-Davidson House, is on the National Register of Historic Places. Menomonee Falls's historic Village Centre is a district of two main streets fronted by 100-year-old buildings. Along with quaint shops and galleries, the Village Centre hosts a calendar of events including holiday parades, farmers markets and free summertime concerts.

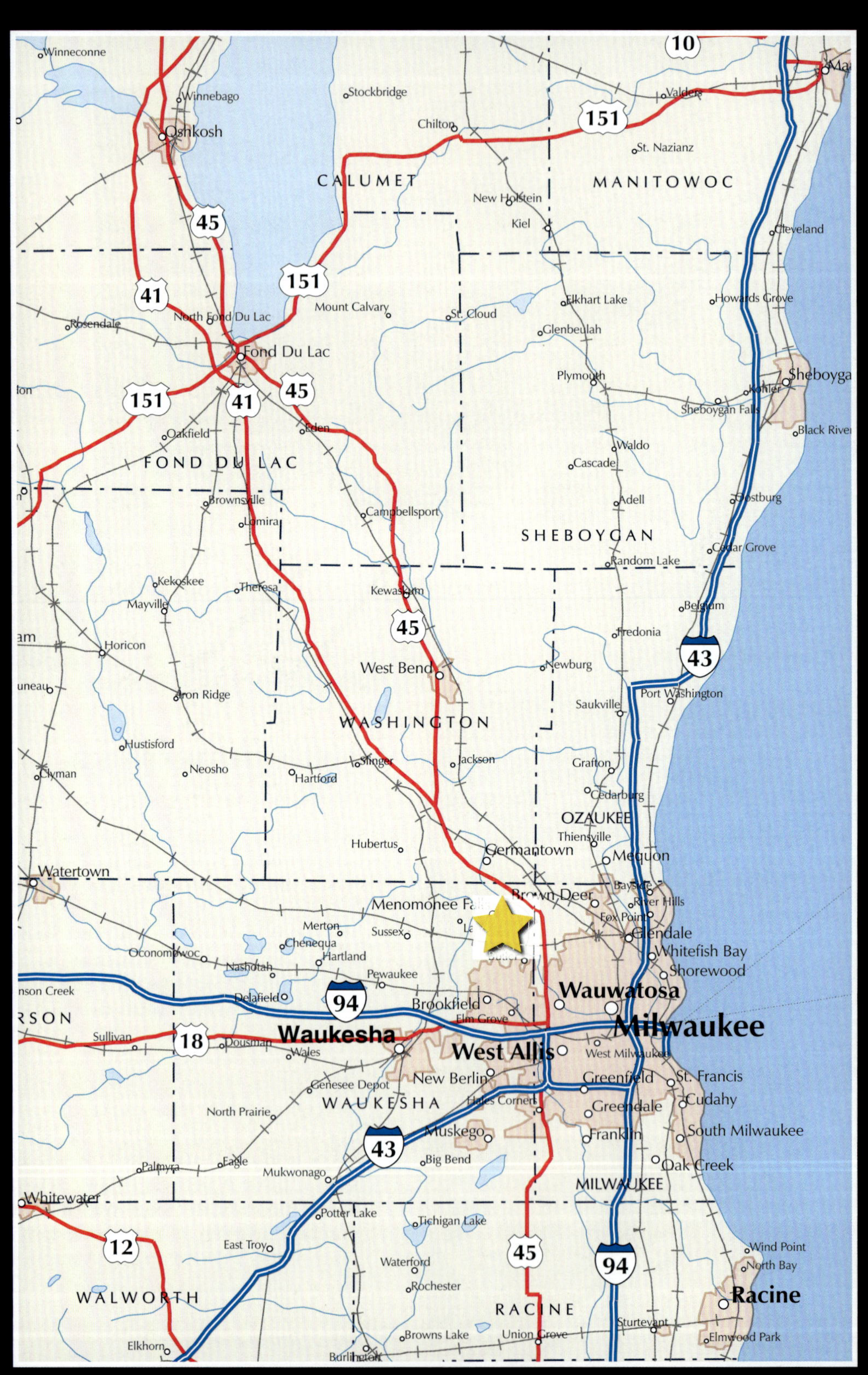

PLACES TO GO

- Old Falls Village
  County Line Road and Pilgrim Road
  (262)-532-4775
- Menomonee Park
  W220 N7884 Town Line Road
  (262) 255-1310

THINGS TO DO

June

- Old Falls Village Days
  Old Falls Village
  (262)-532-4775

September

- The Big Pig Gig
  www.thebigpiggig.com
- Cheery Cherry Fall Fair
  Village Park
  communitymemorial.com/cheery_cherry

The Quilted Basket

ARTS & CRAFTS

Ann and Tom Wanke, owners of the Quilted Basket, provide education, service and loads of quilting supplies to satisfy every quilter's need. Whether you quilt as an outlet for your creativity, appreciate the practicality of warm layers on a cool night or just want to add a decorative touch to your room, the Quilted Basket anticipates your needs. After years of dreaming of their own business, Ann and Tom opened the shop in 2000. They quickly outgrew the original space, and when the opportunity to move to the Four Corners area of Menomonee Falls arose, they took it. Now, the three large rooms provide plenty of space for Husqvarna Viking sewing machines, quilting notions and more than 6,000 bolts of fabric. Colorful quilts and finished garments on display are sure to inspire you to get stitching, but if you wonder where to start, Ann offers sewing and quilting lessons for adults and children, plus special interest clubs and demonstrations by nationally known instructors. Tom keeps your sewing machine running in tip-top condition with service and repair on all brands of machines. Visit the Quilted Basket to find inspiration and supplies for your next quilting project.

N88 W16599 Main Street, Menomonee Falls WI
(262) 251-8791 ***www.thequiltedbasket.com***

Nino's Italian Bakery

BAKERIES, COFFEE & TEA

When you watch through the large picture windows at Nino's Italian Bakery and see Nino Sgroi baking, and when you sample what he makes, you will think that he must have gone to school many years to learn his craft. The fact is, Nino has never taken a single baking class in his life. He is a natural who began hanging out in bakeries when he was a young boy, after moving here from Italy when he was 12 years old. Nino would take it all in while he swept the floors to earn a few dollars. Nino has been running his own bakery since 1970, with 30 years on the East Side of Milwaukee and six years in Menomonee Falls. To create his crusty European breads, he never measures in the conventional way. He applies this intuitive gift to his exquisite wedding cakes as well. Nino learned to make them simply by watching. Nino's wife, Nina, is the artist behind all of the Italian cookies and pastries, including cannoli and biscotti. She also cooks for Italian catering events with her homemade specialties. Nino's Italian Bakery is truly a family business, involving the efforts of Nino, Nina and their daughters, Josephine, AnnMarie and Tina. They also have a wholesale business that distributes their bread and rolls to restaurants and grocery stores. The Bakery also serves sub sandwiches, soups, grilled panini and gourmet coffee, as well as a full-service deli in addition to their homemade baked goods. On Wednesday nights they serve spaghetti dinner with garlic bread (Nina's homemade sauce and meatballs), and Nino serenades his customers with his accordion. Coming soon, Nino's Italian Bakery will be offering mail order Italian cookies for any event.

N88 W16683 Main Street, Menomonee Falls WI
(262) 502-1997
Ninos2000@sbcglobal.net

Kesslers Diamonds

FASHION

Kesslers Diamonds is a company of people driven by their core values, not the bottom line. Richard Kessler's devotion to customer satisfaction was the key that turned the smallest jeweler in southeastern Wisconsin into the largest. Richard was a stranger to the jewelry business when he went to work for a jeweler at age 27. In 1980, he bought a struggling jewelry store and 10 years later, he was still struggling, until a motivational seminar and a philosophical turnabout earned him the gratitude and respect of countless satisfied customers. In an effort to become the most respected name in diamonds in southeastern Wisconsin, Richard lowered prices permanently and placed signs in his window that read, "Don't look for a sale, there isn't going to be one." Next, he stopped trying to be everything to everyone and specialized in diamonds, specifically engagement rings and loose diamonds, although Kesslers is also the place to turn for diamond bracelets, earrings and pendants. He went on to encourage lifelong relationships with clients by instituting Kesslers Miraculous Warranty, an unconditional lifelong guarantee on everything sold at Kesslers. Richard hires employees who care about people, then teaches them the jewelry business. His stores are filled with chairs, so clients can have a relaxing experience. Next time you are in the market for diamond jewelry, visit Kesslers Diamonds with locations in Appleton, Brookfield, Greenfield, Madison and Menomonee Falls. The selection is the largest in the state and the core value of the staff is to build lifelong relationships with each and every client.

Menomonee Falls: (262) 251-4570
Greenfield: (414) 325-9800
Brookfield: (262) 782-6100
Appleton: (920) 749-0000
Madison: (608) 662-9800
www.kesslersdiamonds.com

Pops Frozen Custard

FUN FOODS

There is frozen custard, and then there is legend. Pops Frozen Custard in Menomenee Falls is destined for legend. Sharon Whitman bought the business from the original Pops, John McLees. Her signature sundaes bear the names of some of her favorite people. Consider the Father Fran Eschweiler, a sundae featuring chocolate brownies that honors the community's beloved Catholic priest. Sharon's husband, John, takes credit for the Chubby Hubby. Ann's Joy and Doug's Rocky Road are other hits in a parade of custard treats. Pops is also the place for burgers, sandwiches or a bucket of fish. You'll find Sharon busily working behind the counter. She relishes the opportunity to ask how her customers are doing and wants to know about your experience at Pops. Not long ago, a customer told her about a conversation he had with a flight attendant at Chicago's O'Hare airport. When asked where he was from, the customer said he was from a little place she would not have heard of called Menomonee Falls, Wisconsin. The flight attendant begged to differ saying she knew it well because it was the home of Pops. Sharon invites you to enjoy a friendly and delicious visit to Pops Frozen Custard. You might end up with a dessert named in your honor.

N86 W16459 Appleton Avenue, Menomonee Falls WI
(262) 251-3320
www.popscustard.com

Carmel Builders, Inc.

HOME & GARDEN

Carmel Builders, Inc., emerges from a family tradition of remodeling excellence. In operation since 1979, owner Tom Weiher and his wife, Barbara, carry on a business inspired by Tom's childhood affiliation with his father who ran a one-man remodeling business out of the family home. Carmel Builders is now a recognized and successful business with deep community ties. Barbara is chair of the Chamber of Commerce Marketing Committee, and Tom sits on the board of Milwaukee/NARI, the National Association of the Remodeling Industry. He has received numerous individual awards, including the 2006 NARI National Spirit of Education award. Carmel Builders took part in the 2006 Habitat for Humanity Builder Blitz, constructing a home for a needy family in just over four days. They also had the privilege of working with a team of contractors on the 2005 MBA's Remodeling Homes Reshaping Lives project. The company has developed a reputation for completing projects on time and on budget. Adhering to a strict code of ethics and supported by an expert team of NARI certified craftsmen, Carmel Builders has demonstrated the ability to perform superior remodeling projects and exhibits competence in developing and writing job specifications with the highest standards of excellence. For the peace of mind that comes from working with a company that focuses on quality and integrity, bring your next project to Carmel Builders, Where Excellence is Defined.

N85 W16080 Appleton Avenue, Menomonee Falls WI
(262) 255-2230
www.carmelbuilders.com

In Sync Designs, LLC

HOME & GARDEN

"Remodeling is what we eat, live and breathe," says Christine McDuffie, who owns In Sync Designs in Menomonee Falls along with Dave Battermann. This sophisticated design center stirs your imagination with a tasteful demonstration showroom featuring kitchen and bath designs that could change your relationship to your home. As a one-stop shop for remodeling, In Sync offers design services, products, installation and project coordination. Christine and Dave can also honor your budget with realistic cost projections. They'll come to your home to access your project and work behind the scenes to make sure the pieces of the remodeling puzzle fall into place. With a quarter century of combined business experience, you can count on their judgment, practicality and design know-how. When it's time to change some of the most important rooms in your house, visit Christine and Dave at In Sync Designs.

N88 W16586 Main Street,
Menomonee Falls WI
(262) 251-7756
www.insyncdesigns.net

Krueger's Entertainment Center

RECREATION & FITNESS

Krueger's Entertainment Center has been in the Krueger family for 50 years. The old bowling alley was completely remodeled in 2005 and offers a wide range of recreational activities. The center remains a family affair, owned by Ralph and Sue Krueger and managed by their sons, David and Dan. Krueger's offers organized leagues for bowlers and dart players. It also provides pool tables, a sports bar and a game room. Hall rentals are available for kid's birthday parties and other group events. The 1950s-style drive-up window is gone, but customers can still experience the inside equivalent with choices of sandwiches, burgers and pizza at the pub and the coldest beers in town. The Suds Pub Laundromat right next door offers the convenience of cleaning your clothes while you are having fun. Krueger's inspires nostalgia for good times out of another era. Fortunately, those good times are still in style, which accounts for the fact that business keeps getting better here. Many locals say they would be lost without Krueger's. Visit Krueger's Entertainment Center for the fun of it.

N87 W16471 Appleton Avenue, Menomonee Falls WI
(262) 251-2340
www.kruegersentcenter.com

MEQUON

Located just north of Milwaukee on the shore of Lake Michigan, Mequon boasts majestic lakeshore bluffs, stately homes and expansive open space. Low-density zoning regulations and high development standards have preserved Mequon's rural heritage, leaving half its land undeveloped. Orchards and produce farms dot the area, while many parks and nature preserves offer recreation. The Ozaukee Interurban Trail is a great way to survey the region's woodlands, wetlands, farmlands, plus the Milwaukee River and Lake Michigan. The 30-mile paved trail, which connects the historic downtowns of Ozaukee County, has been designated a Great Wisconsin Birding Trail. In 1839, the first German settlers arrived from Pomerania, seeking religious freedom. They founded Freistadt (Free Place) in the western Mequon Township and built the first Lutheran Church in Wisconsin in 1840. Mequon continues to celebrate its German heritage in an annual outdoor festival called Pommern Tag (Pomeranian Day). The Gathering on the Green is an annual evening of jazz in the park.

PLACES TO GO

- Mequon Nature Preserve
  (262) 338-1794
- Ozaukee Interurban Trail (parking)
  6100 N Mequon Road
- Rotary Park
  3900 W Highland Road

THINGS TO DO

June

- Pommern Tag Outdoor German Festival
  Mequon City Park
  (262) 242-0653

July

- Gathering on the Green
  Mequon Rotary Park Pavilion
  (262) 242-6187

The Chalet Motel of Mequon

ACCOMMODATIONS

The Chalet Motel of Mequon offers travelers award winning accommodations and dining at excellent rates. The motel's owners, Bob Briese and Linda Walsh, have won the Mequon/Thiensville Business of the Year award for their service to customers and the community. The Chalet offers 53 rooms, 35 of which are nonsmoking. All rooms feature complimentary high-speed Internet access, coffee makers, refrigerators and microwaves. Those seeking an even more luxurious experience can check out The Chalet's 14 executive rooms with 32-inch televisions, DVD players and plush mattresses, or the Jacuzzi suite, which features a four seat Jacuzzi whirlpool. The motel is AAA approved and pet friendly in standard rooms. If you're looking for some delicious food, you'll appreciate the motel's restaurant, Señor Sol Mexican Restaurant & Cantina, open for lunch, dinner and cocktails seven days a week. The Chalet is conveniently located less than 15 minutes from downtown Milwaukee and 10 miles from Historic Cedarburg shopping. Concordia University, several area golf courses, and the new Bayshore Towne Center shopping are only minutes away. If you're looking for great accommodations and a home base from which to visit some of Wisconsin's finest attractions, stay at The Chalet Motel of Mequon.

10401 N Port Washington Road,
Mequon WI
(262) 241-4510 or (800) 343-4510
www.chaletmotelmequon.com

East Towne Jewelers

FASHION

With 22 years in the business, East Towne Jewelers owner Mary Seramur knows how to put a little sparkle in your day. Whether you're looking for the newest in designer lines or wish to restore a family heirloom, this Mequon jewelry store is prepared to fulfill your desires. East Towne Jewelers carries the latest in earrings, chains, necklaces, bracelets and pendants from several prestigious designers. For a thin, Swiss watch with timeless appeal, East Towne carries the Cyma line of watches and the more adventurous looking Alfex. You'll find dazzling luxury diamond pieces, enamel by Soho, and a charm line by Pandora. Award winning designers Judith Ripka and Robert Lee Morris add a modern twist to classic styling. Mary brings her love and knowledge of art to the store with her own custom designs, which use gold, silver, platinum and gemstones. Mary has traveled the world to find the best stones and materials to use in her work. She delights in collaborating with the customer to design the perfect piece for an individual's needs and personality. "There is no greater thrill than seeing your personal feelings and ideas come to life in unique, handcrafted jewelry," says Mary, whose designs range from the traditional to three-dimensional avant-garde pieces. Mary can also restore and update your family heirloom so it can be worn with today's styles. Whatever your jewelry fantasy, come to East Towne Jewelers to turn it into reality.

Photo by Quentin Finucan

1515 W Mequon Road, Mequon WI
(262) 241-8007 or (800) 547-8007
www.easttownejewelers.com

Michael I Kim, DDS

HEALTH & BEAUTY

Dr. Michael I. Kim is the classic example of the local boy who became a success in his hometown. Dr. Kim, a native of Mequon, has been practicing dentistry since 1986. He attended Marquette University High School, Marquette University and Marquette University Dental School. After 13 years in Fox Point, Dr. Kim outgrew the location and moved his practice to Mequon in 1999. Dr. Kim believes in involving his patients with their care so they can achieve optimal health. He treats his patients like they are his own family, which may sound like a sales pitch, but it is true. He doesn't use silver amalgam fillings, because he wouldn't use them on his own family. Dr. Kim's office even feels a lot like home, with comfortable, uncluttered rooms that are tastefully decorated. The waiting area is meant to be relaxing and includes a children's area where kids can watch television and play. Even the treatment rooms have televisions on the ceilings to help patients relax. Dr. Kim feels it is important to restore teeth to proper function and aesthetics. Teeth need to look and feel good. Overall health is also important. There is a strong correlation between oral health and the risk of cardiovascular disease and stroke. His quarterly newsletter, which is full of information that will help you stay healthy, even includes a tasty recipe. If you are in need of a dentist who will help you achieve a healthy, beautiful smile, call Dr. Michael I. Kim.

10033 N Port Washington Road, Suite 150
Mequon WI
(262) 241-5558
mikimdds.com

Exteriors Unlimited Landscape Contractors

HOME & GARDEN

Exteriors Unlimited Landscape Contractors creates and maintains elegantly functional outdoor living spaces using the highest quality materials and workmanship. The company, owned by Mike and Doug McConnohie, has installed and managed commercial and residential landscapes since 1981. When you are ready to create a landscape for your home or business, Exteriors Unlimited Landscape Contractors has a talented staff of certified landscape architects, horticulturists, maintenance and landscape technicians ready to help. A staff member sits down with you for a free initial consultation. If necessary, a landscape architect prepares a conceptual drawing and a master plan based on your ideas. During construction, the project manager stays in continuous contact with you from start to finish. Exteriors Unlimited can create the ponds, walls, pavement and plantings necessary to achieve your vision. After your gardens are complete, Exteriors Unlimited can maintain them beautifully with everything from trimming and mowing to fertilizing and pond cleaning. Exteriors Unlimited Landscape has received awards for lighting and landscape design from the National Builders Association and the National Association of the Remodeling Industry. The company has also been featured in *Milwaukee Magazine*. Most Exteriors Unlimited accounts come from customer referrals, a sure sign you will receive quality and attention to detail. Call the professionals at Exteriors Unlimited Landscape Contractors, and have them create a private oasis for you.

6929 W Donges Bay Road, Mequon WI
(262) 242-4884
www.exteriors-unlimited.com

Casa Grande

RESTAURANTS & CAFÉS

Casa Grande in the Mequon Pavilions is a delicious dream come true for both its diners and its owners. Owners Oscar and Reynaldo Castro watched during their childhood as their father, Aurelio, cooked for migrant workers in California and shared in his dream of opening up a restaurant of their own. Unfortunately, Aurelio never got that chance, but Oscar and Reynaldo and many of their siblings are living that dream and share it daily with those who seek a tasty Mexican meal. Aurelio's recipes are alive and well here, with everything from the familiar fajitas, tacos and burritos to one-of-a-kind dishes like the Pollo a la Wisconsin, a salted chicken breast topped with cheese sauce and tortillas. Casa Grande's Cajun tacos, with a combination of pork and chicken, were a big hit at Milwaukee's Mexican Fest recently. Lunch offerings here include traditional huevos rancheros and tostadas. Who can resist a well-made Mexican flan or fried ice cream? The Castros take pride in menu selections made from scratch as well as generous portions and fresh ingredients. The menu changes seasonally. Be a part of the Castro family's dream and enjoy the fabulous fruits of their labors with a visit to Casa Grande.

10942 N Port Washington Road, Mequon WI
(262) 240-9658

Chip and Py's

RESTAURANTS & CAFÉS

With the sounds of light jazz joining the sight of elegant linen tablecloths and the flavors and smells of delicious gourmet food, it's easy to understand why Chip and Py's is renowned for its romantic atmosphere. The Mequon restaurant is named for two dear friends of Richard and Julie Staniszewski, who, along with daughter Amelia Betzhold, own and operate the restaurant, which has been at its current location for the past 15 years. The elegant offerings represent several styles of cuisine, from such Asian-influenced dishes as Siam Shrimp to European fare, including veal piccata or Parisian style lamb chops. For lunch, consider slightly lighter meals, including a steak sandwich topped with mushrooms, cheese and caramelized onions or the Mandarin Duck Breast Salad. Complete your repast with a decadent dessert, such as the cappuccino ice cream pie or molten chocolate cake. The restaurant offers a full-service bar and an extensive wine list. Small tables place you intimately close to your dining companions, and a cozy fireplace in the main dining room adds warmth and romance to winter visits. A luxurious patio that seats 40 is open for fair weather dining from May to November. Two party rooms cater to groups, while live music adds its own charm to Friday and Saturday night dining. Put some romance into your dining experience with a visit to Chip and Py's.

1340 W Towne Square Road, Mequon WI
(262) 241-9589
www.chipandpys.com

Photo by Mark Sadowski

PLACES TO GO

- Governor Nelson State Park
  5140 County Highway M, Waunakee
  (608) 831-3005
- Mendota Park Beach
  5130 County Highway M
- Middleton Historical Museum
  7410 Hubbard Avenue
  (608)-836-7614
- Middleton Train Depot
  1811 Parmenter Street
- Pheasant Branch Creek Conservancy
  4864 Pheasant Branch Road

THINGS TO DO

March

- Madison Antique Show
  Keva Sports Center
  (715) 355-5144

June

- American Girl Seconds and Returns Sale
  www.madisonchildrensmuseum.com/benefitsale

August

- Good Neighbor Fest
  www.middletonfestival.com

MIDDLETON

Middleton is a growing suburb of Madison on the west shore of Lake Mendota. Its scenic environment and dynamic commercial hub go towards explaining why *Money* magazine named Middleton the 7th Best Place to Live in America. Benefiting from close proximity to the University of Wisconsin Research Park, Middleton supports a strong cluster of high-tech, biotech, pharmaceutical and medical research industries. A key commercial development, the Greenway Center, is the site of Wisconsin's first boutique mall, Greenway Station. Middleton's greenbelt offers 1,000 acres of parklands, including beaches on Lake Mendota and the wetlands and woodlands of the Pheasant Branch Conservatory. In its earliest years, the Middleton area was a frequent camping ground for the Algonquin tribe, whose mounds are still observable in the greenbelt. Business kicked off in the Middleton area in 1856 with the establishment of Middleton Station, the first railroad depot between Lake Michigan and the Mississippi River. Middleton built itself around the train depot, which today houses the Middleton Tourism Commission.

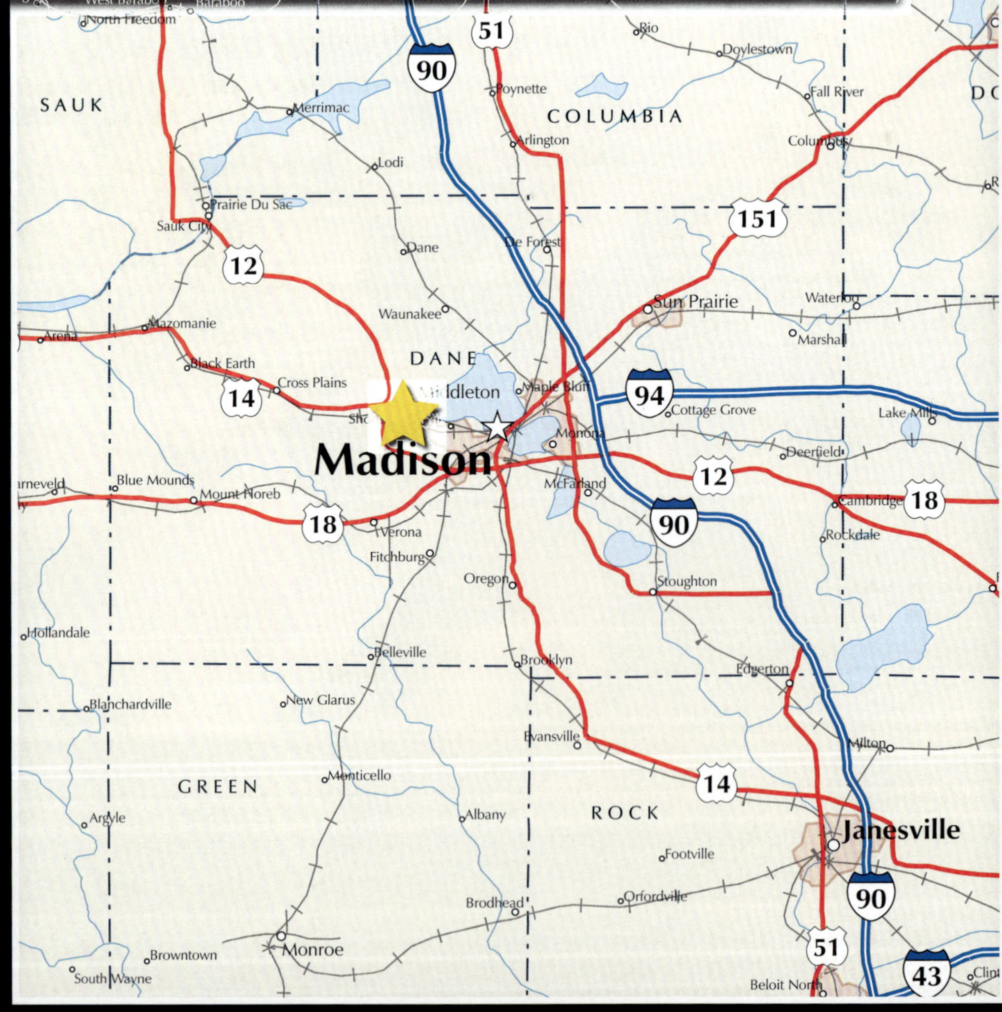

Hilton Garden Inn

ACCOMMODATIONS

With luxurious rooms and amenities plus an appealing location, the Hilton Garden Inn in Middleton is a haven for business and vacation travelers. The Hilton Garden Inn is less than 10 miles from such notable destinations as the State Capitol, the Kohl Center, Camp Randall Stadium and the University of Wisconsin. A free shuttle transports guests to destinations within five miles of the hotel. Adjacent to the hotel is Greenway Station, a worthwhile shopping destination with a varied slate of stores and restaurants all within walking distance of the hotel. Even if you never leave the Hilton Garden Inn, you'll find everything you need. Each room offers complimentary high speed Internet access with secure remote printing to the hotel's 24-hour business center. You'll find two telephones with voicemail and a 25-inch television with premium channels and video games to keep the young and the young-at-heart amused. The hotel offers an enhanced pool area filled with fun water activities and toys, plus a game room and fitness room. Breakfast is as close as the on-site Great American Grill restaurant. Plan your next large gathering at the Hilton Garden Inn where 3,600 square feet of banquet space can accommodate up to 250 people. Business conferences and special events, including wedding receptions, benefit from the hotel's full service catering and audio visual services. Whether you are working or playing, next time you are in Middleton stay at the Hilton Garden Inn.

1801 Deming Way, Middleton WI
(608) 831-2220 or
(877) STAY-HGI (782-3444)
www.madisonwestmiddleton.stayhgi.com

Fairfield Inn & Suites by Marriott Madison West/Middleton

ACCOMMODATIONS

Travelers can rest easy on the thick mattresses, crisp linens and custom comforters at Fairfield Inn & Suites by Marriott. This hotel, serving Madison and Middleton, offers a new and particularly comfortable bed in every one of its 93 rooms and 10 suites. You'll also find complimentary wireless high-speed Internet access, a coffee maker, hair dryer, iron and full-size ironing board. In the morning, treat yourself to the trademarked Early Eats complimentary hot breakfast, which features a Jimmy Dean breakfast sandwich. After a long day of driving or business meetings, the indoor pool, whirlpool and exercise area will have you feeling rejuvenated in no time. If staying in your room appeals to you, you'll be glad to know that many area restaurants deliver to the hotel. Fairfield Inn & Suites is conveniently located just minutes from downtown Madison, the Kohl Center and the University of Wisconsin. Shoppers will appreciate the adjacent Greenway Station with its eclectic mix of shops and restaurants. One meeting room with 288 square feet of space appeals to small groups. Come to Fairfield Inn & Suites by Marriott-Madison West/Middleton for comfort, convenience and a staff that's ready to make your stay the best it can be.

8212 Greenway Boulevard, Middleton WI
(608) 831-1400
www.fairfieldmadisonwest.com

Residence Inn by Marriott Madison West/Middleton

ACCOMMODATIONS

Residence Inn by Marriott Madison West/Middleton has all the comforts and relaxing feel of home along with all of the equipment and amenities a business traveler needs. This 100 percent smoke-free hotel offers spacious studio, one- and two-bedroom suites with complimentary wireless high-speed Internet access and secure remote printing to the hotel's business center. You'll also find fully equipped kitchens and televisions with HBO and other premium channels. Start your day with the complimentary trademarked Hometouch hot breakfast buffet and stay in shape while traveling with an outdoor all-purpose sport court, an exercise room, heated indoor pool and whirlpool. Many local restaurants deliver to the hotel and shopping opportunities abound, including those at the adjacent Greenway Station. For trips within five miles of the hotel, be sure to take advantage of the free shuttle service. The hotel's meeting space will accommodate up to 15 people, and catering services are available. The friendly staff aims to make you feel as comfortable as you would in your own home. During the summer, the manager even holds an outdoor cookout once a week. If you're looking for a homey atmosphere with full services for the business traveler, visit Residence Inn by Marriott Madison West/Middleton.

8400 Market Street, Middleton WI
(608) 662-1100 or (800) 331-3131
www.residenceinnmadisonwest.com

Scott's Pastry Shoppe, Inc.

BAKERIES, COFFEE & TEA

Celebrating 25 years in business, founding owners Jackie and Russell Scott started Scott's Pastry Shoppe, Inc. in 1982. This full-line bakery offers the best donuts, delicious cakes, cookies, brownies, breads, tortes and more. Wedding cakes are a specialty. The Scott's daughter, Dawn, joined them in 1994. In 2005, Russell retired to a support role, leaving the mother-daughter team to run the business. The heavenly smell that greets you at the door is only outdone by the mouthwatering sensations you experience when you eat here. Known in the community for hiring teenagers, don't be surprised to see the young people taking care of customers and keeping the place sparkling clean. Come join the locals over a great cup of coffee, or sit and watch the world go by on the deck overlooking University Avenue. A second location on Airport Road, in the new local airport, is a great place to get a pastry or eat lunch. Jackie Scott holds many awards, and she values giving to her community. In the late 1990s she created a day care for the employee's children, earning the loyalty of her employees. Serving on the local Chamber of Commerce board, technical school advisory board, and spending time in the local elementary schools helps her to really know the customers and to serve them with high quality products, and great service. Whether you live here or are just visiting, Scott's Pastry Shoppe is one of the sweetest places you'll ever go.

6637 University Avenue, Middleton WI
(608) 836-7333
19 W Main Street, Madison WI
(608) 256-7333
8300 Airport Road, Middleton WI
www.scottspastryshoppe.com

MILWAUKEE

Greater Milwaukee is a water lover's paradise and an important port. Quiet, residential neighborhoods are scattered throughout the city. There's nightlife along Water Street and serenity in the 15,000-acre Milwaukee County park system. While Milwaukee is not far from metropolitan Chicago, Wisconsinites have always taken pride in their differences from the Illinoisans, for example by contrasting their transparent politics with the colorful history of their neighbor.

Milwaukee received its name from the Native American word *Millioke*, meaning gathering place by the water. In recent years, Milwaukee has initiated a comprehensive revitalization project concentrated on its waterfront. Many new buildings ornament the lakefront and river banks, together with water-taxi landings, cafes and brewpubs. The Riverwalk, a continuous pedestrian byway, has become the center of city Milwaukee's vigorous cultural scene.

Milwaukee is famous for its many ethnic and music festivals, which represent at least a dozen nationalities and a range of musical genres. By far the largest of these is Summerfest. Listed in the Guinness Book of World Records as the largest music festival in the world, Summerfest attracts as many as 900,000 visitors a year. In former decades, Milwaukee was the number one beer producing city in the world, boasting four of the world's largest breweries. Schlitz inspired one of the best-known slogans in the industry: the Beer that Made Milwaukee Famous. Today the former Schlitz Brewery complex is a business park. While three of the original four breweries are gone, tourists are warmly received at the Miller Brewery and at the 1892 Pabst Mansion, home of the Pabst beer barons.

Visitors can explore Old Milwaukee by strolling through one of the revitalized historic neighborhoods such as Walker's Point and the Historic Third Ward. Walker's Point is home to one of Milwaukee's most notable landmarks, the Allen-Bradley Clock Tower. The tower's four-sided clock is the largest of its kind in the world.

The Historic Third Ward is home to the Milwaukee Institute of Art and Design and the Eisner Museum of Advertising and Design. Its quarterly art event, Gallery Night and Day, attracts thousands of visitors. It is also the site of the Milwaukee Public Market, a year-round gourmet and specialty foods bazaar. Milwaukee's most visually prominent attraction is the Milwaukee Art Museum, with a new wing designed by Santiago Calatrava in his first American commission. The museum includes a *brise soleil*, a moving sunscreen that unfolds like the wing of a bird.

Visitors will notice the many cream-colored brick buildings. During the latter half of the 19th century, Milwaukee produced as many as 15 million of these bricks a year, using two thirds of them in its own construction. These were boom times, when huge numbers of Germans flocked to the city and built its population. The German heritage and influence remains widespread: To this day, there are more than 40 pages of Schmidts and Schmitts in the phonebook, far more than Smiths.

PLACES TO GO

- Betty Brinn Children's Museum
  929 E Wisconsin Avenue
  (414) 390-KIDS (5437)
- Black Holocaust Museum
  2233 N 4th Street
  (414) 264-2500
- Bradley Center
  1001 N 4th Street
  (414) 227-0400
- Broadway Theatre Center
  158 N Broadway
  (414) 291-7800
- Cathedral Square Park
  520 E Wells Street
  (414) 277-0860
- Charles Allis Art Museum
  1801 N Prospect Avenue
  (414) 278-8295
- Discovery World at Pier Wisconsin
  500 N Harbor Drive
  (414) 765-9966

- The Eisner American Museum of Advertising & Design
  208 N Water Street
  (414) 847-3290
- Estabrook Park
  4400 N Estabrook Drive
  (414) 332-6191
- Haggerty Museum of Art
  Marquette University
  (414) 288-1669
- Henry Maier Festival Park and Lakeshore State Park
  200 N Harbor Drive
- Marcus Center for the Performing Arts
  929 N Water Street
  (888) 612-3500
- Midwest Airlines Center
  400 W Wisconsin Avenue
  (414) 908-6001
- Miller Visitor Center
  4251 W State Street
  (800) 944-LITE (5483)
- Milwaukee Art Museum
  700 N Art Museum Drive
  (414) 224-3200
- Milwaukee County Historical Society
  910 N Old World 3rd Street
  (414) 273-8288
- Milwaukee County Zoo
  10001 W Bluemound Road
  (414) 771-3040
- Milwaukee Public Market
  400 N Water Street
  www.milwaukeepublicmarket.org
- Milwaukee Public Museum
  800 W Wells Street
  (414) 278-2728
- Mitchell Park Horticultural Conservatory
  524 S Layton Boulevard
  (414) 649-9800
- Museum of Beer and Brewing
  (414) 265-2337
- Pabst Mansion
  2000 W Wisconsin Avenue
  (414) 931-0808
- Pabst Theater
  144 E Wells Street
  (800) 511-1552

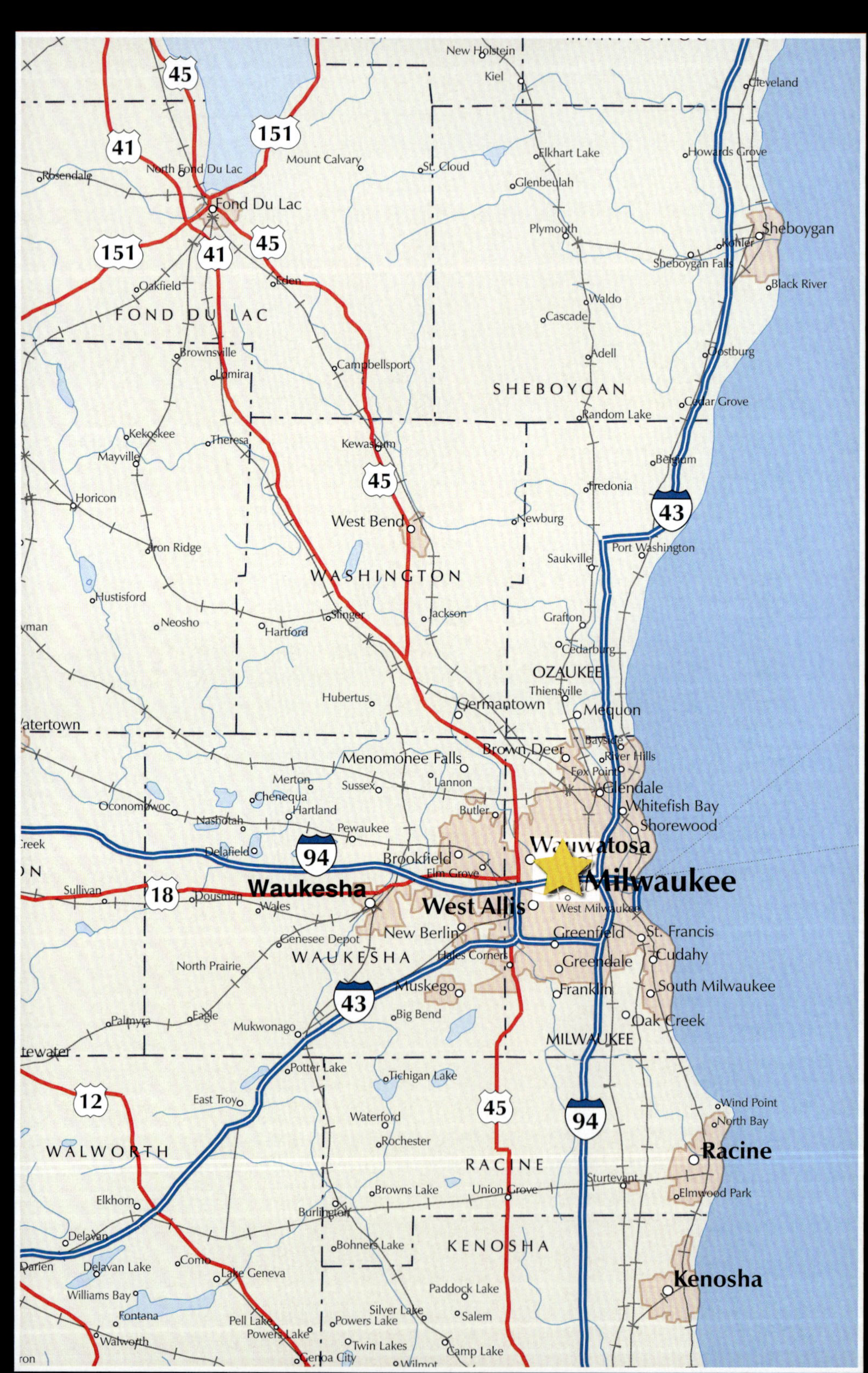

Milwaukee War Memorial

- Pettit National Ice Center
  500 S 84th Street
  (414) 266-0100
- Veterans Park
  1010 N Lincoln Memorial Drive
  (414) 277-0860
- Villa Terrace Decorative Arts Museum
  2220 N Terrace Avenue
  (414) 271-3656

THINGS TO DO

February

- Greater Milwaukee Auto Show
  Midwest Airlines Center
  www.motortrendautoshows.com/milwaukee

March

- St. Patrick's Day Parade & Party
  (414) 276-6696
  www.westown.org

June

- PrideFest
  Henry Maier Festival Park
  www.pridefest.com
- Riversplash!
  Riverwalk
  www.riversplash.com
- Lakefront Festival of Arts
  Art Museum grounds
  (414) 224-3854
- Juneteenth Day Celebration
  Dr. Martin Luther King Jr. Drive
  (414) 372-3770
- Polish Fest
  Henry Maier Festival Park
  www.polishfest.org

June-July

- Summerfest
  Henry Maier Festival Park
  www.summerfest.com

July

- Bastille Days
  Cathederal Square Park
  www.easttown.com/info/Bastille%20Days/bdindex
- Festa Italiana
  Henry Maier Festival Park
  www.festaitaliana.com

Ambassador Hotel

ACCOMMODATIONS

When Rick Wiegand bought the Ambassador Hotel in 1995, the once-elegant facility had fallen into disrepair. Designed by Peacock and Frank, known for their Art Deco theaters, and built in 1927, the hotel was a celebrated place for social events in its glory years. Fortunately, in spite of its decline, none of the original architectural details had been removed or destroyed, and renovation unearthed stunning marble floors beneath green shag carpet and beautifully detailed crown moulding hidden by dropped ceilings. After a multi-million dollar renovation, the Ambassador once again proudly displays original etched bronze elevator doors, elegant chandeliers and terrazzo floors. All 133 rooms come with world-class service and premium amenities, such as down pillows and comforters, upscale Aveda products and 24-hour room service. The Ambassador provides free parking and complimentary shuttle service to metro Milwaukee attractions, such as sports events and theaters. Try superb New American cuisine, such as Thai Curried Rack of Lamb, in the Envoy Restaurant, or delight in the lighter fare at the Caffé Deco coffee shop. Weekends bring live jazz to the Envoy Lounge, where friends can gather for superior libations. Whether you are looking up at the bold Ambassador lettering that shouts from the rooftop, enjoying the modern amenities or the meticulous restoration of architectural elements, you can be sure of one thing—the Ambassador is back and here to stay. Come see for yourself with a stay at this classic hotel from the age of Art Deco.

2308 W Wisconsin Avenue, Milwaukee WI
(414) 345-5000 or (888) 322-DECO (3326)
www.ambassadormilwaukee.com

The Astor Hotel

ACCOMMODATIONS

The Astor Hotel on Lake Michigan is the symbol of elegance, history and charm. Completed in 1920 for businessman Walter Schroeder, the hotel retains many period details. Stained glass, an antique grandfather clock and works by regional artist Francisco Spicuzza welcome you in the lobby. Original brass, laundry chutes and chandeliers set the mood. Guestrooms offer views of the city or Lake Michigan. All suites come with a full kitchen and dining area. Studio apartments and three-bedroom residences up to 3,000 square feet in size are available. If you prefer to have someone else do the cooking, the Astor Street Restaurant can meet your needs. Steak, prime rib and the fish fry are just some of the popular menu items. A delightful Sunday brunch is also available. Special events are no problem at the Astor, which has ballroom and banquet facilities for up to 300. The hotel is ideal for weddings, corporate meetings and parties. If you need a smaller space, consider the Renaissance Room, which can accommodate up to 125. Take advantage of the fitness center and on-site beauty salon so that you look your best before the big event. The Astor is close to the Grand Avenue shops, the Bradley Center and the Marcus Center for the Performing Arts. It is listed on the National Register of Historic Places. Whether you're looking for a place to hang your hat for the night or a furnished apartment to live in, consider the Astor Hotel, a historic treasure and the jewel of Milwaukee.

924 E Juneau Avenue, Milwaukee WI
(414) 271-4220, (800) 558-0200 or in Wisconsin (800) 242-0355
www.theastorhotel.com

The Pfister Hotel

ACCOMMODATIONS

Lose yourself in the elegance and gracious hospitality of a bygone era with a stay at the Pfister Hotel, named by *Condé Nast Traveler* as one of the World's Best Places to Stay. This AAA Four-Diamond hotel first opened in 1893, thanks in part to an elite group of Milwaukee citizens who were dedicated to creating a grand hotel in the heart of the city. Among this group was Guido Pfister, a man well known for his philanthropic endeavors whose untimely death prompted his children, Charles and Louise, to step in and finish the project as a memorial to their beloved father. The stunning hotel features extraordinary architecture and a world-class Victorian art collection. Located just three blocks from the shores of Lake Michigan, the Pfister offers 307 lavishly appointed rooms and suites, a swimming pool on the 23rd floor and Blu, one of Milwaukee's most sophisticated martini and wine bars. Hotel dining includes award winning cuisine from Café at the Pfister and Café Rouge, as well as 24-hour fine dining room service for your convenience. The Pfister Hotel's elegant lobby lounge features a gold trimmed ceiling mural, a live pianist and a striking hearth that has been a community gathering place for over a century. This glorious Old World hotel, with its personable and professional staff, is the ideal place to host gala events, intimate corporate functions and weddings. Enjoy a distinguished hotel experience designed for the 21st century traveler at the Pfister Hotel.

424 E Wisconsin Avenue, Milwaukee WI
(414) 390-3828
www.thepfisterhotel.com

Cream City Ribbon

ARTS & CRAFTS

In 1988, Lorette Russenberger bought a failed ribbon making business with antiquated equipment through an IRS auction. Although nothing about Lorette's background—she holds a Ph.D. in architectural history and has worked in art restoration—appears to be preparation for Cream City Ribbon, her purchase proved visionary as consumers looked to replace plastic ribbon with a natural product. Cream City makes a form of non-woven cotton ribbon that is hard to find, because the equipment to produce it is no longer made. Lorette's equipment was imported from Germany in the 1920s. Instead of using complex weaving equipment to interlace warp and weft, Cream City creates ribbon by laying cotton yarns parallel to each other and bonding them together with adhesive. The adhesive creates a crisp product that holds its shape, can be curled, shredded or printed for good-looking gift packaging. Cream City Ribbon can be custom designed and printed with words or images. The acid and lignin-free ribbon is also ideal for scrapbooking, card making and paper crafts. "Our mission is quality in our product, excellence in our service, value to our customers and respect for the environment," says Lorette. Retailers, manufacturers and events planners can search for a distributor through the website, while others can find Cream City Ribbon at Broadway Paper in Milwaukee or on the website.

(414) 277-1221
www.creamcityribbon.com

Loop Yarn Shop

ARTS & CRAFTS

Knitting and crocheting have become hot pastimes. Paparazzi have spotted Hollywood stars such as Julia Roberts and Russell Crowe knitting in public. The average age of knitters and crocheters is dropping fast. College students and even young children, both boys and girls, are picking up fiber hobbies. Loop Yarn Shop can help you get started and add skills to your repertoire. Loop Yarn Shop specializes in sensual natural fibers, including alpaca, silk, bamboo, cashmere, organic cotton and blends. The store stocks a full range of accessories: needles, hooks, buttons and knitting or crochet bags. Caitlin Walsh, owner of the shop, learned knitting and crocheting from her mother, Patricia, who also instructs and designs for Loop. Caitlin went on to graduate from the Maryland Institute College of Art with a major in fiber. Whether you're a beginner or a master knitter or crocheter, Caitlin and Patricia bring their experience and training to bear to help you find the best fibers and patterns. Caitlin and Patricia design their own patterns and can therefore help customers create truly personalized items. Customers are free to come in, sit down and knit or crochet up a storm. Instructors hold classes for every skill level, from Knit and Crochet 101 to Intarsia knitting and lace crocheting. Come to Loop Yarn Shop for individualized customer service and specialized yarn, instruction and supplies.

2900 S Delaware Avenue, Milwaukee WI
(414) 481-4843
www.loopyarnshop.com

Artist and Display Supply Company

ARTS & CRAFTS

Artist and Display Supply Company stocks just about anything you can imagine for the fine artist or craftsperson. It has been supplying the Milwaukee area since 1936, and occupies a full city block. This store is filled with ideas and inspiration as well as all the art materials to follow through on that inspiration. You can take a class in drawing or painting or choose from a variety of other classes, geared for beginners through advanced students. The shop features demonstrations and a knowledgeable staff committed to opening artistic adventures to everyone, from children through adults. The store also highlights unique gifts and handmade papers. Each holiday is greeted with an unusual collection of ornaments and decorations. An online catalog puts the vast inventory of the store at your fingertips, but only a visit here exposes customers to an exciting and friendly atmosphere that makes browsing the aisles the beginning for many creative projects. The store is open seven days a week, but closed on Sundays during the summer months. Visit Artist and Display Supply Company to put your imagination to work. Ask to meet Erica, the store's mascot boxer dog. Well-behaved dogs are welcome to shop with their owners.

9015 W Burleigh Street, Milwaukee WI
(414) 442-9100 or (800) 722-7450
www.artistanddisplay.com

Melk Music

ARTS & CRAFTS

The staff at Melk Music has been helping people make beautiful music for half a century. Melk Music is a trusted name for new and used instrument sales, rental, repair and restoration. The large selection of band and orchestral instruments include quality manufacturers such as Bach, Buffet, Glaesel and Selmer. Melk Music is the only dealer in Wisconsin to stock Schilke trumpets. You can try out any instrument in the store before you buy it, and peruse the stock of accessories and sheet music as well. Melk Music also provides studios for private lessons by some of Milwaukee's finest music teachers. The repair shop performs general clcaning, maintcnancc, ovcrhauls and custom modifications. New state-of-the-art, ultrasonic cleaning processes are used, which are safer for both the instrument and the environment. The staff can complete most repairs within a week. *Milwaukee Magazine* has again named Melk Music the "best place in town to get your horn fixed." Philip Melk, Sr. and Philip Melk, Jr. established the repair shop in 1956. Now third-generation owner Fred Melk continues to provide customers with quality instruments and repair service. When you visit Melk Music, you and your instrument are always in good hands, whatever your musical needs.

8625 W Adler Street, Milwaukee WI
(414) 771-0900
www.melkmusic.com

The Eisner-American Museum of Advertising & Design

ATTRACTIONS

Elaine Eisner created The Eisner-American Museum of Advertising & Design to showcase the social, historical and aesthetic implications of advertising and design. Opened in 2000, it is the only museum of its kind in the country. The Museum is located in a historic building in Milwaukee's Third Ward. The 10,000-square-foot display space hosts both permanent and changing exhibits. The Eisner celebrates advertising and design from all eras and media, from print to television to computers. You'll see interactive displays for all ages. You can record your own commercial in a radio studio by reading a famous advertisement or singing a commercial jingle. The Eisner can even make an elegant setting for your wedding, corporate gala or business seminar. Smaller meeting rooms are available for luncheons and gatherings. In addition to fostering public awareness of the influential role of advertising and design on society, The Eisner also serves as a resource for design students, advertising professionals and educators. Group guided tours, including school tours, are available. The Museum is dedicated to the memory of William F. Eisner, a mentor to many in the advertising field. Founder Elaine Eisner was William's wife. Come see for yourself how popular culture meets art at The Eisner-American Museum of Advertising & Design.

208 N Water Street, Milwaukee WI
(414) 847-3290
www.theeisner.com

Milwaukee Institute of Art & Design

ATTRACTIONS

The only independent, four-year college of art and design in Wisconsin, the Milwaukee Institute of Art & Design (MIAD) features nationally renowned galleries and a BFA program. The School holds a special position in the life of its students and the community at large. MIAD's two public galleries, the Frederick Layton Gallery and Brooks Stevens Gallery of Industrial Design, are open year-round and committed to the exposition of critical issues in art and design. MIAD was founded in 1974 and is fully accredited to award the bachelor of fine arts degree in 11 majors. Its alumni work as industrial designers, communication designers, illustrators, interior and architectural designers, photographers, sculptors and artists throughout Wisconsin and the nation. MIAD's time-based media major fills a fast-growing and critical economic niche, providing the professionals needed in animation, video and interactive digital media. Nearly 90 percent of graduates are employed within their first year of graduation. Because of the college's community service course requirement, which encompasses research and 50 hours of community service, MIAD graduates enter society with a sense of social responsibility and the ability to transform the world civically, economically and artistically. MIAD also engages thousands of community members annually through its continuing and youth education programs, arts educator institute, and visiting artists' lectures and programs. Through its Visual Resources Design Group, MIAD provides affordable design services to the non-profit community. To visit the college's Third Ward galleries and campus, call the Milwaukee Institute of Art & Design.

273 E Erie Street, Milwaukee WI
(414) 847-3200
www.miad.edu

Canfora Bakery

BAKERIES, COFFEE & TEA

The next time you visit the Milwaukee area, you'll want to discover something that locals already know: Canfora Bakery is the best bakery in town. This family-owned and operated bakery is staffed by Rosa and Carl Canfora. They are joined most days by their daughters Natalie, Bianca and Carla. Since 1981, the Canforas have been serving up a full range of baked wonder, from doughnuts, cookies and canoli, to breads, rolls, tarts, éclairs and many, many specialty desserts, including wedding cakes. Rosa's real whipped cream cakes are regionally famous. The Canforas also lay claim to one of the best deli selections in town, which makes for a busy and popular lunch hour. On Sunday mornings, locals line up for the hot ham and rolls. The Canforas are a close-knit family who treat their employees and customers like family. Carl has worked in bakeries since he was a child. After he met Rosa, she fell in love with baking, as well. The rest, as they say, is history. The Canforas opened their first bakery on the south side of Milwaukee. They moved to Bay View in 1997. Do yourself a favor the next time you're in the area. Visit the Canfora family bakery and treat yourself to the fruits of their amazing culinary talents.

1100 E Oklahoma Avenue, Milwaukee WI
(414) 486-7747
www.foodspot.com/canforabakery

Bella Caffe

BAKERIES, COFFEE & TEA

Bella Caffe in Milwaukee's historic Third Ward gives you plenty of reasons for stepping away from the ordinary. Owners Tim Talsky and Jim Nowlen have made Bella famous with the combination of atmosphere, coffee drinks and lunch options here and are a presence at many community events. They serve a full line of espresso drinks as well as hot cider and fresh squeezed lemonade. Their staff attends seminars to learn the fine points of brewing and tasting. You can enjoy your morning coffee with oatmeal, a fresh bagel, scone or muffin. Lunch features quiches, sandwiches, salads and several soup choices, brought to you by Bella's sister business, the Soup Market. Daily soup specials change and might include African peanut and chicken, tomato bisque or Mardi Gras chili. A dessert of cheesecake or flan is well worth your consideration. If you're coming in before or after a show, bring in your ticket stub for a discount. Bella also offers catering services. The historic building is wonderfully inviting with brick walls, cherry wood counters, high ceilings and huge windows. In Italian, Bella Caffe means *beautiful coffee*. Come on by and discover just how beautiful coffee can be.

189 N Milwaukee Street, Milwaukee WI
(414) 273-5620
www.bellacaffe.com

Photo by Debbie Pagel

Eat Cake!

BAKERIES, COFFEE & TEA

Some of the world's most talented artists are largely self-taught. Jack London taught himself to write, Grandma Moses taught herself to paint, and Debbie Pagel taught herself to bake. The proof of her excellence is available at Milwaukee's Eat Cake! Since 2003, Eat Cake! has specialized in creating cakes for weddings and other occasions. The store's inspiration comes from two segments of Debbie's past. The first was her entrepreneurial stint as a young teen, when she made a few bucks baking special occasion cakes and pastries for her friends. The second was her education in fine arts at the Milwaukee Institute of Art & Design. Debbie combines knowledge from those experiences to create individually designed cakes that reflect the style of the occasion being celebrated. She was once scolded by a customer at a library opening who believed the cake delivery was late. The angry librarian was standing right next to what looked like a stack of books. It was actually the cake. Debbie has also created a replica of Milwaukee's City Hall for a mayoral inaugural, a four-layer cake with each level resembling a different animal skin and a rendition of Edvard Munch's famous painting *The Scream*. Debbie's penchant for adding a new twist to old ideas is evident in her clever motto: From Traditional to Ridiculous, It's All Sublime. Visit Eat Cake! for the rare chance to buy a cake baked by a true artist.

4303 W Vliet Street, Milwaukee WI
(414) 344-3119
www.eatcakemilwaukee.com

Wild Flour Bakery & Café

BAKERIES, COFFEE & TEA

Dolly Mertens, owner of Wild Flour Bakery & Café, wanted to live surrounded by bread. She now has her wish. Since 1996, Dolly, and her husband, Greg, have baked a variety of artisan breads fresh daily. Their son Josh has been part of the business from the start, and such is his feel for dough that Dolly calls him the brains behind the bread. Loaves are hand shaped and baked in a brick oven on a stone hearth. All are free of fat, sugar and preservatives so you can enjoy them without guilt. You'll love the sourdough olive rosemary or cranberry walnut bread. Apricot pecan, jalapeño cheese and rye are also popular. Wild Flour offers rolls, organic breads and specialty homemade cookies, including the popular no-flour Monster Cookies. You'll find seasonal pies and mouth watering mixed fruit tarts. Enjoy a quick bite on the patio or a sit-down lunch of homemade soup, fresh salad, and a hot or cold sandwich on Wild Flour bread. With four locations in the area, plus four farmer's markets in the summer, you're sure to find Wild Flour nearby. *Milwaukee Magazine* says that Wild Flour Bakery & Café has the best bread in town and the *Milwaukee Journal Sentinel* reports it has the best pie. Come taste the award-winning difference for yourself.

2800 W Lincoln Avenue, Milwaukee WI (414) 831-1692
275 W Wisconsin Avenue, Milwaukee WI (414) 298-9858
422 E Lincoln Avenue, Milwaukee WI (414) 727-8145
1205 Milwaukee Avenue, South Milwaukee WI (414) 571-1298
www.wildflour.net

Aggie's Cakes & Pastries

BAKERIES, COFFEE & TEA

Some people ponder great philosophical questions, like whether it's better to be or not to be. Others have slightly more mundane questions, like which place serves the best strudel in Milwaukee. According to *Milwaukee Magazine,* the answer to the strudel question is Aggie's Cakes & Pastries. Aggie's is a second-generation operation with roots in Michigan, where Aggie Purcell's parents opened the family's first bakery in 1977. The Milwaukee shop opened in 2002, and Aggie operates it with the assistance of her brother Nuccio Bongiorno and her mother, Nina. Aggie does all of the baking, with the exception of a delicacy known as Sundays Hot Ham and Rolls. Nuccio is responsible for that one. Aggie's, a full-service bakery, is well known for its eight varieties of fruit dumplings, cheesecakes and cookies. The shop also serves tortes, mini-pastries and pies. The bakery is especially renowned for creating more than 200 wedding cakes per year, complete with toppers and accessories. You'll find banana nut, cherry nut and tiramisu here. Visit Aggie's Cakes & Pastries for baked delicacies from parents who taught their children that baking is an everyday delight.

1800 E Howard Avenue, Milwaukee WI
(414) 482-1288

T.H. Stemper Co.

BUSINESS & SERVICES

As churches tend to the needs of their flocks, so T.H. Stemper Co. tends to the needs of churches. T.H. Stemper's owners, the Stemper family, pride themselves in their ability to furnish an entire church, down to dressing the choir. T.H. Stemper's offers everything a church or person would need to celebrate a religious occasion. That includes everything from liturgical robes to statuary, candles and communion supplies for all Christian denominations. T.H. Stemper is the largest provider of nativity scenes in the entire Midwest. In addition, the company offers restoration of statuary and sacred items such as chalices to deal with years of wear and tear. It also offers a consignment center for churches to resell items they have outgrown. This has the effect of preserving these precious items. T.H. Stemper has often found itself reselling items made by its founder in the company's early years. Thomas H. Stemper founded the enterprise in 1911 when he purchased a bankrupt statuary firm. He later merged it with a religious goods store and incorporated both under the T.H. Stemper name in 1946. Ownership passed to Thomas's sons and then to grandsons Peter, Dan, Joe, John and Jim and their mother, Jean. The Stempers invite churches and individuals to T.H. Stemper for all their religious outfitting needs.

1125 E Potter Avenue, Milwaukee WI
(414) 744-3610 or (800) 686-3610
www.stempers.com

Milwaukee Map Store

BUSINESS & SERVICES

For those of us who have a special fascination with maps, a visit to the Milwaukee Map Store and Service is like a visit to heaven. The retail outlet is filled with old and new maps from every country. Special maps are available for hunting and fishing. Milwaukee Map Store and Service is an agent for the U.S. Geological Survey and can provide any of that service's 52,000 maps. Puzzles, games and educational materials are also on hand. Brothers Quentin, Charles and Jan Swain, the owners, are the second generation of Swains in the map business. Their father had a mapping service as well. Milwaukee Map Store and Service has developed and produced in-house a series of area maps focusing on Wisconsin and the upper Midwest. In addition to the retail business of selling maps and globes, the map service publishes custom maps to meet the specialized needs of businesses and individuals. The service has responded to many unusual requests over the years. One example was a map of Wisconsin showing the distribution of pheasants. Laminating, mounting and framing services are available in-house as well. Map service products are available on-line to those who cannot visit the store. Whether you are a map enthusiast or your interests are strictly practical, a visit to Milwaukee Map Store and Service is an extraordinary experience.

959 N Mayfair Road, Milwaukee WI
(414) 774-1300 or (800) 525-3822
www.mapservice.com

Jerry Mitchell Briefcase Gallery

FASHION

Add an extra touch of elegance to your work ensemble with stately briefcases and organizers from the Jerry Mitchell Briefcase Gallery. Owner and founder Jerry Mitchell escaped from communist Romania and came to the United States for a better life, bringing with him degrees in math, engineering and philosophy, which he used to create profoundly different components for his unique cases. Mitchell, who opened his shop in 1982, now holds a variety of U.S. patents for his varied closures and improvements, including a distinctive modular handle with integrated frame assembly. "Each one is a work of art," says Mitchell, who carefully crafts the briefcases from the finest saddle and European leather with locks and straps of superior design and workmanship. The gallery, located in downtown Milwaukee's historic Third Ward district, also offers custom organizers, satchel bags and classic purses, as well as totes, duffles and drawstring bags. Look for coin purses, cosmetic bags and money clips along with protective lotions and saddle soap to care for your leather products. Rediscover the luxury of leather with finely crafted briefcases and accessories from the Jerry Mitchell Briefcase Gallery, purveyors of the world's best briefcases.

226 N Water Street, Milwaukee WI
(414) 272-5942 or (800) 583-0946

Photo by John Grant

Aala Reed

FASHION

For five years, Laura Lutter Cole worked for a large accounting firm, running the Entrepreneur of the Year program. She watched people with vision, energy and creativity as they started their own businesses. These go-getters became an inspiration to Laura, and in 2001, she joined their ranks and opened Aala Reed. During her time spent in the office, Laura saw men struggle to find contemporary, fashionable menswear that worked well in any setting, from business casual to weekend wear. She took this information to heart when she opened her boutique. Fashion conscious men no longer need to travel to Chicago or New York for the latest designer apparel, because Aala Reed offers lines from many exclusive brands, including Ted Baker of London, Hugo Boss and Gant. In 2006, Aala Reed expanded to offer a women's boutique with versatile clothing that takes you from day to evening, such as dresses and business casual, as well as denim, slacks and shirts. A wide selection of jewelry, shoes, bags and other accessories add the final touches. When browsing the racks, vibrant paintings on the walls are sure to catch your eye. Each one is hand painted by a Haitian artist, and proceeds from the paintings benefit the medical needs of rural Haitians and support the arts in that impoverished country. Enjoy the trip to Aala Reed, where Laura helps men and women fill the gaps in their wardrobes with contemporary fashions for all occasions.

1320 E Brady Street, Milwaukee WI
(414) 226-2252
www.aalareed4men.com

Kloiber Jewelers

FASHION

For the past 80 years, Kloiber Jewelers has been selling and repairing fine jewelry in the downtown Milwaukee area. This long-lived shop was founded by Frank Kloiber and his son Clyde and inherited by Karin Volz and other employees in 2001. Karin became sole owner of the company in June 2006, and with the help of her loyal staff continues to offer the same excellent service and meticulous attention to detail that made Frank and Clyde famous. Kloiber Jewelers offers a full line of fine jewelry made from 14-karat and 18-karat gold, platinum and sterling silver, including wedding sets, engagement rings, necklaces and bracelets. The shop also specializes in diamonds and colored gemstones, as well as corporate gifts, fine watches and clocks and exquisite giftware. This is the ideal place to find the latest designs from such designers as Hidalgo, Claude Thibaudeau and Storywheels. It's also the place to have one of your precious treasures repaired to perfection. The shop has kept meticulous records of every purchase since it opened in 1926 and keeps registered wish lists, helpful tools in choosing gifts for past clients and loved ones. If you require engraving or an appraisal, Kloiber Jewelers has the necessary expertise. Whatever your jewelry needs, come to Kloiber's, where Karin and her staff take their reputation for quality personally.

411 E Wisconsin Avenue, Milwaukee WI
(414) 276-2457
www.kloiberjewelers.com

Photos by John Paul Greco

Roger Stevens Menswear

FASHION

Roger Stevens Menswear features the finest menswear available along with incomparable customer service. Located off the lobby in the historic Pfister Hotel, Roger Stevens is prepared to serve the business professional, the hotel guest who just lost his luggage or the man headed to the ballpark. Owner Steve Schroeder has been providing Milwaukee's best menswear since 1976. A community leader, Steve helped to launch the East Town Association with George Watts, bringing together more than 100 businesses to help spur growth in the East Town area of downtown Milwaukee. Steve was a key player in organizing the first Bastille Days Festival more than 25 years ago and was its executive director for a decade. He takes his business seriously and it is reflected in his shop. Equipped with a full-service tailor shop, Roger Stevens is prepared for same-day alterations. Tailored clothing from Hickey-Freeman, Samuelsohn and Southwick are available off-the-rack and made-to-measure. Other resources include Robert Talbot, Bobby Jones and Individualized Custom Shirts. The level of service makes shopping a pleasure. The staff have been known to meet people at the airport, deliver clothing to a local venue or whatever it takes to serve their customers. They'll consult you on your wardrobe needs and even assist in evaluating your closet. They understand that the clothing you purchase at Roger Stevens is not only a reflection of you, but of their company as well. When it's important for you to look your very best, head to Roger Stevens Menswear in the historic Pfister Hotel.

428 E Wisconsin Avenue, Milwaukee WI
(888) 422-9010 or (414) 277-9010
www.RogerStevens.com

A. J. Ugent Furs

FASHION

For three generations the Ugent family has offered furs of quality and distinction to American and overseas customers. Morris Ugent came from a Lithuanian family of tailors and opened his Milwaukee fur store in 1922. His son A. J. worked for him and opened A.J. Ugent Furs in its present location in 1959. A. J.'s son Rodney is the current owner and runs the store with sister Lori Nashban. Ugent Furs adorns its customers in mink, sable, chinchilla and fox. You'll find luxurious beaver, lynx and raccoon, too, fashioned into full-length and three-quarter-length coats, jackets, capes and other outerwear. The variety at Ugent includes exquisite knitted fur jackets and capes, which use a process invented 20 years ago for a casual, modern style. Sheared fur provides still another look, which resembles the richest velvet. You'll find wool coats here, too, plus shearling and leather coats with fur trim. Such accessories as fur hats, headbands and collars promise to wrap you in luxurious softness and style. Ugent's master furriers hand pick the furs, then fabricate them into top-of-the-line apparel. These experts also repair, restyle, condition and appraise furs, and offer storage in climate-controlled vaults. For furs of unsurpassed luxury and styling, visit A. J. Ugent Furs.

8333 W Capitol Drive, Milwaukee WI
(414) 463-7777 or (800) 544-3877
www.ugentfurs.com

freckle face

FASHION

For fashionable clothing for newborns to eight-year-olds, visit freckle face. Owner Deanna Inniss knows what's happening in children's fashion; she brings her New York City know-how to Milwaukee, with cute, classic styles by new and emerging designers as well as exclusive offerings. The store features clothing from Bluebird and Pura Vida, in addition to attractive footwear not readily available elsewhere. It stocks a complete line of attractive children's bedding. Little ones enjoy the classic books and toys sold at freckle face, and new moms find all the baby clothes and accessories they need. Expectant moms delight in the attractive maternity tees and diaper bags. Though the store is in the kids' clothing business, Deanna treats customers in a manner that's reminiscent of an upscale clothing boutique for adults. Very kid-friendly, freckle face has animal crackers on the counter and a coloring table to keep kids occupied while mom and dad shop. The store hosts several classes for parents and kids, including a Mommy & Me jewelry making class. On winter nights, parents gather to learn to knit while enjoying wine and cheese. For stylish clothing, bedding and toys, visit freckle face.

407 E Buffalo Street, Milwaukee WI
(414) 298-1488
www.frecklefaceboutique.com

HERS

FASHION

HERS is owner Elissa Elser's fashion dream come true. The Milwaukee boutique owner has dreamed of owning a store like this one since she was 16 years old. She earned two college degrees, in fashion design and accounting, to bring her dream to fruition in 2004. When you walk into this store, your fashion dreams will come true, too. HERS, located in the historic warehouse district, offers a large selection of designer women's clothing, ranging from casual jeans and t-shirts to cute party outfits from such designers as Susana Monaco, Louis Verdad and Isabella Fiori. If you're looking for clothes for the boardroom, consider a suit by Philippe Adec or Tom K. Nguyen. You'll also find jewelry, belts, handbags and dresses right off the runways of New York, Los Angeles, Boston and Paris. Expectant mothers can remain stylish with the shop's large selection of fashionable maternity wear. Elissa and her friendly staff will help you find the most attractive styles for your body type. You can also hire a personal shopper here to bring you clothing for your inspection. The personal touch is important to Elissa, who makes a point of learning her customers' names and tastes. Come in to HERS, where fashion dreams come true.

309 N Water Street, Milwaukee WI
(414) 273-HERS (4377)

Ilze Heider Leather Designs

FASHION

At Ilze Heider Leather Designs, you'll see functional purses and small leather accessories that are true works of art. Ilze's studio contains fun and colorful purses and small soft leather accessories, such as checkbook covers, day planners and credit card holders. Ilze's true passion lies in the purses, which range from small basic-black items to large tote bags with pockets in a rainbow of colors. Ilze, who was born in Latvia, employs many Latvian motifs and techniques, such as embossed leather with hand pressed dyed designs. Her work also features Celtic and art deco designs as well as block printing. You can spot a bag with fringe or one decorated with beads. Ilze does not repeat her designs, so all work is one-of-a-kind. Ilze took up sewing in grade school and sold handmade creations to fellow employees at her first job. In 1980, she turned her talent into a full-time business. She moved into a studio space that was as yet unpainted and without electricity. It took plenty of work to turn it into the comfortable site it is today. In addition to the studio, you can also find Ilze's work at regional art shows and in boutiques and galleries nationwide. Look for her designs at the Morning Glory Gallery at Marcus Center for the Performing Arts downtown. For leather handbags and accessories you'll love, seek out Ilze Heider Leather Designs.

133 W Pittsburgh Avenue, Suite 308, Milwaukee WI
(414) 272-4606
www.ilze.com

J. Bird Boutique

FASHION

What is the best place to find something to wear on Friday night? According to the *Milwaukee Sentinel Journal,* it's J. Bird Boutique. The shop takes its name from the childhood nickname of one of its owners, Jennifer Putney. Jennifer's partner is Robert Leschke. At J. Bird, you can find items from emerging and hard-to-find designers. The shop stocks clothing from Lara Miller, Diane Medak, Johnny Was and other names. Trunk shows are a regular event. J. Bird also carries a large variety of casual wear, including jeans, shorts, tanks and t-shirts. The boutique has an array of fancy footwear from Dick and Jayne as well as the British-based J Shoes. Looking for Hanky Panky (the lingerie brand)? You can find it here. Tammy Spice and Jennifer Mog supply jewelry, and Kyle Meyer provides glass goods. All of the jewelry in the store is created by local artists. The store is a fun and comfortable place for women. The helpful staff can assist you in finding the best clothes for your size, shape and budget. If you're looking for a special girls' night out, you can book the store for an entire evening. J. Bird will provide catering and discounts for everyone in your party. Women looking for the best clothing, jewelry and shoes are invited to take wing and fly to J. Bird Boutique.

415 E Menomonee Street, Milwaukee WI
(414) 727-6553
www.jbirdboutique.blogspot.com

Lela

FASHION

Where can you have a glass of wine, let your children feed the pet fish, take a belly dancing class and buy designer clothes and funky accessories? Owners Stephanie Laraine Sherman and Carrie Lee Arrouet put this unique blend together at Lela, located in Milwaukee's historic Third Ward. The partners opened the shop after meeting in a leadership development class and deciding to fulfill their shared dream of owning a business. Their store's name is a combination of their middle names. Lela blends the work of local, new and emerging designers with vintage clothing and designer label consignment pieces. You'll find fashion-forward formalwear, dresses, skirts and sportswear like the items appearing on Chicago and New York runways. Look for flirty formals by local designer Shanel Regier and up-to-the-minute casual wear from Trina Turk and Tibi. You can relax and enjoy your shopping adventure at Lela, knowing your children will find amusement, too. Lela takes part in a huge Milwaukee fashion show every September, which is the Wisconsin equivalent of New York Fashion Week. To help you look and feel great in your purchases, Lela offers Pilates and belly dancing classes. For clothing designs along with a warm and unusual welcome, visit Lela.

321 N Broadway, Milwaukee WI
(414) 727-4855
www.lelaboutique.com

Miss Groove

FASHION

Miss Groove in Milwaukee can dress and accessorize you in a way that is youthful and fun, just like the name implies. From weekend looks to business casual, you'll find high quality fabrics, including denim and tweed, and such offerings as funky sweaters that can be worn in every season. Check out the selection of beautiful jackets, dresses, trousers and hats. Why not add a handbag or some jewelry to round out your new look? Browse the popular Italian leather handbags or take home a Matt and Nat bag. You'll find selections priced to fit any budget, all reflecting the shop's attention to a youthful clientele as well as to those with a youthful attitude. For undergarments, walk across the street to the Miss Groove annex, Casa Bella. This sister shop features clothing by American, Italian and French designers and specializes in loungewear, foundation garments, robes and slippers. You'll see bras in hard to find sizes. A bridal registry is available as well as private shopping dates for men who want to buy something special for their ladies without feeling intimidated. Whether you're shopping for one thing in particular or a whole outfit from bra to bag, come see the experts at Miss Groove and Casa Bella, and you're sure to leave looking your very best.

1225 E Brady Street, Milwaukee WI
(414) 298-9185
www.missgroove.com

Three Graces

FASHION

Located in Milwaukee's historic Third Ward, Three Graces is a contemporary boutique for women's shoes, clothing and accessories. Co-owners Pam Kerwin and Joanne Szymaszek discussed going into business together for several years before finally taking the plunge. The two friends jumped into the fray, because they believed downtown Milwaukee needed a retail outlet for fashion-forward women's clothing. Their outstanding selection of clothing lines, from such designers as Max Studio, BCBG, Three Dot and Joe's Jeans, can meet your needs for a wedding gown, a night on the town or a casual afternoon. Three Graces carries some shoe brands not available elsewhere in Wisconsin. They also offer a separate bridal salon featuring not-so-traditional wedding dresses and gowns with a contemporary look. You can find just the right purse to complete your look and get your jewelry repaired here, too. Pam and Joanne complement their merchandise with an insistence on a high level of service that focuses on making you look beautiful without making you feel besieged by overly aggressive attention. You can reserve the shop for private parties and receive consultation in closet design and wardrobe development. For a look that completes and complements you, visit Three Graces.

207 E Buffalo Street, Milwaukee WI
(414) 273-3350
www.threegracesonline.com

Vieux et Nouveau

FASHION

Vieux et Nouveau (old and new) stocks fashion for the hip woman: contemporary, vintage and handcrafted artisan pieces. Vieux et Nouveau also specializes in fashion to fit women with curves. Owner Heidi Calaway has a background in fashion and strives to offer edgy, fun, fashionable, runway style in sizes up to 15/16. She works very hard to find great pieces that real women can wear. Heidi personally selects items for her store that are often one-of-a-kind, ranging from casual to office to dressy. Professional women with flair shop the boutique for shirts, skirts, dresses and slacks. You can finish your outfit with the perfect handbag, hat or a piece of quality sterling or natural stone jewelry. The service at Vieux et Nouveau is unparalleled. Heidi is more than just a salesperson. She is a fashion consultant. She will help you build your wardrobe and show you how to deploy each piece in many different ways. She offers personal shopping services, career consulting for businesses, hair and makeup referrals and fashion shows. One of her most popular events is the Very Fashionable Shopper, a party at the boutique where you and your friends can sip wine and nibble appetizers while enjoying discounts on shopping. Come to Vieux et Nouveau and let Heidi help you be the best that you can be.

1688 N Franklin Place, Milwaukee WI
(414) 287-9049
www.vieuxetnouveau.com

Boutique Bé bé

FASHION

If your child grows up to become a famous fashion designer, you could credit Boutique Bé bé for planting the seed. Since 1990, parents have been dressing their children in stylish clothing that they would otherwise have to go to Chicago to find. The shop brings in customers from all over the state, who are looking for apparel from Tea, E. Land and Marie Chantal along with German sweaters and coats from Giesswein. Discerning shoppers know that this is the only place in Wisconsin to find the Burberry line of fine clothing. Styles range from funky to conservative for girls up to size 16 and boys up to size 8. Visiting Boutique Bé bé is worth it just to browse the spectacular baby items. For years, families in and around Milwaukee have chosen this store as the place to register for baby gifts. Boutique Bé bé carries baptismal gowns as well as formal dresses for flower girls. Billie Kubly was one of the store's most devoted customers who shopped here for 16 years. When she found out that founder Barbara Hussussian was retiring, she couldn't imagine a Milwaukee without Boutique Bé bé, so she bought the business to keep it open. The half-price sales in January and July are legendary. Start developing your child's sense of style right away by shopping at Boutique Bé bé.

2630 N Downer Avenue, Milwaukee WI
(414) 964-BEBE (2323)

Gilles Frozen Custard

FUN FOODS

For most businesses, change is the key to survival, but in the case of Gilles Frozen Custard, a lack of major change is the formula for success. Milwaukee is full of early stories that mention the icy-cold custard at Gilles. Sixty-eight years later, that same custard, served at the same location, has a large and loyal following. Recently, *Milwaukee Magazine* named the custard the best in the city. Even the ownership has been remarkably stable in this legendary establishment, with just two ownership changes since Paul Gilles opened the restaurant in 1938. In 1977, Robert Linscott, who had worked at Gilles since the early 1940s, bought the restaurant and made it a year-round operation. In 1993, brothers Pat and Tom Linscott, who started working there in their teens, bought it. "If it works, don't change it," says Tim. "People come in and reminisce and I say, 'I remember being here when I was a kid.'" The biggest change at Gilles is the menu, which started out in the early days with hot dogs, root beer and vanilla custard. You can still get a great hot dog here, but you'll also find hot and cold sandwiches, side orders, desserts and 16 custard flavors. Bud Selig, baseball commissioner and former Brewers owner, has stopped in for a hot dog and soda nearly every day for over 29 years. Prepare for cool pleasure seven days a week with a visit to Gilles Frozen Custard.

Photo by Stu Spivack

7515 W Bluemound Road, Milwaukee WI
(414) 453-4875
www.gillesfrozencustard.com

Kallas Honey Farm

FUN FOODS

For three generations, the Kallas family has supplied the finest domestically produced honey to households and commercial operations throughout the Midwest. Founded by Master Beekeeper John P. Kallas in 1941, Kallas Honey Farm is now known as one of the largest family-owned honey packers in the Midwest, processing several million pounds annually. Its flagship brand is available in nearly 30 states. The farm has maintained high standards and supports the American Honey Producers. Kallas Honey Farm offers eight different varieties of honey produced in various regions of the country. Each one has its own flavor, color and aroma derived from the plants the bees were foraging, such as clover, alfalfa or orange blossom. No additional ingredients are ever added. The farm also offers specialty products like natural comb honey, natural raw honey and whipped honey. Kallas has grown into one of the Midwest's premier suppliers of honey as a commercial ingredient. All of these products are certified kosher by the Chicago Rabbinical Council. You will find this honey in nationally known brands, in products such as breads, deli meats, snacks, soft drinks and many others. Kallas Honey Farm ships honey in all sizes of containers, from small gift jars to tanker truck loads. For a difference you can taste, look for honey from Kallas Honey Farm.

(414) 462-3530
www.kallashoney.com

Nikki's Cookies & Confections

FUN FOODS

While working as an international model and living in England, Nikki Taylor tried different shortbreads from English recipe books, but found that nothing compared to the ancestral recipe passed down by her grandmother. Upon returning to Wisconsin, Nikki and partner Bill Danner started a cookie company to market American shortbread cookies. Today, Nikki's product line includes flavored shortbreads, chocolate layered cookies and holiday specialties, including a sugar cookie recipe from Nikki's mother, Eleanor. Nikki's commitment to using wholesome, high-quality ingredients has never wavered; she uses fresh Wisconsin products whenever possible, such as creamy grade AA Wisconsin farmers butter and cranberries. Nikki's products are kosher, all natural and free of preservatives. Widely recognized for their exquisite packaging with eye-catching graphics, Nikki's products are sold in all 50 states as well as Canada, England and Japan. Known for her whimsical cookie cutter shapes, Nikki also offers shortbread cookies dipped in lots of gourmet chocolate and hand-decorated. From chocolate keylime shortbread to Gingerbread Bear Paws, you'll find sweet creations perfect for gift giving and holiday events. Delight your family and friends with a gourmet confection from Nikki's Cookies & Confections. You can purchase Nikki's Cookies online or at various stores that sell gourmet cookies.

(414) 481-4899 or (800) 776-7107
www.nikkiscookies.com

Suzy's Cream Cheesecakes & Distinctive Desserts

FUN FOODS

For the past 23 years Suzy has been on a single quest, to create the very finest cheesecakes money can buy. That's why, with more than 40 variations on the theme of cheesecake, a Suzy's Cream Cheesecake will tempt even the most conscientious calorie counter. A Suzy's cheesecake starts out as a blend of two types of fresh cream cheese. To this is added only pure cane sugar, whole fresh eggs, real Madagascar vanilla and lemon juice. Crusts are made using butter—never shortening—and are hand pressed into each pan just before baking. As for chocolate, the only thing Suzy might add to her Callebaut Belgium Chocolate would be a little heavy cream. When nuts are needed, Suzy uses only the largest pecans and almonds she can find. Suzy started making cheesecakes at her family's white table cloth restaurant in the early 1980s to fill a gap in the dessert menu. After they became so popular that dining room patrons ordered whole cheesecakes to carry out, she opened her own store. Twenty-three years later Suzy's Cheesecakes are available in 18 states, and sold in over 1,000 of America's best grocery stores. If you're looking for an alternative to sending flowers or a fruit basket, Suzy's has been shipping her cheesecakes in brightly colored gift boxes via FedEx for more than 20 years. They will usually arrive in just two days, always cold and packaged with as much detail as she puts into all of her desserts.

5901 W Vliet Street, Milwaukee WI
(414) 453-2255 or (800) 828-1055
1775 E Bolivar Avenue, St. Francis WI
(414) 744-0816
www.suzys.com

Barclay Gallery & Garden Café

GALLERIES & FINE ART

The Barclay Gallery & Garden Café offers fine crafts, food and drink to discerning patrons. The gallery displays handmade crafts from more than 300 top artists. You'll find wood, ceramics, metal and other media fashioned into jewelry, vases, sculpture and other items both decorative and functional. The gallery has one of the largest collections of hand-blown glass ornaments in the region. At the restaurant, you can dine surrounded by beauty. Try a light meal of fresh soup, salad, and a sandwich or spring for a melt-in-your-mouth entrée. The weekend brunch is popular. A take-out coffee area also sells specialty beers, wine and wine accessories. Live music plays at the Barclay several nights a week. Other special events have included Tarot Tuesday, Wine Oh! Wednesday and Fish Fry'Day. Owner John LeBrun plans to add rooftop garden seating and an upstairs banquet hall with more art on the walls. John opened the business to escape the endless meetings, budgetary planning sessions and other demands of his job as senior vice president for a major publisher. He opened the restaurant to ensure that he had plenty of customers for the gallery, and he soon discovered how demanding—but satisfying—the restaurant trade can be. Join the throngs who have made Barclay Gallery & Garden Café one of Milwaukee's most popular destinations. You'll enjoy the visit.

158 S Barclay Street, Milwaukee WI
(414) 347-0500
www.barclaygalleryonline.com

Katie Gingrass Gallery

GALLERIES & FINE ART

The Katie Gingrass Gallery is a contemporary art and fine craft gallery located in the Historic Third Ward of downtown Milwaukee. Since Katie opened her gallery in 1984, she has been at the forefront of hosting exceptional exhibitions of the paintings, pastels and sculpture of regionally and nationally recognized artists. Gallery exhibitions change every other month, and local artists are regularly featured at Coquette Café, a revered French restaurant around the corner from the gallery. The Katie Gingrass Gallery represents fine contemporary craft artists working in ceramic, glass, wood, metal and fiber. Annually, Katie and her staff take fine collectible craft to the SOFA (Sculptural Objects Functional Art), an international art exposition at Navy Pier in Chicago. In addition, the Katie Gingrass Gallery is a Midwestern leader in providing corporate clients with art-related services including commissioned original works of art to fit any specific need. A large selection of art is available in all price ranges with framing, delivery and installation services included. Visit the Katie Gingrass Gallery, located just one block south of the Milwaukee Public Market in Milwaukee's premiere shopping district, or find out at more on its website.

241 N Broadway, Milwaukee WI
(414) 289-0855
www.gingrassgallery.com

Elaine Erickson Gallery

GALLERIES & FINE ART

The Elaine Erickson Gallery focuses on contemporary paintings, sculpture and works on paper. Also featured is an exquisite collection of African art, including masks, statuary, beadwork, textiles and utilitarian items. The gallery was established in 1994 in suburban Milwaukee. In 1998 the gallery relocated to the Historic Third Ward district, becoming part of its vibrant, artistically diverse community. Elaine personally selects all of the artwork represented in the gallery and is dedicated to maintaining a consistent level of quality. New and emerging artists are exhibited along with well-established painters, printmakers and sculptors. Originally educated in accounting, Elaine was hired to do the accounting for a well established art gallery and says, "I knew at that time, that this is the world I would be in for the rest of my career. Owning my own gallery is a dream come true." Elaine is a member of the Milwaukee Art Dealers Association and is very active within the arts community. Visit the Elaine Erickson Gallery today to view great pieces and to increase your understanding of art.

Tom Hoffman—*Oracle*, 7″ x 5″ Oil on Board

207 E Buffalo Street, Milwaukee WI
(414) 221-0613
www.eericksongallery.com

Landmarks Gallery & Restoration Studio

GALLERIES & FINE ART

To say that Landmarks Gallery & Restoration Studio carries a wide selection of fine art and prints would be a gross understatement. Landmarks Gallery carries the work of more than 1,000 artists and sculptors from around the world. This family-run business provides expert framing and restoration services, plus it will locate custom pieces and provide appraisals. When it comes to framing, the shop can accommodate any piece of art or memento, whether it is a tuna tail, a Civil War firearm or suit worn by Buddy Holly or Paul McCartney. Owners Huetta and J.P. Manion opened Landmarks Gallery after their own search for a painting for their home. They found paintings either too expensive or lacking in quality. After visiting a gallery in New England, they decided to become gallery owners themselves. They opened Landmarks Gallery in 1966 and since then have been providing quality framing and restoration services. Their daughter Mary oversees the framing department. All work is done on-site. Landmarks Gallery & Restoration Studio's quality service has earned them notice by Angie's List. Atlantique Exposition's New Years antique show invites them as specialists in restoration. For fine art of high quality at reasonable prices, or for express restoration needs, put Landmarks Gallery & Restoration Studio to work for you.

231 N 76th Street, Milwaukee WI
(414) 453-1620 or (800) 352-8892
www.landmarksgallery.com

Tory Folliard Gallery

GALLERIES & FINE ART

The Tory Folliard Gallery features contemporary art by the region's most accomplished artists. Established in 1988, the Milwaukee gallery focuses on landscape, still life and figurative art, showcasing nationally known painters, sculptors and photographers such as Eric Aho, Tom Uttech, Wolf Kahn and John Wilde. You will also discover works by Fred Stonehouse, Patrick Farrell, Judy Onofrio, Harold Gregor, Gladys Nilsson and glass artist Janusz Walentynowicz. Each month the gallery presents in-depth exhibitions. It is a regular exhibitor at international art fairs in Chicago, New York and Palm Beach. Tory Folliard Gallery is located in a large warehouse space in the Historic Third Ward, seven blocks from the Milwaukee Art Museum and two blocks from the Milwaukee Public Market.

Tory Folliard Gallery Interior Shot with Heads:
Bronze sculptures by Susan Evans and paintings by T.L. Solien

233 N Milwaukee Street, Milwaukee WI
(414) 273-7311
www.toryfolliard.com

Blush Beauty

HEALTH & BEAUTY

Are you ready to put your best face forward? Sarah Brucker, a professional makeup artist, stylist and image consultant, helps Milwaukee clients improve their face value in her trendy new beauty boutique. After freelancing for years in Los Angeles, New York, Las Vegas and Scottsdale, Sarah opened Blush Beauty in her hometown's Historic Third Ward in 2004. Here you'll find more than 30 trendy, upscale lines of cosmetics, fragrances, and skin and body care products, including DuWop, B-Kamins and men's luxury grooming products by Truefitt & Hill. Blush is also the only store in Wisconsin to sell Laura Mercier cosmetics. Sarah focuses on personal attention and product education while showing clients how cosmetics can enhance their looks and teaching them how to apply each product. A unique feature, the Brow Bar, showcases the expertise of esthetician and brow expert Laurel Carraway, who helps clients achieve the best brow shape for their faces. Clients can choose to be inspired by a celebrity's brow shape, if they wish, while sipping a glass of Blush's signature pink champagne. Blush also offers individualized facials in a facial room named Face Couture, plus makeup consultations and makeup application for special events such as weddings or model portfolios. Visit Blush Beauty, one of the hottest cosmetic boutiques in the Midwest, and let Sarah improve your look.

249 N Water Street, Milwaukee WI
(414) 272-1718
www.blushmilwaukee.com

Badalamenti Center for Advanced Aesthetic Dentistry

HEALTH & BEAUTY

Fascinated with the world of science and art, Peter Badalamenti D.D.S. merged two magnificent domains into one unique discipline—advanced aesthetic dentistry. His passion is in transforming the dis-ease of someone's unattractive smile into a beautiful and fully functional work of art. Highly trained in the specialized field of neuromuscular aesthetic dentistry, Dr. Badalamenti performs procedures to fully reposition the jaw, eliminating chronic jaw pain and in many cases headaches, in addition to correcting uneven smiles. Dr. Badalamenti has the skill, experience, critical eye and artistry to design a priceless smile for you without years of braces and painful surgery. To take a client who has either lived with an unattractive smile or has lived with years of neglect because of fear and reverse it all within a short time is tremendously gratifying to him. As a top restorative and implant dentist, Dr. Badalamenti's clients read like a who's who. People in all walks of life often rely on a great smile as part of their public image. Don't let your teeth rob you of the future you deserve. To feel fabulous, look more attractive and have healthy mouth is absolutely magical. Make your appointment today and let Dr. Peter Badalamenti design a smile for you.

9302 W Bluemound Road, Milwaukee WI
(414) 258-3332
www.smileofyourdreams.com

Halo

HEALTH & BEAUTY

Milwaukee hair stylist Diane Lukich understands hair health. She also understands her clientele and knew what she wanted to offer them when she launched Halo in 1994. The salon builds on Diane's philosophy of caring for the whole person and reflects her unique vision for Halo: "If you only use light for yourself, it's absorbed and creates a shadow. If you let it overflow to others it creates a halo." Every staff member at Halo has studied with celebrated stylists and carries a certification in their area of expertise. Halo embraces new technologies and specialized services, including Japanese thermal straightening, micro mist hair treatments and human hair extensions. From precision haircuts to corrective color and perms, the salon staff will help you look your best while ensuring that your hair remains in great condition. Diane can create picture perfect makeup for your wedding day using airbrush techniques. Halo offers nail enhancements and such eye services as permanent eyelash extensions, eyebrow tinting and brow design. Pampering comes standard here, where clients can enjoy tea, coffee or bottled water while indulging in online shopping on a computer provided for customer use. Diane owned several salons before she bought and renovated the Halo building with the help of co-owner and professional building designer Leroy Buth. When you are ready to refresh your look and your spirits, visit Halo.

1221 E Brady Street, Milwaukee WI
(414) 272-4247
www.halohairspa.com

BBC Lighting

HOME & GARDEN

BBC Lighting is a bright idea in more ways than just lighting. BBC will provide your entire family with a memorable shopping experience they will never forget. Browse past thousands of chandeliers, bath lights, outdoor fixtures, lamps and ceiling fans, while munching on BBC's endless supply of free popcorn. The showroom also has a huge display of Casablanca fans, along with an impressive selection of Schonbek and Waterford crystal. Select from all the latest styles of the most prestigious brands and receive BBC's lowest price guarantee. As a major supplier to new home buyers, BBC offers free consultations, storage and delivery. BBC's commercial division specifies lighting for all types of buildings, warehouses, parking lots and athletic fields. Everyone will marvel at the extensive selection of collectibles, including celebrity memorabilia, unusual antiques, rare autographed photos, neons, juke boxes, pinballs, kiddie rides and more. For added entertainment, the kids will enjoy free rides in the six-foot tall Green Bay Packers helmet or on the old-time musical merry-go-round. For an illuminating shopping adventure you are sure to enjoy, come visit BBC Lighting, a Milwaukee landmark.

2015 W St. Paul Avenue, Milwaukee WI
(414) 933-0808 or (800) 533-0406
www.bbclighting.com

Urban Sense

HOME & GARDEN

If you want to make a floral statement that is elegant, fresh, inventive and decidedly out of the ordinary, step into Milwaukee's Urban Sense. Owners Chris Dobs and Dan Block have created a floral, décor and gift boutique that is guaranteed to put the bloom on your shopping trip. Chris is a long-time floral professional and Dan is an architectural whiz. Together they have created a cutting-edge business that offers high-quality plants, arrangements and décor items you won't find anyplace else. They grow many of their plants and herbs in their own greenhouse, and are known for their inventive and reliable handling of special events, including corporate soirées, parties and weddings. Urban Sense is a very contemporary store that offers innovative designs and a collection of artistic and high-quality gifts at very reasonable prices. They are especially known for their European flowers and plants. The next time you are on a shopping trip to Milwaukee, make sure to visit Urban Sense. If you can't make it to Milwaukee, but still want to make a statement, visit their website or call for delivery details.

5911 W Vliet Street, Milwaukee WI
(414) 257-0434
www.urban-sense.com

Marsh Hill

HOME & GARDEN

Marsh Hill owners Mark and Heidi von Hagke have brought the bounty of their European antique treasure hunt back to Milwaukee in the form of European furnishings. With attractive antique pieces from France, Austria, England and elsewhere in Europe, you're bound to find a treasure for your own home. Mark and Heidi pick their merchandise for its quality and palpable sense of history, which promises to add spirit as well as style to your rooms. Marsh Hill offers something for every room in the house, from harvest tables and dining sets to French mirrors, chests, chairs and armoires. Timepiece collectors will appreciate the shop's antique grandfather clocks. The shop also features beautiful Oriental rugs sure to transform any room. Every room in the store is set to help customers envision how pieces can be used in their homes. Marsh Hill is proud of their European contacts, who help Mark and Heidi locate this special inventory. The store's philosophy matches that espoused by Winston Churchill: "We shape our dwellings and afterward our dwellings shape us." Shape your dwelling to your liking with a visit to Marsh Hill.

2045 W St. Paul Avenue, Milwaukee WI
(414) 933-1061
www.marshhillantiques.com

Usinger's

MARKETS & DELIS

For more than 120 years, Usinger's has sought to make America's finest sausage. Usinger's makes its famous sausage from the freshest cuts of lean beef and pork and flavors them with rare spices such as East Indian nutmeg, California paprika and Zanzibar cloves. You can choose from more than 70 varieties of Old World sausage, including andouille, bratwurst and the ever-popular wiener. Sample the blood sausage or liver sausage such as braunschweiger. The shop also carries quality ham, luncheon meat and summer sausage. Usinger's maintains a friendly turn-of-the-century feel with tile floors and marble counters. A mural depicts the traditional German elves who have become the company's mascots over the years. Gift baskets pack tasty sausages together with cheese, crackers and other treats. Usinger's ships anywhere in the United States, and if you're not in Milwaukee you can order the shop's special products from its website. Founder Fred Usinger, a German master sausage maker, arrived in America in 1870 with $400 in cash and his favorite sausage recipes. Within 10 years, he had his own shop and was creating the renowned Old World sausage that bears his name to this day. The brother-and-sister team of Fritz and Debra Usinger are the fourth generation of the Usinger family to keep the tradition going. If you're looking for America's best sausage, come enjoy the traditional family recipes at Usinger's.

1030 N Old World 3rd Street, Milwaukee WI
(414) 276-9100 or (800) 558-9998
www.usinger.com

El Rey Markets

MARKETS & DELIS

The El Rey Markets specialize in Hispanic products. Some have called the first El Rey Market, a combination grocery and restaurant, the real community center of Milwaukee Hispanics. Today, El Rey operates four grocery markets, a new 21,000-square-foot superstore on Milwaukee's South Side and a tortilla and tamale plant. The plant turns out a million tortillas a week. The grocery stores sell them by the box. Long lines of customers eagerly shop for a dizzying array of chiles and spices, tropical fruits and vegetables, and cuts of meat unfamiliar to most Anglos. An aisle is devoted to religious candles. Owners Ernesto and Heriberto Villarreal believe that the combination of Mexican foods and customs with American ingenuity has allowed their business to thrive. They point to their tortilla and tostadita chip making as an example. The recipes come from Mexico, the corn is from Wisconsin and Iowa and the ovens are made in California. El Rey wholesales to almost all restaurants serving Hispanic cuisine in the Milwaukee area. The Villarreals believe that family is key. The two brothers married a pair of sisters, Olivia and Cris, and went into business together in 1978. Everyone in the Villarreal family works in the stores, including children and in-laws. The El Rey Markets employ more than 440 people in a company that began as a tiny family operation. Visit El Rey Markets and you'll find authentic Mexican foods made with the finest ingredients from Middle America.

916 S Caesar E Chavez Drive (16th Street), Milwaukee WI (superstore)
1023 S Cesar E Chavez Drive, Milwaukee WI (Mercado El Rey, the first store)
3524 W Burnham Street, Milwaukee WI (El Rey Plaza)
1433 W Burnham Street, Milwaukee WI (El Rey Nana's)
1320 W Burnham Street, Milwaukee WI (El Rey Food Mart)
(414) 643-1640

Outpost Natural Foods Cooperative

MARKETS & DELIS

Shoppers in Milwaukee care about personal and environmental health and show that caring by shopping at Outpost Natural Foods Cooperative. Outpost provides organically and locally produced goods to the public and to its owners at three locations in greater Milwaukee. It proudly offers Fair Trade products, which benefit farmers and producers worldwide by helping them deal directly with buyers, thus receiving fair compensation for their goods. Outpost Natural Foods also educates the community about choices that have an impact on personal and environmental health and about the philosophy and effectiveness of cooperative business structures. It offers a myriad of foods for special dietary needs along with the services of a nutritionist. The store regularly hosts in-store samplings and workshops as well as outside events. The cooperative, the first certified organic retailer in southeastern Wisconsin, began in 1970 with 100 members who wanted regular access to healthy food. Today, Outpost is co-owned by more than 13,000 community members. Outpost consistently features a full line of natural groceries, organic produce, prepared deli foods and sandwiches. Look for naturally raised meats, fresh seafood, beer and wine, as well as a large selection of personal care items, cards and gifts. The co-op satisfies its customers with efficient, personalized service, carried out in a spirit of fun and genuine cooperation. Come to Outpost Natural Foods to sample tasty foods that support your health and the health of the planet.

100 E Capitol Drive, Milwaukee WI (414) 961-2597
7000 W State Street, Wauwatosa WI (414) 778-2012
2826 S Kinnickinnec Avenue, Milwaukee WI (314) 755-3202
www.outpostnaturalfoods.coop

West Allis Cheese & Sausage Shoppe

MARKETS & DELIS

West Allis Cheese & Sausage Shoppe was saved from closure thanks to the Lutz family and their love of Wisconsin cheeses. West Allis Cheese, originally called Merkt, first opened in 1969. The shop was an area landmark where the Lutz family had always bought their cheese. In 2001, when they heard the store was closing, brothers Mark and Howard Lutz purchased the shop to continue the tradition. Today West Allis Cheese & Sausage Shoppe offers more than 150 varieties of cheese. The store features premium cheese suppliers, such as Carr Valley Cheese and Pleasant Ridge Reserve. Whether it's world champion blue cheese or cheddar that's been aged up to 10 years, you'll find it here. The Lutzes maintain close relationships with their cheesemakers and bring them into the store to meet and share their knowledge with customers. Specialty cheeses range from goat and sheep milk cheeses and spreads to hard cheeses that are available by the pound. West Allis features products by Lake Geneva Country Meats, including such sausage varieties as Bavarian sausage and flavored brats. Cheese and sausage baskets make thoughtful individual or corporate gifts, and the shop creates more than 5,000 Christmas baskets every year. If you love cheese and sausage, come visit West Allis Cheese & Sausage Shoppe at their original location or at their newest location inside the Milwaukee Public Market.

6832 W Becher Street, West Allis WI
(414) 543-4230
www.wacheese-gifts.com

Taste of Wisconsin

MARKETS & DELIS

When the fabulous new Milwaukee Public Market opened in the city's historic Third Ward in 2005, the market asked West Allis Cheese & Sausage Shop to open a store there. Owners and brothers Mark and Howard Lutz, and Mark's wife, Linda, had already featured strictly Wisconsin products at their West Allis store for many years. They quickly decided to showcase their products in the wonderful ambience of the market, where producers come to give out samples and meet customers. Taste of Wisconsin offers a wonderful variety of the most unique Wisconsin taste treats, including jams and jellies, honey and cranberry products. Here you'll find hard-to-locate gourmet items, like Martha's Mustard, Big Butz BBQ Sauce and Stump's Olives, as well as Barbetta's Gourmet Grill Rub and many award winning cheeses. Gift baskets and boxes, available year-round, come pre-packaged or customized. The Lutzes will also work with any budget to create gift packs for individual or corporate gift giving. Taste of Wisconsin offers Christmas baskets, too, and ships anywhere within the 50 states. Whether you're looking for such snacks as cookies, popcorn and sodas or for gourmet treats, including coffee, cocoa and spices, the Lutzes have chosen Wisconsin's best offerings to place here. They invite you to sample the results at Taste of Wisconsin.

400 N Water Street, Milwaukee WI
(414) 289-8333
www.wacheese-gifts.com

Beans & Barley—Deli, Market & Café

MARKETS & DELIS

Beans & Barley—Deli, Market & Café is a truly eclectic full-service health food store with sustainable, organic options for the healthy, educated shopper. Opened in 1973 by Mike Stevens, Beans & Barley set out to improve the health of Milwaukee patrons by offering vitamins, supplements, healthful deli items and groceries that maintained both quality and value. These goals remain in place today under the ownership of partners Pat Sturgis, Patricia Garrigan, Peggy Silvestrini and Lynn Sbonik. From the deli to the 80-seat dining room, you'll find a range of healthful, delicious choices, featuring such housemade specialties as lasagna, burritos, vegetarian chili and vegan soups. Artisan breads are popular here, in addition to the many dessert options and a large selection of carry-out items, including a box lunch to-go. Both the market and café offer beer and wine, including several organic selections. Other beverage choices include espresso drinks, tea and smoothies. Your own recipes will benefit from the organic and special diet foods sold here. Grocery options are numerous, and you'll also find natural health and beauty products. A visit to this modern space bathes you in light and surrounds you with the work of local artists. Let the experts at Beans & Barley show you how the right foods can improve your well-being.

1901 E North Avenue, Milwaukee WI
(414) 278-7878
www.beansandbarley.com

FishAddiction Custom Fishing Rods

RECREATION & FITNESS

Sean Gilles has been making the fishing experience the best it can be since 2001. At FishAddiction Custom Fishing Rods, he can make a custom rod to your specifications, with guides, length, action and power just for you and the specific fish you're trying to catch. Sean began creek fishing with sticks and homemade dough for bait when he was barely old enough to walk. As an adult, he found that no one made the rod he was looking for, so he learned to make them himself. After 10 years of research and development, Sean was able to design truly superior rods. The process of making a rod begins with defining what you need. FishAddiction doesn't even order materials until the customer makes the necessary decisions. It takes about a month, but in the end you walk out with your dream rod. It will capture the exact look and feel that you want, from wooden handles to decals and personal messages. Needless to say, Sean is extremely detail-oriented. He wants to make sure that you leave with the most desirable and reliable rod possible. *John Gillespie's Water and Woods* has featured Sean's work, and so has *Outdoor Wisconsin*. When you're ready to take your fishing to the next level, visit Sean at FishAddiction Custom Fishing Rods. You'll soon have a performance rod that will be the envy of all of your buddies.

1331 W Euclid Avenue, Milwaukee WI
(414) 383-8707
www.fishaddiction.com

Laacke & Joys

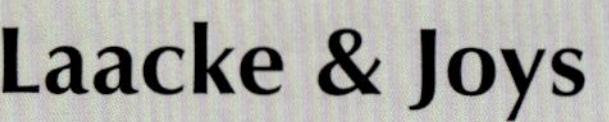

Being outdoors in Wisconsin is one of nature's grandest gifts. Laacke & Joys has everything to make reveling in this gift a supreme experience and 164 years of expertise to prove it. The Laacke & Joys staff members love outdoor sports. If they can't find the perfect outdoor equipment for a sport, they'll manufacture it themselves. The company is the oldest outdoor manufacturer and retailer in Milwaukee. The Joys company began in 1844 as a vendor of ship supplies. The Laacke business was founded in 1887 to make tents. The two companies merged in 1957. Today, whether it is camping, boating or fly fishing products you seek, President Marsha Mather will make sure you have the products you need. When you rent a canoe or a kayak from Laacke & Joys, you can enter the Milwaukee River right from the store. Laacke & Joys can supply you with its own brand of Wildwood tents. Top brand equipment for skiing, snowboarding, camping, backpacking and biking is a necessity for a staff that participates in outdoor sports, and customers can shop here knowing they will be talking with people who understand sporting equipment. Laacke & Joys also carries clothing, footwear and a large in-stock selection of outdoor furniture. Visit one or all three locations, and discover for yourself why Laacke & Joys has been around for so long.

1433 N Water Street, Milwaukee WI (414) 271-7878
19233 W Bluemound Road, Brookfield WI (262) 782-2960
1515 W Mequon Road, Mequon WI (262) 241-4500
www.laackeandjoys.com

MODA 3

RECREATION & FITNESS

Eric Kuester and Christian Deaton live what they sell at the ultra cool snowboard and skateboard shop, MODA 3. The two die-hard snowboarders found it difficult to acquire some brands and limited edition gear in the Milwaukee area, so in 2004, they opened the store, which specializes in snowboarding equipment and skateboarding equipment, plus streetwear appreciated by hip sports enthusiasts. Visible ducting, concrete floors and clean lines give the shop its modern, urban look. Find Burton snowboards and boots for riding the hills, or let Eric and Christian repair and tune your board. A snowboarder often turns to skateboarding during the summer months, which accounts for MODA 3's line of quality skateboards. Clothing from Quicksilver and Obey keep you comfortable while out on the board or just hanging with friends. MODA 3 carries limited edition Nike sportswear and other hard-to-find collector pieces, as well as Nixon watches, backpacks and many accessories. Christian and Eric are admitted sneaker heads, and make sneakers look more like art than footwear, with row after row of shoes displayed on the walls. Stop by in September for Boardfest, a celebration that kicks off the snowboarding season with more than 50,000 pounds of shaved ice and appearances by Olympic stars. Come to one of MODA 3's stores for everything you need to hit the slopes or the pavement.

320 E Buffalo Street, Milwaukee WI
(414) 273-3333
W307 N1497 Golf Road, Delafield WI
(262) 432-1709
www.moda3.com

Barclay Gallery & Garden Café

RESTAURANTS & CAFES

The Barclay Gallery & Garden Café offers fine crafts, food and drink to discerning patrons. The gallery displays handmade crafts from more than 300 top artists. You'll find wood, ceramics, metal and other media fashioned into jewelry, vases, sculpture and other items both decorative and functional. The gallery has one of the largest collections of hand-blown glass ornaments in the region. At the restaurant, you can dine surrounded by beauty. Try a light meal of fresh soup, salad, and a sandwich or spring for a melt-in-your-mouth entrée. The weekend brunch is popular. A take-out coffee area also sells specialty beers, wine and wine accessories. Live music plays at the Barclay several nights a week. Other special events have included Tarot Tuesday, Wine Oh! Wednesday and Fish Fry'Day. Owner John LeBrun plans to add rooftop garden seating and an upstairs banquet hall with more art on the walls. John opened the business to escape the endless meetings, budgetary planning sessions and other demands of his job as senior vice president for a major publisher. He opened the restaurant to ensure that he had plenty of customers for the gallery, and he soon discovered how demanding—but satisfying—the restaurant trade can be. Join the throngs who have made Barclay Gallery & Garden Café one of Milwaukee's most popular destinations. You'll enjoy the visit.

158 S Barclay Street, Milwaukee WI
(414) 347-0500
www.barclaygalleryonline.com

African Hut Restaurant

RESTAURANTS & CAFES

Africa is a land of contrasts comprised of 54 countries, each with its own food and cultural traditions. You can explore a bit of this dynamic continent with Yinka Adedokun at his popular Milwaukee eatery, African Hut Restaurant. Yinka is from the Yoruba tribe of western Nigeria. He came to the U.S. in his 20s and earned both bachelor's and master's degrees from the University of Wisconsin. He and his wife, Moji, opened African Hut in 1993. A few of Yinka's traditional recipes come from his mother, a well respected and much loved restaurateur in the large city of Ibadan, Nigeria. Much of his cuisine comprise of meat dishes and delectable vegetarian offerings. Customers appreciate such specialties as Jollof rice, a mix of vegetables and spices in a tomato base. Yinka and Moji spend up to six hours on the dishes, using traditional methods. African Hut Restaurant serves lunch and dinner six days a week. Yinka also invites schools, culinary classes, civic and corporate groups to the restaurant. He offers presentations on African food and culture through his secondary company, African Presentations, either at the restaurant or at the customer's site. Experience the intoxicating scents and flavors of authentic African cuisine at African Hut Restaurant or have Yinka cater your next event.

1107 N Old World 3rd Street,
Milwaukee WI
(414) 765-1110
www.africanpresentations.com

Crazy Water

RESTAURANTS & CAFES

Savor the flavors of the world at Crazy Water, where chef and owner Peggy Magister uses peak-of-freshness ingredients to create New World fusion cuisine for those with an adventurous palate. Peggy, a Milwaukee native, received her formal culinary training in San Francisco before returning home to launch her career as a restaurateur in 2002. Crazy Water is named in honor of Peggy's favorite Venetian restaurant, Aqua Pazza, and is located in a late 1800s dwelling that has been beautifully restored to retain the original wood floors and bar as well as the original tin ceilings. The eatery features an open kitchen where you can personally watch Peggy create her scrumptious delights, along with two cozy dining rooms, making this an equally ideal setting for an intimate supper for two or a group of friends or business associates. Crazy Water's eclectic menu changes seasonally and includes freshly caught fish and seafood from the Milwaukee fish market and fresh produce from local vendors. Popular menu favorites include the seared peppered tuna with banana salsa and fried won ton chips, the roasted beet salad with raspberry blue cheese vinaigrette, and roasted Costa Rican sea bass served with artichokes in shallot cream. Crazy Water boasts an array of decadent desserts and a choice selection of fine wines from around the world that make an excellent addition to any meal. Open up your mind to a world of culinary possibilities at Crazy Water.

839 S 2nd Street, Milwaukee WI
(414) 645-2606
www.crazywaterrestaurant.com

Three Brothers Restaurant

RESTAURANTS & CAFES

Three Brothers Restaurant treats Milwaukee to fine Serbian cooking in a casual atmosphere. Milun Radicevic and his son, Branko, were captured while working underground to fight the Nazis in World War II. A tribunal freed Branko but sent his father to a German concentration camp. After the war, a local sponsor in Milwaukee brought Milun to the United States, where he and his wife, Milunka, opened Three Brothers Restaurant in 1953. Their three sons, Branko, Milutin and Alexander, fled Yugoslavia in 1956 and joined their parents, who had named their restaurant Three Brothers in anticipation of their sons' arrival. Milun's sons were prepared for the restaurant life, having all worked in the two restaurants Milun had owned in Yugoslavia. Located in an historic building built in the 1800s for the Joseph Schlitz Brewing Company, the restaurant features family recipes from Serbia and Yugoslavia, including goulash and chicken paprika. Branko and Patricia Radicevic run the restaurant now and recommend allowing two hours for dinner, as they use no outside chefs; every dish is handmade by family members. Three Brothers features *burek*, a thin pastry filled with beef and cheese or spinach and cheese, as well as roast goose and roast lamb. Be sure to try the homemade strudel, baklava or *palacinka* with delicious Serbian coffee. The restaurant has been featured in *Gourmet* and *Bon Appétit* magazines. In 2002, it won the James Beard award. Come to Three Brothers Restaurant for authentic Serbian flavor in an unhurried atmosphere.

2414 S St. Clair Street, Milwaukee WI
(414) 481-7530

Butch's Old Casino Steak House

RESTAURANTS & CAFES

Butch's Old Casino Steak House is not just a great place for steak: it's a trip to a bygone era, back to where the original casino and steakhouse once sat in the 1940s. Owner Butch Schettle wanted to recreate the style of the legendary Milwaukee restaurant he once worked at long ago. He starts with the choicest meats available in the best grades. Then he ages and cuts the meat in-house. All steaks are cooked in black cast iron skillets, just as they were in the original steakhouse. Try the 12 or 20-ounce filet, the 24-ounce t-bone, or if you're really hungry, attempt the 32-ounce porterhouse. All meats are served with fresh mushrooms, soup or salad and your choice of potatoes. Fresh Italian bread and a deluxe relish tray will also be at your table for sharing. This would be enough food for most, but if you've been saving up for this meal all day, you might want to try the homemade mozzarella or shrimp cocktail for starters or save room for the homemade cheesecake for dessert. Ask your server for the wine list, or enjoy one of the many imported beers. You can also try Butch's other steakhouse in downtown Milwaukee, The Clock. For the best steaks and seafood and great value for your money, Butch's Old Casino Steak House can't be topped.

555 N James Lovell Street, Milwaukee WI
(414) 271-8111
www.butchsteakhouse.com

Vecchio Bar & Grille

RESTAURANTS & CAFES

Vecchio Bar & Grille translates from the Italian to mean *Old Bar & Grille*, and this classic yet trendy Milwaukee restaurant definitely has a warm, European vibe. Owner Russ Davis grew up in the restaurant business, and when he decided to settle down he gave up photography to establish the restaurant in 1996. Known for its great food, Vecchio Bar & Grille's offerings include juicy steaks, seafood, homemade thin crust pizza and pasta. A wonderful assortment of appetizers, such as creamy spinach dip and crab cakes, set the stage for Vecchio's specialty entrées. The restaurant's famous fondue dinner for two includes a cheese fondue followed by a house salad, a meat platter and creamy chocolate fondue for dessert. The full bar includes an extensive, well-chosen wine list, a great selection of domestic and imported beers and an incredible martini menu that was voted best in Milwaukee. Sunday brunch selections include quiches, eggs Benedict, cream cheese-stuffed French toast and pancakes, all part of the buffet. Enjoy your meal while people watching in the charming outdoor garden area. Host your next event at Vecchio Underground, a private event room that seats up to 50 guests. For great food and drink at reasonable prices and a lively, late-night crowd, come to Vecchio Bar & Grille.

1137 N Old World 3rd Street, Milwaukee WI
(414) 273-5700
www.cafevecchio.com

Broadway Bistro, Broadway Bakery & Café and Gourmet To Go

RESTAURANTS & CAFES

From fine dining, to casual, to catering, you'll find it all at one address. Three companies, Broadway Bistro, Broadway Bakery & Café and Gourmet to Go, share the same Broadway address in Milwaukee, and they aim to serve all of your dining needs. Broadway Bistro provides an elegant indoor and outdoor dining experience. This eclectic American bistro's menu changes each season to allow for the finest fresh ingredients. Everything's made from scratch here. Enjoy luscious lobster crepes for breakfast, a chicken and raspberry salad with gorgonzola and toasted walnuts for lunch, and Sicilian seared tuna topped with tomatoes, onions, olives, capers, pine nuts and raisins for dinner. If you're looking for something casual, pop into Broadway Bakery & Café. Travelers on the go will want to grab a breakfast sandwich or Danish. Or enjoy a steaming cup of cappuccino and any one of many delicious soups, salads and sandwiches on the menu for lunch. There are vegetarian alternatives available. Save room for a cookie or cream cheese brownie for dessert. If you're looking for delicious food for your private party or corporate lunch, Gourmet to Go can bring it right to you. From breakfast quiches to oven-roasted turkey with gravy for lunch, you'll find everything you need. The company offers customized menus for any occasion. Let Broadway Bistro, Broadway Bakery & Café and Gourmet to Go provide you with a great dining experience whenever, and wherever, you want it.

241 N Broadway, Milwaukee WI
(414) 431-2880
www.241broadway.com

Nanakusa Japanese Restaurant

RESTAURANTS & CAFES

Nanakusa Japanese Restaurant owner Richard Kaiser wants people who visit his restaurant to leave full, happy and smarter about Japanese cuisine. An admirer of Eastern philosophy and culture, Richard opened Nanakusa in 2001 to bring a taste of authentic Japanese food and culture to Milwaukee. Diners at Nanakusa have the chance to try authentic Kobe beef, made from animals fed and massaged daily to avoid developing too much muscle. Enjoy this tender delicacy several ways, including cubed and grilled in garlic butter or *No Tanaki* (seared, sliced thin and served chilled with a sauce). Unlike most restaurants in Japan, Nanakusa offers a large menu full of options, including noodles, teriyaki and sushi so good the Milwaukee Sushi Society meets there regularly. You'll also find a list of 70 wines, chosen for their compatibility with Japanese food. Nanakusa is one of only three Japanese restaurants in the world recognized by *Wine Spectator* magazine. Nanakusa carries the largest selection of sake in the state. The restaurant has received rave reviews from both the *Milwaukee Journal Sentinel* and *Milwaukee Magazine*. The décor here features a Japanese minimalist style, where diners experience an intimate eating environment. For a taste of authentic Japanese food and philosophy, come to Nanakusa Japanese Restaurant.

408 E Chicago Street, Milwaukee WI (414) 223-3200 *www.foodspot.com/nanakusa*

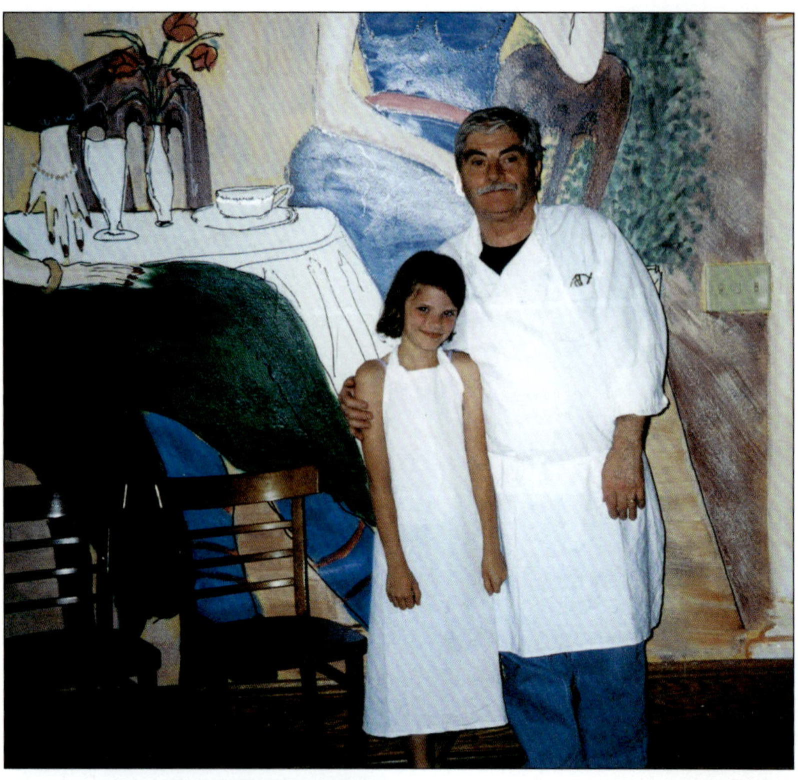

Elliot's Bistro & Bar

RESTAURANTS & CAFES

Ooh la la. Elliot's Bistro & Bar—candlelight, beautiful colors, and a warm, intimate atmosphere accompanied by classic French flavors and aromas are what you will find at this innovative restaurant. The friendly and caring staff know just how to pamper each guest, assuring everyone an enjoyable and memorable dining experience. Elliot's Bistro & Bar showcases Chef Pierre's mastery of authentic classic French cuisine. They were given three-and-one-half stars by *Milwaukee Journal's* food critic, Dennis Getto, and listed as one of the best restaurants in Wisconsin since opening. This is as close to France as you will get in Milwaukee. Chef Pierre has an alluring list of dishes ranging from classic standards like Beef Bourguignon to quiche. Let him come to your tableside with his flaming skillet for a flambé steak *au poive* or a tempting dessert such as crepes. Sample one of the many sumptuous wines with your dinner or have a delicious mixed cocktail created by one of their skilled bartenders. Weekends offer a wonderful brunch complete with six different styles of Bloody Marys. Selections change seasonally and daily. Let Chef Pierre, his wife Deborah and their staff graciously entertain you. Come sample one of Milwaukee's jewels at Elliot's Bistro & Bar. Call ahead for hours of operation or to make reservations for special events and private parties.

2321 N Murray Avenue, Milwaukee WI
(414) 273-1488
www.elliotsbistro.com

Hotch-A-Do

RESTAURANTS & CAFES

Angie Storm started Hotch-A-Do organic bistro in 2006 with the help of her large family. Guests can enjoy her mother Carol's yummy tomato sauce, her father's cookies and her own veggie sandwich. Carol's contributions also include lasagna Hotch-A-Do, cheese potatoes and baked chicken provolone. Hotch-A-Do bistro makes pizza according to a revered Storm family recipe that uses fresh tomato sauce, a selection of natural toppings and real Wisconsin cheese. Some of the other family recipes are grandma Franca's meatball hoagie, brother Will's garlic Alfredo pasta and brother Tim's pancakes. Angie says that customers come first in this family-friendly eatery, and she proves it by offering free wireless Internet, healthy organic foods and a smoke-free environment. A full bar completes the package with its popular Bloody Marys, 18 wine varieties and 15 selections of beer. Where does the name of the restaurant come from? A little girl stands in one spot, swings her arms, repeatedly chants "hotch-a-do," and then performs a world-changing somersault. Her relatives burst into applause. The little girl was Angie, and hotch-a-do still means "Get ready, I'm about to do something big!" You'll agree that Hotch-A-Do is something big after you taste the Storm family recipes.

1813 E Kenilworth Place, Milwaukee WI
(414) 727-2122
www.hotch-a-do.com

Tess

RESTAURANTS & CAFES

"I can't think of a better place to eat dinner outdoors than at Tess," writes *Milwaukee Sentinel Journal* food critic Dennis R. Getto. The critic refers to this Milwaukee restaurant's beautiful garden setting complete with flowers and a fountain. In good weather, you can enjoy your gourmet meal on white linen tablecloths at a back patio. The restaurant also features a quaint dining room that seats 30. Owners Joseph Volpe and Mitchell Wakefield went to school together and seized on the opportunity to create a restaurant that plays to both of their strengths. Joe is the executive chef, and his menus combine the best of French, American and Asian cuisine. The fish stew is especially renowned, with shrimp, scallops, halibut, salmon, mussels and Yukon Gold potatoes cooked in tomato sauce. A tasty crème brûlée makes a simple but elegant finale to your meal. While Joe works in the kitchen, Mitch guides a friendly staff in making sure everything about your dining experience is comfortable and pleasant. The staff is knowledgeable about everything on the menu and can help you pick the right wine to complement your meal. Tess is a favorite place for celebrating special occasions, thanks to its remarkable food and lovely atmosphere. For a dining experience sure to delight all your senses, visit Tess.

2499 N Bartlett Avenue, Milwaukee WI (414) 964-8377

Safe House

RESTAURANTS & CAFES

Since 1966, the Safe House has been a place to come in from the cold and enjoy food and drink. The owner's name is Baldwin, David Baldwin. He's so dedicated to keeping the Safe House secret that the sign on the door reads International Exports Ltd. Once agents enter, a receptionist asks them either to provide a password or put on a small show for the patrons inside who are watching on closed-circuit television. Then, a door hidden by a bookcase swings open. Whether you like your martini shaken or stirred, you'll find it mixed to perfection at the bar. House specials include the Under Cover Girl and the Goldeneye, named for Ian Fleming's home in Jamaica. Pre-mission briefings include Control's Censored Cheese Spread, or start with the Roman Spies Caesar Salad. For a light mission, try the Spy Burger, or go all-out with Chef's Spycials such as tenderloin, ribs or vegetable lasagna. Don't miss the Furtive Friday Fish Fry. You can complete your mission with Bond's Bomb dessert, which comes with a real lit fuse in the chocolate chip ice cream. A telephone booth provides cover for your escape. *Time* and the *Milwaukee Journal-Sentinel* have written up the Safe House, and the History Channel has covered it as well. Your mission, should you choose to accept it, is to enjoy thrills, adventure and great food at the Safe House.

779 N Front Street, Milwaukee WI
(414) 271-2007
www.safe-house.com

The Soup Otzie's

RESTAURANTS & CAFES

Soups are one of life's comfort foods. At the Soup Otzie's in Milwaukee, the choices are plentiful and the customer service is almost as impressive as the comforting quality soups. Owner Joan Otzelberger worked in the restaurant business for years, and soups were her passion. She started the business with brother Tom, sister-in-law Kristi and friend Yvonne Schwartz in 2003. Tom left the business in the spring of 2005 to pursue other interests. The most popular soups are available every day, notably chicken soup with your choice of homemade dumplings or egg noodles and stock made from scratch. Cream of potato, pot roast and vegetarian soups are other daily offerings. Joan makes two specialty soups every day. The menu changes monthly with more than 300 soups served. Unusual varieties include cream of Reuben, shrimp bisque and roasted carrot with pecans. All soups are served with fresh baked bread. The Soup Otzie's passes out samples, so you know what you are getting. Cold sandwiches, hot paninis and summer salads are also on hand. The restaurant prepares fresh, homemade chicken and tuna salad daily. Enjoy the family atmosphere in the dining area or grab a frozen soup to take home. For a delicious soup or other light fare in a warm, friendly atmosphere, bring your appetite and your friends to the Soup Otzie's.

3950 S Howell Avenue, Milwaukee WI
(414) 747-9670

Roots Restaurant and Cellar

RESTAURANTS & CAFES

The merging of great minds often creates great businesses. Such is the case with Roots Restaurant and Cellar, the result of a merger between an organic farmer and a man from a farming family who has 20 years in the restaurant business. High school friends John Raymond and Joe Schmidt had talked about owning a restaurant together for years. They made it happen in February of 2004. Joe is the farmer, growing micro-greens and herbs, vegetables, berries, quince and Asian plums, in addition to the flowers used on the tables. John uses Joe's garden creations to offer a diverse menu with a California fusion flair. The regular menu includes Soy Grilled Tilapia, which includes cashew sticky rice, coconut curry and seared yuzu dressed pea shoots; and San Francisco cioppino, which includes mussels, shrimp, fish, scallops and spices in a fennel-tomato broth. Other menu items change daily. Check the wine list for the perfect complement. Roots Restaurant has been featured in both *Organic Style* magazine and *Bon Appetit.* The upstairs features the restaurant, while the downstairs "cellar" offers a full bar and a more casual dining experience. Eat inside or enjoy the patio during cooperative weather. As the food here takes a little longer to create, take the time to enjoy the views of downtown Milwaukee or the sloping gardens surrounding the patio. For personable and knowledgeable service and whole foods cooked with love, visit Roots Restaurant & Cellar.

1818 N Hubbard Street, Milwaukee WI
(414) 374-8480
www.rootsmilwaukee.com

au Bon Appétit Catering

RESTAURANTS & CAFES

Lebanese cuisine has its own distinct set of flavors and boasts alluring aromas that tease the senses and stimulate the mind until nothing will do but to try a bite. At au Bon Appétit Catering, Chef Rihab Aris uses her culinary ingenuity to create Lebanese meals with French flair. Rihab, the owner, operator and chef, came to the United States in 1990 after fleeing war in her native Lebanon. She has turned her lifelong passion for cooking into a delightful catering and packaged food business, where she can share her native dishes and culture with her American guests. Rihab opened au Bon Appétit as a restaurant in 1991 and quickly gained a loyal clientele who spread the word of her superb eatery throughout the Milwaukee area, earning her a great deal of recognition and a listing among the top 30 restaurants in the city for 13 years running. In October of 2006, the restaurant closed and the catering and packaged food business' were moved to the next level. Rihab offers catering for two to 200 and her own line of prepackaged and bulk items which are available from local grocers and delicatessens. You will find dishes such as *djaj mehshi*, basmati rice with chicken, and *shawarma*, or gyros, made with slices of grilled beef and lamb and tahini sauce. Savor the fusion of flavors from Lebanese food with French and Mediterranean accents from au Bon Appétit Catering.

219 N Milwaukee Street, Milwaukee WI
(414) 223-3222
www.aubonappetit.com

The Soup Market

RESTAURANTS & CAFÉS

When Milwaukeeans want the best bowl of soup, stew or chili in town, there's just one decision they have to make: do they head to The Soup Market's original location in Bay View or to the newer store in the Milwaukee Public Market. The Soup Market serves six kinds of soup everyday. There's always chicken noodle and chicken dumpling, plus three daily specials (one cream soup, one vegetarian and one miscellaneous), along with a different chili every week. Dave Jurena and Tim Talsky are soup geniuses. Everything is made from scratch, with the freshest, most wholesome ingredients (including the noodles and dumplings), and it all tastes more homemade than homemade ever tasted. Their soup forecast might include such mouth-watering concoctions as Cajun-style cheese soup with andouille, white bean chili with grilled chicken, African peanut and chicken, or Portugese stew with linguica sausage. You'll sometimes find the best tasting New England clam chowder outside of New England or a Poblano corn chowder that will make you pine for the great Southwest. In addition to their two retail outlets, The Soup Market supplies soups to more than 15 coffee shops in the metro area, along with quiches, cookies and sandwiches. The next time you visit the Milwaukee area, stop into The Soup Market for a bowl of hearty goodness. It's some of the best soup you ever tasted.

2211 S Kinnickinnic Avenue, Milwaukee WI
(414) 727-8462
thesoupmarket.com

The Wicked Hop

RESTAURANTS & CAFES

It's likely that baseball fans across the nation remember that day in 1982 when the Brewers won the pennant and the term *wicked hop* was coined. Step-brothers and partners Miles and Andy O'Neil certainly remember that day every time they step through the doors of their wildly popular Milwaukee eatery, The Wicked Hop, named in honor of their home team's victory. The Wicked Hop is located in the Third Ward's oldest dwelling, the Merchant Mills fruit warehouse, which was constructed in 1875. The brothers painstakingly remodeled the vintage building right down to the original and distinctive cream-colored city brick. Today the restaurant is open seven days a week and offers an astounding selection of delicious dishes along with a sizeable array of wines, beers and spirits, including more than nine different martinis. The menu offers a variety of your favorite pub-grub foods, such as nachos, wings and freshly made sandwiches, wraps and salads, as well as perfectly prepared entrées that are well above the par. The Wicked Hop also offers succulent burgers made with Black Angus or Kobe beef and a hearty Sunday brunch, which can be enjoyed with such specialty drinks as the Glass Slipper, a 67-ounce Bloody Mary served in a German boot stein. Even if you're not a big baseball fan, you'll feel like you hit a home run when you visit The Wicked Hop.

345 N Broadway, Milwaukee WI
(414) 223-0345
www.thewickedhop.com

Giraffe Ltd.

SHOPPING

Wedding couples in Milwaukee have been counting on Giraffe Ltd. for exceptional wedding invitations since 1986. Giraffe Ltd. offers customers an entire trousseau of exquisite wedding papers, including thank-you notes, reply cards and table cards. Owner Nancy Wood delights in sharing her great taste and knowledge of wedding etiquette with customers. The Giraffe Ltd. selection is expansive; customers can look through the sample books from top line companies, including Crane, William Arthur, Caspari, Anna Griffin, Vera Wang and many others. Personalized, detail-oriented service and exceptional products ensure that customers receive exactly what they need. In addition to wedding invitations, Giraffe Ltd. offers a wonderful assortment of stationery, party invitations and birth announcements that can be personalized and printed in-house. You'll find elegant wedding and shower gift selections as well as complimentary gift wrapping. Upscale gift lines include Mariposa bowls, trays and entertaining accessories, acrylic giftware by Grainware, fabric placemats, ice buckets, waste baskets by Palmer-Smith and metal serving pieces by Armetale. Women's accessories are a favorite and Giraffe Ltd. features the complete line of Vera Bradley handbags, gifts and travel items. The baby section always has the newest trends in gifts as well. For knowledgeable guidance and outstanding selection, come to Giraffe Ltd.

527 E Silver Spring Drive, Milwaukee WI
(414) 332-8900

Rainbow Booksellers for Children

SHOPPING

Rainbow Booksellers for Children is a quaint, beautiful store where parents and children can come to celebrate the joy and adventure of reading. When owner Marye Beth Dugan heard that her favorite Milwaukee bookstore was closing, she bought it and moved to the area in 1994. Marye Beth's mother taught her that children deserve to see beauty and hear full sentences, a philosophy that drives the operation at Rainbow Booksellers. Marye Beth makes a point of reading every book on the shelves. The selection at Rainbow Booksellers ranges from children's reference and history books to adventure stories. You'll find books here for readers of all ages and levels. The eclectic collection also includes many hard-to-find volumes. Those looking for multicultural and bilingual books for children will be delighted at the selection available here. Rainbow Booksellers offers everything at a considerable discount compared to what you'd pay elsewhere. If you can't find what you're looking for on the shelves, the friendly, knowledgeable staff can special-order it for you. The store, which won the prestigious mayor's design award, is every bit an old-fashioned bookstore with nooks and crannies to explore. Marye Beth invites children of all ages to come in and experience the beauty of books at Rainbow Booksellers for Children.

5704 W Vliet Street, Milwaukee WI
(414) 774-7205
www.rainbowbooksellers.org

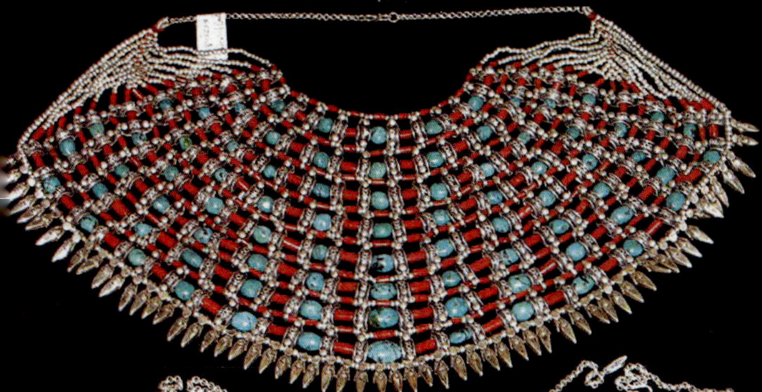

Artasia Gallery & Museum

SHOPPING

If you love Asian art, furnishings and culture, Artasia Gallery & Museum is the place for you. Eli Rosenblatt formerly lived in China as an interpreter, and that is where he met his wife, Pauline. The two started Artasia in 1992 when they began bringing jewelry and clothing from China to the United States. Since then, Artasia has grown to a 14,000-square foot store filled with wares not only from China, but also Tibet, Nepal, Mongolia and Southeast Asia. Eli does all the traveling now, hand-picking items that demonstrate beauty and creativity. You can find antique Chinese stick puppets (over 150 of them), Hmong ceremonial necklaces and Mongolian folk masks. Artasia stocks a vast number of statues in stone, wood and bronze. Popular figures include Buddha, Kuan Yin and even the elephant-headed Hindu god, Ganesh. Sizes range from a few inches to ten feet or more in height. Artasia also has one of the largest collections of antique Chinese folk statues in the world, over 1,200 ranging from the Ming Dynasty to the 20th century. In the store you can play traditional Asian musical instruments, including an eight-foot wide, 10-foot tall Tibetan temple drum. Artasia stocks furniture, from ornate alters to country armoires, ranging in age from new to hundreds of years old. The shop is a gathering place for travelers, students, historians and those who enjoy Asian culture and history. It contains a Chinese tea house where you can sit and meditate with a steaming cup of tea. Whether you're looking for jewelry, religious artifacts, clothing or anything else Asian, come to Artasia Gallery & Museum for a glimpse of authentic style and history.

181 N Broadway Avenue, Milwaukee WI
(414) 220-4292
www.artasiagallery.com

Fruit Ranch Gift Center

SHOPPING

Whether they are delivering to corporate clients across the country or to a very special grandmother across town, each individual gift is made with the same care and quality that has made the Fruit Ranch a tradition since 1935. Started by the family's great, great grandfather as an open-air fruit boat, eventually the business moved to a storefront in Milwaukee and became the Fruit Ranch Gift Center. Fourth generation Owners Teri Gay and Tanya Gearhart are focused on what they do best. Fresh fruit baskets, Wisconsin cheese and sausage boxes, and lovely gift baskets are designed with care by dedicated Fruit Ranch employees. Teri and Tanya are prepared to fill orders as small as one basket or as large as 10,000. While fruit baskets still remain the most popular gift, many fun baskets have been added to the catalog. Some of the most popular theme baskets include Back the Pack for Green Bay Packer enthusiasts and the Let's Ride basket, containing Harley-Davidson licensed items along with cheese, sausage and crackers. The perfect gift to send for the holidays, the Taste of Wisconsin is filled with great foods made in the state and will satisfy the cravings of your out-of-town family and friends. Because the customer always comes first at the Fruit Ranch, custom baskets are not a problem and can contain almost anything. You can choose from sugar-free treats, fresh flowers, mugs and plush animals. Other favorites include the bath and body basket or chocolate lover's basket, which is perfect for the hard-to-buy-for. Whatever the occasion, a gift from Fruit Ranch Gift Center is a beautiful and delicious way to please the people in your life.

6301 W Bluemound Road, Milwaukee WI
(414) 476-9600 or (800) 433-3289
www.fruitranch.com

Decorate! A Holiday Marketplace

SHOPPING

Decorate! A Holiday Marketplace is an amazing four-day winter wonderland of art, crafts and gifts displayed in a boutique setting. This holiday shopping experience contains several themed areas filled with hundreds of presents that include jewelry, florals and original home décor. The November event, which began in 1997, is the creation of Bonnie Loduha, working under the name of her alter ego Bonnie Lynn. Decorate! A Holiday Marketplace takes place within 7,000 square feet of space provided by the Zoofari Conference Center at the Milwaukee Zoo. In addition to Bonnie's latest offerings, you'll find a wide variety of prizes from the area's top artists. You'll see beautiful locally made handbags and clothing. There are wreaths galore, handmade ornaments and other Christmas-wares. Among the most popular items every year are the delectable chocolates from the area's chocolatiers, with free samples, of course. Bonnie's artistic career began one Christmas when she was a young girl. Her mother gave her a box that included scissors, glue, sequins and bits of fabric. That Christmas present sparked her artistic talent. Bonnie says it was, "a gift of endless ideas, untold adventures and a lifetime of imagination." Initially, Bonnie sold her wares at craft shows. Later, major vendors such as Hallmark discovered her work. Bonnie has designed figurines, giftware and décor for Country Life, Russ Berrie and other brands. If you're looking for one-of-a-kind gifts, be sure to mark your calendar for Decorate! A Holiday Marketplace.

9715 W Blue Mound Road, Milwaukee WI
(414) 688-5854
www.christmasvillagebybonnielynn.com

Future Green

SHOPPING

Looking to live a more healthful and socially responsible lifestyle? In this modern world, this type of living is not always easy to find. This is why Lisa and Swee Sim created Future Green, your one-stop shop for organic, Fair Trade and sustainable products in downtown Milwaukee. While working at an organic food store, Lisa saw that the demand for green products reached beyond food alone. Working with several co-op villages and artists around the world, she now seeks out the highest quality Fair Trade items and crafts for Future Green. The superb quality continues with such necessary luxuries as all-organic bedding, nontoxic interior decorating materials and reconditioned accessories for the home. Discover top designer organic clothing for men, women, children and infants. All of their products offer the means of living a wholly pure lifestyle. In addition to global consciousness, Future Green is committed to local community outreach by donations and such awareness-raising activities as organic-clothing fashion shows and free Qi Gong classes. So come explore and spend some time and a shrewd dollar at Future Green, where it's easy being green. Wholesome Products for Pure Lifestyles.

2352 S Kinnickinnic Avenue, Milwaukee WI
(414) 294-4300
www.futuregreen.net

Sprout!

SHOPPING

The owners of Sprout! pride themselves in unusual clothes and special toys that allow adult and child to play together. Toys and clothes are focused on the creative growing child, age newborn to six years, with practicality in mind. Clothes and accessories, such as the Paulina Quintana line, run up to size eight and are available in both casual and dress styles. Plush learning toys are available from Haba, Melissa & Doug and Gus Gutz. Sprout! stocks Ecboo and Hape games. Toys are often classic and educational in nature, such as puzzles, wire mazes and blocks. You can also find books, musical instruments and art supplies. Bring the kids on the weekend to enjoy balloons and free popcorn. Any day of the week the little ones can enjoy one of the three play areas, including a Lego wall. Children can try out many of the toys and games that the boutique sells. Sprout offers free gift wrapping and many special events each month, such as Pirate Day, Kiddie Cocktail Party and a jelly bean counting contest. As parents of a toddler, owners Kristin and Jim Vailliencourt find owning a children's store to be a natural for them. Kristin is a former teacher. Her husband, Jim, a graphic designer, handles logos, newsletters and marketing. Visit Sprout! today and find creative ways to add to your child's early years.

320 E Buffalo Street, Milwaukee WI
(414) 289-0844
www.sproutkid.com

Uhle's Tobacco Company

SHOPPING

Jim and Jeff Steinbock didn't intend to own a tobacco shop when they first began working for Jack Uhle in the 1970s. Jack opened his shop in 1939 and had vast knowledge to pass on to the brothers, who proved ready learners, mastering not only pipe repair and tobacco blending but also a sense of discernment. Jack moved the shop to its present location in the 1950s. He also started a wholesale business in tobaccos and pipes that continues to thrive. In 1982, Jim and Jeff bought the business, continuing Jack's traditions and starting a few of their own. The art of blending tobacco is one of the Steinbocks' strengths, and the company maintains a small factory on the premises for blending fine pipe tobaccos, both aromatic and English blends. After much sampling, Uhle's committed to its own private-label handmade cigar from Honduras, called the Uhle Honduran Blend Cigar. The Steinbocks travel frequently to tobacco producing countries and have developed strong ties with producers there. Uhle's cigar inventory is extensive and includes cigars by Ashton, Arturo Fuente and Davidoff. Jeff developed the J.S. Pipe, which has been a big seller in the store. In 1996, the Steinbocks expanded the shop to include a smoking lounge with leather furniture and humidified lockers for customer storage as well as a room that displays cigars, pipes and pipe tobacco. If you are looking for a smoking experience you'll cherish, come to Uhle's Tobacco Company.

114 W Wisconsin Avenue, Milwaukee WI
(414) 273-6665 or (800) 877-7024
www.uhles.com

Paddy's Pub

WINES, BREWS, PUBS & CLUBS

Pull up a stool and have a pint at Paddy's Pub. Owners Patricia Phillips-Wood and Orlen (Woody) Wood opened the Milwaukee pub in 1996. Patty, a business owner in the area for 20 years, and Woody, who retired from 27 years with the Milwaukee police department, wanted to have a safe and comfortable place for people to come and relax with a friend. You will find an impressive selection of Irish whiskeys and beers, including some hard-to-find varieties. You will also find some unique Irish ice cream drinks. Each experience at Paddy's Pub promises to be different than the last, thanks to four bars and a variety of cozy nooks. One of the bars is made of ornately carved wood and dates back to the 1700s. The two-story pub looks like a castle from the outside and features six-foot-tall stained glass windows on the top floor. Historical paintings and photos adorn the walls. In fine weather, you can enjoy your pint from a stone-walled outdoor patio and garden with five fountains, created by Patty and Woody to delight their customers. Paddy's Pub is available for weddings and other special occasions and can host a party of about 200 people. Woody and Patty offer a catering menu with numerous choices for your event. If you're looking for an inviting place to meet with friends, both old and new, come on in to Paddy's Pub.

2339 N Murray Avenue, Milwaukee WI
(414) 223-3496
paddyspub@earthlink.net
www.paddyspub.net

Vitucci's

WINES, BREWS, PUBS & CLUBS

Friends have been meeting friends at Vitucci's, a family-owned watering hole, since 1934. Before the Vitucci family settled on a cocktail lounge, friends were meeting friends over dinner as early as 1903 at Mike Vitucci's Third Ward restaurant, where Mike became known as the King of the Third Ward. Later, Mike's son, Frank, got involved in the restaurant business. Three of Frank's 12 children, Mike, Myron and Angelo, took over after Frank passed away. The three boys have since passed and the business is now owned by their three widows and operated by Angelo's son Tony. Open evenings every day of the year, Vitucci's full bar offers excellent cocktails, including fabulous martinis. With enough space for 150 people, there's plenty of room to play pool or video games. You can also choose to simply sip a cold one while catching the game on one of five big-screen televisions. Schedule your next private party in the large back room, where there's room for 80 people, and you can arrange catering with Vitucci's or provide your own food. A nostalgic feeling prevails, partly due to a mural that showcases Angelo and his brothers and partly thanks to the different generations who have mingled here. According to people who ought to know, "If you're from Milwaukee, you've been to Vitucci's." Come join the good times.

1832 E North Avenue, Milwaukee WI
(414) 273-6477
www.vituccis.com

Have A Nice Day Café

WINES, BREWS, PUBS & CLUBS

At Have A Nice Day Café, known to locals simply as The Café, people have been getting their groove on since 2000. The dance club's décor is retro, with giant disco balls and fluorescent spattered walls. Celebrity faces are painted on nearly every inch of wall space, and curved booths and lava lamps speak of earlier times. Owner Jake Dehne set out to improve Milwaukee's nightlife, and The Café draws impressive crowds on Thursday, Friday and Saturday nights. DJs spin mostly tunes from the 1970s, 1980s and 1990s. The state-of-the-art sound system and lighted dance floor encourage everyone to bust a move on the dance floor. A full bar features the usual cocktails as well as a good selection of beers. The most popular drink is the signature Happy Bowl, a 64-ounce fish bowl filled with fruity punch and assorted liquors and outfitted with several long straws for sharing with friends. The Café attracts a great mix of men and women, and the strict dress code contributes to an atmosphere of safety. The Café caters both large and small private parties and handles all staffing needs, including a DJ. The winner of AOL City Guide's Best Dance Club in 2006, The Café was also voted Best Dance Club in Milwaukee several years running. Take in Milwaukee's night scene with a visit to the Have A Nice Day Café.

1103 N Old World 3rd Street, Milwaukee WI
(414) 270-9650
www.cafemilwaukee.com
www.myspace.com/cafemilwaukee

The Harp Irish Pub

WINES, BREWS, PUBS & CLUBS

For three decades, the Harp Irish Pub has been one of those special places where, as the *Cheers* soundtrack goes, "everybody knows your name." The Milwaukee pub has been owned by the Wakefield family since the 1970s. It's a comfortable environment, with longtime staffers and customers who enjoy the congenial environment. You'll find an outdoor patio where you can take in the Milwaukee skyline and river while enjoying lunch or dinner and a beverage of your choice. When the weather cools, a cozy fireplace invites sipping some Irish coffee. The casual fare here includes salads, sandwiches and appetizers as well as a locally made bratwurst. The German sausage is as natural in this friendly place as you will be, even if you aren't Irish. The Harp has a citywide reputation for its annual St. Patrick's Day celebration, with celebrants forming a line outside long before the bar opens. In some ways the Harp feels like family, with a loyal clientele that goes back several generations. When you are ready to pull up a stool and say hello to old friends or make new ones, you're ready for the Harp Irish Pub.

113 E Juneau Avenue, Milwaukee WI
(414) 289-0700

Sprecher Brewing Company

WINES, BREWS, PUBS & CLUBS

A Milwaukee landmark since its inception in 1985, Sprecher Brewing Company makes a wide variety of world class beers and gourmet sodas. Sprecher employees gladly give behind-the-scenes, public and private brewery tours. Guests are guided through the history of brewing and the brewery, then ushered into the Old World-style indoor beer garden and tasting tent where they are invited to sample the beers and sodas on tap. Black Bavarian, Pub Ale and Special Amber are popular favorites; Sprecher Hefe Weiss was elected one of the 25 greatest American beers by *Men's Journal* magazine adding to the brewery's list of impressive awards. Sprecher also makes seven gourmet sodas in its brew kettles, including root beer, cream soda, Orange Dream and ginger ale. Sprecher Root Beer has been voted best tasting root beer in numerous polls, and was featured on Food Network TV's *Road Tasted*. A local chef liked its complex flavors so much he developed a prize winning Sprecher Root Beer Barbeque Sauce. Founder Randy Sprecher acquired a love for European beers while he was a soldier stationed in Germany. Upon his return to the U.S., Sprecher taught himself to homebrew the European beers he enjoyed. After working his way through college, taking courses that would help him become a brewmaster and run a brewery, Sprecher completed a special study in fermentation science at University of California, Davis. In 1980 he moved to Milwaukee to become a brewing supervisor at Pabst, where he worked until opening his own brewery. Sprecher Brewing Company is the first microbrewery established in Milwaukee since Prohibition. Drop by for a tour or book a private event where you can taste award-winning Sprecher beers and gourmet sodas in the enjoyable Old World setting.

701 W Glendale Avenue, Milwaukee WI
(414) 964-7837
www.sprecherbrewery.com

PLACES TO GO

- Mineral Point Opera House
  139 High Street
  (608) 987-2642
- Mineral Point Railroad Depot Museum
  13 Commerce Street
  (608) 987-2695
- Orchard Lawn/Gundry House
  234 Madison Street
  (608) 987-2884
- Pendarvis House
  114 Shake Rag Street
  (608) 987-2122
- Shake Rag Alley Center for the Arts
  18 Shake Rag Street
  (608) 987-3292
- Soldier's Memorial Park
  Merry Christmas Lane and Copper Street
- Yellowstone Lake State Park
  8495 Lake Road, Blanchardville
  (608) 523-4427

THINGS TO DO

January
- Winter Carnival
  (888) 764-6894

May
- Six Weeks 'til Summer
  (888) 764-6894

June
- Midsummer Pub Night
  Pendarvis
  (608) 987-2122

July
- Woodlander's Gathering
  Shake Rag Alley
  (608) 987-4499

August
- Iowa County Fair
  www.iowacountyfair.org

September
- Cornish Festival
  www.cornishfest.org

October
- Fall Art Tour
  (608) 987-3201
- Hangin' Day
  (608)-987-3201

MINERAL POINT

First-time visitors to Mineral Point find a town that looks like a quaint European village. This community in the driftless area of southwestern Wisconsin is surrounded by beautiful, natural landscapes. One of the oldest communities in Wisconsin, Mineral Point is listed on the National Register of Historic Places. See Pendarvis House, where costumed guides lead you through a restored miner's settlement and tell the story of early immigration and mining. Wisconsin began in Mineral Point with the inauguration of Henry Dodge as the first territorial governor. Buildings older than Wisconsin itself have been lovingly restored for new uses. Downtown consists of a collection of early commercial buildings ranging from simple limestone cottages to massive Romanesque structures. Art studios and galleries, antique shops and other specialty shops ma ke this quite unlike a typical small-town business district. Mineral Point artists own and operate studios downtown. Once a community of miners, Mineral Point is now a center for the arts.

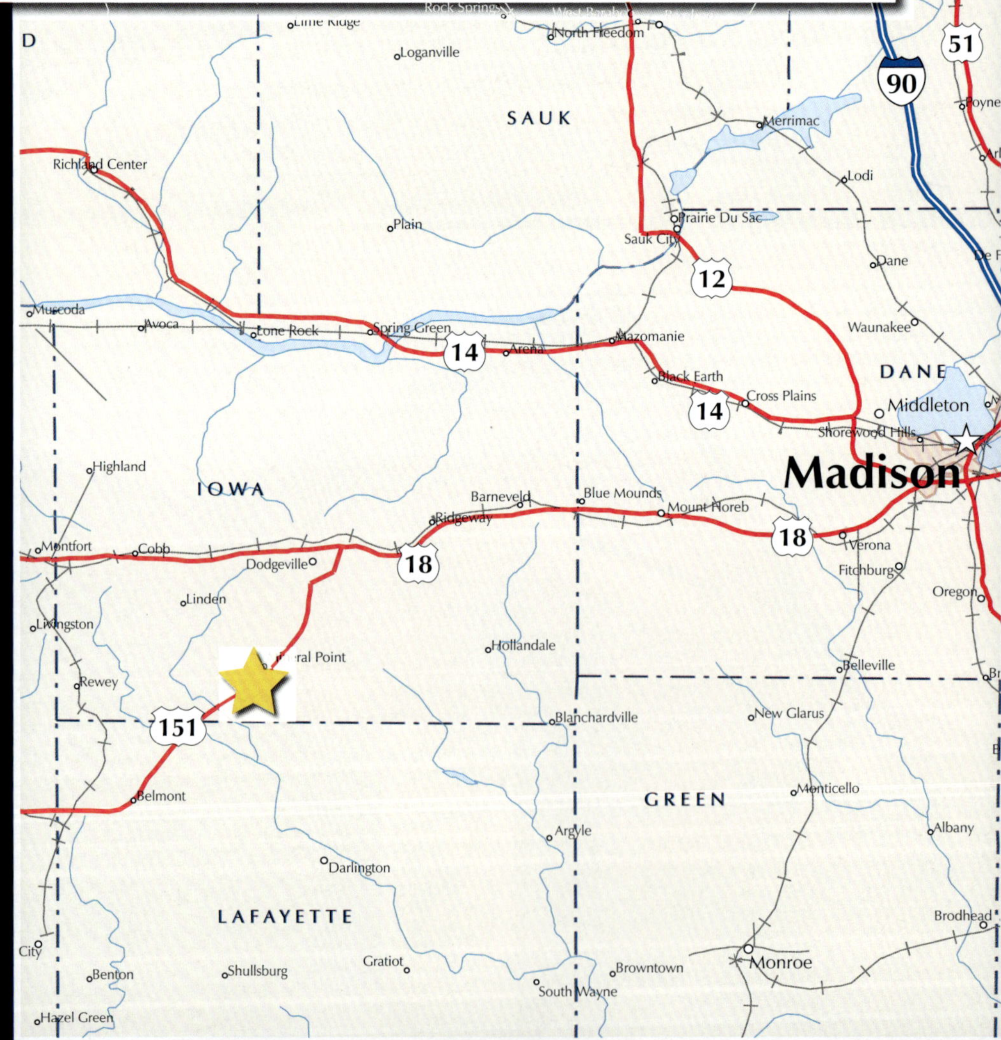

The Cothren House Historic Lodging

ACCOMMODATIONS

Enjoy a relaxing lodging experience reminiscent of a bygone era with a stay at the Cothren House Historic Lodging, a charming bed-and-breakfast housed on the picturesque Cothren Estate. The 1851 limestone house was commissioned by Montgomery Cothren, a lawyer from Brooklyn, New York, who served as a judge on the Fifth Judicial Court for 12 years and was a distinguished member of the committee that brought Wisconsin into the Union. Visitors to this historic estate may choose from two different lodging options, the Cottage at Cothren or the Cabin at Cothren. The cozy cabin was built in 1835 as a pioneer dwelling; it was disassembled and moved to the Cothren Estate in 1977. The cottage originally served as the kitchen for the main house. Today it features two charming rooms, cable television and a private outdoor area. Each morning guests receive a delicious breakfast, brought right to their door, and each dwelling comes stocked with treats and beverages for your enjoyment. The Cothren House recently added an authentic New England style pub in the basement, which is open to guests for wine tasting events and special occasions. The estate's manicured grounds, maintained by Judy Filardo for 30 years, feature several natural, vegetable and flower gardens that make ideal backgrounds for weddings and other special events. Delight in the whispers of yesteryear, while relaxing with modern comforts at Cothren House Historic Lodging.

230 Tower Street, Mineral Point WI
(608) 987-1522
www.cothrenhouse.com

Terrill Garden & Gift Center

HOME & GARDEN

Take a stroll through a Lilliputian Garden of Eden with a visit to Terrill Garden & Gift Center. Opened in 2000 by Larry and Deb Terrill, this family company specializes in full-service landscaping and is dedicated to creating gorgeous, original outdoor spaces using only the highest quality products, such as Rockwood retaining walls and ponds by Aquascape Designs. Terrill Garden & Gift Center's inspiring two-acre plot, originally a football field, is home to a picturesque assortment of quaint bridges, soothing ponds and glorious flora. Larry, who has a background in explosives, and Deb intended to open a small mom-and-pop landscaping enterprise, but ended up with a much bigger operation. Today their award winning business is Iowa County's largest nursery, floral and gift center. Terrill's Floral Impressions department offers an extensive selection of fresh and silk flowers, along with indoor plants and balloon bouquets. As a full-service floral shop, Floral Impressions can work with you to design exceptional arrangements for weddings, funerals as well as special get-well arrangements and fresh bouquets for your home or office. Terrill's is also a great place to find one-of-a-kind fountains, garden benches, wind chimes and goodies for your vegetable garden, along with herbs, stepping stones and original outdoor gifts and décor. Sit back, relax and design the backyard retreat of your dreams with help from the friendly and knowledgeable team at Terrill Garden & Gift Center.

802 Ridge Street, Mineral Point WI (608) 987-3366

Marr's Valley View Farms LLC

MARKETS & DELIS

Four generations ago the Marr family emigrated from Germany to the wilds of Wisconsin where they started a cattle farm that became an enduring legacy for their descendants and a treasured tradition for the community. The 560-acre Marr's Valley View Farms is currently under the ownership of brother and sister team Mike Marr and Lois Federman along with their spouses, Joyce Marr and Doral Frost. The farm raises black Angus cattle, initially feeding the herd grass, then finishing with a grain and corn mix. Marr's beef is guaranteed free from growth hormones and animal by-products, ensuring healthy, wholesome beef. The company offers a range of popular cuts, including New York strips, roasts and ground beef. Other favorites include sliced corned beef and a signature jerky. Pork lovers will delight in Marr's smoked bacon, ribs and sausages as well as the juicy chops. All of Marr's processing is done by Weber's of Cuba City, where it is Wisconsin State inspected and hung to age for a minimum of two weeks, at a temperature of 34 to 36 degrees, in order to promote tenderness and enhance flavor. For those who are interested in stocking up, Marr's offers quarter, half and whole beef and pork purchases. Customers can choose the cuts and packaging they require and pay only for the weight of the meat they take home, a specialty service ideal for families of all sizes. Enjoy quality meat and old-fashioned service with a visit to Marr's Valley View Farms.

21471 S Oak Park Road, Mineral Point WI
(608) 987-3096
www.marrvalleyviewfarm.com

Papa Pat's Farmhouse Recipes

MARKETS & DELIS

Treat your family to a delicious array of farm fresh favorites at Papa Pat's Farmhouse Recipes, where the specialty of the day is always old-fashioned canned goods that look and taste like they are straight from your grandmother's kitchen. Pat Shemak created Papa Pat's with a dual purpose in mind. First, Pat wanted his customers to experience traditional family recipes that date back 70 to 100 years. Secondly, he wanted to provide jobs for individuals with disabilities, in cooperation with the Hodan Center, an organization dedicated to promoting opportunities for work and personal development for people with disabilities. Pat's sister was a client-employee at Hodan Center for 18 years, which led Pat to take a job in the Center's food service department. His own restless creativity led him to Papa Pat's, where he has developed a full line of canned items, many of which can be purchased across Wisconsin and from numerous vendors nationwide. The shop offers 38 products, including relishes, pickles, soups and sauces, along with a variety of jams, butters and pancake mixes. Other favorites from Papa Pat's are the Cornish Chili Sauce and terrific cookie and bar mixes. The company also offers fundraising packages, which are a great way to raise money for your school, church or community organization. Add great foods to your pantry while helping the client-employees of Hodan Center by visiting Papa Pat's Farmhouse Recipes.

941 W Fountain Street, Mineral Point WI
(608) 987-3336
www.papapats.com

Dodge Point Country Club

RECREATION & FITNESS

Enjoy a spectacular game of golf while being surrounded by Southwest Wisconsin's lush and picturesque countryside. Located between Mineral Point and Dodgeville, the Dodge Point Country Club was originally the farm home of Bill Hannah, who built a three-hole course on the property so he could get in a round of golf now and again. In 1947, Dodge Point Country Club received its charter. Today, Hannah's old farmhouse, which has been lovingly restored, serves as Dodge Point's Clubhouse. Current co-owner Tony Pittz's father purchased the property in 1977, and Tony himself has been working at the club since the early 1990s. Tony and his partner, Jay Loop, offer their patrons a casual and thoroughly enjoyable destination that is dedicated to providing optimal service and amenities, including a fabulous restaurant, a pro shop and a driving range with practice facilities. The challenging 18-hole, par-70 course offers scenic rolling hills, tree-lined holes and fast, delightfully tricky greens. Dodge Point accepts reservations one week in advance and requires patrons to wear only non-metal spikes. After a great game of golf, relax with your friends at the club restaurant, where you will be treated to a mouthwatering array of tasty dishes, including hearty sandwiches, juicy hamburgers and tender steaks. Dodge Point further offers banquet facilities that are ideal for weddings, reunions and corporate events, especially when combined with the club's beautifully manicured grounds. Find the fun and relaxation you've been searching for with a day at Dodge Point Country Club.

1771 County Road YD,
Mineral Point WI
(608) 987-2814
www.dodgepointcountryclub.com

Mineral Spirits Saloon & Café

RESTAURANTS & CAFÉS

Savor a taste of history while reveling in the joyful ambience created when fine food and drink combine with true hospitality at the Mineral Spirits Saloon & Café. The original section of the limestone building housing this popular eatery dates back to the mid-1800s, when it served as one of the territory's first stagecoach inns. The vintage dwelling has been the site of numerous businesses over the decades. Pete and Lisa Keller completely renovated the landmark in 2000; in 2005, it reopened as Mineral Spirits Saloon & Café under the ownership of Jeff and Peg Koehler and Sharon Whitford. The café, which is operated by Sharon, offers a healthy menu filled with light but flavorful options as well as a fabulous array of decadent desserts. The saloon carries a full selection of your favorite spirits and a selection of local wines and beers. Local craftsmen designed the large square bar from cherry wood. Comfortable bar stools surround the bar area, and a television above the bar allows guests to keep an eye on the big game. For those who enjoy their meals *al fresco*, Mineral Spirits offers a lovely patio dining section that comes complete with a limestone cave dwelling, called a badger hole, which once housed area miners and today holds a sculpture of three miners. Enjoy exceptional cuisine and old-fashioned hospitality at Mineral Spirits Saloon & Café.

20 Commerce Street, Mineral Point WI
(608) 987-2030
www.mineralspiritsrestaurant.com

The Foundry Books

SHOPPING

If you're interested in learning more about Wisconsin's long and interesting history, from its influence on industry to its patronage of the arts, then head to the Foundry Books in historic Mineral Point. Housed in an old foundry building that predates Wisconsin statehood, this delightful shop brims with rare and out-of-print tomes outlining state history, along with vintage children's books and an assortment of maps, documents and ephemera. The beguiling shop further carries an array of pamphlets, broadsides and county histories, along with other works that are of interest to Wisconsinites and those who enjoy exploring our nation's past. Retired physician Dean Conners started the book shop in 1995, then sold it to Gayle Bull and her late husband, Jim, in 2002. The Bulls choose the business as both a retirement project and as a way to finance their love of books and their book buying habits. Gayle delights in sharing her treasures with her customers and invites visitors to browse as long as they like or curl up with a book in the adjacent garden. In addition to the broad selection of books, Gayle offers the Foundry Boxworks, which specializes in creating book and document reservation boxes, along with memory, decorative and other made-to-order boxes that will be cherished for generations to come. Discover regional cookbooks, Wisconsin authors and a world of other inspiring books with a visit to the Foundry Books

105 Commerce Street, Mineral Point WI
(608) 987-4363
www.foundrybooks.com

The Barn Shops

SHOPPING

Proudly housed inside a stately 1830s barn are 10 engaging shops, filled to the brim with gifts, collectibles and wonders for your home and garden. Jody and Bob Cody purchased the 130-acre homestead in 1996 and transformed the property's 3,500-square-foot limestone horse barn into The Barn Shops. The mannequin known as Grandpa Jo sits faithfully near the door and silently welcomes visitors here, while the Codys happily give tours and gladly answer any questions that may arise. Look for the Woolrich Clothing Shop, where you can find stunning sweaters and outerwear along with great accessories, and the Christmas Shop, where Christmas comes everyday. Other great shops include the Home Accent Shop, filled with clever accent pieces and home décor items, and the Outdoor Garden Shop, where you can find whimsical, practical and downright delightful goodies that suit your yard, garden and outdoor-living lifestyle. The Barn Shops carry Rowe Pottery, baby gifts and fine jewelry, along with great quilts, gift baskets and Hooks world-champion cheeses. In addition to quality products, the Codys dedicate themselves to exceptional, old-fashioned service with a smile, which adds immensely to the pleasure of visiting here. Discover delightful treasures while taking a nostalgic look at Mineral Point's pioneering past with a trip to The Barn Shops.

100 Merry Christmas Lane, Mineral Point WI
(608) 987-2779
www.thebarnshops.net

MONONA

Located just a few miles across Lake Monona from the State Capital, Monona offers all the benefits of a small community with the additional benefits of an urban neighbor. Monona has 24 beautiful parks with over 330 acres of public open space. The Aldo Leopold Nature Center is here as well. With 4.5 miles of shoreline on Lake Monona and the Yahara River running through it, Monona provides residents and businesses a beautiful setting with plenty of activities near and on the water. Each year Monona features one of the largest Memorial Day parades in the area. In addition, the Monona Community Festival spans two days in early July and provides fun for the entire family. Monona contains the site of the former Royal Airport, the center of Madison aviation from 1926 to 1938. The field provided the first passenger air service to Chicago.

PLACES TO GO

- The Aldo Leopold Nature Center
  300 Femrite Drive (608) 221-0404
- Winnequa Park
  Healy Lane

THINGS TO DO

May

- Monona Memorial Day Parade
  (608) 222-8565

July

- Monona Festival
  Winnequa Park www.mononafestival.com

AmericInn Lodges & Suites of Madison South

ACCOMMODATIONS

Whether you travel for business or pleasure, when you check into AmericInn Lodges and Suites in Monona you'll enjoy spacious accommodations with all the comforts you deserve. The welcoming lobby offers a cozy fireplace, comfortable conversation areas and 24-hour front desk service. Quiet Nights, Rest Assured is more than a motto at AmericInn; masonry-constructed rooms block out noise and ensure a restful night's sleep. All 61 rooms feature refrigerators, coffeemakers, small microwaves and hair dryers. Fireplace and whirlpool suites are available, as well as rooms accessible to disabled people. Free wireless Internet access, large televisions with 70 cable channels and guest laundry facilities provide all the comforts of a well-equipped home. The AmericInn meets the needs of families with two-room suites as well as cribs and rollaway beds; children 12 and under stay free with an adult. Whether you're a kid or just a kid at heart, you'll enjoy the indoor recreation area, where you can splash in the sparkling pool or try your luck in the game area. Unwinding in the hot tub, sauna or steam room is a boon to weary corporate travelers. After a great night's sleep, enjoy the free Continental breakfast, which includes make-your-own Belgian waffles. AmericInn welcomes you to the end of the day with a combination of luxury and value.

101 W Broadway, Monona WI
(608) 222-8601 or (800) 634-3444
www.americinnmadisonwi.com

PLACES TO GO

- Browntown-Cadiz Springs State Recreation Area
  Cadiz Springs Road, Browntown
  (608) 966-3777
- Historic Cheesemaking Center
  2108 7th Avenue
- Monroe Arts Center (MAC)
  1315 11th Street
  (608) 325-5700

THINGS TO DO

April

- MAC Taste of Spring
  Ludlow Mansion
  www.monroeartscenter.com/taste-of-spring.php4

June

- Hot Air Balloon Rally
  www.wicip.uwplatt.edu/green/ci/monroe/balloon/about.htm

July

- Green County Fair
  Fairgrounds
  www.greencountyfair.net

August

- Family-A-Fair on the Square
  Downtown Square
  (608) 325-7648

September

- Berghoff and Blues
  www.huberbrewery.com/berghoffandblues

September (even-numbered years)

- Green County Cheese Days
  www.cheesedays.com

November

- Swiss Fest
  Turner Hall
  (608) 325-7648

MONROE

Monroe is the seat of lush Green County. Early farmers raised wheat almost exclusively until a serious oversupply developed in the 1870s. Swiss immigrants helped bring about the crucial shift to dairying. Monroe today is known as the Swiss Cheese Capital of America, and several major cheese plants form the basis of its economy. Visitors can tour the downtown cheese factories and historic buildings on Courthouse Square, which is anchored by a grand, Romanesque courthouse. A drive through Monroe's neighborhoods reveals well-kept homes and flower gardens. Norman Crampton rated Monroe 13th in the country in *100 Best Small Towns in America*. The tranquil countryside outside Monroe makes for scenic afternoon road tours past meandering streams, prairies and tree-lined fencerows.

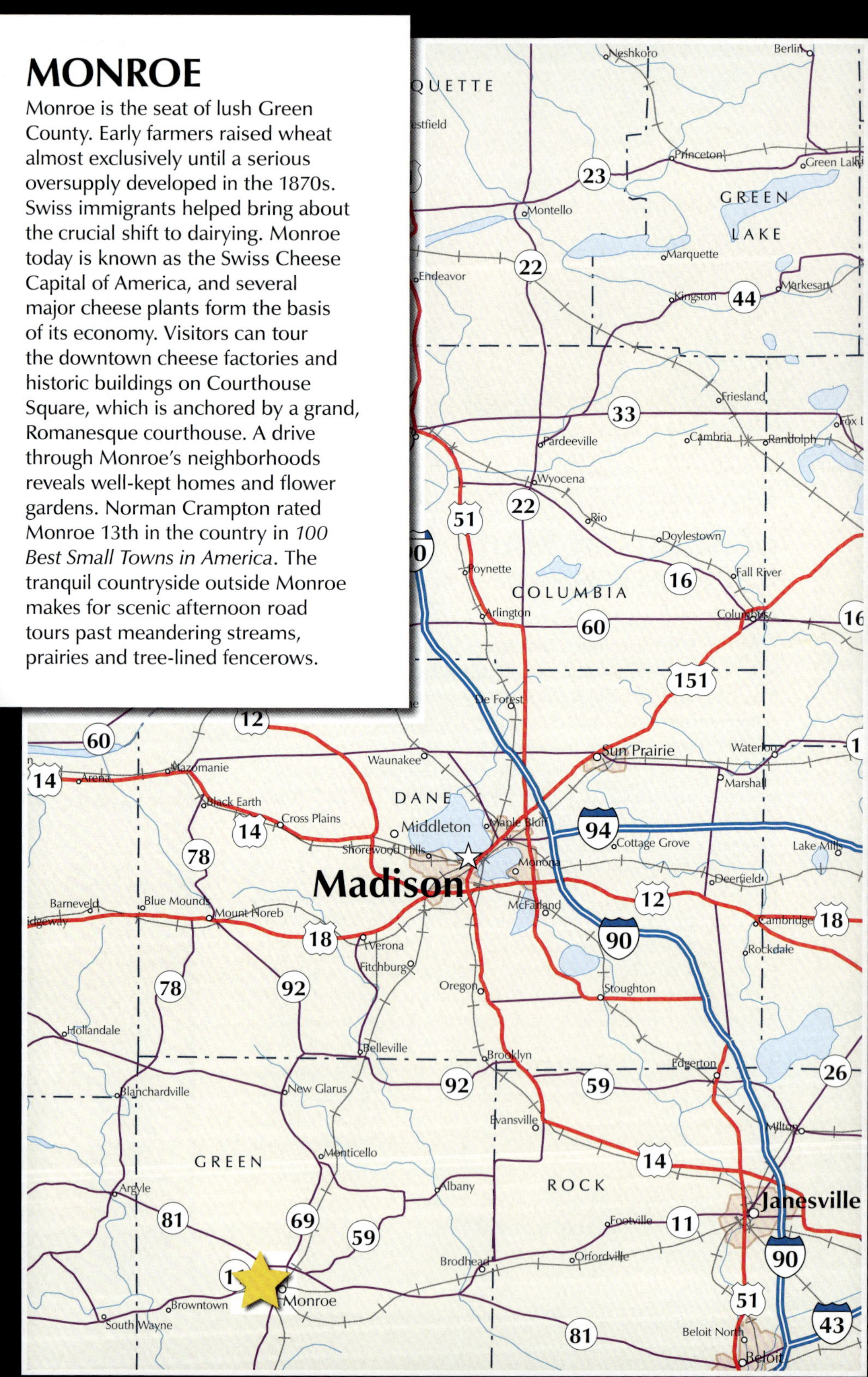

Baumgartner Cheese Store and Tavern

MARKETS & DELIS

In a constantly changing world, it's always nice to find a place that stays the same. One of those places is the family-owned and operated Baumgartner Cheese Store and Tavern, the oldest continuously operating cheese store in Wisconsin. Baumgartner's has been selling cheese since 1931 in a Swiss-style shop in the quaint Swiss community of Monroe. The store features giant murals of Switzerland that make you feel like you're shopping in the Alps. Next door to the popular retail shop you can enjoy great food and locally brewed beer at Baumgartner's Tavern. Baumgartner's features a huge selection of award-winning cheeses, including imported cheeses and numerous varieties made right in Wisconsin. You'll also find specialty foods such as sausage, Landjaeger, mustard and rye bread. The tavern serves great soups, chili, and the best sandwiches in southern Wisconsin. Owners Chris and Tyler Soukup boast that everybody in Green County has made it to Baumgartner's at one time or another for one of their famous sandwiches, and you'll believe it when you see the wall that displays signatures of patrons. If you can't make it to Baumgartner Cheese Store to add your John Henry this season, give them a call. They'll mail your favorite bulk cheeses right to your doorstep. The next time you're in southern Wisconsin, make it a point to visit Baumgartner Cheese Store and Tavern. They're open seven days a week.

1023 16th Avenue, Monroe WI
(608 325-6157

The Joseph Huber Brewery

WINES, BREW, PUBS & CLUBS

Judging by the dozens of awards they have won, the brew masters at the Joseph Huber Brewery seem to have everything under control. Nevertheless, guests on the brewery tour are invited to perform the Huber tradition of rubbing the kettle to ensure a great batch of beer. Founded in 1845 as the Blumer Brewery, the Huber Brewery ranks as the oldest brewer in continuous operation in the Midwest. Its family of beers includes everything from lagers and pilsners to special seasonal brews marketed under the Berghoff, Huber and Rhinelander names. Choosing the best would be impossible, because they have all been racking up bronze, silver and gold medals at beer competitions for decades. A superb beer begins with quality ingredients and then takes its time. In an age when the average brewing time for a beer in America is 14 days, the brewery management at Huber Brewery insists on allowing five weeks for the ingredients to blend together. You will learn all of this and more on the brewery tour. Plus, you can stock up on mugs and t-shirts in the gift shop and, of course, taste the product in the Founder's Tap Room. If you cannot visit the brewery, you should ask for the beer at your favorite liquor store, bar or restaurant. Visit the Joseph Huber Brewery and rub a kettle of great beer.

1208 14th Avenue, Monroe WI
(608) 325-3191
www.huberbrewery.com

Oconto River
Photo by Bob

PLACES TO GO

- Blue Mound State Park
  4350 Mounds Park Road, Blue Mounds
  (608) 437-5711
- Cave of the Mounds
  2975 Cave of the Mounds Road, Blue Mounds
  (608) 437-3038
- Little Norway Museum
  3576 County Highway JG, Blue Mounds
  (608) 437-8211
- Mount Horeb Area Museum
  100 S 2nd Street
  (608) 437-6486
- The Mustard Museum
  100 W Main Street
  (800) 438-6878

THINGS TO DO

May

- Country Jamboree
  Fire Station
  (888) 765-5929

June

- Summer Frolic
  Grundahl Park
  (608) 437-5914

July

- Art Fair and Sons of Norway Kaffe Stue
  88-TROLLWAY
  (888-765-5929)

August

- National Mustard Day
  Mustard Museum
  www.mustardweb.com/mustard-day.htm

September

- Festival of the Mounds
  Blue Mound State Park
  (888) 765-5929

October

- Fall Heritage Festival
  88-TROLLWAY
  (888-765-5929)

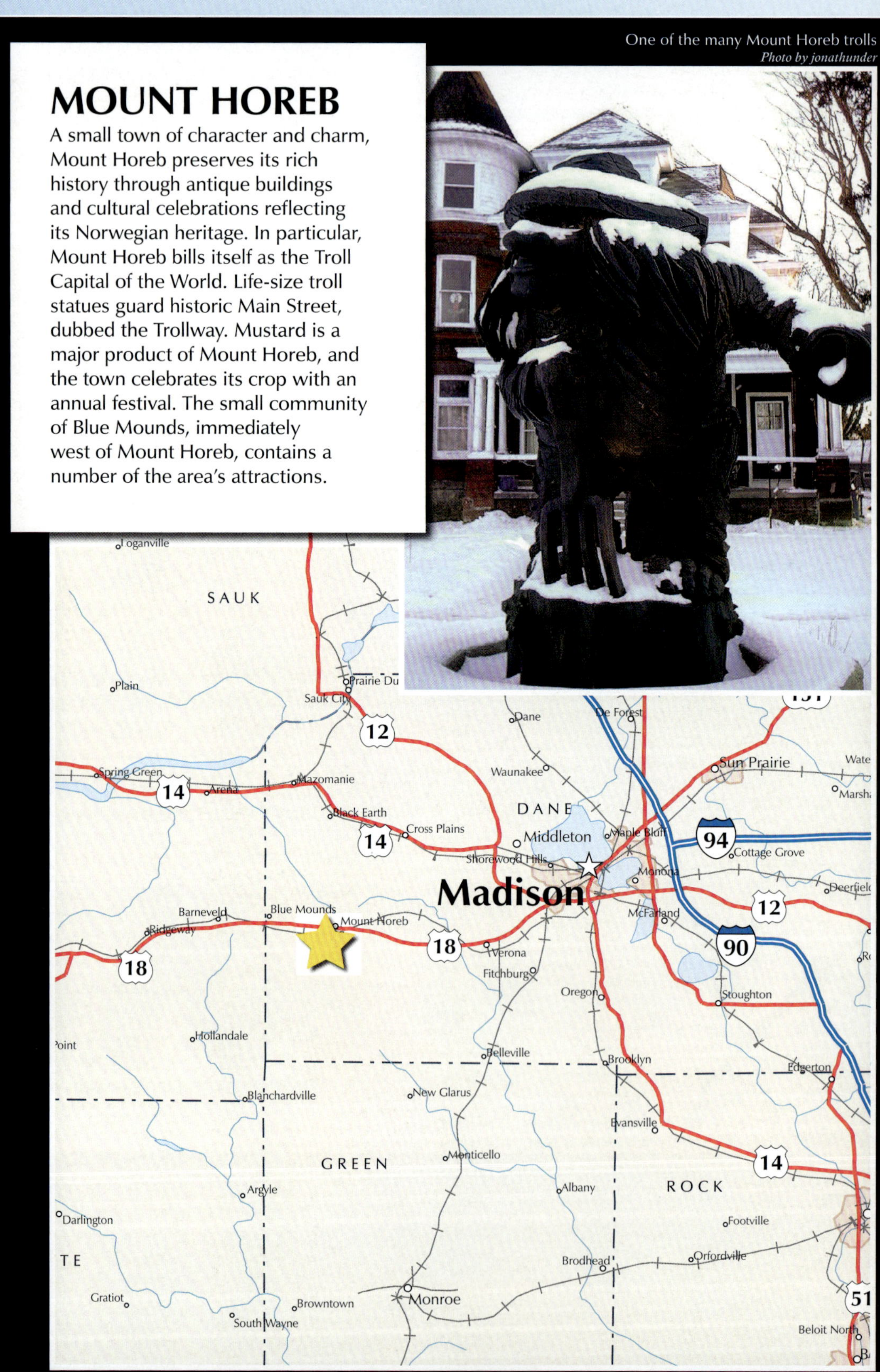

One of the many Mount Horeb trolls
Photo by jonathunder

MOUNT HOREB

A small town of character and charm, Mount Horeb preserves its rich history through antique buildings and cultural celebrations reflecting its Norwegian heritage. In particular, Mount Horeb bills itself as the Troll Capital of the World. Life-size troll statues guard historic Main Street, dubbed the Trollway. Mustard is a major product of Mount Horeb, and the town celebrates its crop with an annual festival. The small community of Blue Mounds, immediately west of Mount Horeb, contains a number of the area's attractions.

Clarence Gonstead Guest Cottage

ACCOMMODATIONS

The Clarence Gonstead Guest Cottage in Mt. Horeb provides an idyllic location for rest and relaxation. Architect Herb Fritz, Jr., who trained under Frank Lloyd Wright, built this stunning 900-square-foot cottage as a guest addition to the main house in 1952. The stone cottage is a beautiful example of Wright's Prairie School styling and sits on a lovely two-acre lot with many mature trees. The property is named after its former owner Clarence Gonstead, a well-known local chiropractor, inventor and author. Phil and Joyce Wall purchased the property in 1993. They have maintained the original features of the cottage, including the cypress walls and ceilings and the large windows. This comfortable suite of rooms includes two bedrooms, a living room with a stone wood burning fireplace and Mission-style furnishings, and a full kitchen stocked with dishes, silverware and cooking utensils. The setting works well for a romantic getaway. Families also enjoy the house, which will sleep up to four. The cottage makes an ideal jumping-off place for enjoying the attractions of the Mt. Horeb area. You'll be close to the America Players Theatre in Spring Green and only five miles from downhill skiing at Blue Mound Park. Those Schwinn Cruiser bicycles provided with your cottage will come in handy for touring the Military Ridge Bike Trail, located just blocks away. For a relaxing vacation in a home of timeless design, plan a stay at Clarence Gonstead Guest Cottage.

602 S 2nd Street, Mt. Horeb WI
(608) 437-4374
www.mthoreb.com/gonstead

Bohn Creek Bed & Breakfast

ACCOMMODATIONS

Bohn Creek Bed & Breakfast is a beautiful turn-of-the-century country home on 10 acres of charming farmland in Vermont Township. Owners Scott and Heather McKay have decorated their home to retain a cozy, farmhouse feeling. The three guest rooms are bright and roomy with polished hardwood floors and vintage furniture. The Vermont room offers a queen bed and can sleep two additional people. The Garden room sleeps two people, and the Futon room is a sitting room with sleeping capacity for one adult or two children. Guests at Bohn Creek join Scott and Heather and their daughter Anya for a breakfast that includes such dishes as eggs Benedict, along with homemade breads, cookies, fresh fruit and coffee. The bed and breakfast is located across from Tyrol Basin Ski & Snowboard Area, which is ideal for guests who ski or snowboard. In the summer, you're welcome to fish for trout from Bohn Creek, which runs along the farmhouse property line. The bed and breakfast makes an excellent jumping-off spot for exploring area attractions. You'll find Cave of the Mounds, Little Norway and the Mustard Museum nearby. You will discover bicycle and hiking trails, a family-oriented fall festival and golfing at the House on the Rock. For a getaway that the whole family will cherish, join the McKays at Bohn Creek Bed & Breakfast.

3506 Bohn Road, Mt. Horeb WI
(608) 437-4085
www.bohncreek.com

Sjolinds Chocolate House

FUN FOODS

If you don't already dream about chocolate, you will after a visit to Sjolinds Chocolate House in Mt. Horeb. Owners Tracy and Chris Thompson and their family opened the shop in July 2006. Yes, you can take home chocolate bars from around the world, but the Thompsons hope you will linger to enjoy your chocolate pastries or chocolate beverages in a pleasant surrounding decorated with Chris' pastel paintings, or come outdoors in good weather. You can savor your chocolate with tea or locally roasted Ancora coffee. The Thompsons use rich Belgian and other gourmet chocolates along with European baking techniques to create such delights a Swedish almond tart or a Danish with a wild blueberry filling. You'll find American-made specialty chocolates here as well as imported chocolates from Columbia, Switzerland and Venezuela. German and Italian confections join Spanish and French chocolates for an international celebration of chocolate in all its many tempting forms. Celebrate an ingredient that has captivated most of the world with a visit to Sjolinds Chocolate House.

219 E Main Street, Mt. Horeb WI
(608) 437-0233

Moonhill Mercantile

SHOPPING

Owner Mary Jane Ellis celebrates the talents of Wisconsin vendors with folk art, gifts and home décor at Moonhill Mercantile. Mary Jane and her husband, James, opened the store in 1994 on Mt. Horeb's historic Trollway. Moonhill Mercantile is Dane County's only Lang Center, featuring all the folk art collections including the entire calendar line, Christmas cards, paper products, mugs and much more from the Lang Companies. Collectors will find folk art figurines and gifts from the Lang Companies, including new and retired characters from the endearing August Moon line. Moonhill is also a Heartwood Creek showplace carrying all the folk art figurines by Jim Shore with their delightful use of color and intricate detail. The stylized figures and flowers in Karen Hahn's Blooming Wild collection celebrate the phases of a woman's life. Fine handcrafted soaps make thoughtful gifts, and Mary Jane looks to a French company, L'epi de Provence, for soaps with irresistible fragrances. The one-of-a-kind furniture pieces made of Wisconsin Bentwood Willow are favorites here as well. Moonhill Mercantile is also your source for Amish candy, made by Miller's Candy Shoppe, as well as fine local jams and jellies. You will find candles, cards, stationery and kitchen items to delight anyone on your gift list. For a carefully selected assortment of gifts for everyday living and giving visit Moonhill Mercantile.

225 E Main Street, Mt. Horeb WI
(608) 437-6346
www.moonhillmercantile.com

Olson's Flowers and Olson's Christmas House

SHOPPING

Bill and Muriel Olson, owners and founders of Olson's Flowers, have been serving the community with premium flowers for all occasions for nearly 52 years. They are the largest Fenton dealer in the state and carry the largest selection of Fenton Art Glass in the Midwest. Next door is Olson's Christmas House, a store that is lovely to visit and fun to shop, featuring Christmas is at its finest. Established in 1979 as a small seasonal shop, Olson's Christmas House has since expanded into a larger year-round store. Here, you will discover a magnificent selection of Santas and fairies by Mark Roberts, Santas and angels by Pipka, and all the villages, accessories, snow babies and accents you desire by Department 56. Look for hundreds of glass ornaments by Radko, Old World Christmas and Inga Glass, a great collection of Byers Choice carolers and beautiful Russian Santas by G. DeBrekht. Possible Dreams, Thomas Kinkade, Jacqueline Kent and Midwest of Cannon Falls are also featured throughout the store. Olson's Christmas House carries many retired collectibles, including some by Leo Smith. Bill and Muriel invite one and all to visit Olson's Flowers and Olson's Christmas House, where the motto is: Don't Start Christmas Without Us.

214 E Main Street, Mt. Horeb WI
(608) 437-3017

Photos courtesy of Fenton Art Glass Company

Scandicrafts

SHOPPING

When Lora Lee had trouble finding work aprons and tool belts in anything other than very masculine styles, she decided to make her own. The result was Scandicrafts, a business newly relocated to Mt. Horeb. Lora is of Norwegian and Danish descent and she honors that heritage by combining *Scandinavian* and *handicrafts* for a business name that is as original as her creations. Her functional fashions include specialized tote bags for dancers and musicians, holsters for massage therapists, and purses and backpacks for students. In addition to her own work, Lora offers a variety of souvenirs and gifts made by other artists. You can find woven and knit items, jewelry, greeting cards and wood carvings, some from Scandinavia and others locally handcrafted. Lora is always open to suggestions for items she can make for you using her large collection of fabrics and trims. For clothing, accessories and gifts that exhibit flair and practicality, visit Scandicrafts.

304 E Main Street, Mt. Horeb WI
(608) 437-2846
www.scandicrafts.biz

The Grumpy Troll Restaurant and Brewery

WINES, BREWS, PUBS & CLUBS

The Grumpy Troll Restaurant and Brewery is located in the historic Mount Horeb creamery building. Built in 1916, it was converted into a brewery and restaurant in 1998. The brewery is located on the main floor of the smoke-free dining room and can be viewed through large windows. Award winning Master Brewer Mark Duchow oversees production in the brewery. The Grumpy Troll offers eight handcrafted beers on tap daily and brews its own root beer. Red Eyed Troll, a mildly sweet and caramel red beer, won the prestigious Peoples Choice award at the 2006 Oregon, Wisconsin beer festival. The beer selections change regularly and feature several IPAs, Stouts, Ryes and Baltic Porters. The complete beer menu is updated regularly on their website. A full lunch and dinner menu, daily specials and kids menu are available seven days a week, featuring burgers, sandwiches, soups and appetizers. Nightly specials include homemade Norwegian meatballs, Friday night fish fry and prime rib every Saturday night. The facility also features a banquet room and sports bar in the spacious upstairs. The beer garden is open all summer for outdoor dining. The Grumpy Troll also sells handmade ceramic mugs, glass containers with their famous logo, shirts, sweatshirts, hats and even growlers and kegs filled with their award winning beers. Owner Doug Welshinger invites you to join him for some beer, cheer and food at The Grumpy Troll Restaurant and Brewery.

105 S 2nd Street, Mt. Horeb WI
(608) 437-BREW (2739)
www.thegrumpytroll.com

Open House Imports

SHOPPING

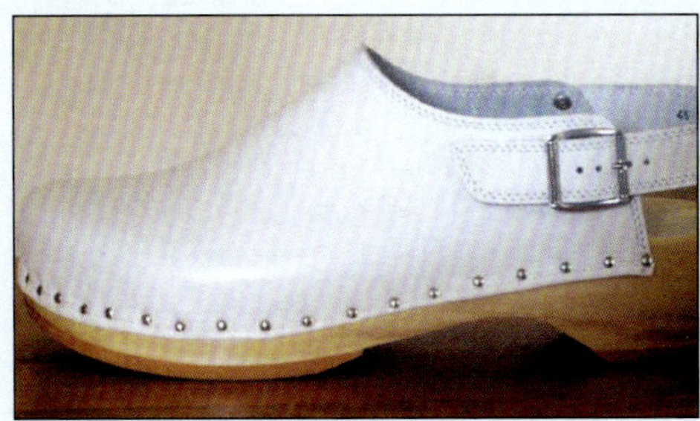

With an authentic Norwegian troll standing guard outside and beautiful art, jewelry and clothing inside, Open House Imports brings Mt. Horeb shoppers a sampling of Norway's finest artistic traditions. The shop opened in 1966 on the street now referred to by locals as the Trollway. Store mascot Troll Odin, with a face only a mother could love, was the first troll along Main Street and stands guard outside the store. One of the chief art forms you'll notice here is rosemaling, a form of painting that originated in Norway in the 1700s and features flowing lines and floral patterns. You will find rosemaling on everything from wooden spoons to wedding chests. You will also find sterling silver Sølje jewelry, the lacy filigree jewelry of Norway. Norway's cherished *Porsgrund* porcelain joins other Scandinavian crystal and china here. Scandinavian clothing is as practical as it is beautiful. Open House carries the Swedish Troentorps clogs, which feature wooden soles and leather tops for long-lasting comfort. A Wisconsin winter gets a whole lot warmer and more stylish with a Dale of Norway sweater from Open House. If you like Troll Odin enough to want to bring one like him home with you, you will find a selection of Tom Clark's gnomes and woodspirits from Cairn Studio. Owner George Sievers invites you to browse through the Scandinavian treasures at Open House Imports.

308 E Main Street, Mt. Horeb, WI
(608) 437-5468 or (800) 236-8811
www.openhouseimports.com

MUKWONAGO

Mukwonago, the Place of the Bear, was once the site of the Bear Clan of the Potowatomi Indians. The first brick house in the area is still standing and is now the Red Brick Museum. Today, the pleasant, rural village has filled up an industrial park, and is a commercial center for the area. Mukwonago offers a beach on the Mukwonago River and access to Phantom Lake. Locals tell the tale of two star-crossed Indian lovers who died on Phantom Lake. According to legend, the drama is reenacted in ghostly form every September 2nd at midnight.

PLACES TO GO

- Field Park
  Highways 83 and NN
- Indianhead Park
  County Highway ES
- Red Brick Museum
  103 Main Street
  (262) 363-6413

THINGS TO DO

June

- Summerfeste
  Field Park
  (262) 363-4380
- Heritage Day
  Indianhead Park
  (262) 363-7758

July

- Croatian Day Picnic
  Field Park
  (262) 363-4380

September

- Fall Festival
  Downtown
  (262) 363-7758

December

- Midnight Magic
  (262) 363-8684

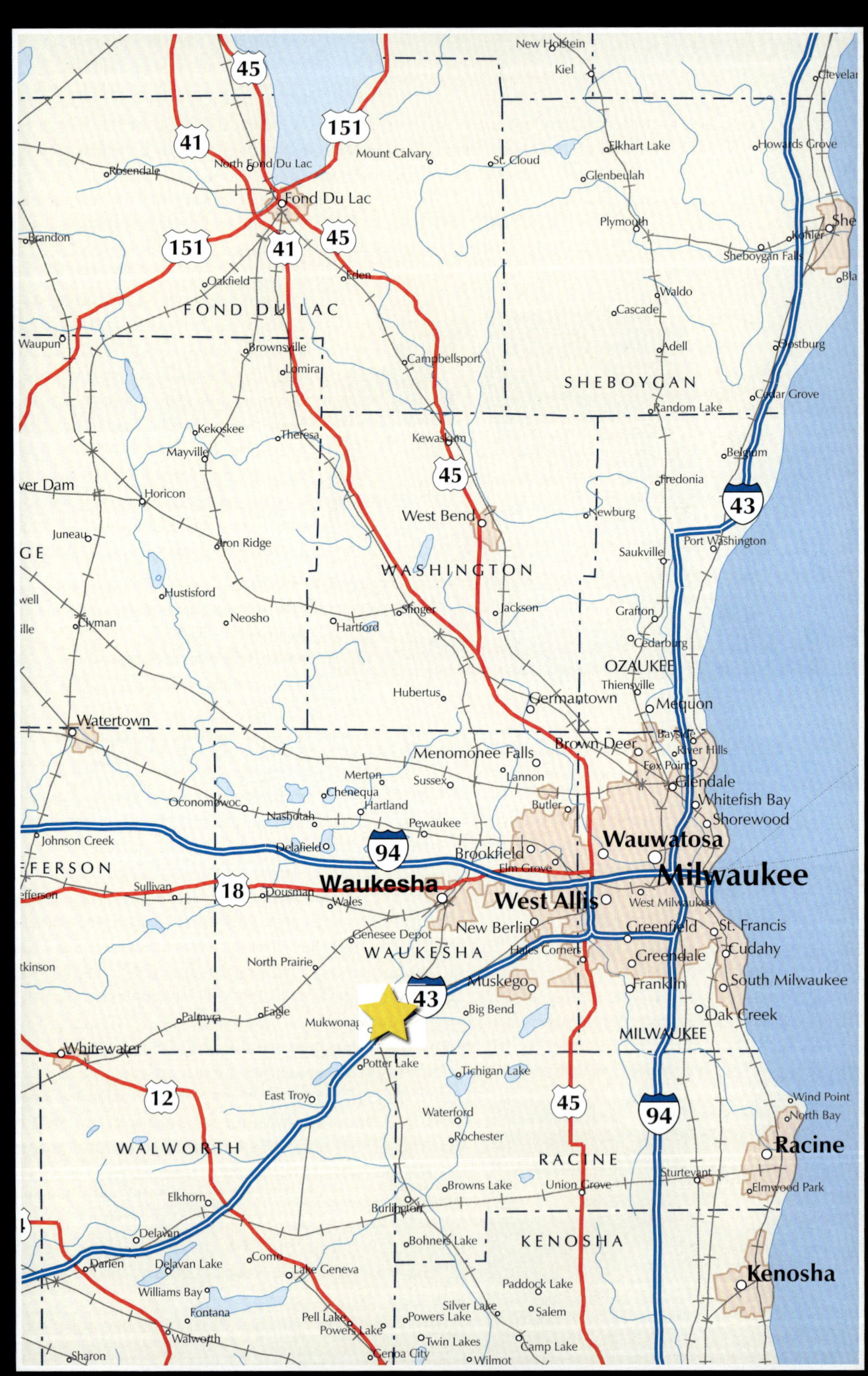

End of the Leash

ANIMALS & PETS

When the doctor said that Susie and Bob Hardaker's dog, Emma, had just four months to live, the Hardakers went to work researching how to provide their Gordon Setter with the best life possible while fighting cancer. What they learned would ultimately inspire them to open End of the Leash, a store dedicated to keeping pets healthy and happy. Through a diet of natural foods and homeopathic treatments, Emma lived 15 months beyond her prognosis. During these months, Susie even developed her own line of healthful treats which she sold to local grocery stores. Susie and Bob are passionate about sharing their experience with their customers and do what they can to help people make educated choices about their pet's diet. End of the Leash sells holistic and all-natural pet foods, organic supplements and homeopathic complexes. You will also find a unique selection of accessories, everything from collars and leashes to bowls and toys. End of the Leash also sells a fun selection of clothing, jewelry and gifts for the pet lover. Emma gave Susie and Bob the knowledge and their flat coat retriever Bradley, who lived for more than 16 years, gave them the proof that diet really does make a difference. For a store committed to your pet's good health, visit End of the Leash.

214 S Rochester Street, Mukwonago WI
(262) 363-3338
www.endoftheleash.com

Stampers Cupboard

ARTS & CRAFTS

Once you enter the quaint atmosphere of Stampers Cupboard in Mukwonago, you are sure to find all you need for paper crafts of all types. Turn your family's photographs and paper memorabilia into treasured scrapbooks and journals destined to become family heirlooms. Nothing says you truly care about someone better than a handmade card. Therese Hennessy opened the popular crafter's destination in 2003, turning her passion for paper craft into a fun and thriving business. The shop offers a wide inventory from more than 100 popular companies with new items arriving every week. This charming shop also offers classes for rubberstamping, scrapbooking, mini albums and all types of other projects. Classes are arranged for groups or individuals and for the young and the young at heart. The classroom is also an ideal place to host your birthday party, baby or wedding shower. Therese created a 1,000-square-foot clubroom where crafters can gather to finish projects and participate in workshops. What sets Stampers Cupboard apart is the friendly and knowledgeable staff members. They are well versed in current paper crafting techniques and are happy to answer any questions that you might have about card making, rubber stamping, scrapbooking or paper craft in general. Relax, have fun and indulge in a hobby that creates lasing memories with a visit to Stampers Cupboard.

555 Bay View Road, Mukwonago WI
(262) 363-5592
www.stamperscupboard.com

Kashmir Music

ARTS & CRAFTS

Kashmir Music sells the guitars, drums and keyboards you need to start your own garage band. Its rental program loans out enough instruments to equip string quartets as well as horn sections. Two hometown guys, Vince Lupo and Trent Winderski, opened the store in 1995 to fill a gap in Mukwanago's retail offerings. Still the town's only full-service music shop, Kashmir Music offers personal small-store service to both the budding musician and the professional. If you break a guitar string, Kashmir Music is the place to find a replacement. It's also where to shop for sheet music, music stands and metronomes. Trent and new co-owner Greg Price keep their prices competitive and offer everything a large music store offers, from equipment to outstanding service. Kashmir Music's roster of instructors currently teaches about 400 students how to play and read music. You can learn guitar, piano and clarinet here, or you can take the voice lessons you'll need to become Mukwonago's next singing idol. Is jazz your style? Is rock or classical music your passion? For a store that covers all the notes, visit Kashmir Music.

200 S Rochester Street, Mukwonago WI
(262) 363-2900
www.kashmirmusic.com

Dragonfly Embroidery

BUSINESS & SERVICES

From spirit wear, to corporate wear, to unique one-of-a kind gifts, Dragonfly Embroidery is the place for you. With a collection of over 14,000 designs to choose from, Kerry Luecht will create a logo that fits your ideas. She also has the capacity to create your corporate logo if needed. She can embellish shirts, jackets, caps and blankets for businesses, school teams, military service members and any special occasion. An interesting job that she completed was for an Air Force Dad who was proud of his son. The final design included USA in large letters with an eagle inside them, and each of the countries below where he had served. Needless to say, he was extremely pleased. Kerry's hardworking partner is her daughter, Erika. She is able to assist you with embroidery and promotional items. You have to love an owner that lists her two cats, Doofus and Squeakers, as employees. They are the store greeters. Kerry remembers when, as kids, they used to call dragonflies the sewing bugs. This is how the business got its name. For your next embroidery job, stop by Dragonfly Embroidery.

305 S Rochester Street, Mukwonago WI
(262) 363-2373

Miller Pharmacy

HEALTH & BEAUTY

Since 1927, the professionals at Miller Pharmacy in Mukwonago have given their patients exceptional personal care. The pharmacists take the time to understand the individual problems of all their patients, and in turn are able to help the patients understand their medications. This service distinguishes Miller Pharmacy from huge, impersonal chain stores and mail order services. Pat Vandehey, the third-generation pharmacist at Miller, is the daughter of Shirley Miller, who continues to participate in the business, and of the late Gerald Miller, a much-loved pillar of the community. Shirley's father, Arthur Stoltz, opened the shop in 1927 on the square in downtown Mukwonago. The soda fountain at the old drug store was a true social center. Needing more space, the Millers moved to a beautiful new building in 1975. Miller Pharmacy offers special diabetes services. The Diabetes Care Center has a wide range of equipment and supplies, including cookbooks and sugar-free candy. The pharmacy provides personalized training on diabetes meters and other products. Miller Pharmacy coordinates a diabetes support group that meets every month. The store also offers a smoking cessation program that meets at the pharmacy. Of course, you can pick up many items other than medical supplies, including Carlton greeting cards and gifts. You'll also find a U.S. Postal Service branch inside the pharmacy. For service Committed to Your Better Health, come to Miller Pharmacy.

801 N Rochester Street, Mukwonago WI
(262) 363-4001
www.millerrx.com

KH Water Specialists, Inc.

BUSINESS & SERVICES

Put the suds back into your daily bath, brighten your laundry, and enjoy a clear, cool glass of fresh water with water treatment services from KH Water Specialists. KH Water Specialists is owned and operated by Kevin and Sue Hellenbrand, who offer a complete line of Hellenbrand water treatment systems, including iron filters, sulfur removal filters, water softeners and reverse osmosis drinking water systems. KH employs a highly trained staff of water treatment professionals capable of servicing all makes and models of water treatment equipment. The company offers a free water analysis and advice concerning which water treatment program will best suit your needs. In an effort to accommodate everyone, KH offers several payment options for necessary equipment, including rental programs with monthly payments and an option-to-buy plan. Kevin grew up in Waunakee, where he worked with his father Jim, who built and developed water softening and iron removal systems for his company, Hellenbrand Water. Kevin opened his own company in 1992 and distinguished himself as a certified water specialist through the National Water Quality Association, an organization that provides continuing education programs to professionals in the water industry and helps them keep abreast of new technologies. KH Water Specialists is a member of both the National Water Quality Association and the Water Quality Association of Wisconsin. You can put a stop to stains in your sink and spots on your glasses by taking control of your water problems with a call to KH Water Specialists.

N9579 County Road ES, Mukwonago WI
(262) 363-4767 or (800) 416-4767
www.khwaterspecialists.com

Mukwonago Jewelers

FASHION

Some jewelry is worn today and forgotten tomorrow, while other pieces go on to become heirlooms. At Mukwonago Jewelers, owner Timothy Davis and his wife, Jane, pride themselves on offering exceptional service and a diverse jewelry collection made from premium materials. Timothy started his college career majoring in molecular biology, but after taking an art class he realized that he possessed a natural talent for art and a special passion for creating jewelry. Tim makes his own platinum castings for the pieces he creates, which is rare in the jewelry business. His gold pieces use 14-karat or higher gold. Over the years Tim has developed his own signature style and design techniques, and his work has been featured throughout southeastern Wisconsin and the United States. He uses a wide variety of diamonds, precious gems and colored stones in his pieces and has gained a loyal following of repeat customers who collect his work. Mukwonago Jewelers accepts many custom commissions and also appraises and repairs existing jewelry. For fine jewelry to be enjoyed today and treasured always, visit Mukwonago Jewelers.

110 Main Street, Mukwonago WI
(262) 363-8932

L'Bri Pure n' Natural

HEALTH & BEAUTY

Admired for its beauty, the butterfly is a fitting symbol for the line of skin care products known as L'Bri Pure n' Natural. Founders Linda and Brian Kaminski chose the butterfly because this creature reveals its beauty only after transforming from a caterpillar. Working with a team of chemists and skin care specialists, the Kaminski's supervised the formulation of a complete aloe vera-based, all-natural line of cleansers, moisturizers and anti-aging products, which help to correct and rejuvenate the skin. The end result is younger, smoother, healthier looking skin. When women look their best, they feel confident, thus achieving L'Bri's overall goal of empowering women so that they may succeed in life. Linda worked for 20 years in the beauty industry, teaching skin care and makeup before launching her own company. She learned from some of the best makeup artists in the field, including world renowned Jacques Lee Pelletier and Steven Tofanetti, who won an Academy award for his work on *Planet of the Apes*. Today, L'Bri Pure n' Natural ships more than 200,000 bottles and jars of skin care lotion, face and body scrub, nutritional supplements and beauty enhancers direct to customers nationwide. Several thousand L'Bri Pure n' Natural independent sales consultants represent the products. L'Bri distributes the skin care products from their company's three warehouses in Mukwonago. The company offers a selection of free samples of its most popular products, which can be requested from the website or by calling L'Bri direct. L'Bri also donates a percentage of their sales each month to the Make A Wish Foundation. To soar like the butterfly to new heights of beauty, try L'Bri Pure n' Natural.

640 Perkins Drive, Mukwonago WI (262) 363-9674 ***www.lbrionline.com***

Won-A-Go Biking

RECREATION & FITNESS

In the 30 years that Won-A-Go Biking has been in business, bicycle styles and technology have changed radically, but owner Andy Fox's reputation for selection, service and reputable repairs has remained constant. Andy started working here as a mechanic in 1977, when he was in high school. He still fixes bicycles today. His other main concern is ensuring that each customer gets the right bike. This means finding a bike that fits a person's height and weight. Just as importantly, it means matching the customer's biking needs to the right equipment. Won-A-Go carries bikes built for comfort, speed or play. Andy stocks bikes and gear from Schwinn, as well as from Trek, a fellow Wisconsin business with a worldwide reputation. Won-A-Go is the place to shop for helmets, water bottles, riding clothes and an array of other biking accessories. Skateboarders know to go here, too, for boards and shoes. When you want to go biking, check out Won-A-Go, which has been keeping Mukwonago on two wheels since 1975.

106 Main Street, Mukwonago WI
(262) 363-4770

The Siege Paintball

RECREATION & FITNESS

The Siege Paintball offers some of the most adrenaline-filled paintball action in southeast Wisconsin. Whether you are a beginner or a seasoned veteran, your visit to the Siege will be fun and memorable. The Siege has five outdoor and two indoor fields. Speedball, an outdoor course, uses giant tires in stacks and standing on end, with a central tire that is eight feet high. Spool and Barrel puts players on their hands and knees for crawling through electrical spools and barrels. Flat Lands offers wooded areas, spools, wood bunkers and a boat. Also known as the big field, it can easily accommodate 40 people. Woodsball is a challenging field, while the new indoor Sup' Air field contains giant inflated obstacles. A second new indoor field, City Street, brings the obstacles of sidewalks, buildings and vehicles into play. The Siege offers a pro shop sporting the latest markers, apparel and accessories. You can stay energized with drinks, snacks and food from the concessions. A $75 membership covers your admission fee for an entire year. Walk-in players are welcome throughout the day. Sessions are not timed, so you can come in when you can and stay as long as you desire. The Siege Paintball lets you enjoy an exciting, friendly and reasonably priced paintball experience in a safe environment. Once you have played, you will be hooked.

S108 W28220 Maple Avenue, Mukwonago WI
(262) 363-9735
www.thesiegepaintball.com

Market Square Family Restaurant

RESTAURANTS & CAFÉS

Enjoy your favorite dishes, perfectly prepared and served with a smile, at Market Square Family Restaurant. Martin and Yolanda Guerrero opened their dream restaurant in 2001 because they love meeting, serving and becoming friends with their patrons. Martin grew up working in his family's restaurant in Mexico City and learned every aspect of the business, from bussing tables and washing dishes to being a line cook and greeting customers, before venturing forth to Wisconsin to open Market Square and forge a better life for his young family. Market Square Family Restaurant is open seven days a week year-round for breakfast, lunch and dinner and features a generous menu filled with scrumptious dishes that are sure to please even the pickiest member of your group. Popular breakfast entrées include fluffy three-egg omelettes and Belgian waffles. For lunch, you can choose from a wide range of sandwiches, burgers and salads. Evening house specialties include roast pork with dressing or tender veal cutlets, as well as chicken parmigiana, savory Athenian lamb chops, homemade pizzas and sensational desserts. The Guerreros offer special menu options for children and seniors, along with diet plates and heart-healthy dishes for those with dietary concerns. Make your next meal a celebration for the senses, highlighted by exceptional cuisine and gracious hospitality, at Market Square Family Restaurant.

1015 County Highway NN, Mukwonago WI
(262) 363-5175
www.marketsquarefamilyrestaurant.com

Whatever Baskets

SHOPPING

Do you need to say thank you, honor a new baby or celebrate a holiday? You can simplify your life by giving a pre-designed gift basket on the next special occasion. Whatever Baskets has a vast assortment of possible baskets from which to choose. They carry sympathy gifts, wedding baskets and table centerpieces. The baskets can contain anything from chocolates to Back to Basics shower gel to flowers and even home tools. Owner Joyce Anderson will have your gift basket delivered anywhere in southeastern Wisconsin or shipped anywhere in the United States. Whatever Baskets can customize your basket by adding anything from a long list of custom items. If you do not see what you want on the list, just ask and Joyce will do her best to find it for you. Joyce was formerly employed by a bank that wanted gift baskets for its customers. She volunteered for the job and enjoyed the project so much that she decided to turn it into a career. Whether you simply need a single basket or have a major corporate order to fill, contact Whatever Baskets and let them help you make your gift giving special.

210 Fox Street, Mukwonago WI
(262) 363-5115 or (866) 845-7847
www.whateverbaskets.com

MUSKEGO

Muskego's three lakes, large forests and abundant game supported a large population of Potawatomi in its early days, who named the area Sun-fish. Today the community continues to enjoy abundant nature and outdoor recreation. Agriculture formed the backbone of the early economy, and the carting of farm products to Milwaukee helped to develop roads between the cities. As Milwaukee residents began to discover the natural beauty of Muskego, a trolley line was opened between the two cities and the first lakeside resorts began to appear. The opening of the Muskego Beach Amusement Park in 1925 and Dandelion Park, which followed, ensured Muskego's place on the map. Though the parks no longer operate, Muskego's beaches continue to attract and the community produces a number of family festivals. During the summer months, the award-winning Waterbugs Ski Show performs free every Wednesday afternoon on Little Muskego Lake.

PLACES TO GO

- Muskego Historical Society
  (262) 679-5990
- Idle Isle Park
  Little Lake Muskego

THINGS TO DO

July

- Historical Days
  Old Muskego Settlement Centre
  (262) 679-2550

August

- Muskego Community Festival
  Veteran's Memorial Park
  (414) 422-1155

November

- Peppermint Fair
  Bay Lane School
  (262) 971-0847

December

- Treasure the Holidays
  Old Muskego Settlement Centre
  (262) 679-2550

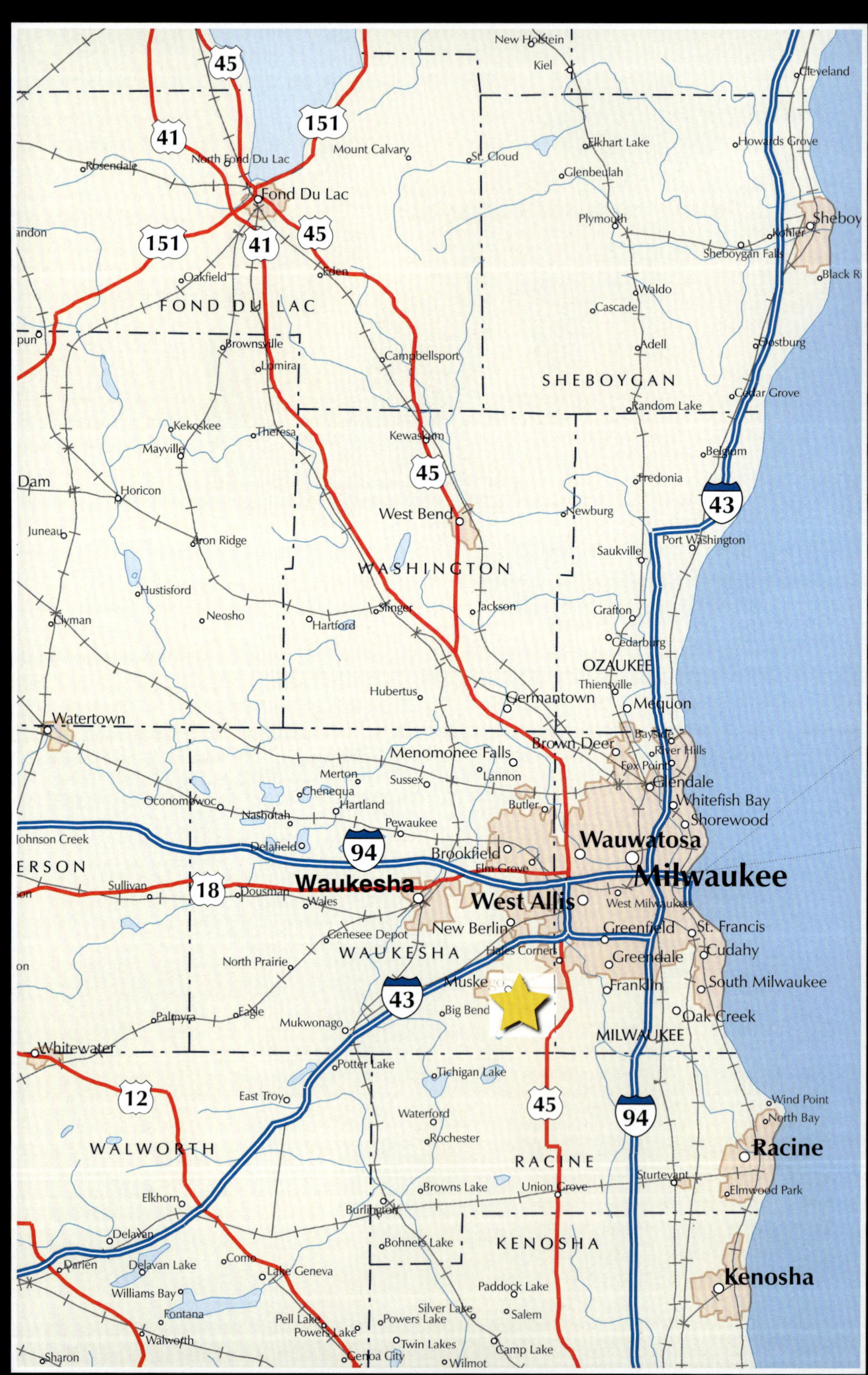

Maxine's Studio of Dance

RECREATION & FITNESS

With a panoramic view of rolling hills and picturesque countryside, Maxine's is truly one-of-a-kind. The studio is housed in a historical century-old barn which adds charm and a warm learning atmosphere. Beyond building confidence through dance, Maxine provides a well rounded education in the stage arts and plenty of opportunities for performance. Students at Maxine's prepare for professional success with classes in pre-ballet, ballet, pointe and jazz, as well as hip-hop, yoga and tap. Musical theater is also a part of the training to develop true dancers. Classes are small, with a maximum of 10 students, allowing for focus on technique and individual growth. Maxine's students have performed locally, nationally and internationally (on cruises). Residents of local nursing homes look forward to the performances that are staged in their facilities. After the nursing home performances, the dancers hand-deliver a carnation to each audience member. Maxine has 35 years of experience. She has danced and studied nationally and internationally. Maxine stages both classic shows and original productions with her husband, Edward Stefaniak, handling props and backdrops. Training at Maxine's provides inspiration and physical development in a friendly nurturing environment.

W182 S8758 Racine Avenue, Muskego WI
(262) 679-1143
www.maxinesdancestudio.com

Alpine Lanes of Muskego and Avalanche Grill

RECREATION & FITNESS

Yes, you can do some serious bowling at Alpine Lanes of Muskego, a state-of-the-art facility with computerized scoring and sleek, attractive lanes enjoyed by both junior and adult leagues. You can also do some serious socializing or bring the family for some food, fun and games. In 1985, Lloyd McIndoe bought the establishment, upgraded the lanes and added bumper bowling, automatic scoring and video games. Lloyd's staff can help you organize a birthday party, corporate event or fundraiser here. Bowlers often enjoy their sport with a cold beer and something to eat. At Alpine Lanes, the Avalanche Grill provides just about anything a bowler could desire, from a cold beer and a fresh burger and fries to baby back ribs, fish and salads. Many believe the handmade pizzas here are the best in these parts. You can pick up an appetizer and a drink to enjoy with your game and continue the fun with a meal in the restaurant. You'll find tables to seat six with holders for your bowling balls, all in an old-fashioned pub setting with rustic knotty pine walls. The grill also offers catering. In 2003, the local Chamber of Commerce named Alpine Lanes Small Business of the Year. Whether you are a seasoned pro or new to bowling, come by Alpine Lanes of Muskego.

S80 W18700 Apollo Drive,
Muskego WI
(262) 679-1250
www.alpinelanes.net

A deer at rest in a Wisconsin park

NEW BERLIN

With its natural beauty and resources and convenience to Milwaukee, New Berlin has become an attractive location for both family and business. The area was primarily agricultural until the 1940s, when residents of Milwaukee began migrating west into the suburbs. Between 1950 and 1960, the town's population tripled. New Berlin's first settler, Sydney Evans, named the town after his hometown, New Berlin, New York. Area residents put the accent on the first syllable of Berlin. The city's historic district converges at Historic Park, which hosts an antique apple orchard. Malone and Valley View parks offer 80 acres each of athletic courts, fields and picnic areas.

PLACES TO GO

- Historic Park
  19765 W National Avenue
- Malone Park
  16400 W Al Stigler Parkway
- Milwaukee Astronomical Society Observatory
  18850 W Observatory Road
  (262) 542-9071
- Valley View Park
  5051 S Sunny Slope Road

THINGS TO DO

July

- Fourth of July Festival
  Malone Park

September

- Prospect Hill Historic Day
  19760 W National Avenue

October

- Applefest
  19760 W National Avenue

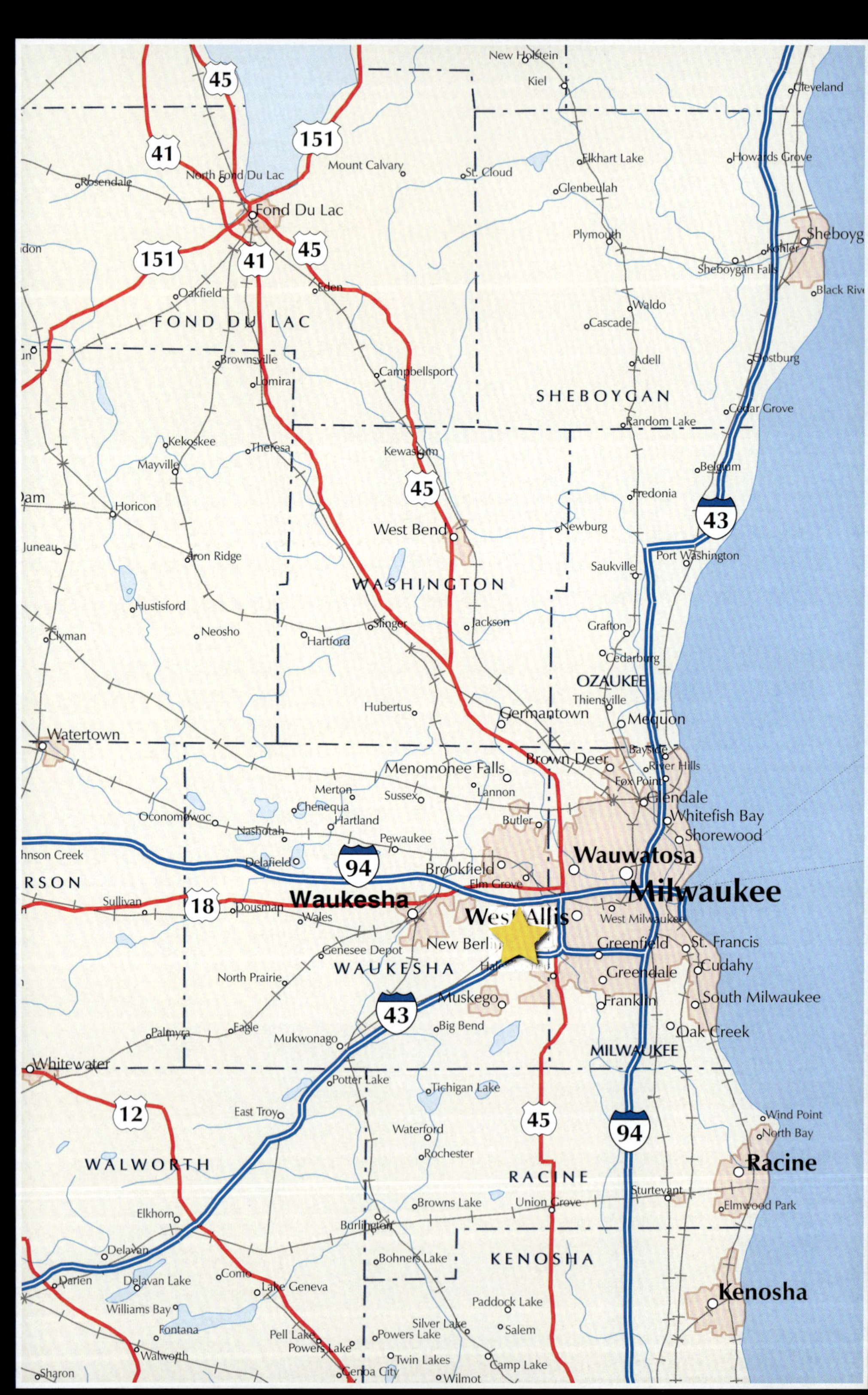

Scrap'n Nook

ARTS & CRAFTS

From rubber stamps to more than 3,000 paper choices, Scrap'n Nook in New Berlin has everything you need to design an elegant or whimsical scrapbook. Linda Barker and her daughter Crystal have been helping customers lay out their memories since 2002, by offering supplies, personal service and classes. Crystal is the expert who designs custom products on the Creative Cutter, a machine that cuts titles and shapes. Crystal, her mom and the staff love helping sororities, sports teams and churches with their custom projects. The café at the front of the store has tables for the customers to use while creating their works and enjoying fresh coffee or tea. This creative zone often makes Scrap'n Nook feel like a workshop or studio. The idea for the business began, sadly enough, when Linda's husband died. Linda and Crystal created a scrapbook for his photos and mementos. Linda went from having no prior interest in scrapbooking to developing an immediate passion for it. Today she shares her enthusiasm not only through her daily work at the store but by organizing the annual bus trip that takes customers to scrapbook stores in other states. Whether you are already hooked on this hobby or just starting, you will enjoy visiting Scrap'n Nook.

14029 W Greenfield Avenue, New Berlin WI
(262) 754-8839
www.scrapnnook.com

Country Sisters

HOME & GARDEN

Country Sisters in New Berlin has what you need to furnish and decorate your vacation cabin. You could also lend a woodsy Up North theme to any part of your home with an Amish chair, antler lamp and pine table. You will get plenty of decorating ideas while visiting Country Sisters, because the store itself is arranged like the inside of a lodge. From the moose and bear prints on the walls to log furniture that invites you to sit down and get cozy, it all looks and feels like your favorite lake getaway. Susan Kirschnik and her sister, Sharon, started selling their wood carvings and gifts at crafts fairs in 1987. They found that they needed a store to keep pace with the interest in their items. Today, Susan runs Country Sisters with her twin sons, Jeremy and Corey. The Kirschniks once made all the items they sold, but success has changed that somewhat. Still, you will find many Kirschnik originals at Country Sisters as well as the work of other Wisconsin artisans. For a shopping experience that evokes trees, wildlife and the rest of the great outdoors, go to Country Sisters.

14220 W National Avenue, New Berlin WI
(262) 784-9631
www.countrysistersllc.com

Four Seasons Sunrooms

HOME & GARDEN

Four Seasons Sunrooms is a trusted name throughout southeast Wisconsin for sunrooms, conservatories and room additions. Al Norgal and his son Scott have the experience that matters when you are considering an addition to your home. Al, who has been in the business since 1965, likes to say that kindness is not a lost art at Four Seasons. He follows these words up with friendly and meticulous service that guides customers through the steps of building a Room With a View that is right for the style and architecture of their homes. The Norgals have perfected their sunrooms through a long process of trial and error at their warehouse and on their properties. Tour the Four Seasons showroom for a look at 10 full-sized rooms. Thousands of photos of previous projects enable you to envision a design for your home while helping you gain a respect for the amount and quality of work that Al, his designers and his crew have performed. Some of Al's carpenters have worked with him for 35 years. Bring sunshine into your life with room construction by Four Seasons Sunrooms, a business with a long track record of reliability and service.

13198 W National Avenue, New Berlin WI
(262) 797-8818
www.sunroomswis.com

Muzic In Motion

BUSINESS & SERVICES

It's hot. It's fun. It's Muzic in Motion. Since 1987, Muzic in Motion has entertained thousands of customers. Todd Scheel and his dedicated staff operate a state-of-the-art facility and provide more than 1,000 shows annually, suitable for weddings, corporate affairs, school dances or sports events. Attention to detail, top-of-the-line sound and light equipment, six hours of music and experienced professional disc jockeys ensure that your reception will be a colossal night to remember. Wedding 101 is the two-hour dress rehearsal for the wedding reception. Enthusiastic staff will walk you through the entire event. Accept Todd's invitation to the next DJ Open House, where you can meet his staff and find out how Muzic In Motion can help you create a celebration beyond your wildest dreams.

2020 S Calhoun Road, New Berlin WI
(262) 797-8880 or (800) 925-8880
www.muzicinmotion.com

Prospect Hill Garden Center

HOME & GARDEN

In a classic case of one thing leading to another, Mike and Patti Backus decided to expand their landscaping business back in 1980 by trying to sell a few plants. Eventually this side venture sprouted into something big, namely the Prospect Hill Garden Center, with 1,800 square feet of retail and 9,200 square feet of greenhouse space on 10 acres of land in the southwest corner of New Berlin. To say that this garden center will amaze you with its array of flowering shrubs, ornamental grasses and 1,000 hanging baskets doesn't even do it justice, because, just for fun, it also has a pumpkin patch, a corn maze and a petting zoo with goats, sheep and a llama. People can purchase common plants in almost any store these days. That's why Mike and Patti aim to please folks who come to their independent garden center to find unusual species. Their selection of tropicals, including banana plants, hibiscus and many varieties of jasmine, is especially strong. Are you tired of the self-serve concept with its lack of help in carrying out cumbersome purchases and its absence of sound gardening advice from a professional? At Prospect Hill Garden Center, staff members are growers, not just sellers, and they are always eager to answer questions and to assist with loading. For a business that just can't seem to stop growing, go to Prospect Hill Garden Center.

19305 W National Avenue, New Berlin WI
(262) 679-2207

New Berlin Hills Golf Course

RECREATION & FITNESS

When the City of New Berlin purchased what is now the New Berlin Hills Golf Course in the 1970s, it wisely let this venerable old course keep being itself. The new owners added some modern upgrades, such as the clubhouse built in 1999, and improved course conditions. However, the overall character of this 100-year-old course remains unaltered and picturesque. Large mature oaks and a river highlight the landscape of this 18-hole beauty. The Root River runs through five of the holes on the front nine, while the back nine plays across a vast and hilly terrain. Tradition is strong at New Berlin Hills, which has hosted several state tournaments and has served as one of the qualifying sites for the PGA Tour's Greater Milwaukee Open. The late legendary Goldie Bateson, recognized as one of the best teachers and players in women's golf, was on the pro staff here for many years and operated the course in the 1950s, when it was a private club. With three sets of tees to choose from and exceptionally well manicured grounds, the excitement and surprises here delight all golfers. The clubhouse features a pro shop and a restaurant, which serves salads, sandwiches and burgers. An adjacent covered veranda is a wonderful spot to relax at the end of an active day. For gorgeous vistas, tradition and tournament-quality challenges, try New Berlin Hills Golf Course.

13175 W Graham Street, New Berlin WI
(262) 780-5200
www.newberlinhills.com

Kat's Café

RESTAURANTS & CAFÉS

Life in New Berlin wouldn't be the same without Kat's Café. Many customers come to this popular spot seven days a week; they even tell the sister and brother owners, Kathy Galanis and Danny Ballos, when they are going on vacation. There must be more than just the fresh, home-style breakfasts, lunches and dinners to make folks feel so good about Kat's. It must be that Kathy really lives by her motto of Love All, Serve All. It's easy to love a place that serves breakfast all day, especially when the choices are as extensive as they are at Kat's, with 17 different omelettes alone. Looming large from among the burger choices is My Big Fat Greek Burger. The menu warns that you had better be hungry for this monster, which puts a Greek spin on a half pound of ground sirloin by adding feta cheese, black olives and gyro meat. Kat's fish and broasted chicken buckets are ideal for takeout. In fact, all menu items are available to-go, which means that you can enjoy one of Kat's thin-crust pizzas and a root beer float while watching your favorite show at home. The only problem is that you can't bring the atmosphere home, too. To eat among friends, go to Kat's Café.

19680 W National Avenue, New Berlin WI
(262) 679-9656

Armeli's Restaurant & Pizzeria

RESTAURANTS & CAFÉS

Tony Armeli isn't out to start some new wave of Italian cuisine. Since 1986, Armeli's Restaurant & Pizzeria has been serving food that would make an Italian grandmother proud. This is the place for spaghetti and meatballs, linguine with clams and lasagna. If the recipe calls for mozzarella or marinara, Armeli's makes it, including a scrumptious garlic crust pizza. You want spumoni cake for dessert? You can get it at Armeli's. The atmosphere is casual, and the fireplace in the round casts a warm glow on a setting that is more like an extended family dining room than a restaurant. The non-Italian portion of the menu offers seafood, steaks and sandwiches. The all-you-can-eat Friday fish fry gets your family off to a festive start for the weekend. If you are passing through New Berlin early in the day, you will want to drop by for the popular lunch buffet. Tony is a visible and gregarious presence at the restaurant, often leading his staff in greeting his guests. Many of his crew have been with him for 15 years or more, proving that working at Armeli's is just as satisfying as eating here. When the urge for classic Italian food strikes, try Armeli's Restaurant & Pizzeria.

16201 W National Avenue, New Berlin WI
(262) 786-6699
www.foodspot.com/armelis

Sunset canoeing

PLACES TO GO

- New Glarus Woods State Park
  W5446 County Highway NN
  (608) 527-2335
- Swiss Historical Village
  612 7th Avenue
  (608) 527-2317
- Chalet of the Golden Fleece
  618 2nd Street
  (608) 527-2614
- Swissland Miniature Golf
  700 State Highway 69
- New Glarus Brewery
  City Track W and Highway 69
  (608) 527-5850

THINGS TO DO

May

- Community Festival
  Downtown
  (800) 527-6838

June

- Heidi Festival
  City Park
  (800) 527-6838

August

- Volksfest (Swiss Independence Day)
  Wilhelm Tell Park
  (800) 527-6838

September

- Schuetzen Fest
  Wilhelm Tell Park
  www.ngschuetzenfest.com
- Wilhelm Tell Festival
  Wilhelm Tell Park
  (800) 527-6838

October

- Oktoberfest
  Downtown
  (800) 527-6838

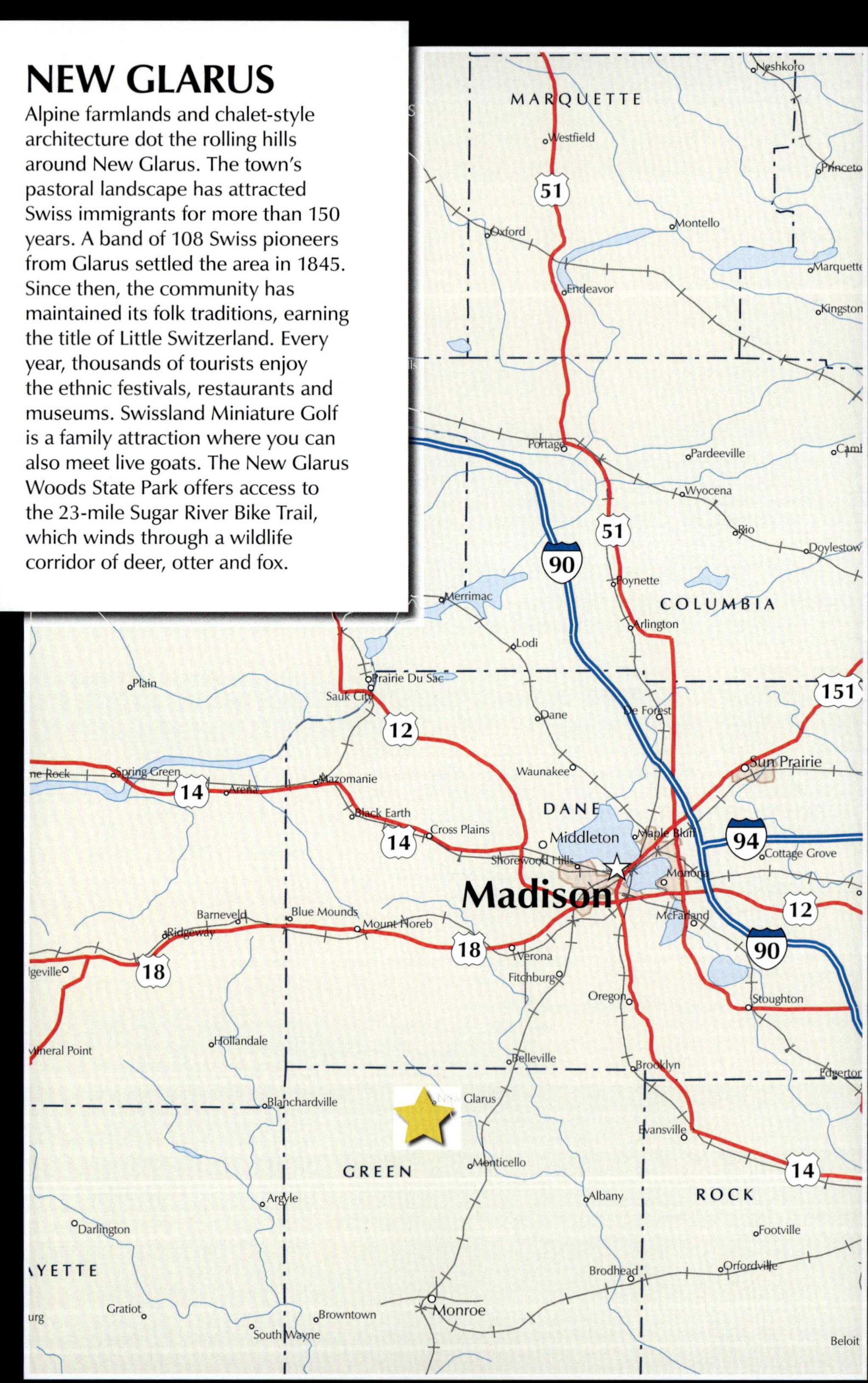

NEW GLARUS

Alpine farmlands and chalet-style architecture dot the rolling hills around New Glarus. The town's pastoral landscape has attracted Swiss immigrants for more than 150 years. A band of 108 Swiss pioneers from Glarus settled the area in 1845. Since then, the community has maintained its folk traditions, earning the title of Little Switzerland. Every year, thousands of tourists enjoy the ethnic festivals, restaurants and museums. Swissland Miniature Golf is a family attraction where you can also meet live goats. The New Glarus Woods State Park offers access to the 23-mile Sugar River Bike Trail, which winds through a wildlife corridor of deer, otter and fox.

Photos © Jerome Mooney Photography

Chalet Landhaus Inn

ACCOMMODATIONS

At the Chalet Landhaus Inn, you can enjoy a vacation in a little Swiss village without leaving Wisconsin. The modern Bernese-style chalet, which has served guests for more than 26 years, welcomes you into its charming atmosphere with a massive stone fireplace, elegant chandelier and comfortable seating in the lobby, sure to entice you to stay a while. The spacious rooms include whirlpool suites and family units with kitchenettes. Business travelers can take advantage of the conference and meeting rooms and then retreat to the large indoor pool and hot tub for some relaxation after work. For vacationers who would like to explore the beautiful surroundings, the chalet is just two blocks from downtown New Glarus and close to two golf courses and the Tyrol Basin Ski Area. Bicyclists love the Sugar River State Bike Trail that is located directly behind the Inn. It is a scenic 23-mile route with a limestone surface, also used for hiking, snowmobiling or quietly watching the abundant wildlife. Start off your busy day of exploring with a hearty breakfast in the on-site Alpine Restaurant. When you return in the evening, the fine dining establishment serves Swiss and American cuisine by a renowned Swiss-trained chef. For a taste of Switzerland in New Glarus, experience the genuine Swiss hospitality and Old World charm of the Chalet Landhaus Inn.

801 Highway 69, New Glarus WI
(608) 527-5234 or (800) 944-1716
www.chaletlandhaus.com

My Friends' House Bed & Breakfast

ACCOMMODATIONS

One of New Glarus' historic landmarks, S.A. Schindler's old house on 6th Avenue, is looking strong and fit as it approaches its 100th birthday. A room in this stately 1911 Tudor-Revival home awaits you at what is now My Friends' House Bed & Breakfast. In one guest room, called My Heritage, old photographs, a hope chest and a quilt-covered bed evoke nostalgia for the days when Mr. Schindler was the president of the Swiss-settled village. Equally rich in personality are the inn's two other guest rooms, My Love, for romantics, and My Garden, a cheerful room overlooking the lovely perennial gardens. Innkeepers Craig & Linda Foreback say that guests come as strangers and leave as friends. The porch, patio, living room and game room encourage socializing, while breakfast might inspire guests to let out a group cheer. A typical meal may begin with assorted Wisconsin cheeses, fruit-topped homemade granola and a fresh baked-good. Next comes an equally beautifully presented second course, featuring a farm fresh egg dish or sumptuous French toast and locally supplied bacon or sausages. Many organic foods are served. New Glarus boasts fine specialty shops and restaurants. Guests can take pleasure in the many festivals held throughout the year. Bicycle enthusiasts appreciate this biking friendly bed-and-breakfast. This area provides endless scenic trails and roads displaying rural Wisconsin vistas. For happy memories in one of New Glarus' finest houses, book a room in My Friends' House Bed & Breakfast.

513 6th Avenue, New Glarus WI
(608) 527-3511
www.myfriendshousewi.net

New Glarus Bakery

BAKERIES, COFFEE & TEA

Savor Old World pastries and original American treats at the New Glarus Bakery, a key member of New Glarus' ethnic community, Wisconsin's Little Switzerland. New Glarus Bakery first opened for business in 1910 and moved to its current location, which was custom built for the bakery in 1913. The site is now a registered Historic Landmark and considered the oldest continually operated bakery in the state, a distinction that was almost lost when the business had to temporarily close for financial reasons. In 2001 Nancy (Weber) Potter had decided to retire from the business after 23 years. The Bakery was then sold and the new owners were unable to maintain it. Former employee Angela Anderson had worked for Nancy and Howard while in high school and had long dreamt of owning the renowned bakery. When she learned that the property was up for auction, she put together a business plan and acquired the necessary financing with the help of friends and a local bank in town. Today, New Glarus Bakery continues the time-honored traditions of making authentic pastries, breads and cookies from scratch, using Old World recipes and the highest quality ingredients. Favorites include the bakery's original hand-rolled nut horns (as featured on the Food Network), and hard-crusted traditional hearth breads baked right on the oven shelves, as well as the famous New Glarus stollen. Enjoy traditional goodies and gracious, personalized service with a visit to New Glarus Bakery, or order online to have your favorite treats delivered to your door.

534 1st Street, New Glarus WI
(866) 805-5536
www.newglarusbakery.com

The Bramble Patch

MARKETS & DELIS

Carol Allen's grandfather would be proud of the awards that her family has been winning for their maple syrup. She sells her syrup, along with an array of gourmet foods and home products, at her store in New Glarus called the Bramble Patch. Her grandfather, Charles, began making syrup in 1889, and the family hasn't stopped since. The most recent award that Carol took home was international: first place for her medium amber maple syrup. Judges from the North American Maple Syrup Council tasted samples from all 19 states and provinces that produce maple products and declared Carol's the best. As if buying a bottle or two weren't reason enough to visit the Bramble Patch, Carol connects customers with the homegrown New Glarus company, Edelweiss Bath & Body, whose soy candles burn clean and long. Other Edelweiss products featured in Carol's store are handmade soaps, shea butters and lotions. She is also proud to carry handmade pottery from the Polish town of Boleslawiec, where pottery making has been a way of life since the 7th century. Gourmet foods with exceptional taste, including teas, salsas and soups, are other Bramble Patch staples. Drop by the Bramble Patch, where family tradition lives on.

526 1st Street, New Glarus WI
(608) 558-8366
www.TheBramblePatch.biz

Maple Leaf Cheese and Chocolate Haus

MARKETS & DELIS

Barbara Kummerfeldt and Steve Wisdom, owners of Maple Leaf Cheese and Chocolate Haus, value the finer things in life. At Maple Leaf, visitors indulge in the flavors of handcrafted fudge, fine wines, cheese made by masters and other gourmet foods. Steve makes more than 200 pounds of fudge each week, employing such specialty flavors as pumpkin, eggnog and toffee nut. Wisconsin is the only state in the United States with a Master Cheese Maker Program, a rigorous advanced education program for experienced cheese makers. All of Maple Leaf's 59 varieties of artisan cheeses come from cheese masters within 50 miles of the store. The Braun Suisse Kase cheese, in particular, holds special meaning to Barbara. It is made from the milk of Brown Swiss cows, the same kind Barbara's dad milked to make ice cream years ago. Barbara and Steve choose wines that pair with the cheeses to highlight their individual flavors. Wine, cheese and fudge demonstrations on the weekends allow visitors to learn more about the products and sample them before purchasing. Barbara and Steve create beautiful custom gift boxes, individualized for the recipient, which may include coffees and teas, candies or other gourmet goodies. Follow your taste buds to the Maple Leaf Cheese and Chocolate Haus for the rich tastes of gourmet foods.

554 1st Street, New Glarus WI (608) 527-2000 or (888) 624-1234
www.mapleleafcheeseandchocolatehaus.com

Argue-ment Golf Course

RECREATION & FITNESS

Golfers of all skill levels are put to the test on the Argue-ment Golf Course, though this nine-hole par 36 course provides an especially welcoming environment for beginners. The folks who run this family owned and operated course have a sense of humor and a helping attitude, both of which are evident in the booklet that they hand each golfer who tees up here. Players at the first hole are warned that "a wide landing area invites you to risk being sloppy off the tee. Don't fall for it!" It's like having an amusing caddie that you can carry in your pocket. Instructions for the third hole, called the Abyss, advise a calm approach to the blind tee. Just "aim for the yellow center flag," they say, "and let it fly into the unknown . . . It's the second shot that's the knee knocker." Even the most experienced golfers will need some help negotiating the difficult sixth hole. "Par here is a wonderful achievement," states your pocket caddie. "Birdie, a near miracle." Will you rise to the challenge? While you are being entertained and coached, take a moment to appreciate the beautiful rolling countryside. The owners have gone to great lengths to provide a picturesque experience, even channeling the water system to incorporate a waterfall into the course. For the ingredients that all add up to a fine day of golf, play the Argue-ment Golf Course on Argue Road today.

N9603 Argue Road, New Glarus WI
(608) 527-6366
www.arguementgolf.com

Edelweiss Chalet Country Club

RECREATION & FITNESS

Rolling hills and beautiful views make a delightful setting for golf at Edelweiss Chalet Country Club in New Glarus. This semi-private golf club boasts a proud history of membership involvement that included getting the necessary funds together in 1990 to build a nine-hole addition to the original 1968 course. From the forward tees measuring 5,400 yards to the back tees measuring almost 6,700 yards, Edelweiss can be enjoyed by players of all skill levels and abilities. Since the club is semi-private, it offers a wide range of membership classifications that are sure to suit your needs. Tee times are also available to the public seven days a week. Everyone enjoys shopping in the extensive pro shop for apparel and accessories. After a round of golf, unwind with a cocktail on the outdoor patio or in the full-service bar. Come enjoy the Friday Night fish fry that will be sure to please your palate. Let Edelweiss Chalet Country Club be the host for the wedding of your dreams. Their banquet room has many large picture windows to give your meal the perfect backdrop. These windows are also a favorite setting for photos, with the golf course in the background. Edelweiss Chalet Country Club has something for everyone, so if you are in the area stop by and check it out.

W4764 Edelweiss Road, New Glarus WI
(608) 527-2315
www.edelweissccc.com

Photos © Jerome Mooney Photography

Chalet Landhaus Inn

RESTAURANTS & CAFÉS

At the Chalet Landhaus Inn, you can enjoy a vacation in a little Swiss village without leaving Wisconsin. The modern Bernese-style chalet, which has served guests for more than 26 years, welcomes you into its charming atmosphere with a massive stone fireplace, elegant chandelier and comfortable seating in the lobby, sure to entice you to stay a while. The spacious rooms include whirlpool suites and family units with kitchenettes. Business travelers can take advantage of the conference and meeting rooms and then retreat to the large indoor pool and hot tub for some relaxation after work. For vacationers who would like to explore the beautiful surroundings, the chalet is just two blocks from downtown New Glarus and close to two golf courses and the Tyrol Basin Ski Area. Bicyclists love the Sugar River State Bike Trail that is located directly behind the Inn. It is a scenic 23-mile route with a limestone surface, also used for hiking, snowmobiling or quietly watching the abundant wildlife. Start off your busy day of exploring with a hearty breakfast in the on-site Alpine Restaurant. When you return in the evening, the fine dining establishment serves Swiss and American cuisine by a renowned Swiss-trained chef. For a taste of Switzerland in New Glarus, experience the genuine Swiss hospitality and Old World charm of the Chalet Landhaus Inn.

801 Highway 69, New Glarus WI
(608) 527-5234 or (800) 944-1716
www.chaletlandhaus.com

Photo © Jerome Mooney Photography

Photo © Jerome Mooney Photography

New Glarus Hotel Restaurant

RESTAURANTS & CAFÉS

In 1845, immigrants from Switzerland founded the village of New Glarus. Now, more than 160 years later, the food, dress and atmosphere of the New Glarus Hotel Restaurant continue to keep the Swiss traditions alive. Hans Lenzlinger, the restaurant's owner, provides a welcoming space inside this historic 1853 landmark for diners to enjoy authentic Swiss fare. Sit in front of the large stone fireplace or at the indoor balcony overlooking picturesque downtown New Glarus. Servers wearing colorful dirndls, traditional full skirted dresses, bring tantalizing plates of Swiss specialties, such as geschnetzlets, thin slices of veal served with a white wine sauce, and kaesechuechli, baked cheese pie. The beef fondue bourguignonne is a New Glarus Hotel Restaurant signature dish. Guests dip cubes of raw beef into copper fondue pots of bubbling oil, then dip the cooked morsels into a variety of homemade sauces. The Sunday brunch buffet offers an elaborate spread, which includes roesti, a salad bar and dessert table. On Friday and Saturday nights, live bands play polka and other catchy tunes while patrons get out on the dance floor. Dine at the New Glarus Hotel Restaurant and take part in the traditions of Switzerland.

100 6th Avenue, New Glarus WI
(608) 527-5244 or (800) 727-9477
www.newglarushotel.com

Roberts' European Imports

SHOPPING

Located in New Glarus, America's Little Switzerland, Roberts' European Imports offers you a treasure trove of authentic Swiss, Austrian and German imports. Stop in and enjoy this eclectic collection of tradition, from leaded stained glass sheilds, to dirndls and cowbells. Roberts' also offers a variety of fondue pots, burners, forks and cookbooks for meat fondue, cheese fondue, chocolate and other tasty fondue recipes. This shop features German-made *bräzeli* irons used by Swiss bakers to prepare the traditional Swiss holiday cookie of the same name. And from the tradition of herdsmen in Alpine meadows of old, Roberts' brings to you a variety of *raclette* grills to prepare meals of melted cheese, grilled potatoes, pickles and onions. In addition, you'll discover Swiss lace and watches, Victorinox knives, home accessories, traditional folk wear, music CDs, alpine prints, Langenthal China, German cuckoo clocks and other delights. Roberts' brings you the sights and sounds of Switzerland—the very flavor of the Alps. If you are unable to visit Roberts' in person, shop online for their full line of imported European products. You'll be glad you did. Roberts' European Imports—since 1946, your Swiss Store in the USA.

102 5th Avenue, New Glarus WI
(608) 527-2417 or (800) 968-2517
www.shopswiss.com

OAK CREEK

Located along the western shore of Lake Michigan, Oak Creek enjoys suburban tranquility with metropolitan conveniences. The community comprises 22 distinctive neighborhoods, each defined by its own physical and cultural features. Vegetable farms dot the surrounding regions, while a diverse industry supports the town. The Oak Creek Power Plant serves the additional function of being one of the few successful nesting places of the endangered Peregrine Falcon. Oak Creek citizens find outdoor recreation at the city's parks and lakefront. During the warmer months, the Community Center hosts an outdoor concert series. The Oak Creek Historical Society maintains a complex of five 19th century buildings and a museum.

PLACES TO GO

- Oak Creek Historical Society
  (414) 764-0567
- Henry Miller Park
  315 E Groveland Drive

THINGS TO DO

July

- Independence Day Celebration
  Downtown

August

- Pig Roast
  Henry Miller Park

Eugene Eder

The Eder Flag Manufacturing Company

BUSINESS & SERVICES

The Eder Flag Manufacturing Company believes that American flags should still be made in the U.S.A. The Eder family has been in business since 1887, and owner Eugene Eder carries on family traditions passed down through the generations. From humble beginnings making pillows, hunting jackets and rag dolls, Eder Flag has become one of the largest manufacturers of flags in the United States. Quality and pride are very important here. All flags are made in-house, whether they are Old Glory, armed forces, maritime or college flags. All flags come in a variety of fabrics and sizes to fit any purpose, from paper toothpick flags to 50-by-100 foot banners. Eder makes holiday and religious flags, flags from around the world, custom flags for Fortune 500 corporations and flags bearing family crests. It makes millions of flags each year. The company is the nation's largest supplier of flagpoles, with nearly 900 models available. It also offers the largest selection of flagpole ornaments. The company made the ornaments for the top of the flagpoles at the United Nations and the flag held by firemen at the World Trade Center after the 9/11 terrorist attacks. Stop by the retail store for flags and gifts bearing the Stars and Stripes. Show your pride in your country, school, military service or other fellowship with an American-made flag from the Eder Flag Manufacturing Company.

1000 W Rawson Avenue, Oak Creek WI
(414) 764-3522 or (800) 558-6044
www.ederflag.com

PEWAUKEE

Pewaukee sits on the eastern tip of Pewaukee Lake at the mouth of the Pewaukee River. The lakefront is the heart of the community, providing for a wide variety of water sports as well as Pewaukee's major industry, sailboat and yacht equipment. During the summer months, citizens enjoy free music concerts every Wednesday afternoon on the lakefront. Downtown Pewaukee is a quaint shopping district. Visitors can view remnants of early Pewaukee at the home of Asa Clark, the town's first settler.

PLACES TO GO

- Clark House Museum
  206 E Wisconsin Avenue
  (262) 691-0233

THINGS TO DO

January

- Fire & Ice Winter Festival
  Lakefront Park
  (262) 691-7275

June

- Pewaukee Beach Party
  Lakefront
  (262) 695-1492

July

- Taste of Lake Country
  Lakefront
  (262) 695-9735

Positively Pewaukee

ATTRACTIONS

Contact Positively Pewaukee to find out what this thriving Wisconsin community has to offer. Positively Pewaukee is a nonprofit, volunteer-driven organization dedicated to fostering and promoting the economic growth and revitalization of Pewaukee. It oversees architectural guidelines for the downtown area, a charming row of shops, restaurants and service businesses designed to look like a vintage Main Street. Its visitor guide to downtown is available at the Positively Pewaukee office or throughout the town. Positively Pewaukee also organizes events that provide fun and bolster civic pride. Taste of Lake Country is one such event, held the last Friday and Saturday in July. Plan your trip to Pewaukee around this celebration to sample the cuisine from local restaurants and enjoy music and other family entertainment. Positively Pewaukee also invites you to register for the Run to the Beach in June, to participate in the scarecrow contest and the Pewaukee Halloween Fun Fest in October, and to attend Waterfront Wednesdays for summer music on the lakefront. If you are new to the area, joining Positively Pewaukee is a great way to meet people and get involved with the community. Whether you are just passing through or moving here to start a new chapter in your life, get in touch with Pewaukee at Positively Pewaukee.

120 W Wisconsin Avenue, Pewaukee WI (262) 695-9735 *www.positivelypewaukee.com*

Photo by D.J. Herda

Pewaukee Veterinary Service

ANIMALS & PETS

When your pet is ill, injured, or needs wellness care, you want veterinarians you can count on to treat the patient with compassion and dignity. You'll find this and more at Pewaukee Veterinary Service, including state-of-the-art medical technology and specialists in innovative methods of animal care. Randy Schuett, who founded Pewaukee Veterinary Service in 1976, is joined by his twin brother, Jeff, in providing complete life health and wellness care to cats and dogs including orthopaedics, dentistry, endoscopy and surgical services. Their well rounded team of caregivers includes veterinarians Tom Hirth and Greta Grittinger, who handle domestic pets and exotics, as well as Eli Larson, who sees a wide variety of pets. Ann-Margret Morgan completes the medical team with certifications in veterinary acupuncture and complementary medicine, such as spinal manipulation and holistic therapies. Expect a level of care that uses the latest advances in endoscopy and ultrasound technology, digital dental x-ray, anesthesia and heart monitoring in all surgery suites. Pewaukee Veterinary Service is not only known for its level of veterinary medical care, but also for its Canine Rehabilitation Center, featuring many types of rehabilitation therapies including hydrotherapy, which uses an underwater treadmill system. The staff is just as top notch as the facility and happy to serve their clients and their pets in all areas of the hospital as well as the pet boarding and grooming business. For veterinary care that is truly both cutting edge and compassionate, come to Pewaukee Veterinary Service.

N29 W23950 Schuett Drive, Pewaukee WI
(262) 347-OPVS (0787)
www.pewaukeeveterinaryservice.com

TLC University

BUSINESS & SERVICES

Debbie Sonnemann, Cheri Otto and Dawn Sukowski, co-owners of TLC University, share a common passion for providing a nurturing environment for children. They became partners when Dawn and Cheri, already co-owners of a daycare center, needed to find a new location for their business. Debbie, who earned a bachelor's degree in early childhood education, started working for TLC when her daughter was an infant and then bought the business in 1995. The three women had previously shared staff and worked together comfortably, so they joined forces and began scouting for a new location. After finding a building, they designed their portion of it to reflect their vision of an ideal childcare center and reopened in September 2005. Dawn, who always wanted to be a teacher, takes charge of the kitchen by cooking most of the meals. Cheri learned childcare with hands-on work at a day care center while attending school as an elementary education major. Debbie, Cheri and Dawn wear many hats, sharing responsibilities and working together to keep costs reasonable and quality high. Their staff members are state certified and work with children from infancy through age 12. The school groups children by age and keeps class sizes small. TLC schedules ample learning opportunities each day, but also allows plenty of free play and individual creativity. The school provides nutritious breakfasts, lunches and snacks. For tender, loving care in a homelike atmosphere, bring your children to TLC University.

1343 E Wisconsin Avenue, Suite 115, Pewaukee WI (262) 691-8800

Judi Welch Signs

BUSINESS & SERVICES

As the sole proprietor of Judi Welch Signs, Judi has been able to expand her abilities as well as her business, allowing for creative flair and a one-of-a-kind look that is often lost in larger companies. Over 25 years, Judi has become well-known for her boat name paintings that can appear on anything from a 15-foot fishing boat to a 60-foot yacht. Some of these boat names include work for celebrities, for example, Ray Alan's *Sugar 34*, Mike Holmgren's *Five Ladies* and Mark Chumura's *Super Chewy*. In 1996, Judi was given the opportunity to team up with other sign shops and paint buses for the 1996 Olympics in Atlanta. In 1995, she helped work on the entrance field to the College Football Hall of Fame at Notre Dame. It is because of her unique style and capabilities that Judi has participated in so many projects. With signs handcrafted from conception to design to implementation, Judi Welch Signs is a distinctive full service business. Let Judy take your idea and turn it into customized reality. As her slogan says, It's All in the Technique.

Pewaukee WI
(262) 691-9520
www.judiwelchsigns.com

Tim's Carpentry

HOME & GARDEN

Tim's Carpentry uses reclaimed and recycled building materials to add charm and beauty to your home. Tim Steep and Kathleen Randolph Steep worked for years in the restaurant business. In a moment of soul searching, Kathleen asked Tim what he would choose to do if he could do anything in the world. Tim immediately replied that he would become a finish carpenter. Within three weeks of that fated conversation, Tim found an apprenticeship with a carpentry business. He learned the craft for five years before setting off on his own to change the way people build homes.

The Steeps strive for green buildings that use environmentally sound construction methods and reuse building materials, thus reducing the need for new raw materials. The benefits of green buildings extend beyond environmental consciousness to reduced energy costs and added comfort, as with radiant floor heat, an efficient heating method that offers the luxury of stepping onto a warm floor on a cool morning. Because much of the salvaged material comes from older buildings, built in a time when such items as doors and mantles were hand carved, the materials can also add character to a space. If you like the idea of environmentally friendly remodeling but are unsure how to proceed, Kathleen's skills as a designer will help with the planning stages, and Tim's building skills will see the job through to completion. Come to Tim's Carpentry to make your home, and the world, a more beautiful place.

162 Sussex Street, Pewaukee WI
(414) 507-7752

All Things Organized

HOME & GARDEN

If you are afraid to go up into your attic because you might get buried under all of the stuff you have piled there, then you need to contact Patty VanWilligen at All Things Organized. If your messy office has become the butt of your colleagues' jokes, then maybe it's time you got serious and let a professional organizer bring order to the chaos. All Things Organized provides hands-on organizing services designed to meet each client's specific needs. What's more, Patty strives to teach, encourage and motivate her clients to remain organized in the future. Patty worked in the corporate world for 19 years, so she brings a high level of professionalism to her new career as a clutter buster extraordinaire. Since starting All Things Organized in 2004, she has straightened up many homes and businesses. She shares her ideas for organizing at seminars, too, and is a member of the National Association of Professional Organizers. Even well organized people can feel overwhelmed when preparing to move out of one home and into another. Patty can help take the stress out of that daunting task. If you are ready to reduce the mess in your home or workplace, call Patty VanWilligen at All Things Organized.

995 Zachary Court, Pewaukee WI
(262) 352-4332
www.allthingsorganizedwi.com

designXchange

HOME & GARDEN

The proprietor of designXchange, Katie Guindon, loves the hunt. Using her discriminating taste to choose home décor pieces from around the world, she fills her small consignment boutique with wonderful and interesting items. "We live in a disposable society where things are constantly changing," says Katie Guindon, "but there will always be people looking for originals of lasting value." For those people, designXchange offers a place to buy and sell home décor, furniture and accessories. From salvaged ceiling tins, one-of-a-kind works of art, and stained glass panels, to armoires, jewelry and handmade handbags, you can uncover the perfect items for your home or an unforgettable gift. Whether it is new or a gently used classic, "I am always looking for the best pieces," Guindon says. "Big box stores represent the ordinary. My small boutique provides the extraordinary." You will find new surprises everyday at designXchange. You can discover trendy contemporary pieces as well as classics. Even the building, which was a one room school house from 1874, is historic. See what you can find and learn how to mix old and new at designXchange. Call or visit the website for more information.

N34 W24041 Capitol Drive, Pewaukee WI
(262) 746-9477
www.designXchange.biz

RCI, Remodeling Center Inc.

HOME & GARDEN

The approach at Remodeling Center, Inc., or RCI, is a careful balance of creative design and the know-how to orchestrate every stage of a residential remodeling job. An RCI experience begins with a thorough design and estimation phase, where RCI works with your wish list to develop design solutions for you. RCI skilled craftspeople are experts at enlarging and updating kitchens to maintain important original elements while incorporating innovative and fully functional new layouts and equipment. They can also thoughtfully plan and execute a master suite, a family room or any project from one room to an entire house. Their stellar remodeling jobs and home additions display a wide spectrum of styles, thanks to careful attention to individual style preferences. RCI has been honored by national and regional associations devoted to remodeling, earning numerous awards for workmanship, attention to detail and historical renovation. RCI is affiliated with Remodelers Advantage, a select national group dedicated to successful business practices. The company builds function and great design into its projects while striving to give each client an enjoyable experience. When you need a building project from the design stage through to completion, come to the award winning professionals at Remodeling Center, Inc.

N35 W21100 Capitol Drive, Suite 6,
Pewaukee WI
(262) 781-8053
www.rcidesignbuild.com

Before

After

Pilates on the Lake

RECREATION & FITNESS

At Pilates on the Lake in Pewaukee, owners Debbie Orlando and Ronda Heppe know that how you stand can affect the health of your entire body. They follow in the footsteps of early 20th century body fitness pioneer Joseph Pilates, who taught a program of movement that strengthens abdominal and back muscles with mind and body control. "It's really not just a workout; it's a lifestyle change," says Debbie, who teaches people to align their bodies for optimum health. The fully equipped studio, which offers private and group sessions with highly trained instructors, opened in January 2006. Debbie holds a gold certification from the Pilates Method Alliance, the highest standard in the field. Programs include private and semi-private sessions that can address individual needs and equipment classes that expand upon mat work for a full-body workout. The Pole, Reformer and Chair classes benefit professional athletes, people recovering from injury and anyone seeking coordination and core strength. Instruction can be tailored for dancers, women before and after childbirth, or people with such disabilities as scoliosis or multiple sclerosis. Ronda and Debbie donate to Trek 100, a 100-mile bicycle ride that funds research for childhood cancers. They are also sponsors of the Sprint for Spina Bifida, and a major sponsor of the Susan Komen Race for a Cure. For a lifetime of balance, strength and flexibility, schedule a workout with one of the certified, professional instructors at Pilates on the Lake.

161 Wisconsin Avenue, Pewaukee WI
(262) 695-2262
www.pilatesonthelake.com

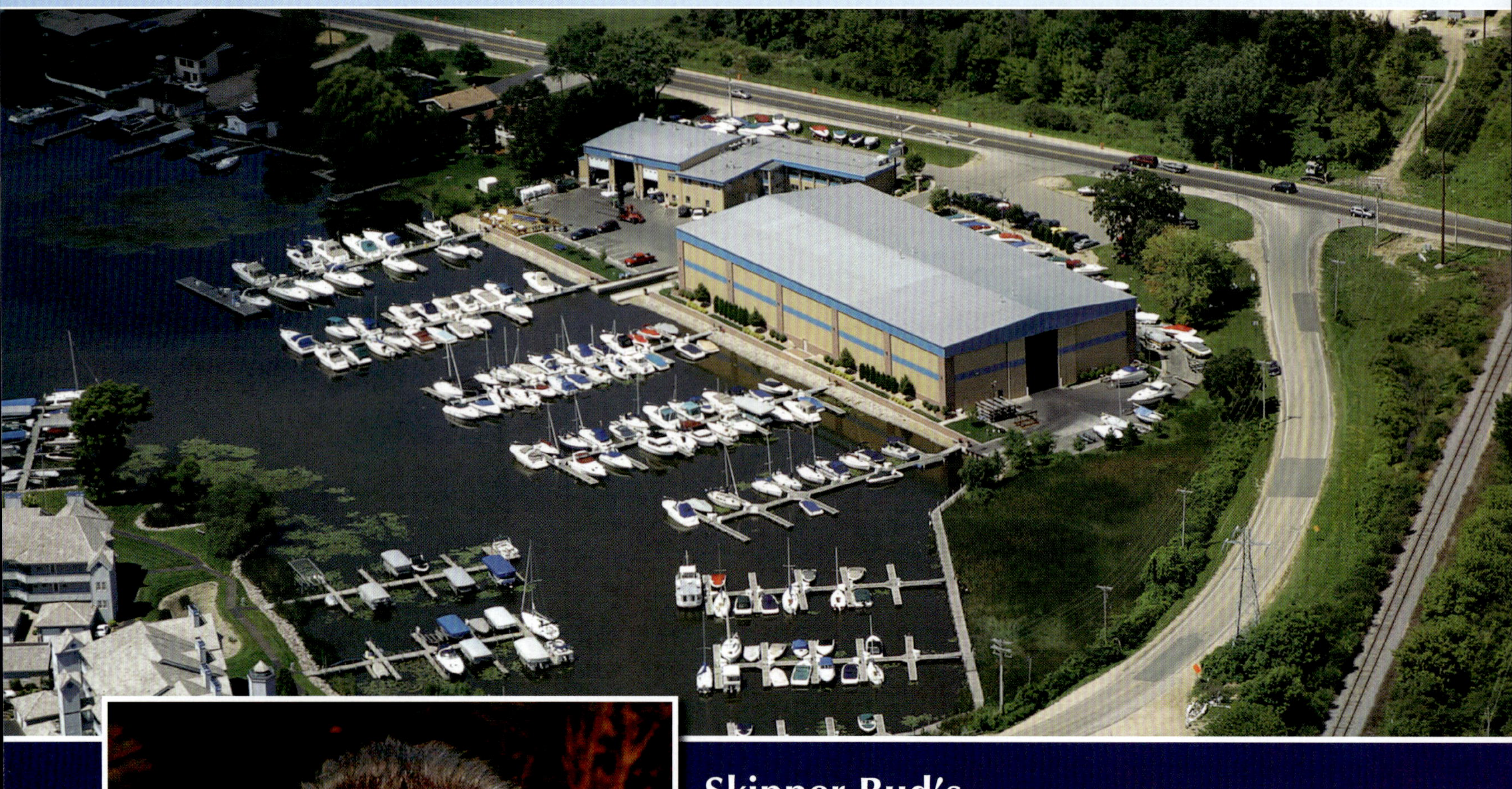

Skipper Bud's

RECREATION & FITNESS

If life on the water is your passion, begin making your dreams come true with a trip to Skipper Bud's. Family run and operated, Skipper Bud's has made a name for itself as one of the two leading boat dealerships in America by offering its clients everything from small family runabouts to luxury yachts. For all their success, the owners would be the first to tell you that Skipper Bud's is less about selling boats and more about developing relationships with customers. A customer-first attitude is what took Skipper Bud's to the top of the boating business. Top-of-the-line brands, such as SeaRay and Four Winns, and boats by small specialty manufacturers like Carver are all displayed in a state-of-the-art showroom. Normally, you'll find at least 50 boats on the floor at any one time. Skipper Bud's also sells used boats. A highly trained staff can help you pick out the right boat for your needs as well as educate you on its proper use and care after purchase. Most Skipper Bud's stores are located next to marinas that are also operated by Skipper Bud's, a convenience that allows you to handle many aspects of boat ownership from one location, including purchase, maintenance and storage or slip rental. At Skipper Bud's, the staff understands your dreams and expectations. So come on down to Skipper Bud's where staff members Deliver the Dream as their motto promises and let you spend your time making great memories.

1030 Silvernail Road, Pewaukee WI
(262) 544-1200 (Pewaukee)
(608) 246-2628 (Madison)
(920) 746-8200 (Sturgeon Bay)
www.skipperbuds.com

Transition Cycle and Body Mechanics Endurance Sports Center

RECREATION & FITNESS

With its parks, trails and landscapes, Waukesha County provides many outdoor recreation possibilities. Transition Cycle can help you live the active life in Waukesha through personal training, cycling and massage therapy. The experts at Transition have an average of 15 years of experience in helping beginners and competitive athletes meet their goals. Clients can train to build strength, flexibility and endurance either one-on-one or in small groups. Transition offers state-of-the-art training equipment, including an Endless Pool that allows you to swim in place against a constant current while coaches monitor and adjust your form. Pat Mueller and his coaching staff provide the motivation and guidance to maximize fitness while minimizing the chance of injury. Transition's massage therapists provide a critical component of recovery and relaxation. John Huenink and his bicycling staff lead cycling groups and help fit cyclists to the right equipment. Transition carries top-brand bikes, guaranteed to stand up to regular use. Whether you're hitting the trails, the water or the weights, check out the expert guidance and resources at Transition Cycle.

161 W Wisconsin Avenue, Pewaukee WI
(262) 264-0070
www.transitioncycle.com

Harken Yacht Equipment

RECREATION & FITNESS

In the sailing world the name Harken is synonymous with innovative yacht equipment. Sailing enthusiasts from around the globe rely on Harken-designed winches, blocks and sail handling systems. Pewaukee is the corporate headquarters for a company that received the DAME Award of the Decade in recognition of its engineering breakthroughs. When it received this high honor at the Marine Equipment Trade Show for the period of 1990 to 2000, Harken topped 700 other marine equipment companies. This industry trendsetter maintains its worldwide influence with offices in Italy and France, as well as Australia, England and Sweden. Harken supplies its equipment to dealers and to the largest boat builders around the world. Every boat in America's Cup and the around-the-world Volvo Ocean Race sports at least some Harken equipment. The company's tradition of innovation began when Peter Harken developed fittings for sailboats that were noncorrosive and required no lubrication. Perfect for the marine environment, these fittings debuted on the gold and silver medal winners at the 1968 Olympic Games in Acapulco. Peter and his brother Olaf have run the business from its Pewaukee location since 1971. For innovation that sets the standard for marine equipment, trust Harken Yacht Equipment.

1251 E Wisconsin Avenue, Pewaukee WI
(262) 691-3320
www.harken.com

Adventure Rock

RECREATION & FITNESS

As one of the few gyms in the United States built exclusively for rock climbing, Adventure Rock can concentrate its efforts on an extraordinary rock climbing experience. Its sculpted wall makes Adventure Rock a valuable complement to outdoor climbing and an important training ground. Adventure Rock boasts over 11,000 square feet of climbing surface, up to 35 feet high. The facility is open to the public seven days a week and memberships are also available. Adventure Rock offers numerous classes where you can learn knot tying, belaying and rope handling, take part in a family-oriented session or improve your bouldering ability. Adventure Rock hosts 40 to 45 birthday parties a week. Sleepovers are popular as well. Boy Scouts and Girl Scouts use the facility to earn climbing badges, while corporations and other groups address issues of leadership, teamwork and problem-solving through the Team-UP program. Ready for true outdoor climbing? Adventure Rock organizes trips to Devil's Lake State Park in Baraboo, a stunning site with sheer rock walls. Advanced climbers learn to set top anchors to ascend these walls. A final service is Adventure Rock's three 25-foot-high portable rock walls, which can be trucked to any event. Adventure Rock is jointly owned by two enthusiastic sportsmen, Ken Chmielewski and John Robinson. For the time of your life, visit Adventure Rock.

21250 W Capitol Drive, Pewaukee WI
(262) 790-6800
www.adventurerock.com

Piano Blu

RESTAURANTS & CAFÉS

When two couples, Ed and Amy Seckinger and Greg and Jane Howe, opened Piano Blu, they envisioned a restaurant with several fun and innovative areas for dining and live entertainment overlooking beautiful Pewaukee Lake. The first floor features the main dining room with a large fireplace and main bar, a private piano lounge, outside patio and main sound stage area that houses a seven foot grand piano. The mood in the restaurant on the first floor stays upbeat with nightly entertainment that ranges from a single piano player early in the evening to smooth jazz, R&B and dance bands on Fridays and Saturdays. If you desire a more intimate setting, you can request to have dinner upstairs in the Rhino Room. This includes another dining area, a private wine room and a bar and lounge. The Rhino Room is the perfect spot to watch the sunset over the lake while enjoying caramelized sea scallops, teriyaki salmon or filet mignon in a Madeira mushroom sauce and a nice bottle of wine from the extensive wine list. The rhino head mounted above the fireplace is said to symbolize the spirit of entrepreneurship and following your dreams. This multifunctional setting accommodates an intimate dinner for two, a large corporate sit-down dinner for 50, or private cocktail event for up to 75 people. Piano Blu is equipped with state-of-the-art audio and video capabilities, and is perfect for combining business with pleasure. Whether you are planning your next event or just dreaming of a night of dinner and dancing, consider Piano Blu.

179 W. Wisconsin Avenue, Pewaukee, WI
(262) 691-0200
www.PianoBlu.com

Kahunas Beach Club and Tiki Bar

RESTAURANTS & CAFÉS

If you dream of getting away to a tropical paradise, there is no need to head to the airport. Just make your way to Kahunas Beach Club and Tiki Bar, where the luau décor, Hawaiian music and island-inspired food make you feel as though you are on vacation. Owners Steve and Mardi Smirl opened Kahunas in 2005, after Mardi's travels around the world provided the inspiration for a tropical-themed restaurant. From the cool pastels of the wall-sized beach mural to the hand carved tiki fountain, the restaurant invites you to hang loose. Steve operates as head chef and enjoys creating new recipes with a tropical twist. Start your island adventure with one of the many *pupus*, or appetizers, including Nana Maria's Platanos, fried plantains served alongside fresh mango salsa. The crabby patties, tender crab cakes made with real crabmeat, are one of Kahunas' signature offerings. Entrées, or *kau kau*, include coconut shrimp with a sweet chili sauce, fish tacos with chipotle lime tilapia and Caribbean red snapper served with lemon coriander aioli. If your dining companions share your adventurous spirit, try the Diamond Head, an enormous drink made of Parrot Bay rum, triple sec and fruity flavors served in the hula girl volcano bowl. Did we mention it arrives flaming? Come to Kahunas Beach Club and Tiki Bar for island hospitality, tasty cuisine with a tropical flair and summer fun year-round.

W279 N2221 Prospect Avenue, Pewaukee WI
(262) 695-8303
www.kahunasonline.com

The Invitation Hideaway

SHOPPING

Why send plain invitations for your special event? Custom designed invitations from the Invitation Hideaway allow you to personalize your message with a stylish keepsake that all of your guests will want to save. Owner Tammy Yundt runs her store as a studio, using her art background to design a look that is right for each customer. The Invitation Hideaway offers a large selection of handmade papers, vellums and cardstock as well as the accessories that embellish and complete the package, such as eyelets, ribbons and envelopes. Tammy says that it's always fun and exciting to work one-on-one with brides as they prepare for their big day. In and around Pewaukee, folks have counted on the Invitation Hideaway for birth announcements, shower invitations and those all-important thank you notes. Tammy has created menus for restaurants and programs for theaters. Stop in today to see how the Invitation Hideaway can personalize your event.

227 Oakton Avenue, Pewaukee WI
(262) 746-9176
www.invitationhideaway.com

PLEASANT PRAIRIE

Pleasant Prairie is in the extreme southeast corner of Wisconsin, bordering on Illinois, Kenosha and Lake Michigan. The area was a center of Indian activity in pre-pioneer Wisconsin, and remnants of Indian culture abound. Some of the earliest traces, found in the Carol Beach area, make up one of the highest-quality archeological sites in the country. Several natural historic sites, such as the Chiwaukee Prairie and the Kenosha Sand Dunes, lie undisturbed in Pleasant Prairie. Modern Pleasant Prairie is one of the five largest manufacturing municipalities in the state. The beautifully landscaped LakeView Corporate Park, a major development, employs more than 8,000 people. Pleasant Prairie's annual triathlons draw scores of athletes from across the Midwest. Tourists flock to the Jelly Belly Candy Company to take the Jelly Belly Express train tour.

PLACES TO GO

- Keno Family Outdoor Theatre
  9102 Sheridan Road
  (262) 694-8855
- Jelly Belly Candy Company (tours)
  10100 Jelly Belly Lane
  (262) 947-3800
- Prairie Springs Park
  9900 Terwall Terrace
  (262) 947-0437

THINGS TO DO

July

- Danskin Women's Triathlon
  Prairie Springs Park
  (262) 947-0437

August

- Pleasant Prairie Triathlon
  Prairie Springs Park
  (262) 947-0437
- Prairie Family Days
  Prairie Springs Park
  (262) 947-0437

Seebeck Gallery

GALLERIES & FINE ART

Some art belongs in museums, some art belongs in designer living rooms, but at Seebeck Gallery, the art belongs wherever you live or work. Owners Jon and Victoria Seebeck believe in art that you can live with. They love to see a customer connect with a particular piece. They provide a whimsical and approachable space in Pleasant Prairie with natural light and 14-foot ceilings. The gallery, open since 1992, represents more than 100 local, regional and national artists and craftspeople. Pieces for sale include breathtaking art glass, a wide assortment of jewelry, original oils and watercolors. Artistically designed home accents include lamps, mirrors and tables. The ceramics are functional as well as beautiful. Jewelry, candlesticks and wind chimes are among the many gift items available. The gallery regularly helps companies visually enhance their work environments. Whether the workplace requires original art or posters, the gallery can match the personality and budget of every client. Seebeck Gallery also provides on-site custom framing services. You can choose from a broad range of available frames or rely on the gallery's innovative ideas. Jon has vast experience as a picture framer and Victoria has a graphic design background. The skilled staff at Seebeck Gallery is always friendly and ready to help. Stop by Seebeck Gallery for arts and crafts that belong in your life.

9020 76th Street, Pleasant Prairie WI
(262) 942-8888
www.seebeckgallery.com

LakeView RecPlex

RECREATION & FITNESS

It takes vision to imagine a rolling park, spring-fed lake and recreation center in place of a gravel pit and cement processing plant. This was just the vision the village president and village administrator of Pleasant Prairie made a reality. Prairie Springs Park and Lake Andrea rest on 825 lush acres and are home to ball fields, play areas, a 2.3-mile running path, nature trails, beach and other outdoor treasures. Nestled along the shore of Lake Andrea, you'll find a true gem, LakeView RecPlex. RecPlex is a giant recreation complex offering several main activity areas: an aquatic center with lap lanes, current channel and indoor water park, an expansive field house, a state-of-the-art fitness center with a sixth-of-a-mile suspended running track and an ice arena, complete with two NHL-sized rinks. RecPlex offers discounted program fees, free ice-skating and many other benefits to its 13,000 members. Visitors are always welcome at RecPlex, which boasts two concession areas, childcare and experienced personal trainers. RecPlex also offers massage therapy, racquetball, therapeutic recreation programs for disabled people, year-round sports, fitness and childcare programs, and facility rentals for parties and meetings. This two-story, glass building treats you to breathtaking views, luring you outdoors to the jogging path, beach or picnic grounds. Every summer, RecPlex hosts two major triathlons and Prairie Family Days (an old-fashioned family festival with food, activities and music). Visit Prairie Springs Park, Lake Andrea and RecPlex in Pleasant Prairie, and discover a great place to live, work and play.

9900 Terwall Terrace, Pleasant Prairie WI
(262) 947-0437
www.recplexonline.com
www.pleasantprairieonline.com

Ray Radigan's Restaurant

RESTAURANTS & CAFÉS

Ray Radigan's Restaurant may belong to Ray's son Mike these days, but Mike knows "Radigan's will always be my Dad's place." He's proud of that legacy and of the traditions that make Ray Radigan's worth the hour's drive from Milwaukee or Chicago. Sure, you can get a steak and good service in either town, but the unrelenting care that goes into every moment of the customer experience here is pure gold. It's not one thing; it's everything that sets this 1933 Kenosha classic apart—the dry-aged prime blue-ribbon beef, the remarkable wine cellar, the tables with fresh flowers and two layers of white linen, the extraordinarily efficient and obliging waitstaff, and the private dining rooms. Ray need not have worried that the service would decline after his death. The mob bosses, local politicians and traveling businessmen who once frequented Radigan's would be as pleased as today's diners. Radigan's long litany of celebrity guests includes Mohammed Ali, who once downed the restaurant's famous 28-ounce T-bone, but got a thumb's down from his trainer when he ordered the homemade banana cream pie. Radigan's eclectic menu features favorite entrées of the past and present; reflecting upon this, Michael quoted a Chicago food critic saying, "Where can I get oysters Rockefeller, veal schnitzel and lobster Thermidor on the same menu?" It is Michael's philosophy of detail, detail and detail that is truly the life blood of this restaurant, which promises and delivers the quality of an era long gone. Ray Radigan's Restaurant, a Tradition of Dining Excellence Since 1933.

11712 S Sheridan Road, Pleasant Prairie WI
(262) 694-0455
www.foodspot.com/rayradigans

PLACES TO GO

- Festival Park
  5 5th Street
- Racine Art Museum
  441 Main Street
  (262) 638-8300
- Racine Heritage Museum
  701 S Main Street
  (262) 636-3926
- Racine Zoo
  2131 N Main Street
  (262) 636-9189

THINGS TO DO

April

- Racine.org Running Festival
  www.racinerunningfest.com

June

- Harbor Fest
  Festival Park
  www.harborfest.org

July

- Great Midwest Dragon Boat Festival
  Samuel Meyers Park
  (262) 884-6400
- Salmon-A-Rama (fishing fest)
  Festival Park
  www.salmonarama.com
- Italian Festival
  Festival Park
  (262) 681-9968 ext. 243

August

- Taste of Racine
  Zoo
  (262) 634-2391
- Armenian Fest
  Festival Park
  (262) 639-6076

September

- Great Lakes Brewfest
  Festival Park
  www.greatlakesbrewfest.com

RACINE

Racine is on Lake Michigan at the mouth of the Root River, and its name is the French word for root. Racine was a factory town almost from the beginning and a major industrial center for much of its history. Johnson Wax was a major employer. Today, business and culture continue to thrive in Racine, with the waterfront serving as the site of many festivals throughout the year. The city's architectural assets include two buildings designed by Frank Lloyd Wright: the Johnson Wax headquarters and the Wingspread Convention Center. Racine also claims to have the largest North American settlement of Danes outside of Greenland, and is particularly known for its Danish pastries.

Wind Point Lighthouse

Wilson's Coffee & Tea

BAKERIES, COFFEE & TEA

Step beneath the lofty ceiling, make your away across the polished wood floor, and enter a world of exotic coffee regions and tropical hillsides covered with tea plants. Wilson's Coffee & Tea opens the door to new horizons in brews, beans and leaves. Wilson's is the only coffee shop in Racine with a coffee roaster, and the delicious aroma of roasting coffee envelopes you as you try to choose from a variety of blends. The Wilsons pride themselves on the diversity of their coffee offerings and have a knack for finding the finest beans from around the world. Sample a steaming cup of Costa Rican La Minita or Brazil Mogiana. Savor coffee from Panama, El Salvador, Yemen or Kenya. Tea fanciers will be equally satisfied with a choice of more than 50 varieties. Take a break from English Breakfast and try a pot of Temple of Heaven green tea or Ceylon Ruhuna. Mingling with the delicious aroma of coffee is the luscious scent of Diane's baked-from-scratch pastries. Augment your afternoon tea or morning mug with a muffin, scone or tart. If you're out shopping, you can always drop by for a sandwich or a salad or order up a Cherry Jubilee latté or a Dreamsicle soda. Take home bulk coffee or shop for such gift items as thermal carafes to keep coffee hot and fresh, coffeemakers and decorative teapots. Whether you are a tea fanatic or a coffee connoisseur, visit Wilson's Coffee & Tea to find your perfect blend.

3306 Washington Avenue, Racine WI
(262) 634-6611
www.wilsonscoffee.com

Photo by Ted Wilson

Remington-May Workshop Gallery

GALLERIES & FINE ART

Artist Kate Remington of Remington-May Workshop Gallery works in an unusual medium. Her concrete animals are particularly expressive and engaging; her dogs, frozen in the midst of characteristic activities, pull at every heartstring. The sculptures lend themselves to homes and gardens as well as public places. They have a pleasing organic quality, and many of the pieces, including seats, bird baths and planters, are functional as well as delightful. Often, they tell a story. In addition to her own pieces, Kate displays work by other artists, choosing pieces that speak to her. The Racine gallery is a true working studio where visitors can watch the process of creation. It is located in a historic building with high tin-covered ceilings and tin wallboards. Large windows admit generous amounts of sunshine. Kate has always been artistic. She started with dance and theater and later took up drawing. Her etchings and paintings hang on walls all over the Chicago area, and her patrons include Mayor Richard Daley and the Vatican. Kate also spent time in the business world until her mother made her promise to work exclusively on her art. As a sculptor, Kate is actually carrying on a family tradition. Kate's family members are the closest living relatives to the famous Western sculptor, painter and writer Frederic Remington, whose works span from the late 19th century to the early 20th century. For striking sculpture and more, stop by Remington-May Workshop Gallery.

613 6th Street, Racine WI
(262) 619-1647 ***www.remingtonmaystudio.com***

The Red Pony

HOME & GARDEN

Owners Kate Cole Buffington and David Mitchell travel between their homes in Pondicherry, India and Wisconsin to import the beautiful pieces on display at The Red Pony. Kate and David enjoy educating their customers about the culture and history of each piece. Their mission is to import one-of-a-kind furnishings from India in the hope that the exquisite craftsmanship evident in these pieces will help promote an understanding of the beauty and depth of Indian culture and history. During the Colonial period, British, French, Portuguese and Dutch colonialists brought their furnishings to India. Local craftsmen were commissioned to make copies of these European pieces in teak, rosewood, satinwood and other indigenous hardwoods available at that time. When colonial rule ended, most of these treasures fell into misuse. Kate and David select and restore these treasures to their original luster. These exquisite pieces are much sought after in Europe, yet are little known in the United States. The Red Pony heirloom furnishings selection includes desks, vanities, cupboards, tables and secretaries. You will also discover items such as sundry boxes, mirrors, silks, statues, doors, columns and more. Visit The Red Pony and open yourself to a new world of beauty.

202 Fifth Street at Main, Racine WI
(262) 498-4290
www.redponyfurniture.com

Braun's Specialties

MARKETS & DELIS

Braun's Specialties in downtown Racine brings together Old World gourmet treats and Wisconsin's finest flavors. From their carefully selected downtown location, Tom and Pat Braun tempt customers with a rich selection of homemade bratwurst, sausages, stuffed pretzels and tangy mustards. This garden of gourmet delights offers Wisconsin cheeses, honey, and locally brewed and imported beer. With the advantage of more than 30 years in the wine business, Tom Braun has managed to put together a veritable wall of wine from across the United States and from 11 countries. He will happily recommend the best selection to set off your next party or special dinner. Coffee from Door County, teas, cigars and chocolates line the aisles of the store's three shopping rooms. Everyone loves receiving a gift basket filled with precious food delicacies. The Brauns can help you design a gift basket filled with such prized selections as special oils, herbs, seasonings and pastas. Braun's Specialties provides all the ingredients for extraordinary entertaining, from specialty foods to handpainted martini glasses, wine goblets and candles. If you're presenting a plate of hors d'oeuvres, planning a picnic or hosting a holiday feast, make sure you explore the bounty at Braun's Specialties.

345 Main Street, Racine WI (262) 633-5806

Dimple's

SHOPPING

One of the many things you can say about Dimple Navratil is that she certainly knows jewelry. In fact, her namesake store, Dimple's, offers one of the largest selections of silver jewelry in Wisconsin. In order to secure her impressive assortment of quality merchandise, Dimple frequently travels back to her home country of India. Her knowledge of the Indian market enables her to offer attractive prices to her customers. She also adds to her eclectic selection by importing products from other far-flung Eastern lands. Dimple and her husband, Denis, are heavily involved in the Racine community and take part in fundraising efforts for hospitals in Wisconsin, Illinois and Indiana. Dimple's is by nature a friendly store with staff members that know not to crowd their customers, but will lend a hand or a word of advice when you want it. The wide selection of curiosities from countries such as India, Nepal and Tibet allows patrons to select items that fit their own tastes and interests. You might find a silk sari, paper lanterns or an art object. To experience 4,000 square feet of treasures from around the world, visit Dimple's.

416 S Main Street, Racine WI
(262) 619-1780

Dover Flag & Map

SHOPPING

All visitors eventually find their way to Dover Flag & Map, where owners JoAnne and John Labre serve as unofficial ambassadors for Racine and the surrounding lake country, passing out maps and area restaurant guides to those experiencing this charming corner of Wisconsin. JoAnne and John have festooned their shop with tasteful displays of maps, flags and nautical gifts. Novelty flags, the flags of various countries and states, team flags and decorative banners cater to a variety of interests. Dover will even make a custom flag to your specifications. The flag shop got started when the Labres found themselves unable to locate a flagpole and began selling poles and flags from their home. Later, they opened a small storefront and added maps and navigation charts to their inventory. Today, people from around the world seek them out for custom projects, such as parade banners, wedding hangings, family crests and company logos. Whether you want to fly a flag with the name of your boat or find a route from here to there, make Dover Flag & Map a stop on your travels.

323 S Main Street, Racine WI
(262) 632-3133 or (800) 204-0075
www.doverflag.com

Uncorkt

WINES, BREWS, PUBS & CLUBS

It's unusual to find a retail wine establishment that feels like an authentic winery, but Sherry and Tim Etes have created just that at Uncorkt in Racine, a classy place to enjoy a glass of wine or to buy a bottle to take home. "Wine is all we do," say the couple, and they have developed the expertise to accompany their very specific focus. Ask them to discuss wine, and you'll be impressed with their comprehensive understanding of what is often a fundamentally confusing subject. Sherry knows the ins and outs of the wine business, thanks to years of professional experience. You'll enjoy your wine with them in a welcoming environment that features brick walls, slate floors and high ceilings. The presence of a rapid chiller allows Uncorkt to chill any bottle in about six minutes. Each week, it offers new small batch fine wines for you to try before you buy. Try the weekly themed wine classes or schedule your next party or corporate event for up to 50 people at the Uncorkt banquet room. Chill out with one of Sherry's or Tim's picks, and shop for quality stemware and wine accessories while enjoying the casual atmosphere and superior wines at Uncorkt.

211 6th Street, Racine WI
(262) 632-WINE (9463)
www.uncorkt.com

Photo by Jon C. Bolton

Photo by Jon C. Bolton

George's Tavern

WINES, BREWS, PUBS & CLUBS

A way station, refuge and musical hot spot, George's Tavern in downtown Racine has catered to the social and mealtime needs of locals and wayfarers alike for 60 years. Owner David Popoff, son of one of the original owners, keeps this lively landmark jumping with regularly scheduled events. Connection to the community is one of Popoff's priorities. His annual cribbage tournament always draws a crowd, and the chili cook-off encourages chili chefs to compete for an engraved plaque on George's Chili Wall of Fame. Drop in once a month and enjoy Spotlight on Racine, a live talk show featuring local celebrities and other notables. Every week, George's is the spot to enjoy live music in an eclectic range of styles. Swing by to catch the tunes and find out why Racine's *Journal Times* selected George's as the best live music club in the county. Thirsty patrons can choose from domestic and imported beers, ales and lagers to wash down a hearty roast beef sandwich or a slice of homemade pizza. After dinner, try a game of darts or pool. If you need a special place for a party or gathering, George's has a spacious room for your event, and the staff will take care of the details. This mainstay of downtown Racine has been in the Popoff family for decades, so you'd expect a sense of tradition to permeate the surroundings, and it does. Come to George's Tavern, where old comrades and new fans find good food, fun and friends.

1201 N Main Street, Racine WI
(262) 632-6469
www.georges-tavern.com

SALEM

Salem, in Kenosha County, is at a nexus of ten lakes that provided major ice harvesting enterprises to settlers in the late 1800s and early 1900s. The boarding houses of these businesses provided the hotels that later became lakeside resorts. As one of the smaller villages in the area, Salem remains a quiet, hidden getaway, oriented around its parks and waterfronts. Salem contains the Village of Paddock Lake, a sub-community built around the lake that offers premium real estate and a growing reputation as one of the best places in America to live and raise a family.

PLACES TO GO

- Fox River Park
  Highways F and W
  (262) 857-1869
- Richard Bong State Recreation Area
  26313 Burlington Road, Kansasville
  (262) 878-5600

Breezy Hill Nursery

HOME & GARDEN

Breezy Hill Nursery in Salem has gained a reputation as one of the finest nurseries in the Midwest. With more than 600 acres of hardy trees and shrubs and a 16,000-square-foot greenhouse filled with annuals and perennials, you are bound to find the landscape items you need here. Breezy Hill is actually three businesses in one: a commercial and residential landscape design company, a retail garden center and a supplier of premium nursery stock. The residential and commercial landscaping service provides six designers and two CAD technicians to make your dreams come true. The retail center offers garden supplies, bird baths and fountains, plus outdoor lighting and irrigation systems. In season, it stocks Christmas trees, poinsettias and pumpkins. The retail shop relies on the nursery stock business, because Breezy Hill grows 90 percent of the plants and trees that it sells. This keeps prices competitive, and the nursery also guarantees its plants for a year. Breezy Hill sells trees that are up to six inches in diameter at the trunk and weigh up to two tons each. Fortunately, it will move and plant trees. The wholesale operation sells plants and trees to businesses all over the United States. Owners Jerry and Colleen Epping invite you to Breezy Hill Nursery, home of quality plants and services.

7530 288th Avenue, Salem WI
(262) 537-2111
www.breezyhillnursery.com

SLINGER

Slinger lies in the headlands of Kettle Moraine, where millions of years ago, glaciers passed through carving the land. The Kettle Moraine State Forest is a beautiful glacial remnant landscape of kames, kettles and eskers. Powder Hill, a large glacial kame, offers a great hike and view. The area also contains some of the richest farmland in the state, which attracted many immigrant German farmers during the early 1800s. Baruch Schleisinger Weil purchased some of the best land and dubbed it Schleisingerville. He built a large store and dwelling on the corner of Main and Franklin streets. Brewers soon discovered the advantages of the area, which offered freshly cut winter ice from Cedar Lake and lumber sawdust of oak, maple and elm for packing. Sometime in the 1920s, the town shortened its name to Slinger, a nickname that was already in common use.

PLACES TO GO

- Kettle Moraine State Forest
  Pike Lake Unit
  (262) 670-3400
- Little Switzerland Ski Area
  105 County Road AA
  (262) 644-5020
- Slinger Super Speedway
  240 Cedar Creek Road
  (262) 644-5921

Uptown

AUTO

In 1946, when Irving Pentler founded Uptown, he placed a great deal of importance on customer satisfaction and offering drivers a choice of exceptional vehicles. Now, more than 60 years later, Irving's son Glen and grandson John remain true to Irving's vision as they carry on the family business. If you are tired of squeezing the kids and all of their gear into a little car, perhaps a Lincoln Navigator from Uptown Lincoln Mercury in Milwaukee is just the ride you are looking for. In Slinger, a sporty Corvette from Uptown Chevrolet will make heads turn as you drive by. A Jeep Commander from Uptown Chrysler Dodge Jeep looks just as good covered in mud after an adventurous backcountry drive as it does on the showroom floor. Year after year, each dealership continues to prove its quality, earning awards, such as General Motor's Mark of Excellence and Chrysler's Five Star certification. Uptown also offers service and parts departments as well as a complete body shop to keep your car looking and running like new. Find your next vehicle at any of the three Uptown dealerships, where more than 60 years of experience in the auto industry promise a satisfying ride on your next set of wheels.

Uptown Lincoln Mercury
2111 N Mayfair Road, Milwaukee WI
(414) 771-9000
Uptown Chevrolet
1101 E Commerce Boulevard, Slinger WI
(262) 644-8800
Uptown Chrysler Dodge Jeep
1111 E Commerce Boulevard, Slinger WI
(262) 644-8400
www.uptownmotors.com

Kettle Moraine Coffee Co.

BAKERIES, COFFEE & TEA

Ask Karen Dreisow and her daughter, Wendy, how things are going at Kettle Moraine Coffee Company, and they will tell you that today is great and tomorrow will be even better. The second phase of a business that began in 1999 is in full swing. The days when Karen ran a coffee shop combined with a florist business are over. With Wendy on board, Karen now focuses all of her energy on giving people more of what they want in a coffeehouse, starting with a great product. However, the homemade baked goods and a full menu of hot and cold drinks are just part of what brings folks here. Boasting a lively community atmosphere and wireless Internet access, Kettle Moraine is waiting to become your favorite place in Slinger to hang out. What's more, a line of coffee cups, travel mugs and gift baskets give it an identity all its own. Don't be surprised if Kettle Moraine becomes a household name some day, because the Dreisows are dreaming big. Kettle Moraine's own signature coffee, roasted on location, is the next phase. When Karen and Wendy close their eyes, they can imagine Kettle Moraine coffeehouses in all parts of Wisconsin and the United States. Drop by Kettle Moraine Coffee Company, where there's excitement in the air, along with the aroma of fresh coffee.

310 E Washington Street, Slinger WI
(262) 644-9510
www.kettlemorainecoffeeco.com

Busy Bee Learning Tree

BUSINESS & SERVICES

Learning to care for the community around them is only one part of a child's day at Busy Bee Learning Tree in Slinger. Kids learn about math, science, group skills and the need to be good to others with projects such as collecting food from neighbors and taking it to the local food pantry in their wagons, leaving flowers planted in Dixie cups on doorsteps, or making cookies and delivering them to a local nursing home. Visiting exciting places including the zoo, county fair and museum, and walking trips to the local bank, bakery and dentist, help the Busy Bee teachers incorporate lots of hands-on activities and investigating by the kids, keeping their days both interactive and fun. It all adds up to a learning experience that lays the foundation for future community membership and participation. For your young community member, consider Busy Bee Learning Tree.

204 Slinger Road, Slinger WI
(262) 644-6211

STOUGHTON

Stoughton is a historic village with Victorian architecture and a rich Norwegian heritage. T.G. Mandt, born in Norway, established the first of several wagon works that became Stoughton's most important industry during the early 19th century. Mandt sponsored men from Norway to come with their families to build the wagons. Stoughton honors Syttende Mai, the Norwegian holiday celebrating Norway's independence from Denmark, with a colorful gala featuring Norse costumes and performances by the world-famous Stoughton Norwegian Dancers. Stoughton claims that its early Norwegian immigrants invented the coffee break, which Stoughton also commemorates in a festival. Stoughton's charming main street offers antique and specialty shops, galleries and wine bars in old cream- and red-brick buildings dating to the mid-19th to early 20th centuries. The Chamber of Commerce offers several walking tour guides that will take you by the town's many architectural landmarks.

PLACES TO GO

- Lake Kegonsa State Park
  2405 Door Creek Road
  (608) 873-9695
- Mandt Park
  811 S 4th Street
- Stoughton Opera House
  381 E Main Street
  (608) 873.6677
- Viking County Park
  2525 County Highway B

THINGS TO DO

May

- Syttende Mai Folk Festival
  Downtown
  (888) 873-7912

July

- Stoughton Fair
  Mandt Park
  www.stoughtonfair.com

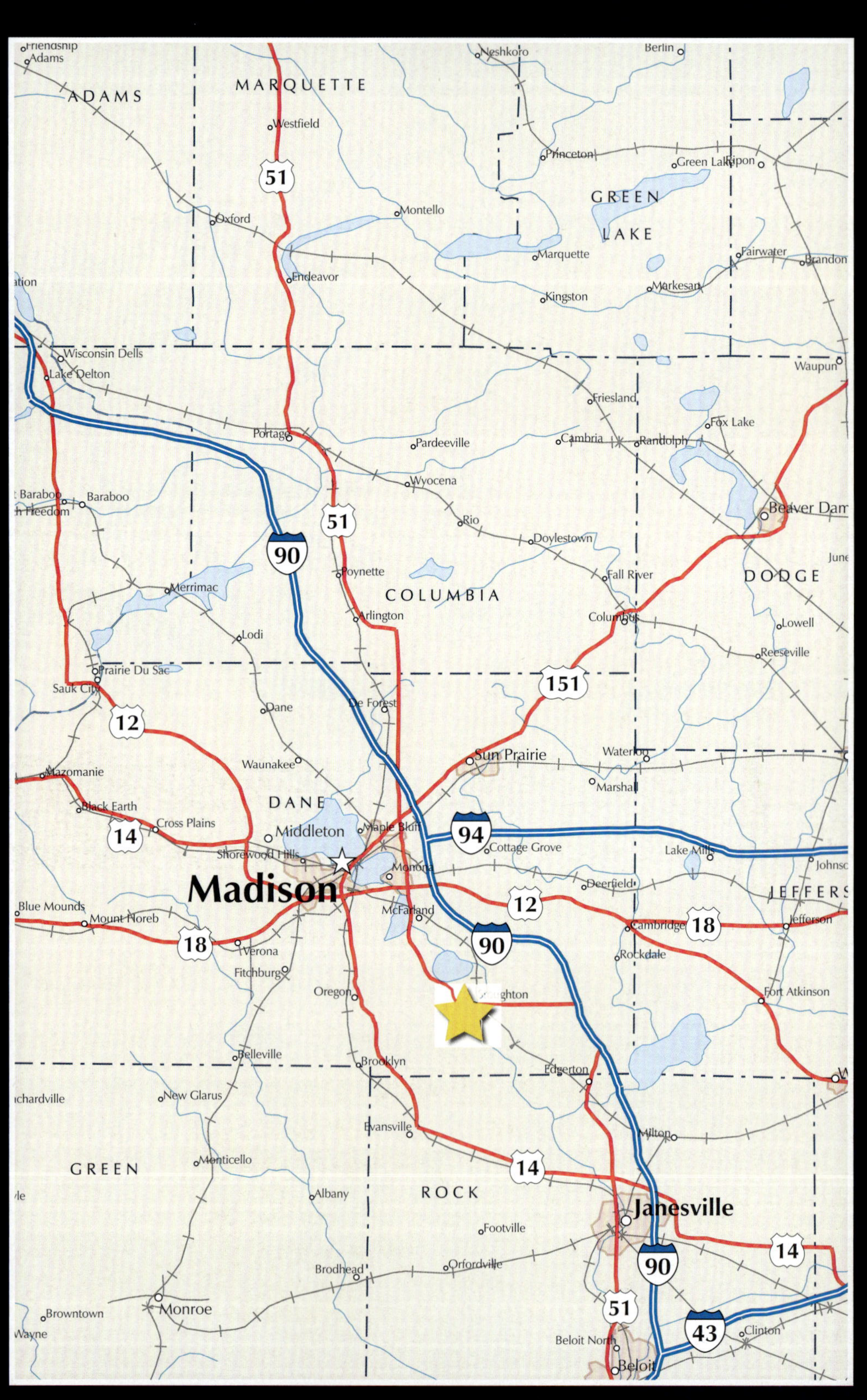

Altemus Corners House Bed & Breakfast

ACCOMMODATIONS

Altemus Corners House Bed & Breakfast lies on 120 acres of beautiful countryside just 25 minutes from Madison. These days, it shelters city folks who come to savor the simplicity and slower pace of rural life. Nickolas Altemus III, of Pennsylvania Dutch stock, built the Federal style brick home in the early 1870s. Marge Stokstad, proprietor of the bed-and-breakfast today, is an artisan who refurbishes antique lamps, crafts custom lampshades and paints in oils. She also supplies the inn with fresh flowers and produce from her farm down the road. Now completely refurbished, the bed and breakfast offers four bedrooms and three guest bathrooms. Period furnishings and handmade Victorian lampshades in every room enhance the original woodwork and layout, and hand-painted murals enliven the elegant dining room. The generous front porch with a gazebo is the ideal spot to enjoy a leisurely breakfast, which includes pancakes, meat, Danish kringle and farm-fresh fruit in season. Guests enjoy air conditioning, a music room and several sitting areas for relaxing and savoring homemade desserts and beverages in the evening. For a taste of history, down-home hospitality and old-fashioned ambience, book your next getaway at Altemus Corners House Bed & Breakfast.

1345 Tower Drive, Stoughton WI
(608) 695-0693
www.altemuscornershouse.com

Fosdal Home Bakery

BAKERIES, COFFEE & TEA

Since 1949, Fosdal Home Bakery has made life a little sweeter for Stoughton residents. The bakery, which originally started in a home, doubles as a deli and a small town coffee shop where locals gather in the morning. "It's about the people," says owner Joseph Crubaugh, a third-generation baker. Joseph attributes the warm and friendly atmosphere to great customers and employees. Known for its authentic Norwegian pastries, the bakery features rosettes, krumkake and sandbakkel and will even ship lefsa to customers via overnight delivery. Other popular pastries include kringles, Danish and Fosdal's famous double chocolate donuts. Expect to find all things sweet and tempting here, from muffins, fritters and scones to Bismarks, croissants and pecan rings. A variety of bars, breads and cakes, some made with real whipped cream, round out the bakery offerings. Fosdal Home Bakery's light lunch options include hot or cold sandwiches on freshly baked breads and flaky pot pies known as Cornish pasties. Daily bread specials and homemade broth or creams soups are popular; the bakery even has a hot line number to call for the soup of the day. Fosdal Home Bakery does an extensive wholesale business within a 60-mile radius of Stoughton and Joseph serves on the board of the Wisconsin Bakery Association. Come on in and enjoy freshly baked treats at Fosdal Home Bakery, Here to Make Life a Little Sweeter.

243 E Main Street, Stoughton WI
(608) 205-9213 (soup hotline)
or (608) 873-8977 (wholesale)
www.fosdalhomebakery.com

Quill & Brush Gallery and Frame Shop

GALLERIES & FINE ART

The Quill & Brush Gallery and Frame Shop in Stoughton is the premiere frame shop in the Madison area. For more than 23 years, Vern Strutzel has been framing artwork and every manner of personal memorabilia, from diplomas and certificates to artwork and sports mementos. Vern has seen his share of adversity over the years, losing his wife to cancer and his home to a tornado. But Vern has persevered, earning a reputation for quality and customer service that keeps people who know him coming back. The Quill & Brush purchases art from all across the United States, Canada and Europe, and from local artists, such as popular Wisconsin painter Steven Kozar and others. Vern enjoys featuring nature and wildlife art, as well as artwork that is reflective of family, but his selection is diverse and wide-ranging. He carries originals as well as prints, and he will work with you to find the frames that will display your artwork to the best possible advantage. The next time you are in the Madison area shopping for art, call Vern at the Quill & Brush Gallery in downtown Stoughton.

143 E Main Street, Stoughton WI
(608 873-8211

Gwen's Frame Shop

HOME & GARDEN

If you are looking for a way to redecorate your home or business without doing a complete remodel, call Gwen Dawdy at Gwen's Frame Shop in Stoughton. Gwen is a makeover specialist with the eye of an artist. Gwen specializes in taking a space, any space, and finding ways to make it work. She will use your existing furniture or artwork and find ways to pull things together. She'll make art recommendations if you are looking for something new. Sometimes her ideas will be as simple as changing the color of your matting or altering wall colors. If you're building from scratch, she'll help you choose colors and materials for floors, counters, cabinetry, carpeting or tile. As you can see, Gwen's Frame Shop is much more than a frame gallery. The shop carries more than 3,000 frame samples and museum-quality materials for collector pieces and antiquities. She and her staff offer canvas stretching, needlework and a computerized mat cutter. But Gwen's talents carry her far beyond framing, matting and picture hanging. People who are selling their homes often come to Gwen for ideas that will help their property sell more quickly. People who are building a new home or office seek her advice on color selection and placement. Party planners will often call for help in staging their event. Gwen's Frame Shop is the place to go in Stoughton when you need ideas that will make your personal space shine.

175 E Main Street, Stoughton WI
(608) 877-1900

Stoughton Garden Center

HOME & GARDEN

Stoughton Garden Center, Stoughton's oldest family-owned business, has been enhancing landscapes since 1864. Currently run by Gary and Nancy Dvorak, the garden center supplies everything needed to make your gardening experience enjoyable and rewarding. Knowledgeable staff members can assist you in choosing from hundreds of products, including fertilizers, tools and a full line of Weber grills. They'll load your vehicle with such bulk landscape supplies as decorative stone, topsoil or bark mulch, or they can deliver the products. The garden center is your headquarters for water gardening needs, from plants and pumps to fittings and fish. The center also offers an extensive array of statuary and fountains. Stoughton Garden Center fills four acres with healthy nursery stock and guarantees every tree it sells for two years. If you're not a do-it-yourselfer, the center's experienced landscape professionals can install everything for you. You'll find 20,000 square feet of greenhouse space with thousands of annual bedding plants. The center also pioneered the Pillow-Pak, which are flowers grown in a pouch. Its European moss baskets make delightful additions to a porch. During the holidays, the garden shop sells ornaments and poinsettias and converts into a fantasyland of fully decorated live and artificial trees, wreaths and garlands. Start your gardening project with a visit to Stoughton Garden Center.

1471 Highway 51, Stoughton WI
(608) 873-9602

Catfish River Arts & Antiques

HOME & GARDEN

A visit to Catfish River Arts & Antiques is an opportunity for inspiration. The Stoughton shop carries the work of 40 area artisans and specializes in late 19th century to mid 20th century furniture. The gallery's owners, Richard Sneider and Stephen Nashold, were so dedicated to presenting these pieces in the perfect place that they spent three years restoring the building, which first opened as a department store in 1898. The two opened their shop in late 2001, and in 2002, the Madison Trust for Historic Preservation presented Catfish River with the Historic Preservation Award. The gallery specializes in Arts & Crafts furnature and mid-century modern pieces. You will also find some Victorian and Art Deco items here. Attractive room settings allow customers to see how the pieces work together. The shop also carries many architectural artifacts, including items from the renovation of the state capitol. Artisan work ranges from hand thrown, intricately decorated pottery to etched marble tiles. You will find hand forged metal home accessories, including bird feeders, rain gauges and lanterns, as well as photography. Rich and Steve and their friendly staff enjoy the rapport they've built with customers. Regulars come from as far away as New York and San Francisco to browse through the unique offerings. Come to Catfish River Arts & Antiques for quality furnishings and fine art to beautify your home.

154 W Main Street, Stoughton WI
(608) 877-8880 or (877) 771-8880
www.catfishriver.com

Stokstad Century Farm

MARKETS & DELIS

The Stokstad Century Farm comes by its name honestly. It's been a Stokstad family holding since 1881 and has sustained the family with numerous crops over the decades. A roadside stand here is well known throughout Dane, Jefferson and Rock counties. Customers come from miles around to buy flowers and vegetables grown here. Present owners Eric and Marge Stokstad are full-time farmers, raising everything from crops, such as alfalfa and tobacco, to vegetables and flowers. They live on the property in a Victorian home that was built by Eric's great-grandparents, Lars and Ingeborg, in 1890. The Stokstad Century Farm house is filled with antiques and surrounded by flowerbeds planted by the ancestral Stokstads when the home was new. From May to November, the roadside stand keeps long hours seven days a week so that you can take advantage of such farm-fresh crops as asparagus, green beans, tomatoes, squash and pumpkins. You can also buy fresh and dried flower bouquets. Those who grow their own crops will appreciate the tractors and tractor implements for sale on the premises. Marge refurbishes antique lamps and crafts Victorian lampshades. You can order custom shades or view ready-made lamps, lampshades and lamp parts by appointment. For produce from a family with deep roots in Wisconsin's farmland, visit Stokstad Century Farm.

305 Highway 51, Stoughton WI
(608) 877-0387

Cheesers

MARKETS & DELIS

Cheesers, a charming cheese shop located in historic downtown Stoughton, has featured Wisconsin and imported cheese and gourmet foods since 1995. When Marie Karay and Peg Schuett purchased the business in 2005, they expanded the product line, but continued to carry old favorites. Marie and Peg now display more than 100 varieties of cheese beneath an ornate tin ceiling in a quaint turn-of-the century building. Every week, Cheesers picks up fresh cheese from local cheesemakers and dairies. Three quarters of their cheese is Wisconsin-made, usually within an hour of the store. Famous for its Deppelers Baby Swiss, a full cream Wisconsin Swiss that recently won international recognition, Cheesers also features specialty cheese from around the world. Samples are available and personalized service includes cheese cut to order. Also available weekly are fresh, squeaky cheese curds, a uniquely Wisconsin phenomenon. The shop supports locally made products of biscotti and honey, as well as Wisconsin-produced pancake syrup, jams, jellies and coffee. Take a stroll through the special Scandinavian section for lingonberries, flatbrod and other delights. Cheesers also serves the Cheesecake Factory's meltingly rich cheesecake on fine china. Enjoy dessert and coffee in the garden-style sitting area, complete with the bubbling sounds of a small water feature. With a nod to Stoughton's Norwegian heritage, Cheesers themed gift packages include Treats from Norway, Let It Snow and Taste of Europe. Order a delectable gift box and have Cheesers ship it for you. Delight yourself or your friends with a gift of cheese or gourmet food from Cheesers.

183 E Main Street, Stoughton WI
(608) 873-1777
www.cheesers.com

Photos by Gary Walker

Nordic Nook

SHOPPING

Nordic Nook, a gift store, is a labor of love that celebrates Norway, the bond between mother and daughter and the blending of two families that traveled from the Old World to the new. Owner Patrice Roe shares responsibility for running the business with her mother, Ardis Gyland, who is a first-generation American and the store's manager. Patrice married into the Roe family, which can claim to be among the original Norwegian settlers in Stoughton, instrumental in building the historic Opera House that opened in 1901. Many of the store's customers say a visit to the Nordic Nook is like a visit to Norway, filled with familiar sensations that conjure up memories of their Nordic heritage. The store is a source for fine Scandinavian wares, including arts, crafts and clothing. Offerings include plates and dishes crafted with the Norwegian decorative painting known as rosemaling, as well as crystal, china, linens, iron and leather items. Other items of interest include dolls, figurines, jewelry and pewter ware. In addition to offering fine merchandise, the Nordic Nook holds several Norwegian celebrations throughout the year, including a Norwegian Constitution Day observance in May, a midsummer's eve celebration in June and a fête celebrating the Land of the Midnight Sun in October. For an opportunity to buy fine Scandinavian goods while enjoying a truly Nordic experience, visit Nordic Nook.

176 W Main Street, Stoughton WI
(608) 877-0848
www.nordic-nook.com

The Stolen Heart

SHOPPING

Looking for home décor, original gifts and jewelry? Just south of Madison lies the Stolen Heart, located in a charming turn-of-the-century building in the heart of historic downtown Stoughton. Nancy Hurt's unique boutique overflows with everything from posh gifts to primitive decorations and crafts. An entire wall of finely crafted clocks shares shop space with an outstanding selection of vintage signs that can be personalized, and that's just the beginning. Expect to find lamps and chandeliers, quilts and beautiful accessories from well-known names like Vera Bradley and Laura Ashley. The Stolen Heart features Hickory Hill furniture and displays an occasional antique piece as well. The exquisite jewelry selection includes beautiful baubles from Lunch at the Ritz and Jolie, as well as bracelets with a wide selection of charms you can personalize with names and birthstones. Grace your home with gorgeous linens from Pine Cone Hill and Bella Nolte, handsome rugs from Company C or wall art that includes signed prints on canvas from Christy Repasy. The Stolen Heart also hosts events, parties and classes on a regular basis. Sign up online for fairy ring, needle felting and ribbon art classes, or learn clutter-busting tips from professional organizer Nancy Kruschke McKinney. From distressed leather handbags to festive holiday décor, when you want items that will steal your heart, visit the Stolen Heart.

154 E Main Street, Stoughton, WI
(608) 873-9444
www.thestolenheart.com

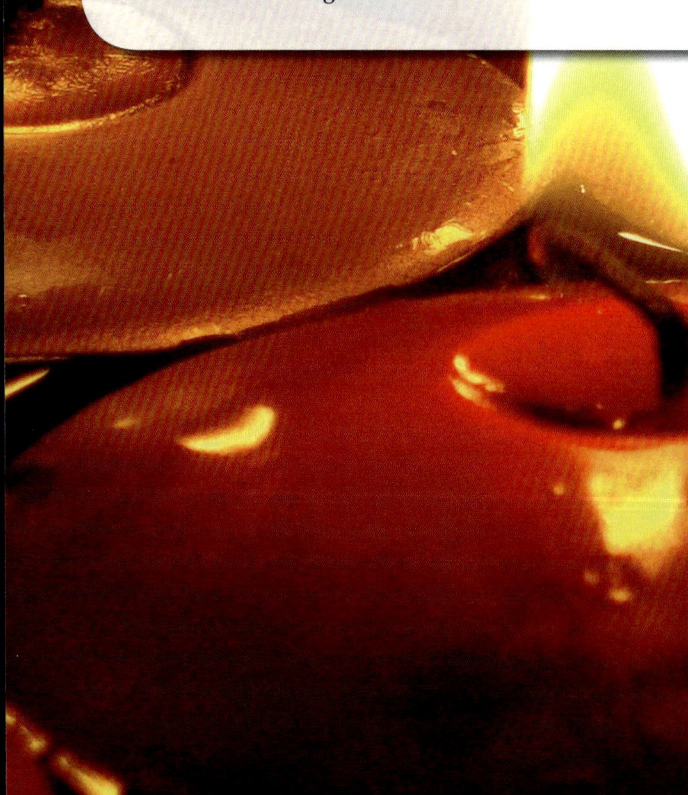

Clock Tower Gifts

SHOPPING

Clock Tower Gifts, in historic downtown Stoughton, pays tribute to its community's heritage by offering traditional Norwegian crafts, such as woodcarvings and rosemaling. The gift boutique, open since 1992, sells wall art, custom florals and the Heritage Lace line of window accents and table linens. Shop owners Becky Greiber and Lou Ann McHugh support local and American businesses. They carry Jim Shore's line of Heartwood Creek collectibles including Santas, snowmen, angels, nautical and all of his other creations. Jim has also teamed up with the Lang company to create cards, journals, photo albums and baskets. Whether you're looking for a keepsake box or scented candles, you're sure to find it here. Clock Tower Gifts is a Silver Paw dealer for the Boyds collectible line and carries of all their current line of plush and resin bears, as well as many retired pieces. They also carry an extensive collection of the Willow Tree angels and figurines. At Clock Tower Gifts, it's always Christmas upstairs, where you'll find festive decorations year-round. Sports fans will appreciate the Badger and Packer merchandise. The friendly staff will gladly help out with suggestions and free gift wrapping. The inventory changes often, so there's always something new to discover. Becky and Lou Ann host several community events, such as Ladies Shopping Night, which features wine tasting and holiday fun in the fall. They also celebrate Syttende Mai in May and Victorian Holiday in December with on-site demonstrations. For gifts from a community-spirited store, visit Clock Tower Gifts.

120 E Main Street, Stoughton WI
(608) 873-6699
www.clocktowergifts.com

PLACES TO GO

- Canal Station Lighthouse
  (920) 743-5958
- Door County Maritime Museum
  120 N Madison Avenue
  (920) 743-5958
- Miller Art Museum
  107 S 4th Avenue (in the Library)
  (920) 746-0707
- Potawatomi State Park
  3740 Park Drive
  (920) 746-2890
- Sherwood Point Lighthouse
  (920) 743-5958
- The Farm
  4285 Highway 57 N
  (920) 743-6666
- Whitefish Dunes State Park
  3275 Clark Lake Road
  (920) 823-2400

THINGS TO DO

May

- Festival of Blossoms
  (920) 743-4456
- Fine Art Fair
  Sawyer Park
  (920) 743-6246

July

- Jefferson Street Festival
  (920) 743-6246

August

- Door County Fair
  www.doorcounty.org/fair

September

- Sturgeon Bay Harvest Fest
  (920) 743-6246

STURGEON BAY

Sturgeon Bay is the seat of Door County, a constellation of small towns on the Door Peninsula, which *Money Magazine* has called one of the top 10 vacation destinations in North America. Sturgeon Bay's recently refurbished waterfront includes city walkways, beaches and the impressive new Door County Maritime Museum. The Door County Trolleys offer tours of the local scenery, lighthouses and ice cream shops. Downtown offers charming stores, fine restaurants and several galleries. Whitefish Dunes State Park, which runs along the shores of Lake Michigan and Clark Lake, contains wetlands, sand dunes and beech forest. It is home to eight Indian villages listed on the National Register of Historic Places. At Potawatomi State Park, visitors can climb a 75-foot observation tower for a panoramic view. At The Farm, you can visit animals, feed their babies, and enjoy nature trails and amusement rides.

Bridgeport Waterfront Resort

ACCOMMODATIONS

You will find Bridgeport Waterfront Resort near the bridge in the center of Sturgeon Bay, close to quaint shops and award winning restaurants. A waterfront walkway connects the resort to city parks that provide sandy beaches, tennis courts and playgrounds. Suites here feature views of the water or the city and one, two or three bedrooms, all with whirlpool baths. Larger suites have fireplaces, complete kitchens and private decks. Bridgeport is an ideal destination for a romantic getaway or business travel, and it is especially attractive for family vacations with its many on-site recreational amenities. Enjoy a sauna, a fitness room and both indoor and outdoor heated swimming pools. Have you ever jumped through a waterfall? You can do just that at Bridgeport's heated outdoor pool. Kids love the indoor splash park with a slide and interactive water games plus a play park with tubes, tunnels and a ball pit. Business travelers can use the business center and access wireless Internet in their suites. Bridgeport also offers three conference rooms with wireless Internet, audiovisual equipment and facilities for groups of five to 72. Bridgeport Waterfront Resort suites are also offered for sale, fully furnished, as condominium units. You can enjoy your condominium as a vacation home and also place it in the rental program. For a relaxing time by the water, visit Bridgeport Waterfront Resort.

50 W Larch Street, Sturgeon Bay WI
(920) 746-9919 or (800) 671-9190
www.bridgeportresort.net

Acme Bead Company

ARTS & CRAFTS

Enter the whimsical world of Beth Ruth when you walk through the doors of the Acme Bead Company, established in 2002. An artist for most of her life, Beth studied art and advertising before finding her niche producing fun jewelry design kits and beaded products. Located in the heart of beautiful Door County, the store offers an exceptional selection of beads and beading supplies for everyone from beginners to professional jewelry designers. You will find books and kits, along with tools for making your own beadwork. Beth's inventory of thousands of hard-to-find beads, including sterling, crystal, seed and glass lampwork beads, grows weekly. Walk through her curiosity shop enjoying the tunes of Billie Holiday, and let your eyes light up at the artistry. You can also order neon signs in colors of your choice and find vintage beaded jewelry. A visit to Acme often involves a greeting from Mavis, Beth's boxer, or from bead boy Scott Wieland; they are not for sale. Check out the website for new products and coupons. Beth invites you to enjoy the lighter side of life at Acme Bead Company whenever you pass through Sturgeon Bay.

41 W Maple Street, Sturgeon Bay WI
(920) 559-7446
www.acmebeadcompany.com

Schopf's Hilltop Dairy LLC

ATTRACTIONS

At Schopf's Hilltop Dairy, a working dairy farm that welcomes tourists, you can see how the cattle are cared for and how milk is produced. Start your tour via the live, moveable video camera, which allows you to see where the cows eat and sleep. You will see the automatic cleaning system, drive-through feeding and the luxury cow mattresses. Next, move on to the milking parlor that allows the staff to milk 80 cows an hour, keeping the cows comfortable all the while. As the cows are milked, you can watch through a 28-foot glass window that is necessary to maintain the high sanitation levels. Staff members shower and change clothes every time they enter or leave the cattle compound. In the main showroom, more glass windows let you monitor the flow of milk from the parlor to the cooling and holding facility. After the entertaining and instructive tour, you can stop at the Dairy View Country Store for Door County memorabilia, fudge made at the farm and goodies from local farmers. At the end of your visit, try the delicious homemade ice cream at the Dairy View Country Store Ice Cream Parlor. From late summer until the end of October, visit the farm's Dairy View Corn Maze that features a different theme every year. Schopf's Hilltop Dairy and Dairy View Country Store are closed January through March. At any other time of the year, the Schopf's Hilltop Dairy barn doors await your visit.

5169 County I, Sturgeon Bay WI
(920) 743-9779
www.dairyview.com

Photo © 2004 Len Villano

Door County Maritime Museum

ATTRACTIONS

Board a real Great Lakes fish tug, explore a 137-year-old lighthouse and discover Sturgeon Bay's rich shipbuilding history at the Sturgeon Bay, Cana Island and Gills Rock locations of the Door County Maritime Museum. Throughout history, the waterways of Door County played a significant role in the development of local and interstate commerce and culture. The museum salutes the lighthouses, shipwrecks and shipbuilders of the area. The Sturgeon Bay museum displays exhibits on the history of Sturgeon Bay's shipyards, which produced fishing trawlers, navy vessels and some of the world's finest yachts. Exhibits show scale models of boats and ships built in Sturgeon Bay, including half-hull, corporate and folk art models. A chronological history of shipbuilding includes an exploration of the Indian dugouts and birch bark canoes of the mid 1800s, the lumber schooners that plied the Great Lakes in the late 1800s, and present-day shipbuilding in Sturgeon Bay. The Sturgeon Bay museum is open year-round and features a gift shop with a maritime theme and beautiful facilities that can be rented for meetings, private parties or corporate receptions. In 1971, the museum opened the Cana Island Lighthouse, one of the most photographed of Great Lakes lighthouses. The museum opened Gills Rock in 1975 with a focus on commercial fishing and shipwrecks. Cana Island and Gills Rock are open from May to October. Step back in time with a visit to all three Door County Maritime Museum locations.

120 N Madison Avenue, Sturgeon Bay WI
(920) 743-5958 ***www.dcmm.org***

Photo © 2004 Len Villano

Hat Head

FASHION

Bob and Bonnie Spielman, owners of Hat Head, confess they are hat fanatics at heart. As Door County's headwear specialists, they have gathered together a mind-boggling collection of headgear that promises to cure the worst bad hair day. You'll find sizes to fit every noggin, prices to fit every budget, and styles for every taste. Looking for a boonie, a bucket, a bandana or a bomber? Red Hat women and mad hatters alike both find the adornments they seek at this distinctive shop. Look for straw hats, sun hats, fishing hats and fun hats. Does a derby suit one day and a driving cap the next? Western hats, leather hats, fedoras and fleece are just some of the possibilities at Hat Head. You'll also find plenty of caps sporting the logos of your favorite teams. Look for the brands hat lovers prefer to flaunt, such as Stetson, Tilley, Kangol and Zephyr. Hat Head offers custom embroidery for one hat or 100 hats. Services here include a program to help chemotherapy patients keep their heads covered. Bonnie and Bob opened the first Hat Head in Fish Creek in 1997 and the second in Sturgeon Bay in 2005. They invite you to have fun trying on a few hats in either Hat Head store.

27 N Third Avenue, Sturgeon Bay WI (920) 746-1514
4149 Highway 42, Fish Creek WI (920) 868-2371

T. Simon Jewelers

FASHION

Tricia Simon opened T. Simon Jewelers 10 years ago and now features the largest display of diamonds and gemstones in Door County, from the ordinary to the extraordinary. Located in downtown Sturgeon Bay, T. Simon Jewelers showcases many exclusive designer pieces, including pieces crafted by Tricia herself. Tricia started out in goldsmithing and jewelry repair and still provides in-store goldsmith work, including repairs, remounts and custom designs. T. Simon Jewelers offers a large selection of slides, diamonds, gemstone rings, bridal sets, pendants and earrings. Love is the fire behind many jewelry purchases, and T. Simon keeps lovers supplied with diamond anniversary bands, engagement rings and wedding bands. The T. Simon staff members are never happier than when they have brought a smile to a customer's face with excellent customer service and quality merchandise. When you are in the market for jewelry, turn to T. Simon Jewelers.

69 S Madison Avenue, Sturgeon Bay WI
(920) 743-2206

Great Blue Herons nesting

PLACES TO GO

- Angel Park Speedway
  (608) 837-5252
- Georgia O'Keefe Family Farmstead
  County Highway T
- Historical Museum
  115 E Main Street
  (608) 837-2915.
- McCarthy Youth and Conservation Park
  4911 County Highway T
- Patrick Marsh
  Highway 151 NE
- Token Creek County Park
  6200 U.S. Highway 51, Deforest

THING S TO DO

February

- Groundhog Day Celebration
  St. Albert's Church
  (608) 837-4547

June

- Strawberry Fest
  Colonial Club Senior Activity Center
  (608) 837-4611
- Taste of the Arts Fair
  Sheehan Park
  (608) 837-4547

August

- Sweet Corn Festival
  Angell Park
  (800) 400-6162

SUN PRAIRIE

Sun Prairie is an attractive and thriving Madison suburb. As the fastest growing city in Wisconsin, it provides a balance of affordability and a high standard of living for 25,000 residents. Visitors will find charming neighborhoods, a historic downtown shopping district and more than 32 parks, equipped with baseball diamonds, outdoor skating rinks and a skate park. The first white men to visit the area were a party of 45 that President Martin Van Buren had commissioned to build a state capitol in Madison. The group traveled for days in the rain until finally emerging into sunshine at the edge of the prairie, where they carved the words Sun Prairie into a tree. Sun Prairie still retains the aura of a hidden haven and consistently ranks as one of the top places in America to live. The village has celebrated Groundhog Day since 1886 and officially since 1948. Jimmy the Groundhog calls the shots on whether Sun Prairie lives up to its name.

National Midget Auto Racing Hall of Fame

ATTRACTIONS

Located in the famed Pavilion at Angell Park in Sun Prairie is the National Midget Auto Racing Hall of Fame. The Hall of Fame is dedicated to preserving the history and heritage of midget auto racing, while at the same time recognizing and inducting into its ranks outstanding people within the sport. The Hall of Fame, established in 1984, is expanding its activities and designing a permanent historical display. Inductees into the hall of fame include Indy 500 winning drivers such as A.J. Foyt, Parnelli Jones, Johnnie Parsons, Troy Ruttman, Sam Hanks, Roger Ward and Bill Vukovich. But famous drivers aren't the only ones included in the Hall of Fame. Famed Chief Mechanic George Bignotti, who wrenched numerous Indy 500 winning cars, and winning car owner Bob Wilke are inductees, too. Numerous NASCAR stars such as Tony Stewart and Jason Leffler are among many others who comprise the current 116 members of the Hall of Fame. Enjoy racing at Angell Park from late May to Labor Day. A special two-day racing event is held each year near the fourth weekend of August. It's held in conjunction with the induction ceremonies and draws some of the biggest names in midget auto racing. Each inductee is presented with a distinctive bronze plaque commemorating their accomplishments which is placed on display in the Hall of Fame for the public to enjoy. Make it a point to see the Hall of Fame.

511 Maynard Drive, Sun Prairie WI
(608) 837-5252 ***www.worthyofhonor.com***

Firemen's Angell Park Speedway

ATTRACTIONS

Are you looking for something exciting to do on a Sunday evening that the whole family can enjoy? Attending a midget car race at Firemen's Angell Park Speedway is just the ticket. The park where the speedway is located opened in 1902 and Angell Park Speedway has been racing since 1946. Owned by the Sun Prairie Volunteer Fire Department, the focus is on family friendly entertainment. There is no charge for children under age 12 when they are accompanied by an adult. The track is a one-third-mile clay oval that is used exclusively for midget races. Many top name NASCAR stars have driven at Angell Park Speedway over the years including Tony Stewart, Kasey Kahne and Jeff Gordon. Angell Park Speedway is also home to the National Midget Auto Racing Hall of Fame, so plan enough time to take a tour before the racing begins. Some of the high points of the racing season are Memorial Day, the annual Hall of Fame Classic two-day race event that features the two top midget racing groups in the nation, and the Firemen's Nationals that take place on Labor Day each year. Races are scheduled from mid-May to Labor Day, so come join the fun and action at Firemen's Angell Park Speedway.

County Highway N, Sun Prairie WI
(608) 837-5252 (racing hotline)
www.angellpark.com

Sun Prairie Volunteer Fire Department

ATTRACTIONS

For a city the size of Sun Prairie, population 25,000, to have a full-scale volunteer fire department is rare. It is one of the few left in the state and provides fire protection not only for the city of Sun Prairie, but also the surrounding communities of Bristol, Burke and the township of Sun Prairie. During fire prevention week, in October, the Volunteer Fire Department hosts an open house with a free pancake breakfast. The fire department is the sole owner of 60 acres of land that houses the legendary Angell Park Speedway and Hall of Fame. The firefighters are also the official escorts for Jimmy the Groundhog when he does his yearly prognostication every February 2. The fire department was first organized in April 1891 with 22 men; today there are 45 members, three of which are women. The department made its first motorized engine purchase in 1927 and currently has nine vehicles: one heavy rescue squad, two tankers, two brush trucks, a 100 foot aerial platform and three engine pumpers. The fire district covers 96.5 square miles, making Sun Prairie one of the largest cities in the state to rely solely on volunteers for fire protection (even the chief is unpaid). For the past 115 years the department has had no firefighter deaths while in the line of duty. Sun Prairie Volunteer Fire Department is a great organization that invites all to support its growth and the continual protection of the district.

135 N Bristol Street, Sun Prairie WI (608) 837-5066

McGovern's Inn and Irish Pub

RESTAURANTS & CAFÉS

Three generations have nurtured and improved the family-owned McGovern's Inn and Irish Pub, a Sun Prairie landmark that beckons residents and tourists. In 1935, Al McGovern bought an acre of swampy land at Main and Bird Streets that contained a bar. After World War II, his sons began improvements and opened the first 10-room motel in town. Today, the inn is known for its down-home hospitality, providing 52 rooms and seven corporate suites. Each suite is named after a local or nationally known artist, such as Sun Prairie born Georgia O'Keeffe or Maggie Schuckert. The establishment attracts many famous people, thanks to its quality food and service. Notable visitors through the years have included well known musicians and Wisconsin baseball players. The restaurant has a reputation for providing the best burgers and live entertainment in town. The prime rib is outstanding, and the soups are made from scratch. Summertime brings seafood boils, live music and beer tasting events. You can choose to eat lunch or dinner indoors, in the sunroom or on the deck. McGovern's Inn and Irish Pub offers services to satisfy just about everyone, including three bars, three large-screen televisions for watching your favorite sports events and complimentary high-speed Internet access. The McGovern family invites you to visit McGovern's Inn and Irish Pub, where that swampy farmland long ago became a Sun Prairie entertainment and lodging hub.

820 W Main Street, Sun Prairie WI
(608) 837-7321 or (800) 837-7321
www.mcgoverns.biz

Firemans Angell Park Speedway, 1950

SUSSEX

The village of Sussex grew up on the banks of limestone quarries that still operate today. The Wisconsin Central and Northwestern railway lines that bisect the township once hauled the stone away. Several original stone buildings survive. Much civic life is concentrated in the village parks and trails. Sussex Village Park, with sports fields, open spaces and summer activities, is a charming place to embark on the Bugline Trail, which travels past the impressive limestone pits on the former Pacific Railroad right-of-way. Sussex earned tourism fame in 1924 when a local canning factory adopted Kewpie as its logo, thus participating in one of the most popular and long-lived fads of all time. Kewpie fans from around the world continue to pilgrimage to Sussex in search of Kewpie items to add to their collections. In recent years, Sussex has initiated a comprehensive development plan that has already created 4,000 new jobs and opened new residential, commercial and industrial sites. The local high school is home to Charger Robotics Team 537, a nationally known, multiple-award-winning group dedicated to preparing today's youth for the jobs and industries of tomorrow.

PLACES TO GO

- Ausblick Ski Hill
  W260 N6395 Mary Hill Road
  (262) 246-3090

THINGS TO DO

March

- Kettle Moraine Geological Society Gem and Mineral Show
  National Guard Armory
  (262) 246-6684

August

- Sussex Antique Power Show
  Sussex Village Park
  (262) 246-3600

September

- Dozer Day
  Halquist Stone Quarry
  www.dozerday.com

Amy B. & Co. Salon/Spa

HEALTH & BEAUTY

You can look at Amy B. & Co. in Sussex as a salon and spa catering to women's good health and beauty, or you can see it as a studio of artists working together to turn each guest into their latest masterpiece. "From the time you walk into Amy B. & Co. until the time you emerge on the other end of your visit, you'll feel more relaxed and looking better than you ever thought possible," says owner Amy Brissette. To accomplish this mission, Amy hires the most dedicated and creative people she can find, people who commit themselves to their profession through constant training. Amy's team offers the latest trends and techniques in hair, skin and nail care. A massage therapist works to relieve stress, improve blood circulation and ease muscle tension. Spa experts awaken dull, dry skin with such treatments as the sea salt body glow polish, which uses aromatherapy sea salts and essential oils to refine and improve skin texture. Amy reminds her clients that she posts monthly specials on her website and that Amy B. & Co.'s salon and spa packages make perfect gifts for brides, teens and wives. Come to Amy B. & Co., and leave feeling like a living, breathing work of art.

N64 W24678 Main Street, Sussex WI
(262) 820-2600
www.amybandco.com

Seigo's Japanese Steak House

RESTAURANTS & CAFÉS

Experience authentic Japanese cuisine while feasting your eyes on an exciting culinary show filled with lightening quick moves and flashing utensils at Seigo's Japanese Steak House. This lively dining venue was founded in 1982 by Seigo Hidaka, a Japanese native, and is now owned and operated by longtime friend and past employee Kenny Shimokawa, also of Japan. Each specially created seating area holds eight to 10 guests, although the restaurant can accommodate groups of up to 20. Each group has its own personal chef, who uses his advanced culinary skills to expertly prepare savory dishes right before your eyes. The personal chefs are as engaging as they are skillful and strive to entertain you through a variety of dashing knife tricks and food-related stunts, such as flying shrimp and flaming onion volcanoes. Besides the popular grill demonstration meals, such as the filet and shrimp or filet and lobster combos, Seigo's Japanese Steak House also offers a sushi and sashimi bar. All of Seigo's choices are prepared using fresh, high quality ingredients. The restaurant features two dining rooms and banquet facilities, along with a large bar and private dining area for special occasions, making Seigo's the ideal place for corporate dinners, anniversaries and birthdays. Enjoy a dinner show the like of which you've never seen before with a visit to Seigo's Japanese Steak House.

N64 W23180 Main Street, Sussex WI
(262) 820-8600
www.foodspot.com/seigos

TREVOR

Trevor is the southernmost city in Kenosha County, on the border with Illinois. The semi-rural region is a popular lake resort area within an hour's drive of Milwaukee. A former railroad town, Trevor grew up alongside the tracks of the Wisconsin Central line a few miles from the Camp Lake depot. Proximity to Camp Lake and the Twin Lakes, as well as a smattering of smaller lakes, makes water access one of the chief benefits of living in Trevor. As one of the last cities in the Kenosha County lakes area to be discovered by developers, Trevor is currently enjoying a real estate boom. Visitors can enjoy the attractions of neighboring Wilmot and Twin Lakes while returning at day's end to the quietude of non-touristed Trevor. The multi-use Fox River State Trail runs through Trevor from Green Bay to Greenleaf.

PLACES TO GO

- Western Kenosha County Historical Society Hall and Twin Oaks Rural Schoolhouse
  25905 114th Street
  (262) 862-2635

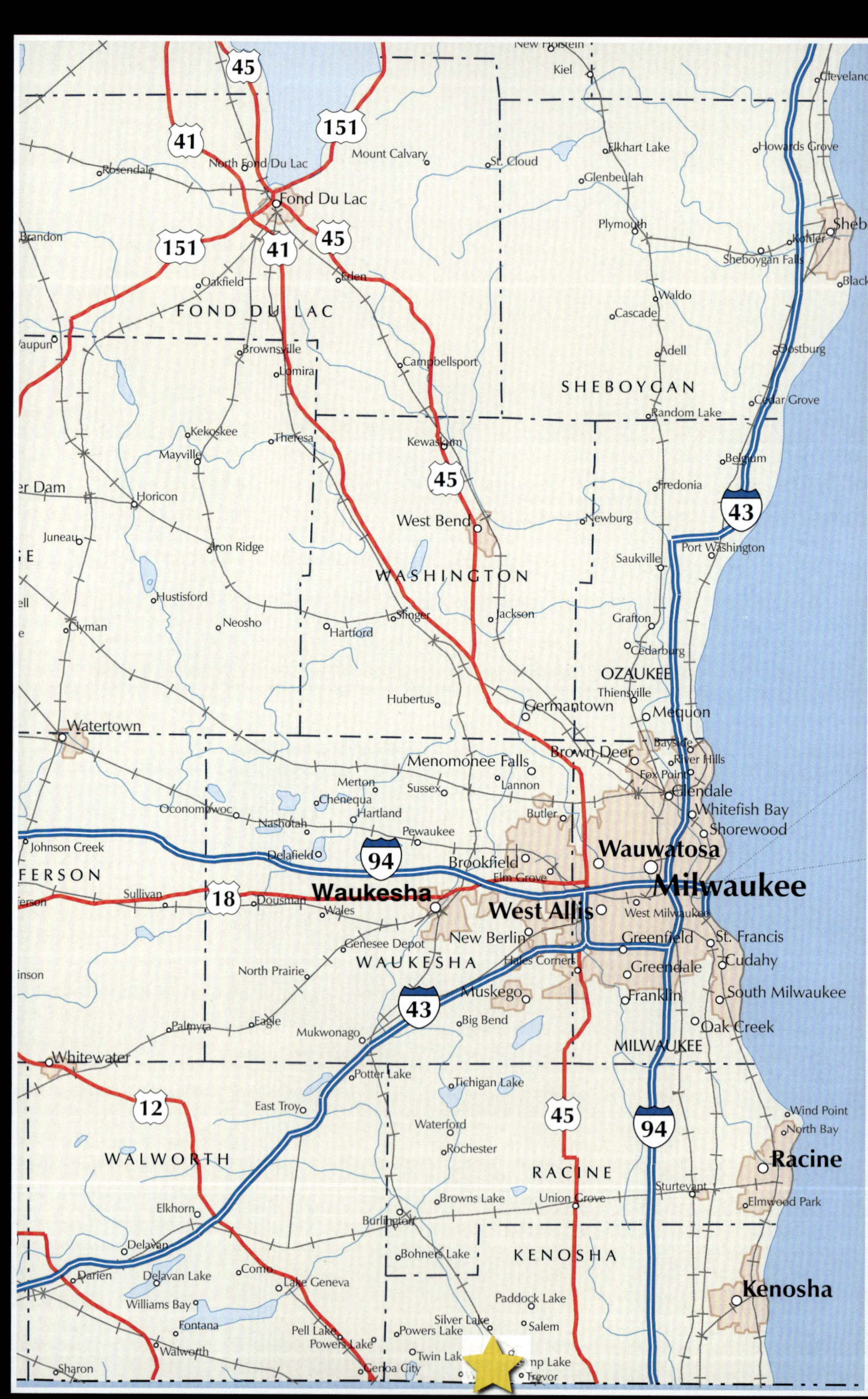

Promised Land Park

RECREATION & FITNESS

Capture the Flag is a classic paintball game and just one of many possibilities for play at Promised Land Park, where Rick and Diann Pinter and their four children have devised a variety of team-based challenges on 53 acres of woods, hills and plateaus. Promised Land is proof that kids can have fun in a Christian environment and is a popular destination for youth groups. The Pinters call their games scenario games, because each features a setting, a plot and a mission. You could be part of the U.S. Special Forces trying to diffuse a nuclear device or marooned on Outlaw Island, fighting criminal villagers for food. Games like Hillbillies and Survivor require strategy and teamwork. Groups need reservations and usually stay all day. The Pinters provide lunch and all necessary equipment for one fee. Referees keep track of points, and a winning team receives a trophy and a group photograph. A spring fed pond offers opportunities for swimming, kayaks or paddleboats. Six miles of hiking trails and set-ups for archery and volleyball further the possibilities for wholesome good times. Rick brings just the right set of skills to this enterprise. He is an inventor, an electrical engineer and a former CIA agent. He also teaches Sunday School and takes a strong interest in teenagers. For activities approved by teens and their families, take your church group or club to Promised Land Park.

29039 Wilmot Road (Highway C), Trevor WI
(262) 694-1540 or (262) 862-7219
www.promisedland.com

TWIN LAKES

The village of Twin Lakes sits at the top of the twin lakes Mary and Elisabeth on the Illinois border. The first European settlers, the Ineson family, arrived in 1837 and named the lakes after their twin daughters. The lakes, which span nearly 1,000 acres, attracted ice harvesters historically and vacationers today. The village's permanent population of 5,300 expands by about a third during the warmer months. In July, Twin Lakes hosts Country Thunder USA, a big-time country music festival that has attracted such luminaries as Faith Hill, Tim McGraw and Keith Urban.

PLACES TO GO

- Country Corn
  11909 Richmond Road
  (262) 215-6166

THINGS TO DO

July

- Country Thunder USA
  Shadow Hill Ranch
  www.countrythunder.com

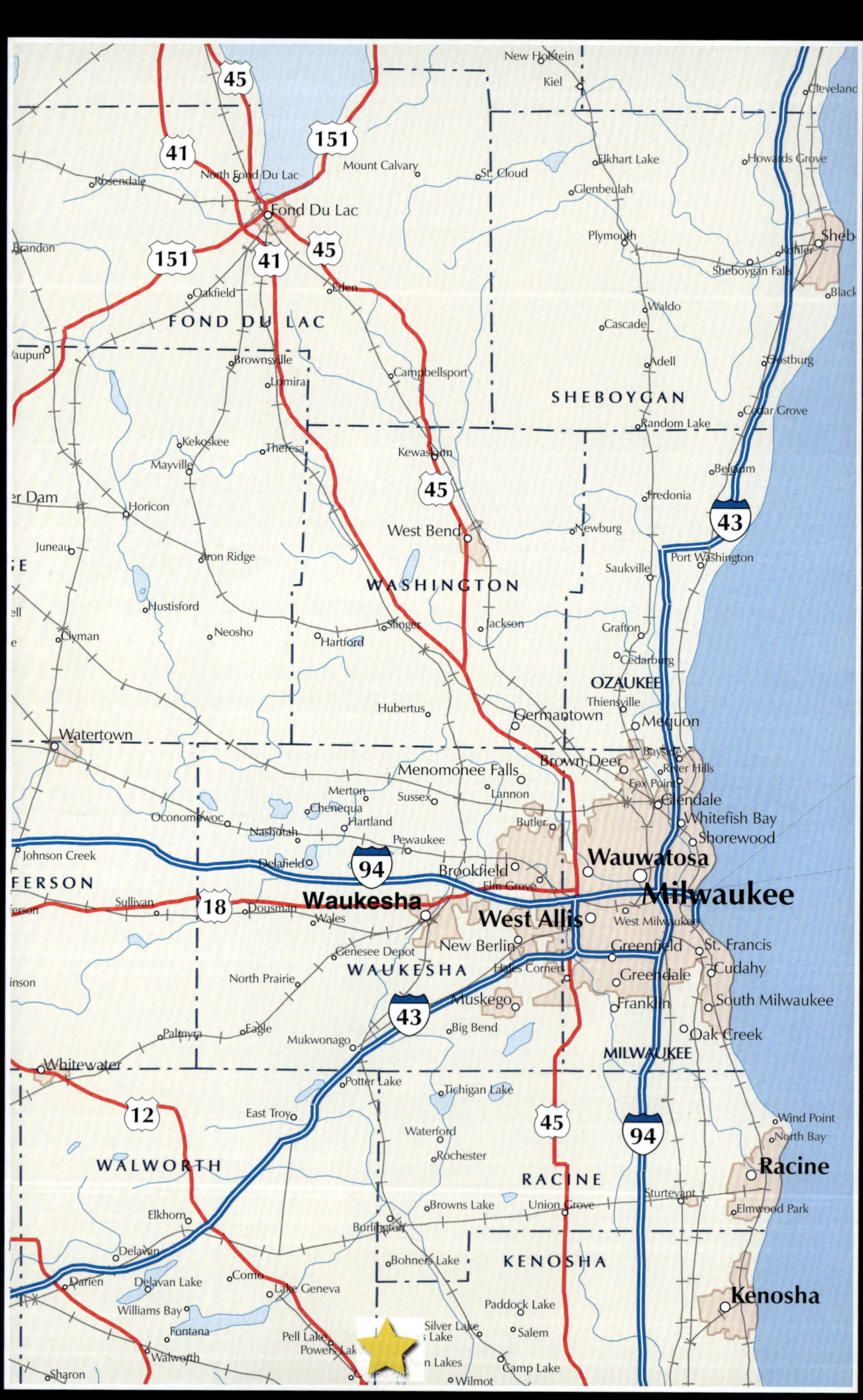

Shadow Hill Ranch

ATTRACTIONS

In business since 1992, Shadow Hill Ranch is a 40-acre campground with a natural bowl that provides an outstanding setting for musical concerts. The Twin Lakes property is one of the country's premier venues for camping and listening to music with room for up to 60,000 people. It's one of three such properties owned by Graham Brothers Entertainment; the others are in Arizona and Texas. Summer events here include Country Thunder USA with its card of top country music entertainers. Keith Urban, Tim McGraw and Charlie Daniels have all played here. You'll find indoor restrooms, a full-service bar and food vendors along with several seating and camping options. Reservation choices include lawn seating with the chairs provided, seating in the VIP area without meals or VIP seating with catered meals. VIPs can also buy alcoholic beverages at a discount. During the four weekends of October, families look forward to Halloween Hollow and Terror Trail. These special events feature an enchanted forest with more than one million twinkling lights, interactive outdoor children's activities and private campfires with make-your-own s'mores kits. Terror Trail is a mile and a half pathway packed with Hollywood special effects and mechanical creatures. For fall fun with the family or a camping event packed with musical entertainment, plan a visit to Shadow Hill Ranch.

2305 Lance Drive, Twin Lakes WI
(262) 279-6960
www.shadowhillranch.com

VERONA

Verona, a fast-growing suburb of Madison, is a verdant residential community within a mile of the city's businesses. Verona sports several golf courses, parks and scenic trails. Badger Prairie Park serves as the central trail junction point, offering access to the Military Ridge Trail and the Ice Age National Scenic Trail, one of only eight national scenic trails in the United States. The Ice Age Trail follows a serpentine course through Wisconsin's world-renowned glacial features. The Military Ridge State Trail runs right through downtown Verona, following the former Chicago and North Western Railway line between the neighboring towns. The packed limestone trail is accessible to cycles, snowmobiles, skiers and even motorized wheelchairs. Verona fosters cultural and performing arts programs through the Verona Area Performing Arts Series.

PLACES TO GO

- Badger Prairie Park
  6720 U.S. Highway 151
- Eagles Nest Ice Arena
  103 Lincoln Street
- Hometown U.S.A. Community Park
  111 Lincoln Street
- Prairie Moraine County Park
  1970 County Highway PB
- University Ridge
  9002 County Highway PD

THINGS TO DO

June

- Hometown USA Festival
  www.veronahometowndays.com

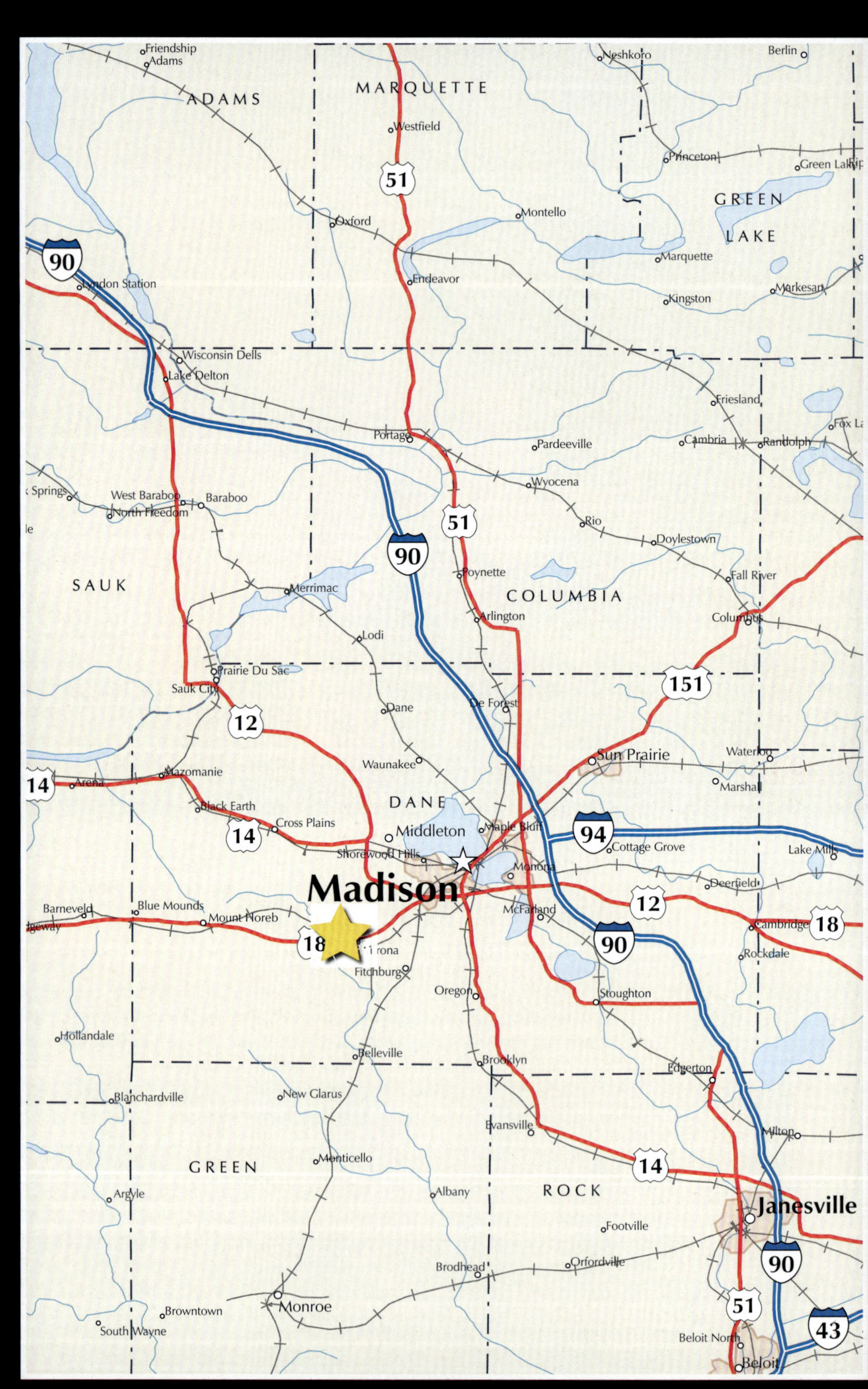

The Sow's Ear

ARTS & CRAFTS

There are 38 million knitters in America and the number is growing. Even so, it's fair to say the concept of a knitting café is unusual. The Sow's Ear is a major hit that attracts an eclectic clientele. Co-owners Mo Brown and Amy Armstrong have a winning formula that combines serving bakery goods, salads and espresso with selling flamboyant novelty yarns and organic cottons and wools. Although the business concept is unusual, this is not a location limited to buying your knitting needs or satisfying your hunger. Customers are known to find fellowship over coffee and to knit the morning away. The Sow's Ear knocks the notion that knitting is the exclusive purview of the older generation. Classes entice students from seven to 80, and enterprising young people coalesce into youth knitting groups. *Better Homes and Gardens* has recognized the owners for their part in revitalizing knitting. Housing activities in a Victorian era house is a perfect fit for a business that seamlessly blends the past with the present. You will be a fit even if you have never knitted a stitch in your life. The Sow's Ear is especially friendly to beginners. Stop by the Sow's Ear to knit, drink coffee and meet people with common interests.

125 S Main Street, Verona WI
(608) 848-2755
www.knitandsip.com

Pure Essence Salon and Spa

HEALTH & BEAUTY

With two small children, Julia Ace may not get much time to pamper herself, but she knows just how to care for others. At Julia's Pure Essence Salon and Spa, patrons receive a beauty experience rich in customer service, with several extra touches that really make you feel special. Pure Essence opened in 2001 and later became an Aveda Concepts Salon. Aveda skin care products use only pure essence oils and certified organic plant and flower ingredients to rejuvenate your skin. The salon's signature Elemental Nature facial is a customized treatment based on your skin type. Elemental Nature massages are also personalized, using a variety of massage techniques and your favorite Aveda aromas. Come in for a new haircut, color or style and enjoy a complimentary head, neck and shoulder massage during the transformation. The spa manicure and pedicure include a soothing paraffin dip and a relaxing scalp massage to make you feel great from head to toe. If you are ready to wow guests at your next event, come in for a makeup application or learn how to apply makeup with a private lesson. Visit Pure Essence Salon and Spa today and let the talented stylists and massage therapists care for you.

104 E Verona Avenue, Verona WI
(608) 848-4050

Hawks Landing Golf Club

RECREATION & FITNESS

Enjoy playing at Hawks Landing Golf Club's 18-hole championship 2006 Course of the Year, designed to challenge and accommodate all golfing levels. Open to the public, the course layout provides four sets of tees, 65 bunkers, water features, native grass areas throughout, and a 395-yard, all-grass range. There's separate chipping, pitching and an 18,000 square foot putting green for you to practice your game. Hawks Landing Golf Club ranks as the finest golf facility in an area rich with great golfing. *Madison Magazine* rated it Best of Madison for 2005 and 2006. *Golf Digest* rates it with four-and-one-half stars as Best Places to Play. A writer for *Midwest Golfing Magazine*, who recently played the course, heaped overall praise upon the "stellar course conditions, first-class amenities and a majestic links-style layout that screams, 'You've got to come back for more.'" He, like everyone who plays the course, was intrigued by the 18th hole. At first look, it is a grueling 550-yard uphill par five, but becomes memorable as the fairway winds past an old silo and ends on the green outlined by a three-tiered waterfall. This delightful signature hole will, as the writer stated, "make you forget your bogey or worse." The experience awaits you at Hawks Landing Golf Club.

88 Hawks Landing Circle, Verona WI
(866) 848-HAWK (4295)
www.hawkslandinggolfclub.com

University Ridge Golf Course

RECREATION & FITNESS

The complete list of awards and accolades for the University Ridge Golf Course is too long to cite in its entirety. It is sufficient to say that this course is rated by every major golf publication in the United States as among the best public courses in every category that matters, including beauty, design, amenities and the challenge it presents. Designed by Robert Trent Jones II, University Ridge has hosted NCAA championships, Big Ten championships and state high school championships. In addition to 18 of the prettiest and most challenging holes in the country, the golf course has first-rate practice facilities. University Ridge is owned by the University of Wisconsin and is the home course of the Badgers. It spreads across the beautiful rolling hills and bowls typical of the Kettle Moraine, the place where the mighty Wisconsin glaciers finally settled down and melted two million years ago. The front nine meanders over lush grasslands, while the back nine is carved out of the densest of Wisconsin's woodlands. The clubhouse, featuring a golf shop, dining room and hospitality tent, is the perfect place to host your next charity or corporate golf outing. If you fancy yourself as a golf enthusiast, this is a course you will want to play. Come to University Ridge Golf Course and enjoy an exceptional golf experience.

9002 County Road PD, Verona WI
(608) 845-7700 or (800) 897-4343
www.universityridge.com

House of Flowers

SHOPPING

Since 1996, House of Flowers has been making customers feel special. Owners Sally Rossmiller and Darren Viatowski are the only florists in Dane County licensed by the American Institute of Floral Design. Sally and Darren, along with their fun and friendly staff, bring a personal touch to delightful tropical arrangements and impressive wedding floral designs. Nothing beats the surprise on a person's face that comes with a gift of flowers delivered right to their door or office, and House of Flowers will deliver up to 20 miles from the Verona shop. In addition to flowers, you will also find a large selection of gifts for every budget, a selection of silk and dried options and numerous European dish gardens. Three times a year, in spring, fall and at holiday time, the shop holds an open house, with floral design classes, many deals and terrific design ideas for the season. The annual summer tent sale is another opportunity to sample flowers and gifts from House of Flowers at a discount.
Sally and Darren believe in the kind of customer service that earns loyalty. They also believe in giving back to the Madison community by supporting several nonprofit organizations and staying involved in local charity work. Visit House of Flowers & Gifts to decorate your home, give a gift of flowers or select a special treasure for someone special.

101 N Main Street, Verona WI
(608) 845-8111 or (800) 869-5080
www.veronaflowers.com

The Purple Goose

SHOPPING

The children's clothing, women's jewelry, gifts and other funky accessories at the Purple Goose are at once hip and practical, making life easier for moms while keeping up with the latest styles. Owner Halley Jones, who accurately describes the Purple Goose as a boutique with city style and hometown charm, opened the shop inside a historic brick home in 2005. The store is user-friendly, and Halley declares that the Purple Goose breaks some of the standard rules of boutique shopping. For instance, the shop encourages moms to bring their kids and offers a fun play area with story and craft times to keep them busy while you shop. Instead of a strict no beverage policy, patrons are welcome to browse while enjoying a cup of java. A portion of the store is an eco-boutique and carries many items that are earth-friendly, sustainable or natural. Fuzzibunz cloth diapers benefit baby's bottom and the environment, and organic cotton clothing embellished with vintage materials is both comfortable and stylish. Old bicycle parts transform into funky pieces of art, like the sprocket wall clock and bicycle chain picture frame. A line of Green Glass tumblers and goblets, made in Wisconsin, uses recycled wine bottles to produce beautiful one-of-a-kind glasses. Come browse through the eclectic offerings at the Purple Goose and leave with fun new treasures and a smile.

400 W Verona Avenue, Verona WI
(608) 845-2368
www.shopthepurplegoose.com

PLACES TO GO

- Black River State Forest
  910 State Route 54 E, Black River
  (715) 284-4103
- Jellystone Park
  1500 Jellystone Park Drive
  (888) 386-9644
- Wisconsin Cranberry Discovery Center
  204 Main Street
  (608) 378-4878

THINGS TO DO

June

- Cranberry Blossom Tour Day
  Cranberry Discovery Center
  (608) 378-4878

September

- Warrens Cranberry Festival
  Downtown
  www.cranfest.com

October

- Wetherby Cranberry Company Public Harvest Day
  www.freshcranberries.com

December

- Christmas Open House
  Cranberry Discovery Center
  (608) 378-4878

WARRENS

Warrens sits among the densest concentration of cranberry marshes in the country. Wisconsin produces about half of the nation's cranberries and Warrens is the center of the industry. Warrens also produces much of the cranberry harvesting machinery used in the United States. The cranberry, in short, is the source of Warrens' special charm. Visitors will find a colorful range of cranberry products, from breads and cheeses to soaps and lotions. Warrens is also one of the few communities producing cranberry glass, a rare red glass created from gold chloride through a delicate, small-batch mixing process. The town's major attraction is the annual Cranberry Festival, which is one of the biggest festivals in the country, drawing 100,000 tourists and 1,500 vendors each year. Throughout the year, bed and breakfasts in Warrens do a steady business among those who enjoy the natural beauty of the region, a wooded constellation of lakes, rivers and streams. In addition to fishing and water sports, Warrens offers three full-circle bike/auto tours, ranging 20 to 30 miles, past cranberry marshes, sphagnum moss beds and Great Blue Heron nesting spots.

Cranberry Lake Village

ACCOMMODATIONS

Imagine waking up every morning to a sunrise over Cranberry Lake. Picture yourself in a community of timber homes nestled on a hillside among 100-year-old pine trees, a place where you can take your family to rejuvenate, relax, and spend quality time with one another. You can have all of that and more if you purchase a home at Cranberry Lake Village, an imaginative concept unfolding in conjunction with Yogi Bear's Jellystone Park in Warrens. At Cranberry Lake Village, you can choose from five different styles of stand-alone timber homes: the Whooping Crane Villa, Trumpeter Swan Villa, Golden Eagle Villa, and Goldeneye Villa. These single-family homes are loaded with amenities, and range in size from 1,105 square feet to 1,830 square feet. Owners enjoy all the fun at the indoor water resort. The resort also offers a great selection of rental units that are perfect for family getaways and sleep up to 12. If you are looking for a home away from home, a place where the kids will want to return year after year, look into the fabulous opportunities available at Cranberry Lake Village.

1500 Jellystone Park Drive, Warrens WI
(888) 386-9644
www.cranberrylakevillage.com

Jellystone Park Camp-Resort and Three Bears Lodge

ACCOMMODATIONS

Relive the happy childhood memory of Yogi Bear and his sidekick Boo Boo at Jellystone Park Camp-Resort and Three Bears Lodge. This family destination dreamland was created 35 years ago by the Pedersen family. Many families come back year after year because this very well could be one of the happiest places on earth. Now owned by Edward Van Der Molen, Jellystone Park features Yogi's Water Zone. Under the watchful eye of fully staffed lifeguards enjoy Blazin' Ol' Blue, the famous 400-foot high waterslide, a wave pool, two hot ponds, paddle boats and a variety of other features. The other water park, Cranberry Lake Water Zone, has two waterslides, paddle boat rentals and a world-class skate park. There are a multitude of campsites including rustic tent camping and full RV hook-ups. If sleeping under the stars is not for you, the Three Bears Lodge has all of the amenities to make your visit more than memorable. The Three Bears Lodge hosts a conference center, a full-service restaurant and an indoor water resort that's complete with Yogi's Picnic Splash, another wave pool, tube slides, indoor and outdoor hot ponds, the Lazy River, plus a water wars balloon game. There are a variety of cabins as well as villas that are custom designed with your family's comfort in mind. You can also wander beautiful hiking trails, find the relaxing fishing pond, or play a game on one of two mini-golf courses. If you'd like to treat your family to an adventure they'll never forget, come to Jellystone Park Camp-Resort and Three Bears Lodge, places where the laughter and the happy memories of childhood will last a lifetime.

1500 Jellystone Park Drive, Warrens WI
(608) 378-2000
www.jellystonewarrens.com

PLACES TO GO

- Brandt/Quirk Park
  800 Carriage Hill Drive
- Octagon House and First Kindergarten
  919 Charles Street
  (920) 261-2796
- Riverside Park
  850 Labaree Street
  (920) 262-8080
- Washington Park
  635 S 12th Street
  (920) 262-8080

THINGS TO DO

June
- Watertown Outdoor Art Festival
  Riverside Park Island
  (920) 261-2992

August
- Watertown Riverfest
  Riverside Park
  www.watertownriverfest.info

September
- Rock River Wine Fest & Craft Show
  Labaree Street
  (920) 261-9460

October
- Watertown Fall Festival
  Downtown
  (920) 261-5185

WATERTOWN

Watertown lies in a quilt of farmland in the Rock River Valley, where the river bends in a horseshoe shape. Settlers placed the original village site inside the horseshoe in 1836, using the river to power sawmills. The riverfront downtown of Watertown is one of the largest and most architecturally significant historic districts in the state. Shoppers will find a host of antique shops, a 1950s-style diner and a cobble-stoned village of shops inside one of Watertown's oldest buildings, the Market Specialty Shopping Mall. A popular landmark is the 1854 Octagon House. This 57-room home features a long spiral staircase and an ingenious cistern system to supply water. Watertown has a significant German heritage. In 1856, immigrant Margarethe Schurz established the first kindergarten in America. The building now stands on the grounds of the Octagon House. Watertown's German-Americans also established one of the first open-air markets in the country. The weekly Fair Day Farmers Market continues in Watertown today.

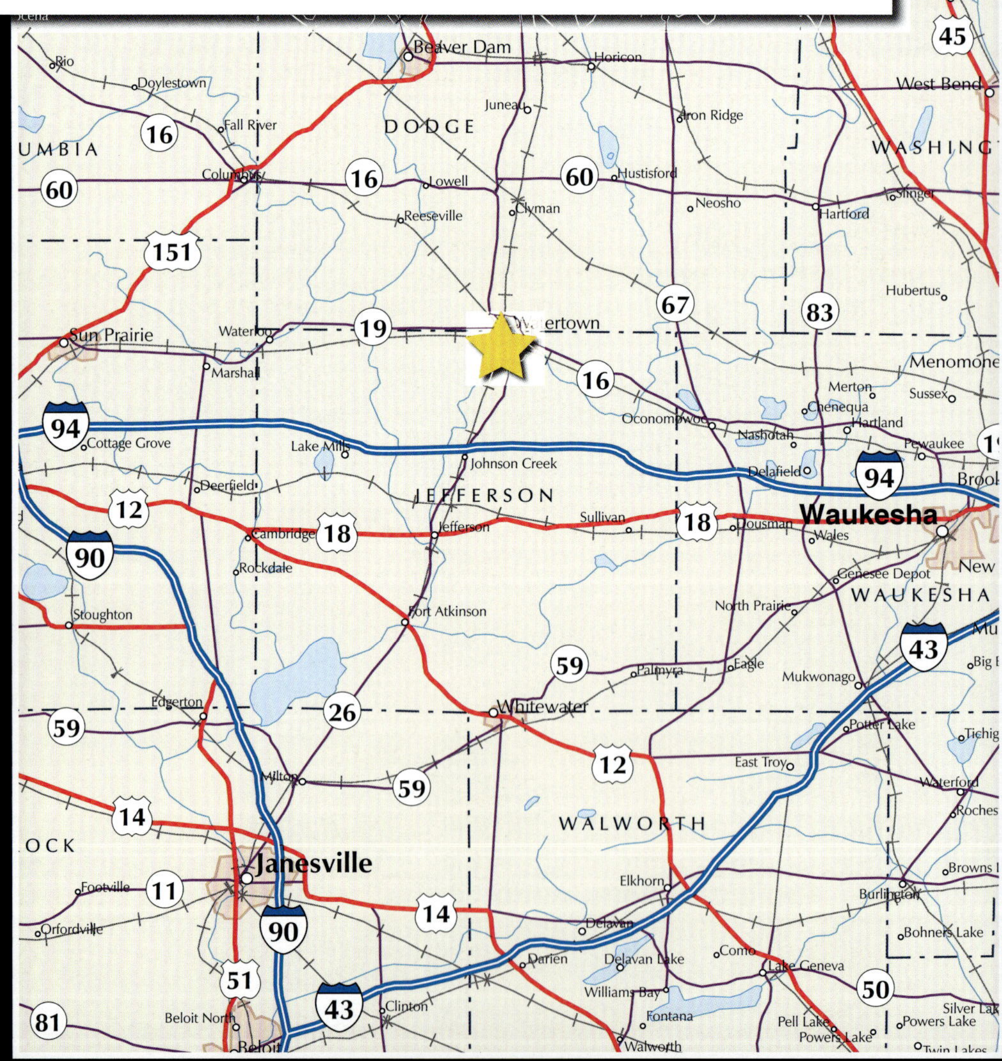

River Bend RV Resort

ACCOMMODATIONS

Owners of recreational vehicles can look forward to a well rounded vacation escape on the shores of the Crawfish River at River Bend RV Resort. Just 60 miles west of Milwaukee and 45 miles east of Madison in scenic Watertown, River Bend RV Resort is a private member-owned resort with more than 600 RV spaces and amenities galore. An amazing 8,000-square-foot water park features two 350-foot water slides and a kiddie pool, complete with swings and a whimsical snail slide. Indoor and outdoor whirlpool spas round out the water features. An activity center provides planned daily events for kids of all ages, including fishing and boating on the river. Try tennis, basketball or miniature golf, or practice your swing at the driving range. River Bend hosts annual events, such as a Civil War reenactment, a Hawaiian luau and a Tom Sawyer fishing contest. If you are interested in becoming a member, River Bend offers the pride of lifetime ownership with two ownership options. Undivided Interest Ownership allows camping privileges by reservation and full access to all resort offerings. Condominium ownership provides year-round camping privileges on your deeded lot plus the ability to sell or bequeath your ownership. If you are looking for a fun-filled getaway where you can make cherished family memories, take a drive out to Watertown. You can dine in River Bend's first-class restaurant and take a tour of the grounds. Then reserve your spot at the River Bend RV Resort on Wisconsin's Crawfish River .

W6940 Rubidell Road, Watertown WI
(920) 261-7505
www.rbresort.com

St. Bernard's Catholic Church

ATTRACTIONS

Founded by a handful of determined Irish pioneers in 1843, the landmark St. Bernard Catholic Church in Watertown counts approximately 1,100 families in its present congregation. Martin Kundig, the first priest here, had high hopes for the fledgling church when he wrote, "I doubt not that great numbers of Catholics will settle here. How the Germans would marvel if they could only see this land." While the current parish buildings, built in 1873, 1883, 1890 and 1892, are all named in the Wisconsin State Register of Historic Places, the members of St. Bernard's have a present-day mission. They strive to live and proclaim the good news of Jesus Christ with a vision of doing God's work by serving the needs of others, especially the poor and vulnerable. The school serves about 160 students and offers an extended daycare program for children before and after school. Children who do not attend the school are encouraged to join Faith Formation classes to learn about the church and its teachings. Whether you are a committed Catholic or a curious newcomer, St. Bernard Catholic Church invites you to worship here and explore the religious, educational and community opportunities available to you and your family.

114 S Church Street, Watertown WI
(920) 261-5133
www.stbern.org

Fine Details Automotive Detailing

AUTO

Fine Details Automotive Detailing was established in 2000 by owners and operators Ken Stolar Jr. and Mike Steggall. With an eye for perfection and a heart to serve people, they started their business cleaning, shampooing, waxing and buffing cars, trucks and SUVs. Seven years later, they have broadened their practice to detailing show cars, semi-tractors, motor homes, boats and airplanes, and have a crew to detail vehicles at auto shows and auctions. They also install truck accessories, vinyl graphics, pin-striping, and XM/Sirius radio and car stereo equipment. The showroom at Fine Details displays all kinds of car stereo upgrades such as CD players, speakers, subwoofers, amps and plenty of installation supplies for the do-it-yourselfer. With more than 25 years of professional experience, Ken and Mike know you will be pleased to have you vehicle serviced at Fine Details. Whether it's a high quality hand-wash or a complete vehicle renewal, they strive for excellence and 100-percent customer satisfaction. They make it easy and convenient for you to keep your vehicle clean and looking like new with free local pick-up and delivery. Isn't it time to protect your investment and visit Fine Details Automotive Detailing to see what they can do for you?

508 W Main Street, Watertown WI
(920) 206-9999

Dave's Turf & Marine

BUSINESS & SERVICES

Leni Kahler grew up with motors: lawn mower motors, tiller motors, chainsaw motors, boat motors, all kinds of motors. And she came by that experience honestly, because it was her dad, working in the family basement, who started what was eventually to become Dave's Turf & Marine back in 1949. It started as a saw-sharpening business. Dad opened a shop in 1950 on Fourth Street, where he began fixing chainsaws, go-carts, lawnmowers and other power equipment. He did pretty well, too. By 1959 he had earned enough respect from his customers that he was able to build a new place on West Spaulding. Dave Kahler came on the scene in 1961, and in 1966 bought a piece of the business that now bears his name. Today, Dave and Leni continue the 53-year tradition in a business that has expanded far beyond dad's original vision, but which still offers his personalized attention. Their large indoor show room on East Gate Road, which opened in 1988, displays 27,000 square feet of new boats, used boats, and an array of power equipment that would give any gearhead pride. They carry Dixie Chopper and John Deere, Princecraft and Warrior. They sell and service Mercury, Evinrude and Johnson. They're on a first-name basis with Ariens, Briggs & Stratton, Jonsered and Tecumseh. They even sell trailers, docks and lift equipment. The business has come a long way from the old saw sharpening shop in the basement, but the underlying philosophy is the same: individual attention to individual needs, which is why Dave's Turf & Marine has been named one of the top 10 dealers in the state of Wisconsin. So whether it's the lawn or the water that is calling your name, head to Dave's. He and Leni will be able to help.

W2755 E Gate Drive, Watertown WI
(920) 261-6802
www.davesturf.net

Watertown Budget Print, Inc.

BUSINESS & SERVICES

Steve Hill has always been interested in printing. Below, you can see him demonstrating an old Franklin press for Dousman, Wisconsin grade school students in 1960. Steve's father was a printer in Chicago. In 1982, Steve and his wife, Donna, purchased Watertown Budget Print, Inc. Staff members here are highly experienced. Head Pressman Zsolt Bajnoc, for example, has been with the company for more than 16 years. Budget Print can handle printing jobs as simple as new business forms or as complicated as an array of full-color corporate identity pieces. The shop gives each job the individual attention it deserves. It provides superior customer service, fast delivery and a high-quality finished product. The Budget Print staff will visit business people at their workplaces to give free no-obligation estimates. Quotes are also available online. Pickups and deliveries are free. Budget Print's primary service area encompasses Dodge, Jefferson, Waukesha and Milwaukee counties. The shop can help you develop custom graphic designs and offers desktop publishing and typesetting services. You'll also find a full-line of bindery services, including folding, drilling and laminating. When you need fast, high-quality color copying, Budget Print has the machines to get the job done. For quick turnaround at a reasonable price, consult Watertown Budget Print, Inc.

107 S 5th Street, Watertown WI
(920) 261-4005 or (800) 729-0728
www.budgetprintonline.com

Maranatha Baptist Bible College

BUSINESS & SERVICES

Founded by Dr. and Mrs. B. Myron Cedarholm, Maranatha Baptist Bible College is housed on 79 acres. This regionally accredited fundamentalist Baptist College, which requires a Bible Core curriculum and focuses on liberal arts degrees, prepares students spiritually and academically to serve the Lord. Their mission is to provide a comprehensive college education, set in a nurturing environment, which is founded on valuable Bible theology true to the Baptist heritage. Serving the Lord while in college is encouraged and facilitated. Students take 30 hours of Bible study and 40 hours of liberal arts studies in addition to program requirements. The faculty/student ratio is 1 to 14, providing for extensive interaction between students and their instructors. MBBC's 32 fields of study include business education, mathematics and speech education. Ministry opportunities include campus hospitality, work at Ethan Allen boys' juvenile correctional facility and nursing home work. Nearly 200 students participate in the athletic programs, including NCCA Division III teams in baseball, basketball, football and soccer. For the musically inclined student, MCCB has an orchestra, band and traveling chorus. For a college experience that provides the foundation for a rewarding career in the ministry, and a marriage and family life based on Christian principles, visit Maranatha Baptist Bible College.

745 W Main Street, Watertown WI
(800) MBBC-WIS (622-2947)
www.mbbc.edu

domani salon & spa

HEALTH & BEAUTY

"I want people to forget their problems," says Tricia Voigt, owner of domani salon & spa. " I want everyone to feel like they are queens or kings." Tricia and the team at domani believe that the better you look, the better you feel, so they have created an environment to foster maximum beauty and total well-being. The professionals at domani salon are committed to keeping abreast of the newest techniques in haircutting, coloring treatments and perming. Makeup specialists can create a whole new you by using industry secrets and proven techniques. Waxing and electrolysis are available, as are manicures and pedicures, which, if you like, can include a hot stone treatment. Domani spa offers a variety of specialty facials, including peels and collagen treatments. Consider one of the spa's four unique Aromasoul massages: Oriental, Mediterranean, Indian, or Arabian. Massage therapists here also specialize in a series of massages designed especially for new mothers and mothers-to-be. Mud wraps and body treatments include services targeted at alleviating stretch-marks and cellulite. The ultimate indulgence is the replenish day escape package which combines a wrap, facial, and massage for renewal of the mind, body, and spirit. Domani is Italian for tomorrow, a fitting name for the forward-thinking spa. Let domani salon & spa renew your spirit today while bringing health and beauty to your tomorrows.

1149C Boughton Street, Watertown WI
(920) 262-8333
www.domanisalonandspa.com

Y's Way Flooring

HOME & GARDEN

We demand a lot from our flooring. We want it to be beautiful, comfortable, durable and easy to maintain. The experts at Y's Way Flooring in Watertown understand the attributes of various flooring products and can walk you through the possibilities. Owners Mike and Dan Yenser promise results that live up to their slogan, Always Fabulous Underfoot. Whether you are looking for carpeting, vinyl, laminate, ceramic or hardwood, Y's Way has the proven product line and the personnel to meet your needs. An experienced staff delights in helping customers coordinate different products, styles and colors. Begin the selection process with a tour of the Y's Way showroom. This well arranged space is artistically designed to assist you with your decision-making process while allowing you to visualize the finished product. Y's Way routinely works with homeowners, corporations and private businesses. The staff understands the advantages and disadvantages of various flooring materials, so you can be assured you made your choices with all the necessary facts. Y's Way does everything it can to meet your timing needs. They will coordinate the details of the installation procedure with local professional installers who are efficient, dependable and proud of their work. Put a floor under you that lives up to your demands with a visit to Y's Way Flooring.

809 Station Street, Watertown WI
(920) 261-7160 or (800) 841-1788
www.yswayflooring.com

Heritage Homes

LIFESTYLE DESTINATIONS

Say goodbye to cutting the lawn and shoveling snow, and say hello to comfortable retirement living and good fellowship when you move into Heritage Homes in Watertown. A ministry of the Lutheran Home Association, Heritage Homes welcomes individuals of all faiths. A community atmosphere exists among the Heritage Homes' residents like no other. Enjoy a game of billiards, grab a book from the library and read it in the fireside lounge, or build something in the workshop. Much like a self-contained village, Heritage Homes even boasts its own country store and a beauty and barber shop. Residents stay entertained with a full schedule of special events and activities throughout the year. A pastor visits weekly to lead Bible classes in the meditation chapel. Built in 1997, Heritage Homes offers one and two bedroom apartments with a choice of four spacious floor plans. For a faith-based haven for active, independent seniors, consider Heritage Homes, where the care of the soul is the soul of care.

700 Welsh Road, Watertown WI
(920) 206-9448
www.tlha.org

Star Karate America

RECREATION & FITNESS

It's hard to beat the attraction of a program that promises to build and encourage self-esteem, self-confidence, self-discipline and self-defense capability. Rick Krueger focuses on these qualities at Star Karate America in Watertown. Rick started taking martial arts classes in 1980 and received a black belt in 1985. He is a two time state champion in the lightweight championship division and a member of the United States Martial Arts Hall of Fame. Rick's martial arts experiences were the beginning of a dream. He and his wife, Virginia, made his vision a reality when they opened Star Karate America. By building confidence and discipline in young people, Star Karate hopes to build tomorrow's community leaders. The basic program, white through green belt, teaches the fundamentals of martial arts. The Masters Club, green through black belt, guides the committed student through the nine levels of training to gain a black belt. Leadership training is available for advanced students who want to make martial arts an integral part of their lives. Star Karate contributes to the safety of young people by teaching Stranger Danger and Bully Basics in the school system. They also offer defense courses as a service to the community. Rick and Virginia hope to instill confidence and discipline in all of their students, so that whatever path they choose in life they will be able to Stand Up, Stand Proud and Stand Out.

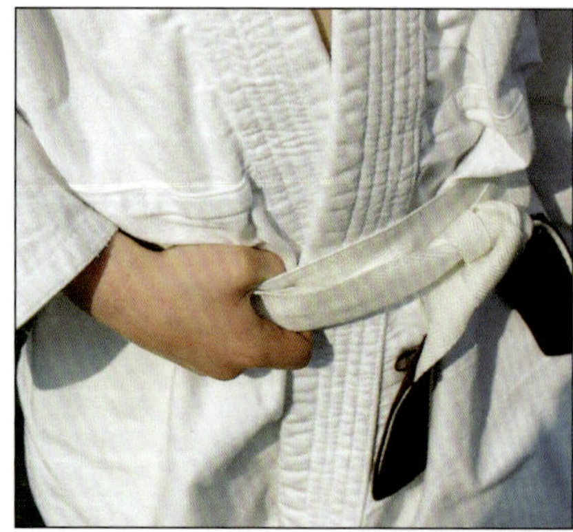

806 West Street, Watertown WI
(920) 206-8883
www.starkarate.com

Photo by Randen Pederson

PLACES TO GO

- Cutler Park
  321 Wisconsin Avenue
- Prairieville Park
  2507 Plaza Court
  (262) 784-4653
- Waukesha County Historical Society and Museum
  101 W Main Street
  (262) 521-2859

THINGS TO DO

June

- Taste of Summer Music Festival
  Expo Grounds
  (262) 896-8490
- Fiesta Waukesha
  Frame Park
  (262) 547-0887

July

- Waukesha County Fair
  Expo Center
  (262) 544-5922

August-September

- Wisconsin Scottish Fest/Highland Games
  Expo Center
  (262) 548-7200

September

- Waukesha Artfest
  Cutler Park
  (262) 547-1522
- Apple Harvest Festival
  Retzer Nature Center
  (262) 896-8007
- Country Fest Outdoor Craft Fair
  Cutler Park
  (262) 542-0166

October

- Craft Fair USA
  Expo Center
  (414) 321-2100

November

- Christmas Walk and Parade
  Downtown
  (262) 549-6154

WAUKESHA

Meaning *by the little fox*, Waukesha is a handsome, historically prosperous community on the banks of the Fox River. Its reputation as a resort and retirement area traces back to the late 19th century, when Colonel Richard Dunbar claimed that the local spring water had healed his painful diabetes. Waukesha became widely known as the Saratoga of the West and enjoyed a brief tourism and population boom that got the economy on its feet. Today Waukesha's population hovers around 7,000. The community enjoys a thriving arts district, several universities and more than 900 acres of lush parklands. The maiden years of the 21st century saw a 16-million-dollar redevelopment of the city's downtown River Corridor, which included the construction of the beautifully landscaped Riverwalk. One of Waukesha's oldest attractions is Waukesha Beach, an amusement park on the southern side of Pewaukee Lake, which originally opened in 1910.

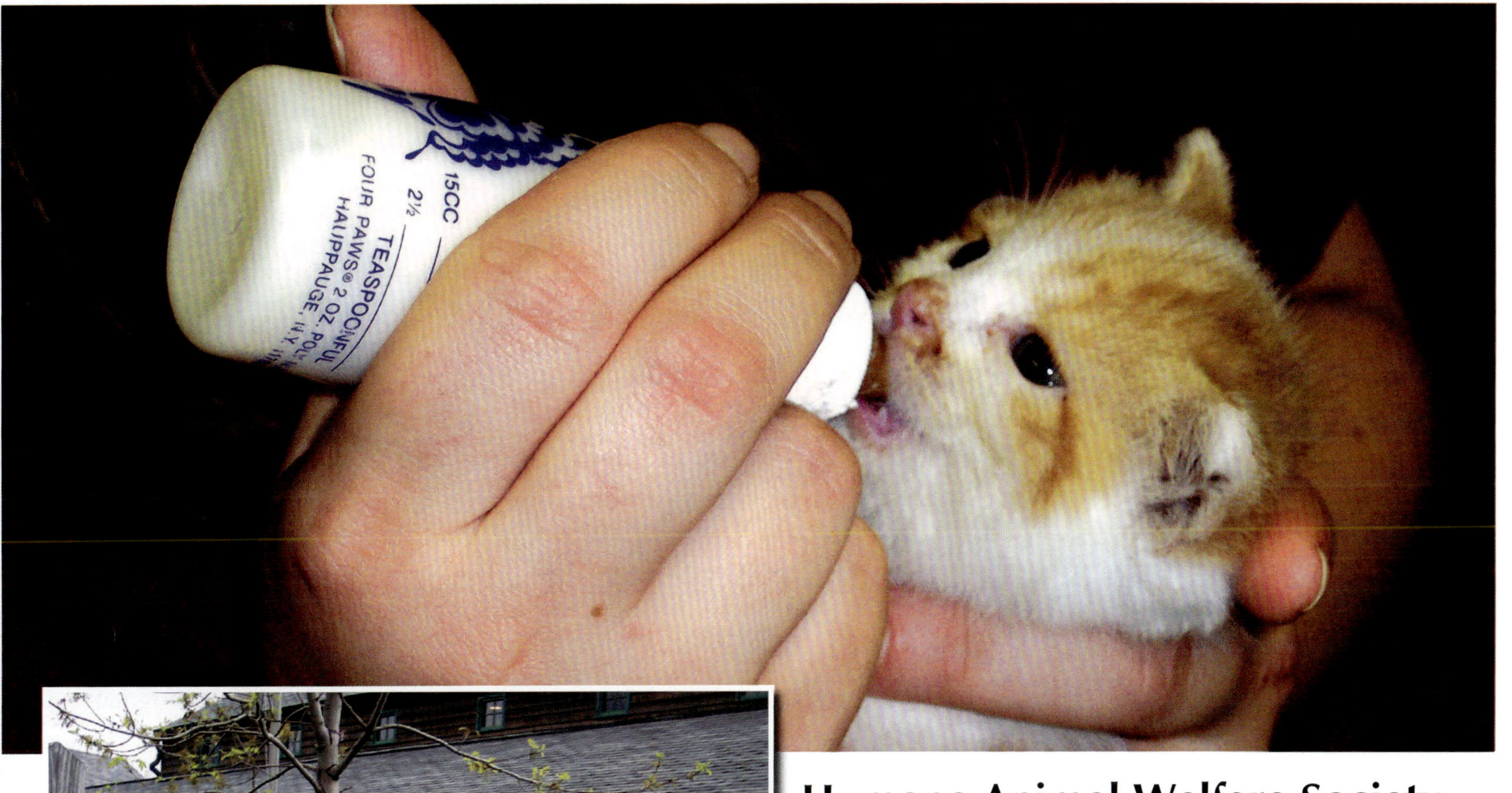

Humane Animal Welfare Society

ANIMALS & PETS

In 1965, residents and area veterinarians were instrumental in forming a nonprofit humane society in the farming community of Waukesha. Before that, area residents had to travel to Milwaukee to find quality care for lost, stray and unwanted animals. Since then, the Humane Animal Welfare Society, known as HAWS, has grown to serve over 6,000 animals each year. Generous donations from animal lovers continue to help the society expand its educational programs and services. HAWS serves 28 of the 37 municipalities in Waukesha County with a remodeled 16,000-foot facility operating under national standards. HAWS provides a lost and found service, adoption services and a has licensed wildlife rehabilitator on staff. HAWS also helps with wildlife capture and safe relocation, provides domestic and wild injured animal rescue and offers 24-hour emergency first aid care. The humane society provides a variety of educational programs, training classes and volunteer opportunities. It cooperates with many organizations, including law enforcement and youth groups. The volunteers and staff at the Humane Animal Welfare Society invite you to Bring Home Your Best Friend.

701 Northview Road, Waukesha WI
(262) 542-8851
www.hawspets.org

Frank's Sewing Center

ARTS & CRAFTS

The knowledgeable staff at Franks Sewing Center has been helping customers discover their creativity and build sewing expertise since 1973, when Frank Kruchoski opened the doors in downtown Waukesha. In 1994, Frank's grandson Brad Kleman took over the business. After a few successful years, Brad knew it was time for some changes. These changes included adding more employees, including Jean Rozek, the embroidery specialist and Wendy Rieves, the quilting specialist. Next, it was time to expand the showroom. A location was discovered right across the street, which allowed Frank's to expand to a four times larger space. In this 7,800-square-foot facility you will find inviting displays of Baby Lock, Elna and Janome sewing machines, sergers and embroidery machines in all price ranges and skill levels. Frank's also has a large selection of sewing and quilting notions including threads, rulers, books, patterns, quilt batting, sewing furniture from Horn of America and Grace quilting frames. You'll be tempted to try your hand at projects galore with Frank's vast selection of ready-made samples to inspire you and helpful classes held in a full-sized classroom. Another feature is the extensive service department, which services all makes and models of household sewing machines. Frank's latest venture is opening its notions4sewing.com website, which allows customers online access to the stores popular sewing and quilting notions. So if you want to learn anything about sewing, embroidery or quilting, visit Frank's Sewing Center, where creativity and state-of-the-art equipment make a great combination.

272 W Main Street, Waukesha WI
(262) 547-7774
www.frankssewingcenter.com
www.notions4sewing.com

Otto's Fine Art Academy, Inc.

ARTS & CRAFTS

It is never too early or too late to free your inner creativity. Curt and Monica Otto developed Otto's Fine Art Academy in Waukesha in response to their combined passion for encouraging talent and confidence through the arts. Preschool lessons for children ages three-and-a-half through five begin with a focus on shapes, simple drawing and basic color techniques. This is an excellent preparation for children up to 12 years old who enter the academy's children's program. The academy encourages children to learn at their own pace as they tackle still life drawing and progress through watercolor and oil painting. The teen program emphasizes drawing from real life and developing more advanced drawing techniques using pencil, pastels, charcoal, watercolor and oil painting. Adult classes welcome the beginner, the experienced artist and the curious. The Ottos will customize a program to fill your needs. Curt and Monica love watching their students build self-esteem as they learn to express themselves through a variety of art media. Summer camps for children ages five to 12 last one week and follow the same basic structure as the regular programs. How about an extraordinary alternative to the usual birthday party? A birthday party at Ottos's starts with an hour devoted to learning drawing techniques and creating individual pastel pictures to take home. The second hour is for cake and gifts. Unleash your inner artist by trying a free no-obligation introductory lesson or giving a gift certificate to Otto's Fine Art Academy.

396 W Main Street, Waukesha WI
(262) 970-9524
www.ottosartacademy.com

Photo courtesy of Carroll Studios

Waukesha Civic Theatre

ATTRACTIONS

In the summer of 1957, a transplanted New Yorker named Irvin Ware brought his theatrical know-how and enthusiasm to Waukesha. With only that in hand, Ware contacted a number of local, similarly minded people, formed a board of directors, and the Waukesha Civic Theatre came to life. The Theatre has been through many changes since that time with shifting buildings and staff, coming to rest at its current and latest incarnation on West Main Street in historic Waukesha. The building combines historic charm with a very modern theater facility. Production quality is comparable to professional theaters. The schedule of events for the year includes six main stage productions and one holiday production. Two PlayMakers productions bring daytime shows to children. These original shows rely on school curricula and themes and ideas relevant to children of various ages. The facility is also used by several outside production companies and presents two to five concerts a year. Coming soon are performing classes for adults. "We provide quality, live entertainment and educational programs that challenge, enrich and entertain both participants and audience members," says John Cramer, managing artistic director. Don't miss your opportunity to experience all that Waukesha Civic Theatre has to offer.

264 W Main Street, Waukesha WI (262) 547-4911 ***www.waukeshacivictheatre.org***

Photo by Rick Vollbrecht

Retzer Nature Center

ATTRACTIONS

Retzer Nature Center in Waukesha offers a place to enjoy and learn about the natural environment of southeast Wisconsin. Visitors amble along five miles of hiking trails, which wind through woodlands, wetlands and prairies. The Adventure Trail, a paved path, provides an introduction to native Wisconsin birds, plants and animals with 30 interpretive stops along 800 feet of trail. Brown's Boardwalk Trail takes the curious through a marsh and fen habitat. Trails are open to the public from sunrise to 10 pm seven days a week year-round, at no charge. Part of the Waukesha County Park System, the nature center occupies land donated by Florence Retzer for the purpose of conserving the scenery and wildlife of this area for the enjoyment of future generations. Naturalists conduct programs inside the Retzer Environmental Learning Center on topics ranging from animal tracks to insect biodiversity. A popular attraction in the exhibit area is the 700-gallon tank of native Southeast Wisconsin game fish. The Charles Z. Horwitz Planetarium features sky shows inside its domed theater. Come to Retzer Nature Center for a long hike, or pass a few peaceful moments at the rain and butterfly gardens. An escape into nature awaits you.

S14 W28167 Madison Street, Waukesha WI
(262) 896-8007
www.waukeshacountyparks.com

Stay Tuned

AUTO

For upgrades to all of your car's audio, visual or security systems, you need Stay Tuned. The shop specializes in installing high-end sound systems. That is, really high-end systems; its clients have won national competitions for sound installations provided by Stay Tuned. Owner Fred Felch places few limits on the type of auto installations Stay Tuned will do and lives by the slogan: You have a dream; we can make it a reality. Stay Tuned installs in-dash and rear seat video systems and navigation systems. After installation, staff members provide coaching on how to use these sophisticated devices. Stay Tuned's meticulous sunroof installations are the choice of Wisconsin's most discriminating new car dealers. Stay Tuned can also provide custom leather upholstery, wheels and tires to complete your car's new look. Stay Tuned even installs performance parts with the same dedication to quality it brings to all its other services. An unfortunate side effect of a Stay Tuned upgrade is that your car becomes more attractive to thieves, so the shop offers the industry's best remote start and alarm systems. Stay Tuned guarantees all installation work for a full half century. When you are ready for the look, the sound and the performance you've always dreamed of having, visit Stay Tuned, where dreams come true.

1603 Manhattan Drive, Waukesha WI
(262) 542-TUNE (8863)
www.staytunedaudio.com

Cybros Bread for Life

BAKERIES, COFFEE & TEA

In 1969, Richard and Delores Cyrus purchased a bakery with the goal of producing bread that would truly be the staff of life. They renamed it Cybros Bread for Life and began baking. Paul Geboy started working for Cybros in the 1980s, and Debi Brook came on board in 2002. When Delores retired in 2002, Paul and Debi purchased Cybros to continue the tradition of manufacturing healthful and delicious cookies, breads and rolls on the Waukesha premises. Cybros products are uncommon because they contain golden wheat berries that are sprouted, pressed through a special sieve and then mixed directly into the dough. The berries never pass through the milling and refining process that turns grains into flour, so the nutrients that nature put in the grains remain in the bread. According to nutritionists, sprouting the grains increases the vitamin content of the seeds by as much as 500 percent. Sprouting begins to transform the starches into simple sugars, which makes the sugars more digestible and the vitamins and minerals easier to assimilate. Cybros bread is extremely low in fat and is made without hydrogenated fats, saturated fats, oils or shortening. It contains just the natural oil from the wheat berries and no preservatives. Only honey and molasses sweeten the sprouted breads. Cybros also offers a selection of baked goods that are free of gluten, wheat and dairy products. Look for Cybros Bread for Life products in finer grocery and health food stores across the country.

417 Barney Street, Waukesha WI
(262) 547-1821 or (800) 876-2253

Waukesha State Bank

BUSINESS & SERVICES

Carl Taylor had a vision for Waukesha State Bank that continues to influence his son Don, vice-president and former president, and grandson Ty, president. While banks were going bankrupt in the 1930s, Carl was buying bank equipment at auctions. This man of Cherokee Indian descent, born in a sod house in the Oklahoma Territory, had already worked his way through college to become a professor of speech at the University of Wisconsin, as well as a part-time preacher. In 1944, he opened Waukesha State Bank and pledged to serve the blue-collar workers of Waukesha while also caring for his employees and rewarding his stockholders. Waukesha State Bank is one of the few remaining private banks and a tribute to Carl's far-sighted belief in Waukesha's economic growth. It prides itself on supporting community projects such as the Fox River Development, and its top officers still have their desks right in the bank's contemporary lobby. Unlike other respectable banks of the 1940s, Carl led the way in consumer banking by lending money not just to rich people and businesses, but to everyday citizens. He emblazoned the words, The Bank of Friendly Service, on his front windows and set out to make the hardworking and thrifty citizens of Waukesha his customers. The bank went on to become the first bank in the state to fully computerize and the first bank in southeast Wisconsin to install a drive-up window. Come to Waukesha State Bank, where all customers are VIPs.

100 Bank Street, Waukesha WI
(262) 549-8500
www.waukeshabank.com

Rose Ann's Maids

BUSINESS & SERVICES

Find time for the important things in life, like family, friends and fun, with a little help from Rose Ann's Maids. This full-service, family owned and operated cleaning company was established in 1987 by Rose Ann Dowdle, who saw the need for such a business in the Waukesha area. In 1988 her daughter Kaylene Dowdle, general manager, joined Rose Ann and in 1999 her granddaughter, Shanna Rose Pease, entered into the business as office manager. All employees at Rose Ann's Maids are licensed and bonded, and the company assigns a maid to each client so that you do not have someone new entering your house each time. The focus of the business has always been to create and retain customers, and the company does this by providing reliable, dependable service that is convenient and non-intrusive. Rose Ann's Maids offers both weekly and bi-weekly service, as well as special move-in or move-out packages and seasonal cleanings. The maids bring all of their own equipment, including vacuums and company approved stepladders. Additionally, the maids use biodegradable and OSHA-approved cleaning supplies. Cleaning schedules include two parts, a general cleaning of the entire house and a total cleaning of one room each session. After each appointment, the maids leave a signed receipt that indicates which room received a total cleaning, the date of the next cleaning and which room will receive a total cleaning on that visit. Live your life, and leave the cleaning to Rose Ann's Maids.

818 W St. Paul Avenue, Waukesha WI
(262) 549-3838

J & S Carpet Cleaning

BUSINESS & SERVICES

When Tony Marotta thinks carpets, he thinks clean. Tony's dad, John, started J & S Carpet Cleaning in 1972, and for more than 30 years, the company has offered top-notch carpet, upholstery and drapery cleaning. In 2001, Tony and his friend and partner, Doug Pike, bought the business, keeping a family tradition alive. J & S employs a one-of-a-kind 12-step process in which your carpet is inspected, vacuumed, treated, dried and even groomed for visual appeal. The last and most important step in the process is a final inspection by the customer. Years of wear can result in wall-to-wall carpet becoming loose and buckled. J & S can fix that problem with a special power stretcher that makes carpet as tight as new. The company can also repair carpet. Upholstery undergoes a similar 12-step process that's certain to add to the life and beauty of your furniture. Draperies and curtains can stay right where they are, because J & S knows how to clean them while they hang. Oriental rugs and loose-woven area rugs benefit from the services at the J & S plant in Waukesha. Many of these rugs are particularly challenging to clean, because they have been designed to camouflage dirt. One study found that a 9 X 12 area rug could actually hide up to 87 pounds of dirt. Freshen your environment with a call to J & S Carpet Cleaning.

1710 Arthur Court, Waukesha WI
(262) 547-6633
www.jandscarpet.com

Jim, Leanne, Joan, DeeDee and Steve

Soft Water

BUSINESS & SERVICES

Water in southeast Wisconsin tends to be much harder than in many other parts of the country and may contain high levels of iron. Melvin and Marion Meyer founded Soft Water in 1946 to solve water quality problems at a reasonable price. The business remains family owned and operated to this day. Soft Water manufactures its own water softeners using the highest quality parts and materials. Likewise, Soft Water offers only the best system for filtering out iron and sulfur with the Iron Curtain from Hellenbrand. For removing a variety of additional impurities, Soft Water sells the Microline reverse osmosis drinking water system. The company provides a salt delivery service that automatically brings new salt to your door at exactly the right time. Each installer is a master plumber with at least 12 years of experience. Rely on Soft Water for your water treatment and service needs.

1344 White Rock Avenue, Waukesha WI
(262) 547-3366
www.softwater.com

The Caring Place

BUSINESS & SERVICES

The Caring Place is a nonprofit community organization dedicated to wellness and enhanced life for adults who require assistance with daily living. The Adult Day Center enriches the lives of older adults by providing socialization and health services. Families and caregivers receive respite while care giving. Field trips create stimulating adventures, while everyday programs provide a purposeful and entertaining social environment. The Caring Place also offers the Meals on Wheels program. A clinical dietician supervises the preparation of the meals. Friendly volunteer drivers stop by to visit while delivering the meal. Director Mary Kapke speaks highly of the staff and the loyal volunteers who make The Caring Place an enriching and positive experience. The Caring Place invites you to give a worthwhile gift to yourself and others by volunteering. Visit them on the web or call today.

810 N East Avenue, Waukesha WI
(262) 542-6388
www.caringplacewaukesha.org

WEBZ Sunset Printing & Graphics, Inc.

BUSINESS & SERVICES

WEBZ Sunset Printing & Graphics, Inc. is a full-service print shop that can assist you with all of your company's communication needs. Named as one of Waukesha's best-kept secrets, Sunset Printing was purchased in 2004 by Colleen Weber. Colleen took this little print shop and added many new services to provide exceptional customer service and quality. WEBZ Sunset Printing & Graphics can create everything from full-color brochures and newsletters to posters, banners and blueprints. It can handle anything from oversized copies and business cards to letterhead, invitations and menus. Other services include signs, vehicle graphics and promotional items, such as plaques or t-shirts. WEBZ is your expert for binding, cutting and lamination. The team at WEBZ also assists with any pre- and post-press issues that may arise and offers end-to-end fulfillment on every project, from design and production to postal mailings and UPS services. WEBZ is able to handle jobs of any size, making it as ideal for individuals and small business owners as it is for large companies and organizations. Whether you're designing wedding invitations for 20 or a monthly newsletter for thousands, trust all of your communication needs to the experts at WEBZ Sunset Printing & Graphics, serving Waukesha County for over 16 years.

530 W24670 Sunset Drive,
Waukesha WI (262) 549-9535
www.webzsunsetprint.com

Mack's Frozen Custard

FUN FOODS

Mack's Frozen Custard has been an area favorite for more than 30 years. It offers a wonderful, family-friendly atmosphere along with great food and a delicious and creamy-smooth concoction, frozen custard. Owners Bill and Steve Nagata have completed the first phase of renovating the classic 1950s-style walk-up custard stand to include indoor and outdoor seating and a new kitchen with a fire-stone hearth oven. They plan to add a drive-thru in the near future. The newly expanded menu has something for everyone. Find New York-style pizza, specialty sandwiches such as Malibu chicken or Philly cheesesteak, salads, wraps and a kid's menu. As good as the food is, it is the custard that made Mack's famous. The custards are made fresh daily and come in vanilla, chocolate and a special flavor of the day. Try chocolate cherry amaretto, turtle, café caramel or grasshopper. These amazing flavors are just a sample of what drives people to come back night after night, year after year, even in the crazy days of winter. How long has it been since you've tasted a banana malt, chocolate shake or a shared banana split? For busy families on the go, Mack's is conveniently located with ample parking in a quiet neighborhood away from the hustle and traffic. Mack's Frozen Custard is where great food and great fun make great memories.

789 W Moreland Boulevard,Waukesha WI
(262) 547-2080

Gallery 1

GALLERIES & FINE ART

Waukesha is an innovative town, with colleges, Wisconsin's first online high school and a city-wide WiFi network. With this kind of character, it is no wonder it is also home to Gallery 1, which has collected more than 50 national and international awards for its framing services. A massive inventory of selections includes striking examples such as frames made of whale harpoons or snake skins. In addition to framing, Gallery 1 carries fine art prints and originals. The shop displays an impressive collection of original 3D art, including Ramona Audley's wildly colored animal sculptures and Bill Koelpin's bronzes. Gallery 1 specializes in conservation framing. Staff members frame fine art, stretch needlepoint and build 3D shadow boxes. Barbara Kocher, wife of artist Bill Kocher, owns Gallery 1 and has established a family atmosphere with the staff and customers. The store has served several generations of artists and art lovers, and customers quickly become friends. All framing is done on site. Nothing is too challenging for this shop. All of its passionate creations are very reasonably priced, and the gallery is open seven days a week. Gallery 1 has been able to expand to a branch store in Delafield. Choose a piece of art in the gallery or bring your own treasured work to Gallery 1. Then see what it can do.

507 E Broadway, Waukesha WI (262) 542-6010
3201 Golf Road, Delafield WI (262) 646-2400

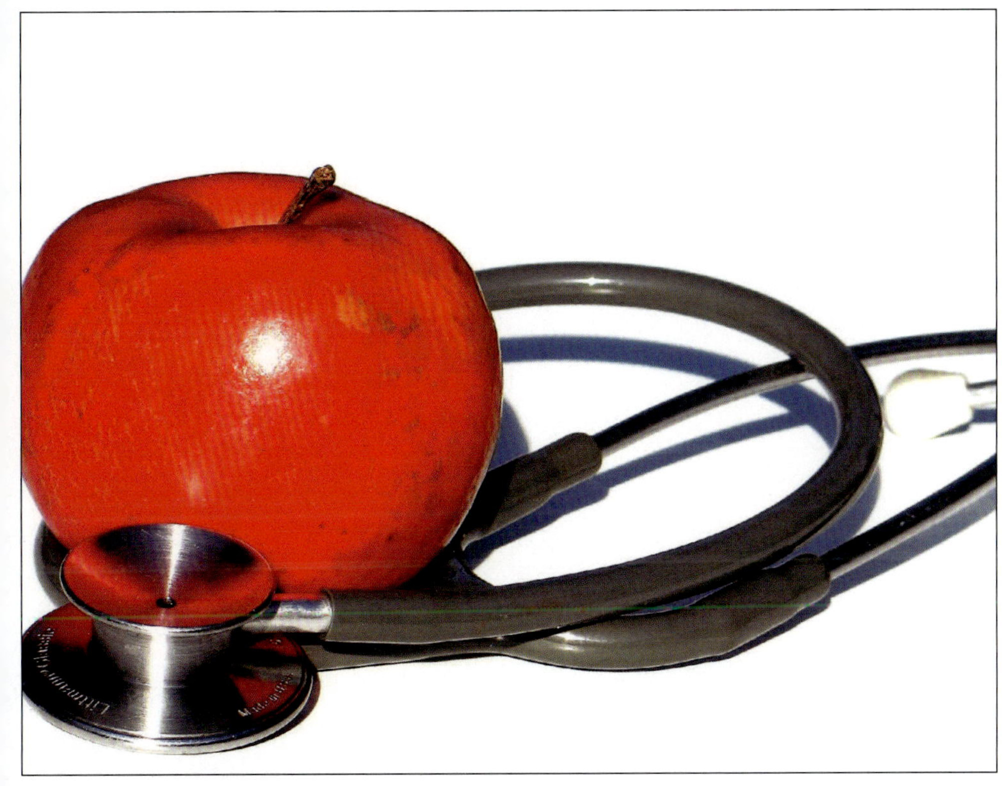

Lake Country Hygienic Center

HEALTH & BEAUTY

Lake Country Hygienic Center (LCHC) works with dietary improvement and detoxification to promote good health, believing that we must not be encumbered by conventional ignorance. Staff believe in education, in arming you with the information you need to make responsible decisions for your health and the ones you love. LCHC provides enzyme valuation, visceral palpatory exams, muscle regeneration therapy, reflexology, kinesiology and colon hydrotherapy. It provides a variety of classes in the natural health field, and supervises and implements deep cleansing protocols to assist the body in regenerating for optimal function. It also provides iridology assessment and classes. LCHC uses all of these resources to help the individual achieve optimal health. Lake Country Hygienic Center has offered classes in the U.S. and abroad. The staff attributes the majority of its expertise to real life experiences dealing with dis-ease of the body.

W240 S6103 Highway 164, Waukesha WI
(262) 521-1799
www.mlchc.com

Russ's and Four Seasons

HOME & GARDEN

Russ's Mulch & Top Soil can provide every service your lawn and landscape requires, directly or through its affiliates. Russ Kulik founded the business in 1965 and sold it to Brian Hanson, one of his best customers, in 2003. Brian was the longtime owner of Four Seasons Landscaping and Maintenance, which continues on as an affiliated company. Today, you can get mulch, topsoil and clean fill at Russ's, as well as landscaping or snow removal services from Four Seasons. Russ's sells bark and seven other varieties of mulch, including Enviro-Mulch and chemical-free playground chips. Brian can spread the mulch for customers, and because of his years of experience, he can answer any questions about what is appropriate for a customer's yard. Four Seasons strives to be the most reliable landscaping service anywhere, and it offers a broad range of landscaping techniques. Brian's philosophy is that each landscape is unique, and each client should have a personalized plan to fit the specific needs of the landscape. Four Seasons installs sod and provides maintenance services, such as mowing, pruning, fertilizing and weed control. Four Seasons' snow removal service for commercial and residential customers uses high performance equipment to ensure the quickest response. Brian's loyal customers know that he values honesty above all other virtues. If you have a home or business in the area, visit Russ's Mulch & Topsoil and Four Seasons Landscaping and Maintenance to keep your outdoor spaces functional and beautiful.

1500 N Springdale Road, Waukesha WI (Russ's) (262) 798-7998 or (262) 798-3960
1535 Brian Court, Brookfield WI (Four Seasons) (262) 938-0444
www.russmulch.com

Signature Lighting

HOME & GARDEN

Since 1978, Signature Lighting has been an important resource for homeowners, electricians, designers and builders. Its handpicked selection of high quality, distinctive merchandise will help set the tone for any home or business. The large showroom with attractively arranged vignettes invites shoppers to experience a vast array of fixtures, accent furniture, rugs and artwork in an attractive setting that both compliments the products and inspires the shopper. The dedicated lighting consultants stress attention to detail, personal service and individualized attention to all customers. President Lyn Schulz has devoted her life to the business and has assembled an impressive staff extensively trained in everything from residential to commercial projects. They have a simple philosophy, which is to treat you as you would like to be treated. That is what has been keeping customers coming for decades. Signature Lighting won the impressive Arts Award for Best Lighting Showroom in the Midwest Region in 2003. Whatever style or budget, you can put your signature on it at Signature Lighting.

1707 Highway 164, Waukesha WI
(262) 542-2229
www.signaturesshowroom.com

Steinhafels Furniture

HOME & GARDEN

Steinhafels Furniture store offers Wisconsin's largest selection of fine furniture, designed to fit your life, along with superior service and a history of excellence that is more than 70 years in the making. Family patriarch "Honest" John Steinhafel and his partner Arthur Mueller opened the company's first store in 1934. Within 10 years, John became the store's sole proprietor and began instilling a sound work ethic in his children that would guide the business through second-generation ownership. Today Steinhafels Furniture is under the ownership and guidance of three third-generation Steinhafels: John's grandson Gary, president; cousin Mark, chief operations officer; and Gary's sister Ellen Steinhafel-Lappe, chief financial officer. By following the same business and life principles set forth by their grandfather, Gary, Mark and Ellen have successfully ushered in a new era of growth and prosperity for the company while retaining the same friendly and personalized service that keeps generations of customers coming back year after year. They are also dedicated to giving back to the community and work with more than 70 area charities. Steinhafels offers the largest selection of quality furniture in Wisconsin, beautifully displayed in their bright and inviting showrooms. Steinhafels has six convenient locations, in Waukesha, Milwaukee, Greenfield, Madison and Kenosha, and offers next-day local delivery and other fabulous benefits, such as a 30-Day Happiness Guarantee. Make every room in the house your favorite room, quickly and easily, with Steinhafels Furniture.

W231 N1013 County F,
Waukesha WI (corporate office)
(262) 436-4600 or (866) 351-4600
www.steinhafels.com

Shabahang & Sons Oriental Rugs

HOME & GARDEN

Enrich your home with an exquisite and masterfully made Oriental rug from Shabahang & Sons Oriental Rugs of Waukesha. Founder and Owner Jalal Shabahang began working in the family business in Isfahan, Iran when he was 17 and opened the Milwaukee store in 1980 with his brothers. In 2000, he and his sons, co-owners Behzad, Ben, and Bruce, added a Waukesha location. For more than 25 years, the Shabahangs have cultivated a reputation for excellence based on their dedication to both their artisan vendors and their loyal clients. Shabahang & Sons has thousands of rugs on display, each of which has been hand selected by the Shabahangs who personally look at hundreds of rugs for each one that they ultimately choose for the company. The family has developed relationships with the artists that create the rugs and can tell the clients where a rug originates and details of its history, based, in part, on the diversity of each region's weave, patterns and colors. The Shabahangs are highly trained and happily do all of the legwork for their clients to ensure that the clients get only the highest quality products. The showroom covers two floors and 6,600 square feet, all of which is beautifully lit, making it a welcoming environment. You will find rugs that are new, semi-antique, or antique and that range in size from a dainty doormat to grand, palace-sized pieces. Easily add elegance and quality to your favorite room with Oriental rugs from Shabahang & Sons.

160 Kossow Road, Waukesha WI
(262) 717-1111
www.shabahangandsons.com

Action Power Sports

RECREATION & FITNESS

If speed, mechanical performance and heart-racing action are the ingredients you demand from your outdoor sports, Action Power Sports in Waukesha wants to talk to you. This locally owned and operated business recently moved into a brand new 18,000-square-foot facility with more than 130 vehicles on display. The striking showroom boasts a large-screen projection television that shows ATVs, motorcycles, snowmobiles and watercraft in action, a surefire way to spread the fever for sports that challenge you and your machine to take on the outdoors. Action Power Sports specializes in Honda and Suzuki motorcycles and ATVs. The store also stocks Honda scooters and the hard-to-find Honda watercraft. Whether you want to race or simply put some thrills into your land or water adventures, you will want to talk to owner Tom Spielmaker, who is passionate about the sports you can pursue with these vehicles. His dealership brims with quality accessories, including a large selection of helmets and a full line of on and off-road clothing. You will find low prices on tires and a well trained staff to introduce you to the world of sports vehicles. The repair department, which supplies motorcycles to area technical schools and training facilities, can work on almost any bike and also services snowmobiles and watercraft. These vehicles are cost effective, too, often getting 30 to 40 miles per gallon. When your inner daredevil goes looking for action and power, start your explorations with a visit to the experts at Action Power Sports.

202 Travis Lane, Waukesha WI
(262) 547-3088
www.actionps.com

Spring City Aviation

RECREATION & FITNESS

Have you ever wanted to fly through the skies, skillfully guiding a plane to its destination? Spring City Aviation can provide you with that opportunity. Owner Brian Behrens piloted his first solo flight at age 16, even before he could drive a car. The urge to fly is in Brian's blood. He takes over Spring City Aviation, located at the Waukesha Airport, from his father. Brian has parlayed his education at Embry Riddle Aeronautical University to include teaching; he also flies for Midwest Airlines. SCA gears its training to recreational and business flying. It offers a private pilot ground school three times a year and an instrument ground school once a year with the goal of thoroughly preparing students for the required written test. Full-time certified instructors train at the student, private, instrument, commercial and instructor levels. Call to set up a discovery flight and meet with a flight instructor, who will answer your questions and give you all the information you need to start your lessons and prepare for your first solo flight. If you dream of mastering the skies, launch that dream at Spring City Aviation.

536 Northview Road, Waukesha WI
(262) 547-8988
www.springcityaviation.com

Prairieville Park

RECREATION & FITNESS

With their children grown, Bill and Linda Gustafson looked for a way to indulge their love of miniature golf and to meet a community need for quality family fun at the same time. In 1995, guided by Providence, the couple built a pristine place with lovely waterfalls for Prairieville Park, a center with an 18-hole adventure-style miniature golf course, batting cages and bumper cars. A family outing at Prairieville Park, located between Brookfield and Waukesha, is sure to amuse everyone in your party. The golf course is both challenging and beautiful, framed by creeks, a mountain and flowers. You can sharpen your batting ability at one of the five batting cages that offer pitching speeds for baseball and for both slow and fast pitch softball. Playfully pursue each other in the gas-powered bumper cars. The cars have inflatable tubes that make them bounce and spin and provide great fun for anyone who is at least 44 inches tall. Visit the gift shop for Packers or Badgers gifts, Cheeseheads and Wisconsin souvenirs and collectibles. Hit the snack bar for hot dogs, pizzas, smoothies or cotton candy. A trip to the ice cream parlor rounds out your adventure. A private party room is available by reservation for birthday parties, group parties and company outings. Bill and Linda invite you to enjoy a mini vacation with your family, a group or a date at Prairieville Park.

2507 Plaza Court, Waukesha WI
(262) 784-GOLF (4653)
www.prairievillepark.com

Merrill Hills Country Club

RECREATION & FITNESS

Located on 200 picturesque acres, Merrill Hills Country Club offers prime golf, dining, tennis and swimming facilities for families. Originally known as the Waukesha Country Club, the club was founded in 1929 on farmland owned by the Merrill family. Since day one, golf has been a prime focus here. Merrill Hills features a 72-par, 18-hole championship golf course. It's a moderately difficult course with fast greens and narrow fairways. A state-of-the-art practice facility offers ample drive and long iron space as well as greens for chipping and putting and bunker practice areas. Recently resurfaced tennis courts are a pleasure for all tennis lovers. Private and group lessons are available from an expert staff. You can also get competitive in five different adult club championships held each summer. The Olympic-size pool is a favorite place for families to cool off on a summer day. Children aged six to 14 can join a swim team that competes in June and July. Coaches work with everyone from novices to accomplished swimmers. The clubhouse, remodeled in 2002, offers both casual and formal dining opportunities in its luxurious dining rooms and lounges. The Merrill Room has earned a five-diamond rating from AAA. For sporting and social opportunities your entire family can enjoy, consider membership at Merrill Hills Country Club.

W270 S3425 Merrill Hills Road, Waukesha WI
(262) 548-1100
www.merrillhills.com

Swimtastic Swim School

RECREATION & FITNESS

With an approach that builds confidence and self-esteem in addition to a love of the water, Swimtastic Swim School offers swim lessons for people of all ages. Smart Fish Swim in Schools is the motto of this Waukesha-based business, which opened its doors in 1999 and includes several franchises in Wisconsin, Illinois and Nebraska. The business started small, with owner Susan Wainscott offering swim lessons to children in her neighborhood. When the business outgrew Susan's home pool, she opened the current facility, built especially for swim lessons. The water and the air outside the pool are both kept at 90 degrees. The pool's 25 feet of steps give students a seat in the water. Certified Swimtastic instructors work with children starting as young as six months and adults of any age. You can choose from one-on-one private lessons, semi-private lessons with two students per teacher, or group lessons with four students per teacher. A water slide and palm tree shower are part of the fun. Every week, the school creates a new theme with changes to the décor and swimming toys. An observation area, complete with coffee, allows parents to observe a youngster's progress. Swimtastic can be rented for birthday celebrations. Let the caring professionals at Swimtastic Swim School make swimming a safe and pleasurable experience.

900 Tesch Court, Waukesha WI
(262) 549-SWIM (7946)
www.swimtastic.com

Heffernan Wellness Center

RECREATION & FITNESS

In Sanskrit, the word *yoga* means union. At Heffernan Wellness Center in Waukesha, students learn to use yoga to unite mind, body and spirit in ways that improve the health of all three. From the age of 11, owner P.J. Heffernan has had an interest in Eastern exercises and philosophy. After sustaining injuries as a martial artist, he took an interest in yoga, first discovering its benefits at the University of Wisconsin in Milwaukee. Since then, P.J. has made routine trips to India and studied under authentic Indian gurus. He began teaching out of his home, then remodeled his current location to provide an ideal environment for both meditation and physical activity. The center contains beautiful wood floors and ceilings, a fireplace and large, open spaces. P.J. teaches Ashtanga yoga, an energetic aerobic style of yoga. *Ashtanga* means eight limbs, referring to eight steps that involve everything from living virtuously to reaching an altered state of consciousness. P.J. offers private lessons in addition to twice-daily group classes. Ongoing classes, offered on a drop-in basis, benefit the novice as well as the advanced pupil. P.J. is a licensed jiu-jitsu instructor and also teaches this form of self-defense. He has two massage therapists on staff. Improve your health with instruction at Heffernan Wellness Center.

1826 E Main Street, Waukesha WI
(262) 524-9222
www.heffernanwellness.com

Aztalan Cycle Club Inc.

RECREATION & FITNESS

Hot racing action isn't always easy to find, but you can find it at Aztalan Cycle Club. This club is one of the oldest and strongest cycle clubs in the Midwest and that means they attract big boys and their big toys. The first class MX tracks draw great rider turnout and fierce competition. The first track is a one-and-a-quarter mile, European style outdoor motorcross venue. It is well designed and offers plenty of big air for spectators. At this track you will find a first rate backwards falling gate, a full track watering system, professional announcing and fantastic food at the concession booths. Track number two is a quarter-mile, oval red clay track called Azzie. It is recognized as one of the best tracks in the Midwest and will run quads and motorcycles on seven dates this year. Every September the Aztalan Cycle Club, which is owned and operated by club members, sponsors a Senior National Race. In October the club donates all proceeds from the Memorial Race to charities, such as the American Cancer Society and the Parkinson's Research Foundation. A special two-day event in July attracts pro riders from all over the country and includes a pro-amateur competition on the short track. If you're looking for the best racing action in the Midwest, you will find it at the Aztalan Cycle Club.

N6643 Gomoll Road, Waukesha WI
(414) 297-9367
www.aztalancycle.com

PLACES TO GO

- Lowell Damon House
  2107 Wauwatosa Avenue
  (414) 273-8288
- Annunciation Greek Orthodox Church
  9400 W Congress Street
  (414) 461-9400
- Mayfair Mall
  2500 N Mayfair Road
  (414) 771-1300

THINGS TO DO

May

- Gem, Mineral & Fossil Show
  Hart Park
  (414) 771-8668

July

- Wauwatosa's Independence Day Celebration
  Hart Park
  (414) 479-8988

September

- TosaFest
  (414) 453-0649

WAUWATOSA

Nestled in the lush Menomonee River Valley, Wauwatosa has a distinct European feel, brought by the first European settlers in 1835. Its tree-lined streets, cream-colored brick buildings and pedestrian-friendly shopping centers are reminiscent of a European village, and the town retains a charming historic district at its heart. Its name is the Potawatomi word for firefly. In recent decades, western Wauwatosa has become an edge city with an important commercial district anchored by the upscale Mayfair Mall, which features two artificial indoor rivers. Wauwatosa also contains Milwaukee County's Regional Medical Center, which includes the Medical College of Wisconsin, Children's Hospital of Wisconsin and one of two level-one trauma centers in the state. Landmarks in Wauwatosa include the Annunciation Greek Orthodox Church designed by Frank Lloyd Wright and the Washington Highlands, a residential neighborhood designed in 1916 by renowned city planner and architect Werner Hegemann. Listed in the National Register of Historic Places, Washington Highlands has earned national renown for its use of Garden City design concepts and is also an oasis of Revival, Craftsman and Prairie architecture.

McPets

ANIMALS & PETS

For pet supplies, healthy foods and education, you can trust the experts at McPets. Owner Pam Haefner has been involved in animal adoption efforts for years and has managed the annual Wisconsin Doberman Rescue. Her husband and co-owner, Mic, has years of retail experience. The Haefners opened the doors of McPets in 2002. They stock leashes, collars, toys and personalized identification tags. Here you can pamper Fido or Spot with a new pet bed or spoil your Persian with a brush. Rawhide chew toys are a necessity for new puppy parents who want their shoes and furniture to remain off limits. McPets offers the popular USA Rawhide brand. Fresh butcher bones and other treats will show your dog you care. Herbal remedies can help with minor ailments. You will also find a great selection of natural foods plus gifts for the pet lover. At McPets, education is a high priority. Pam and Mic will help answer your questions, whether your pet is new or a longtime member of the family. Customers can learn how to raise healthy pets and keep them healthy and happy throughout their lives. The shop also promotes pet rescue by offering a discount for customers who offer proof of adoption. Cat, dog, lizard or fish, the Haefners want your pet to live long and prosper. Let McPets help you with your best friend.

6817 W North Avenue, Wauwatosa WI
(414) 476-8640
www.mcpets.net

Richard Bennett Tailors

FASHION

Richard Bennett Tailors has been literally at the cutting edge of tailoring techniques since Elmer Miller opened the first of a set of Richard Bennett Tailors stores in Wauwatosa in 1961. Today the store concentrates its efforts at one location, offering exclusive men's ready-to-wear and specializing in custom-made suits and dress shirts. In the early days, the store used photometric custom fitting technology to send precise measurements to the tailors. In 1980, just as photometric technology became obsolete, Elmer's son David came on board, and the shop switched to a system of manual measurements that featured many try-on jackets. In 1994, Dave became president of the company and keeper of the promise, We Suit You Better, which is a matter of family honor. You can choose from hundreds of fabrics for your tailored clothing, and Richard Bennett will keep track of your choices and measurements. In addition, Richard Bennett carries Burberry clothing and accessories, Lacoste for men and women, St. Croix Knits, Bills Khakis and sportswear from Tommy Bahama, Haupt, Riscatto and Scott Barber. The store's deep-toned wood paneling showcases everything the well-dressed man could desire, from suits, sweaters and slacks to shoes, shirts and socks. You'll find cuff links and ties, too. The store takes an active role in the community and donates to many charities. For clothes that fit your body and your lifestyle, visit Richard Bennett Tailors.

2500 N Mayfair Road, Wauwatosa WI
(414) 774-4850
www.richardbennetttailors.com

Heinsight

FASHION

Looking for something in leather that's just your style? Heinsight, a leather boutique in charming Wauwatosa, specializes in creative leather apparel. The leather handbags, coats and hats are nicely showcased against original brick walls just behind a quaint, historic storefront. Owner Cindy Hein Westin went from loving her home economics classes in high school to involvement with the theater costume department in college and later began doing alterations for friends. After working in custom leather repairs, she moved her sewing studio from her home to its present location in 1997. Soon, she added retail items to her custom work, and today she offers the best of both worlds to her customers. Cindy crafts jackets with distinctive details, such as hand lacing and perforations. Her hats feature detachable leather flows. Her fashion-forward creations incorporate shearling and soft, quality leathers in fun, trendy colors. This gifted fabric artist can create just about anything you can imagine, and she also repairs and redesigns items you already own. Cindy also shops for quality ready-made items to add to the mix at her boutique. For original, top quality leather apparel and accessories that will set you apart from the crowd, Cindy invites you to Heinsight.

7609 Harwood Avenue, Wauwatosa WI
(414) 456-9211

Winters Group

HEALTH & BEAUTY

Winters Group in Wauwatosa is a one-stop shop for the home of your dreams. This progressive group can help you articulate your ideas for design, construction or remodeling, help you refine them, then see the project through to completion. They employ architects, designers, builders, remodelers and other craftsmen. The team concept means they can provide you with a project that will enrich your life as well as enhance the value of your home. Over the years Winters Group has racked up numerous awards for quality workmanship. Whether you need a kitchen remodel, an addition to your home, or a complete historical renovation, their design/build approach will assure that you'll get the best possible quality and value for your money. When the construction is finished, their interior design team can help you choose materials, paint and decorating options that will put the finishing touches on your project. To make your home even more of a treasure, consult Winters Group.

7772 Harwood Avenue, Wauwatosa WI
(414) 771-6202
www.wintersgroupllc.com

The Innovators Salon and Spa

HEALTH & BEAUTY

Patricia Guzman first opened The Innovators Salon and Spa in 1987. Pat's people-oriented service and focus on customer satisfaction led to a growing clientele. Needing more space, in 2002, the salon moved to its current Wauwatosa location. The full-service salon specializes in hair color, including highlights, lowlights and firelights. Pat and her staff are professionals, dedicated to innovative services. Staff members continue their education on a regular basis and can offer the latest hair cutting and coloring techniques. The Innovators Salon and Spa also offers a wide range of spa services. Develop a glow in the tanning bed; receive manicures and nail enhancements, restorative facials and waxing services. The Innovators Salon and Spa has a certified massage therapist on location who provides therapeutic relaxation massage, trigger-point release, pregnancy and sports massage, as well as other modalities. Like the hairdressers, the massage therapist participates in ongoing training to keep abreast of the most up-to-date techniques. The Innovators Salon and Spa has a down-to-earth staff that contributes greatly to the clean and friendly environment. For services that will accentuate your lifestyle, visit The Innovators Salon and Spa.

10600 W Bluemound Road, Wauwatosa WI
(414) 774-6818
www.innovatorssalonandspa.com

St. Camillus

LIFESTYLE DESTINATIONS

As we age, our need for health services may change quickly and alter our ability to remain independent. The St. Camillus continuing care retirement facility in Wauwatosa has been addressing the needs of elderly residents since its founding in 1931. The campus, which features 288 apartments for independent living, a skilled nursing facility, assisted living and home health options, is a project of the Roman Catholic Order of St. Camillus. The Order devotes itself worldwide to serving the poor, the sick and the elderly with a sense of compassion and love. Here, elderly residents find the comfort, security and friendships they need to stay vital and independent. Residents can live in their own apartments and enjoy community amenities, such as a lovely lobby with an atrium, grand piano and fireplace. When needs change, this sparkling state-of-the-art facility provides the necessary level of care, including a 76-bed skilled nursing facility and assisted living with round-the-clock staffing. The St. Camillus facility can also arrange for homemaking, companion care or the services of a home health aide. In the spirit of St. Camillus and the order that he founded, the staff here sees every human being as a special creation of God and worthy of their care and loving concern. If you are seeking a retirement facility that caters to your physical, spiritual, social and emotional well-being, visit the St. Camillus campus and learn more about life in this caring environment, where people come first.

10101 W Wisconsin Avenue,
Wauwatosa WI
(414) 259-6333
www.stcam.com

The City Market

RESTAURANTS & CAFÉS

The City Market isn't really a market. It's a café. Actually, it's three cafés, with two locations in Wauwatosa and one in Shorewood. It has three locations because one wasn't enough for a place this good. The City Market is what some might call a casual, upscale bakery-style café. They serve breakfast, lunch and dinner, with bottomless cups of coffee and bakery cases filled with housemade specialties just begging to be eaten. City Market serves breakfast all day long. They make their own granola. They make the best, most authentic scones in the region. They serve your food fast. And they do it with style. The City Market offers an airy and inviting atmosphere. They offer more than 10 varieties of artisan breads every day, along with a winning assortment of sandwiches, soups and salads. The open-face egg panini with potatoes is highly recommended, unless you prefer an egg scrambler, which comes with whatever you choose. Co-owners Julie Hollingsworth and Jeff Swanson have hit on a recipe for success that has made The City Market one of the area's favorite eateries, the kind of place that is as popular for families as it is for business lunches. Stop into The City Market next time you have a taste for good honest food at a good honest price.

8725 W North Avenue, Wauwatosa WI
(414) 453-0000

The Little Read Book

SHOPPING

In a time when national chains and big-box stores are swallowing small, independently owned bookstores, the Little Read Book has thrived for more than 20 years. It might be the friendly staff that keeps people coming back, or it could be the book selection and charming atmosphere, where you're welcome to browse for hours. If you ask most of the people in Wauwatosa though, they'll all agree that the success of the Little Read Book is because of owner Linda Burg. Her staff knows that without Linda the terrific atmosphere that's always been the heart of the Little Read Book wouldn't exist. Linda started the bookstore as a way to honor her mother, who instilled a lifelong love of books in her. "My mother was always reading. She always had a book in her hand or with her," says Linda. Though it started in a tiny space, the Little Read Book has now grown to three times that size and carries not just books, but personal gifts, cards and children's novelties. Linda and her staff strive to offer knowledgeable book recommendations, whether you are seeking a best-seller or a hard-to-find treasure. Linda believes in giving back to her community in a big way too. She hosts a preschool story time monthly and offers school and church discounts as well. When you're in Wauwatosa, be sure to stop by the Little Read Book, and browse through Linda's rooms filled with books and love.

7603 W State Street, Wauwatosa WI
(414) 774-2665
www.littlereadbook.com

Celebrate Wisconsin

SHOPPING

Since 1983, Celebrate Wisconsin has been the state's premier source of gifts celebrating almost every aspect of the Badger State. Nickname aside, most people associate Wisconsin with its most famous product, cheese. Celebrate Wisconsin embraces the state's dairy identity with plenty of cow collectibles and shelf after shelf of everything cheese, from erasers and coasters to those cheesehead hats that fans wear at Green Bay Packers' games. But it's not all cheesy at Celebrate Wisconsin. You will find calendars evoking the beauty of the state and books about its history and most famous recipes. From Milwaukee frozen custard and bubbler mugs and T-shirts to custom gift baskets filled with tasty Wisconsin treats, Celebrate Wisconsin is your one-stop gift shop. Located in the Mayfair Mall, Celebrate Wisconsin is simply brimming with wonderful gift ideas and souvenirs for all ages.

2500 N Mayfair Road, Wauwatosa WI
(414) 258-7553
www.celebratewisconsin.com

Red lighthouse on northside of Kenosha
Photo by Richie Diesterheft

PLACES TO GO

- City Hall Gallery
  7525 W Greenfield Avenue
  (414) 302-8200
- International Clown Hall of Fame
  640 S 84th Street, Suite 526
- Wisconsin State Fair Park and Exposition Center
  640 S 84th Street
  (800) 884-FAIR (3247)
- West Allis Historical Society
  8405 W National Avenue
  (414) 541-6970

THINGS TO DO

March

- Indian Summer Festivals Winter Pow Wow
  State Fair Park
  (414) 273-2680

May

- Cinco de Mayo
  State Fair Park
  (414) 389-6000

June

- West Allis Western Days
  State Fair Park
  www.westerndays.com

July

- National Street Rod Association Milwaukee Nationals
  Wisconsin Exposition Center
  (901) 452-4030

August

- Wisconsin State Fair
  State Fair Park
  (800) 884-3247

September

- Harvest Fair and World Beef Expo
  State Fair Park
  (414) 266-7000

November

- Holiday Folk Fair International
  State Fair Park
  (414) 225-6225

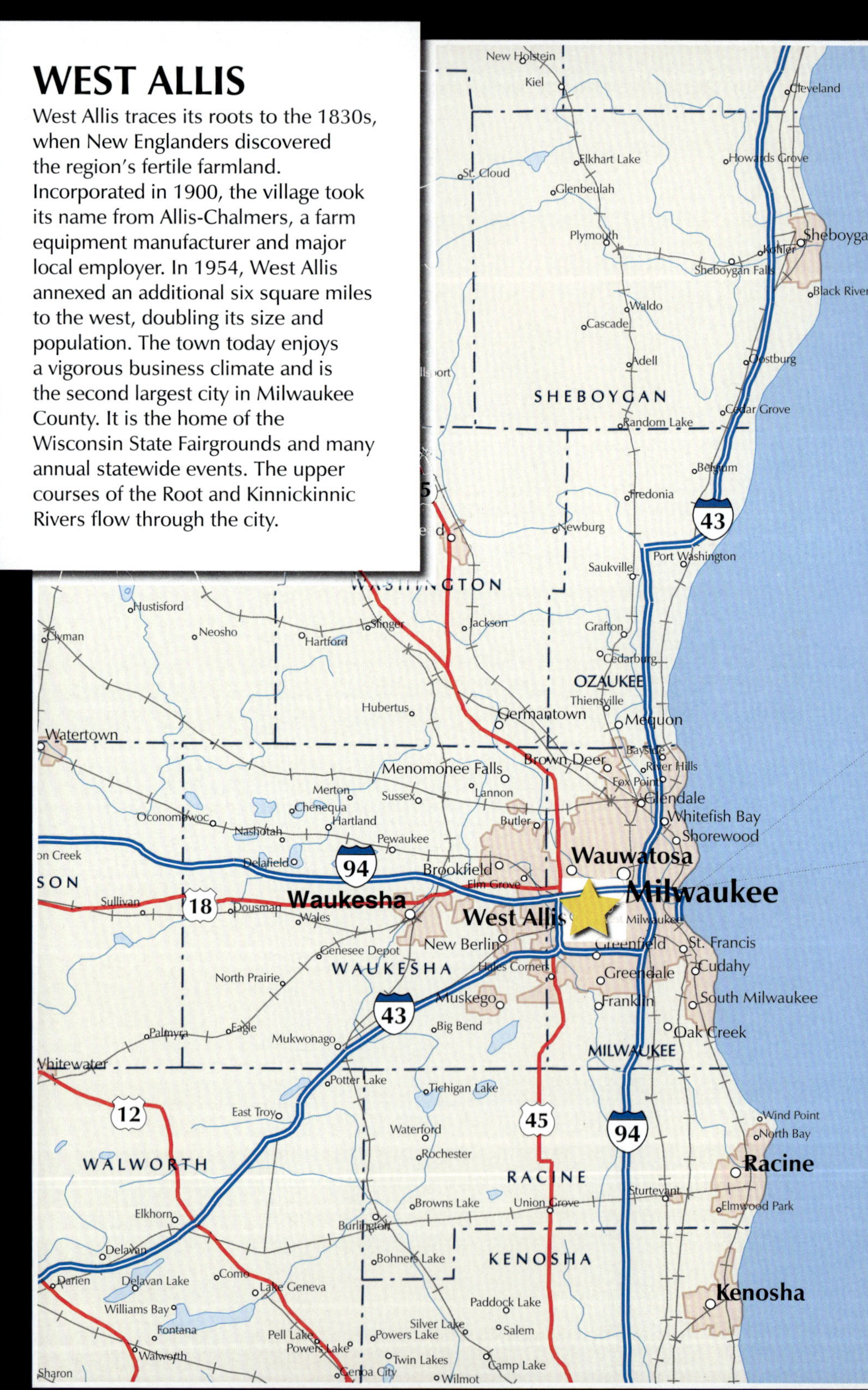

WEST ALLIS

West Allis traces its roots to the 1830s, when New Englanders discovered the region's fertile farmland. Incorporated in 1900, the village took its name from Allis-Chalmers, a farm equipment manufacturer and major local employer. In 1954, West Allis annexed an additional six square miles to the west, doubling its size and population. The town today enjoys a vigorous business climate and is the second largest city in Milwaukee County. It is the home of the Wisconsin State Fairgrounds and many annual statewide events. The upper courses of the Root and Kinnickinnic Rivers flow through the city.

West Allis Cheese & Sausage Shoppe

MARKETS & DELIS

West Allis Cheese & Sausage Shoppe was saved from closure thanks to the Lutz family and their love of Wisconsin cheeses. West Allis Cheese, originally called Merkt, first opened in 1969. The shop was an area landmark where the Lutz family had always bought their cheese. In 2001, when they heard the store was closing, brothers Mark and Howard Lutz purchased the shop to continue the tradition. Today West Allis Cheese & Sausage Shoppe offers more than 150 varieties of cheese. The store features premium cheese suppliers, such as Carr Valley Cheese and Pleasant Ridge Reserve. Whether it's world champion blue cheese or cheddar that's been aged up to 10 years, you'll find it here. The Lutzes maintain close relationships with their cheesemakers and bring them into the store to meet and share their knowledge with customers. Specialty cheeses range from goat and sheep milk cheeses and spreads to hard cheeses that are available by the pound. West Allis features products by Lake Geneva Country Meats, including such sausage varieties as Bavarian sausage and flavored brats. Cheese and sausage baskets make thoughtful individual or corporate gifts, and the shop creates more than 5,000 Christmas baskets every year. If you love cheese and sausage, come visit West Allis Cheese & Sausage Shoppe at their original location or at their newest location inside the Milwaukee Public Market.

6832 W Becher Street, West Allis WI
(414) 543-4230
www.wacheese-gifts.com

Kegel's Inn

RESTAURANTS & CAFÉS

Kegel's Inn has offered the best in German and American cuisine since 1924. The restaurant serves more duck than any other restaurant in the Milwaukee area, due to a house special, the boneless roast duck. The potato pancakes are the best anywhere and the breading on the enormously popular Friday fish fry is perfect. *Wiener schnitzel* is another winner. Other offerings include *Hasenpfeffer*, or rabbit stew. Award winning desserts are also available, plus a full bar with a menu featuring imported beers on tap and other selections. Austrian born John and Anna Kegel opened Kegel's as a speakeasy during the days of prohibition, offering 20-cent whiskey and 15-cent homebrewed beer with a free meal. Prohibition was tremendously unpopular in beer loving, German Milwaukee. When beverage alcohol became legal again in 1933, the Kegels immediately went legit. A little over a year and a complete remodel later, the business reopened much as it is today. Brothers Rob and Jim Kegel, the most recent family members to operate the inn, keep up the standards set by their parents and grandparents, and the result is universally positive reviews. In addition to the traditional menu, the Kegels continue to preserve the heritage of the original building. Hand-painted murals cover the walls, stained glass and leaded windows give light and an original trap door behind the bar holds beer. For a truly historic experience and a meal you'll talk about long after you leave, visit Kegel's Inn.

5901 W National Avenue, West Allis WI
(414) 257-9999

Oniomania

SHOPPING

Oniomania is the technical term for an affliction suffered by many of the most interesting people. It means "the irresistible urge to buy things." Andrea Kopan, a jewelry artist for more than 13 years, is an unabashed oniomaniac, which is probably why her store, Oniomania, is such a hoot. Oniomania is one of the most eclectic boutiques you will ever peruse. It's full of handmade, one-of-a-kind adornments crafted by artists from Wisconsin and elsewhere, including Andrea and her partner, Dale Dehmlow. Oniomania, billed as "a unique experiment in adornment," carries a large and varied selection of items, including jewelry, purses, pajamas, stained glass, mosaic mirrors, painted furniture, umbrellas, fiber art, pewter and natural soaps. Located across the street from the bustling West Allis Farmer's Market, Oniomania is a great place to shop for gifts. Prices are very affordable, and both Dale and Andrea will fill you in on the backgrounds of the artists who make the pieces they sell. The next time you have an irresistible urge to buy cool things, don't fight it. Instead, head on over to West Allis and visit Oniomania, a true shopper's delight.

6430 W National Avenue, West Allis WI
(414) 727-9797
oniomaniawi.com

WHITEFISH BAY

Located on the scenic bluffs above Lake Michigan, Whitefish Bay enjoys a small town atmosphere within six miles of the attractions of Milwaukee. Native Americans and fishermen were among the first settlers, until Milwaukee beer baron Captain Frederick Pabst realized the commercial potential of the location in 1889. The Pabst Whitefish Bay Resort put Whitefish Bay on the map, drawing as many as 10,000 tourists a day over a century to enjoy free concerts in the beer garden, ride the Ferris wheel and stay at the Bellevue hotel. Today, Whitefish Bay is primarily residential, with a business district on Silver Spring Drive. The town enjoys several fine parks and swimming beaches. Klode Park, on the lakefront, offers tennis courts, soccer fields, a community-built playground and ice-skating in the winter. A picturesque trail winds from the park to the beach. If you prefer to avoid the crowds, try the smaller beach at Big Bay Park. Old Schoolhouse Park, across from the public library, features a botanical garden.

PLACES TO GO

- Klode Park
  N Shore Drive
- Big Bay Park
  N Palisades Road

Bay Bakery

BAKERIES, COFFEE & TEA

The Bay Bakery specializes in premier wedding cakes and French pastries. After a consultation, Bay Bakery custom decorates every wedding cake to suit the taste of the bride and groom. *Milwaukee Magazine* has called the bakery's creations the best cakes in Milwaukee. Dany and Virginie Olier, owners of the shop, have added an array of exquisite French pastries such as éclairs, chocolate Ganache and fruit tarts to the Bay Bakery's traditional line of wedding cakes. The Oliers bake all goods from scratch on the premises and Dany insists on using real butter in all his concoctions. It's the most expensive alternative, but clearly provides the best flavor. The Meredics, a family of German bakers, began making wedding cakes at Whitefish Bay in 1932. Dany and Virginie bought the shop from the Meredics in 1995. They are French, so the Bay Bakery is a true pan-European enterprise. Dany acquired his baker's expertise in an upscale Milwaukee hotel and was anxious to strike out on his own when the Bay Bakery became available. Stop by anytime for the fabulous pastries, and then let the Bay Bakery put the finishing touches on your special day.

423 E Silver Spring Drive, Whitefish Bay WI
(414) 332-5340
www.baybakery.com

Gallery 505

GALLERIES & FINE ART

Gallery 505, a contemporary fine art gallery, offers spirited original art from around the world as well as museum quality framing. Tom Harris purchased Gallery 505 in 1993 after working in the gallery's frame shop while putting himself through college. While working for the previous owner, he learned how to blend colors and use framing to make art stand out as the focal point in a space. The frame shop features more than 1,000 samples of high-end, premium frames. Tom and his creative staff preserve your keepsakes and fine art with archival matting and special glass designed to block UV rays. All work is guaranteed and performed on-site, so nothing ever leaves the shop. Tom is fully licensed and bonded. The dynamic gallery space, a 2004 addition, employs color blocking in rich, bright colors to show off vibrant original artwork. Sculpture, prints and glass art are represented as well as oil, watercolor and acrylic paintings. Client services include art rental and art trial periods, where customers can take artwork home to see how it looks in their space. Residential and corporate consultations assist customers in selecting appropriate art or framing to enhance their homes or businesses. The gallery also performs installations and provides free delivery. Clients may rent Gallery 505 for wine tastings, office parties or other events. For outstanding original art and preservation framing, visit Gallery 505.

505 E Silver Spring Drive, Whitefish Bay WI
(414) 962-6302
www.gallery-505.com
www.tgfuwfb.com

Armin and Pauline Koch

Armin Koch Furniture & Design

HOME & GARDEN

In 1954 Armin and Pauline Koch opened a small furniture store on Farwell Avenue in Milwaukee. Ten years later they moved to a bigger space in Shorewood, and five years after that, their son, Jim, joined the business. Armin passed away in 1974, after 22 years at the helm of Armin Koch Furniture, but the business continued under the guidance of Pauline and Jim. They moved to their current location in Whitefish Bay in 1982, and two years later, Jim's wife, Diane, joined the company. Pauline passed away in 1997, and today the company is run by her grandchildren, Jon and Laurie. For 55 years, Armin Koch Furniture has been providing steady, reliable service and merchandise to generations of households. When Armin started the business, he did it with $500 and four card table sets. Today the company carries furniture for every room in the house, and features a full-service design center staffed by expertly trained designers. They carry custom entertainment centers, custom area rugs, a huge selection of upholstery fabrics, custom window treatments, and every style of office décor available. Things have changed over the years at Armin Koch Furniture & Design, but one thing has remained constant. A member of Armin's family is always on hand and intimately involved in making sure customers get the attention they've come to expect from the area's best family-owned furniture store.

615 E Silver Spring Drive, Whitefish Bay WI (414) 962-0320 *www.arminkoch.com*

Elements East— Fine Asian Furnishings

HOME & GARDEN

Elements East gives customers the chance to make the clean and simple lines of antique Asian furniture a part of their lifestyle. The Whitefish Bay store's owner, Alicia Urban, lived in China and Taiwan, where she developed a love for Asian culture and design. She and partner Therese Armbruster bring some of that culture back to the Milwaukee area with pieces they hand select in rural China and Indonesia. The two travel to Asia several times a year, visiting out-of-the way markets, private homes and warehouses to find the most unique and eye-catching items. You'll find 100-year-old antique hand carved chairs with a lacquer sheen enhanced by time. Tables, lighting and statuary feature hand-cast metal and stonework plus elegant joinery. The vast majority of pieces at Elements East have a story to tell as most are between 80 and 250 years old. Alicia and Therese assure the artistic integrity of the pieces by making sure any necessary restoration work happens in the country of origin. An on-site feng shui consultant can help you determine the proper pieces and placements for your home. For furnishings that capture the Asian spirit with their simplicity and attention to detail, visit Elements East.

109 E Silver Spring Drive, Whitefish Bay WI
(414) 332-3530 ***www.elementseast.com***

Placesetters

HOME & GARDEN

Owner Mara Riteris founded Placesetters in 1977 with several other women and still loves finding tasteful table accessories for her customers. Every nook and cranny at the Whitefish Bay store bursts with hand picked, quality items at different price points. Serving pieces, glassware and an array of fine linens make colorful tabletop statements, while candlesticks, vases and centerpieces provide tasteful accents. Expect to find plenty of clever ideas you can use at home, especially from the shop's spectacular seasonal displays, themed for holiday entertaining. Christmas sees the entire store transformed into a winter wonderland, with window displays that showcase holiday ornaments and other décor. Customers from all over Wisconsin and out of state come to Placesetters for Mara's carefully selected gifts. Mara credits her longtime staff with much of the store's success, including employees who've been with her for up to 25 years. They cheerfully provide personalized service and knowledgeable answers to your questions. Special orders are welcome, and Placesetters offers local delivery, gift cards and free gift wrapping. Whether you need an elegant china service for eight or an upbeat platter to liven up a holiday table, start your search with a visit to Placesetters.

501 E Silver Spring Drive,
Whitefish Bay WI
(414) 962-1060

WILLIAMS BAY

Williams Bay, a village on Geneva Lake, is a favorite upscale vacation and retirement spot. Largely unsettled until the 20th century, the lake area saw an explosive housing boom in later decades as city folk increasingly discovered the quiet, relaxed lifestyle and natural beauty of the region. The population of Williams Bay has doubled within a span of 30 years. If you're visiting Williams Bay, you will find yourself drawn to the Lakefront, where the rolling lawns of Edgewater Park serve as the site of various community festivals throughout the year. The public boat launching facility at Williams Bay Beach will set you on your course for a day of fishing, waterskiing or sailing. The Lakefront in Williams Bay is also the site of the Yerkes Observatory of the University of Chicago. The observatory's refracting telescope is the second largest in the world.

PLACES TO GO

- Yerkes Observatory
  373 W Geneva Street
  (262) 245-5555

THINGS TO DO

February

- Winterfest
  Edgewater Park
  (262) 245-2720

July

- Art by the Bay
  Edgewater Park
  (262) 275-5567

Details...in the Bay

HOME & GARDEN

Details...in the Bay holds all the little treasures that add up to make a big impact on the appearance of your home. Following a longtime dream, Joey Coleson opened the store, which features a view of the lake, in 2003. Here you can find home décor and gifts and then learn how to pull the details together to create a warm and inviting space. Shabby chic signs by Danielson Design add whimsy to your walls, imparting such words of wisdom as *Paradise found* and *Life is good on Lake Geneva*. Vintage postcards of Williams Bay get a new lease on life as tumbled Italian marble coasters. A series of cookbooks with matching CDs ensure you always have the right mood music, whether for a romantic dinner or a festive wine tasting. Details also offers workshops on a variety of topics, ranging from organizing your closet to vintage paper crafts. Regular shoppers mark their calendars for the Paris Flea Market, a special event held on the first Sunday of each month, when you can find great bargains on closeouts and one-of-a-kind items. Visit Details...in the Bay for an eclectic mix of items sure to add personality to your home.

88 N Walworth Avenue, Williams Bay WI
(262) 245-9150
www.detailsinthebay.com

Daddy Maxwell's

RESTAURANTS & CAFÉS

For more than 20 years, people have craned their necks for a better view as they drive by the igloo shaped building in Williams Bay. Inside this unique piece of real estate, Daddy Maxwell's serves outstanding home-style meals at an affordable price. In 1987, Marshall and Janette Maxwell purchased the old Artic Restaurant building and named their new business after Marshall's father. The menu offers pages of family recipes. One of the most popular breakfast items is the French batter pancakes served with butter and syrup, or you can have them with blueberries, strawberries or bananas. Other legendary entrées include the crab and spinach omelette and the eggs Benedict. Check the board up front for the day's specials or the weekly fish specials, as they are always changing. Many celebrities have dined at this noticeable landmark, and the restaurant recently earned a place in best-selling author James Patterson's novel *Sam's Letters to Jennifer.* Janette attributes much their success to the fantastic employees. After Hurricane Wilma struck in 2005, six employees (including the owners) were stranded for 14 days in Cancun, Mexico. Janette says that the employees back home worked overtime to make sure the restaurant ran smoothly and they did such an awesome job no one was the wiser. Though many things have changed in the world over the past 20 years, you can still count on great food, personable service and the memorable ice block architecture of Daddy Maxwell's. Come celebrate two decades of great food in one of Williams Bay's favorite hangouts.

150 Elkhorn Road, Williams Bay WI (262) 245-5757

Sunset on Lake Geneva

WILMOT

Wilmot is a small, pleasant community near the Illinois border. It is named for the Wilmot Proviso, a congressional proposal during the Mexican-American War that purposed to ban slavery in any territory acquired from Mexico. Situated on the Fox River, Wilmot developed by harnessing the power of the river, first to support a flourmill and later to generate electrical power. Today Wilmot is famous for skiing. Wilmot Mountain is the closest ski resort to Chicago and one of the most popular in the region. Wilmot Mountain's world-renowned ski school draws students from all over for the best in ski lessons.

PLACES TO GO

- Wilmot Mountain Ski Area
  11931 Fox River Road
  (262) 862-2301
- Wilmot Speedway
  Fairgrounds
  (262) 279-3892

THINGS TO DO

August

- Kenosha County Fair
  Fairgrounds
  www.kenoshacofair.com

September

- All Breed Dog Show and Obedience Trial
  Fairgrounds
  (262) 654-4831

Wilmot Mountain

RECREATION & FITNESS

Walter Stopa was pretty sure his instincts were right when he judged a hill outside of Wilmot to be suitable for a ski area. The year was 1938, and when 300 skiers showed up for opening day, Walter knew for certain that he had something. To this day, the Stopa family continues to run Wilmot Mountain, still the closest ski area to Chicago and the Chicagoland suburbs, though much else has changed. Visitors now have their pick of 25 runs catering to varying skill levels and accessed by eight chair lifts and three rope tows. Snowboarders are welcome at Wilmot Mountain, with the Terrain Park offering thrills to more experienced boarders. Back in the old skiing-only days, enthusiasts lined up to grab onto the single rope tow, powered by a tractor motor. Then, after taking their run, they huddled in the 25-square-foot warming hut, heated by a cooking stove. Today, the main lodge offers a more spacious setting for relaxation and socializing, while the cooking stoves at Wilmot Mountain do what they were designed to do, namely prepare food for the many patrons of the Iron Kettle Restaurant, the Pizza Barn and two pubs. The ski school offers lessons for all ages, beginning with a program for children four to eight called Winter Wonderland. The Wilmot Ski Patrol, 200 volunteer members strong, has twice received the National Patrol of the Year trophy. Make Wilmot Mountain, the site of exhilaration and fun for nearly 70 years, your winter playground.

11931 Fox River Road, Wilmot WI
(262) 862-2301
www.wilmotmountain.com

PLACES TO GO

- Circus World Museum
  550 Water Street
  (866)-693-1500
- Devil's Lake State Park
  S5975 Park Road
  (608) 356-8301
- H.H. Bennett Studio & History Center
  215 Broadway
  (608)-253-3523
- Mirror Lake State Park
  E10320 Fern Dell Road
  (608) 254-2333
- Mt. Olympus Water & Theme Park
  1701 Wisconsin Dells Parkway
  (608) 254-2490
- Noah's Ark Waterpark
  1410 Wisconsin Dells Parkway
  (608) 254-6351
- Parsons Indian Trading Post & Museum
  370 Wisconsin Dells Parkway
  (866)-281-8704
- Ripley's Believe It or Not Museum
  115 Broadway
  (608)-253-7556
- Rocky Arbor State Park
  S U.S. Highway 12
  (608) 254-8001

THINGS TO DO

January

- Flake Out Festival
  La Crosse Street Festival Site
  www.wisdells.com/events/flakeout.cfm

May

- Automotion (car fest)
  Noah's Ark Waterpark
  www.wisdells.com/events/automotion.cfm

June

- Taste of the Dells
  Downtown
  (800) 223-3557

September

- Wo-Zha-Wa Days
  www.wisdells.com/events/wozhawa.cfm

WISCONSIN DELLS

Stunning scenery and more than 80 attractions make Wisconsin Dells a national tourist destination, swelling the steady population of 3,000 by thousands more throughout the year. The city takes its name from the Dells of the Wisconsin River, a spectacular glacially-formed gorge featuring striking sandstone rock formations along the riverbank. Early landscape photographer H. H. Bennett put the Dells on the map beginning in the 1870s with his widely distributed stereoscopic photographs. Today visitors can take any number of guided tours of the area, whether by boat, train or horse-drawn wagon. Specializing in family attractions, Wisconsin Dells bills itself as the Water Park Capital of the World, boasting 18 indoor and three outdoor water parks, including the biggest of each kind in the nation. The Dells River District is the downtown shopping mecca, known for its fudge, distinctive architecture and scenic RiverWalk. In the summer, the Dells River District is live with free entertainment, including street-side musicians, clowns and jugglers.

Trappers Turn Golf Club

RECREATION & FITNESS

Beauty, drama and challenge await you at scenic Trappers Turn Golf Club in Wisconsin Dells. In an area carved by glaciers thousands of years ago, this 27-hole-facility features a combination of woodland holes, rolling mounds for a Scottish flair, rock canyons and beautiful Mystic Lake. Trappers Turn has a reputation as a golf lover's paradise. Challenging to the advanced golfer, yet offering a design that is more playable and fun, the 27 holes created by Andy North and Roger Packard allow everyone to enjoy a great game. The beautiful Southern Classic clubhouse facilities can accommodate your outing, meeting or special gathering. The full-service restaurant offers a variety of menu choices for golfers on the turn or for those looking to unwind after the round. Hotel packages can make your dream golf getaway a reality. Awarded five stars by the *Chicagoland Golf Magazine* and four-and-one-half stars by *Golf Digest's* Best Places to Play, Trappers Turn Golf Club has hosted several Wisconsin PGA Championships and the 1998 Wisconsin State Open (won by PGA tour star Steve Stricker). Come see why Trappers Turn Golf Club has been consistently ranked as one of the top courses in Wisconsin.

652 Trappers Turn Drive, Wisconsin Dells WI
(608) 253-7000 or (800) 221-TURN (8876)
www.trappersturn.com

Marley's—A Taste of the Caribbean

RESTAURANTS & CAFÉS

As they would say in Jamaica, "Bring da family, mon." Families are always welcome at Marley's—A Taste of the Caribbean. This Wisconsin Dells restaurant simulates the carefree fun of a Caribbean island, complete with palm trees, thatched-roof huts and plenty of island specialties, like crab dip, jerk chicken and sautéed grouper. Owners Jeff and Marci Morris opened Marley's in 2000, combining Caribbean food and drink with playful entertainment for a restaurant that's made a name for itself by inviting guests to come for the food, stay for the fun. The 200-seat restaurant is locally popular year-round and gets extra-busy in summer with visitors from Noah's Ark next door. Families can follow a meal at Marley's with a half-price deal on mini golf at Marley's Shipwreck Lagoon. The Lagoon also invites baseball and softball players to try out the batting cages. The Friday fish fry, Saturday prime rib special and a kid's menu add further enticement. At night, Marley's becomes a very lively nightclub with weekly Hawaiian tropic swimwear competitions in the summer, a karaoke night and live entertainment. A large dance floor, pool tables and darts keep diners entertained long after they have finished their delicious Caribbean fare. From Packers to politicians, just about everybody appreciates Marley's, as close as you can get to a Caribbean cruise while remaining in Wisconsin. Take a break from the ordinary at Marley's—A Taste of the Caribbean, and you'll soon be saying "Ya mon, no worries."

1470 Wisconsin Dells Parkway, Wisconsin Dells WI
(608) 254-1800
www.marleysclub.com

Essen Haus German Restaurant

RESTAURANTS & CAFÉS

Enjoy a true taste of Germany with a visit to Essen Haus German Restaurant, where Eat, Drink and Be Merry is more than a motto; it's a way of life. Robert Worm founded the original Essen Haus in Madison in 1984. He has since made quite a name for the place with recognition as the Best of Bars by the Food Network and as one of America's Top Tasty Destinations by *Martha Stewart Living* magazine. Robert's second Essen Haus is part of the delightful Bavarian Village and Chalet complex in the heart of downtown Wisconsin Dells. Here you can view the German glockenspiel that reenacts the Pied Piper of Hamelin legend every half hour and tour the outdoor biergarten. When you're finished with your tour, head inside Essen Haus for an authentic German meal served up by friendly staff members dressed in traditional German attire, complete with dirndls and lederhosen. Specialties of the house include the roast pork, along with the Wiener schnitzel, hühner schnitzel, and the wurst teller, a combination sausage plate featuring bratwurst, Thuringer and knockwurst. Essen Haus German Restaurant is proud to be the nation's largest seller of German draft beer in the United States and offers 12 traditional German beers on tap, as well as an extensive selection of domestic and imported beers and Weissbier bottles. Treat yourself to an authentic German meal without leaving the country by visiting Essen Haus German Restaurant, a Wisconsin tradition.

414 Broadway, Wisconsin Dells WI (608) 253-7766
514 E Wilsonstrasse Street, Madison WI (608) 255-4674
www.essen-haus.com

Index by Treasure

A

B

C

Index by City

V

W